CORE STUDIES

FOR

BTEC NATIONAL

**PAUL CALLAGHAN
TOM HARRISON
JOHN ELLISON
JEFF HINDMARCH
TONY GOUGH**

WITH CONTRIBUTIONS FROM
BERNARD CALLAGHAN

Faculty of Administrative and
Business Studies
New College Durham

Illustrations by Paul Henry

BUSINESS EDUCATION PUBLISHERS
1986

To Richard John

Published in Great Britain by Business Education Publishers,
Leighton House, 17 Vine Place, Sunderland, Tyne & Wear.

Tel: 0783 674963/091 5674963

ISBN 0-907679-16-1

Printed in Great Britain by
City Printing Works (Chester-le-Street) Ltd.,
Broadwood View, Chester-le-Street,
Co. Durham DH3 3NJ.
Tel: 0385 883255

PREFACE

This book covers the units forming the common core of BTEC National courses. These are:

People in Organisations

Finance

The Organisation in its Environment

It provides students with a broad integrated examination of the wide range of human, financial, economic and legal aspects which are essential to the study of modern organisations. It has been written in a way which makes it simple for students to obtain a thorough understanding of the concepts, language and practice of organisations.

The book adopts an integrated and inter-disciplinary approach to each of the core areas and is written in a lively and accessible style. The content of each chapter is developed through a series of problem based assignments set in an organisational context, which collectively form the basis for active student centred learning. As a single, substantial information source, it provides an essential learning resource for all BTEC National students. The book has been designed to be used in conjunction with the 'Abbotsfield File — a business in action', the series of case studies also written by Callaghan and Ellison.

A free lecturer's manual is available from the publishers by colleges which adopt the book for student use.

ACKNOWLEDGEMENTS

The production of this book has involved the contributions of many people who all deserve our immense thanks. These include Denise Blenkhorn who helped with the business aspect of the project and with Kathryn Martin who typed the original manuscript. Sheila Callaghan and Lilias Smith helped with the administration and continually offered much needed encouragement. Particular thanks go to Wendy and Tony Matterson who read the drafts of the Finance Section and contributed invaluably by ensuring that it reflected current professional accountancy practice. Gillian Callaghan, Peter Miller and Bernard Callaghan spent many hours proofing the manuscript and considerably improved its style and clarity. Paul Henry's illustrations are an obvious testimony to his unique talent and imagination.

Thanks are also due to Dalgety plc, Birmingham City Council, Grand Metropolitan plc, London and Scottish Marine Oil plc, the BOC group and HMSO for the inclusion of their excellent examples of data presentation. Part of the book was originally written for the NALGO Correspondence Institute and we offer our thanks for the use of this material.

Our sincere gratitude goes to everyone at City Printers in Chester-le-Street. Specifically we must thank Dorothy Robson who typeset the book with her usual accuracy and good humour. Gary Henderson and Caroline White produced the artwork with skill and flair. Len Smiles cheerfully helped to print the book and Mildred Read put it together. Don Henderson provided help and most significantly, we must thank Allen Stoddart whose continued hard work and confidence in the project have been unequalled.

Finally we must apologise to our families and loved ones for neglecting them during the time it has taken to produce the book. Our thanks are but a small return for their patience and understanding.

Any errors or omissions that remain are the responsibility of the authors.

PC
TH
JE
JH
TG

Durham
August 1986

CONTENTS

PEOPLE IN ORGANISATIONS

THE ORGANISATION IN ITS ENVIRONMENT

People in Organisations

Chapter 1

PEOPLE AND ORGANISATIONS

THE CHARACTERISTICS OF HUMAN BEHAVIOUR

If you were asked to describe the main features that characterise the behaviour of human beings how would you respond? You might reply that the task is impossible because you cannot be sufficiently objective. You might say that the behaviour of mankind is simply too complex to reduce to a list of characteristics. Nevertheless, whilst recognising that all people possess their own individual behavioural, as well as physical characteristics, it is still possible to observe certain qualities and characteristics that mankind has consistently displayed from generation to generation. For instance it would be difficult to dispute the statement that man is highly social, inventive, warlike and artistic. The list could go on and on. Each behavioural trait is of course merely one component of a complex whole. Whether we are referring to an individual, or to an entire society, it is never accurate to select a single aspect of behaviour and present it as though it represents a complete and exclusive description. We might describe a friend as an extrovert, yet know that there are certain social situations he or she tries to avoid. We might hear it said of the Germans that they are hard working, or of the American that they are materialistic. Nevertheless we may know Germans or Americans who in no way correspond to such a broad generalisation of the character of their entire nation.

The fact is that generalisations, whether applied to Germans, or Londoners, women or black people, or any other group that can be given a simple label, always distort the reality which is the complexity of our social structures. Therefore they ought to be treated with caution. In fact the way individuals or groups of individuals behave is not always predictable. It is a complex combination of natural characteristics and developed responses. These developed or learned responses result from the specific environment in which people live and work. In many circumstances the environment is constantly changing. People have to adapt to such change if they are to integrate successfully within society. Change is implicit in all aspects of life, from the social to the economic, and the scientific to the political. Some changes can be resisted, but in the main change has an irresistable power about it. It is a process of evolution.

If we return to the question that was posed at the beginning of this chapter we might observe that, subject to the considerations introduced above, two further characteristics of human activity are the capacity to communicate and the desire to organise. The concept of man as a communicator is one which is readily apparent. The idea of man as an organiser is perhaps not so immediately obvious, yet a moment's reflection will reveal that man has an innate capacity for organising, and creating organisations. Social organisations hold societies together. Political organisations control them. Business organisations manage the use of their resources.

THE FORMATION OF ORGANISATIONS

Man is a social creature, generally choosing to live in groups or communities rather than lead an independant existence. Such communities are held together by common aims, interests or principles. If these change the community will invariably adapt. If they disappear altogether the community itself will probably disintegrate, its members perhaps reforming subsequently into new communities.

For a community to exist as a separate entity, it must develop a structure in which each member has an identifiable role, whether of a formal or informal kind. In this way the community acquires coherence, and may be regarded as an organised and distinct group. By this we mean that the individuals combine to form a more complex whole in which people are connected to each other through membership of the group. Whether people are conscious of it or not, their lives are dominated by their membership of a variety of groups or communities. For the majority of people the most immediate of these groups is the family. Then there are circles of friends and acquaintances. There are the clubs and societies that a person belongs to, the organisation that he or she works in, the local community — city, town or village — of which he or she is a part, and of course the much larger community he or she belongs to comprising all the individuals of a nation.

Indeed it is possible to go further and talk of membership of a broader community still, the EEC, of which our country, and hence we as individuals, are all members. The following observations can be made about membership of groups:

(a)   generally the larger the number of individuals that make up the group the less will be each individual's influence and control over it. In a family the parents will perform a dominant role in bringing up the children when they are young. But the same person in the role of an employee in a large organisation has far less influence over the operations of the organisation than over the running of the family's affairs;

(b)   membership of a group inevitably involves identifying the nature of an individual's role within it, that is the rights and responsibilities that go with membership;

(c)   the group will usually have a purpose for its existence. It has already been said that communities evolve because they possess communal aims and interests. For example the ECC has stated economic, political and, to a lesser extent, social objectives. A business organisation, whether it comprises two people operating as a partnership, or a multinational public limited company with thousands of employees, will always have a set of objectives. So while the purpose or rationale of the group will vary from one to the other, there must always be some kind of objective or the group will not survive;

(d)   the group will have a structure, in other words it will have an organised framework which holds it together. In the case of a business organisation the form this structure takes is of particular importance. If it is not suitable the organisation cannot operate efficiently or effectively. The need for a suitable organisational structure is examined in more detail later.

Thus it is man's nature to associate, and in the very act of associating it becomes necessary to produce organisations of one sort or another to meet the needs of man.

THE NEED FOR COMMUNICATIONS

It was pointed out earlier that communicating is a highly significant feature of human activity. It enables people to develop relationships, and is necessary in the formation of any kind of organisation. When communications and organisations are considered in terms of the relationship between them, it is not difficult to appreciate that an inadequate communications system hinders the success of the organisation in meeting its objectives. It may help to examine this relationship by means of an analogy between the organisation and the human body. The body, like other living things is made up a highly complex collection of individual components which are designed to work together in harmony. The human body is a product of evolution and has adapted to meet the environment in which it exists. People are clearly not identical. Differences occur that allow individuals to accommodate the wide range of climatic conditions in the inhabited parts of the world. Some racial groups have blood which has adapted to life in high altitudes, or skin colour to cope with extreme sunlight, or heavier layers of fat to withstand the cold. In the same way organisations adapt to cope with the specialised environments within which they have to work. A nuclear power station is not just superficially physically very different from a building society headquarters. It is also intrinsically different for the nature of its operations give rise to risks which are unique to it. To cope with these risks it has to develop specialised physical and administrative mechanisms.

Successful organisations are those which are able to adapt to their environment. The human body has many functions and capabilities. It can walk, run, talk, manipulate and observe. To achieve these actions commands must be given to the various organs and limbs which are capable of carrying them out. The commands come of course from the brain, and are passed as minute electric pulses through the nervous system. They are picked up by the limb or organ to which they are directed by the brain. In simple terms this is the communications network of the body. The system also works in reverse. Instructions received through the senses are passed back by the same route to the brain, where they are interpreted, and acted upon.

Exactly the same process is at work in an organisation. It too has a 'brain' made up of those responsible for controlling the activities of the organisation. The 'brain' may be the club committee, the board of directors of a company, or the councillors of a local authority. Decisions that are made at that level are then communicated to the appropriate part of the organisation to carry them out. When the board of directors decides that company spending needs to be reduced the message is passed to all the departments of the company. When the full council decides to implement a decision to build new council offices the relevant departments are informed. Once the instruction has been received it merely remains for it to be carried out by the department or individual concerned. However, as with the human body, failures of any part of the system of communication can have a marked effect upon an organisation's performance. This breakdown may originate within the mechanism by which messages are transferred, or with the recipients to whom the messages are directed, or even in the brain itself — those who control the organisation. Such possibilities are considered in more detail later.

TYPES OF BUSINESS ORGANISATIONS

In order to best examine how these breakdowns can occur, and how they can be remedied, it is first necessary to look briefly at the different types of business organisation. There are a number of methods of classifying business organisations. Probably the two most common ways are by reference to economic criteria, and by reference to legal status.

Economic Criteria

Here the organisation is being viewed in terms either of how it is financed, or what its stated objectives are. Thus a major classification of organisations using these criteria is into organisations in the public sector and those in the private sector. Essentially public sector organisations are those which are financed and controlled by the state. They may have a variety of objectives but often these will include providing some service or benefit to society. Private sector organisations are owned, financed and controlled by a private individual or groups of individuals. Their objective is usually to make profits. These distinctions are discussed in some detail in chapter 18.

Legal Status

The law places emphasis upon the procedure that has been followed for creating the organisation rather than the purpose for which it has been formed. Legally there are two important classifications to be aware of. Firstly, a distinction is drawn between corporate bodies, (that is registered companies and statutory corporations, such as local authorities and nationalised industries) and non-corporate bodies (called unincorporated associations). Secondly, an important distinction is made between private registered companies and public registered companies. These classifications are examined in more detail in chapter 18.

The reason why legal status is a relevant consideration in examining an organisation's communication system is that the law recognises certain rights and duties on the part of the individuals who control business organisations, and indeed on the part of the organisations themselves if they are corporate bodies. These rights and duties are important when considering an organisation's communications system since it is normally by using the system that they are carried out. If it does not work properly then legal obligations may be overlooked, resulting in consequences that range from contracts that cannot be enforced, claims for damages, fines and even imprisonment, and the dissolution of the business organisation. Two examples will illustrate this.

The Health and Safety at Work Act 1974 imposes a duty upon organisations to provide for the health and safety of their employees "as far as it is reasonably practicable". This involves developing a safety policy to operate throughout the organisation, supported by a set of procedures to ensure that the policy is effectively implemented. Safety representatives are appointed, a safety committee formed, accident report forms prepared, and the workforce informed of the arrangements. The consequences of an organisation failing to make these arrangements work effectively can be a fine. Ultimately power is available to the Health and Safety Executive to issue prohibition notices which have the effect of closing the whole or a part of the plant until specified safety precautions have been taken.

The Employment Protection (Consolidation) Act 1978 grants the right to all employees not to be unfairly dismissed. The Act sets out a number of grounds for dismissal. If any one of these grounds can be established to the satisfaction of an industrial tribunal, then the employer's dismissal of the employee is capable of being regarded as fair. But in every case the industrial tribunal must also be satisfied that the employer acted reasonably in dismissing the employee on the particular ground relied on. In employment it is common to find employees keeping poor working hours — arriving late or leaving early. One of the grounds for dismissal under the 1978 Act is misconduct and poor time keeping is normally regarded as misconduct. However it would generally be regarded by an industrial tribunal as being unreasonable of an employer to dismiss an employee on such grounds without first giving an oral and then a written warning that if the misconduct continues the employee will be dismissed. Thus for an employer to act successfully within the law it is vital to establish a system which is capable of dealing with staff who are guilty of misconduct in a way that ensures that the employer's view of the conduct is being effectively communicated to the employee concerned. So for instance if the employee was not made aware that bad timekeeping was regarded as misconduct and was not warned, the company would find it difficult to convince an industrial tribunal that the dismissal was fair.

The examples given above apply to all larger organisations, whether corporate or not. Sometimes the specific legal nature of an organisation places particular demands upon it in communication terms. For instance a partnership is required under certain circumstances to contain the names of the partners on all its business correspondence (letters, invoices, orders, receipts and written demands for payment), and display prominently in the business premises a notice containing its name, the name of all the partners and an address at which documents can be served on a partner. On the other hand a registered limited company has a public file kept on it, which the company is obliged to complete and keep up to date by supplying the Companies Registry with details of its internal rules (its Articles) its principal external features (the Memorandum of Association) and an annual statement of its financial affairs in the form of an annual return. A local authority is obliged to give public notice of its meetings, generally allow the public and the press access to its meetings and most specifically of all, to keep minutes of its meetings which are available to electors for inspection and copying.

Of course many of the legal demands placed upon organisations prompt the organisation to act in a way it would not necessarily voluntarily undertake. It may see them as an unnecessary and costly intrusion into its private affairs. Nevertheless the consequences of non compliance encourage it to comply.

ESTABLISHMENT AND MAINTENANCE OF A COMMUNICATIONS SYSTEM

In a sense legal constraints impose demands upon the communication system of an organisation. It is of course in the interests of any business to establish and maintain an effective communications system. Returning for a moment to the earlier analogy of the human body it will be clear that damage to the nervous system can reduce the responsiveness of the body to the orders from the brain. Where the damage is of a relatively minor kind, such as a broken arm or leg, it will be possible to adopt short term measures to cope — taking time off work, obtaining the assistance of family and friends to cook, shop or do the washing. Where the damage is of a major kind, causing a permanent breakdown of some part of the system, such as a paralysis, then measures must be taken to accommodate in the long term the changes that this brings about.

In terms of an organisation, failures in the communication system may be of both the minor and the major kind. For instance it may be that as a result of key personnel or equipment being out of action on a temporary basis the system suffers an information blockage; perhaps accounts are not being prepared, or material cannot be photocopied, or letters are not being answered. However when the member of staff returns to work, or the machinery is repaired, the system reverts to its normal operation, and the damage is not significant. But where the damage is of a major kind the effects on the organisation can be devastating. A couple of examples will illustrate this.

Firstly, suppose a large organisation has an unionised workforce. The management is firmly of the opinion that unions in general are against the best interests of the company. The unions on the other hand regard the management as reactionary and unwilling to allow worker participation. In such circumstances there is a serious danger that the entrenched views of either side will make it more difficult to operate the organisation. There could be a total breakdown in labour relations. This will rapidly lead to industrial action and loss of production.

Secondly suppose a business becomes aware that many of its competitors are diversifying their product range. They are also using new methods of production that are less labour intensive. These place heavy reliance upon new technology and technological processes. The newspaper industry provides a good example of a major switch in recent times from old traditional working methods and equipment to new technology and working practices. Despite the business being aware of the changes that are taking place, its own organisation structure is such that:

(a) staff have no adequate opportunity to express their views about the need for change;

(b) information received by the organisation from external sources describing the changes taking place within the industry are not acted upon because they are not understood or do not pass to the appropriate personnel;

(c) monitoring and evaluation procedures within the business are non existant, or not adequate to signal to the business that it is becoming increasingly non competitive.

Gradually, through a combination of factors that collectively represent an inadequate communications structure within the business, it is becoming increasingly ineffective in the market place, its market share will drop, and it will eventually go out of business. In the labour relations example the parallel with the human body is the brain instructing the body to go to work, or do the shopping, and the body being unwilling to respond. In the example of the business failing to adapt to change, the cause is not so much unwillingness as physical inability. It is like the brain telling the legs to run when they are hardly fit enough to walk, or perhaps the senses simply not appreciating the messages they are receiving.

ESTABLISHING A COMMUNICATIONS SYSTEM

It follows that all organisations must address themselves to the design and introduction of a system of communication which is responsive to the particular needs of the organisation, and which recognises the organisational structures within which it should operate. When a business is being set up it may well be that considerations of establishing a communications network within it take a secondary place to the creation of departments or sections to fulfil specific functions in the organisation, for example a production department, or sales department and an accounts department.

To build a business around a communications network would be a case of letting the tail wag the dog. However as is indicated earlier if the organisation structure does not pay heed to the vital role of communications within it, it is unlikely to operate satisfactorily. To recap, the communication process involves three distinct components:

(a)   the individual or group giving the instructions or information;

(b)   the individual or group receiving it; and

(c)   the mechanism by which the transfer takes place.

Communications and information systems are considered in more detail in chapter 3. For the present it is useful to identify some of the main considerations to be borne in mind when examining a communications system against the backdrop of organisational structures.

(a)   The Composition of the Organisation

In nearly all organisations a division is drawn between those who manage (i.e. the managers or 'management') and those who carry out the instructions of the management (the workforce). Only in the smallest organisations is it likely that such a division will not exist. In addition however there are the owners of the organisation. The owners may also be the managers, for instance the directors of a family business run as a private limited company will also act as its directors, but in large organisations the owners may be quite distinct from the managers, but having the ultimate power to control them. This is the case in a public limited company. The mechanisms that enable the owners to exert control over the mangers, and which enable the managers to report to the owners on the performance of the business are an important feature of the communications system. In the case of public limited companies it is at company meetings, notably the annual general meeting, that the interaction between owners and managers is most pronounced.

Local authorities provide an alternative model in terms of their composition. They are not owned in the sense in which organisations in the private sector are owned. They are controlled by the elected members who sit as councillors. The members decisions are carried out by the officers and staff of the authority. The members themselves are accountable to the electorate; the ratepayers who have voted them into office. It is important that there is effective communication between these groups. For instance when a committee of the authority makes a decision through the passing of a resolution, the decision is recorded and the responsibility for its implementation is transferred to the appropriate department. In the department a senior officer — the local authority 'manager', instructs staff to take the necessary action required by the council. This in turn may involve communicating with the inhabitants of the district served by the council; for example publishing details of a new by-law or notifying individual owners that a planning application has been approved or rejected.

(b) The Aims and Objectives of an Organisation

All organisations have aims and objectives, even if they are not explicitly stated. It is for instance implicit that an organisation will do all it can to remain in existence, other than in those cases where it has been formed for a specific purpose which has now been fulfilled. The general desire to survive is not restricted solely to private and public sector trading organisations. The abolition of the metropolitan counties in April 1986 was preceded by strenuous attempts on the part of these councils, both inside and outside Parliament, to remain in operation. Aims and objectives are set:

(a)   by senior managers of organisations; and

(b)   by Parliament, in the case of state owned industries.

The failure to communicate aims and objectives to the workforce can produce the following effects:

(a)   employees are unaware of the broader context within which they are working. Suppose management in an organisation which is threatened with closure devises a survival package. This aims to hold down wage rises for the next three years with the objective of avoiding redundancies, making the business more cost effective, and anticipating a growth in demand by that time. If the workforce is denied access to this information, and is merely informed that the company is not prepared to accept an increase in its wage bill, much greater resentment is likely than if management provides a reasoned account of its longer term strategy.

(b)   employees are not encouraged to identify as essential components of the organisation. This really is an extension of the point made above. Companies that convey the importance of the individual to the work of the organisation as a whole, generally enhance motivation, but inevitably must in so doing divulge the aims being pursued by the company. These may be production figures for the next month, or year; statements concerning product quality; or perhaps the desire to improve and extend the product range. An indirect way of communicating the last example to the workforce is by means of a system which encourages staff to suggest ways of improving and developing products and systems using suggestion schemes, or discussion groups.

One of the major causes of conflict between management and workforce is the lack of a well established set of objectives for the working group (i.e. the whole of the organisation or section of it) to achieve.

A method of attempting to overcome this management by objectives, that is a systematic approach to management which involves fixing objectives for the organisation and the individual. The use of this approach involves managers in producing an action plan which should include:

(i)   establishing the objectives of the business in every significant area of its operation;

(ii)   assigning these objectives to individuals, providing them with a time scale and quantifiable targets;

(iii)   agreeing action to be taken. This involves the manager discussing his objectives with his staff, and vice versa;

(iv)   carrying out the agreed action; and

(v)   reviewing the performance of the action.

One of the benefits of management by objectives is that it can significantly improve the system of internal communications. The objectives of organisations are considered in some detail in chapters 7 and 18.

(c)   The Management Structure of the Organisation

Management structures vary from organisation to organisation, but one of the basic principles of good management is the need to lay down and clearly define lines of authority. This has the effect of identifying the relationship between superiors and inferiors and should ensure that individuals are clear as to whom they are accountable.

Large and small scale organisations

By now it should be clear that in the working life of any organisation communications perform an indispensible role in maintaining its effectiveness by acting as the mechanism enabling the components part of the structure to knit together as a unified whole. It is of course simple advice to tell managers that the organisation they control will only run as efficiently as the communication network permits. It is much harder to advise on an appropriate type of network to suit the needs of the organisation, or to diagnose a lack of efficiency as the result of a failure of communications. Thus a high level of absenteeism in a particular department may be recorded as being due to illness. The true cause may be a reluctance on the part of staff to keep a good attendance record because they find their section head an intolerable superior. The superior may lack the social skills necessary to cope with the job. Perhaps he or she is rude, or arrogant, or patronising or excessively authoritarian in dealing with the staff. Management however may not be aware of the communications breakdown in the section. Instead they will seek some rational explanation for the absenteeism. They may believe that the cause is the physically or mentally demanding nature of the work being performed or just the general poor health of people in that section. In such a case the underlying problem — a superior whose capacity to deal with others is poor — becomes compounded by the inability of management to recognise it. This in its turn suggests an inadequate supply of information to the managers.

The Factors affecting the Suitability of a Communications System

What then are the factors a manager should be advised to pay attention to, when considering the suitability of the communications system operating in his or her organisation? The most obvious is the scale of the organisation. The scale of an organisation can be a reference to:

(a)   its annual turnover or the level of revenue which is a measure of its financial importance;

(b)   its physical size. The buildings or the plant that it uses will reflect the nature of the work it carries out and the productive capacity involved. An aluminium smelter demands a substantial plant size to accommodate it. If the existing plant is running at full capacity, but is still not meeting demand the plant must be physically expanded if the demand is to be met. A large scale organisation of this type may be compared with an organisation that has a similar financial turnover but requires a much smaller physical site to do so. A good example is provided by the high technology "sunrise" industries producing computer software and hardware.

(c)   its workforce. Some commercial and industrial activities are highly labour intensive, which means they employ large numbers of staff, whilst others can operate with very low staffing levels. A useful comparison is provided by organisations in the energy sector. Despite widespread reductions in its labour force in recent years British Coal (formerly the National Coal Board) still relies heavily upon manpower to operate its mines. There have been substantial improvements in coal extraction methods as the industry becomes more mechanised. However each ton of coal produced still needs face workers and supporting staff. The Central Electricity Generating Board on the other hand produces electricity at atomic power stations manned by small numbers of skilled staff. This is achieved through the use of automated high technology control and monitoring systems which merely require supervision by power station staff. In the non-industrial sectors similar comparisons can be drawn. In the Health Service for example the number of administrators has been reduced, as computerised systems have been introduced, yet the patient care carried out by the medical staff remains labour intensive. Technological developments in that field have helped to improve the standards of health care, rather than reduce staff numbers.

The scale of an organisation is important because it is an indication, in crude terms, of the amount of communications activity which will take place. It would be misleading to suggest that there is a precise relationship between the type of communications network appropriate to an organisation and the financial, physical or human scale of its operations. It is nonetheless obvious that an organisation employing 200 staff requires a system of control such as a personnel department which would clearly not be needed by a business employing 20 staff. Similarly an organisation with a turnover of £5 million a year is likely to need a larger financial department than one with a turnover of £50,000 a year, even if both use essentially similar financial and accounting systems.

One further point may be added on the topic of scale. This compares the public and private sectors. Organisations in the private sector range from one man businesses occupying a single room and having a small income to massive multi-nationals. The public sector on the other hand includes few small scale organisations. Even the smallest local authorities in England and Wales employ over 100 staff.

THE STRUCTURE AND OPERATION OF THE ORGANISATION

In addition to the scale of the business enterprise the management must also pay attention to:

(a) the structure of the organisation; and

(b) its operating methods.

(a) The Structure of the Organisation

There are a number of overlapping structures in any organisation. There is the financial structure, the legal structure and the organisational structure. Of these the financial and legal structures are dealt with in chapters 12 and 18 in more detail, and here we can simply note that both have implications for the communications system for instance the process of holding meetings in registered companies is regulated by statute, and thus such companies are obliged by their legal structure to conduct their business according to externally imposed rules. The organisational structure of a business is concerned with the co-ordination and grouping of related activities to achieve the organisation's objectives.

The successful business will have divided its activities into a logical sequence and have allocated each such division sufficient resources to adequately perform its function. The responsibilities for each section of the business must be clearly defined and the authority to undertake such responsibilities must be delegated to the appropriate section. The overall organisation must ensure that there is co-ordination between the various aspects of the business and that clear lines of communication have been established. However the organisational structure must retain sufficient flexibility to allow it to adapt to change.

The need for a formal organisation structure is to ensure that each individual is able to identify his or her position within the organisation. Employees should be aware of their own responsibilities, to whom they are directly accountable and for whom they bear a managerial or supervisory role. A further advantage of a formal structure is that it should allow management to develop areas of specialism and expertise within the organisation.

Almost certainly informal structure will also develop within an organisation as a result of personal relationships, work patterns and practical expediency. Such informal structures are to be encouraged unless they conflict with the efficient operation of the business.

Most organisations have a pyramid structure in which authority and responsibility extend downwards in a hierarchical pattern. Senior management make the executive and policy decisions. They have the overall responsibility for the success or failure of such policies and have the authortity vested in them to allow them to carry this out. As you move down the pyramid, status, responsibility and authority decreases.

Most organisations have a pyramid structure

It is usually possible to identify two forms of authority in an organisation:- i) line; and ii) functional. Line authority is the direct relationship between a superior and his or her subordinates. It is shown on an organisation chart by a vertical line indicating direct authority. Functional authority indicates the responsibility for specialist functions in an organisation. So for example the personnel department is responsible for that sphere of the organisation's activities relating to the workforce in all of its departments. Organisation charts are an attempt to record the formal structure of the business showing some of the relationships, the downward flow of authority and responsibility and the main lines of communication. They have the advantage of forcing senior management to clearly define organisational relationships. They are a useful introduction to the organisation for outsiders, particularly new employees, and they can form a starting point from which management can initiate change or evaluate the strengths and weaknesses of the organisation. However they can quickly become out of date as personnel and operational relationships change and they often introduce a degree of rigidity into the organisation as people feel that they are constrained by the defined limits of their position in the organisational chart.

In terms of both line and functional authority the simplicity or complexity of the organisation chart will be a reflection of the scale of the organisation. The organisation charts given below provide a comparison between two private sector organisations, one a professional partnership, the other a large private limited company.

An organisation chart for a professional partnership

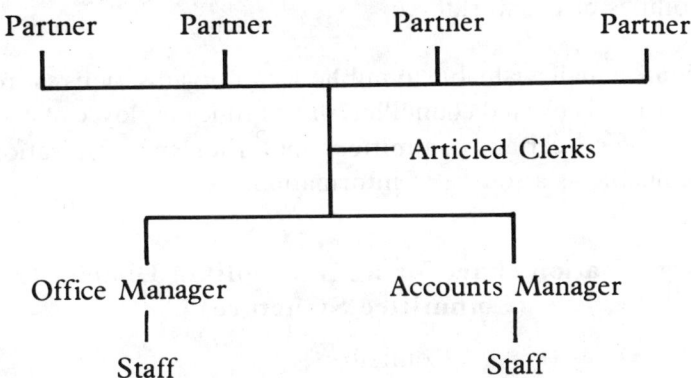

An organisation chart for a large private limited company (*Southern Electronics*)

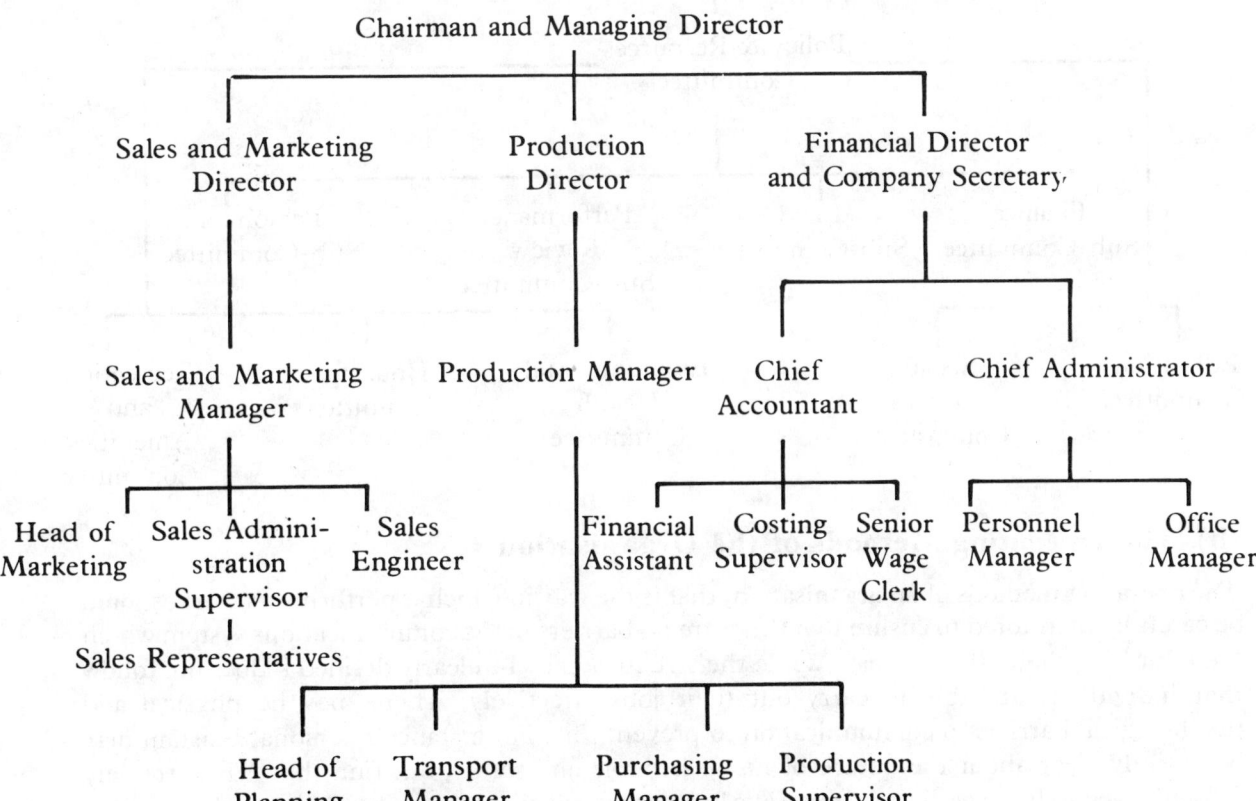

The value of an organisation chart is that:

 (a) the task of preparing it enables the individual components of the organisation to be brought under review;

 (b) an assessment can be made of the relationship of each component part of the organisation to the others;

 (c) management must consider the authority required by individuals within the structure to carry out their responsibilities adequately;

 (d) it assists staff in locating their role and status within the organisation.

Thus organisation charts, by identifying lines of authority and responsibility, can be of great assistance in the improvements of the communication system by managers. They may for example reveal that an existing structure is such that it inhibits change and development in the organisation, perhaps where it becomes apparent that research and development work is spread too widely and is not co-ordinated. As mentioned earlier the structure should be carefully monitored to ensure that it does not become out dated and begin to introduce rigidity into the roles and responsibilities of the workforce.

Organisation charts are equally valuable to public sector organisations as are those in the private sector. For instance a newly elected councillor, or full time employee of a local authority with a responsibility for servicing certain committees may find an organisation chart of the kind included below invaluable as a source of information.

**Organisation chart for a Metropolitan District Council
(Committee Structure)**

Council

Policy & Resources Committee

Finance Sub-Committee Land Sub-Committee Performance Review Sub-Committee Personnel Sub-Committee

Education Committee Social Services Committee Environmental Health Committee Housing Committee Recreation and Amenities Committee

(b) The Operating Methods of the Organisation

The operating methods of an organisation, that is the way in which it performs its work, should be carefully monitored to ensure that there are no barriers in the communications system which are inhibiting their effectiveness. While the structure may be clearly defined it does not follow that individuals are able to carry out their jobs effectively. There may be physical and psychological barriers to communication to prevent this. For instance a personal assistant may be entirely clear about the nature of his or her role and status, but find that it is extremely difficult even to liaise with their boss. The boss is never available when needed, and the assistant finds that the job cannot be adequately performed because he or she lacks authority to make decisions in the absence of the boss. There are many barriers to communication and they are considered in chapter 3.

Particular attention should be paid to the support systems of the organisation. These make up a sub-system of the broader communications system operating within the organisation, and they include administrative, clerical and technical services. It may help to identify the types of support each of these services can provide.

(i) Administrative Support

Administration is an aspect of management. A manager is essentially someone responsible for directing the workforce in carrying out their work so as to ensure that as far as possible the policies of the organisation are being met. Managers often have specific responsibilities, as can be seen in the company organisation chart shown earlier. Without people to co-ordinate and control the work of the organisation, it could not operate adequately. Not surprisingly administrators are a part of all medium and large scale organisations. They may even have a role in smaller ones as was seen in the partnership organisation chart.

(ii) Clerical Support

Clerical support covers such jobs as filing, typing, handling mail, reproducing information, and switchboard work. All these tasks may be performed by a single office or department, usually called a General Administrative Office, or just a General Office. In practice this could be just a room or perhaps a suite of rooms or even various 'nooks and crannies' located within a building. When we think about 'the office' we all usually have some set ideas about what activities are carried out there.

The major activity of all offices is to act as a communications centre. By this is meant the place which is responsible for coping with information of all kinds. This information could be verbal such as a telephone call or in writing such as in the form of a letter. In larger organisations, staff working in such offices may be given titles which reflect their specific role such as telephonist, receptionist, secretary, director of administration, filing clerk, clerical officer, reprographics operator, typist or clerk. In smaller organisations office staff are usually engaged upon the same type of work function, but often have to perform more than one of these tasks without being given a formal title. They may simply be described as 'office workers'.

The function of all offices is to deal with information. The distinguishing feature between different offices are the ways in which each organisation decides to arrange its formation and its communications functions. Since there are many different types of businesses it follows that the clerical procedures an organisation chooses to operate should be purposely developed to cope with its own particular needs. This involves establishing a process whereby a continuous flow of data is constantly being dealt with. This process can be broken down into separate components. Consequently in relation to the processing of information the procedures of the office can be identified in the following stages:

The Collection of Source data

This involves the office collecting together information it has received from many different sources; both from outside the organisation and also from within it. At this stage all these separate pieces of information are termed the 'source data' because they have been merely received and nothing has yet happened to them. When source data is received into the office, staff need to register or reference the contents so that appropriate action can be taken, where necessary. Registering all data is important so that there is always on hand, in permanent form, a record of data received. Once recorded the information needs to be stored safely. This involves operating an appropriate storage system whereby data can be quickly accessed when, and if, it needs to be worked on.

The Processing of Source Data

Data is accessed from storage so that it may be processed. 'Processing' is merely a term used to describe the kinds of operations which might then take place, before it becomes technically known as information.

The act of processing may involve merely sorting out data, or it may involve the need for some form of action to be undertaken. It may be that new data needs to be compared with old data, or that some kind of analysis has to be carried out. How the information is produced obviously depends upon what it is needed for. For example data may be translated onto forms or documents, statistics may be required, reports or summaries may be needed. When data is already in the form of information it may be that it merely needs to be re-stored for reference purposes; or that a means of distribution is required so that further actions/decisions can be taken.

The Distribution of Information

Information (processed data) may need to be transmitted to a particular destination. Those who are to receive the information could be located inside or outside the organisation. Such a distribution may involve the production of simply one copy of the information of it might be that multiple copies are made. The information could be produced in a number of different forms; written, typed, printed or by using a computer-based medium.

The information and communications function should be considered together and in so doing the role of documentation in transmitting data/information within an organisation can be examined. Written material, and especially the use of forms are the focus of any organisation's communications system.

If the purpose of such a flow of documentation is categorised within an organisation then its objectives would be:

    (i)   to pass on information;

    (ii)   to pass on instructions;

    (iii)   to gather information;

    (iv)   to record information;

    (v)   to conduct business.

An immediate response to the question 'why are forms used?' would possibly be that they save time and effort and as such are a quick and convenient way of fulfilling the five objectives outlined above. Once a form has been designed, a standard procedure can then be adopted. This means that the same form is always available for use by staff.

The use of such documentation has certain distinctive advantages. Standardised forms ensure that the same information is sought every time, as the headings on the form act as a prompt for answers. However there are two drawbacks here. One is that in the design of the form there may be a weakness in that there are insufficient or inaccurate headings. This can mean that not all the information needed is incorporated by the person filling in the form. The second drawback is that when a person completes the form he or she may be restricted to responding only to those headings given. Despite these problems, forms do ensure that information is collected in a uniform way, for instance headings are in the same place on every form. This makes it very much easier to collate and compare information once it is obtained. The use of forms is further considered in chapter 5.

The procedures adopted by an 'office' to carry out the information/communication functions are again dependent upon its nature and departmental structure. An organisation may adopt exclusively manual systems which would mean that all these functions are operated by individuals using the minimal amount of machinery. Therefore upon receipt into the organisation, data would be recorded, processed, stored and made ready for distribution and passed on within the office, all by hand. It is unusual for organisations to operate totally manual systems. In many smaller organisations it is usual to find a combination of manual and mechanical procedures. This means that the organisation performs its operations using basic equipment such as type-writers, telephones, calculators and some form of 'copying' machine. Other organisations, whether they are large more 'forward-thinking', or merely because of necessity, may have introduced electric or electronic systems to aid information/communication flow. The significance of electronic procedures will be stressed throughout all of the sections of this book.

Storing and Recording Information

To operate efficiently an organisation will need an effective filing system. The system must ensure that:

(i) there is a suitable place for the storage of records;

(ii) that these records are kept safely;

(iii) that data/information is easy to locate, select and retrieve.

If the recording and storage of data is considered in a wider context, it is important to realise that each organisation will choose those systems best suited to its own individual needs. Remember also that there is a wide variety of equipment on the market and it is constantly being improved and up-dated by manufacturers, to meet both new demands and competition from rival suppliers.

It may be helpful to dispel a common myth. If an organisation uses 'manual' systems then it tends to attract the label of being 'old fashioned', especially when measured against businesses installing new information technology systems. An organisation may in fact judge that its existing systems are more than adquate to meet its needs, so why the need for change? Perhaps the company feels that it is too small to justify technological change. More significantly perhaps it believes that the cost entailed in introducing electronic systems would be prohibitive, both in terms of buying new machinery and in releasing staff to undertake training courses. Many businesses appreciate their lack of expertise when considering the introduction of new systems and so consequently opt to stay with those systems which have been tried and tested and proved to be reliable. Neither must it be over-looked that staff may view with concern any move away from their own traditional working practices.

There are a range of systems available for recording and storing information. They include:

(a) **Manual Systems:** these rely upon different types of filing equipment, and may use different methods for performing the filing work. Papers, letters, documents, plans and other types of material to be filed can be organised by using alphabetic, numerical, geographical, subject and chronological arrangements. In any filing system whatever the methods and equipment used it is essential that the system is simple to operate, so that relevant information can be accessed by the users of the system quickly. It should also be remembered that a system that is simple to operate for those familiar to it may be difficult for the uninitiated to make much sense of. Producing a filing manual may help to overcome this. In addition the following points should be borne in mind. The system should ensure that:

(i) attention is paid to the whole filing process. This involves the way in which materals for filing is collected (perhaps on a weekly basis from individual departments); the way in which it is examined to ensure it has been released for filing and determine under which heading it should be filed (a process known as indexing); whether cross referencing is necessary, in other words the possibility of the paper being searched for under more than one heading; the accurate filing of material, for many hours can be involved in futile searches for incorrectly filed material; the transfer of material when the transfer date, if any, has been reached. It may be for instance that after a certain time departmental files are transferred to a centralised filing system; the disposal of material when appropriate.

The storage of material that no further reference is ever likely to be made to simply wastes space, thus files often contain a date after which they can be destroyed. Confidential waste should be shredded.

(ii)   all papers on the same subject should be filed together, and the file maintained as a complete record. This means that it should contain, in addition to correspondence and other business communications, records of important telephone conversations and discussions.

(iii)   the files should be maintained in a good physical condition. An inappropriate method of storage, or heavy use of a file can cause physical deterioration.

(iv)   access to files should be restricted to authorised staff, and only authorised staff should be permitted to carry out the initial filing work.

(v)   the system should use a mechanism for ensuring that files or parts of files which are removed from it are charged out to the user, so that it is possible to trace a file that has not been returned.

Among the different types of filing equipment the following are the most common:

vertical filing: using filing cabinets, which contain files in drawers. It is common to find that each drawer uses a suspended file, which is a continuous chain of pockets running the length of the drawer. This system avoids individual files falling into the bottom of the drawer, and makes access easier if the drawer has not been overfilled.

horizontal filing: using cabinets which are low but wide. Horizontal filing is used mainly for storing drawings and plans.

lateral or open shelf filing: in which the filing unit is similar to a bookcase, enabling files to be placed side by side along the shelves. This system is useful where box files are maintained by the organisation.

rotary filing: using a circular unit of varying height and circumference which can be rotated by the user to quickly gain access to a file. The wedge shaped spaces within these units make them ideal for storing book files and ring binders.

An efficient, effective and economic filing system is essential to any organisation, for the information it contains is the stored memory of the organisation.

(b)   Photographic Systems: usually these involve photographing papers and documents and transferring them onto film (for example 8 mm) using a microfilmer, hence this system is known as microfilming. The film is stored in round metal containers and can be accessed by viewing it through a scanner which can select individual frames. The scanner may be able to project a full sized image onto a screen.

In libraries, microfiche systems are used as a method of storing information, as an alternative to card indexing systems. A viewing machine is able to present the fiches (large plastic sheets containing closely printed and highly detailed information) on a screen, and the user is able to obtain information by scanning each individual fiche using a control lever across a reference grid. Microfiche has found application in other areas as well as libraries. For instance garages use such systems to locate individual parts for the repair of motor vehicles.

(c)   Electronic Systems: these are being used increasingly as the most versatile and cost effective method of storing information, although the application of computer based information systems goes well beyond the mere storage of information. Information technology is considered in chapters 4 and 20 and here a brief summary of the equipment used and its application will suffice.

In an office the item of equipment likely to create the greatest impact is the word processor. A word processing system contains four basic components:

    (i)   a keyboard and a display unit, for use by the operator;

    (ii)   a printer, which can produce a printed copy of the information called 'hard copy' (letters, documents, financial statements and such like) which is fed into it using the keyboard;

    (iii)   the internal memory; and

    (iv)   the text storage media.

Modern processors are capable of dealing not only with the use of characters for storage or retrieval (i.e. words and numbers) but also all types of data for a range of processing purposes. Such mini-computers are now available at low cost.

The applications of computer based information systems provide the clearest statement as to why they have revolutionised administrative and clerical work over the past few years. Using the system standard letters and documents can be prepared, stored, retrieved and amended as appropriate. No longer does a typist have to laboriously type over and over again the same letter or contract. In addition the system has a data-base which is really a sophisticated file stored magnetically on tapes or disks. Not only can such a system contain large quantities of information (the data) in a compact form, but it can also enable people to access the data base and rapidly extract from it information according to different permutations or sequences. An example may help to explain this. Suppose a data-base in a large organisation contains details of thousands of people including their sex, age, date of birth, income, number of dependents and so on. Using a computer facility it becomes possible to obtain information on, say, the number of men between the ages of 40 and 45 who have more than two dependants and are earning less than £10,000 per year. Using traditional manual methods to extract this information would be very time consuming, but with the assistance of a computer data base the task becomes relatively simple. To assist in the task of extracting information in this way, information retrieval packages are available. These are standard programs written in computer language.

THE COMMUNICATION SYSTEM IN OPERATION

We can conclude this examination of the relationship between the structure of an organisation and the communication system operating with it by briefly tracing the process involved in employing staff and the implications this has for the communications network. Obviously employing people is only one of many tasks involved in business operations, but it serves as a useful example because it provides a clear illustration of how far communications infiltrate processes. Large organisations, structured on functional lines will have a personnel department responsible for all staffing matters. The communication aspects of the employment of a new member of staff are likely to emerge in the following sequence:

    (i)   a department identifies a vacancy and notifies the personnel officer of the details of the vacancy;

    (ii)   a job advertisement is prepared by the personnel department in accordance with the details provided. The advertisement probably follows a 'house style'. Decisions must be made on whether national or local advertisements are needed, and the possibility of approaching the local employment register and job centres to identify likely applicants who are available for work;

(iii)   enquiries are received and application forms are sent out. Care should be given to the design of the forms. They should be simple to understand, and provide the organisation with the information it requires in advance to produce a short list. Information about the organisation, and a job description should accompany the application form. It may also be wise to provide details of conditions of service;

(iv)   appropriate staff meet to produce a short list. A representative of the appropriate department will be involved together with a representative of the personnel department;

(v)   the shortlisted applicants are notified of the time, date and place of the interview. Arrangements must be made to appoint and brief the interview panel;

(vi)   the interviews are held. The panel should be aware of the social skills involved in conducting an interview. For example interviewees should be put at their ease as far as possible, and the panel members should encourage interviewees to give of their best.

(vii)   a decision is made on the basis of the interviews as to the appropriate interviewee for the job. The interviewees are notified of the outcome of the interviews;

(viii)   the successful applicant is told when to start work, who to report to, and where to report. A contract of employment is prepared and signed by both sides;

(ix)   any additional information relevant to the new starter is provided — for instance details of an induction programme, health and safety procedures, and so on.

The effective integration of a suitable person for the job into the work of the organisation depends upon the quality of the process identified above.

ASSIGNMENT — THE ORGANISATION

Choose an organisation with which you are familiar. This could be the organisation you work for, or your local authority, or the college you are studying at.

TASKS

1. Collect any available information that describes the structure of your chosen organisation, and from this produce an organisation chart displaying either the line authority within the organisation or its committee structure.

2. Investigate the operation of the communications system within your chosen organisation, to enable you to produce an information sheet for distribution to all the staff of the organisation, which describes:

   (a) the method used by the organisation for receiving and storing data;

   (b) the system of administrative and clerical support it operates; and

   (c) the method it uses for distributing information.

DEVELOPMENTAL TASK

3. Prepare some outline notes on the material you have produced under task 2 that you could use to present a short talk. The talk would be given to other members of your group, and would:

   (a) describe the administrative system operated by your organisation; and

   (b) introduce your ideas on how the system might be improved.

ASSIGNMENT — SOUTHERN ELECTRONICS' INDUCTION PROGRAMME

You work for Southern Electronics, a large electronics manufacturing company employing over 400 people at its main plant. The organisation chart for the company can be found earlier in the chapter. For some time it has been felt by the Personnel Director that new starters employed in the administrative area of the organisations work receive an inadequate introduction to the activities of the organisation.

The issue has been raised at a Board Meeting and the Personnel Director has passed on to you the memorandum contained below:

SOUTHERN ELECTRONICS LTD.

MEMORANDUM

From: Personnel Director

To: Personnel Assistant

Date: 13 October 19xx

Ref: Induction Programme

At a Board meeting held on 12 October 19xx it was resolved that, "The Personnel Director be instructed to prepare a one day induction programme to be compulsorily attended by all new administrative staff joining the company from 1 January 19xx."

I have a number of ideas as to the form this programme could take, but I would like you to provide me with your own thoughts. Please draft some suitable material and submit it to me for my consideration.

TASKS

1. Draw up a one day programme, structured to provide a new starter with an opportunity to examine the physical and organisational structure of the organisation.

2. Prepare an information sheet that could be given to new staff at the end of their induction programme, providing them with:

    (a) a statement of the company's communication policy;

    (b) an outline of how grievance procedures are dealt with by the company;

    (c) the sports, recreation and leisure facilities provided by the company;

DEVELOPMENTAL TASK

3. Prepare a discussion document which examines whether induction programmes have any value for new employees, or the organisation they work for.

Chapter 2

ORGANISATIONS AND COMMUNICATIONS

FORMS OF COMMUNICATION

One of the most striking characteristics of human behaviour is the extent of man's ability to communicate. Equally notable is the diversity of the methods used to communicate.

BODY LANGUAGE

Our facial expressions indicate our emotions, demonstrating happiness, boredom, anger and pain. Our whole bodies often express our feelings and so we physically distance ourselves from people who we regard with disapproval. Similarly we draw closer and become attentive to those we like. The way a person stands can express dejection or confidence; folded arms are an indication that someone is not at ease. Hands and fingers are highly expressive instruments for displaying our views. They may display gestures of welcome and friendliness as well as disgust and contempt.

All these forms of communication are a type of language usually called non-verbal communication or more normally 'body language'. Whilst this form of expression often comes from a conscious effort at representing ourselves to others in a chosen way, sometimes people are largely unaware of the messages they are communicating. In the same way it is possible to obtain a very distinct impression of someone else's view of another person, even though they have attempted to disguise their true feelings. Everyone is aware of having met somebody, often at a social gathering, who superficially is friendly and interested, but who we feel is merely putting on an act. These feelings can often cause us confusion, bearing in mind that we have no concrete evidence to support our intuition.

In fact all people behave in this artificial way from time to time, presenting what is called a "public face", which may bear little resemblance to what they are actually like. For instance at an interview we will try to create an image of being confident and calm, probably the last things we are actually feeling. We may also behave physically in ways we believe are appropriate to our position at work. For instance we may let the boss out of the lift first, even though it would be easier to get out first ourselves.

Like other languages, body language can be ambiguous. The smile of a colleague may be one of genuine warmth at seeing us; it might also be the self-satisfied expression of someone who knows that he has just been promoted in preference to us. Like other languages it can also be misinterpreted, and sometimes simply not understood at all.

ORAL COMMUNICATION

As well as communicating in gesture, we also communicate orally. The range of oral communication is enormous. The English language for example contains hundreds of thousands of words. Thus, through speech, individuals communicating with each other can attain levels of

. . . *'body language'* . . .

awareness quite impossible simply using body language. Speech, in the sense of a common oral language shared between people, enables complex ideas to be tangibly expressed and discussed. Through such dialogue man has attempted to understand himself and his physical environment.

Although the absence of speech would not prevent us from communicating effectively by other means, for most people talking is the most comfortable method of expression. It is immediate, it provides an infinitely variable range of choices to convey all our messages, and of course it is rapid. How often have we heard it said, in response to a particular problem, "if only I could get to talk to him, I'm sure we could sort it out." How common is it to find that talks are arranged between two sides in a disagreement as the method of sorting out differences; unions and employers, to settle wage demands and employment conditions, nations with other nations to discuss economic strategies and more arms control. Even our system of government, the Parliamentary system, reflects the significance of discussion and debate, for the word 'Parliament' means a place for speaking. Clearly we have an inherited belief in the value of oral communication.

WRITTEN COMMUNICATION

The final method of communicating which we need to examine is written communication. Strictly speaking, writing is the use of physical symbols to represent words. Words are the sounds which make up speech. But this definition can be broadened to include other forms of physical representation, such as diagrams, graphs and charts; in other words all types of visual representation. All forms of numerical representation can be included under this heading as well.

It is said to be man's ability to pass the accumulated knowledge of the past from one generation to the next by means of written sources that that has brought us to our present state of economic, social and technological development. It is certainly true that the technological achievement of sending men to the moon and controlling nuclear energy could not have occurred by passing on the enormous body of scientific knowledge through word of mouth. This would be physically impossible. But it is equally the case that these developments, together with most other aspects of the social and scientific environment would not have been possible without man's capacity for organisation.

It is these twin themes of communication and organisations which this chapter examines.

THE IMPORTANCE OF INFORMATION

What is the purpose of communicating? The answer seems to be to impart information. Each form of communication mentioned so far has as its underlying purpose the transfer of information, for instance our emotional condition, or the financial condition of the organisation we work for. Transferring information is the way we pass on knowledge to others. Information is the raw material of communication. Effective communication is therefore realised when knowledge being transferred is received and understood by whoever it is being directed at.

Receiving information is a function of physical transmission, thus the radio stops broadcasting whilst the transmitter is being repaired. Understanding is an activity of the mind, involving a comprehension of the information. You may know that the theory of relativity is expressed by the equation of $e = mc^2$, but have absolutely no perception of what this actually means. Of course we do not always need to understand information that comes our way in order to do our jobs. A person employed in an industrial process may know that the machine must be switched off if certain faults develop and respond to this task admirably, whilst having no understanding of what the cause of the fault is. Generally, however, it is an asset to understand rather than merely know. Not only does an understanding increase interest and therefore concentration, but it can also enable people to respond positively and effectively in their work. Take two quite distinct examples. The machine operative who knows how to use his machine and understands the nature of the complete production process could recommend improvements in the production process. An employee who knows that his application for promotion has been unsuccessful, but has not been told the reason for the management decision may not work at his best because of his lack of understanding and frustration.

CHARACTERISTICS OF INFORMATION

Information has a number of identifiable characteristics, some of the most important of which are outlined below.

1.   Information covers all forms of knowledge, from hard facts such as a set of monthly sales figures to abstract ideas, for example the concept of liability;

2.   Information can be exchanged in a variety of ways, ranging from high technology communications system that use satellites to transmit messages from one part of the world to another, to the simple use of speech and questions;

3.   Information is received using our senses, primarily those of sight and hearing;

4.   The medium in which information is expressed is closely related to its content, its purpose and its intended audience, for example the evening news bulletin on television uses speech, graphics and visual images to effectively inform the viewer;

5.   Information may be transmitted erratically and in an unplanned way, such as a person's response to an unexpected telephone call, or be communicated in accordance with an overall plan or system such as the information system operating within an organisation;

6.   Certain types of information may require an element of investigation, search or enquiry, for instance to perform a statistical calculation to establish an average monthly wage for a group of workers it would be necessary to find out how much each man earned in the period and then work out the average. Alternatively information may already exist in a recorded form, such as in the files of the finance department;

7. Information can be stored and different methods may be used to do this, including files of paper, computer disks and microfiche;

8. Enormous quantities of information can now be transferred from one part of the world to another through the use of technology, for instance when one computer 'talks' with another.

In the context of the industrialised and commercial world the collection, handling and storage of information is an essential part of the successful operation of any business. Without adequate information, when data arrives too late, is insufficiently detailed or even too detailed, management cannot operate effectively. The place of information systems in the operation of business organisations is examined in the next chapter.

COMMUNICATING INFORMATION EFFECTIVELY

There are a number of reasons why it is essential for organisations to be effective in their communications, for instance:

1) To aid decision making

2) To enhance the organisation's reputation

3) To ensure the effective operation of the organisation's systems.

1.   To aid decision making

Effective decision making is founded upon obtaining and interpreting all appropriate information. Without such information decisions are likely to be a product of guesswork or speculation. Managers require accurate, relevant and up to date information to act rationally and competently. Imagine a large manufacturing company deciding to invest in expensive new manufacturing equipment without first identifying whether it can afford the equipment and physically accommodate it within the existing plant. The person taking the decision will need to know how much loss of production will result while it is installed, which personnel if any have the skills to operate it and whether the market can absorb the higher output of goods produced using the new machinery. No rational company would contemplate such a course of action without first obtaining information to provide the answers to these questions. Nor would a local authority attempt to raise its rates, close a school, or build council houses without its officers first seeking all the data necessary to advise the members of the alternative courses of action available, and the consequences of pursuing them.

Whether the decision making takes place in a commercial company or a public body the decision makers ultimately have to account to the people they represent — shareholders or ratepayers. If they are to come across as professionals in the eyes of such people it is essential that managers have access to all the information appropriate to their responsibilities. Nothing is as damaging to a manager's reputation as a public recognition that he was unaware of important information. You may have noticed how often in Parliament members try to embarrass their political opponents by revealing information that the opponent was unaware of.

2.   To enhance the organisation's reputation

Effective external communications enhance the reputation and image of the organisation. This results in the growth of goodwill between the organisation and its customers and clients. For instance an organisation which unduly delays in responding to customers enquiries or complaints or where the telephone is never answered, will develop a poor standing in the eyes of its existing and potential customers.

3.   To ensure the effective operation of the organisation's systems

If internal communications are effective, systems within the organisation operate smoothly, for example its financial system, stock control and personnel functions. As a result, deficiencies and

Effective external communications . . .

problems can be identified quickly and remedial action taken. In consequence product and service standards can be maintained and staff morale kept high. Two examples will illustrate this. Firstly, a slack system of stock control can result in orders being lost and long delays in delivery occuring. Secondly, an inefficient personnel department that fails to recognise and act upon an employees grievance could be responsible for an escalation of the problem into an industrial dispute.

To summarise, poor communications result in lack of information, dis-information, misunderstanding and confusion. To help overcome such undesirable consequences, an organisation should pay close attention to all forms of communication. In practice this means selecting, collating and presenting the data to be communicated in a suitable format. This may be a report, a balance sheet, a letter or a chart. In fact as we shall see, part of the skill of communicating is to choose the most suitable format to transfer the information. Once the format is selected further skills are required of the communicator to use the format in the manner it demands. Usually accuracy will be important, but sometimes style and tone as well, for instance when writing a letter or sending a memorandum.

YOUR ROLE AS A COMMUNICATOR

In our daily lives and particularly in our jobs we must all assume the role of a communicator. Because of the importance of communications we all need to be aware of the skills required.

Being aware of the sources of information

To obtain data you must be aware of the main sources that can be drawn upon, for instance within the organisation where records and files are kept and how they can be accessed. Outside the organisation you must be able to use the information facilities of libraries, government departments, local authorities and so on. Sometimes there are legal obligations to make available to the public specific types of information. The Companies Registry in Cardiff holds files on all registered companies. These can be examined on the payment of a small fee, and can provide a valuable source of information, such as a company's annual accounts. The Local Government (Access to Information) Act 1985 imposes upon all local authorities the obligation of providing details of meetings, agendas and minutes which are available for public inspection. It also requires a local authority to publish certain information such as a register containing the names and addresses of all its elected members.

Being aware of the purpose and message of the communication

You must also be conscious of:

(a)   the content of the message, for instance is it an order, a piece of advice or merely "for information only"; and

(b)   the method of communicating it, for instance should you write a letter or pass the message by telephone.

Your decision will be influenced by the size of the target audience, whether the message is urgent, physical factors such as the design of the work place, and also cost.

The essential test of your ability as a communicator is whether you are understood. But we should remember that there are always two sides to communication, the person giving the message and the person receiving it. Just as it is important that your communications must be understood, you will also need the skills involved in receiving information and being able to take appropriate action on it.

THE SKILLS OF COMMUNICATING

We give, receive and exchange information all the time, whether at work or outside working hours. All this involves communication skills. It is a curious fact that most of us will only be vaguely aware of how successful we are at using our communication skills. Usually it is only when something goes wrong that we recognise the weakness of our communication, for instance when we are told "I am sorry but I don't follow you," or when we fall back on the expression "Know what I mean?", or perhaps when a senior in our organisation calls us into his office, and, holding a report we have prepared for him, tells us, "This is simply not good enough." In fact the only time during which communication skills are specifically developed and formally assessed occurs during our education. Even then there may be significant areas of communication that are not a part of the curriculum. For most of us using a telephone, speaking publicly and filling in forms are abilities acquired from personal experience. We seem to survive this lack of formal training, although how well we cope is sometimes more difficult to estimate.

You may find it useful to calculate roughly how much time you spend daily in communicating and therefore the importance of this activity to you. The type of work you do obviously affects the extent of your communications activity; a factory worker on the shopfloor engaged in manual work is likely to spend far less time communicating during working hours than an administrative employee working for the same organisation, although during their leisure hours the difference will probably be less marked.

The major activities of communicating are reading, writing, listening and speaking. Of these it tends to be the oral activities which receive least attention during our school careers. Perhaps this is because the nature of oral communications makes it more difficult to assess than a letter or an essay which clearly has a more permanent form. The elements of communications are all essentially inter-connected. The writer expects his words to be read, whilst the reader will read to discover the writer's message. The speaker addresses his words to the listener intending that they be heard, whilst the listener tries to understand the speaker's message from the words he or she hears. Specifically it might seem that the skills of reading and listening are less demanding than those of writing and speaking. This is not so. Reading and listening can only successfully be achieved by high levels of concentration. As communicating is a two way process it is not possible to realistically divorce the skills of the person transmitting the information from the person receiving it. A person who has good communication skills is both a good speaker and a good listener. But they do not always coincide. You will probably have met someone who is an excellent listener, responsive and attentive, but who is unable to string two words together themselves. Or the individual who is a compulsive talker but is unable to recognise when they should listen and take notice of others. The more highly developed are your communications skills, the more effective you are as a potential communicator. The most accomplished public address however may come to nothing if the audience is made up of people whose concentration threshold does not last longer than five minutes. The bulk of the speech or lecture passes them by. Some of the most important aspects of good communicating are identified below:

(a) Speaking and listening

A speaker should:

    (i)   have a wide vocabulary and choose from it with care;

    (ii)   use the correct pronunciation of words;

    (iii) deliver sentences at a reasonable speed;

    (iv) vary the intonation of the delivery;

    (v)   maintain some eye contact with the listener, allowing the listener the opportunity to intervene whenever this is called for.

A listener should:

    (i)   concentrate on the words used by the speaker;

    (ii)   interject to clarify points of difficulty or confusion but in a way which does not break the speaker's flow;

    (iii) maintain attention by looking at the speaker;

    (iv) respond non-verbally to what is being said — nodding to signify understanding or approval, or smiling to provide encouragement.

(b) Writing and reading

A writer should:

    (i)   express ideas and information in a form which is grammatically correct;

    (ii)   write legibly;

    (iii) edit and correct the written material before issuing it;

    (iv) employ sound vocabulary;

    (v)   ensure correct spelling.

A reader should:

    (i)   check words that he or she is not sure of by using a dictionary;

    (ii)   read at a reasonable speed so as not to lose the sense of the message;

   (iii)   try to summarise the main points mentally as they appear;

   (iv) where necessary 'skim' material. (Skimming is considered later in the chapter.)

Of course these points about communication skills are general guidance only. For example if you are engaged in taking down notes whilst a speaker is giving a lecture, you are simply providing yourself with a record of the major points that are being made. As long as the notes are only for your personal use any method you use to express them is acceptable if you understand it. Often people develop their own shorthand for note taking purposes.

Of course these points about communication skills are for general guidance only. For example if you are engaged in taking down notes whilst a speaker is giving a lecture, you are simply providing yourself with a record of the major points that are being made. As long as the notes are only for your personal use any method you use to express them is acceptable if you understand it. Often people develop their own shorthand for note-taking purposes.

THE CONVENTIONS OF COMMUNICATING

So far we have concentrated on skills, but we cannot ignore the importance of convention when we are considering methods of communicating. Convention is concerned with generally accepted practice, and in the business world it plays a very important part both in verbal and written communication. Let us consider an example of a verbal convention. In many areas of employment it is still the convention for employees to use the formal methods of address when speaking to seniors — either "Sir" or "Mister, Mrs or Ms". It might not constitute insubordination to speak to a senior using his or her christian name, but it would certainly be unfavourably received. In the same way the use of slang expressions in a conversation with the managing director or chief executive will not generally improve one's career prospects. Convention is more significant in the written word, especially in business letters, notices and reports, that is in formal written communications. It would not for example, present a very convincing picture of a well run organisation if the company decided to dispense with the use of punctuation in its business documents. It might also give rise to a great deal of confusion. As grammatical convention is so important it is considered in more detail below.

GRAMMATICAL CONVENTIONS AND SENTENCE STRUCTURE

The most basic component of written language is the 'word'. We talk of the words used in a language as its vocabulary. Whilst a single word can convey a meaning, in order to express complex ideas and the relationship of things to each other, we use sentences. Sentences are made by linking words together. A sentence should be complete in itself and convey a question, a statement or a command. To create a sentence the writer must follow certain rules which are referred to collectively as the rules of grammar.

GRAMMAR

The aim of grammar is to ensure that the words of a sentence are arranged so that together they convey a single meaning. If they are capable of bearing more than one meaning the sentence is ambiguous and accurate communication is lost. For example consider the sentence, "The sales manager told the production manager that his department was a disgrace to the company." We do not know from this which department is a "disgrace to the company." A further example is the sentence, "Applications are invited from men over twenty five years of age or women." Can female applicants be under the age of twenty five?

Slight changes in the grammar of a sentence can completely alter the meaning of the sentence, so it is important to pay careful attention to the words being used. For instance compare the sentences:

"**Only** I wrote to the company."

"I **only** wrote to the company."

"I wrote **only** to the company."

"I wrote to the company **only**."

By moving the word 'only' through the sentence different meanings emerge. In addition a single word can be stressed by printing it in italic form in order to emphasise the sense in which the word is being used, although this is a printing convention rather than a grammatical one. Usually a sentence can be recast to emphasise its meaning, and in doing so possibly remove ambiguity as well. Using one of the examples above "I only wrote to the company" we do not really know whether the writer is emphasising the means by which he communicated with the company, or whether the company is the only organisation which has been treated in this way. Compare the meaning of the following alternatives, "It was only the company I wrote to," and "To the company I only wrote."

THE COMPONENTS OF A SENTENCE

There are eight different parts of speech which can be used to form sentences. These are:

    (i)   verbs;

    (ii)   nouns;

    (iii)   pronouns;

    (iv)   adjectives;

    (v)   adverbs;

    (vi)   prepositions;

    (vii)   conjunctions; and

    (viii)   interjections

(i) verbs

The words in a sentence each perform different functions. Verbs are words indicating the state or the action of a subject and are sometimes referred to as 'being' or 'doing' words. The most common verbs are "to be" and "to have". Verbs can be used in different senses to signify the time at which the event they describe occurs, thus "I talked" (past tense), "I am talking" (present tense) and "I shall talk" (future tense). They can be used actively and passively to convey different emphasis, for instance "The Government cuts civil servants pay." Here "cuts" is used actively and as it immediately follows "government" it emphasises that word. This could alternatively be expressed as "Civil servants pay is cut by the Government." This sentence now emphasises who has suffered the cut rather than who is responsible for it.

(ii) nouns

Nouns are words that name a person or place or thing. If the thing is tangible, with a shape and volume, such as a factory, an individual or a manufactured product then the noun is a concrete one. If the thing is intangible, such as quantity, a value or an attribute (for example Justice or Information) the noun is said to be abstract. Collective nouns are used to describe a group of things, for instance a 'firm' of accountants. It is important not to refer in the same sentence to a group as a single entity and then as a collection of individuals, thus, "The management took their places and it then commenced its business."

(iii) pronouns

Pronouns are used instead of nouns to identify a person or a thing already mentioned or known from the context of the sentence. There are personal pronouns such as "I" or "you" and "they", and interrogative pronouns such as "who", "what" and "which".

(vi) adjectives

Adjectives describe nouns; "the large warehouse", "the green folder", "the main entrance." An error to be avoided is the use of superfluous adjectives. Examples might include "a major disaster" or "a noisy disturbance". In fact the use of adjectives as a complete contrast to the nouns they are describing can be used to humourous effect — "a quiet disturbance". (This figure of speech is known as an oxymoron.)

(v) adverbs

Adverbs describe verbs, for instance "the workforce is slowly learning the skills," or "she often calls," or "the shop was closed simply because of the power cut". In these examples the adverbs are "slowly", "often" and "simply".

(vi) prepositions; (vii) conjunctions; and (viii) interjections

Prepositions describe directions or position ("in", "on", "under", etc), conjunctions join words together ("and", "or") and interjections are exclamations ("oh!" and "ah!").

Which of these eight parts of speech appear in a sentence obviously varies according to the message the writer is seeking to convey, and the tone and style which is being used. However all sentences must consist of a subject and a verb. This can occur with just two words, such as "I called," or "Richard paid." In both cases there is a subject, the individual performing the action, and a verb indicating the activity of the subject. Some verbs require an object as well as a subject to make proper sense. We are left wondering in the case of the caller whom, why, and how he called.

A group of words without a verb is referred to as a phrase. A phrase may make sense even though it lacks a verb, for instance, "Mr. J. Owen — Quality Control Supervisor.

PUNCTUATION

The purpose of punctuation is to:

    (a)   provide tone and expression to the written word; and

    (b)   provide pauses to help the reader grasp what has been said before moving on to the next idea or set of ideas.

Different types of punctuation provide the writer with alternatives for achieving these purposes. Although grammatical rules certainly exist for the use of correct punctuation, probably the best guide to punctuation is the writer's own sense of what feels right. This often becomes clear when reading back over the written material. In oral rather than written communications the speaker has greater control over punctuation using gestures, expressions, tone of voice and pauses. For example pauses can be lengthened to heighten the emphasis on what has just been said.

The full stop

The full stop is the single most important component of punctuation. It is used to end the sentence. It also appears in some abbreviations, for instance Mr. Smith, and R. Smith J.P. When does a sentence end? Perhaps the most helpful advice is to think about how the writing would sound if it were being spoken. Where would the breaks come? Bear in mind that people often manage to produce longer sentences when they are speaking than would look or feel right if seen in written form.

The comma

A comma is used to mark a short pause within the sentence. Short sentences are helpful to the reader. They are easy to follow. Used excessively however, they restrict the writer's style, and create an impression in the readers mind of travelling in a jerky car. Whilst a straightforward writing style assists the reader's understanding, the longer sentence may be necessary to closely link related ideas. It is then that the comma becomes useful. It should be borne in mind that over enthusiastic use of commas may hinder the reader's understanding rather than help it.

The main uses of the comma are:

(a) in lists, as a means of separating items;

(b) to report direct speech, as for instance in the following sentence. The secretary said, "The office has been busy all day."

(c) to mark the end of a clause. "In reply to your letter of 24 May, I have now spoken to the people concerned."

(d) As a substitute for brackets. "The clerical assistant, a man of fifty-five, took early retirement."

(e) to enable adverbial phrases to appear in the middle of sentences. Words like "however" and "nevertheless" are adverbial phrases.

The semi-colon

Sometimes a writer needs to introduce a longer pause than a comma, but does not wish the sentence to end. To achieve this the semi colon is used. The three situations in which it is usually employed are:

(a) to stress the separate identity of listed items. "The file included: the client's name; his date of birth; his previous employment experience and details about his state of health."

(b) to emphasise a conjunction. "We are not happy about your attitude to time-keeping; nor do we intend to alter your working hours."

(c) to act as a conjunction by joining two related things. "The word processor is a valuable asset; it has revolutionised our office procedures."

The colon

The colon can be used in a number of different ways. It is used:

(a) to introduce a list, hence its appearance above;

(b) as a means of dividing a general idea from the explanation. "Spirit duplicators are unsatisfactory: they are messy, smelly and difficult to use."

(c) to contrast one idea with another. "Economic expansion creates jobs: economic decline reduces them."

Brackets

These are a method of providing additional information in the form of an aside. "Mrs. Black (Company Secretary) spoke at the meeting." Often brackets (known technically as parentheses) can be replaced by commas. Which method is the more appropriate in the last sentence? As a means of introducing a note of confidentiality, however, brackets can be most effective. "You may recall me telling you (when we met over lunch last week) that the merger is likely to go ahead."

Dashes

The dash is another device for introducing a pause, and creating emphasis. Dashes lose their impact if they are used too frequently. When a dash is introduced in a sentence the phrase or clause following it should end with a dash — or a full stop.

The Apostrophe

An apostrophe is used to indicate possession. Compare the following three sentences:

"The council's duty is a statutory one." (One council)

"The councils' duty is a statutory one." (More than one council).

"A statutory duty is imposed upon councils." (All councils, but no apostrophe is needed because there is no possession by the councils. It is a simple plural).

An apostrophe is also used where one word is a contraction of two, thus "don't" (do not) and "it's" (it is). Note the two senses of "its" i.e. "Its quality is excellent," and "It's of excellent quality."

Quotation marks

Double quotation marks are used to indicate directly reported speech. The supervisor said, "The morale of my staff is high." Single quotation marks are used for titles, for instance 'The Economist'. They are also used in written directly reported speech to indicate quotations used by the speaker. The supervisor said, "The morale of my staff is high, and the foreman said to me yesterday 'it's because of the recent government order' ". There are two ways of reporting speech; directly as in the example above, and indirectly. Indirect, or reported speech, involves describing past events. In reported speech the statement above would read, "The supervisor said the morale of his staff was high and that the foreman had told him the previous day it was due to the recent government order."

GENERAL GRAMMATICAL CONVENTIONS

The following should be noted:

(a)   do not split infinitives, thus the expression "to boldly go where no man has gone before", should read "to go boldly . . ."

(b)   be consistent in the use of words within a sentence. Do not, for instance, write, "One never knows if the photocopier will work, and you simply cannot rely on it." Use either the form "one" or "you" in both instances.

(c)   some words consist of pairs. When one is included in the sentence, so must the other, for instance "neither, nor", "either, or" and "not only, but also."

(d)   be clear about the use of "who" and "whom". "Who" is used whenever it is the subject of the verb, thus "The accountant who prepares my accounts," whereas "whom" is used where there is a preposition governing it. One says "to whom?", "for whom?" and "whom is it for?"

Paragraphs

Just as words combine to form sentences, so sentences combine to form paragraphs. A paragraph contains a group of sentences related to the same idea or ideas. When the idea or topic changes a new paragraph should begin. The pause between one paragraph and the next signifies the change of content. The use of paragraphs involves care, whilst a paragraph that is too long can cause the reader difficulty in coping with larger blocks of information, paragraphs that are too short are disconcerting and confusing.

INTERNAL AND EXTERNAL COMMUNICATION METHODS AND FORMAT

We have already examined in this chapter methods of communicating through the use of written, verbal and non verbal means. In the case of written communications we have seen that an essential element to achieve effectiveness is in an awareness of grammar. Next we need to consider the methods and formats that can be used to convey information. Before doing so, however, it is important to recognise that business communications has two distinct aspects to it. On the one hand there are the communications within an organisation — its internal communications: on the other there are the external communications. In a sense it is artificial to split up the communication activity of an organisation in this way. The skills of communication are essentially the same whether a person is dealing with his fellow employees or his organisation's customers and clients. However different needs are met by the use of different methods and the internal information demands of an organisation do not necessarily coincide with the external demands it recognises. For example most external dealings tend to be formal, whereas internal information transfers, especially verbal exchanges, are often of a less formal kind. In addition the formats used for the purpose of giving, receiving and exchanging information vary widely according to the nature and content of the information, who is providing it and who is receiving it. Thus the means used to arrange an interdepartmental football competition are unlikely to share much in common with designing and implementing a feasability study on company relocation. This is particularly so if the study has to be presented to the entire board in the form of a fully documented formal report, accompanied by an oral presentation. Similarly the way in which an organisation responds in communication terms to a letter of complaint from a customer, is unlikely to be the same as the treatment given to a grievance raised by an employee concerning conditions of service.

THE METHODS OF INTERNAL COMMUNICATION

Conveying information involves making a number of decisions. It is of course necessary to know what the content of the information is. This may not always be as simple as it seems. If the communicator is a part of the information chain it is possible that such a person may be confused about the message to be transferred, having failed to receive it clearly. If a senior issues you with a vague instruction to, "Tell the staff about the safety arrangements", you will need to ascertain the following points: which safety arrangements?; which staff — all of them or some of them?; where are the safety arrangements described?; why is this communication necessary — perhaps a legal obligation or a policy decision? Whatever the reason it is difficult to place communication of information in context if there is no apparent purpose in transferring it; what precisely is it that the staff need to be told? When you are the initiator of the communication it will be easier to obtain answers to most of these questions; you will presumably know why you need to transfer the information for instance!

Having ascertained what the information is, why it needs to be transmitted and who needs it, a choice must then be made as to how it should be transmitted, that is the method of delivery. In its simplest form this involves asking:

    (a)   should the method be formal or informal? and

    (b)   should the method be verbal or non verbal?

Most of the physical means available to transmit information are capable of being used either formally or informally. Letters, reports, speeches and instructions can all be delivered in a style and tone which reflects strict conventions or alternatively a relaxed and more individual approach. However, many communications have to be fitted into prescribed formats allowing for no choice. All organisations rely on the use of forms to simplify and standardise information flows. A company may for instance use standard form contracts to trade under, accident report forms to detail accidents occuring at work and invoice forms for billing customers. Sometimes such forms must comply with statutory requirements. For instance information regarding the insurance of premises and the ownership of a business must be displayed publicly in a standard form. Thus a distinction needs to be drawn between circumstances where an organisation:

(a)   chooses to use a form as part of its internal communications system. An example is the use of forms to obtain and record employees personal details;

(b)   is obliged by law to provide information, without a particular format being prescribed, for instance the requirement that employers provide employees with written details of the contract of employment that exists between them; and

(c)   is obliged by law to provide information using a prescribed format.

Examples include the use of application forms, for instance to register with the Data Protection Registry to store personal records on computer or the Director General of Fair Trading to provide credit facilities to customers.

The following are amongst the most common means used to physically transmit information internally: memoranda, notes, notices, reports, accounting statements, files, agendas, minutes, telephone conversations, meetings, public address systems and face to face contact. Evidence suggests that for the average employee involved in administrative and clerical duties, a breakdown of the working hours he or she spends using different methods of communication will reveal around three quarters of that time spent in oral communications (i.e. speaking and listening).

FORMS OF INTERNAL COMMUNICATION

THE MEMORANDUM

The memorandum is a very common means of transferring information in written form within the organisation. Memoranda may be handwritten, although usually they are typed. The style is generally to keep to short sentences, without the use of paragraphs, for the main purpose of the memorandum is to convey a brief message.

The layout of the memorandum is standardised, and most organisations will use memoranda that have pre-printed headings and carry their business name. The memorandum will indicate from whom it has come, to whom it is addressed, the date, a reference or heading, and who, if anyone, has received copies. The originator should keep a copy of the memorandum. If several copies are being sent a tick is placed against the names of each individual receiving one, to indicate that this is his or her copy. Copies should be sent to individuals, in addition to the addressee, who need to know the message being sent. It may, for example, be courteous to keep a superior informed of a matter which is being dealt with by a member of his or her staff. It also gives the superior an opportunity to intervene if he is concerned about the way the matter is being dealt with.

Clearly it is important for an employee who uses a memorandum to be familiar with the organisation's structure, and so be aware of who within it, ought to be given a sight of the communication. Whilst it is unnecessary to circulate all communications between staff, it should be recognised that key personnel within a section or department may be unable to perform their jobs satisfactorily if they are not provided with essential information, and "kept in the picture".

A memorandum does not need to be signed, although the originator may initial it. Nor does it need compliments such as "Dear Sir", or "Yours sincerely."

The main uses of the memorandum are:

(a) to issue an instruction, for instance, "please attend the meeting to be held at . . . ";

(b) to record a fact or series of facts that the recipient should be made aware of, thus "I attended the meeting as you instructed";

(c) to put forward suggestions. An example could be, "I would suggest that in future you deal with the clients in a more tolerant way," or "I feel it would help the department if extra time were made available for staff meetings";

(d) to express a point of view, thus "In response to your comments at the meeting last week, I take the view that the major priority of the department is cost cutting."

It has already been noted that the initiator should keep and file a copy of each memorandum. Like any written communication its great value is that:

(a) it provides a permanent record for the initiator; and

(b) it is valuable evidence of any action taken if a dispute arises. Indeed it is useful to follow up important oral exchanges by means of a confirmatory memorandum whenever possible.

An example of a memorandum is given below:

ABBOTSFIELD LTD.

MEMORANDUM

To: Mr. G. Baker

From: Mrs. J. Bruce   Reference: JB/AC

Copies to: J. Adams   Date: 23rd May 1986.
            P. Hudson (for information)

Subject: **Staff Briefing**

Confirmation has been received from head office that the Briefing meeting will take place on 6th June. Please attend.

Usually a memorandum form is small in size and this physically prevents messages from becoming too wordy.

INSTRUCTIONS

Whilst a memorandum may be used to pass on instructions, there are also other commonly used written methods. For instance staff may receive an instruction manual. This might contain information on the operation of equipment used in the place of work. It could also describe the action to be taken in the event of an accident at work, or the procedure to be adopted by a member of staff who is unable to report in for work.

Simple instructions may appear on equipment, or in the office or plant to identify what action should be taken in the event of fire. The method which is used is obviously largely determined by the specific context. For example it would be appropriate to give to all new starters a plant diagram indicating the location of fire exits with general instructions on the action that should be taken if a fire were to occur.

Instructions are used to:

(a) require the recipient to act in a certain way, for example, "In the event of a generator failure you should report the matter to the plant manager immediately";

(b) restrain the recipient from acting in a certain way, thus, "Under no circumstances should unauthorised staff enter the research and development unit";

(c) simply tell a potential user how to use an item of equipment — "To operate press button A, select the appropriate file and type your message."

In expressing instructions, style is very important. The imperative form should be used when the instruction has to be complied with, for instance, "Enter all new client details on Form 5A" or "You must enter . . . ." Since failure to observe an instruction may give rise to disciplinary proceedings it is essential to use such expressions as "must", "ought" and "should". Such language will make the recipient fully aware of the nature of the obligation that is imposed when a written instruction is personal rather than directed towards the workforce generally. The use of imperative language may appear to be authoritarian. "Telephone the Sales Director and pass on my congratulations," as an instruction given to a secretary, is likely to result in the Sales Director receiving a less enthusiastic message than if the secretary received the instruction prefixed with "please", although even with the addition "please" the instruction is still clearly a command.

As with all forms of communication the method and the delivery should always reflect the context, and in the case of instructions it is essential that they be expressed both clearly and logically. This may involve sequencing the instructions as a list of numbered points, rather than combining them all, in no particular order, as a general statement. For instance a set of instructions to a market researcher engaged in field work might read:

1. Greet the interviewer with the time of day — "good morning" etc.

2. Introduce yourself and the name of the company.

3. Show evidence of your identity.

4. Briefly explain the nature and purpose of the survey.

5. Explain that the survey will last only ten minutes, and the information obtained will be of great value.

Presented in this way the interviewer can learn the instruction sequence and consequently relate to the interviewee as an efficient professional, whereas a muddled set of instructions could result in a messy presentation and a refusal by the interviewee to be interviewed.

INTERNAL PUBLICATIONS

Large organisations find it helpful to regularly publish a bulletin or magazine for distribution to all members of the workforce. Bulletins are usually cheaply produced, whilst magazines are often glossy and attractive, reinforcing the reputation and status of the organisation. Such magazines are limited to very large companies, such as Shell and I.C.I., but whether it is a magazine or a mere bulletin that is used such a publication is a useful way of passing on information that is:

(a) purely personal — weddings, retirements, deaths of staff etc.,

(b) organisational — changes in personnel, company trading activity, new systems being introduced, and so on.

NOTICE BOARDS

Notice boards are one way of communicating generally within an organisation. They are invariably split into sections dealing with a range of topics, from sport to Union meetings.

Some organisations make use of a display board. This may be restricted to information on one topic, but may be placed strategically so as to gain maximum impact. For instance a display board concentrating on health and safety matters might be located at the entrance to the staff canteen where employees queue up for meals.

The advantages of a notice board is in its:

    (a)   cheapness;

    (b)   ability to be kept up to date easily; and

    (c)   accessability.

They do however suffer from certain drawbacks including:

    (a)   the possibility that some staff ignore them altogether;

    (b)   the likelihood that staff maybe selective and only examine those sections of the board which are of interest to them;

    (c)   the fact that notices inevitably lack detail because of the physical limitations of the board;

    (d)   the tendency for the board to become overcrowded which can cause people to ignore it because of the poor visual presentation of material.

SUGGESTION BOXES

Suggestion boxes are used very successfully by some organisations as a method of encouraging employees to put forward their own ideas on all aspects of the organisation's business such as improvements to the company's products, or its systems. They have the advantage of improving employee involvement in company affairs, and in the case of the best ideas may produce savings for the company. It is common to offer cash payments for ideas which are accepted. Despite appearing to be a modern way of communicating within a large organisation where the individual's voice might not otherwise be heard, suggestion schemes have in fact been in existence for at least one hundred years.

REPORTS

Reports may be made verbally, but are usually written. A report is a document which examines a specific topic or topics in order to:

    (a)   convey information;

    (b)   report findings;

    (c)   put forward ideas and suggestions.

In addition a report will usually make recommendations upon which action can be taken.

There are many ways of classifying reports. This is a reflection of the variety of activities they are used to consider and the differing contexts in which they are used. The most common classifications are:

(i) Formal and Informal Reports

Formal reports are more detailed and require greater structure and subdivision. Informal reports are usually shorter, less structured and more generally used.

(ii) Routine and Special Reports

Routine reports are a common feature of most industrial and commercial organisations. As their name suggests they are produced as a matter of internal routine as part of the information system of the organisation. For example a routine report would be a report on sales figures produced by the sales department, or an annual report dealing with trading activity for each fiscal year. Routine reports are generally standardised.

A special report is a "one-off", dealing with a non-routine matter. This could be an evaluation of the performance of a group of employees, a report of a conference attended, or an enquiry into the restructuring of the entire organisation. Because a special report is not concerned with a routine issue its structure will not be standardised. It will however be based upon terms of reference. These are simply the set of instructions given to its author(s). Furthermore the format of the report is likely to follow the sequence identified below:

(a) a statement of the terms of reference of the report. These will specify its objective or objectives;

(b) a statement of facts or arguments, set out logically, regarding the subject being investigated;

(c) the identification of viable solutions to the problem, giving the respective strength and weaknesses of each course of action. This stage is usually referred to as the "findings";

(d) the recommendation, supported by appropriate reasons.

In addition detailed information may be contained in appendices, included at the back of the report. The body of the report will contain references to the appendices, but the text will be prevented from becoming too detailed by including the appendix material separately.

The more structured nature of a formal report reflects the greater detail of the information contained in it, and is likely to consist of;

(a) a title page;

(b) a contents page;

(c) a summary of the recommendations;

(d) an introduction (containing the terms of reference);

(e) the information on which the report is based;

(f) conclusions;

(g) recommendations;

(h) appendices;

(i) references to information sources relied upon, for example the use of books, papers and other reports which are listed in the reference section of the report with their titles, their author and where they can be located.

It should be stressed that even the so called 'informal report' is essentially a formal document for it must observe certain conventions of layout. Representing as it does a work of research, argument and recommendation, a report provides its author with a significant test of his or her communication skills. It is certainly possible that an individual's reputation may be enhanced or seriously damaged by the quality of the report they produce. The report may circulate amongst a range of senior staff throughout the organisation, be discussed at meetings, and be filed for public reference. Whatever its progress it will carry the author's name.

What then are the skills needed by the report writer?

There are essentially three of them, and clearly they overlap.

(a) SKILLS OF PREPARATION

It is impossible to proceed without being entirely clear as to the reasons for the report. Having established these reasons it is then possible to identify the recipients of the report. There may in fact be a distribution list already in existence. Sources of information need to be identified and relevant information gathered from them, which must then be evaluated, so that it can be classified. Since information makes up the core of any report it is helpful to remember that the way in which it is used will depend upon the purpose of the report. The information may simply need re-presenting. For example if the report is to provide a list of the highways which the local authority must repair, once the basic information has been gathered, the task is to express it in a clear, concise way.

It may however be that an explanation is required, thus a report upon the implications of the Companies Act 1985 or the Insolvency Act 1986 could not stop short at simply regurgitating the provisions of these statutes once they had been obtained. The report would also need to comment upon their effect.

Finally a report may involve original thought by its author where he or she is obliged to make proposals, for example report on possible designs for a new stock control system. Here objectivity is called for in weighing up the pro's and con's of the alternatives.

There are many points to bear in mind, but above all the report should read as a document which is clear, concise and relevant. It is also useful to be aware of the broader implications of the report, for instance is its subject matter an issue that is the subject of conflict between your senior and another member of the organisation.

(b) CONSTRUCTING THE REPORT

Having obtained all the raw data considered necessary for inclusion within the report, the next step is to consider how the report should be constructed.

Layout is particularly important in formal reports, since these will contain a considerable body of detailed material which needs to be carefully structured to avoid repetition and satisfy the need for clarity and coherence. It should be remembered when writing a report that, as with any form of written communications a permanent record is being created. Whether a written communication is filed depends upon its importance as a record for the organisation, but reports will invariably be filed as they represent research which may prove valuable to the organisation in the future.

The report should clearly indicate the arrangement of material within it. Patterns used for reports may vary according to their subject matter and purpose but as a general guide the arrangement will be likely to adopt the following order:

(i) an introduction.

This will seek to establish not only the purpose of the report and the authority under which the author is acting, but also the author's name, for whom the report has been prepared, and what its subject matter is, if this is not apparent from the statement of its purpose. It should, of course, also be dated.

In a long report the introduction could usefully include a list of the main section headings, as a form of index.

(ii) background.

Sometimes it is necessary to trace the background or history of events which have lead to the preparation of the report. In doing so the writer is providing the reader with a perspective that helps to set the report in context. If background information is not essential to obtain a proper understanding, but is still felt to be of value, it can be inserted as an appendix.

(iii) data.

It is upon the data or facts which the report contains that the writer will be seeking to present the alternative arguments concerning the reports proposals. It is essential therefore that this information is accurate, and preferably supported by a reference to its source. If data is of a detailed or technical kind it should be contained in an appendix or appendices, and simply be summarised in the body of the report. If this is not done the reader may find it difficult to grasp the salient features of the data or factual material being presented. The types of detailed and technical data referred to above could include statistical information, specialised material such as an economic model or statutory regulations, and financial data. Indeed most reports will inevitably examine the cost implications of any proposals they contain, unless these attract no additional costs.

(iv) analysis.

This is likely to be the most intellectually demanding aspect for the writer, for it involves presenting arguments for and against the proposal(s) of the report, in an objective way. It therefore requires the writer to perform a critical analysis of the data set against the context of the purpose for which the report has been prepared.

(v) conclusion.

The conclusion may include a summary of the main aspects of the report. It will certainly present the recommendations of the writer, and if these are detailed they should be individually listed.

(vi) appendices.

It has already been suggested that in the interests of producing a readable report which flows, appendices are an invaluable way of incorporating important data which would otherwise get in the way. If appendix material is used it is essential that it is accurately referenced and cross-referenced in the body of the report to offer the reader a layout which makes access to the information as straightforward as possible. It is most frustrating for a person who is discussing a report in a meeting to spend unnecessary time thumbing through it to locate a particular section or statement, on which he or she wishes to comment. To help overcome this headings and numbering should be used.

HEADINGS

These should be as simple and brief as possible. A general heading or title will be given to the report as a whole, and the remainder of the report will carry main headings, for instance "conclusions", with the text under these main headings broken up by sub headings, such as, "Financial implications,", "Personnel implications," and so on.

NUMBERING

Not only should each page be numbered, but also the paragraphs of the text, unless the report is very short. Thus each main heading might be given a prefix letter, "A", "B", "C" etc, each sub heading within it a prefix number "1", "2", "3", and each paragraph an additional number. In this way any paragraph within the report can be located quickly with the existence of an index, cross referencing page number to paragraph references. Thus an individual paragraph would appear as "B.1.7."

(c) WRITING THE REPORT

The usual style to adopt is one which aims to be clear and brief. It should also be straightforward, although the writer should be conscious of the political implications of the report within the organisation, choosing words with care so as to avoid unnecessary friction. The text must also be relevant. Readers of the report will lose patience if they have to wade through material which is superfluous.

Report writers should avoid using jargon and clichés, for instance:

> Avoid   "At the present point in time", and use "now".
>
> "An all-time high" is better expressed as "a peak", and
>
> "Insofar as it concerns this company higher productivity would be occasioned by maximising employer/employee participation levels," would be more understandable if it read "Higher company productivity would result from effective industrial relations."

When the report is produced it is often useful at this stage to seek the comments of colleagues, especially superiors, on its style, presentation and content.

BUSINESS MEETINGS

The experience of most employees, irrespective of whether they work in the public or the private sector, is that the further up the organisational ladder they climb the more meetings they are required to attend. They may have to prepare documents for meetings, attend and speak at meetings, and take notes at meetings. The fact is that 'the meeting' is generally regarded as one of the most appropriate ways of enabling views to be aired, shared and discussed, and in this way to arrive at decisions. Those who have experienced meetings soon become aware that the efficient and effective use of a person's time is not always realised by attending a meeting.

A recent training film for business managers conveys this message humourously. The entire working day is spent attending meetings, which leaves no time to prepare for them, so this work has to be carried out at home. As a consequence most of the staff attending the meetings are so tired that they fall asleep.

meetings . . . meetings . . . meetings . .

(i) Agendas

Whether a meeting works successfully often depends upon the way in which the Chairperson conducts it, but it is more likely to be successful if every member knows in advance when and where the meeting is to be held, and the nature and order of the business. If reports or other written documents are to be considered at the meeting these should be issued in advance, rather than 'tabled' (that is first presented at the meeting itself). The document used to inform staff of a meeting is called an agenda. An example is given below.

Meeting of the Policy and Resources Committee to be held on Thursday 24 May 19xx, commencing at 10.30 a.m., in the Board Room.

AGENDA

1. **Apologies for absence**

2. **Minutes of the last meeting**
    To approve the Minutes of the last meeting held on Thursday 22 April 19xx (copy enclosed)

3. **Matters arising**

4. **Report of the Resources Sub-Committee**
    To consider the report of the Resources Sub-Committee on Office Equipment required (copy enclosed)

5. **Any other business.**

                                                                    15 May 19xx

---

(ii) Minutes

It will be noticed that the second item on the specimen agenda refers to the minutes of a previous meeting. Minutes are records kept of the business of meetings. They include not only decisions made by the meeting, but also the discussions which lead to any decision. Minutes are in fact a type of report. It is usually the responsibility of a secretary appointed by the members of the meeting to keep a record of the proceedings as members discuss issues and reach decisions. It is then the Secretary's responsibility to prepare formal minutes from this record. The minutes will be typed and distributed to members of the meeting, usually accompanied by the next agenda. Minutes are of particular value when the meetings which they record are regularly held, as for example in the case of a local authority committee which meets each month. In such an arrangement the first proper business of the meeting is the approval of the minutes of the last meeting.

This process has the effect of reminding members what was previously discussed and decided, enabling them to check whether agreed action has been taken, allowing them the opportunity to accept (or reject) the minutes as an accurate record of the previous meeting. As with other written records minutes should be clear, precise, and as concise as possible, but without losing essential accuracy, if they are to be approved as a true account of the previous meeting. The style of writing appropriate to minutes is to keep sentences short. It is not necessary to link one point with another where reference is made to the statements of individuals speaking in the meeting indirect or reported speech should be used. Finally, for reference purposes, a system of numerical recording should be used against each minuted item. An example of a set of minutes is set out below:

Highways Committee

20 February 19xx (7.15 - 8.00 p.m.)

217 Members present — Councillor Blake (Chairperson), Councillor Askew (Ms.), Coleman, Clarke (Mrs), Lawes, Smith, Smythe (Mrs), Williamson and Young.

218 Apologies for absence — Apologies for absence were received from Councillor Martin.

219 Minutes — The Minutes of the meeting of the Committee held on 26 January 19xx were approved as a correct record and signed by the Chairperson.

220 Report of the Chief Highways Officer. The report of the Chief Highways Officer dated 14 January 19xx (ref. no. CHD/1/86) was received and approved. The report examined the use of high intensity lighting for major road junctions.

221 Ashford Road Roundabout Improvements — The committee considered the planned improvements to the Ashford Road Roundabout and the recommendation of the Chief Highways Officer's report.

Recommended That provision be made for the installation of high intensity lighting in the layout of the Ashford Road Roundabout Improvements Scheme.

It should be noted that there is a statutory obligation for local authorities to keep minutes of their proceedings, and that these minutes are made available for public inspection. Consequently local authority minutes are formally framed, sometimes providing full details of motions and amendments which were put to council meetings.

ABSTRACTS OR SUMMARIES

A further type of internal communication in written form is the abstract.

Anyone who has administrative and clerical responsibilities deals with written material constantly. In a managerial post, in order to cope efficiently, a person will find it necessary to reduce or condense much of the written material they are faced with. Letters, reports, memoranda and other communications are being generated on a daily basis and if every word has to be read the manager is likely to develop a steadily increasing backlog of uncompleted or untouched work that fills the in-tray. There are two ways in which this difficulty can be overcome;

(a)   by improving personal reading techniques;

(b)   by requiring subordinates to summarise material.

(a) The manager may use techniques to improve his or her reading skill

To do this it is necessary to become aware of the different levels of reading. These are skimming (or scanning), 'normal' reading and in-depth reading. Which level a person uses depends firstly upon having a proficiency in all three. Having acquired this it becomes possible to adopt whichever technique is best suited to the time available for reading the material, and the nature of the material itself. Most people read at the normal level without difficulty, for normal reading is reading for pleasure: reading a newspaper, a magazine or a novel. The rate at which the material is understood at this level will generally not matter. If however the material being read is hard to understand because the ideas it expresses are difficult to grasp or the vocabulary used is largely unfamiliar, there is a tendency to read it superficially. In depth reading involves spending time in working towards an understanding of difficult material. It is an equally valuable skill for the student! In the working environment constant change means that even experienced staff face reading challenges from time to time. A clear example of this is the effort made by people experiencing for the first time the language of computing. Thus in-depth reading is very much a part of working life. By its nature it is a slower process than normal reading and can consume large quantities of the manager's limited time.

Certainly there is a loss of efficiency when, after ploughing through a body of complex written material, it is realised that none of it was really relevant after all.

To help avoid this problem, and to generally improve reading speeds, the technique of skimming is used. It is a technique with which most people are familiar, although success in using it does not automatically follow from knowing about it. It involves glancing through material, paragraph by paragraph, to gain a feel for the content. Then the reader may return and re-read the material thoroughly if the content is relevant and time permits, or simply to rely upon the general impression obtained. In the latter case this may be enough to enable the reader to participate effectively at a meeting, or telephone a customer, or perhaps interview applicants for new jobs.

(b) A manager may instruct subordinates to abstract or summarise the material.

These two expressions are essentially the same, and summarising is an activity familiar from school days when it was called 'precis.' It involves the process of writing a shorter version of a communication, whether the orginal is oral, (for example the discussion of a meeting which are converted into minutes), or written (such as a lengthy report).

The task of summarising may become necessary at any time. A superior may call a member of staff into the office with the instruction, "Can you provide me with a written summary of the developments in our negotiations with the Council over the planning application for the new factory?" Or perhaps an internal telephone call may be received for the employees superior from a senior member of the organisation who simply instructs, "Will you pass on the following details concerning the Bridgewater Contract?", and then narrates a sequence of events.

Three skills are vital to summarise properly:

(i) A thorough understanding of the material is vital in order to produce an effective summary. Your ability to understand unfamiliar material was assessed at school in comprehension exercises.

(ii) Selecting the essential points from the material. There must be no alteration to the factual content and no additions to the material made. The main theme and major factual components should emerge from the information selected, and arguments that have been used.

(iii) Writing the summary clearly and, of course, concisely. If this is not achieved the whole purpose of the summary is defeated. Textual material can be condensed by using a single word to replace a group of words, and by reducing sentence (and hence paragraph) length.

Some examples may help to illustrate this process.

"The chairman of the company in his address to the members of the meeting, informed them that the way in which the company conducts the business of buying and selling is by getting straight on with the job, rather than unduly time wasting and prevaricating."

This long-winded statement can be reduced to:

"The company chairman told the meeting that the company trades promptly,"

Similarly: "It was explained to the foreman that his services were being dispensed with," becomes "The foreman was told he was sacked."

A summary should read as a whole, rather than as a collection of disconnected sentences. To achieve such unity involves maintaining a logical sequence to the ideas being expressed in the passage, and exercising care in the linking of sentences. A wide vocabulary will clearly help.

EXTERNAL WRITTEN COMMUNICATIONS.

Since organisations exist to meet the needs of customers and clients they spend a significant proportion of their time communicating with them. But external communications do not stop there. Whether an organisation likes it or not it has to deal with outside bodies and individuals which impose demands upon it, for instance, it must deal with the Inland Revenue when assessing its corporation tax, the Department of Health and Social Security in making national insurance contributions and the local authority when paying its rates. It also enters into relationships with:

(a) its suppliers, from the local electricity board for its power supplies to printers for its stationery;

(b) its advisers, including accountants and lawyers;

(c) the bank;

(d) the landlord from whom it may rent its property;

(e) the trade union, whose members it employs.

Obviously communication between the organisation and this diverse range of outsiders takes place in many different ways.

Often communications will be oral. These take place over the telephone or by meeting face to face. For the moment, however, we are concerned with the methods used to communicate in writing, whether the organisation is the initiator or at the receiving end of the process. The major form of external written communication is the business letter.

BUSINESS LETTERS

There are a number of reasons why it is essential for business letters to meet high standards of communication. For instance:

(a) outsiders invariably judge an organisation by the letters it writes, especially if they have not dealt with it in any other way, thus a business letter performs a public relations role;

(b) the letter may be designed to convey an instruction, for instance to a bank, and it could be financially harmful if it is misinterpreted;

(c) a letter may give rise to legal liability, for instance if it is defamatory, or where it constitutes an offer or an acceptance in contractual negotiations.

It should also be borne in mind that the contents of a letter may be widely circulated, if, for example, it is a letter to a newspaper editor explaining a company's reasons for closing a local plant or perhaps responding to public criticism. In such circumstances the construction of the letter is particularly important. Not only are there public relations to be maintained (or perhaps restored) but also the tort of defamation to be considered, for unjustifiable statements that harm the reputation of an individual or an organisation may be actionable and result in the writer paying substantial damages as compensation.

The purpose of the business letter

In commerce and industry business letters are used for many different purposes. The writer needs to be quite clear about the purpose of the letters he or she is writing, for what it says and how it says it reflects who the recipient is and why the communication is being made. It is not difficult to appreciate that the letter a company writes to another company apologising for a delay in supplying goods will be in a very different tone from that it writes to its bank complaining that the bank has wrongfully dishonoured a cheque drawn by the company. Similarly a local authority housing department might be expected to respond by letter to a request for information about the availability of a council house somewhat differently than it would to a council tenant's statement that unless a different rent collector is appointed the tenant will assault the existing rent collector next time he appears.

The type of letter that an organisation writes in terms of its content, style (formal or informal) and tone (friendly or restrained) reflects the purpose of the communication. Whatever the purpose is however, it should always be borne in mind that the use of business correspondence is a means of avoiding a time consuming and unnecessary face to face meeting. It also provides both parties with a permanent record of the arrangements they have made.

TYPES OF BUSINESS CORRESPONDENCE

The main types of business corrrespondence are:

    (a)   letters requesting and providing information;

    (b)   letters of complaint;

    (c)   circulars and standard letters;

    (d)   references and testimonials.

These are now considered.

(a) Letters requesting and providing information

For many organisations these types of letters make up a substantial proportion of their business correspondence. This is perhaps even more the case for public sector organisations, such as local authorities, than for private sector ones. Local authorities receive many requests for information relating to the services they provide. If the letter is requesting information it is essential that the writer has first clearly established in his own mind precisely what he wants to know. For example suppose a company was to write to a local authority in the following way:

>   "Please let us know of the grants that you offer."

Such a request is most unhelpful. The council needs to know what specific need the enquiry is related to. The company may be interested in grants for setting up a new business, or for taking on additional staff, and so on. Presumably the company is clear about the purpose for which the grant is being sought, so this should be clearly expressed in the letter.

When a letter supplies information the writer should seek to ensure that it is written in a form which is understandable to the recipient. This may seem a very obvious requirement, but often staff who have worked in a particular department for a long time are so familiar with procedures and technical expressions that they forget that outsiders do not share this knowledge. Equally it may be obvious from the content of the letter of request that the writer faces particular difficulties which should be recognised when responding to it. Many examples can be given. The letter may indicate that the writer has great difficulty in communicating and so very simple language should be used in writing a reply. It may be evident that the writer is distressed, for instance a pensioner worried about his inability to meet the rates demand, or a single parent anxious about the housing conditions for his or her family. In such circumstances whatever information is provided should be accompanied by some general words of support, although of course one should beware of making promises that it may not be possible to keep.

In business situations, perhaps the most common type of written enquiry is that from a wholesaler or a retailer to a manufacturer requesting information on prices and specifications of goods, availability, trade discounts and so on. The reply to such an enquiry will usually be a letter of quotation. As with any letter of enquiry the writer should be courteous, set out the questions clearly and in sufficient detail, and include any further information that is relevant to the enquiry, for instance that the matter is urgent.

The reply should deal with each question raised accurately and completely and should reflect a tone and style which indicates a genuine desire to be of service. This may, for instance, involve providing additional information which was not requested but which will clearly be helpful to the enquirer. Finally it is in the interests of the organisation sending the reply to do so as soon as possible. In the case of a commercial organisation this can only enhance its reputation, and it may well result in an order being placed.

An example of a letter of enquiry, with a reply is given below.

Jones Bros.
Electrical Contractors
56 Bridge Street
Blackburn

13 October 19xx

Dear Sir,

We understand that you manufacture a complete electronic security system for use in domestic properties, which has recently received a Design Centre award.

Would you kindly send us details of this system, together with an indication of trade terms, and let us know how soon you are able to deliver following receipt of an order.

Yours faithfully,

Peter Wilson

Peter Wilson

for Jones Bros.

Owen and Collins Ltd.
Electrical Supplies Manufacturers,
Unit 27
Avonwell Industrial Estate
Bristol.

Owen and Collins Ltd.
Electrical Supplies Manufactures,
Unit 27, Avonwell Industrial Estate
Bristol.

15 October 19xx

Dear Mr Wilson,

Thank you for your enquiry concerning our award winning 'Sensitron' security system. The system has already been fitted in over 10,000 homes since it was introduced in March this year.

I enclose a brochure which fully describes and explains the system. The brochure contains fitting instructions, and we recommend installation by a qualified electrician.

A price list is included in the brochure; we can offer a discount to trade customers of 10% on list price for accounts settled within seven days. Goods are despatched within 2 days of receipt of orders.

I also enclose a catalogue containing other products we manufacture, which I hope you will find useful.

If you require further help my sales staff will happily deal with any points over the telephone (Bristol 772731, extension 20), or arrange to visit you.

Yours sincerely,

Richard Meek

Sales Manager

Messrs. Jones Bros (Attention of Mr. Wilson)
Electrical Contractors
56 Bridge Street
Blackburn.

(b) Letters of complaint

A letter of complaint will invariably be based upon a grievance held by the complainant. An organisation may receive such letters; it may also need to write them itself. Often when the complaint comes from an individual the letter will reflect strong emotional feelings. These may be quite justified, yet be most unhelpful in constructing a letter which is appropriate to its purpose. Thus such a letter should not be abusive, threatening (if it is the first letter that has been written) or contain allegations which it may not be possible to substantiate. Rather it should set out the facts as the writer understands them, avoid irrelevancies, and be polite. For instance it is good practice to make it clear in the letter that the writer anticipates a favourable response to the complaint if it is found to be established after enquiry. These observations are of particular importance when an organisation is making the complaint. Compare the following examples of letters of complaint sent by an organisation to a customer:

Example 1.

"Dear Sir,

We refer to the as yet unpaid sum of £378 owed to us by you. We find it intolerable that we should have to write to you demanding payment of your bill. It is our policy to vigorously pursue claims against our debtors, and since you have chosen to ignore this debt we shall have no alternative but to commence legal proceedings unless payment is made forthwith.

We should point out to you that this company is not run as a charity, even though you obviously believe that it is.

Yours faithfully"

Example 2

"Dear Mr. Smith,

We are sure that there must be some good cause for your delay in settling payment of your account Number 876413. If we can assist in any way in overcoming any difficulties you may have we should be glad to do so. If so, would you either call in, or give us a ring as soon as possible.

It may be that you have already made payment, in which case we apologise for inconveniencing you.

Yours sincerely"

Example 3

"Dear Mr Smith,

We have received no reply to our reminder of the non payment of your account. We must now regretfully point out to you that unless we hear from you as to the position within the next seven days, we shall have to consider taking steps to recover the amount.

Yours sincerely"

If it is discovered that a complaint is justified, it will be necessary to write a letter of apology, offering to make amends. This may involve financial compensation or adjustment, the replacement of goods, or an indication that an employee in the organisation has been disciplined.

Of course the examination of the complaint may reveal that it is totally without foundation, or there is some real doubt about its justification. In this case it will not be appropriate to make an offer of amends, unless in the case of a genuine doubt the organisation chooses to maintain goodwill by making perhaps a token gesture.

Whatever the circumstances letters responding to criticisms must be very carefully constructed. If the criticism is well founded the response should admit the error using restrained language, thus "upon immediate enquiry it became clear that an administrative error resulted in your goods being misdirected. Please accept the company's apologies for the inconvenience you have been caused". It would be excessive, for example, to add "You may be assured that this will never happen again," for even in the most efficient organisations errors can and do occur and there can be no guarantee that a similar problem might not arise in the future.

If the organisation does not believe the complaint to have any foundation it is still necessary to provide a response, and the question arises as to how this should be framed. Since the organisation will doubtless wish to maintain goodwill, as future orders may depend upon maintaining a sound relationship with the customer, it is vital that the customer is not made to feel foolish. It may help if the response is sent out under the signature of a senior member of staff, to signify the importance the organisation attaches to the criticism.

An example of a reply to an unfounded complaint is given below.

> "Thank you for your letter of 20 April 19xx. I am very sorry that you felt you received discourteous treatment when our accounts department contacted you by telephone regarding your bill. I have spoken to the member of staff you dealt with and put to him your complaint.

> I am satisfied that he dealt with the matter correctly, however I am glad you drew my attention to your concern, since we value good customer relations, and are always prepared to investigate customers'criticisms or complaints.

> I hope the matter is now satisfactorily cleared up, and that we can remain of service to you in the future."

Whilst there is doubt about the substance of the complaint there is clearly no need to provide an admission of responsibility or an apology. Nevertheless in the interests of goodwill, which in turn reflects upon the reputation and good name of the organisation, it is important that the response reflects the concern of the organisation and recognises that the writer of the letter of complaint is genuinely upset or annoyed. The letter might read as follows:

> "I am sorry to learn of your annoyance at the refusal of the department's refuse collectors to remove the kitchen units that are in your rear yard. The refuse collection teams are under instructions to collect all refuse on their weekly visit which in their opinion can be physically lifted and safely carried on their vehicles.

> It is however sometimes necessary to arrange for a larger refuse vehicle to collect specific items. Such an arrangement will need to be made in this case.

> If you would kindly contact this office (extension 225) letting us know when it would be convenient to remove the kitchen units immediate arrangements will be made to do so."

Finally it should be noted that letters of complaint should be dealt with promptly. This of course is true of all business correspondence, however in the case of complaints it may take time to carry out an enquiry. Thus it is essential to notify the complainant as soon as the letter of complaint is received that the matter is being dealt with, for example:

> "Thank you for your letter indicating that your account has been overcharged by £874. The matter is being urgently investigated and we should be able to give you a full reply within fourteen days."

To summarise, complaints are an inevitable outcome of administrative, commercial and industrial activity. Complaints may or may not be justified, but the manner in which organisations respond in writing (and indeed orally) to them, may in the view of the customer or the rate payer be as important as the product or service itself.

(c) Circulars

These are sometimes referred to as 'standard letters', but strictly speaking a circular is used almost exclusively for advertising purposes, whereas standard letters may fulfil a variety of purposes, for example inviting job applicants to attend for interview, or inviting customers to a company presentation. In the case of a standard letter, whilst the bulk of the information it conveys is standard, some provision will need to be made for the non-standard aspects of it. Thus a standard letter inviting applicants to attend for interview might read:

"You are invited to attend an interview for the post of . . . .

The interview will be held on . . 19xx, at Crown House, High Row, Carlington, commencing at . . . . . am/pm.

If you are unable to attend would you please contact the personnel department as soon as possible."

Such letters can be stored on a word processor, and the blanks, including the name of the interviewee, completed as appropriate for each separate occasion.

Circulars are addressed "Dear Sir or Madam," "Dear Elector" and so on, whereas most standard letters will contain the salutation "Dear Mr. Jones", "Dear Ms. Peters," etc. Referring to the recipient's name creates a more personal impression than using the expression "Sir" or "Madam" but it will not usually be possible to personalise a circular because of the large number of copies involved. Since a circular is aimed at selling a product, a service, or, as in the case of an election, a person, it should be designed to:

(a) create an instant impact — perhaps through the use of a headline, or photograph, or the dramatic use of colour;

(b) encourage the recipient to read it — a 'lightweight' text using simple language and a style appropriate to the message should achieve this. A prospective local government candidate, for example, will not try to sell him or herself in the same way as a new toothpaste!

(c) be memorable — achievable very often using a slogan or some catchy advertising 'copy'.

(d) References and Testimonials

All organisations are called upon from time to time to write references and, to a lesser extent, testimonials. A reference is a statement, usually produced as a letter but sometimes completed on a standard form, which is:

(a) provided for a future employer (company, college etc), by someone who has knowledge of the applicant; and

(b) contains a statement of the applicant's qualities and abilities. These may be qualities of character, or abilities related to work performance.

A testimonial is a letter of commendation, written either by the employer or by some other person or body with whom the applicant has had dealings. A major distinction between a testimonial and a reference is that a reference is sent direct from the person providing it to the person requiring it, whereas a testimonial is held in the possession of the applicant who sends a copy of it in support of a job application. Not surprisingly prospective employers value references more highly than testimonials, for a testimonial can be easily forged and tends to highlight the strengths of the applicant at the expense of his or her weaknesses.

When an organisation, or indeed an individual, is required to provide a reference it may recognise a moral obligation to be as open and honest in its assessment as possible. In consequence it may quite honestly make statements which it believes to be true, but which are in fact not true. The law recognises that a person has a right to protect his or her reputation, and an action can be brought for damages under the tort of defamation where such reputation has been harmed by an untrue statement of a defamatory kind. The defence of priviledge exists to strike a balance between the need to protect reputations and allow freedom of expression in a communication made between a person acting under a moral obligation to provide a reference and a person having a professional interest in receiving it. If an organisation writes a letter of reference containing untrue statements about the applicant, then provided the reference was issued without malice, the existence of priviledge will provide a complete defence to the organisation.

A letter of reference usually follows a traditional layout and an example is included below.

James Clark: 6 South Green, Stainmore, Essex.

I have known the above for over five years, and I am very happy to write in support of his application for the position of clerical officer.

He joined this company as a sales clerk, and after three years was promoted to his present position as a sales assistant.

He has shown a conscientious and mature attitude to his job and can work well with others, although recently he has found difficulty in working with one of his colleagues with whom he has had a number of disagreements. He is an ambitious young man whose career prospects are limited in this organisation by the lack of promotional posts available.

I have every confidence that if his application is successful you will find him to be a valuable addition to your staff. I will certainly be sorry to lose him. Please contact me if you require any further details

Yours faithfully

James Deighton

Company Secretary.

A final note on references. Firstly there is no legal obligation upon an organisation to provide one. Secondly the permission of a referee should be sought before his or her name and address are included on the application form. In cases where an appointment needs to be made rapidly, it is possible that the referee will be telephoned to provide an oral reference, and it does not assist the applicant if the referee is not prepared. In any case there may be reasons why a referee will decline the invitation to act in this capacity.

The layout of a business letter

The general layout of a business letter says something of the organisation which has written it. If the layout is pleasing to the eye and contains at a glance the major information the recipient requires — who the sender is, when it was sent, and what it is concerned with — the recipient is encouraged to regard the organisation sending it as an efficient one. Thus it is not just a case of satisifying standard business conventions when writing a business letter. It has to do with providing a communication in a form which advertises a chosen image for the organisation. The point has already been made that the content of a letter should always be presented courteously. It is sometimes said that the 'ABC' of efficient and effective business letters is accuracy, brevity and clarity. But looking beyond content there are other features of a letter which make an impact on the reader:

    (i)   the design of the printed letter head;

    (ii)   the quality of the paper;

    (iii)   the style and quality of the typewriter or printer head used;

    (iv)   the positioning of the text within the space available; and

    (v)   the use of margins.

A well written letter that meets the requirements of accuracy, brevity and clarity may nevertheless be let down if the letter head is out of date and has to have typed amendments made to it, the paper is thin, and the text is cramped onto a page that is too small, or located at the top of a page leaving a large gap below it.

Having made the observation that a business letter should be regarded in its totality, covering content, style and layout, it is useful to identify the conventions that a business letter should observe. These include:

(a) the senders' name and address.

If the letter does not contain a printed letter head, the sender's address should be included in the top right hand corner of the first page, and the sender's name at the end of the letter.

(b) the date.

This appears after the senders address, and is usually inserted on the right hand side of the page. The month should be written in full to clearly distinguish the date from any reference included in the letter.

(c) the salutation or greeting.

It is usual now to use the recipients name whenever possible, thus "Dear Mr. Green". When the recipient is named in this way the letter should be ended "Yours sincerely". If the greeting "Dear Sir" or "Dear Sirs" is used the letter should close "Yours faithfully." If the letter is written to someone the writer knows well it will begin "Dear Paul" and may end "With best wishes." Letters to a newspaper editor begin simply "Sir".

(d) title or subject line

This is an underlined heading which briefly indicates the subject of the letter. Although not essential it can be very helpful for the addressee, for example it allows the appropriate file to be quickly found.

It is a particularly useful device therefore when dealing with accounts and policies, when the number or reference can be inserted as a heading.

(e) the writer's name.

This appears after the close, and is usually in the form of a signature. It is common practice to print the name beneath the signature, and to indicate the status of the writer, for example "Senior Housing Officer", or "Company Secretary". Sometimes the letters "p.p" are used against the signature. This carries a specific legal meaning and indicates that the signatory is empowered to sign on behalf of another person or the organisation itself.

It is common for less senior staff to be allowed to sign letters, and in this case the indication of the signatory's status will include who he or she is acting on behalf of, thus "Assistant Marketing Manager, for Marketing Manager". Sometimes a personal assistant may sign a letter under specific authority. If so the following form of words should appear "Dictated by Mrs. Pearce and signed in her absence."

(f) references.

The purpose of using references in business letters is to link subsequent correspondence on the same subject matter with the file, and also to ensure that a reply can be directed to the right department or individual. It is therefore a means of ensuring that correspondence is dealt with promptly, and that the author of the letter can, if necessary, be traced. This is obviously more important in larger organisations than small ones.

Usually two references are provided. They appear as "Your Ref:" and "Our Ref:" enabling both the sender and the recipient to link the letter to their respective filing systems. The normal practice is for the initials of the person signing the letter to appear first, followed by an oblique, and then the initials of the secretary/typist. Longer references may refer to the file number or the department.

(g) enclosures.

Very often the enclosure is of more value than the covering letter which accompanies it. It is vital to indicate that a letter includes enclosures, as a reminder to whoever prepares the letter for posting. Common devices are asterisks and stickers, but the most common method is to type "Enclosure", "Encl." or "Enc." at the bottom left hand side of the letter.

(h) the recipient's name and address.

This may appear either at the top left hand side of the letter beside the date, or alternatively at the bottom left hand side, below the senders signature.

TELEX

Telex is a system of written communication used primarily by industry and commerce. The message is transmitted using a teleprinter, and the telex user is given a Telex number, which acts like a telephone number. A telex directory is also provided. Telex facilities are operated by British Telecom.

The advantage of using telex is that:

    (a)   the message can be transferred virtually instantaneously;

    (b)   a written record is kept of the communication;

    (c)   messages can be sent at any time, so provided the recipient's teleprinter has been left on it is possible to pass a message from the United Kingdom during working hours to New Zealand while the staff of the organisation are at home in bed because of the different time scale.

    (d)   errors typed out on the teleprinter can be easily identified by inserting the word "error" and then retyping the correct message.

Because the use of telex facilities is costly (charges are based upon time rather than number of words) the message should be terse but understandable. Normally grammatic rules are dispensed with. An example of a telex message would be:

> "MANAGING DIRECTOR VANDOR P.L.C. ARRIVING 17.30 FRIDAY 31ST OCTOBER. PLEASE MEET. ARRANGE BOARD MEETING FOR 20.00 SAME DAY. MAIN AGENDA ITEM JORDANIAN CONTRACT. CIRCULATE FINANCIAL REPORT 86/2/A IN ADVANCE. BOOK HOTEL ACCOMMODATION ONE NIGHT"

THE USE OF FORMS

One final aspect of the written communications used by organisations needs to be considered; the use of forms. This topic can be dealt with under three headings:

(a) the nature and scope of forms;

(b) the design and layout of forms;

(c) specific types of forms.

(a) the nature and scope of forms

We live in an environment of forms. The major social events of our existence are recorded on them such as births, marriages and deaths. We complete them for licences, insurance policies, job applications, property purchases, credit transactions, membership of organisations and so on. They invade every aspect of our lives, and if we work in an administrative job the likelihood is that processing of forms will be the main aspect of our job.

What is a form and why is it necessary? A form is simply a document of a standardised type, prepared in advance and used as a means of eliciting information from the person completing it. This is achieved by including instructions indicating the nature of the information being required and leaving spaces or blocks where it can be inserted. As with any type of information gathering mechanism the skill in obtaining an accurate and comprehensive response lies in designing appropriate questions and presenting them in a suitable layout. Nevertheless it should be remembered that there may be considerable skill involved in effectively completing a form as well.

Individuals and organisations alike are constantly exposed to a bombardment of forms to be completed, nevertheless many organisations find it useful and necessary to produce their own forms. These may be used as part of an internal system of communication, such as stock records and computer input forms, or as an aspect of external communications, for instance application forms, market research surveys, and questionnaires used to test consumer satisfaction with products and services. A local authority will use many types of forms to obtain relevant information ranging from grant application for loft insulation to planning applications and forms detailing council house applications. No doubt you will have completed an enrolment form at college when you joined your course; perhaps you applied for a grant by completing a form; probably you were required to complete further forms for your course tutor when you attended your first class meeting. The advantages of using a form to obtain and record information are:

(a) the information obtained can be precisely tailored to the needs of the organisation by the use of suitable questions;

(b) the information is provided in a standard order which assists the processing of it;

(c) unnecessary correspondence can be avoided; and

(d) detailed information can be rapidly accessed.

It might also be added that the effective use of forms in an organisation can save time and money, however these benefits can be offset by the over enthusiastic use of forms generating irrelevant and unnecessary information that the organisations has to cope with. Thus an initial question to be asked prior to designing a form is whether it is really necessary. Perhaps there is a simpler way of obtaining the information. Even if this is so the fact remains that the form is a major tool of communication for all types of organisations. It is an indispensible mechanism for obtaining information, and monitoring processes and activities.

(b) the design and layout of forms

The design and layout of forms is a skilled task, often carried out by specialists. Essentially it involves constructing the appropriate questions to which answers are being sought, and ordering them in a suitable way. Sometimes an existing form may be amended to meet the requirements of the form designer.

The following issues need to be addressed in producing the form.

(i) the instructions to the recipient.

It helps to remember that a form involves two way communication. The recipient should be clear how the form should be completed, to whom it should be returned, when it should be returned by, and perhaps what purpose it serves the organisation seeking to obtain the data. A valuable general instruction is to indicate that no part of the form should be left unanswered, and that questions that do not apply to the recipient should be answered "Not applicable".

(ii) the questions.

Questions can be framed in different ways, but as long as they are clear and precise it is simply a matter of design preference as to the method used. An example of different approaches is the use of direct and indirect questions, thus "What is your reason for seeking this job?" (direct), "Reason for application" (indirect). The language of each question should be kept as simple as accuracy permits, and it should never be necessary for the recipient to spend time working out what a question means. If a question inevitably involves the use of a technical expression, a note of explanation should be provided, preferably as close to the question as possible. The designer should be aware of the types of reader who will complete the form, to ensure that its language reflects the most basic level of literacy that any reader may possess. A questionnaire for completion by lawyers would probably use a wider range of vocabulary than would be desirable in a form to be completed by nine year old school children.

(iii) the responses.

It should be absolutely clear how the recipient is required to respond to the questions. Common methods of response include: "Please place a tick in the appropriate box," "Please answer 'yes' or 'no', and "Please state briefly your reasons." If the recipient is confused it is possible for the answer given to be the opposite of the correct one. When a written or typed response is asked for sufficient space should be made available.

(iv) question sequence.

This should be logical. An application form for a job might commence with a section dealing with the applicant's personal details: name; age; marital status; number of dependants. It would then require information on qualifications and work experience. This would be followed by a section identifying the applicant's interests and hobbies, a section specifying referees, and finally a section enabling the applicant to identify the questions which make him or her suitable for the post.

(v) processing considerations.

Sometimes the information obtained needs to be collated for the preparation of statistical returns or survey reports. It may be that the organisation is seeking to identify trends and general patterns rather than use information obtained on an individual basis. If this is so it is vital that the information is presented in a way which is as easy as possible to process. If the information is to be processed electronically then the capacities of the data processing equipment used will need to be considered when the form is produced. In such cases instructions may be of vital importance: the machine may be unable to pick up and 'read' anything other than black ink or print.

(vi) legal implications

Many forms are the direct product of statutory provisions. Applications to renew business leases, to provide information for the Registrar of Companies, to register as an elector, to complete an income tax return, and to tax and insure a motor vehicle all involve the completion of forms that are required by statute. Often criminal penalties can be imposed if the information provided is known to be false. In the case of insurance proposals the proposer (the applicant) is under a positive legal obligation to provide information materially relevant to the risk to be insured, even if this is not asked for on the form. An organisation insuring its premises against fire is likely to find the insurance company avoiding the policy if it discovers that the organisation is knowingly employing a convicted arsonist. It will be no defence to the organisation to say that the policy did not ask "Do you have in your employment any convicted arsonists? If so please give details."!

(c) Specific types of forms.

The variety of forms in common use is so vast that it is impossible to give anything other than a very general description of what they include. It may however help to identify the broad categories into which they fall. These categories relate to the purpose of the form and clearly the content of the form will usually reflect the purpose or objective the organisation has in using it.

Thus forms are used:

    (a)   to keep records — financial; personnel; statistical and so on;

    (b)   for applications — for jobs; grants; hearings before an industrial tribunal;

    (c)   for making orders or bookings — goods from a supplier; a package holiday; a credit transaction; internal requisitions;

    (d)   to monitor processes and make assessments — stock records; the evaluation of product quality; work sheets; income tax returns;

    (e)   for carrying our surveys (usually by means of questionnaires) — consumer reaction to a new product; the Census.

ORAL COMMUNICATIONS

Having examined in some detail the written methods used by organisations in the communication process, we must conclude by looking at the oral methods of communication that organisations use. These include: the use of the telephone; dictation; verbal presentation of reports; interviewing and meetings. It should be recalled that oral communication involves not only the skills of speaking but of listening as well. A communications system is ineffective if its staff are poor listeners, and research evidence suggests that most people listen at a 25% efficiency level. Poor listening can result in work being retyped, orders being misdirected and meetings being rearranged.

The larger and more complex an organisation becomes the more important it is for those operating the communications system to guard against it becoming too unwieldly. When oral messages are being transferred the larger the number of employees involved in the chain of communication the greater is the danger of the message becoming distorted. The story is told of the message being sent along the trenches during the First World War which began its life as "3000 Germans advancing on the West flank. Send reinforcements" but ended up as "3000 Germans dancing on a wet plank. Send three and fourpence".

A good listener is someone who:

    (a)   concentrates on the speaker's delivery without being distracted by external or internal factors (noise and daydreaming for example; or the speaker's habits)

    (b)   is not emotionally affected by the statements the speaker makes;

(c)   listens to everything that is being said, rather than concentrating on main points, or homing in only when the speaker sounds more interesting;

(d)   recognises that people are able to take in words much faster than they can be spoken, and develops a strategy for overcoming the spare time this disparity provides. Note taking is a useful device for doing so. Obviously the nature of the subject matter is a significant factor. If the speaker is using complex language and sophisticated concepts the spare time for other thoughts the listener may have is likely to be very limited.

STYLES OF ORAL COMMUNICATION

As a general proposition oral communications are either formal or informal. Informal speech is largely used in our social and domestic relationships. The language used is abbreviated for we know each other well, and lengthy explanations are not called for. Compare a chat you might have with a close friend, with the casual conversation you might have with a stranger at a business function, to assess how much the language you use varies according to the recipient.

Formal speech is appropriate to the work environment where the speaker represents the organisation, and therefore delivers his or her words with more care and precision, in a carefully structured way. Clearly a telephone conversation with a business customer does not warrant a style or tone which is over familiar or excessively casual. A personal telephone call to a friend however is quite a different matter.

The nature of oral communications is affected not only by the purpose of the statements being made, the formal/informal distinction, but also by the physical distance between the parties involved. In face to face communications the physical proximity of the parties enables much closer awareness to develop through the use of forms of non-verbal communication such as facial expressions and other forms of body language, whereas more distant communication, for example the use of the telephone, effectively eliminates the use of non verbal signs and emphasises the importance of the language being used.

The significance of these elements of formality/informality, and physical distance lies in the different social rules which govern oral communications. For instance in face to face communications we tend to respond in different ways to the people we are dealing with according to our perceptions of what they expect of us. You might feel it quite out of order to crack a joke with your Head of Department, whereas you do this all the time with colleagues of the same grade as yourself. Status then is an important factor in the self determination of what is and is not acceptable oral expression. So too is the reaction we identify from what we say to others. If the Head of Department leads the conversation by telling a joke we may feel this is a suitable opening for a humourous anecdote that it would not otherwise have seemed appropriate to tell.

Thus it is not true to say that being physically close necessarily produces a less formal approach to oral communication, nor that it is impossible to communicate informally over a distance (for instance phoning a friend.)

This interrelationship can be described diagramatically:

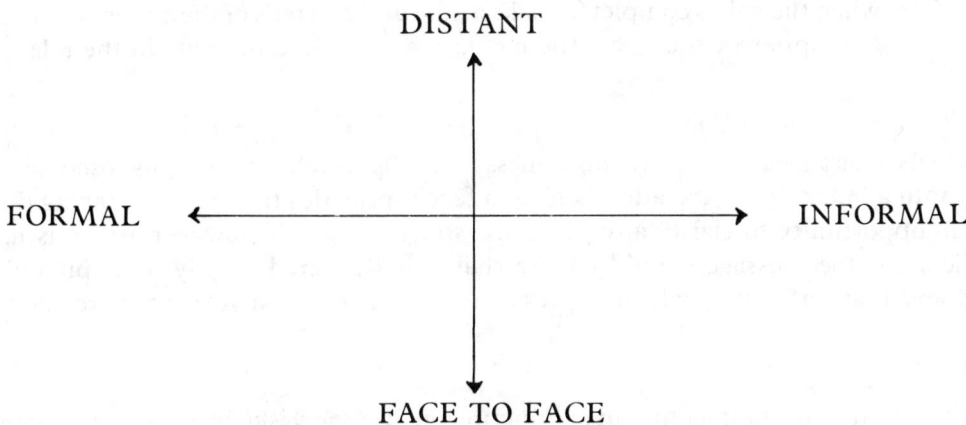

Different oral communications can be placed within any one of the four quadrants according to where they lie on each axis. An example is given below:

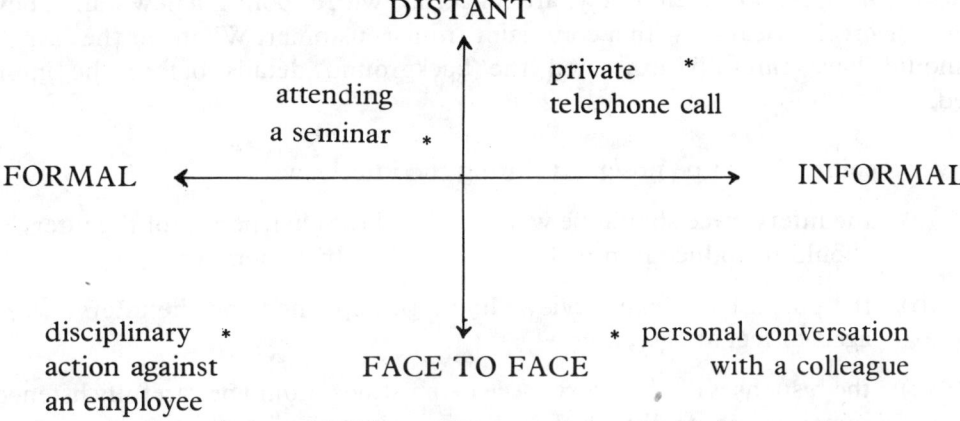

METHODS OF ORAL COMMUNICATION

The Telephone

Within most organisations the telephone is a vital tool in the business of communicating. It is important not just as a link with customers and clients, but also as a means of communicating internally through the organisation if it is equipped with a PABX system.

When making a telephone call it is necessary to think out what needs to be said in advance. If the message is long or complex it is especially important to be sure that it has been received and understood by the person at the other end of the line. Asking for the message to be repeated is useful. This can identify confusion that may arise over the sounds of words which are similar. An order for "Fifty" can easily be mistaken as one for "Fifteen" for example, and "Miss Carr" may end up as "Miss Garr". Obviously it helps to speak as clearly as possible into the mouthpiece of the telephone. The following points should be followed when using a telephone:

(a) when making or receiving a call the identity of the parties should be established at the outset;

(b) a pad and pen or pencil should be immediately to hand in order to avoid keeping the other party waiting;

(c) the parties should speak as clearly as possible: often telephone conversations are conducted in very noisy environments which makes it difficult to distinguish the voice on the telephone from other extraneous sounds;

(d) avoid keeping a caller waiting for long periods whilst information is being sought: it is far better to arrange to call back;

(e)   when the call is completed make a note of the details of the conversation and take appropriate action (pass the message on, or place the note in the relevant file).

Dictation

Dictation is used as a means of conveying a message orally which is to be transposed into writing — usually into a letter. If the dictation is face to face it provides the secretary taking down the message an opportunity to clarify any problems straightaway. If however a tape is made the person dictating the message should ensure that it is delivered clearly, that punctuation is identified and that difficult words or expressions such as unusual surnames are spelt out.

Interviews

Probably the most important feature in conducting an interview is to be properly prepared. The interview room should be laid out so that the interviewer and the interviewee are close enough to be able to hear each other properly. The interviewer (or the panel) should have examined the application prior to the interview and have identified a systematic approach to the questioning of the applicant. Of course not all interviews are concerned with appointing new staff. They may be disciplinary or involve dealing with a complaint from a customer. Whatever the case the interviewer should have carefully examined the background details before the interview is conducted.

The following points should be observed during the interview:

(a)   the interviewee should be welcomed and the chairperson of the interview panel should introduce him or herself and the other members;

(b)   the purpose of the interview should be explained and the interviewee encouraged to feel at ease;

(c)   the responses of the interviewee to questions should be carefully listened to. It is important not to disturb the interviewee's train of thought and to monopolise the conversation. The questions themselves should be pertinent, and a note should be kept of points that need to be remembered as the interview proceeds;

(d)   the interview should be concluded when the interviewers have received the information they need.

The situation should be summarised. If it is possible to do so any decision which has been reached should be communicated. Alternatively it should be explained that a decision will be communicated at a later stage, and an indication given as to when this is likely to be.

It is courteous to thank the interviewee for attending, and in the case of a job application for which a decision can be made after the interviews have been completed, it is a human gesture to provide the unsuccessful applicants with some brief words of reassurance.

ASSIGNMENT — A LETTER FROM MRS HARRIS

The Housing Department of Centwich District Council has received the following letters:

26 Nantwich Grove
Macclesfield
Cheshire

27 May 19xx

Dear Sir or Madam,

My nephew's council house is terrible. I've never seen anything like it in my life. I keep telling him to complain to you but he won't so I have to. My house is as bad. Can you do something about it? My husband has been off work and laid up with his back for weeks and I don't know where the rent is coming from. It makes me feel like suicide. I'm nearly sixty one and Harry is fifty nine. If nothing happens soon I'm going to the newspapers.

Yours sincerely

J. Harris (Mrs)

Cheshire Chronicle
Print House
Stockport

28 May 19xx

Dear Sir,

Following a complaint received by this newspaper from a Mrs J. Harris of 26 Nantwich Grove, Macclesfield, concerning the condition of her council house, a reporter and a photographer visited her home.

This lady's story is very disturbing. I am writing to inform you that I will be carrying the story on the front page of next Friday's edition of the Chronicle. I will of course be happy to publish any response you care to make to the story.

Yours faithfully,

Bruce Wilson

Bruce Wilson (Editor),

Director of Housing
Centwich District Council
Council Offices
Centwich.

5, Stoke Terrace,
Macclesfield
Cheshire

29 May 19xx

Dear Sir,

I understand that my aunt, Mrs J. Harris, has written to you, making a number of complaints. I felt I ought to point out to you that I am entirely satisfied with my council accommodation, and that my aunt is at present being treated by her doctor for depression.

Yours faithfully,

Mick Williams

TASKS

In your capacity as a housing assistant you have been asked by your head of section to consider these letters.

1. Draft a letter in reply to Mrs Harris's letter in which you attempt to deal with her complaint.

2. Draft a letter in reply to the letter from the Editor, in which you attempt to persuade him not to publish the story concerning Mrs Harris.

3. Draft a letter in reply to the correspondence from Mick Williams in which you suitably acknowledge him for the information he has provided.

4. Write a memorandum to the Director of Housing alerting him to the situation that has arisen concerning Mrs Harris.

5. Imagine that you are a reporter on the Cheshire Chronicle: Prepare a newspaper article to be carried in the next edition covering Mrs Harris' story.

ASSIGNMENT — GEE'S SUPERMARKET

Following the merger of Gee's Supermarkets, with the Constance Food Store group, the first board meeting of the new company, G & C Foods Ltd. resulted in a number of important changes being implemented. One of them was the establishment of a personnel department. Previously neither company had operated a personnel department, but had left personnel matters to individual departments to sort out for themselves.

You have been transferred to this new department, where your job involves you working as a senior assistant to the Personnel Office, Anne Robinson. After your initial meeting with Ms Robinson, at which a variety of issues were discussed, you received the following internal memorandum from her:

From: Personnel Officer

To: Senior Personnel Assistant   Date: 9 June 19xx

Re: **Establishment of Standardised Materials**

I have given thought to our conversation on the need for standardised letters and forms to meet the functions of the new department. I am satisfied that we cannot standardise job adverts, however please provide me with drafts of the following:

Forms:
— a job application form that all job applicants would have to complete (I would want it to contain sufficient information to enable me to use it as an employee record form)
— a staff appraisal form to record job performance

Letters to fulfil the following tasks:
— invite applicants for job interviews;
— inform an applicant that he/she is not being called for interview;
— inform an interviewee that he/she is not being offered the job;
— offer the job to the successful interviewee;
— issue a formal warning to an employee guilty of misconduct stating that dismissal will result from a repetition of the conduct complained of;
— issue a dismissal;
— inform an employee that he/she is being made redundant.

I am aware that this is a substantial task but would ask you to complete it as a matter of urgency.

TASKS

1. Draft the forms and letters requested in the memorandum, using a content, tone and style appropriate to each of them.

2. write a memorandum to the Personnel Officer indicating that you expect the work to take considerable time to complete.

DEVELOPMENTAL TASK

3. Obtain examples of some of the above documents, letters and forms used by public and private sector organisations in your area. Compare these in order to produce a dossier containing a single example of each document, letter or form which combines the examples of best practice in each.

Chapter 3

INFORMATION SYSTEMS

INFORMATION TRANSFER

Any organisation, whether it is a small business with only a few employees or a multi-national company with a staff of thousands, is involved in a continuous process of information transfer. This will include communication with outside individuals and organisations. Orders may be placed, demands for payment made or letters of complaint received. These are all examples of external information transfer.

Internally, information is passed from superiors to subordinates and vice versa. Instructions are given, advice sought and praise and criticism handed out. In fact everywhere we look in an organisation we see information transferred in a wide variety of forms: orally; in writing; electronically or even in the non verbal message conveyed by the shake of the head as the boss informs the supplicant worker that his pay rise has been refused.

If this activity were to stop the organisation would be unable to function, for information is as as essential a resource as its workforce or its capital equipment. Denying it this information would be like restricting the flow of oxygen to the human brain: at first it works less efficiently but finally it stops working altogether. For many organisations it is the failure of the information system itself which may produce this distorting effect. This is because the system does not function efficiently and thus creates a blurred picture to the 'brain' of the organisation, in other words the individuals who manage it are not receiving the right information. Obviously it is of vital importance to the organisation that such a situation is avoided at all costs. Later in this chapter we will be examining some of the symptoms which ineffective or inappropriate information systems reveal, and then considering how the causes of such problems can be dealt with.

Our immediate task however is to examine the nature and scope of "information transfer", in order to gain some idea of why this information transfer process is so vitally important. The first observation that can be made concerns the nature of the process, and involves us in looking at the functions of communication.

WHY DO WE COMMUNICATE?

If you reflect for a moment on the major aspects of your communications with others and examines what your reasons or motives are for communicating, you are likely to come up with a list that is longer than simply "to seek or give information". For example it may be that you are merely being sociable, for instance inquiring after someone's family or it may be that you are providing psychological support to a friend or colleague who has a particular problem. Your communications could also have a mercenary or commercial motive such as trying to persuade someone to buy your car. These then are only some of the purposes underlying our communications with others.

In a sense all of the examples given above have relevance to organisations. We can recognise that a workforce will be well motivated if its members enjoy satisfactory social relationships with each other. If the organisation's personnel department is able to provide psychological support to workers who need it, they may be able to achieve their full work potential once again. In the same way that you may be trying to sell your car, all commercial organisations are trying to sell their products or services and are thus in the business of persuading customers to buy. Furthermore within an organisation managers may spend time trying to persuade staff to improve their timekeeping, change their working practices or increase their output.

When the underlying purpose of a communication is social, psychological or persuasive it is not always easy to measure how successful it has been, for it does not necessarily have a tangible end product. Your friend may be pleased that you asked her about her family, your colleague consoled by your words of help or the buyer persuaded to part with his money. But other factors may have played a part. The purchaser may have bought the car irrespective of your persuasion! However in the case of transferring information the success of the transfer process can be guaged by assessing whether the recipient has acquired the knowledge or information and it is in a form which is understandable.

Next we need to consider why it is necessary to transfer the information in the first place. It is only by considering who is passing on the information, to whom it is directed and its nature that it is possible to decide whether the information transfer is necessary at all. For this purpose a distinction may be drawn between the internal and external communications of the organisation.

THE SCOPE OF INFORMATION TRANSFER

(a) Internal Communications

The structure of an organisation, refers not only to the physical environment in which the staff work, but also to its social and psychological environment. By this is meant such factors as the respective positions and the authority and status of staff. It is the organisation's structure which will influence the flow of information within it. For instance in a small organisation with only one boss, who likes to know everything that is going on, all the important information will be directed from or to that individual. In a large organisation its functions will certainly be separated and dispersed. The managing director or chief executive will wish to be made aware only of information relating to major issues and will not normally be bothered to deal with every message of a trivial nature or to sign every letter that leaves the organisation.

To determine the effectiveness of the process it is necessary to ascertain whether the right information gets to the right person at the right time or if there is some structural barrier to communication which needs to be identified and overcome. Appropriate organisational structures are those which recognise that information flows are necessary for the smooth running of the enterprise. Furthermore the processes used for satisfying the informational needs of the organisation must be suitable. For instance, when an accident occurs in the production process at work, there should be an existing procedure of which all staff are aware to cope with the situation. The procedure will involve not only the completion of an accident report form which is designed to enable all the information relevant to the incident to be recorded, but also to identify the departments of the organisation which should receive a copy of the report. There is little point in circulating the report to all departments; the sales department would have little use for such information. Certainly for those departments that do require it, the report will have failed to do its job if the information it contains is ambiguous, unclear, or positively misleading.

(b) External Communications

It is important that the organisation is alert to the communications it has with outsiders. The organisation must be able to respond appropriately to information it receives and also be aware that the information it gives out will affect the value of its reputation with the outside world.

Therefore such information needs to be transmitted intelligibly.

Two examples may help to illustrate the significance of these aspects of the organisation's external communications. Most large organisations keep detailed computer records. These include lists of customers and their addresses, staffing records with previous employment histories, disciplinary action taken — perhaps even convictions. To cope with the danger that misuse of this information can cause to individuals, the Data Protection Act 1984 was passed by Parliament with the support of the government. The Act obliges data users to register with the Data Protection Registrar if the data files they keep fall within the scope of the Act. Failure to do so can result in fines up to £2000. When an organisation receives advance notification of such legislative provisions it will arrive as information coming into the organisation. It must have a system developed for passing the information, in an appropriate form, to the relevant personnel, so that they are aware of the change, and can comply with the law.

Our second example relates to the output of information. Imagine the chaos and the damage to the reputation of a bus company whose published timetables contain inaccuracies about times, routes and destinations. Again there is a vital need to ensure that the organisation communicates accurately and intelligibly to its recipients, using a suitable format.

. . . . imagine the chaos and the damage to the reputation . . .

AN INFORMATION PROCESS IN PRACTICE

It is useful at this stage to briefly sketch information processes in practice. Let us take two familiar organisations, firstly your own local authority, and secondly the college at which you study and examine how their information needs are interlinked.

Your local authority, whether it is a district, county metropolitan borough or London borough, will employ a workforce of many hundreds. They administer and perform the various duties and functions which by law the council must carry out. These operations are financed by grants provided from central government and income derived locally from rates, as well as from other sources such as council house rents. For this financial relationship to work there must be detailed flows of information between the local authority and central government to establish revenue needs. Thus it must provide central government with details of the number of children of school age, old people and disabled citizens in its area.

Furthermore there needs to be communication between the authority and its ratepayers to establish how much they will be required to contribute in rates for the coming financial year. This takes the form of a rate demand from the authority, containing information that tells the householder how much income the authority needs, where it is coming from, how it is calculated and how it is to be spent.

Let us suppose that the authority is one obliged to provide education services. The Education Department will consist of administrators responsible for ensuring that school and college buildings are physically maintained and that staff are employed and paid for teaching in those institutions. The education department must therefore compile and maintain detailed records of the physical and human resources that it controls. It must ensure that it regularly updates any changes to these resources and feeds back information to schools and colleges through head teachers and principals. This takes the form of education budgets.

At the same time the schools and colleges themselves will be disseminating information in a variety of ways. They will be publishing prospectuses, listing the courses and subjects they offer, detailing examination results, and advertising extra mural activities. They will be informing new students and pupils of their timetables and gathering data about them using a variety of formats, such as enrolment forms and record cards.

Your college will have a committee structure designed to enable it to operate efficiently and effectively. Committee members require notice of meetings and agendas; records will need to be kept of the meetings that are held and important decisions communicated to those who are affected by them. Information will be passed down from the college management to the teaching staff detailing changes in employment conditions, training opportunities and internal promotions. Information will be passed up through the committee structure from the staff to the management, identifying examination performance, reports of meetings and conferences attended.

Thus if you stop for a moment to consider the organisation in which you work, the local authority whose area in which you live or the college at which you are studying, and examine the work it does, you may begin to appreciate the enormous amount of time and effort that is devoted to the business of giving and receiving information. It is very much like a production process. An organisation can only function satisfactorily if its members operate as a team, working together to meet the aims and objectives of that enterprise. It is inevitable that there must be information systems to assist the workforce in obtaining a clear view of what they need to know to do the job, whether it is in respect of the nature of their role, or simply who to contact to obtain a particular file. If the system is deficient, the members of the organisation are starved of the knowledge they require to perform their work. Like a computer controlled production process that has been incorrectly programmed there can be little hope that the end product will be what was originally intended.

AN INFORMATION POLICY

Much of the business of managing an organisation is directed towards ensuring that its policies are effectively implemented. The term 'policy' is very wide. In its broadest sense it refers to the general aims of the organisation and is often framed as organisational and individual objectives. Organisational objectives can be drawn in both economic and social terms. For example a business may establish a corporate policy which spans the next five years, which indicates planned areas of expansion and anticipated levels of growth. Equally the policy may include more specific individual objectives set for personnel within the organisation. They may emerge out of a job description, or be a target or task set by a superior, such as a monthly sales target. Furthermore because of its underlying importance a general policy statement on communications is likely to emerge in any examination of the objectives of the organisation. Such a statement will not be an end in itself, but simply the means by which the other objectives can be satisfactorily met.

Lying at the heart of any information system are two fundamental issues. These are the need to:

1. ensure that the organisation receives the information it requires to operate efficiently and achieve its objectives;

2. ensure that this information is received by the appropriate member of staff.

A failure to cope with these may have dramatic results. For example the failure to notify shop stewards of a change in working practices may result in the workforce taking industrial action. Alternatively the failure of the Social Services Department of a local authority to recognise signs of child abuse may be the result of the complex communications problems of co-ordinating the various organisations and individuals potentially involved such as schools, doctors, social workers and the police. Such communication failure may have harrowing consequences. Therefore it is obvious that an information system should be established which tackles the two problems outlined earlier. Thus it is necessary to examine these two related but nevertheless distinct aspects of the communications process: who communicates with whom and what is being communicated.

1.   Who communicates with whom?

In a sectionalised or departmentalised organisation much of the work going on relates essentially only to a specific department and usually the larger an organisation is, the more functionally departmentalised it becomes. In such circumstances there may be neither the time nor the need for individual employees to be aware of those activities of the organisation which fall outside their own work responsibilities. Therefore information transfer should be limited to those who need to know. For instance in a legal department the systems and procedures used, and the information being passed between the staff may be of no concern or interest to the sales department or the research and development department. Top management will certainly be concerned that the legal department conducts its work efficiently. However it may not interfere with the departments methods of working. It is for the section head to be responsible for such matters as its use of secretarial support, the telephones and the telex, written correspondence and face to face meetings. Therefore the lines of communication at a functional level are often established by department or section heads.

However people in more senior posts acting in a controlling capacity need to take a much broader view. This is necessary to enable them to co-ordinate the work of the staff they are responsible for, and so achieve a satisfactory integration of this work with the activities of the rest of the organisation in order that it operates as an integrated whole. Their information needs will be to monitor and review the progress of the organisation's aims and objectives.

Thus in large organisations there will be lines of communication, paths along which information passes backwards and forwards. These lines of communication may be downwards (communications from a superior to a subordinate), upwards (subordinate to superior) or horizontal (communications between people of similar status). Even an organisation employing a small number of staff, such as a small retailer, is likely to have identifiable lines of communication which follow this pattern. How formal or informal these lines of communication are often depends upon the size and type of the organisation. In a local authority for example, the range and complexity of work being carried out, together with the large number of employees performing it, leads to an essentially formal and clearly defined organisational and communications structure. It is unlikely that a junior clerical assistant will have direct access to the chief executive. This would be less likely in the case of a building site where a much more informal communication structure is appropriate to the type of team work the job involves.

. . . a more informal communication structure . . .

2.   What is being communicated?

The information content of an organisation's internal communications is wide ranging and will vary according to the type of work being carried out. Nevertheless all organisations require basic systems dealing with such matters as financial records. The following list includes some common examples:

Work rules; orders and instructions; grievance and disciplinary procedures; contracts of employment; accident reports; sales records; financial statements; statistical data, stock control records, and so on.

These examples are essentially related to the internal aspects of communications and fall within the expression "control"; they are all control mechanisms in the hands of managers.

It is important that some system of inter-departmental communication should be devised which identifies how the information is to be passed and to whom it should be directed. For instance in most organisations, internal memoranda will frequently be used to act as a form of internal communication. To use it you need to know how it can be physically transferred and to whom it should be properly addressed. There may be many individuals who should receive it and they need to be identified in advance. You should also keep a copy of the memo on an appropriate file. It is a written account of your action.

At the centre of such interdepartmental activity will usually be a general office. The function of the general office has already been examined in chapter 1. However we will briefly reconsider its role in the organisation. Its role will involve:

(a)   providing information to organisations and individuals in the outside world;

(b)   receiving incoming information and processing it;

(c)   keeping central records;

(d)   providing the organisation with data for control purposes; and

(e)   often providing administrative support services such as reprographics, secretarial services and telex facilities.

Such an office is involved in information processing, receiving, storing, retrieving and passing on information. Many of these tasks can be carried out admirably using a computer based information system.

Additionally there are the external communications of the organisation, involving relationships with the outside world. These include those it supplies or buys from, and those to whom it is responsible legally and economically. We have already seen that one of the aims of communications is often to persuade. In practice the dissemination of information by an organisation may involve an attempt to convince the recipients that the company's product is worth buying or that the local authority is providing a valuable service to its ratepayers. In other words the information process often forms part of a marketing strategy. This is true not only for external communications but internal communications as well. When management inform the shopfloor workers that the recession prevents the payment of a wage increase this year, they will doubtless try to convince the workforce that there is no alternative. If the management's powers of persuasion are poor they may well face a labour dispute.

As one aspect of its external information processes the organisation will issue or receive communications that are purely informative, with no hidden persuasive component, such as invoices, rates demands, general correspondence, and a wide range of other documentation.

Having identified both the extent of the lines of communication and examples of the nature and content of the information being transferred it is finally possible to describe the information system or systems of an organisation. However, whether or not the systems operate as an effective and coherent whole can really only be answered by returning to our earlier discussion of objectives and determining how successfully these are being met.

In practical terms the way to ensure that the organisation's information transfer is satisfactory is by adopting appropriate formats. Thus it is important to bear in mind who the recipient is, what the information consists of and the purpose of the communication. But like any other system, regular monitoring is essential to prevent the existing system from losing its capacity to cope with demands that steadily change. If your organisation is unaware that its competitors are processing data ten times more quickly than it is, it will soon find itself becoming uncompetitive through its lack of cost effectiveness. The reason why the competitors are able to process information more quickly may be that they have invested in an appropriate computer system while your organisation has retained its traditional manual systems.

ELEMENTS IN THE DESIGN OF AN INFORMATION SYSTEM

We have already noted that larger organisations will often acknowledge the major role played by communications by adopting a communications policy. Such a policy is likely to describe the purpose of the communications activity and the importance management attaches to it, but it will not usually be a detailed statement describing the system. It is more likely to be a statement of the organisation's philosophy than a practical guide on how to implement and operate a communications network.

This is not to suggest communications policies are cosmetic shams and of no real value. On the contrary they can be instrumental in creating the ethos or atmosphere of the workplace. Most of us quickly gain a sense of the social climate of an organisation when we enter its building. Sometimes we will be aware of a cold impersonal attitude of its staff to us or perhaps just a feeling of indifference. Alternatively a warm and helpful approach will be immediately apparent. This social climate is also a reflection of the measure of staff contentment with their working environment, both in physical terms such as pay, accommodation, equipment, canteen facilities etc, and in psychological terms for example workers' job satisfaction, their quality of relationships with fellow employees, and their perception of their role.

. . . the social climate . . .

A major contributor to the quality of the working environment is the communications system operating within it. Since such systems are pervasive, infiltrating every aspect of work, it is essential that they are effective. Breakdowns in communications damage not only business efficiency but staff morale. Consequently a policy that both emphasises the overall importance of good communication, and states how this objective is to be realised is beneficial in the following ways:

(i)   the mere existence of such a policy suggests that management is aware of and receptive to the role of communications in the organisation, and that planning and decision making throughout the undertaking should take place mindful of the communications issues involved;

(ii)   it lays a foundation upon which to build a more detailed communications network specifically related to information flows;

(iii)   as a consequence of (i) and (ii) the organisation's internal operations run effectively because relevant data is available when and where it is needed and staff consultation procedures are improved; and

(iv)   attention is paid to developing good public relations and thus enhancing the image of the organisation in its external relations.

The factors that a communications policy might identify to deal specifically with communications as they affect employees personally include:

1.   The importance of good employer/employee relations
In a large organisation this is achieved by a personnel or welfare officer taking responsibility for the handling of:

(a)   disciplinary measures;

(b)   employees grievances;

(c)   the monitoring of career development;

(d)   personal problems, such as illness, or the death of a member of the employee's family.

2.   The need for machinery to enable consultation to take place between management and workforce;

3.   The importance of providing induction for new starters, and of keeping staff generally informed about the organisation and what is happening within it.

Putting such a policy into practice goes a long way towards ensuring that good industrial relations can develop and, more broadly, that employees are happy in their job.

4.   The cost of an information system
Clearly the process of communication costs money. A large part of an organisation's man hours are devoted to it, and thus it needs to be as cost effective as possible. This can be achieved by using suitably trained staff and appropriate equipment. In large organisations experts are sometimes brought in to examine the needs of the system and suggest ways of improving it and making it more efficient and cost effective.

Costs may be viewed in absolute terms, that is the operating costs to the organisation of both its internal and external communications systems. This can be done by assessing the man hours involved, the equipment which has to be bought and specific costs such as computer time for data processing or telephone or telex charges. It may also be looked at in relative terms by comparing one approach with another, for instance by evaluating the operating costs of a telex system as opposed to telephone usage.

Absolute costs are essentially policy considerations to be determined by senior managers, making budget allowances and identifying areas in which savings can be made. In both public and private sector organisations restrictions are often placed upon outgoing telephone calls requiring that all but urgent calls be made during the cheaper periods of the day.

Determining relative costs involves careful costing exercises. It may be that replacing typewriters with word processors will increase efficiency, but there may be training costs and a larger initial outlay. There may also be the job of convincing older staff of the benefits of the new methods. A comparison is often made between the cost of a telephone call as against a letter. To arrive at a proper conclusion not only must one consider the time factor involved, but hidden costs such as maintenance of the typewriter, the salary of the typist and so on.

An information system will often emerge out of a general statement of organisational policy. In smaller organisations, however, it will invariably be considered without reference to broader communications policy. In fact many information systems, whether the enterprise is large or small, are not actually the product of an overall design at all, but simply the outcome of piece-meal developments as the organisation has evolved. In consequence the system may be ill-suited to the enterprise it serves, containing unseen barriers to communications. In the design of an information system it is vital to be aware of the ways in which barriers to communications occur.

IDENTIFYING BARRIERS TO COMMUNICATION

Such barriers are the consequence of poor system design and are either physical or psychological. They result from a very wide range of causes, some of which can be easily identified and resolved, especially when the solution to the problem involves elementary changes to the design of the system. Other barriers, especially those caused by negative attitudes, require time and delicate handling.

DESIGN FAULTS.

These include:

(a) Incompatible organisational structures.
For example a problem could arise in an organisation, where the personnel department deals with disciplinary matters and the heads of section handle the personal problems of staff under them. Because these matters are separately dealt with this could prevent a connection being made between, for instance, abusive behaviour at work and personal problems at home. In other words the link between cause and effect is not recognised.

(b) Imprecise descriptions of roles and responsibilities.

Staff should be clear about the tasks they are required to perform, to whom they are accountable, and the extent of their responsibilities.

(c) Lack of supervision and/or training.

Effective supervision can identify difficulties facing members of the workforce which prevent them from performing their jobs effectively. Training programmes can help to overcome these.

(d) Ineffecient or inappropriate information systems.

For instance an appraisal of the reprographics work carried out could reveal that the existing facilities are too slow or not sufficiently cost effective.

(e) Mechanisms for evaluating the system are inadequate or non-existent.

In order to discover whether or not a system is functioning properly it has to be reviewed and faults diagnosed and cured. Thus an analysis of the system by a professional outsider such as a management consultant or a systems analyst is a valuable tool. This is especially so when the size of the organisation makes it impossible for the managers to rely on essentially informal structures for control. As growth occurs there is a tendency towards greater division of labour and this in turn requires an increase in the physical size of the workplace. The obvious impact this has upon a communication system is to force it to become more formalised so that it can cope with the more complex communications patterns that develop.

PHYSICAL BARRIERS

(a) Inadequacies in the geographical layout of the workplace

Many people are employed by organisations in which a number of physically separated buildings are administered as a single entity. This situation is often the result of superimposing a new organisational structure upon existing sites which were not designed to cope with it. Many schools and colleges are based on split sites as a result of educational re-organisation. For instance two schools half a mile away from each other and previously quite separately administered are now being operated as a single administrative unit because of an amalgamation. This problem may also be encountered where an organisation occupying a single site expands its operation as growth takes place. Limitations of space and money can result in an overall building plan that is not conducive to effective communications between departments. Sometimes in a single office complex, such as the administrative block of a local council, the physical re-arrangement of departments so that those most closely interrelated are placed beside each other, can have a marked effect upon improving communications efficiency.

(b) Inadequacies in the provision of equipment

This may be due to a lack of investment in updating existing equipment, such as typewriters and photocopiers. Management may fail to realise the potential of new systems and the value of the electronic office in improving performance. It can be as simple as failure to regularly service equipment causing it to break down, or the inability of staff who use equipment to realise its full potential. Thus the boss may prefer to dictate letters orally to a secretary, rather than use a dictating machine because he is intimidated by technology. The capacities of the audio-typing facilities, the equipment and the trained audio typist are thus being wasted.

(c) staff problems

The most obvious difficulty that can occur in this respect is quite simply a problem of under-staffing. If the manpower needed to operate the information system is not at full strength the system cannot work satisfactorily.

ATTITUDINAL BARRIERS

These may occur at any level within the hierarchy of the organisation. It may be helpful to note that there are usually two clearly discernable elements in the social/psychological climate of the organisation. There is the official line of command which is found by looking at the administrative arrangements for the organisation, for instance how it is structured and what the job descriptions of individual staff contain. This is referred to as the "authority hierarchy" and it can be set out in the form of an organisation chart. This will almost always reveal a pyramid design to the power structure of the organisation.

At a more subtle level there is what is referred to as the "status hierarchy". This is less to do with rank than with the earning of respect. Of course it is often the most powerful individuals in the organisation who are also the most respected. However such respect may be related more to their power to 'hire and fire' than to any belief in their integrity and capability. It does not always follow that you will automatically approach senior staff when you are seeking help or a favour. Instead you turn to the long serving employee whom everybody agrees knows the system inside and out and can use the contacts developed over years of service to "get things done".

Having briefly identified these aspects of authority what attitudinal barriers can exist? They include:

(a) Employee problems

These may be the result of an individual's own personal attitudes. These include phobias, such as the fear of the radiation levels emitted by visual display units or basic prejudices against the opposite sex or people from different racial or cultural backgrounds. Alternatively the fault may lie with management. An employee's lack of training may affect his ability to perform effectively an allotted responsibility. This failing may not be the fault of the employee but instead be the result of the management's inability to recognise the need for training or to appreciate the skills appropriate to the task. Similarly an employee who is apathetic and demoralised may be ineffective in his work. Such behaviour may stem from the fact that the job is not intellectually or physically stimulating. This should be recognised by the management and acted upon. Perhaps the employee should be offered a clearer and more challenging career structure.

(b) Managerial failures

Certain management styles generate significant barriers to communication. Different types of organisation operate different styles of leadership. An over autocratic, or highly paternalistic approach, or maybe a general indifference to the interests of the workforce can have a marked adverse effect on the performance of employees. It is important that managers recognise the needs and aspirations of their employees to help overcome such problems as the lack of motivation mentioned earlier. Any communications system in an organisation relies heavily upon the consultation procedures between management and workforce. It is equally important to delegate. Bottlenecks can occur when an individual in the enterprise is trying to cope with a workload that is too heavy; the consequence is often that information is provided too late — or not at all.

(c) Personality conflicts

Closely associated with these communications barriers are the personality conflicts that can often occur. In the narrowest sense these may involve the personal dislike of one member of staff for another. This becomes an issue when both individuals must communicate and transfer information. Such information in the hands of an individual can be used as a means of asserting power over others. This may take the form of retaining the information until a vital meeting and then using it to embarrass or disconcert the other person. It may involve "forgetting" to pass on a message. At its most extreme it may involve refusing to deal with the other person other than

. . . *adopt a stereotyped image of each other* . . .

through an intermediary. Such behaviour can be very damaging to the business, especially as "sides" in the dispute can develop, compounding the problem and creating an emotionally charged atmosphere that is not conducive to the free flow of information.

In a broader sense, such conflicts may involve the personality or culture of larger groups of people. We are all familiar with the notion, sometimes real, often apparent, of the entrenched approach of management and unions in dealing with each other. Both sides may adopt a stereotyped image of each other as representing the conflicting values between which there is no common ground. Group conflict may even occur between departments, between the shopfloor and the supervisors, or between skilled and unskilled workers. Inter-union disputes could also be another cause of group conflict.

ASSIGNMENT — OWEN PRINT LTD

Owen Print Ltd is a private limited company employing over 90 staff spread across six departments; Sales and Administration, Finance, General Office, Production, Technical and Despatch.

The company is an old family business that has rapidly expanded its production over the past five years. It is operated from two sites in the market town of Hereford. The main site houses the production, technical and despatch departments. A new building, first used four years ago when expansion forced the company to increase its accommodation, houses the other three departments.

As a family business the company is run on rather old fashioned lines. It is autocratic. Of the four directors three are members of the family. The Chairman and Managing Director is Cecil Owen; his son Colin and daughter Madelaine are also directors, and Barry Grant, who is not a member of the family, is the remaining director.

Cecil Owen still sees the company as it used to be many years ago; a small business in which everybody knew each other and he knew exactly what was going on everywhere within the company. He is still referred to by older employees as the 'gaffer', and if they have problems Cecil Owen is always willing to hear them. But he is not a man who likes labels for people, and most employees have no formal job descriptions. Nor does the company have any formally stated aims and objectives other than those contained in its Memorandum of Association.

Barry Grant, as well as being a director, is also Company Secretary and in overall charge of the Sales and Administration Department, Finance and the General Office.

Recently Mr. Grant has become increasingly anxious about the inadequacies of the communication/information system operating within the company. He has identified that:

- (i)   new and existing staff are often unclear about their role within the company;

- (ii) no single individual has responsibility for personnel matters;

- (iii) the physical and organisational structure of the company is not conducive to effective communication;

- (iv) savings could be made in the general office by switching to the use of word processors instead of typewriters.

In relation to point (iv) he has provided you with the following figures:

General Office employees   3 secretarial staff

Each work 9 a.m. - 5 p.m., 5 days per week (with one hour for lunch)

Costs using existing equipment:

1. Average costs of producing a letter £2.40p

2. Average cost of producing other typed material: £1.56 per page.

      Average time involved in   1.   :   30 minutes

                                       2.   :   20 minutes

Costs using word processing equipment:

Cost of purchasing each individual word processor   :   £800

1. Average cost of producing a letter: £1.25p

2. Average cost of producing other typed material: 85p

      Average time involved in   1.   :   15 minutes

                                      2.   :   10 minutes

Each week an average 150 letters and 150 other documents are produced.

TASKS

1. You are an employee of the company directly responsible to Barry Grant. You have been asked to produce an informal report for Mr. Grant that he can present to the next meeting of the Board of Directors. In the report you should take each of the points (i), (ii) and (iii) raised by Mr. Grant and indicate:

   (a) Why it appears that the problem exists?

   (b) Why it represents an unsatisfactory position for the company in information terms? and

   (c) How the situation might best be overcome?

2. Furthermore Mr. Grant requires you to provide him with a set of calculations to indicate how many months it would be before the word processing equipment, if introduced, would pay for itself in savings.

DEVELOPMENTAL TASK

3. Draw up an outline strategy for selling the idea of the introduction of an information technology system throughout Owen Print Ltd. This should include an introductory talk to be given to staff by Mr. Grant, and a letter from the company to all staff explaining the personal and organisational benefits of introducing such a change.

ASSIGNMENT — CASTLE ENGINEERING

Castle Engineering Ltd is a medium sized company engaged in the production of industrial ball bearings and employing 200 staff. The Managing Director, John Castle, recently decided to retire in order to concentrate on the reduction of his golf handicap. His replacement was his son-in-law, Philip Barlow.

The two men held widely differing views on the treatment of the workforce. John had tended to distance himself, adopting a 'superior' attitude in keeping with his aloof personality. The only occasions on which John spoke to the workers was to announce redundancies.

Philip was determined to break this tradition. On his first day he called all employees to a meeting in the staff canteen. He addressed the workforce and the main emphasis of the speech was his desire for "the company to grow and to make even larger profits".

Following the meeting, Philip made a tour of the various departments. He spoke to Darren Hunter the junior warehouseman, and told him to "keep up the good work" as there was a "bright future for enterprising young men".

During the remainder of the visit, and in particular in the production area, Mr Barlow was surprised to be greeted with at best a lack of enthusiasm, at worst open hostility. He asked Rupert Castle, the Production Director and son of the ex M.D., to speak to the production workers to discover the reason for this unrest.

Rupert had unfortunately inherited his father's aloof manner, and was not particularly popular having been appointed Production Director at the age of 22 on gaining a degree in Sociology from Keele University. He had the added disadvantages of being extremely introverted and having an unfortunate habit of mumbling when speaking to large groups. As a result, he was unable to gain any response from the workers, who virtually ignored his address.

Following these incidents, Philip Barlow has asked the Personnel Department to report on the problems which have been encountered.

TASKS

In your capacity as an administrative assistant within the Personnel Department you have been asked to assist in the preparation of this report.

1. Advise your departmental head in the form of a memorandum as to possible reasons for the adverse reaction to Mr Barlow's address.

2. The lack of response to Rupert Castle's request for information also troubled Philip Barlow, and he was eager to know why this had occurred. Mr. Barlow has called your office while you were at lunch and asked you to ring him back in relation to this problem. Prepare some brief notes which will enable you to talk to Mr Barlow on this matter.

3. The conclusion of the report to Mr Barlow has to suggest possible changes which would prevent a reoccurence of these episodes. Prepare this section of the report.

4. At lunch the following day you overhear an argument between Darren Hunter and the head warehouseman, Bill Blyth. Darren was contesting that Bill, as an 'old man', was finished and might as well retire now. You report this conversation to your section head who suggests that you interview both Darren and Bill together to clear the air. Prepare some notes which will assist you in carrying out this interview.

DEVELOPMENTAL TASKS

5. Role play the telephone call between Mr Barlow and yourself as the personnel assistant as outlned in task 2.

6. Undertake a role play exercise in which you simulate the proposed interview referred to in task 4.

Chapter 4

INFORMATION TECHNOLOGY

One of the most exciting developments in recent years has been the growth of the technological revolution. This has come about as a result of the evolution of micro electronics. Its impact is being felt in all aspects of life. Many of the mundane tasks which were previously undertaken by hand can now be carried out more quickly and efficiently by using machines. Domestic appliances such as washing machines and televisions are now controlled by micro chips. Each time you make a deposit or withdrawal from your bank account an electronic machine will register the transaction. Booking a holiday or monitoring the heart beat of a new born baby can now be carried out much more effectively using a computer. The applications are endless. In chapter 20 we examine some of the wider uses of new technology both in the home and at work. In this chapter we will concentrate on one specific aspect of the technological revolution — information technology.

THE DEVELOPMENT OF INFORMATION TECHNOLOGY

Information technology involves the use of computer based systems to store, process and transfer information. It has evolved as a result of developments in two distinct areas:

(a) computing;

(b) telecommunications.

Clearly we have had a telephone network for several decades and computers have been in existence since the late 1940s. However the important advance in recent years has involved the linking of the two. In other words being able to transfer information quickly and effectively from one computer to another using conventional telephone lines, satellite links and optic fibre cables. The establishment of this link has led to a communications revolution which has wide implications for the way in which organisations communicate both within and between themselves. While in this chapter it is only possible to be able to briefly outline the main applications of information technology it is hoped that this will be sufficient to spark your interest and encourage you to find out more about this rapidly developing area. We will begin by considering the uses of information technology as a means of improving an organisation's internal communications system.

THE USE OF INFORMATION TECHNOLOGY WITHIN THE ORGANISATION

THE ELECTRONIC OFFICE

Increasingly you will hear the term 'electronic office'. This involves the performance of many clerical and administrative tasks by a set of computers or other electronic equipment which are linked together into a 'network'.

A NETWORK

This means that the machines are connected using an internal telephone line or a simple cable. The network allows the machines to:

(i)   share resources; and

(ii) share information.

(i)   Sharing resources

To operate a computer you need the computer itself (known as the central processing unit or CPU), an input device (such as a keyboard, a disk drive or a tape recorder), a monitor or visual display unit (VDU) and an output device (for example a printer, monitor or disk drive). Each of these pieces of equipment is expensive and a 'stand alone' system which is completely self contained will require all of them. A network system will mean that individual users can share some of the equipment. So for example one central CPU may be linked to a number of terminals each with its own monitor but without a disk drive or printer. A user will access the machine through the terminal but will need to go to the central printer for 'hard copy' output. This type of network is known as a 'star' network and is shown in the figure below.

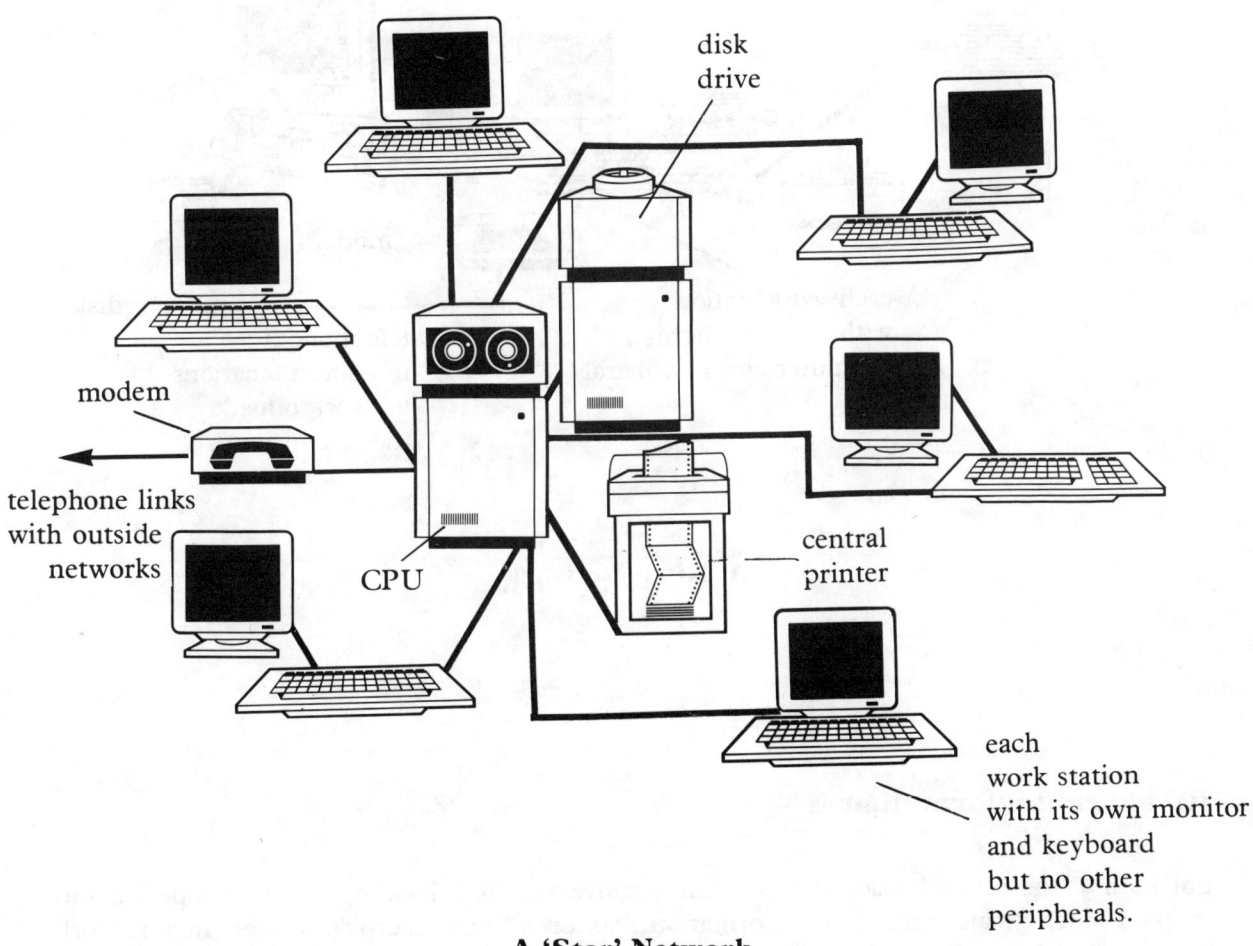

A 'Star' Network

Alternatively a number of micro computers each with their own CPU can be networked together. In this way they can transfer information held on one machine to another almost instantaneously. This allows each to be used either independantly or as part of the network. Such a network is known as a 'ring' network and is shown in the figure below.

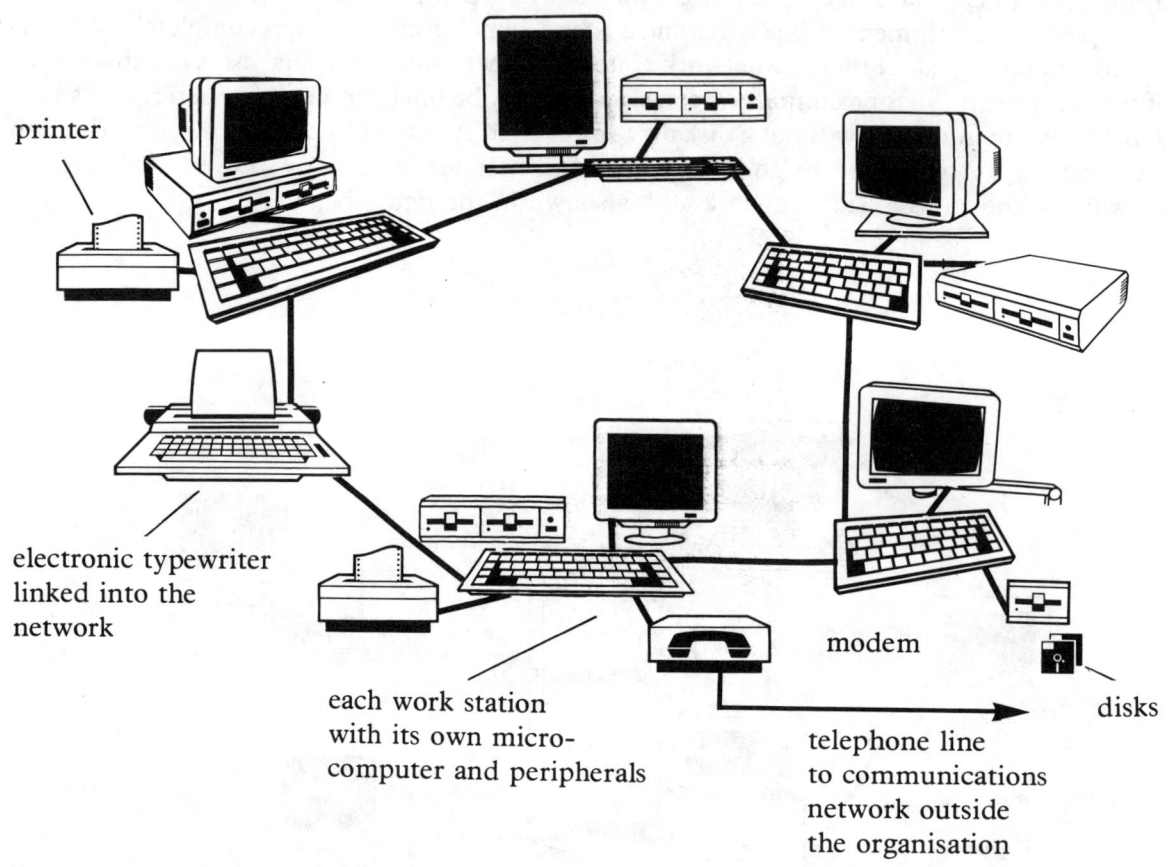

printer

electronic typewriter
linked into the
network

each work station
with its own micro-
computer and peripherals

modem

telephone line
to communications
network outside
the organisation

disks

A 'Ring' Network

(ii) Sharing information

For both of the network examples mentioned above a major advantage is that it is possible to access a much greater amount of information than on a single micro computer. In a network system which has only one large CPU, the memory of the machine will be considerably larger and it may be linked to a hard disk system. These are large capacity storage units holding magnetic disks somewhat similar in appearance to a stack of gramophone records encased in a removable pack. They hold many more times the amount of information than the floppy disks used by mico computers. However they are expensive and most organisations would find it uneconomic to have a hard disk drive for every computer terminal. Thus by networking the terminals most efficient use can be made of such equipment.

If a number of micro computers are networked together they can transfer information held either in the memory or from an individual floppy disk.

THE USES OF A NETWORK

If a number of machines are linked this will reduce the document and paper flow within the organisation. There has ever been the suggestion of the 'paper less' office. An example may illustrate how this can be achieved.

If goods are delivered into the organisation it is the normal procedure for the receiving department to complete a Goods Received Note. Copies of this are then sent to the purchasing department, the accounts department and to the stores. In other words a considerable amount of paper work is generated. If instead the goods receipt is entered into a terminal which is networked to the rest of the organisation, the information that the goods have been received is immediately recorded on the central data base. This can then be accessed by any other authorised department through its own terminal. Thus the information can be made available to everyone who requires it in one simple data transfer.

The applications are numerous. Imagine every memo which is sent, every notice circulated or report copied in a large organisation. Clearly the physical movement of paper is enormous. If instead the initiator of a memo simply input the message into a terminal and then directed the machine to transfer it electronically to every named recipient via the information technology network then the reduction in the amount of paper transferred is obvious.

Other aspects of information technology within an organisation such as word processing and data processing are examined in chapter 20.

THE USE OF INFORMATION TECHNOLOGY OUTSIDE THE ORGANISATION

EXTERNAL COMMUNICATIONS SYSTEMS

Organisations must communicate externally as well as internally and in this respect information technology can play an even greater role in improving the efficiency of an organisation's communications. This is because data can be transmitted around the world in a matter of seconds. So for example a bank deposit made in London can be credited to a bank account in New York in less than a minute. Thus trading transactions or money transfers can be carried out speedily so opening up the world as a possible immediate market.

Financial organisations such as banks now make extensive use of such technology allowing them to deal in all the money markets of the world from a London office.

The transfer of business information can also be of vital importance. A British company dealing with a Swiss organisation may wish to be kept informed of any changes in their trading partner's share value in Switzerland. Such information can now be transferred within seconds. Reuters, the news agency, developed networks to get the news from around the world to Fleet Street and other newspaper centres as quickly as possible. These links are now used to transfer business information to paying clients much more than to relay the latest cricket score from Australia or the news of a flood from India.

ELECTRONIC MAIL

Increasingly organisations are using information technology networks as a means of transferring messages. British Telecom has an electronic mailing system which allows messages to be passed from computer to computer throughout the world.

SOME IMPLICATIONS OF THE INFORMATION TECHNOLOGY REVOLUTION

It has been suggested that the information technology revolution will further divide the world between the 'haves' and the 'have nots'. However in this case the distinction will be between those countries which are information 'rich' and those which are information 'poor'. By this is meant that the developed nations and particulary the USA will dominate the electronics and IT industry. In order to make advances in this field vast amounts of money must be invested in research and development and only the rich countries can afford to do this. Yet as development gathers pace the rich countries expand their lead in this field while the poor countries fall farther behind. Even comparatively rich countries like Canada are worried by the advances being made by their American neighbour. The Canadians fear that developments will cost them investment and jobs. An American multi-national may have offices in Toronto. In the past it had to employ many Canadians to administer its affairs. Today however as information technology allows the transfer of data quickly over long distances, it can centralise its administration in its New York office. The central computer can then relay the required information such as wages, invoices and so on to Toronto by telephone line. The consequent loss of employment is clearly worrying to the host nation. It is not too difficult to imagine American multi-nationals doing the same thing in the UK. The loss of administrative jobs at such companies as Fords and General Motors by such a policy would be substantial.

Nevertheless the information technology revolution presents a challenge which Britain should not avoid. The developments in the new fourth generation of 'thinking' computers will provide limitless potential for man's inventiveness in terms of the scope of its applications.

ASSIGNMENT — UPDATING THE SYSTEM

Jayston International Freight and Transport Limited is a small company based in Loughborough specialising in the transportation of high value freight, both within the United Kingdom and Worldwide. Its business has grown dramatically in the last ten years particularly as a result of the expansion of the European market with the growth of the EEC. It has a head office staff of twenty eight and has used a manual system of office administration registering incoming freight, organising transportation to destinations, recording deliveries and invoicing and verifying payment from customers. It has built up its business through a well thought out marketing strategy advertising in yellow pages, local newspapers and specific trade journals. The managing director, Jim Mutton, is confident that the business can be further expanded by increasing advertising expenditure and extending the number of pick up locations to cover the whole of the UK. He proposes a national advertising campaign and realises that it is essential to increase the efficiency of the Loughborough head office if this objective is to be achieved.

If the expansion is to be successfully undertaken Mr Mutton believes that the company will have to improve its administrative procedures and install some form of computerised system. You are currently employed as an administrative assistant to Mr Mutton and he has asked you to undertake a feasibility study of his plans for computerisation.

TASKS

1. Prepare an informal report for Mr Mutton in which you consider the possibility of introducing some form of computerised system into the organisation. In the report you should outline the advantages of the 'electronic office' and the possible difficulties which the company may encounter in any such change over from the current manual systems.

2. As an appendix to your report produce a diagram showing the type of computer network which could be introduced into the organisation. Clearly label your diagram showing both the equipment which could be used and the departments of the organisation which could be included in the network.

DEVELOPMENTAL TASK

3. Research the implications of the Data Protection Act 1984 for organisations using any form of computerised records.

Chapter 5

DOCUMENT SYSTEMS AND PROCEDURES & THE PRESENTATION OF DATA

In earlier chapters we have examined some of the types of information that an organisation may need and we have seen tht one of the most important is the business document. In the first part of this chapter we will examine some of of the business documents employed by an organisation and the procedures which accompany their use.

PURCHASING DOCUMENTATION SYSTEMS

There are usually a number of distinct stages in the purchase of any goods or services by an organisation and each of the stages requires the appropriate documentation. To illustrate these stages we will use the example of an accounts manager who wishes to buy a new micro computer for his section.

(i) The Purchase Requisition

If the accounts manager has the authority to initiate such a purchase, he will issue a purchase order requisition. This is a request to the purchasing department asking for the piece of equipment which is required. At this stage the manager may have a particular make of machine in mind which will meet his requirements. If this is the case he should specify this on the requisition form. Alternatively he may have a specific task in mind that can be accomplished by any of a range of machines, such as the ability to handle spreadsheets, in which case he may not specify a particular model but allow the purchasing department to choose the best purchasing option available. The date when the machine is needed would also be shown on the requisition as this will give some indication to the purchasing department of the urgency of the purchasing procedure. An example of the requisition which could be used in this case is shown on the next page.

(ii) Letters of Enquiry

When the purchasing department receive the requisition they will begin to make enquiries to find the most suitable supplier. Such enquiries may involve relatively simply tasks such as looking through suppliers catalogues and advertisements; they may take the form of telephone enquiries to establish such details as price, specification and delivery or they may use a formal letter of enquiry which asks potential suppliers to give details of the goods and conditions they offer. If the potential order involves substantial expenditure and there are a large number of possible suppliers, the purchasing department may decide to advertise and ask for tenders or quotations. Legally such letters of enquiry or advertisements constitute the organisation's invitation to treat. The legal aspects of the purchasing process are considered in detail in chapter 21.

A PURCHASE REQUISITION FORM

SOUTHERN ELECTRONICS PLC			
PURCHASE REQUISITION			

Requisition Number: 37129		**Date:** 27 Oct. 19xx	
Description	Reference	Quantity	Price (if known)
IBM Personal Computer	IBM PC	1	

Initiating Department   Accounts

Cost Code   AC179

Signature......T Richards...........

Position   Accounts Manager

Authorised by   D.Heslop   D. Heslop

Position   Accounts Director

(For Purchasing Dept. Use)

Order No.   **Date Order Placed**.........................

Supplier...

(iii) Quotations or Tenders

Potential suppliers who become aware of the organisation's requirements may submit a quotation or tender. This will normally constitute the supplier's offer and will include such details as the specification of the goods, the price, delivery dates and other details such as the provision of guarantees.

(iv) Placing the Order

When the buyer has examined all the potential offers to supply the product, he will select the most favourable and issue a purchase order. This is the organisation's acceptance of the supplier's offer. It will have a separate purchase order number. The order will confirm the price, the delivery date required and any other terms or conditions which the buyer wishes to include in the contract. It will be signed by someone with sufficient authority to sanction the amount of money which is being spent. It is important that a copy of the order is forwarded to the accounts department for they will not pay the forthcoming invoice unless they can verify that an official order, which has an acceptable order numbr, has been placed. Larger organisations will often have standard conditions of contract which they expect all suppliers to accept. In certain circumstances the supplier may have made his offer on his own standard terms. Conflict could arise if the purchaser's standard terms differ substantially from those offered by the supplier. This problem will normally be resolved through negotiation, but if there is still a dispute the law would determine the terms which would apply if a contract had been entered into. Again this aspect is considered in chapter 21. An example of an order form is shown on the next page.

(v)   The Acknowledgement

Most suppliers will immediately acknowledge the order and this will allow the buyer to confirm that the terms have been formally agreed. It will also act as a check that an order has been received by the supplier.

(vi) The Advice Note

It is standard practice for a supplier to send a buyer an advice note when the goods are despatched. This acts as a warning to the buyer that the goods are in transit and also permits the buyer to prepare its good received department for the imminent arrival of the goods.

(vii)The Delivery Note

When the goods are delivered, a delivery note will be attached which has been made out by the supplier. This should clearly specify the goods which are being supplied. A copy is normally signed by the receiving organisation and then retained by the carrier of the goods as proof that the goods have been delivered. Because of this it is important that the receiver checks the goods which are specified on the delivery note. Any discrepancy should be notified immediately to the buying department and on the delivery note itself.

(viii) The Goods Received Note

Once the goods have been checked it is normal procedure to produce a goods received note. This is an internal document which records the acceptance of the goods into the organisation. A copy is held by the goods receipt department, a copy is passed to the purchasing department and a copy is sent to the accounts department. The goods can then be held in stock or as in the case of the micro computer we are considering, passed immediately into the user department.

(ix) The Invoice

The supplier will now bill the buyer using an invoice. This is the demand for payment for the goods supplied. The buyer will check the invoice agains the original order form and the goods received note and, if all three tally, payment will be authorised. If there is a discrepancy the accounts department will usually ask the supplier to rectify the matter. If the buyer has been

A PURCHASE ORDER FORM

SOUTHERN ELECTRONICS
Sheraton House
Southlea Trading Estate
Southampton

Tel: Southampton 793695   Telex 479152

VAT Registration No: 326 1604 72

PURCHASE ORDER

Purchase Order No.   713287

Date: 3 November 19xx

Your Quotation/Tender Reference: 37/FT/19

To: Datafile Ltd.
147-149 Solent Street
Southampton

Please supply the following goods. Standard terms and conditions given overleaf.

Description	Reference	Quantity	Price
IBM Personal Computer	IBM PC	1	£1278.00
		VAT	£191.70

Delivery Date required: 15 Nov: 19xx   **Total Order Value**   £1469.70

W. Maxwell

W. Maxwell
Purchasing Officer
for Southern Electronics

asked to pay too much the supplier will be required to issue a credit note which will allow the buyer to reclaim the difference either in the form of new goods or simply to pay the appropriate amount. If the buyer has been asked to pay too little then the supplier will issue a debit note to make up the difference.

(x) The Statement

Many organisations will not pay for goods as they are bought but prefer to wait until the supplier issues a monthly statement which itemises all the purchases made in the month and requests payment of the total sum still owing. Payment on statement simplifies the number of financial transactions between the buyer and seller and is sometimes used to advantage by the buyer as it delays payment.

STOCK CONTROL DOCUMENTATION SYSTEMS

Most organisations need to carry stock. If the organisation is involved in manufacturing it must hold stocks of components and raw materials. A retail organisation must hold stocks of goods to meet consumer needs and even an organisation in a service industry such as a local authority housing office or an insurance company must keep stocks of the stationery it uses. In chapter 15 the importance of stock from a financial management viewpoint is discussed. There we recognise that holding too much stock is unnecessarily adding to the costs of the organisation, while holding insufficient stock can result in production delays, loss of sales or other operational failures.

The organisation needs therefore to keep appropriate stock records which monitor not only the movement of stock into and out of the organisation but also help to maintain minimum and maximum stock levels. This is usually achieved by the use of some form of stock record card. An example is shown in the figure below.

ABBOTSFIELD FURNITURE LTD.

Item: Number   — 7138   Max Stock 250
       Description — $5^1/_4$ inch Floppy Disks   Min Stock 50

Date	Receipts			Issues			Balance
	Quantity	Invoice No.	Supplier	Quantity	Requis-ition	Section	
							62
27/5/86	180	300486	Datafile				242
28/5/86				10	94172	Accts	232

A Stock Record Card

The card shows the maximum and minimum stock levels which the organisation wishes to hold for that particular item. These levels are determined by the regularity of use of the item within the organisation and the speed with which stock can be replaced by suppliers.

So in the example used, if the organisation finds that it uses approximately 30 floppy disks a week and that it takes a maximum of 7 working days to get new supplies it may decide never to hold less than 50 in stock for if it did it might find itself out of disks before they could be replaced from the supplier. Furthermore the organisation has decided on a maximum stock level of 250. It does not wish to hold more as it will simply be tying up cash in unproductive stock. Yet it has found that if it buys 150 disks in bulk at one time from its supplier it is offered a substantial discount.

Movements into and out of the stock room are recorded on the card as they occur. Receipts are logged showing the date, the supplier and the invoice number. Issue of stock is shown with the appropriate requisition number and the department or section which has received the goods. With each transaction the balance of stock is adjusted and it is the responsibility of the stock control clerk to re-order once stocks are running close to the minimum stock level. The amount ordered should keep the stock held below the maximum stock level.

PRODUCTION CONTROL

If the organisation is involved in manufacturing it will require some system to monitor and control production. Normally the activities of the production department are determined by the level of orders the organisation has received or anticipates receiving. Production can be initiated from three sources:

  (i)   a special individual order placed by a customer;

  (ii) anticipated demand leading the marketing department to initiate production;

  (iii) stock levels running low resulting in the stock controller requesting the production of additional stock.

If the organisation has a regular level of sales in a stable market then it is likely that production will be maintained at a steady level with no fluctuation in activity rates. However some markets tend to be less stable and so the marketing department must work closely with production planning to adjust production to meet demand.

It is the responsibility of the production planning section to co-ordinate production and to do this it must order sufficient materials either from the stores or from outside suppliers, through the purchasing department, to meet the production department's requirements.

As some raw materials or components may need to be bought in, the production planning department must anticipate the necessary lead time required to place such orders. By 'lead time' we mean the time taken between initiating the orders and the delivery of the goods.

Once the appropriate raw materials are assembled, the production department should ensure the production schedules are met. This requires the monitoring of progress and output and motivating the staff if necessary. This aspect of management is considered in chapter 8. A diagram may help to illustrate the production process. This is shown on the next page.

WAGES AND SALARIES PROCEDURES

Any employer must recognise that an efficient wages and salaries system is essential to maintain the continued co-operation of the workforce. They must be paid the appropriate amount due and also they must be paid on time. It is also the employer's responsibility to make the correct deductions from employees wages of Pay As You Earn, Income Tax and National Insurance Contributions.

The first step is to determine the individual employees gross pay. This may be fixed at the same level per week for a year or depend on the amount of overtime the worker has completed that week. Conversely there may be a reduction in gross pay for any time off work for which pay must be deducted. Many employers use a time card or a clock card system which records the employees attendance at work. Other employers tend to leave it 'on trust' and accept the hours the employees claim.

Once gross pay has been established the employer must calculate the tax and national insurance payments due and deduct them from gross pay. These are then forwarded to the Collector of Taxes who distributes them accordingly to the Inland Revenue and the Department of Health and Social Security. Employers are required by law to keep detailed records of all

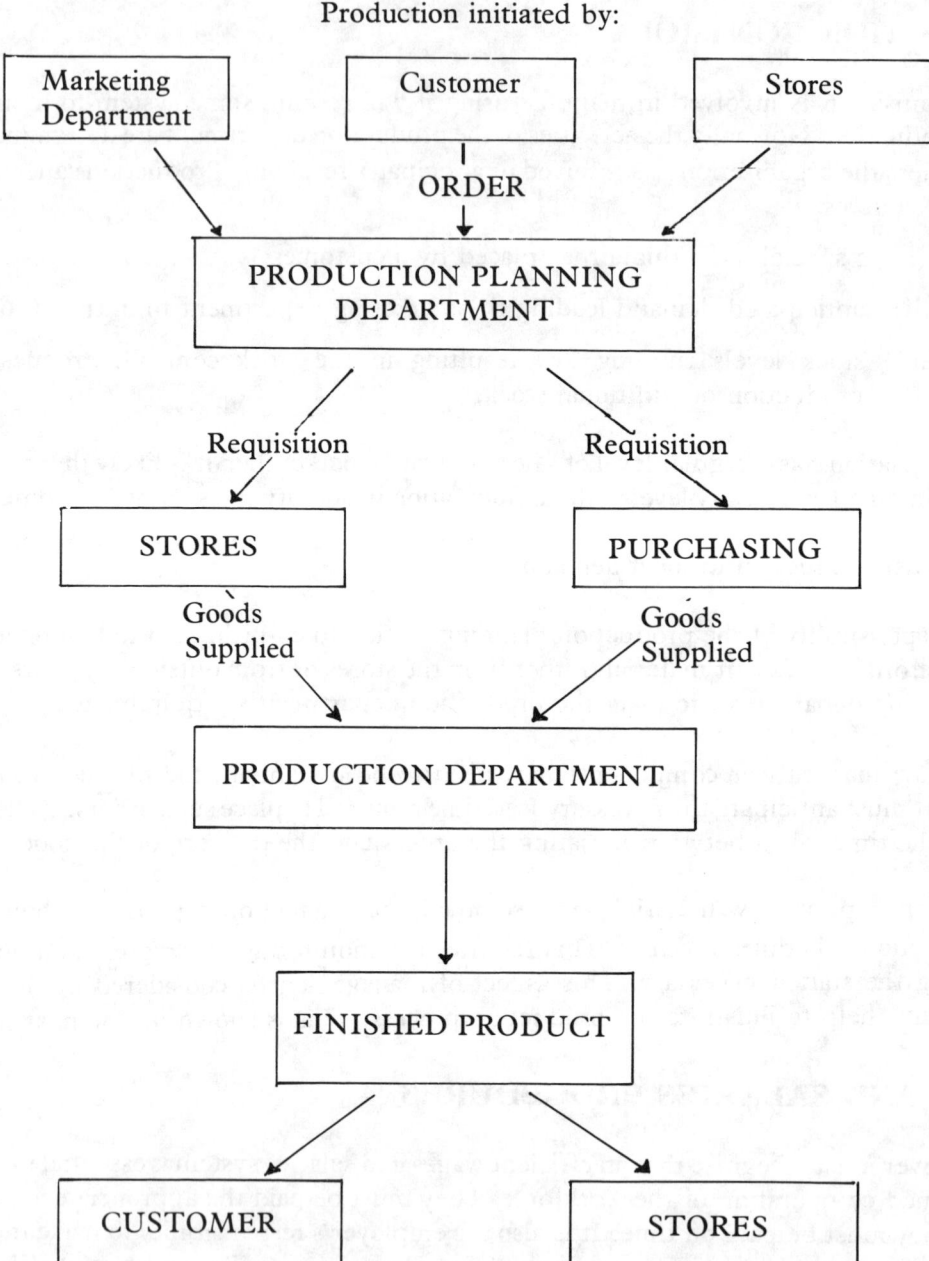

The Production Process

Production initiated by:

employees who are paid over the statutory minimum for national insurance contributions. Such records will provde a basis for wages and salaries analysis and also allow the employer to produce a P60 which is a statement given to each employee at the end of a tax year showing the amount of wages, tax and national insurance paid in the year. If an employee leaves for any reason before the end of the financial year the employer must provide a P45 which details tax and national insurance payments for the financial year up to the date at which the employee left. The figure on the next page illustrates the stages in the wages process.

Stages in the Wages Process

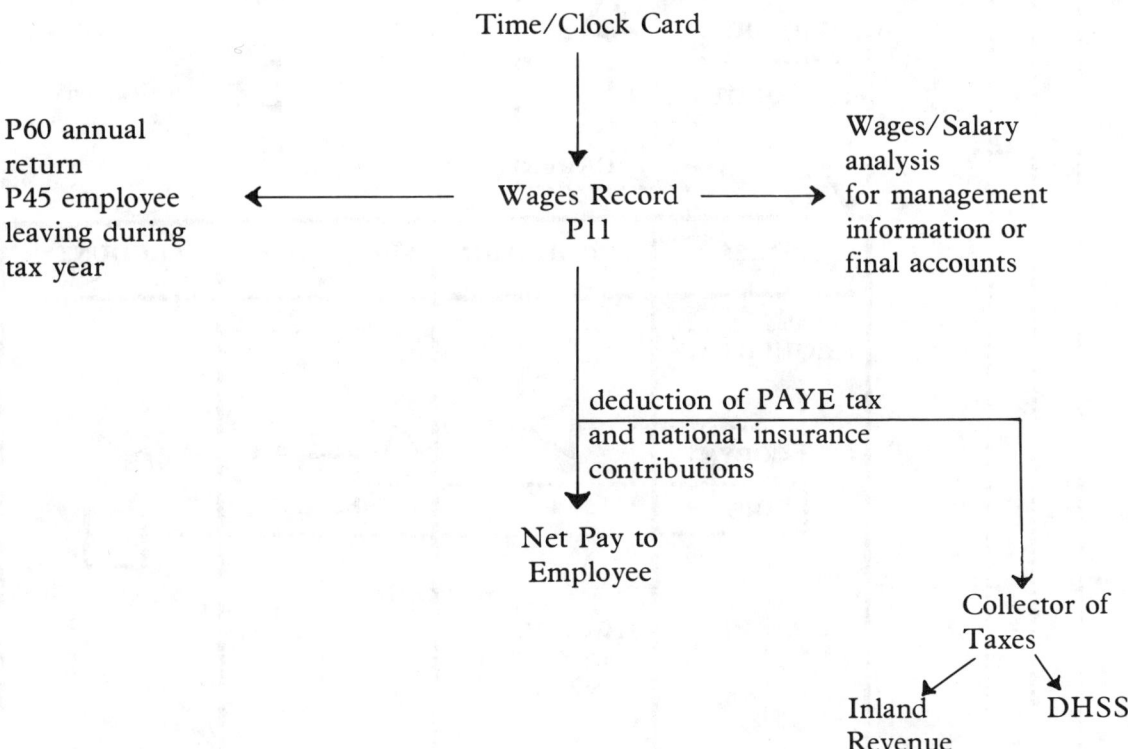

THE CONTROL OF THE FLOW OF DOCUMENTS

As we have noted an organisation will generate an immense number of documents. It is important that the flow of documents is controlled so that the organisation does not become overwhelmed by paper. It is necessary therefore that appropriate systems are employed to control the flow. There are a number of techniques which can be used but here we will concentrate on the application of document flow charts.

DOCUMENT FLOW CHARTS

This will illustrate the flow of documents used in a particular procedure. It should identify the documents which are used and the departments which initiate them, take action because of them or receive a copy for filing or future action.

To illustrate a document flow chart we have traced the procedure a manufacturing company may use from the point at which it receives an inquiry from a customer, through production and despatch until it receives final payment for the goods.

Steps in the Document Flow Chart for Sales

(i)   Customer sends a letter of inquiry (1) to the sales department.

(ii) Sales department replies with a quotation (2).

(iii) Customer places an order using his official order form (3).

(iv) Sales department raises a sales requisition (4) for the goods and passes the

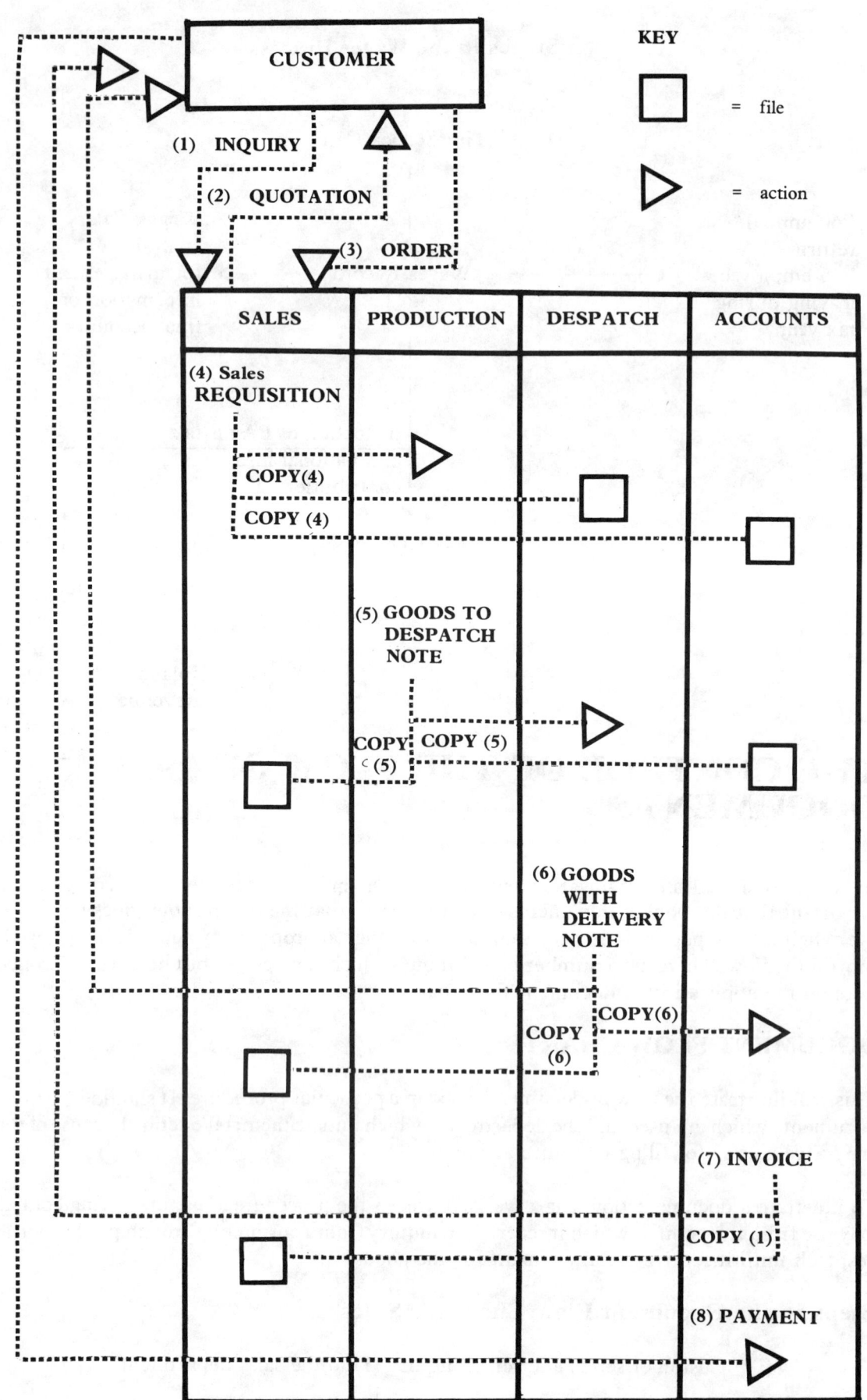

DOCUMENT FLOW CHART FOR SALES

original to the production department. Copies are sent to the despatch and accounts departments which are filed awaiting further action.

(v)   Production department manufactures the goods and transfers them to the despatch department. Included with the goods is a goods to despatch note (5). Copies of this are sent to the accounts department and sales department for filing.

(vi)   Despatch packages the goods and sends them to the customer with a delivery note (6). Copies of the delivery note are sent to the accounts department and sales department.

(vii) Accounts department checks the delivery note (6) with the sales requisition (4) and the goods to despatch note (5). If all three tally, an invoice (7) is sent to the customer with a copy to the sales department.

(viii) Once the customer has received the goods and is satisfied that they correspond to his order, he will send a cheque in payment (8) to cover the invoice (7). On receipt of the payment, the accounts department will verify it against the invoice and if it is satisfactory will process it through the customer's account.

Note the Sales Department receives copies of all the internal documentation. This is because it is the customer's link with the organisation and so, should some delay occur in processing the order, the sales department may be asked by the customer to check the progress of the order.

Clearly it is possible to prepare flow charts for all the important procedures within an organisation. In identifying the flow of documents in this way management is able to identify potential delays and hold ups in a process. If the procedure is not working as it should it may be that some department is not receiving a copy of a document which it requires to play its part. Alternatively from a flow chart it is possible to isolate unnecessary document flows. For instance in our example there would be no need for the production department to receive a copy of the invoice which the accounts department sends to the customer. Thus unnecessary waste or duplication of documents can be eliminated.

THE PRESENTATION OF DATA

This part of the chapter will introduce you to some simple methods of data presentation. There is a great deal of information communicated in the form of statistics and we shall examine some of the different ways in which these statistics are shown.

It is important that you are able to support your written arguments with a clear and concise presentation of quantitive information, and be capable of interpreting data which is given to you in a quantitative form.

The objective which you should set yourself when using a statistical presentation is that the meaning you wish to convey should come across in the most clear and precise manner.

In order to achieve this, you should:

(a)   be aware of the audience to which your work will be shown — it may be necessary to adjust the amount of data or its complexity to meet the needs and understanding of the target audience;

(b)   never overcomplicate data presentation;

(c)   always seek to include the appropriate amount of detail to convey your message adequately.

TABLES OF FIGURES

Data can be presented in tabular form in a variety of ways. Perhaps one of the most useful and also the simplest to present and interpret is the frequency distribution. This indicates the frequency with which a certain value or range of values occurs in a particular set of data.

The table below is a frequency distribution. It shows an analysis of ordinary shareholdings for a major public limited company, Dalgety plc.

Dalgety PLC

Shareholder information

Analysis of ordinary shareholdings at 30 June 1984

	Number of holdings	Shares held	% of total shares
By category of shareholder			
Individuals	41,757	22,320,463	28
Banks, nominees and other corporate bodies	4,447	39,297,297	51
Insurance companies	298	10,000,488	13
Investment companies and pension funds	180	6,015,769	8
	46,682	77,634,017	100
By size of holding			
1–250	17,659	2,046,715	3
251–500	11,387	4,380,902	6
501–1,000	11,325	8,372,456	11
1,001–20,000	5,923	14,153,260	18
20,001–100,000	260	13,368,189	17
100,001–500,000	117	26,234,369	34
500,001– and over	11	9,078,126	11
	46,682	77,634,017	100

(Source: Dalgety plc, Report to Shareholders, 100th Year, 1884-1984)

This table is a grouped frequency distribution in that it does not seek to list the precise shareholding of every shareholder of the company but groups them into appropriate classes. So, for example, there are 17,659 shareholders with 250 shares or less. This is a useful means of presentation but care must be taken in chosing the appropriate class size. For instance if the company had chosen a class size in this instance of, say, 5 (for example 501-505, 506-510 etc) it would have found that it had too many classes for the range of shareholdings it sought to present.

Similarly the company could have chosen very large class sizes (for example, less than 20,000 shares and greater than 20,000 shares). The table below illustrates how this would look.

By size of holding	No. of Holdings
less than 20,000 shares	46294
greater than 20,000 shares	388
Total	46682

In this instance the table may give us too little information for any real level of analysis.

The original Dalgety table also breaks down the distribution by characteristics of the shareholders. In this case by the type of shareholders they are (Individuals, Banks, Insurance Companies and Investment Companies).

This form of breakdown is extremely useful if you wish to emphasise a characteristic rather than a quantitative measure.

GRAPHS

Information can be presented in a variety of graphical forms. They are often used to show changes in a particular variable over a period of time: they could, for example, illustrate differences between countries, authorities or organisations.

In this section we will use some excellent graphs from the City of Birmingham's Annual Report and Accounts. This local authority is particularly imaginative in the way it presents information to its ratepayers.

The two graphs used give a clear visual impression of two important social indicators. The first illustrates changes in births, deaths and population for the city over the period. The second shows the increasing trends in the City's housing waiting list.

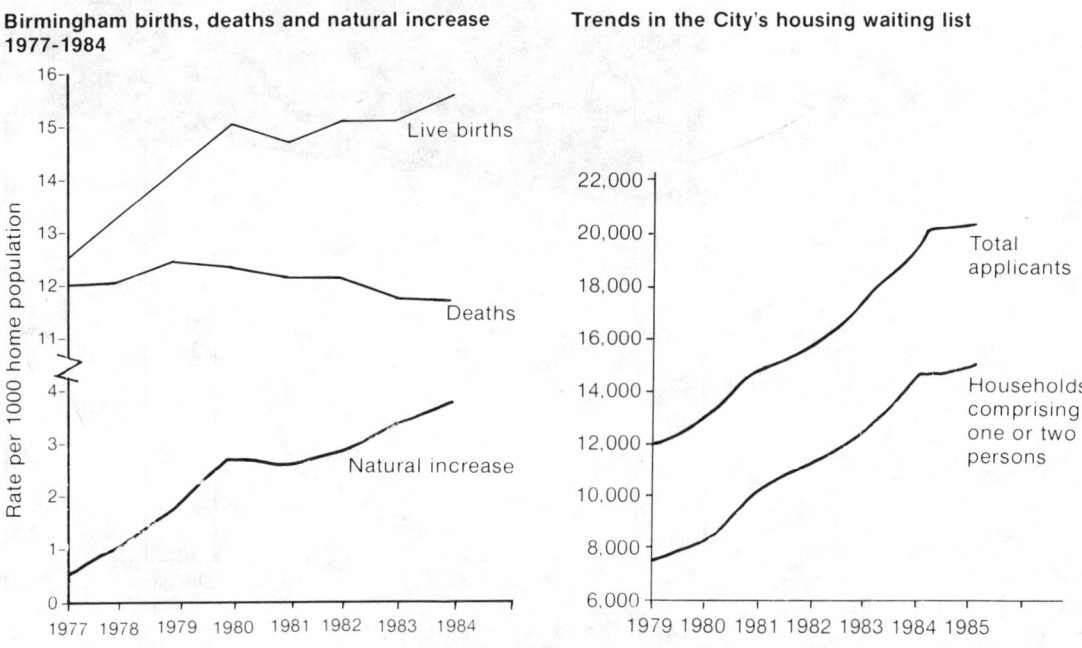

(Source: City of Birmingham Report and Accounts, 1984-85)

Where it goes – public spending by function

Public spending in the United Kingdom by function

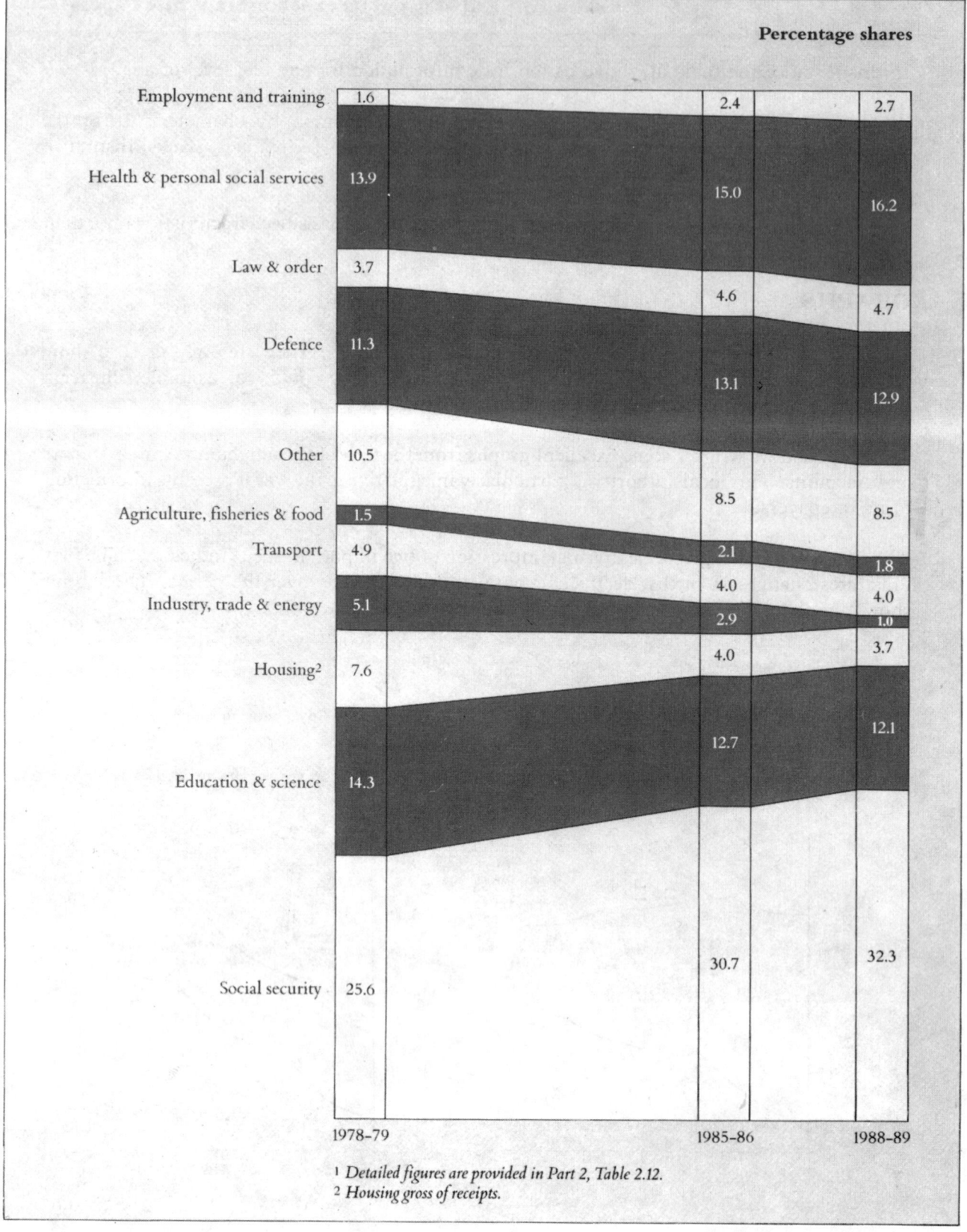

Percentage shares

	1978–79	1985–86	1988–89
Employment and training	1.6	2.4	2.7
Health & personal social services	13.9	15.0	16.2
Law & order	3.7	4.6	4.7
Defence	11.3	13.1	12.9
Other	10.5	8.5	8.5
Agriculture, fisheries & food	1.5	2.1	1.8
Transport	4.9	4.0	4.0
Industry, trade & energy	5.1	2.9	1.0
Housing[2]	7.6	4.0	3.7
Education & science	14.3	12.7	12.1
Social security	25.6	30.7	32.3

[1] Detailed figures are provided in Part 2, Table 2.12.
[2] Housing gross of receipts.

(Source: The Government's Expenditure Plans 1986-87 to 1988-89)

One factor to beware of when presenting information in graphical form or when interpreting it is to be sure that the scale of the axes does not make the data look more or less dramatic than it is. For example in the graph showing the housing waiting list trends if the scale of the vertical axis had been doubled the already difficult position could have been made to look much worse. Similarly by halving the scale of the vertical axis the trend could have been made to look much less worrying. It is important therefore, not to use scales which either exaggerate or underplay a trend. Often, of course, the use of graphs such as this is to reninforce points made in writing. It is possible then to adjust the graph to emphasise these points.

Other types of graphs are also used in emphasising particular trends or comparisons. For example, if you wish to illustrate how a change in the make-up of a particular total has occurred over time, it is possible to use a strata graph.

The figure on the facing page is a strata graph showing public spending in the UK by function. It clearly shows the trends in spending by central government in specific areas over a ten year period. So, for example, Housing has fallen from 7.6% of the total in 1978-79 to a projected figure of only 3.7% of the total in 1988-89, while Social Security spending has risen dramatically as a percentage from 25.6% to 32.3% over the same period. Strata graphs are an excellent means of illustrating changes in the make up of a total over a period of years.

BAR CHARTS

Bar charts are used to compare different categories by presenting them in columns or rows of different height or length. Each category is diplayed discretely and usually each column or row is of the same width.

The bar chart on the next page shows an analysis of the activities of Grand Metropolitan PLC, a major company involved in a wide range of activities ranging from its ownership of Watney Mann and Truman Brewers, Berni Inns, Mecca bookmakers, Express Dairies and Inter-Continental Hotels to the production of a wide diversity of food and drink. (They even sponsor Tottenham Hotspur Football Group through their ownership of the Holsten Pils UK rights). The chart breaks the group's activities into specific categories and shows how each contributes to overall turnover, trading profit and capital employed. Further analysis of these terms is undertaken in chapter 16.

Bar charts need not necessarily be horizontally presented. Often a more emphatic effect can be achieved by showing them vertically, at an angle or in some other form. The next figure is an excellent example of this, again from Birmingham City Council. They are showing how the council will spend its revenue and how this revenue is raised. At a glance the ratepayer can see that £317m or 43% of the total budget will be spent on education, similarly that £224 or 30% of all revenue must come from the rates and that £96m or 43% of rate revenue is raised from domestic ratepayers.

Grand Metropolitan PLC

Analysis of
Group
Activities
expressed as percentages

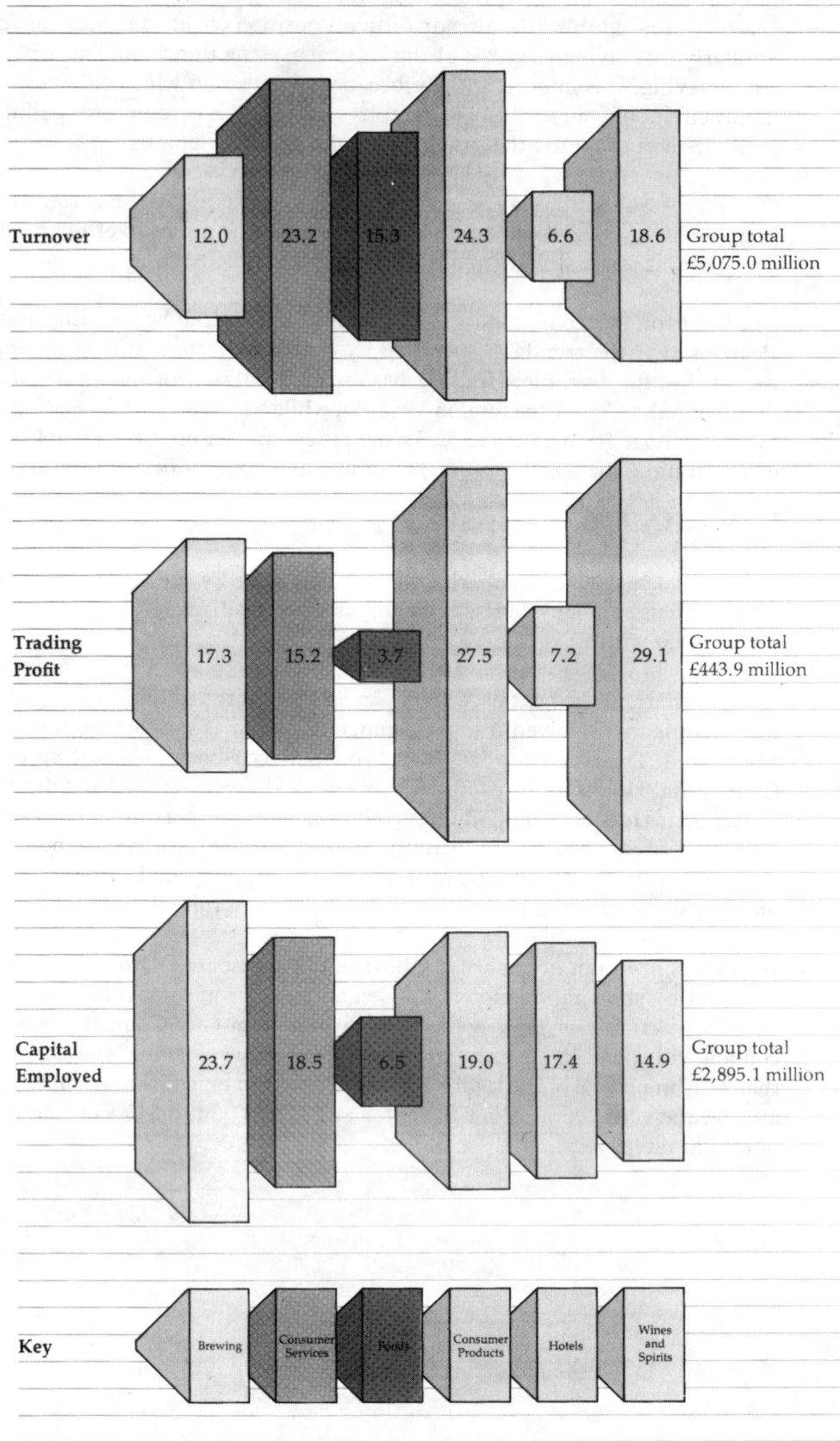

Turnover 12.0 23.2 15.3 24.3 6.6 18.6 Group total £5,075.0 million

Trading Profit 17.3 15.2 3.7 27.5 7.2 29.1 Group total £443.9 million

Capital Employed 23.7 18.5 6.5 19.0 17.4 14.9 Group total £2,895.1 million

Key Brewing Consumer Services Foods Consumer Products Hotels Wines and Spirits

(Source: Grand Metropolitan Annual Report 1984)

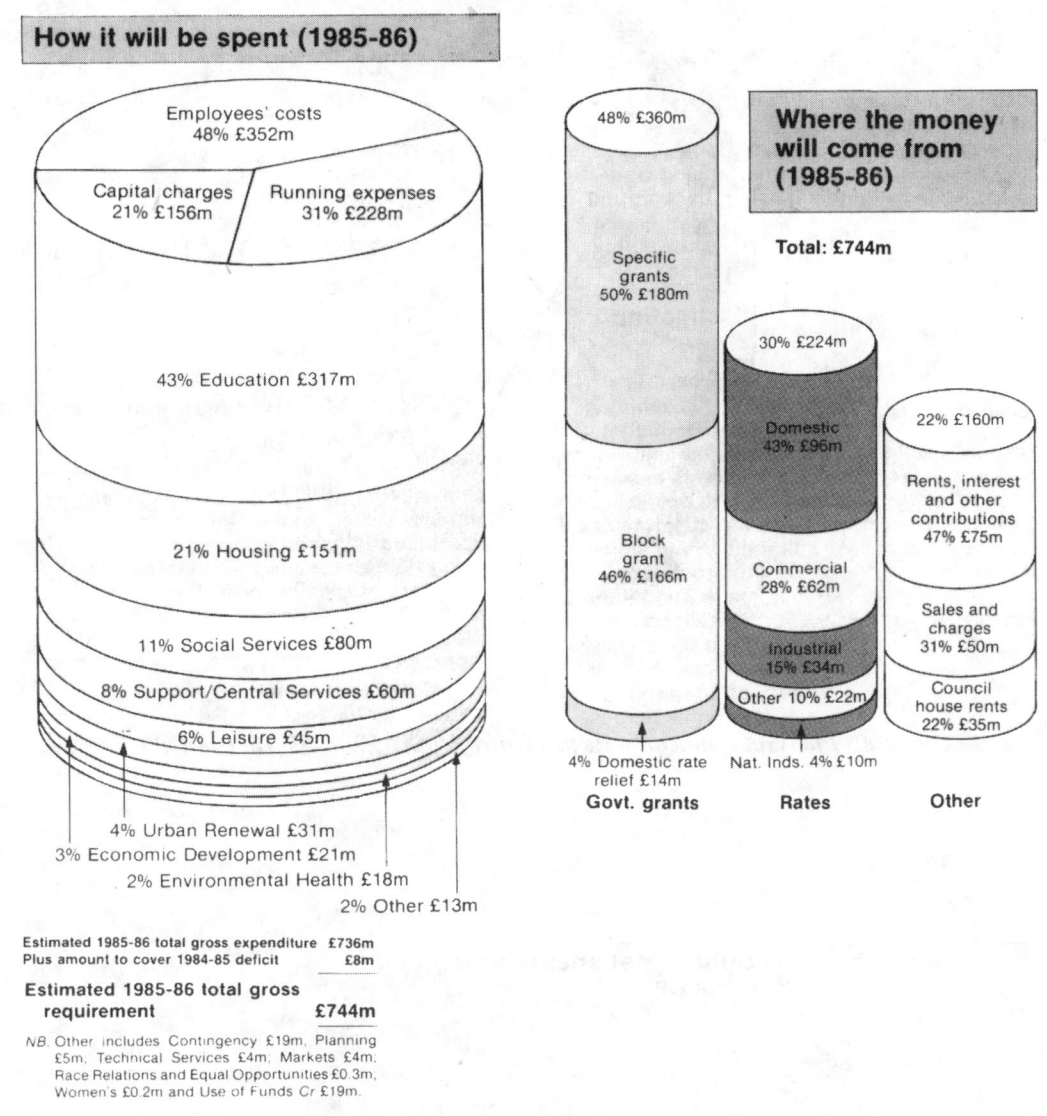

Birmingham Spending and its financing

How it will be spent (1985-86)

Employees' costs
48% £352m

Capital charges
21% £156m

Running expenses
31% £228m

43% Education £317m

21% Housing £151m

11% Social Services £80m

8% Support/Central Services £60m

6% Leisure £45m

4% Urban Renewal £31m
3% Economic Development £21m
2% Environmental Health £18m
2% Other £13m

Estimated 1985-86 total gross expenditure £736m
Plus amount to cover 1984-85 deficit £8m

Estimated 1985-86 total gross requirement £744m

NB. Other includes Contingency £19m, Planning £5m, Technical Services £4m, Markets £4m, Race Relations and Equal Opportunities £0.3m, Women's £0.2m and Use of Funds *Cr* £19m.

Where the money will come from (1985-86)

Total: £744m

48% £360m
Specific grants 50% £180m
Block grant 46% £166m
4% Domestic rate relief £14m
Govt. grants

30% £224m
Domestic 43% £96m
Commercial 28% £62m
Industrial 15% £34m
Other 10% £22m
Nat. Inds. 4% £10m
Rates

22% £160m
Rents, interest and other contributions 47% £75m
Sales and charges 31% £50m
Council house rents 22% £35m
Other

(Source: City of Birmingham Report and Accounts, 1984-85)

PIE CHARTS

A pie chart is a form of visual presentation which breaks down a total figure into its different components. The two pie charts on the next page illustrate spending in the public sector. The larger pie chart is for the central government and shows for instance that the government plans to spend £14.3 billion on Education and Science in 1986-87. The smaller chart is for Birmingham. Here, the education budget takes by far the largest share of net spending, £234 or 63%. (This may confuse you as this does not tally with the figure for Birmingham's education spending shown earlier on the bar chart. In fact the bar chart is for 1985-86 while the pie chart is for 1984-85. It is important to read what the chart says as well as studying the graphics.).

With a pie chart we may include the actual figures, (as for the central government's spending plans) percentages of the total or both (as in the Birmingham pie chart) if it is thought that this adds to the understanding of the diagram.

Planning total by department in 1986-87

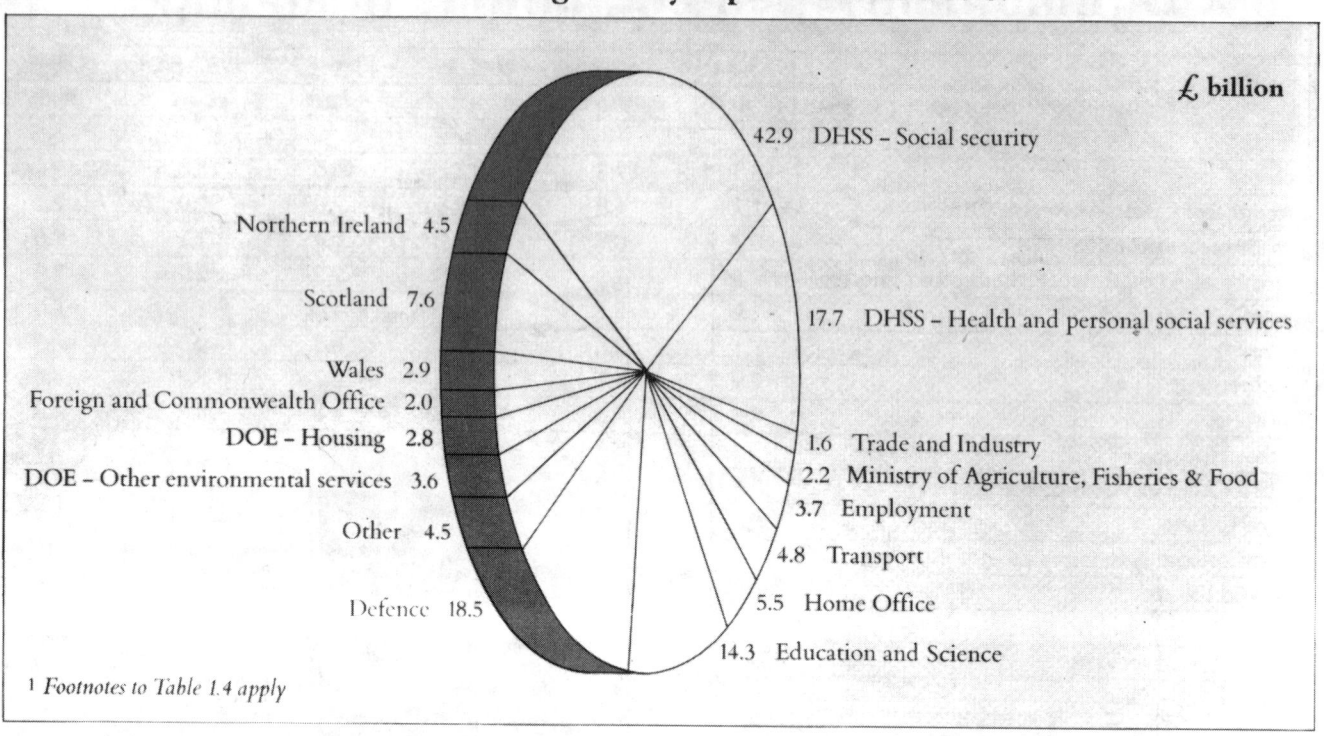

£ billion

42.9   DHSS – Social security

Northern Ireland   4.5

Scotland   7.6

17.7   DHSS – Health and personal social services

Wales   2.9
Foreign and Commonwealth Office   2.0
DOE – Housing   2.8
DOE – Other environmental services   3.6

1.6   Trade and Industry
2.2   Ministry of Agriculture, Fisheries & Food
3.7   Employment

Other   4.5

4.8   Transport

5.5   Home Office

Defence   18.5

14.3   Education and Science

1 *Footnotes to Table 1.4 apply*

(Source: The Government's Expenditure Plans 1986-87 to 1988-89)

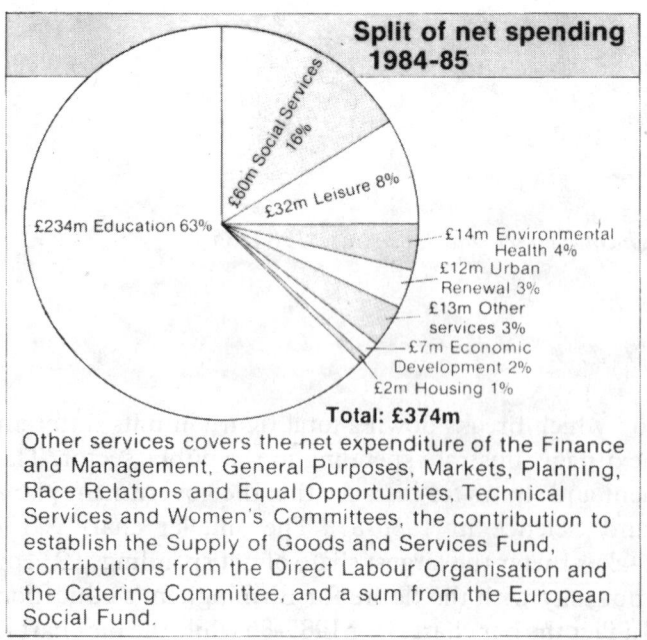

Split of net spending 1984-85

£60m Social Services 16%

£32m Leisure 8%

£234m Education 63%

£14m Environmental Health 4%
£12m Urban Renewal 3%
£13m Other services 3%
£7m Economic Development 2%
£2m Housing 1%

Total: £374m

Other services covers the net expenditure of the Finance and Management, General Purposes, Markets, Planning, Race Relations and Equal Opportunities, Technical Services and Women's Committees, the contribution to establish the Supply of Goods and Services Fund, contributions from the Direct Labour Organisation and the Catering Committee, and a sum from the European Social Fund.

(Source: City of Birmingham Report and Accounts, 1984-85)

PICTOGRAMS AND CARTOGRAMS

Two further types of diagram which may be useful are pictograms and cartograms. These use small pictures of variables which the presenter seeks to illustrate or a map in which particular features of countries or regions are displayed. Care must be taken not to make these look too decorative or fancy because this may distract the reader from the points to be made.

The first figure we will use is a pictogram from London and Scottish Marine Oil plc. It imaginatively illustrates their increases in oil well drilling activity (gradually building up the oil rig over the time period) and also the increase in the company's annual production of oil shown by the oil barrels).

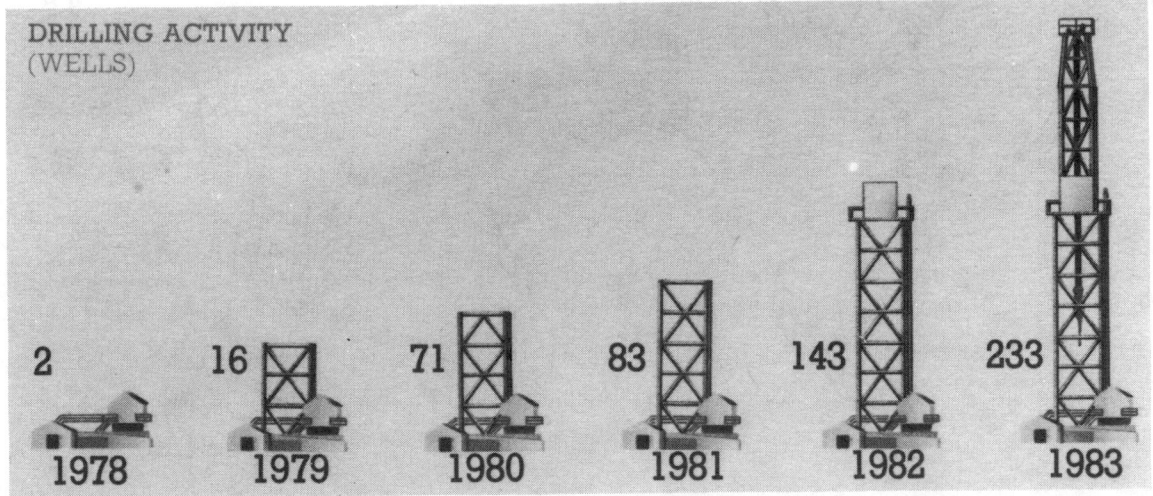

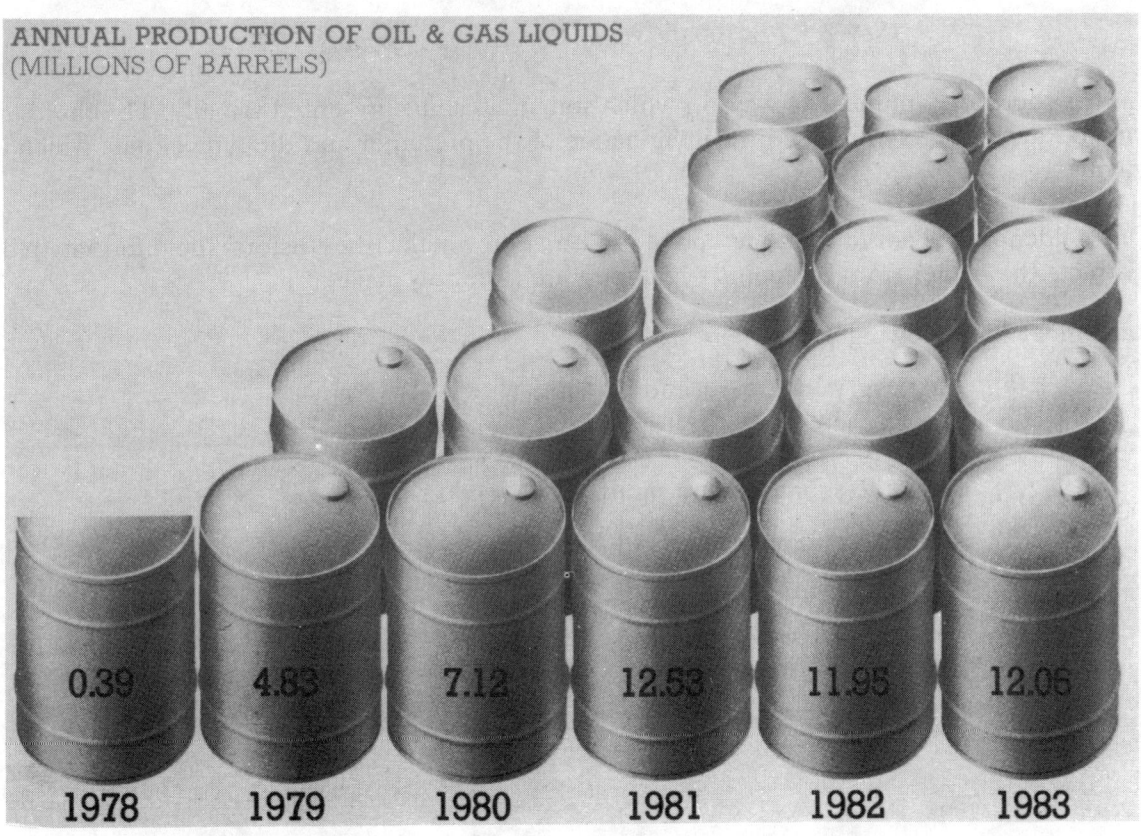

The final figure in this chapter is a cartogram from the BOC group. BOC (or British Oxygen) is a major British mulit-national company with activities in more than 50 countries in the world. It illustrates this and the importance of each area to the company's activities vividly in the figure.

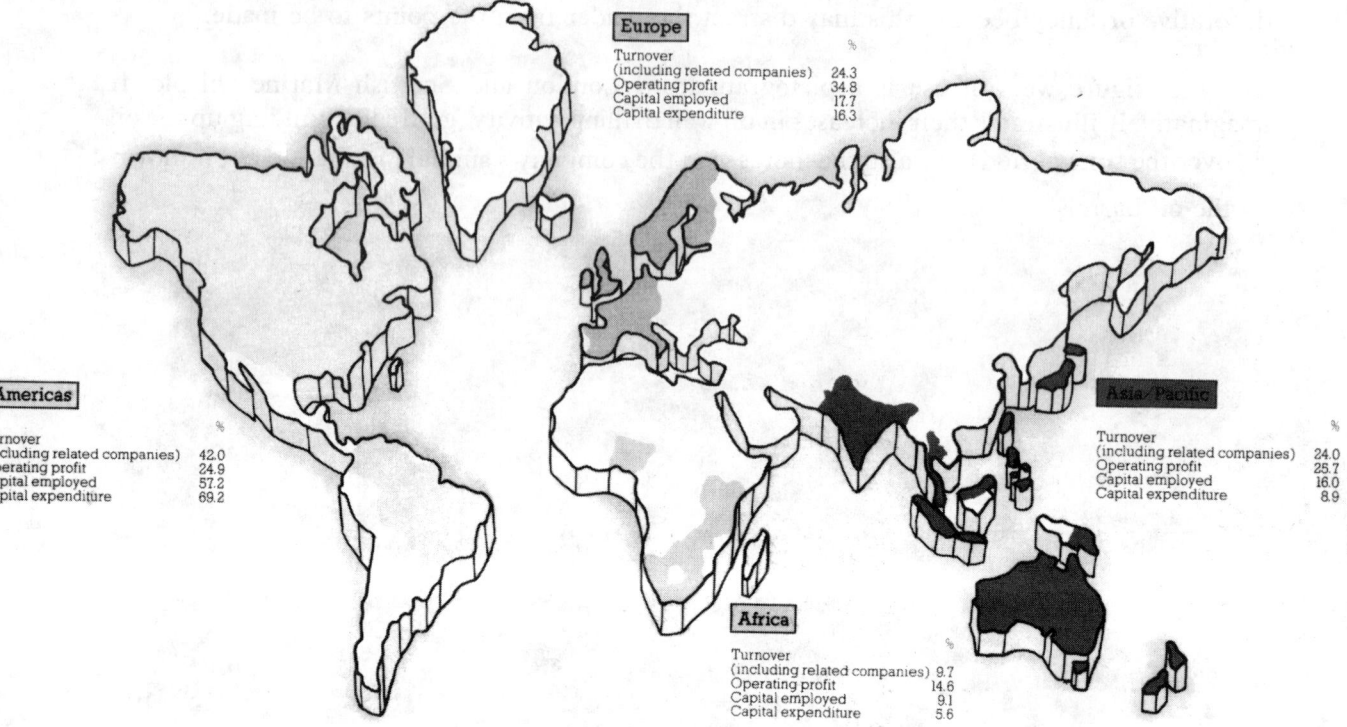

Europe
%
Turnover
(including related companies)   24.3
Operating profit   34.8
Capital employed   17.7
Capital expenditure   16.3

Americas
%
Turnover
(including related companies)   42.0
Operating profit   24.9
Capital employed   57.2
Capital expenditure   69.2

Asia/Pacific
%
Turnover
(including related companies)   24.0
Operating profit   25.7
Capital employed   16.0
Capital expenditure   8.9

Africa
%
Turnover
(including related companies)   9.7
Operating profit   14.6
Capital employed   9.1
Capital expenditure   5.6

(Source: The BOC Group, Report and Accounts 1983)

Clearly there are a number of ways in which statistics can be presented visually. The choice of method depends very much on the imagination of the presenter and the type of data which is involved.

One golden rule is not to use a method of presentation which either distorts the information or distracts the reader from the point which you are trying to make.

Remember the following points:

(a)   keep everything clear and concise;

(b)   always give the figure or table a title;

(c)   show the source of any figure or table;

(d)   label all component parts of the figure or table.

ASSIGNMENT — PURCHASING MADE EASY

"The trouble with trying to buy anything in this place is that the system is so complicated" said Harry Edwards one day over coffee. "If I could only understand the purchasing procedures I'm sure I could run the office more smoothly." Harry is the Marketing Manager for Teeschem Ltd, a large chemical company based in Cleveland. He has recently been appointed to the company and has moved from a small business in which purchasing office supplies was simply a matter of asking the firm's accountant if there was money available in the budget and placing the order. In Teeschem, however, the company is such a large organisation that strict control has to be maintained over all aspects of the company's spending. Harry approached Jim Sunley, the Purchasing Manager of Teeschem and asked for some guidance. Jim, in his usual friendly way, tried to explain the system as simply as possible. "You raise a purchase requisition for the goods you require and pass it to us in the purchasing department. If you are not sure of the best supplier or the best price we will find these for you. We then place an order. Of course we keep you informed by sending you a copy of the order when its placed. We also send a copy to the Accounts department as they will have to pay the bill. When the goods are received into the company, we are notified with a goods received note and again you will get a copy to say the goods have been received. If there is any problems with the goods when they are received this is noted both on the delivery note and on the goods received note. You can then arrange to have them brought up to your office. When the invoice comes in from the supplier, it is checked by the invoice verification section and if everything is OK then it will be paid by accounts. Is that clear enough?" Harry nodded but in a way that indicated that he had only vaguely grasped the system. Jim reflected on Harry's problem and decided to do something about it.

TASKS

1. You are a clerical assistant in the purchasing department of Teeschem. Jim knows that you have a good understanding of the system. He has asked you to prepare a 'step by step guide to purchasing' which can be circulated throughout the organisation. Bearing in mind that this will be used by all grades of staff, prepare this guide using simple and concise language.

2. Jim is concerned that the purchasing process is not overcomplicated. He wishes to be sure that there is not a duplication of documents 'floating around the organisation'. He has asked you to prepare a document flow chart similar to that shown earlier in the chapter but which is applicable to the purchasing process. Prepare this flow chart for Mr. Sunley.

DEVELOPMENTAL TASK

3. Try to obtain copies of the documents used by any organisation in your area. Identify the common aspects and from them produce a standardised purchase order and invoice form.

ASSIGNMENT — PRESENTING THE BUDGET

Presenting information to the ratepayers in a manner which is understandable and acceptable has always been a problem for Northdownshire County Council. In recent years the opposition parties on the council have severely criticised the way in which the annual rate demands have been presented to the authority's citizens. The County Treasurer has been asked by the Chairman of the Council to try to improve things for the coming year (1986/87). He has prepared the budget for the coming year and it is as follows:-

	1986/87				1985/86
	Gross Expenditure	Government Grants for Specific Services	Charges for Services	Net Expenditure	Net Expenditure
	£m	£m	£m	£m	£m
Education	165.8	8.1	17.0	140.7	136.2
Fire	8.1	—	0.7	7.4	7.0
Highways and Transportation	27.7	4.8	4.9	18.0	17.1
Police	36.1	15.4	5.3	15.4	13.6
Social Services	33.8	0.1	9.0	24.7	22.4
Other Services	17.2	3.5	2.9	10.8	10.1
Contingencies	20.7	2.4	2.2	16.1	10.7
Total Expenditure	309.4	34.3	42.0	233.1	217.1
Less: Government Block Grant				121.6	116.9
Use of Balances				0.2	4.9
Ratepayers' Contribution				111.3	95.3
Each 1p on the precept raises				£565,035	£566,953
The precept is therefore				197p	168p

[handwritten note in left margin: 4th Feb]

TASKS

[handwritten: In the]

1. You are employed in the Treasurer's Department of Northdownshire County Council and have been asked by your section head to prepare some examples of graphical presentation which may be included in the forthcoming county report and budget. Your section head has suggested that you should include at least one bar chart and one pie chart and also that you should show not only the 1986/87 breakdown but also some comparison with the 1985/86 figures. He has also encouraged you to use some imagination in the way you present the data and has mentioned the use of pictograms or other forms of visual presentation. Prepare a range of charts and diagrams which may be used.

    [handwritten in left margin: one other imaginative chart]

2. As part of the central government's budgetary measures the council's grant for the year has been cut from 48.7% of expenditure to 46.4%. This has meant that the council has had to increase its rate by a greater percentage than would have been the case had the grant remained constant in real terms. The Council has decided that the reasons for the rate increase should be made clear to the ratepayers. Your section head has asked you to draft a short paragraph of not more than 250 words explaining the situation. Prepare this draft.

    [handwritten in left margin: Central Govt has reduced its funds]

DEVELOPMENTAL TASK

3. Obtain a copy of the rate demand or annual budget and report for your local authority. Analyse it from the point of view of data presentation and prepare appropriate graphs or charts to illustrate the authority's expenditure and revenue.

Chapter 6

PERSONAL RELATIONSHIPS AND THE SOCIAL ENVIRONMENT

There are few households which have not at sometime experienced a member of the family coming home from school, or work, the club or the pub, and launching into a bitter attack upon someone who has upset them. Such attacks usually begin with the words "Do you know what so and so did today?!," followed by an emotional retelling of the incident that has so affected them. Unhappy experiences of this kind tend to be conterbalanced by the more pleasurable encounters with others. The school pupil returns home to announce, "The headteacher told me I did really well in class," or one friend tells another over a drink, "The boss had me in and told me a promotion is on the way". It is clear that the contact we have with others can produce emotional highs and lows, whilst in between the two extremes lie the majority of our personal exchanges with others.

In the working environment the quality of these face to face exchanges, and indeed of our relationships with other employees generally, is of importance not only to us personally, but to the organisation as well.

In this chapter we examine personal relationships within the workplace, to assess the significance of the role they play. By way of introduction, consider the situation described below.

> John was the manager of a section within an organisation. He was nearing retirement age and seeking early retirement. He was one of the longest serving staff in the organisation and as well as earning respect through his status, was also respected as someone who knew the business inside out. Moreover most staff regarded him as a gentleman because they found him to possess honesty and integrity. He respected the confidences of staff, and could always be approached by an employee with a personal or professional problem.
>
> His leadership style was persuasive rather than coercive, and his orders and instructions were delivered in a way which sought to avoid confrontations. When these arose with staff they were dealt with as an issue for joint discussion rather than unilateral managerial action. In total John enjoyed good personal relationships with all his staff.
>
> When he retired he was replaced by Richard, who had joined the section eighteen months previously with a reputation as a high flier. Richard had proved extremely able at his work, although he distanced himself from most staff and was therefore not a popular figure with his colleagues. He made his name with senior staff through his initiative and drive, and he was for them the obvious choice for promotion.

This was not a view shared by staff of the same status in the organisation as Richard, most of whom had longer service with it than he did. When the promotion was announced considerable resentment was felt. This resentment was re-inforced by Richard's style of leadership. One of his first steps on taking over was the complete reorganisation of the section. This was completed with a minimum of consultation and announced by Richard at a meeting of the section staff at which he brushed aside all criticisms of the new system, making it clear that staff who were unhappy with the arrangements should look for work elsewhere. Within six months in his new role Richard was the head of a section that was organised with great efficiency, but in which the morale of the staff was far lower than it had been in John's day, a period most of them looked back on with nostalgia and affection.

The point of this scenario is simply that personal relationships, and the social climate of the organisation play a vital role in the quality of life of the organisation. You may care to reflect upon the situation described and consider both the short term and long term implications of the replacement of John by Richard for the business they worked for.

PERSONAL RELATIONSHIPS IN THE WORKING ENVIRONMENT

People at work find themselves in an environment which forces them to develop personal relationships with other employees. In any business the staff have to work together as a team, if for no other reason than that as the individual components making up a larger whole, they have to communicate with each other to maintain any sort of contact with the organisation they belong to. It is simply not possible for an individual working for an organisation to be totally outside its communication network. It may be helpful to recall the analogy developed in chapter 1, of the organisation as a human body, a living organism made up of separate components which when combined form the complex whole. Any part which ceases to function, or does not function properly, is likely to have an effect upon the whole body. How significant the effect will be depends upon the importance of the particular component in question. We know that the body cannot function without a brain or heart, and we are equally aware that a body can be maintained with one lung or a single kidney. In much the same way individual employees are more or less important to the organisation as a whole depending upon the functions they perform. But whether their function is vital to its total operation, or merely ancilliary to it, if they do not mesh into the internal communication network then they cannot be regarded as contributing anything to it. If the analogy is taken a little further it can be seen that components which malfunction are sometimes positively harmful to the organisation as a whole. Thus in the same way that a hormone imbalance can totally affect a person's judgment by distorting the nature and quality of messages passing to and from the brain, so too an accountant who produces incorrect management information or a sales director who erroneously over-estimates future market growth is adversely affecting the organisation he or she work for. Is it then that when one talks of personal relationships within an organisation, this is simply another way of referring to any form of communication between staff? Or is it appropriate to see personal relationships as something more substantial than the connection between members of staff who occasionally send internal memoranda to each other or speak briefly over the telephone to each other?

In order to answer this question it is essential to remember that the process of communicating is a human activity. People communicate within organisations primarily to pursue the work of the organisation, but the organisation itself is, after all, a collection of individuals joined for a common purpose. Thus an organisation can be regarded as a social group with its own unique social identity created, maintained and developed by the complex interrelationship of the people who make it up. These people, as members of the group, may well be conscious of their group identity, especially if the organisation they work for deliberately encourages such an awareness. Japanese and American companies for instance, use various techniques and strategies for developing in their staff high levels of loyalty and even affection for the employer. Company songs, social functions which all of the family can attend, sports facilities, welfare benefits, and a generally paternalistic approach towards the well-being of staff both inside and outside work are methods of developing in each individual employee the belief that he or she is part of a closely bonded community. In cases where this effect occurs, individuals are likely to experience a sense of belonging, in the same way that they will probably already 'belong' to other groups: the family, for instance, or the local football or cricket team, or perhaps a political party. The benefits to the employer are likely to be a dedicated workforce anxious for the organisation to prosper, whilst the benefits to the employee are both material (for example generous sickness or invalidity payments) and psychological (for instance the feeling that he or she is needed and recognised by the organiation).

Most people have an innate need to pursue a common goal or share a common identity with others, for reasons that include security, social acceptability, competitive drive or simply gregariousness and these are considered in more detail in chapter 9.

THE SOCIAL MOTIVATION TO WORK

Realistically however, it has to be said that most people who are working are doing so primarily to earn a living rather than as a way of spending time with others. We go to work to gain income from which to live, rather than as a means of engaging in social activity. Nonetheless for many employees the social aspects of their work do meet a fundamental need. It is not unknown for the pools winner to continue working for the same employer even though the economic reason for doing so no longer exists. Thus we can conclude that the social dimension of a person's work is a vital element in the study of organisations. It is vital for two reasons. Firstly, the purely personal one that the individual possesses a feeling of well-being if personal relationships at work are successful. Secondly, because if staff relate to each other in a socially harmonious way the internal patterns of communication within the organisation work smoothly and efficiently. Disharmony can disrupt these patterns.

What we must now discover is something about the nature and quality of this social dimension that exists within the organisation. In order to do so it may be helpful to summarise what has been said so far. The following propositions have been put forward:

1. Organisations are made up of people who taken together possess a group identity;

2. This group identity gives rise to a social unit;

3. For the unit to function coherently its members need to communicate with each other.

To these initial propositions can be added some additional ones:

4. The social environment is only one of a number of different dimensions appraent in a study of organisations;

5. There are many methods of communication used in organisations;

6. There are different reasons for communicating;

7. Organisations need to be sensitive to the needs of the individual and the group.

For the remainder of this chapter we shall explore the meaning of these additional propositions, in order to gain an appreciation of the importance of personal relationships and the social environment to the operation of the organisation.

THE SOCIAL ENVIRONMENT

The social environment of the workplace is a way of describing in broad terms the nature and quality of all the relationships between the members of the workforce. Thus it involves considering the rules, procedures and principles which at any given time regulate an organisation in its capacity as a society; that is as a society of workers.

The following characteristics can be identified within the social environment of most organisations:

1.   THE EXISTENCE OF RULES AND CONVENTIONS

In common with all societies the social structure of the workplace is regulated by a mixture of formal rules and informal rules and conventions. These may be initiated by the organisation from above, that is passed down from senior management to the rest of the organisation. Alternatively they may emerge as a form of custom and practice amongst the staff; in other words convention. Generally rules are supported by sanctions, invariably legal and economic ones, to ensure compliance. Convention however relies upon the consensus support of the workforce. The following examples will clarify the distinction:

> **(a)   formal rules:**
>
> an employer may specify that if an employee is late for work twice in one calendar month he or she must be formally interviewed by the section head; if an employee has a grievance concerning another member of staff the matter can only be dealt with through the machinery of the organisation's formal grievance procedures.
>
> **(b)   informal rules/conventions:**
>
> within an organisation it may be accepted that all junior staff refer to senior staff by their style i.e. "Mr" or "Mrs X"; holiday rotas are arrived at by negotiation; the working day finishes half an hour earlier on a Friday.

Whilst most people accept the need for both formal and informal rules of the kind noted above, it is important to recognise that rules that are introduced without consultation and which are perceived by employees to be unfair or inappropriate may lead to resentment and attempts at undermining them. Generally people respond more favourably when they have had an opportunity of at least being able to express their own points of view, even if they are not ultimately taken up.

2.   DIFFERENT SOCIAL GROUPINGS

Unless an organisation is very small it is usual to find that staff will form a variety of sub-groups. For instance the managers of a business may tend not to mix socially at work with their inferiors (for instance at lunch or over coffee), but keep within each others company at such times. There may be many reasons for such behaviour, such as:

> (a)   a belief that it is necessary to distance themselves in order to avoid discipline problems arising through over-familiarity;
>
> (b)   the view that they have little in common with their subordinates;
>
> (c)   an assumption that this is a way of asserting their status superiority;
>
> (d)   the fear that they may reveal confidential information;
>
> (e)   the expectation that they can be compromised whilst they are off guard. For instance where the junior member of staff buys the boss a drink in the pub at lunchtime, and then asks if he can leave work early.

Other sub-group identities may be based upon all the staff of a particular clerical grade, ex-school friends who work for the same employer, the committee members of the company's social club, and so on.

3. THE GRAPEVINE

It has already been said that ideally management should consult with staff, especially staff leaders such as union representatives, prior to introducing changes. Often the most valuable information can be gained by 'off the record' face to face discussions. The less willing an organisation is to release information to the staff the more likely it becomes that informal communication networks will develop. People have an insatiable desire to know what is going on and become frustrated, anxious and angry if they believe vital information is being withheld. This may be anything from a belief that redundancies are imminent to the expectation that their boss is leaving.

Information passing through informal channels is said to pass through 'the grapevine'. Grapevine networks tend to operate horizontally, that is occur between staff at the same or approximately the same level of status throughout the organisation. The danger of the grapevine is that it can spread entirely erroneous information which adversly affects the performance of those who come into contact with it.

There are three types of informal communications networks.

(a) the parallel network

Here a person who is centrally placed in the organisation and able to obtain confidential or interesting information passes it on to his or her acquaintances. Administrative and clerical support staff invariably are well placed to act in this way.

(b) the casual network

This involves a person obtaining the information accidentally, and passing it on by word of mouth to someone else who does likewise. Such a communication chain may involve many people, and the more there are, the greater are the chances that the original statement will be distorted.

(c) the cluster network

Here the originator of the rumour passes it on to two or three others, each of whom passes it on to two or three more.

There may be cases in which the management or the workforce find it useful to set a rumour in motion. If twenty redundancies have to be made, the pill may not seem as bitter if a week before the formal announcement the rumour gets about that fifty redundancies are planned.

4. CHANGE

The social environment is dynamic and is subject to continual change. Sound leadership qualities are needed by managers to introduce and carry through any sort of change which personally affects staff.

Changes may be brought about either by internal or external factors. For instance an organisation may decide that it is economically desirable to relocate. This change, carrying with it substantial social upheavals for staff who may have to move house and change their children's schools, is a purely internally generated change. Tact, persuasion and understanding are social skills demanded of the manager in such circumstances.

Equally a local authority may find that its rate support grant is cut, obliging it to look for economies in its staffing levels. It may cope with this externally precipitated change by redeploying staff, providing early retirement schemes, and issuing redundancy notices. Again the personal impact of this strategy upon the staff involved requires sensitivity to the needs of the individuals affected and the staff as a whole.

METHODS OF COMMUNICATION

This topic has already been considered in some depth in chapter 2. Here we can note that the decision as to a suitable method of communication to meet the needs of the particular occasion is one which can be easily overlooked by the overworked administrator, or simply not appreciated and in consequence great damage can be done.

Consider the following examples:

(a) An administrative assistant has been given the task of producing a formal report on some aspect of the work of her company. She spends a considerable amount of time researching and writing up the report, including a number of evenings working at home. Her superior indicated when she gave her the task that if she performed it thoroughly it could mean a promotion. The day after she completes the report she receives an internal memorandum from her superior which simply states. "I acknowledge receipt of your report, which due to recent management rethinking is no longer needed."

(b) At the office Christmas party the Office Manager gives a speech before all the office staff. One of the staff present is 62 and has urged the company to let him continue working until the age of 65. After discussion the company has agreed. At the end of his speech the Office Manager concludes, "and I am pleased to say that Harry is being given early retirement. Quite a Christmas present, eh, Harry!"

(c) One of the senior staff of a company comes bursting into the typing pool where there are ten typists at work. In his hand is a letter typed by one of the typists who has only just started working for the company. "This is a disgrace, and you are a disgrace. You are not fit to work here. Type it again!" he shouts across the room to the typist, at the same time screwing up the letter and throwing it on the floor.

In the first example above, the tactless communication of her superior is likely to produce a reaction in the administrative assistant which at best sees her superior as insensitive and unreliable and at worst leads her to look for a new job.

In the second example the Office Manager's public address is clearly inappropriate, for at least two reasons. Firstly it indicates a possible weakness in the channels of communication in the organisation, and secondly it demonstrates a lack of sensitivity on the part of the Office Manager regarding the time and place for a statement of this kind to be made. Let us consider these two issues in turn. To begin with the Office Manager appears to have received misinformation from the company, since Harry has negotiated to stay on. Alternatively the company may have changed its mind about the early retirement, without telling Harry, which is inexcusable. But quite apart from the question of how well informed the Office Manger actually is, and even assuming the information is correct, it is doubtful whether the speech at the office party is, in the circumstances, a suitable occasion to reveal that Harry is leaving. He may regard the matter as confidential; something which he would want to tell colleagues about in his own time. He may be sensitive about his age. At very least it would be wise to alert him in advance of what is going to be said, so that he is given an opportunity to give or refuse his consent to it.

In matters of a personal nature it is most important to guard against making them public, certainly at an inappropriate time and place. This holds true whether the information is revealed expressly, as in this case, or if it is allowed to leak out. In organisations where other staff are "in the know" about a personal matter before the individual who is directly affected (promotion, disciplinary matters, redundancy and so on), not only does the individual concerned feel angry, hurt and possibly humiliated, fellow staff are also likely to sympathise with that person, and perhaps see their organisation as one which is insensitive to the feelings of its staff. The lack of trust and confidence this can create is harmful to the type of relationship between employee and organisation that is needed if the employee is to give of his or her best.

In the last example the criticisms that can be levelled at the senior member of staff are that:

(i) he has publicly humiliated the typist;

(ii) he has made no allowance for the fact that she is a new starter;

(iii) he has revealed himself in the eyes of a member of staff to be someone totally lacking in manners and grace in an ill-tempered response to an incident to which he seems to have totally over-reacted. It is unlikely that either the typist in question or the others in the typing pool will give of their best to this member of staff in the future. Indeed as someone lacking in self control it may have been purely by chance that his outburst did not include a sexist comment such as "You women are all the same!" (assuming the typist to be female!), resulting in them refusing to work any further until an apology has been given. Unnecessary oral confrontation of this sort are usually counterproductive and should be avoided.

REASONS FOR COMMUNICATING

It is not possible to guage the appropriateness of the method used to communicate without considering what reason or function the communication is seeking to fulfil. Since communicating is a two way process it is necessary to examine not only the aim or intention of the person initiating the communication, but also the perception of the person receiving it. For instance when a senior member of staff says to a junior employee, "Your looking rough today. I doubt whether you are fit for anyhting," the employee may take this to be a way of issuing a rebuke, whilst the intention of the senior was simply to be sociable and sympathetic. It is easy for messages to be misinterpreted.

It is possible to classify the reasons for communicating as seen from the initiator's standpoint, into four separate catagories of intention:

(a) to give or obtain information;

(b) to encourage or persuade;

(c) to indicate sociability; or

(d) to provide psychological support.

Clearly these categories can and do overlap. For instance when one colleague says to another, "There is a quicker way of working out your figures, if you would like me to show you," the statement falls under (a) and (c) above, whilst when a supervisor tells a junior employee, "Although you did not receive the promotion you performed very well in the interview, and you should apply for Mrs Wilkins position when she leaves next month," catagories (a), (b) and (d) are each involved.

PERSUASION

Each of the categories referred to demands different skills on the part of the initiator to be effective. For example giving information requires precision of presentation, whilst persuasion, which is a skill in itself, will usually involve the communicator in using a wide repertoire of devices to achieve the desired effect such as a change in belief or attitude. Persuasive powers are valuable to all those in positions of power and authority, such as managers and politicians, whilst they are equally necessary to anyone engaged in the business of selling goods or services, such as advertisers, sales staff and so on. Some of the issues associated with persuasive powers are:

(a) **the choice between 'hard sell' and 'soft sell'.**
This is the choice whether to put pressure on people, or whether to create an impression of unbiased neutrality. The door to door salesman is traditionally associated with the 'hard sell' approach. Advertising companies using television commercials to increase the sales of products often rely upon subtle techniques to persuade. Within an organisation persuasive tactics used on staff are likely to rely on both methods;

(b) **the use of argument.**
The construction and delivery of an effective argument is a highly developed skill, which may involve using legal, economic, financial, political or moral principles in support of the argument or perhaps relying on expert opinions. Thus an employer may attempt to convince the staff of the need for individual economies or greater output by arguing a financial case, or by presenting the findings of an investigative body into the work of the organisation, such as the report of a systems analyst.

(c) **style of presentation.**
Whether the approach is hard sell or soft sell, and whatever argument is being relied upon by the persuader, the style of presentation must be carefully considered. This involves identifying the character of the audience or individual and tailoring the approach accordingly. It is really a case of adapting the approach to meet the needs or requirements of the recipient. For example is humour likely to be a successful device; what is the social background of the individual or group; is the audience partisan?

It may not be felt that in communicating with the intention of being purely sociable, very heavy demands of skill are placed upon the communicator. In organisations the status heirarchy can sometimes have the effect of stifling this form of communication, for a superior will sometimes feel that fraternising with junior staff is a recipe for future discipline problems, and may also erode his or her status. As between staff at the same level, sociability usually helps to create close bonds of group identity with the result that individuals will be most prepared to work together as a team.

Finally a word about psychological support. Whilst it is appropriate to provide words of comfort and assistance to those who have experienced a personal trauma, there are clearly occasions when specialist advice and help is needed. A large organisation which seeks to meet its obligations towards the staff by providing them not only with a source of income, but also with an environment that is emotionally and socially supportive, will operate a personnel department to cope with such issues as family bereavement, illness and related personal problems.

THE NEEDS OF THE INDIVIDUAL AND THE GROUP

Under this final heading we can consider some of the points that the manager should bear in mind when dealing with the management of the workforce:-

(a) the workforce is a group, and will perform most effectively when its individual members are encouraged to see themselves as a cohesive self supporting team. Teamwork relies heavily upon leadership, and a good leader is someone whom the group can respect;

(b) individuals working for the organisation have particular needs which should be identified and recognised. An employee will usually be seeking both personal and career development and a system for enabling this development to be monitored through regular employer/employee dialogue is valuable;

(c) adequate physical and psychological rewards both to groups and individuals should be given to mark achievement and encourage further development;

(d) the climate of the organisation should be carefully monitored. For instance, organisations in which there are group rivalries, or where excessive competition is encouraged or the rewards system is considered to operate unfairly will possess a climate of disharmony that is not compatible with an efficient and effective business unit.

In practical terms the manager can introduce systems to assist in the task of managing human resources. These generally include machinery for staff consultation, grievance disputes, and induction programmes. The working timetable should be designed to enable staff to meet together as groups to discuss problems and issues. Ideally the communications network should be structured so as not only to meet the direct resource requirements of the organisation, but also to meet the needs of the staff as people. Thus events such as anniversaries, births, and promotions should be 'picked up' within the system and celebrated. For most people such rituals are part of the culture of our society and there is no reason why the working environment should not encourage them.

It has been said that a good manager is a person who has a clear picture of the organisation in his or her mind. Such a mental picture is one which needs to be heavily focussed on the staff of the organisation, the resource that makes the organisation work. Management has considerable control over the social environment of the workplace, and must always be mindful that a work-force which operates as a socially cohesive unit will work far more effectively for the organisation than will one in which there is division and conflict.

But it should be remembered that, in common with other aspects of organisation in its environment, the social environment is volatile and dynamic and consequently subject to constant change; personal relationships as we know from our own personal experience have to be worked on, and this is as true of the relationships we have at work as of those we enjoy with our family and friends.

ASSIGNMENT — MOVING SOUTH

Following a decision to reorganise its manufacturing operations, the head office of Redwell Ltd contacts the managers of the company's plants in Belfast, Bolton and Wolverhampton informing them of the decision of the Board of Directors to close down these plants in order to locate the entire manufacturing base at the main site near Rochester in Kent.

The Board, through Head Office, has provided the respective managers with details of the effect the relocation will have on staffing levels at the three plants. Staff over the age of 55 are to be offered early retirement and minimum lump sum payment of £5,000, whilst all remaining staff are to be offered jobs at Rochester, with a flat rate payment of £1,500 available to cover removal and additional expenses.

The managers of the respective plants are now faced with the task of implementing the change. Head Office has indicated that it should be handled sensitively. The time schedule for relocation is six months. Unfortunately the Manager at Belfast has found that a rumour of the closedown has been passing around his plant and staff are convinced there are to be widespread compulsory redundancies.

TASKS

You work in the personnel department at the company's Head Office and have been required to visit each of the plants to assist their managers and staff in 'selling' the change to the workforce.

1. Because of the situation you decide to visit Belfast first, followed by visits to Wolverhampton and Bolton. In advance of your visits to the Belfast and Wolverhampton plants produce a written strategy which you can put to the managers of these plants, in which you identify a schedule or programme to be followed by them to:

    (a)   introduce the facts of the relocation to the staff; and

    (b)   deal with individual issues arising from the change.

2. The Bolton manager has asked you to assist in conducting interviews with two members of his staff who are not keen on moving South with the company. Both employees are regarded as valuable members of the workforce and the manager is anxious that the company should not lose their talents. Prepare a list of arguments that you might use as a method of persuading these employees to remain with the company, and move from the North West to Kent.

DEVELOPMENTAL TASKS

3. Role play an exercise in which you give an oral presentation to the rest of the group where you speak to them about the changes planned by the company, and encourage them to remain loyal to the company.

4. Prepare some outline notes for a brief speech in which you are to mark the early retirement of one of the company's employees at a staff party given to mark the closure of one of the company's plants.

Chapter 7

THE EFFECTIVENESS AND EFFICIENCY OF AN ORGANISATION

THE NEED FOR OVERALL EFFICIENCY

For any organisation to operate effectively and efficiently, every individual employee and every department must work together as a co-ordinated whole. Each part of the organisation must seek to attain a similar high standard, for if there is one weak element in the system it will tend to undermine the rest. For example, even the best planned organisation using the latest technology will prove ineffective if the workforce is badly trained or motivated. Conversely, as one often sees with successful football clubs, when all the elements work together in harmony the end result can be greater than just the sum of the individual parts. 'Synergy' is the name given to this beneficial outcome. For example, a well motivated worker in a good group can spark off ideas or suggestions for improvements that can be developed and refined by his fellow group members. The workers in the group are not simply carrying out their tasks, they are in fact improving the organisation's chances of success by inspiring change through innovation.

Therefore in this chapter we will be examining the way in which management can make the organisation more efficient and more effective and achieve a degree of synergy by monitoring and improving the individual elements which make up the organisation as a whole. In doing this we must bear in mind that to be successful an organisation must produce goods or services which meet the needs of customers. Therefore it must improve the management of its productive resources so that this objective can be achieved in the optimum way.

AN IDEAL MODEL OF AN ORGANISATION

To achieve commercial success an organisation must not only produce a product which the customer wants, it must also ensure that its internal operations are managed efficiently. There are many examples of companies with products which are in great demand from consumers but which have been unable to organise their production and internal operations effectively. The Sinclair computer company had a product which was a market leader but it was plagued with production delays which deterred the potential customer and eventually led to Sinclair being taken over by Amstrad, its major rival. Thus the internal management of an organisation must be efficient, effective and designed to benefit the organisation as a whole.

One way to help to ensure that these objectives are achieved is to design an ideal model of an organisation against which we can compare real organisations. This may then be used by an organisation to guide it step by step in achieving its objectives and eventual consumer satisfaction. This 'ideal model' may be unattainable in real life. However the model could form a rational basis on which organisations could attempt to operate. Also the model may be used for comparison if some part of a real organisation has problems. For example, if the demand for an organisation's products is falling, then perhaps it should analyse the characteristics of its products and compare these with current customer needs. This may show that customer demands or tastes have changed and are no longer in line with the organisation's product. This analysis would indicate that the organisation had moved away from the guidelines given in the 'ideal model'. Reference to the model may also suggest possible corrective action the organisation should consider. Thus the model we will present is both a prescriptive aid to designing an organisation's operations and a diagnostic tool in solving management's problems. We should therefore be able to assess or evaluate the organisation's progress by reference to the model.

We can construct a 'general' model for any organisation. However if we were to consider a specific organisation a more detailed model may have to be designed. This is necessary as the detailed workings of any particular organisation must be suited to its own specific objectives. For example the detailed operating system of a service organisation, such as the Education Department of a Local Authority, will necessarily differ from that of a production organisation, such as a brick making company. However the 'general' model may be similar for both. For example both attempt to meet customer's needs, operate organisation structures designed to provide the necessary service and make use of trained and skilled personnel. They will both have objectives, targets, policies, plans, programmes and budgets designed to encourage efficiency and effective operation.

We will begin by considering the most important feature that will make up the design of a 'general' model. It is necessary to decide how these features should best fit together to achieve overall co-ordination. In the following section we will consider the important features of the model, their significance, and how they may be assessed or evaluated.

The following figure shows a possible 'general working model' of an organisation and reflects the aims of the organisation through its internal operations.

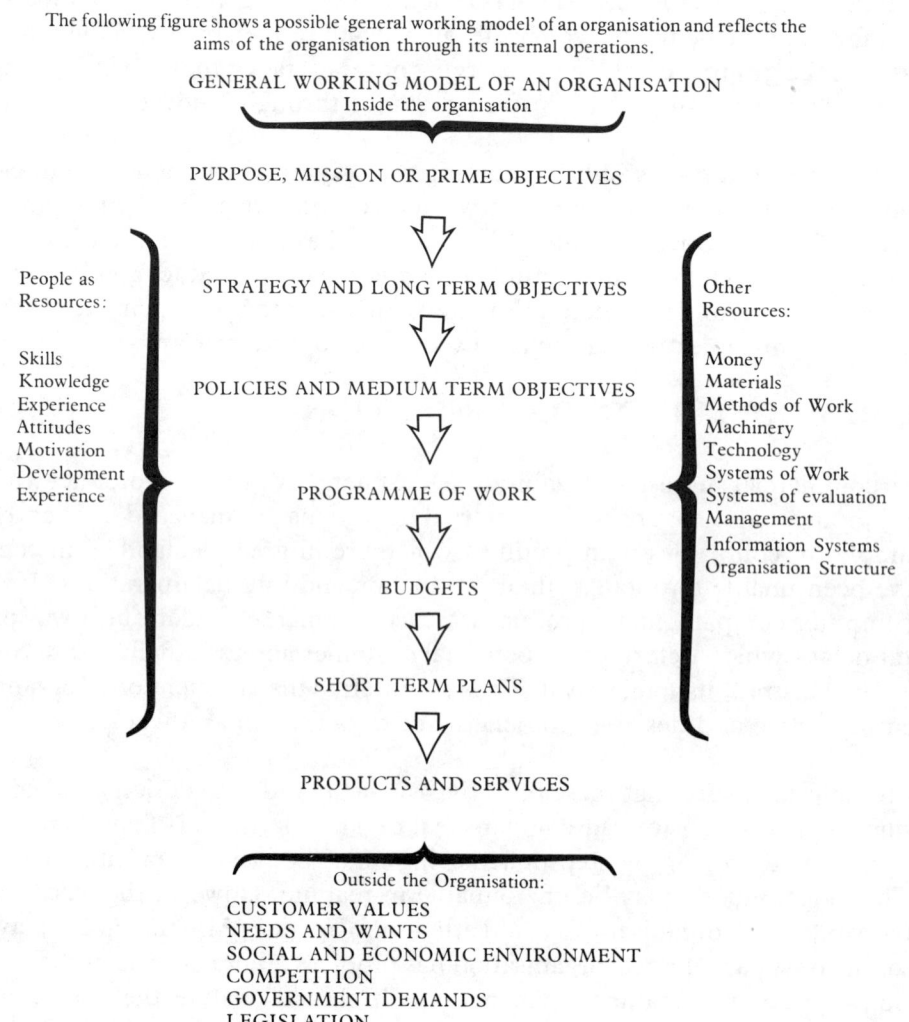

GENERAL WORKING MODEL OF AN ORGANISATION
Inside the organisation

PURPOSE, MISSION OR PRIME OBJECTIVES

People as Resources:

Skills
Knowledge
Experience
Attitudes
Motivation
Development
Experience

STRATEGY AND LONG TERM OBJECTIVES

POLICIES AND MEDIUM TERM OBJECTIVES

PROGRAMME OF WORK

BUDGETS

SHORT TERM PLANS

PRODUCTS AND SERVICES

Other Resources:

Money
Materials
Methods of Work
Machinery
Technology
Systems of Work
Systems of evaluation
Management
Information Systems
Organisation Structure

Outside the Organisation:
CUSTOMER VALUES
NEEDS AND WANTS
SOCIAL AND ECONOMIC ENVIRONMENT
COMPETITION
GOVERNMENT DEMANDS
LEGISLATION

THE PURPOSE, MISSION OR PRIME OBJECTIVES OF AN ORGANISATION

The prime objective of any organisation is to meet the needs of its customers or clients. This statement is equally true for a public service or organisation such as a local authority who must satisfy the wants of its citizens, as it is for a private sector enterprise which can only survive by adequately catering to the demands of its customers. Therefore in setting its prime objective the organisation should identify two elements:

(i)   Customer or Client Needs

(ii)   The Specific Type of Customer or Client.

(i)   Customer or Client Needs

An organisation usually tries to determine the needs of its customers or clients by using some form of market research. Many private sector trading organisations operate a marketing policy which is determined by its market research findings. Its marketing policy seeks to anticipate, stimulate and satisfy the need of the customer. Market research is an attempt to identify these needs and the extent to which they are currently satisfied or can be met through the introduction of new products. Public Sector service organisations also try to satisfy customer needs, but often they will tend to rely on information gathered by elected members, some limited population surveys or, as in the case of the National Health Service, analysing medical statistics.

For many consumer products such as food and detergents, market researchers are employed by suppliers to continuously question selected samples of the public, regarding their preferences for the organisation's products and those of their competitors. There is a continuous effort to produce new products or services which anticipate new or changing customer demands. How successful an organisation is in meeting its customers needs is sometimes assessed by their product share of the market, which is usually expressed as a percentage of total market sales. Thus a company which has managed to achieve a dominant market share is usually the producer which has most accurately assessed the demands of its customers. For example, Amstrad recognised that there was substantial demand for a cheap word processor which was simple to use and was in the reach of even the smallest business. Its success in this field reflects the shrewdness of its managers in recognising this need and filling it with their products.

A large market share is not the only measure we have of assessing a company's success. Sometimes organisations who only have a relatively tiny share of the total market can still be successful by serving a small but highly profitable segment of the market. For example Rolls Royce or Morgan sell comparatively few cars but have limited direct competition in their small segment of the car market and thus show excellent profits.

Alternatively in a highly competitive market in which the total sales are relatively static or perhaps even declining, many organisations are deemed successful if they manage to survive over a long period of time.

(ii)   The Specific Type of Customer or Client

In determining its prime objectives an organisation must be careful to clearly identify the particular type of customer it seeks to supply. Often this may be obvious. The Health Service attempts to provide health care for all. A housing department provides accommodation to those who are homeless or in substandard housing. However, for commercial producers, identifying the segment of the market which it will attempt to cater for may be crucial in achieving its long term success. If Rolls Royce's prime objective is to produce 'the Best Cars in the World' then only the wealthiest customers are likely to be interested and it will have to adjust its product marketing accordingly.

CHANGING THE ORGANISATION'S PRIME OBJECTIVES

From time to time an organisation must examine its prime objectives to see if they are still relevant and meet present customer needs. As a consequence of such an examination the whole direction of the business may be revised. Japanese camera manufacturers once set out to produce cheap replicas of the most expensive cameras in the West. However their reputation for quality grew and well known Japanese camera manufacturers, such as Nikon, now produce a product that is equal to any of their competitors.

THE SUCCESS OF THE PRIME OBJECTIVES

To assess the success of the prime objectives of an organisation it is necessary to judge how well it meets its customer needs since they are so closely inter linked. Thus profitability, market share, innovative ability or sheer long term survival may be all good indicators. Often the values that the organisation's owners or managers believe to be important are incorporated into its stated prime objectives and this will be further reflected in the way the organisation operates. For example if an organisation's stated purpose is to be a leader in new technology, then a large proportion of its profit must be retained and spent on research and development.

CORPORATE STRATEGY AND LONG TERM OBJECTIVES

An organisation's top management must ensure that its long term objectives are set in accordance with its fundamental statement of purpose. Often such long term planning of objectives is called corporate strategy. Corporate strategy differs from planning in that it sets broad targets, such as the expected level of profit over a long period of time and in so doing may require that the organisation employs new resources or changes those it currently uses. Such strategy must be much more concrete that the rather vague philosophy and values stated in its prime objectives. For example if Rolls Royce has the prime objective of producing the 'best car in the world' the company must decide how this can be best achieved. The organisation must decide whether it is going for the fastest, largest, most luxurious, most expensive or most reliable car. You could perhaps compare the strategy of Rolls Royce with that of another luxury car manufacturer such as Porsche. Clearly the German car manufacturer has chosed to emphasise the speed of its product, while you will not see the speed of a Rolls Royce stressed in its advertising. Instead it may emphasise the fact the the only thing that you can hear when driving a Rolls at 70 mph is the ticking of the clock, a clear indication of a luxurious ride.

These objectives must be revised regularly to ensure that they are still relevant. Design, price, output and achievable profit may have to be modified in line with changing demands. So for instance, Mercedes have decided to move down into the small car market as a way of catering for a wider customer market. Yet if Rolls Royce decided to adopt the long term objective of making large quantities of small cars, this surely would not be in keeping with their stated purpose and so may not be successful in the long run, as their product would be less exclusive.

IBM originally made business machines such as time keeping clocks etc. Then they sold off their original business to concentrate on their new objective of producing computers. From an assessment of customer demands it became clear that in only supplying the hardware (the computers) the company was not adequately meeting consumer needs. The software (programs or systems) for use with their machines then became a major part of the business. As the use of new technology expanded customers demanded more help in solving their business problems and so problem solving 'packages' of machines and software were then devised. Thus it could be said that the original objective, which was simply to produce machines, has been modified to the long term objectives of solving customers business problems.

The length of time needed to accomplish the long term objectives or strategic plans of an organisation can vary from 5 to 25 years or more. Launching a new model of car may take up to five years from initial conception. The building of a new District General Hospital has taken up to 15 years from the original discussions. Let us suppose that British Rail wished to electrify all the railway lines in the country. This would have to be a very long term objective if it were to be achieved without massive spending in one year or huge losses incurred in scrapping diesel stock. If this changeover was completed gradually it may be completed more economically. This would be true especially where maintenance demanded a complete overhaul of existing networks. Yet it could still take up to 25 years. The assessment of success for an organisation's corporate strategy can then often only be measured in terms of its long term financial position, market share, or range of services produced over a similarly long period of time.

POLICIES AND MEDIUM TERM OBJECTIVES

More concrete proposals are likely to be stated in an organisation's medium term objectives. Examples of medium term objectives may be the level of profit expected from a particular investment project of the type and scope of goods and services to be produced. Guidelines for managers may also be laid down to help them in the task of achieving these objectives. These guidelines are often called 'policies'. An example could be the Safety Policy every organisation must have if it is to conform to the requirements of the Health and Safety at Work Act 1974. Whilst Marks and Spencer display signs stating their policy of mainly buying goods of British manufacture, not all organisations are as open as this regarding their policies because of the need for commercial secrecy of simply poor communication of their policies.

PROGRAMMES OF WORK

So far we have concentrated on the functions of top management in determining the overall objectives and policies of an organisation. However it is middle management who must determine the programmes of work to achieve these objectives. This really involves the day to day operations of the business. It would cover such issues as how the product or service should be produced on an operations basis or the part that each department or section is expected to play in the overall production process. Such tasks may appear less important and yet as we stressed at the beginning of this chapter it is vitally important that all elements of the organisation should work effectively and efficiently. Thus programmes of work should be clear and co-ordinated if the organisation is to achieve its objectives.

SHORT TERM PLANS AND BUDGETS

Long term objectives (or strategies) may take five years or more to complete and individual programmes from one to five years. Short term plans and budgets must be established to manage the operations of the organisation within the current and coming year. They must also be broken down into shorter periods for the first line managers. First line managers deal directly with the workforce and have to interpret management wishes which are stated in the plan and ensure that they are carried out by the workforce. Of course all the previous objective setting and planning may come to nothing if the workforce are not sufficiently motivated to satisfactorily carry out the plan! We consider the problem of staff motivation in chapter 8.

THE MANAGEMENT OF THE RESOURCES REQUIRED TO ACHIEVE AN ORGANISATION'S OBJECTIVES

At this point we will deviate slightly from the stages of our 'general working model' of the organisation to consider the management of the resources that are needed to achieve the stated objectives. In chapter 19 an organisation's resources are classified as land, labour and capital. However for the purpose of decision making by management an alternative classification is often employed. Resources are sometimes stated as the 4 "M's" — Manpower, Money, Machines and Materials. However other scarce and valuable items are used as inputs into this production process. Examples include methods of working, such as good systems and techniques, land and buildings, the skills of the workforce and even time and ideas.

MANAGEMENT OF RESOURCES TO ACHIEVE EFFECTIVENESS AND EFFICIENCY

The management of an organisation must ensure that its objectives are met by using the resources it has at its command in the most effective and efficient manner. An effective manager is one who has achieved the objectives that he has been set in the time allowed. For example, a refuse disposal team may have the task of emptying every dust bin in a given area each week. If this objective was achieved could the team leader claim to have been 100% effective in carrying out his task? Certain questions should be asked as to how the task was organised. Did he use too many men in each crew or was the budget overspent because of the need for overtime payments in order to complete the task in the week? If this was the case it may be that the efficiency of the operation was less than ideal even if it was effective in achieving the task objective.

A major problem in assessing efficiency is that it can only be expressed as a measure in comparison to some other method of working. For example if we examine the time it took to complete the task of clearing the bins we may find that it took 5 days to complete in one week and yet with the reorganisation of the methods employed, it may only take 4 days in the following week. It could be said that there had been a 20% improvement in efficiency. However we still cannot identify the ultimate level of efficiency. Consequently it cannot now be stated that the operation is 100% efficient if there is still room for improvement.

VARIETY OF STANDARDS

When considering the efficiency or effective use of resources we must also realise that there may be a variety of standards to be set, all of which may be equally important. It would be unwise to halve the time taken to clear the bins if most of the rubbish was left on the householder's front step! It is not just the quantity of work done that is important, there is also the aspect of the quality of work such as meeting the standards of value or performance needed. Often such measures of quality are more difficult to assess accurately but they can be just as important. From the customers point of view they may be even more important. Ask the householder who has to sweep up every time the dust bin has been emptied!

In a production process the original material used must also be up to the standard required to ensure the quality of the final product. You cannot make silk purses out of sow's ears, as the saying goes. But it is also true that if the skills of the workforce, the management systems and the methods and machines used are inadequate then you cannot efficiently and effectively make silk purses out of pure silk either.

A further problem facing managers is that of determining the standard required for each part of the work and explaining it to the workforce. If the process requires a mechanical part to be machined then a technical description of the dimensions to be achieved may be sufficient such as 10cms ± 1cm. However it is much more difficult to explain to workers the standard of service required. For example how do you accurately explain and later assess the standard of nursing care to be provided or an acceptable standard of dealing with a customer. Such assessments often require subjective judgements on the part of managers who have experience of the quality of the product or service that is likely to satisfy the customer or client.

PRODUCTIVITY MEASURES

One method employed is to use productivity as a measure of efficiency. This involves determining the actual output or production achieved and dividing it by the input of resources needed to produce it. Let us use the example of a coalmine. Suppose coalface A produced 120 tons of coal

. . . variety of standards . . .

in a shift while coalface B produced 80 tons. Obviously coalface A has a higher output or production. But how efficient was coalface A in the use of manpower? Coalface A used 60 men and thus their productivity was 120/60 = 2 tons per man shift. Coalface B used 20 men and therefore their productivity was 80/20 = 4 tons per man shift. If we compare the two, Coalface B appears to be more efficient. However the management of the mine may seek a reason for this discrepancy in production and it would not be surprising to find that coalface A had more difficult working conditions. The men may work equally hard but more manpower is needed to overcome the inherent geological problems. Coalface A is more effective in producing coal (120 tons) but less efficient in the use of manpower (2 tons per man).

IMPROVING PRODUCTIVITY

In most instances an organisation will seek to maintain or increase its volume of production or service while constantly increasing its productivity. It is a bit like swinging a tiger by the tail, it would be very dangerous to stop and let go. Clearly if a competitior gains a productivity advantage this could be turned into a commercial advantage by reducing price and so attracting customers.

One major argument for improving productivity is that it is less wasteful in the use of resources. Costs can be reduced by making savings in the manpower required to produce a specified level of output.

As an example we will take the case of a shirt manufacturer. Let us suppose that to produce 1000 shirts the company faces labour costs of £1000 or £1 per shirt. However with the introduction of sophisticated computerised cutting machines, the same labour force now produces 2000 shirts at no extra cost. The labour cost per shirt is now only 50p. If they were sold at the same price, there would be 2,000 x 50p or £1000 extra profit. This could be available for distribution among the shareholders in higher dividends or among the employees in the form of a pay rise. Perhaps the selling price could be reduced which would benefit existing customers or attract new buyers for the company's product. If every organisation in Britain was able to increase its productivity then the whole country would benefit.

PRODUCTIVITY PROBLEMS

There appear to be many benefits to be gained from an increase in productivity. Improved productivity, superficially at least, appears to be the key to business success. Unfortunately when productivity increases this does not always means that a manufacturer can increase his sales correspondingly. In our example the increase in productivity may have adverse effects for the workforce. Half the shirt workers may be made redundant if the previous sales figure of 1000 shirts cannot be improved. As a result of the increased productivity, the employer only needs half as many workers to produce the same level of output. The unions therefore may argue that it is against their own best interests to improve productivity at a time when demand for the product is not increasing. However if all the workers were kept in a job, the comparatively low productivity may mean that the product is no longer competitive. Consequently the organisation would start making a loss and could eventually go out of business altogether, with all the workers losing their jobs.

METHODS OF IMPROVING PRODUCTIVITY

Potentially it is possible to improve productivity in any of the organisation's productive resources. The possibilities range from using better materials, implementing improved methods of work, acquiring better machinery or adopting new technology. It may simply mean encouraging the workers to work harder. Some employers use incentives such as bonus payments to increase productivity. Others ignore these 'carrots' and offer the 'stick' of threatened dismissal. In the long run it may be difficult to continually make people work harder and constantly improve productivity using such methods, for there is a physical limit to the amount people can produce and no amount of incentives or threats can get them to work harder.

Generally the biggest increases in productivity have come from new technology and new machinery. Automation and robotics have meant that fewer people are needed in car factories to produce the same output of cars. Automation means that machines can stamp out an endless stream of parts with little human attendance and robot arms can handle spray guns or welding equipment and mimic human movements in a tireless fashion. This helps to explain why jobs in the manufacturing sector have decreased in recent years.

The service industries however are one area in which the use of manpower is increasing. These are areas which often offer a personal service and so it has not been so easy to replace manpower with machinery. They are said to be labour intensive. Consider the possibility of replacing manpower in a very personal service such as the National Health Service. It is often not desirable. Nevertheless even in such service industries there are areas where manpower can perhaps be used more efficiently. Improved technology means that previously slow laboratory tests are now carried out at greater speed by a computer aided analytical machines. New office technology ranging from computerised records of patients and the use of word processors may allow many savings to be made in hospital administration.

PERFORMANCE INDICATORS

Management often seeks to compare the relative efficiency of different parts of the organisation, discover weaknesses and then seek improvements. Crude measures such as the output of coal per man can give British Coal some indication of the performance and productivity of the different mines and coal faces. Stores can measure the sales output or turnover of items per metre on shelf space. Faster turnover may mean a more efficient and profitable use of the store's shelf space. The National Health Service uses performance indicators such as the average length of stay of patients in a hospital for a given ailment. It also compares the number of staff employed per patient between different hospitals. These indicators do not automatically suggest that one hospital is operating inefficiently but may signal the need for further management investigation. If the investigation produces acceptable answers then no action need be taken. For example teaching hospitals may have more staff per patient, since the training needs of their medical students must also be met.

BUDGETS AND BUDGETARY CONTROL

The main system employed by organisations to evaluate the use of their resources is the use budgets and budgetary control. Each budget constitutes the planned use of resources for the coming year or some other period. Every type of resource could appear in the budget: manpower, materials, machines etc. Each item is expressed in monetary terms to enable comparisons. Therefore if one department requires new machinery while another asks for new personnel, the overall effect of each alternative on the organisation's total budget can be compared in terms of how much each will cost. Each department is usually given an individual annual budget and together these individual budgets form the budget for the enterprise as a whole. The organisation may seek to apply some overall measure of financial constraint and make each department justify any increase in its resources. Clearly in times of severe financial constraints with cutbacks in spending, departments may find themselves competing for the reduced sum of money available to the organisation.

Such budgets are plans for the future. Middle and lower management are responsible for keeping to their budgets once they have been agreed. It is the responsibility of top management to ensure that each department's budget is reasonable and the resources which have been allocated will be used in a way which will achieve the objectives of the organisation.

Budgets are not only plans, they are also 'tools' to allow the measurement of performance of a department or section. If a department budgeted to spend £120,000 on labour costs in a year, then this could be considered to be £10,000 per month. If in one month this varied and became for example £15,000, this variance of 50% overspend would justify management investigation. If there was good reason for the variation then no action need be taken. However it may mean that the department may have to trim its labour costs in later months or that extra finance would have to be found by cutting back elsewhere and the added extra labour cost accounted for in the overall plans. Budgets and budgetary control systems thus provide a means of planning for those resources which will be needed in the future and form the basis of management control over the use of resources. The importance of budgets and budgetary control is considered in detail in chapter 16.

PERSONNEL RESOURCE COSTS

One problem which faces the management of any organisation is the need to value the work performed by its workforce. What is meant by the familiar expression "a fair day's work for a fair day's pay"? This problem is often of crucial importance for usually the most expensive and important resource of any organisation is its personnel. The organisation needs systems for assessing the value of the work done by an individual and so allow it to provide suitable rewards to encourage their continued employment. There are essentially two systems generally used.

1.   Job evaluation in which the job or position is assessed.

2.   Merit rating where the value or merit of an individual is assessed and rewarded.

JOB EVALUATION

An organisation should determine and evaluate the worth of any job within it and try to allocate pay in relation to its value. Many methods have been attempted but all have their critics. The two main methods are:

       (i)   ranking; and

      (ii)   points rating.

(i)   The Ranking Method

This determines which job in the organisation is most important and then ranks all other jobs in order of importance below it. Such a method is not easy to complete in any objective way. For example how would you compare an office supervisor with a production supervisor?

(ii) Points Rating

The other more popular method is the 'points rating' method. Here points are allocated according to how the job equates to several important factors, for example responsibility for people, responsibility for finance, skill and education required. The points for each category are then totalled and the job is graded according to the number of points. By such means jobs in an employer's offices or in the factory can be awarded points in the same way and so can be graded and rewarded comparably.

Pay Bands

Having carried out job evaluation it becomes possible to assess appropriate pay levels. Pay bands are established. Jobs with similiar points, for example 100 - 150 points, may fall within the same 'pay band' and attract the same salary. Any change in the 'Job Specification', that is the detailed description of the job or position the employee holds, may move the job into a different pay band.

MERIT RATING

This approach can be more controversial than job evaluation and is not always readily accepted by trade unions. Here an individual worker is assessed and his performance is then graded. It does however, have major difficulties in implementation. For example two people doing a similar task on the same pay scale may adopt different approaches to the job. The performance of one may be considered by the manager to be only just satisfactory while the other may be judged to be outstanding. Unless there is a quantitive measure of output such as the number of units produced in a day, such a comparison may be based on subjective judgement by the manager. Furthermore to reward the person judged to be outstanding, an increase in wages called a 'merit award' may be given.

The problem arises in finding an objective method of determining how good people are at their jobs. The pay award ought not to be made on the mere whim of an individual. Some organisations lay down a set of criteria against which people are rated every year. Examples of the criteria used include attitude to work, how well objectives are met and even time keeping. Such criteria are identified in advance and then an individual manager decides how well a member of staff measures up to them. For example the worker may be graded as being less than satisfactory, satisfactory, good, or outstanding. Often the manager discusses the rating with the individual worker before it is submitted to senior management to try to encourage improvement in the future. High ratings naturally attract higher pay awards. This measure of the 'worth' of an individual could be the basis for the establishment of a plan for the improvement of the individual concerned. This may include training where it is needed.

Job evaluation and perhaps merit rating could be said to be an attempt to judge what is a 'fair day's pay'.

Merit Rating

WORK STUDY (METHOD STUDY AND WORK MEASUREMENT)

Basically 'work study' is an attempt to objectively find the best method of working and to measure the amount of work that is required to complete a particular task. There are two main approaches to work study:

    (i)   Method Study

    (ii) Work Measurement

(i) Method Study

Method study uses a variety of techniques to find the best method of doing a job. The work to be done is studied. Trials are carried out and the method which achieves the desired results in the shortest time is usually chosen. Wasted effort can thus be eliminated. For example, nurses in a ward may walk backwards and forwards between a fixed drug cabinet and the patients to administer medicines. This is tiring and unproductive movement. A lockable drugs cabinet on wheels could be unchained when needed and pushed between patients. One problem of method study techniques is the possibility of oversimplifying any job so that it becomes monotonous and boring to the workers who may then lack motivation in their work.

(ii) Work Measurement

Work study practitioners are trained to study a job of work and determine how long it should take a trained worker to complete a task. The various components or elements of a job are determined. A simple example could be picking up a cardboard box, packing a number of components, adding packing material, sealing the box and putting it onto a conveyor. For each box packed, a stopwatch can be used to determine the time taken. However workers could be slow or quick in their movements. The problem for the person timing the task is to decide whether the work is being carried out quickly or slowly. This is called rating, and is a skill requiring practice to agree the time taken for each movement to a British standard. Taking into account the rating, by determining the time taken and the rest allowances, a standard time for any job could be fixed and this is measured in 'standard hours' or 'standard minutes'.

A worker could be given a variety of jobs where the standard times were known for each. These could be added together and, under bonus conditions, the manager may expect 8 standard hours work to be achieved in an 8 hour day. This would usually mean a bonus payment for the worker involved. The actual amount of bonus would vary depending on how closely the set target was achieved. If more measured work, for example 9 standard hours, is completed in a day then a greater bonus would be paid. The bonus is usually calculated over a working week. It is not always necessary to pay bonuses which are separate from the normal weeks pay as the workforce may agree to meet some target of measured work for an agreed level of pay.

Work study provides a method for estimating in advance how long a job will take and measuring the productivity of work completed. It can thus provide a measure of efficiency.

Work study could been seen as an attempt to determine what is a 'fair day's work'.

VALUE AND THE CUSTOMER

In the above sections we have concentrated on examining how management may assess the efficiency and effectiveness of the work process. Finally we return to the general model which was established at the beginning of the chapter. If you turn back to the model you will see that the final element is the product or service which is produced. The production process may be as efficient as is humanly possible but if the final product does not meet the needs of the customer then all the effort involved in producing it is wasted. In the final analysis it is the customer's measure of performance which is most important. All the individual tests and measures which have taken place may be of little importance to a customer. The customer may be more interested in the overall quality, value or reliability of the final product. This is true for both manufactured goods and for services. It is unlikely that a purchaser will enthuse about the beauty of a car's interior design if the engine keeps on breaking down. The holiday maker will not sing the praises of the travel company, even if the transport and accommodation were good, if all his baggage was lost on the journey. Consider how you would feel about the quality of patient care if you arrived at a hospital with an appointment at 11 a.m. and you were not attended to until 3 p.m. and your X-ray pictures had been mislaid. The level of quality throughout the whole product or service must be of the same high standard if the customer is to be satisfied. It is the value of the total package which is all important.

The public is also likely to assess how well an organisation has used its resources, by how well the goods or services meet customer needs. If the producer and customer have different ideas as to what is valuable then the product or service is less likely to be well received. Car manufacturers producing expensive and sophisticated suspension systems will not succeed commercially if the customer preferred instead that the extra cost had been spent on a radio, sunroof and cloth upholstery. What the customer sees or perceives as value for money is important to the customer. Certain British motor cycle manufacturers persisted in producing large 'hairy' machines for a dwindling number of large 'hairy' motor cycle enthusiasts. Those seeking cheap, easy to use transport, looked elsewhere, to Japanese manufacturers, for what they considered to be good value to them.

A certain paint manufacturer considered that the emulsion paint it sold was better than the competition. The basis for their claim was on the results of a 'scrubbability' test. Their paint resisted severe scrubbing with water much better than others. But how attractive was this claim to the potential customer, in fact how often does a householder scrub walls or ceilings? In fact the manufacturer's claim for the product was largely irrelevant to the needs of the customer and as you can imagine the paint manufacturer did not end up being successful.

Organisations must continue to improve their technical and economic effectiveness and efficiency in the use of their resources. Competition does not stand still and consumer values can change. The organisation must determine its own internal measures to meet its own values and standards. However, the organisation will only survive if its customers demand the goods and services which it produces. Thus how successful an organisation is in the use of its resources is determined ultimately by the customer, and it is through the customer that the ultimate survival of the organisation will be determined.

ASSIGNMENT — THE DRIVERS BONUS

John Carr is the owner and Managing Director of a small but successful laundry in Leeds. The company employs over 300 people in its two plants near the city centre. He has recently appointed a new Production Manager, Tom Lawson, with the main priority of improving productivity and increasing the company's competitiveness. As the first part of his programme to improve productivity Tom used the services of a firm of management consultants to design a productivity bonus scheme for the transport section of the company. This bonus scheme was the first of its kind to be introduced into the company and if it proved successful then a larger scheme encompassing all the laundry workers was envisaged for introduction at a later date.

The transport section has had the same ten drivers for over eight years. They have always worked as a team and any absenteeism has been covered by the others agreeing to do overtime without any trouble. The drivers had previously been paid on a day rate basis. Their basic rate paid a weekly wage of £110 but with overtime and the 'Christmas bonus' this averaged out at about £160 per week over the year. Once the productivity bonus scheme had been introduced Tom Lawson announced his pleasure at its success. The company had taken on several new contracts with commercial organisations and the drivers were handling 78% more work. Their wage (including bonus) now averaged £180 per week and no overtime was necessary.

However, in spite of the newly rearranged work routes and the work study based times, the drivers felt that some of the routes were harder to complete than others in the times allocated. At first the men switched routes between each other to equalise earnings but this created arguments about the relative inequalities. Later they 'modified' time sheets so that time saved on 'easy' journeys was balanced out with the extra time needed to complete some of the 'harder' journeys. This gave a constant bonus payment each week. Mr Lawson turned a blind eye to this 'creative' time-sheet completion as he knew that the journeys were still being done. Usually the drivers rushed to return to their Depot, and chatted to the other drivers, drank tea and completed their time-sheets.

After three months of the scheme, John Carr spoke to Tom Lawson and agreed that the bonus scheme seemed to be more productive but there had been complaints. Customers had said that the drivers were not interested in listening to suggestions or complaints. Furthermore the vans were dirty, even though the bonus scheme allowed for cleaning time. The drivers approached John Carr suggesting that the time-sheets were unnecessary. They preferred to return to a day rate of £110 plus a fixed bonus of £70. This would save completing time-sheets, allow time for cleaning, listening to customers and still keep to present schedules. Mr Carr felt sympathetic with the drivers. Mr Lawson had reservations but promised to investigate the matter, discuss it with his staff, and reply by next Monday.

TASK

1. You are employed as Tom Lawson's assistant in the production department of the company. He has asked you to prepare a report on the new bonus scheme in which you consider the following issues:

   (a) the rationale for the new bonus scheme;

   (b) the problems identified in running the scheme;

   (c) alternative suggestions for changes to the scheme and the relative merits and demerits of such alternatives;

   (d) recommendations for changing the scheme.

DEVELOPMENTAL TASK

3. Discuss in groups the pros and cons of bonus schemes generally from the viewpoint of management and workforce.

ASSIGNMENT — THE TYNE WEAR CASTING COMPANY

The Tyne Wear Casting Co. Ltd. is a long established organisation based in South Shields employing a workforce of 550. It produces a variety of castings, mainly for other organisations to use with their products. Its largest sales are to car and lorry manufacturers, who buy engine and brake castings from the company for assembly in their own plants. These components are made on sophisticated automated machinery. This allows the company to meet the huge quantities needed by their customers. Great care is taken to ensure that each casting is nearly identical to others of the same type and specification. Each mass-produced casting, individually makes only a small profit but, because of the large numbers sold, the business remains profitable. In addition to its general castings work the company still retains a Sand-casting Foundry which deals with small quantities of 'specials' which are 'tailor-made'. This is the type of work for which the company was originally founded and it is still an important aspect of the company's work. Each of these special castings is sold at a relatively high price and profit. The Foundry is fairly self-contained, with its own management, salesmen and workforce. In some ways the production of good sand-casting is almost an art rather than a science and skilled and experienced staff are essential. Most of the people working there have long service with the company. They are proud of their skills and tend to look with disdain on the mass-produced items produced by the rest of the company. There is in fact little communication with other parts of the organisation. Some of the castings produced in the factory are designed to hold axle bearings. Thus, after casting, the side made to hold the bearings is machined to very exacting measurements. This means that the 'inside' of the casting is polished and gleaming, while the 'outside' is of a very rough looking appearance. Paul Carter, the Works Manager, had a series of castings shot blasted a number of times each time with a different grade of shot. Each improved the appearance of the cating in a different way. However, this operation was expensive, especially using one particular grade of shot-blasting. Once completed one set of the shot blasted castings shot blasted a number of times, each time with a different grade of shot. Each improved the appearance of the casting in a different way. However, this operation was expensive, by tiny hammers and this was the finish favoured by Paul Carter and many others. On Monday afternoon it was the not the favourite finish of the Foreman, David Bell. The castings had been made for an important new customer, but the shot-blasting was taking much longer than it should. The shot was not identical to that originally used and the Quality Control Manager would not agree that the finish achieved matched that of the original they kept and he believed that keeping to laid-down standards was most important. The workforce were grumbling that all this delay would spoil their bonus as it was interrupting the smooth flow of production. The Sales Office demanded action as they had promised the customer delivery on Monday and they wanted to be seen as reliable.

Mr Carter refused to send out any material which he believed did not match the high standard for which the firm was famous.

John Bell was the cousin of the foreman, as well as the salesman dealing with this order. He 'unofficially' called on David and took one of the disputed castings to the customer. The customer was puzzled by all the fuss and delay. He said that the castings were used on coal rail-wagons and their long-life and trouble-free performance were what he wanted and the appearance was unimportant. The castings were sent to the customer as soon as John Bell returned to the Foundry. If they had been delayed one day longer the business would have been lost.

TASK

1. You are employed as a management trainee by the Tyne-Wear Casting Co. Ltd. You have been told to produce a project on the above situation to be presented for discussion at a future management meeting. In the project you should:

   (a) identify and describe the values held to be important by the various individuals in the situation;

   (b) analyse the various problems which arose in the situation;

   (c) suggest ways in which such problems could be prevented from recurring.

DEVELOPMENTAL TASK

2. Undertake a role play exercise where the management meeting is simulated.

Read chapter 7

— Page — 139 Customer or Client needs
       148 Value and the customer
       137- An Ideal model of an organisation

3rd March

Chapter 8

PEOPLE IN THE ORGANISATION

THE IMPORTANCE OF PEOPLE IN THE ORGANISATION

Essentially an organisation is a structured system which uses its resources to provide goods or services to customers or clients. The managers of an organisation may often find themselves heavily involved with such matters as financial control, methods of work, design and specification, material purchasing and control, operational programmes and all the administrative and managerial tasks that seem so necessary to the running of a modern organisation. However the most important resource an organisation has is the people that it employs, and therefore adequate management time must be allotted to meet their needs.

It is possible to examine the importance of an organisation's personnel from several differing viewpoints. These are:

1. The Financial Approach

2. The Altruistic Approach

3. The Potential Approach

4. The Productivity Approach

5. The Development Approach

1. THE FINANCIAL APPROACH

There appears to be a continuous debate in the media concerning the need for all organisations to implement financial cutbacks, limit budgets, lower costs and set competitive prices. All point to the need for careful control of the organisation's spending. If that is the case, then priority must therefore be given to the resources which normally make up the largest share of an organisation's costs. Most organisations, and especially those in the service sector, are 'people intensive' and 65-75% of their total budget may be taken up by staff costs in the form of wages, pensions, employee facilities, etc. This is by far the largest element in their costs and therefore demands priority attention. Take the case of the National Health Service with a budget in excess of £15 billion per annum. More than £10 billion of this is spent on personnel costs, which means that it must seek value for money from each employee.

2. THE ALTRUISTIC APPROACH

A very high proportion of an employed person's time awake is spent at work. Therefore there is an argument that it is only morally right that work should be interesting and satisfying. The employer should be altruistic in his attitude to his employees. However the question is what should a job provide? Everyone has their own ideas but most would include a reasonable wage or salary, interesting and challenging tasks, meeting and working with other people, some chance to display initiate and demonstrate worth, and an opportunity to 'get on'.

Some people's jobs do contain these elements and their work becomes a central life interest. Work often overlaps into their leisure time and some activities can blur the distinction between work and leisure. There are many examples of this such as friends discussing anecdotes from work and social activities connected with the place of work.

However the opposite is also true for many other jobs. Some jobs are designed for 'efficient working' with easily learned, repetitive tasks being carried out as a small part of the productive process. People work in a strictly ordered manner and so have little opportunity to display initiative. Such jobs treat people like machines. It would be gratifying to suggest that this type of working has been replaced by employers who were keen to improve good human relations. Unfortunately this has not happened despite the fact that machine-like jobs are best carried out by machines. There have never been greater opportunities to automate repetitive productive processes by introducing new methods and machines or replacing human movements entirely by machines for tasks such as spot welding or simple assembly.

It is important to design jobs in which people can use new technology such as word processors and computer aided design to remove some of the repetitiveness of certain processes and allow people to carry out those tasks which need the flexible approach of a human being.

3.   THE POTENTIAL APPROACH

Engineers, by improving design, have managed to extract more power from engines of a similar basic design. For example, a 2-litre car engine in the early part of this century could produce only 40 brake horse power (b.h.p.) while today a 2-litre family saloon can produce around 115 b.h.p. and a 2-litre racing car engine over 400 b.h.p. In other words the engine had the potential to produce more power and skillful engineering managed to bring out this greater capability. The same may be said about the way in which people are managed. We may ask whether the 'potential' of an organisation's workforce has been fully tapped. An organisation with 1000 employees has 1000 brains at its disposal. The organisation should use the potential of its workforce to develop new ideas about work methods, the products the organisation manufactures or the service it provides.

Many organisations have tried to capitalise on this potential by allowing employees a greater opportunity to participate in the decision making process when it affects their work. Varying methods are used, ranging from the organisation encouraging suggestion schemes in which individuals can propose improvements or amendments to their work, to discussion meetings which aim at group problem-solving. Such approaches enable a greater breadth of experience and skill to be brought to bear upon an organisation's problems. This may constructively change the way in which management and the workforce co-operate and may improve human relations if the benefits of such improvements are felt by the employees. This in turn could lead to a more co-operative attitude between management and unions and so benefit industrial relations.

4.   THE PRODUCTIVITY APPROACH

If the cost of manpower his high, it needs to be paid for by high output. At the turn of the century F.W. Taylor wrote a book called 'Scientific Management' which proved to be extremely influential. He and his associates suggested that only high productivity could solve the problem of providing high wages while maintaining low average labour costs per article produced. For omer would benefit. If this resulted in higher sales for the product then more profit would be generated for the organisation and this in turn would lead to higher dividends for the shareholders.

The problem is essentially the need to motivate the workforce so that higher levels of output can be achieved by the same number of workers. F.W. Taylor believed that money was the major incentive to increase production and his 'scientific management' approach therefore attempted to find the best method of working and reward the workforce if they could achieve this. The workforce were expected to follow rigidly the prescribed method of working and, if the specified levels of output were achieved, then bonus payments were paid as an incentive. This method of payment allows the worker greater control over his work and wages. One major problem with this approach is that specified levels of output may be set unfairly high. This can be the cause of poor industrial relations leading in some cases to industrial action in the form of strikes and go-slows. Management are never sure what a new job will cost until disputes over bonus levels are settled. Modern work study methods seek a fairer approach to setting targets of work. However as we have already mentioned, if the work which employees are required to perform is simple and repetitive this will not provide a great deal of job satisfaction and so financial incentives may not in themselves be sufficient to motivate the workforce.

There are many motivational theorists who believe that peoples' needs and wants from work are much wider than merely monetary rewards. F. Herzberg believed that the conditions under which people work must be sufficiently attractive to prevent worker dissatisfaction. Such conditions include the organisation's policies, procedures and rules, pay and pay increases, the type of supervision and the working environment enjoyed by the worker. However he believed that these alone would not necessarily lead to a high degree of motivation. Consequently Herzberg suggested that each individual's job must be designed to incorporate those factors which will give positive job satisfaction. These factors include the following:

    (i)   the need to structure the job so that workers are allowed to make decisions for themselves;

    (ii)   employees should be able to see their own achievements and not simply regard their work as merely an insignificant part of the whole productive process;

    (iii)   they should receive recognition for their work achievements;

    (iv)   they should have clear individual responsibilities;

    (v)   when jobs are initially designed or altered some measure of 'job enrichment' should be included. (Job enrichment is considered later in the chapter).

5.   THE DEVELOPMENT APPROACH

All organisations need to keep up-to-date account of the value of the business enterprise. As we see in chapter 14 this takes the form of their annual balance sheet where the value of the organisation's assets and liabilities are expressed in financial terms. The organisation would wish to see improvements in its balance sheet position from year to year. However one asset which is not included in the balance sheet is the organisation's workforce and yet as we have already noted this is often the organisation's most valuable resource. Therefore an efficient manager will wish to evaluate the worth of his workforce on a regular basis by undertaking an audit of the skills and experience of the organisation's employees. He may then attempt to ensure that the 'value' of the organisation's employees increases each year by enhancing their skills and abilities through training and staff development.

PERSONNEL MANAGEMENT

We have already established that the manner in which employees are treated is of the utmost importance to the successful management of any organisation.

It is clear therefore that those involved in the management of staff must be assisted in the way in which they carry out this function. To help achieve this objective many organisations now have separate personnel departments. The responsibility of these departments is to help and give assistance to managers in the organisation on all aspects of personnel work. This may include advice and guidance on such matters as safety, health and welfare, recruitment, termination of employment, job specification and matters related to industrial relations and collective bargaining. The role of the personnel department is considered in more detail in chapter 1.

MANPOWER PLANNING

As we have already noted in chapter 7 it is a function of the organisation's senior management to decide overall policy and objectives. An important aspect of this is the establishment of a personnel policy and personnel objectives for the organisation as a whole. This is often referred to as the manpower plan. A long term strategy is needed for the organisation and the manpower plan is an integral part of this overall corporate strategy.

Manpower planning may be defined as the means by which an organisation may plan its future employee requirements. This will involve determining the number and quality of employees that will be required in the future. Obviously the organisation's requirement for manpower will be set by the anticipated future demand for its product or service and as such is part of the long term development of the organisation. Clearly it is important to ascertain whether or not this future demand is capable of being met by the present workforce and, if it cannot, then there is the need to establish plans to ensure that the present staff can be trained or developed or that new employees can be recruited to fill the gap.

THE AIMS OF MANPOWER PLANNING

In order to survive, every organisation must meet its own needs and demands for employees. This may be expressed under the following headings:

(i)   Recruitment
The organisation must ensure that the right kind of employee is attracted. Thus its recruitment policy is determined by its specific manning needs.

(ii)   Experience
Well trained and experienced employees must be encouraged to stay with the organisation. This is achieved by ensuring that there is the appropriate working environment, career structure and adequate rewards.

(iii)   Task performance
Each employee must carry out his or her duties and responsibilities in an efficient and effective way and the employer must be able to monitor this and rectify any deficiencies in its employee's performance.

(iv)   Motivation
Employees must be motivated so that they will do more than just carry out instructions. For the organisation to grow and survive it must have employees who are willing to extend themselves in their work tasks and use the full range of their skills to seem improvements.

THE USE OF MANPOWER PLANNING IN GUIDING MANAGEMENT DECISION MAKING

Manpower plans can guide management decision making in a number of respects. These include: recruitment; staff and management development; training, involving an assessment of the number and categories of staff who require training; anticipating the need for redundancies; productivity bargaining; improving industrial relations; estimating labour costs; health, safety and welfare; accommodation requirements; and disciplinary procedures.

THE NEED TO UPDATE THE ORGANISATION'S MANPOWER PLAN

The manpower plan will need updating at various intervals as a result of changes in:

(i) new technology

To maintain a competitive position the organisation must adapt to changes in new technology. This may mean updating the skills of existing employees or hiring new employees with new skills. New technology may require changes in the methods of work as well as the equipment which is used. This may also involve a corresponding change in the attitude of the workforce to new technology.

(ii) government intervention

The government may introduce new legislation which will require a modification of an organisation's manpower plans. A contemporary example is the change in female compulsory retirement age contained in the Sex Discrimination Act 1986.

(iii) new organisational goals

Changes in market conditions may often force an organisation to rethink its business strategy. This could mean a major revision of its manpower requirements. For example the decline in the need for more merchant shipping has led to shipyard closures.

(iv) the changing needs of society

The public's ideas, tastes and needs all tend to change. Such change may cause an organisation to grow or decline. For example tobacco firms have been forced to diversify into the manufacture of other products as smoking has become less socially acceptable. This has obviously meant a reduction in the number of workers in the tobacco industry.

THE TIME SCALE OF MANPOWER PLANNING

Planning by its very nature involves the anticipation of future events. The further we project into the future the less certain is our plan. Therefore we can divide manpower planning into different time scales.

Short term manpower planning

Planning up to 1-2 years ahead provides for the personnel needs of the organisation in its present form. Examples are the replacement of people who retire or training programmes for new starters.

There should be adequate data available to use in forecasting such short term changes. The organisation should have job descriptions of all existing staff and personnel records will indicate the age of individuals to anticipate retirement. Often a computer system is used to hold a data base for personnel information. This enables information, such as the identification of workers within a given age range, to be obtained very quickly.

Long term manpower planning

If an organisation looks further ahead, such as over the next 2-5 years, there will obviously be a greater degree of uncertainty. However, the training of certain employees such as accountants or engineers may require a considerable amount of such forward planning. Also if the organisation is involved in long term projects it will have to anticipate its manpower needs in advance and allow sufficient time to recruit or train appropriate staff.

Long term manpower planning attempts to provide for the personnel needs of the organisation as it may develop in the future. This has to take into account any new objectives the organisation may wish to pursue. To achieve this the needs of both direct and indirect workers may be taken into account. If for instance, a hospital decided to provide a new service such as bone marrow transplants, not only would doctors and nurses (regarded as direct staff) be required but also vital ancilliary staff (regarded as indirect staff) such as laboratory scientific officers, administrators, porters, and others.

New technology which requires new skills is always difficult to predict with any degree of accuracy. Predictions of the current developments in new technology have been that workers in the future may have to change their skills at least three times in their working career.

INDUSTRIAL RELATIONS

By industrial relations we mean the relationships which exist between the organisation and its workforce. Every organisation should attempt to develop good industrial relations as the effects of industrial action can be severely damaging. As organisations increase in size individual bargaining between a manager and an individual worker becomes no longer practical. In such circumstances the trade unions will undertake this role on behalf of individual workers. This is referred to as 'collective bargaining'. With the development of 'white collar' or staff unions managers and workers will sometimes find themselves in the same union and clearly this may tend to complicate the roles each play. A climate where good communications and morale are present is usually conducive to good industrial relations.

The effects of poor industrial relations may damage industrial output and confidence in British industry and so government agencies have been established to assist in the practice of industrial relations. The most important of these is ACAS (the Advisory, Conciliation and Arbitration Service). Codes of Practices designed by ACAS are intended to assist the promotion of good industrial relations. The importance of industrial relations is examined in some detail in chapter industrial relations. The importance of industrial relations legislation is examined in some detail in chapter 19.

PEOPLE AND MOTIVATION

One of the major objectives of an organisation's recruitment policy should be to attract the type of personnel which it believes has good potential for development. It is then necessary to ensure that new staff are sufficiently well treated to encourage them to stay with the organisation. For example most employees would expect fair salaries and decent conditions of work. Organisations must ensure that staff are trained to carry out their duties and responsibilities in a reliable way. However it may be insufficient for employees to merely carry out their assigned tasks. To ensure that an organisation will grow, will seek new methods to improve effectiveness and efficiency, and will be able to cope with crisis and challenges in a manner which creates improvements needs active and creative and well motivated employees. To survive the challenge of competition, an organisation needs continual innovation and improvement. Primarily ideas for change must come from the organisation's staff. Thus the important aim of achieving a well motivated workforce likely to inspire change should be incorporated into every personnel policy.

The process of achieving a well motivated staff is not a simple one. People are complex and very much individuals. Unlike machines, they do not always 'think' or act in the same way. Thus the aim of this section is to consider the ways in which employees can be motivated and examine the factors, methods or processes which are of importance in achieving this.

A MOTIVATION MODEL

Organisations hope to achieve their goals and satisfy the needs of their employees at the same time. Thus the management seek to ensure that organisational goals are achieved by suitably rewarding sound work performed by their staff, who are then recognised as achievers. The following figure is a model which demonstrates this approach.

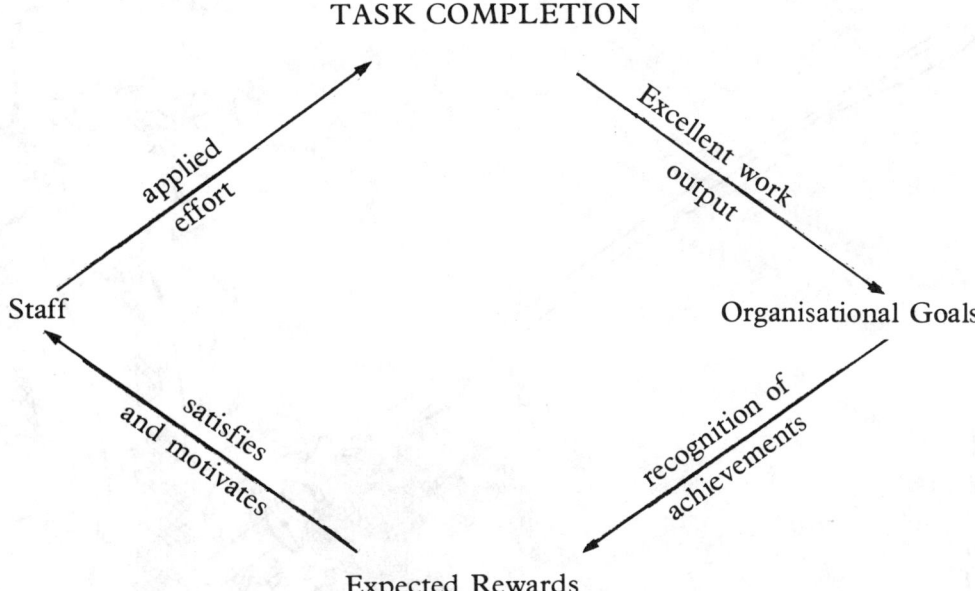

TASK COMPLETION

Staff

Organisational Goals

Expected Rewards

This is of course an ideal model which may never be fully achieved in the real world. However it could be used to analyse and test the 'needs and rewards system' of an organisation to judge how effectively it operates.

The model could also be used by management to formulate questions which must be answered in a real organisational situation. The answers could form the basis for decisions leading to corrective action. Examples of the questions that management might address are:-

1. Do they know all the needs of staff and the rewards the staff expect?

2. Have they ensured that the staff are aware of the tasks they have been set and the type of effort to apply in order to achieve task completion?

3. Have they ensured that staff have the knowledge, skill and experience that is needed?

4. Are they satisfied that staff have a full understanding of what goals must be achieved?

5. Have they ensured that staff receive recognition for their efforts when these goals are achieved?

6. Have they identified whether the rewards that staff receive are those which are expected by them?

7. Are they satisfied that the rewards the staff receive are sufficient to motivate them to continue to give a sustained effort?

REWARDS

From the model, it is obvious that the needs of staff and the rewards that the organisation gives, are at the heart of the motivation process. The rewards that different organisations offer are many and varied. Some organisations have attempted to apply what is commonly known as the 'carrot and stick' approach! Put simply, a donkey is likely to move forward if tempted with a carrot in front of its nose. The alternative is to apply a stick to its other end, which may give a similar forward motion. Such treatment, suitably modified can be used with people. Thus a boss may offer the 'carrot' by encouraging his production workers to reach higher output targets by offering a weekly bonus depending upon the targets being reached. He may also use the 'stick' by dropping veiled threats to his production supervisors that, "if the quality drops, changes will have to be made around here"!

the 'carrot and the stick' approach . . .

F.W. Taylor, suggested that all that a workforce wanted was a chance to earn more money, and nothing else was important. He devised financial incentives schemes which offered large bonuses to workers for increased output. The problem was to find a scheme which was 'fair' to both management and workers. Today many schemes are based upon measured work systems devised by work study practitioners. No one suggests that money is not important, but may question whether it is the only important reward that people seek from work.

People differ in the priority they give to the rewards they expect or receive from their work. Nevertheless there is evidence to suggest that the following factors appear on most people' list of priorities.

The factors are money, performing useful and interesting work, using a full range of abilities and skills, avoiding being bored, meeting people, working with people, obtaining a sense of achievement, having achievement recognised, promotion, security, fringe benefits and paid holidays.

THE ROLE OF MONEY AS A MOTIVATOR

It is not always clear what value money has as a motivator for any particular individual at work. For example the Health Service and other organisations have voluntary workers who do not receive money for their services but still give of their best.

Even pools winners have been known to return to work because they miss the social environment or the work activity. On the other hand there are those who take dangerous jobs or tasks, which many would avoid, mainly because of the high pay such jobs carry. Thus money may have minimal effect or a considerable one depending on the individual. In fact for the majority of employees, money is one of several important factors in motivation.

FINANCIAL INCENTIVES AS MOTIVATORS

Financial incentive schemes which pay a money bonus for extra output have been used for many years. The most successful are based on a system that simply pays more money for more work. In other words, the striking of a bargain that balances pay with effort. Of course the 'rate' that links money to effort should be objectively assessed, and recognised and accepted by both management and workforce. Previously it was the practice to adopt what were referred to as 'piecework' methods. These were based on rates of pay which were arbitrarily determined. The methods used were often the source of bitter argument. It was even suggested that some organisations actually produced less due to the time wasted in industrial action caused by piece rate disputes. Nowadays work study measurements, undertaken by trained practitioners are used to fix the rate of pay for a specific task. These have been found to be more accurate and acceptable to the workforce.

Many organisations have found that up to 30% extra output from the same workforce can be achieved after incentive schemes have been applied. A bonus which is paid weekly allows the workers to see quickly the benefit of their greter endeavours.

When the bonus payment does not immediately appear in the worker's pay packet after the additional work has been performed, the extra income is not as closely associated with the extra work done. Because of this the incentive value of the bonus scheme diminishes.

A similar problem exists when the bonus is linked to a more general output of the organisation rather than directly to the individual's own efforts. For example clerical workers in British Coal may receive a bonus based upon the fluctuating output of faceworkers. The reason behind this is that the clerical work is a necessary service to achieve the output of coal. It is however only indirectly linked to the physical productive process.

To summarise the two major factors that management should be aware of in introducing bonus schemes are:

      (i)   the need to pay bonuses as quickly as possible after they have been earned;

      (ii)   the problem of attempting to tie the bonuses of those who are not involved in physical production to the output levels of the organisation as a whole.

WORKFORCE CONTROL

It is possible to view the effect of incentive schemes from a different perspective. Incentive schemes allow workers to partially determine their own output and so regulate their own pay. Such decisions were traditionally the province of management but in such circumstances can now be decided to some extent by the individual worker. Allowing some element of discretion in work methods or delegating decision making powers to staff may further increase the level of motivation.

There is a possibility that bonus levels may fall if output cannot be sustained for a reason which is outside the control of the workforce. This is a fear that some workers guard against, by deliberately 'hiding' extra output and so not claiming the full bonus due each week. In this way they can add 'extra' output when it is needed. Consequently bonus levels will often show an unnaturally even level for considerable periods of time.

The workforce may also arrange between themselves an artificial 'ceiling' above which bonus levels are not allowed to rise. They will do this because they fear that unusually high bonus levels may attract unwanted attention from senior management. The workforce may even fear that the management may reduce their basic rate of pay and so they could end up working harder for smaller rewards. If, for any reason the level of bonus drops, some individuals may view this as management's fault and believe that without the bonus the workforce is being exploited. This view may colour their attitude towards management and result in a lack of trust in future pay negotiations. In fact the bonus system may come to highlight the 'them and us' divide.

A further advantage of the changeover to a bonus incentive system of working is that such a change may highlight 'hidden' problems within the organisation. Often the increased level of output of the workforce may reveal inadequacies in other parts of the organisation's productive process. The purchasing, supply and storage of raw materials may have appeared to have been adequate in the past. Previously a hold-up in supplies to the factory floor may have been welcomed by the workforce as an unofficial break from the demands of production. With the introduction of the incentive scheme, any failings in the material supply system will be emphasised by the increased demands of the workforce for extra output. The foreman may discover that both the higher management and the workforce are chasing him to get supplies 'to the right place at the right time'.

Management and management systems are expected to ensure that materials, methods, specifications and services are adequate to enable the production or direct workers on bonus to carry out their tasks with the minimum of interruption.

1.   INCENTIVE SCHEMES FOR DIRECT WORKERS

Production or direct workers are usually tied to schemes which provide an early 'feedback' on their progress by paying the bonus a week after it is earned. There are various types of bonus schemes that are used in organisations, all of which have benefits and disadvantages. The main types of scheme are:

> (i)   piece work;
>
> (ii)   measured day work;
>
> (iii)   high day rate schemes.

(i)   Piece Work

The oldest type of scheme is the piece-work system, so called because a bonus is paid for each 'piece' of work produced. Usually the price paid for each 'piece' of work is settled by 'negotiation' which may often result in bitter arguments between management and workforce. The modern version is referred to as the 'straight proportional scheme'. This is determined by work study methods based on 'standard hours' worked and is judged to be a fairer system. The bonus which is paid is directly proportional to output which has been objectively rated.

(ii)   Measured Day Work

'Measured day work' has replaced earlier bonus schemes in many organisations. It has the advantage of maintaining a steady output and stable bonus, which is of benefit to both management and workforce. The bonus is paid on an agreed output of work which, with certain safeguards, the worker agrees to maintain. Such agreements are usually reached after employees have had some experience of bonus working.

(iii) High Day Rate Schemes

Here the workforce is expected to produce levels of output which are predetermined by management. Often the pace of work is dictated by the speed of machinery or a conveyor with which the worker must keep pace. An attraction of such a scheme to the worker is that it provides a higher than average rate of pay which does not fluctuate. Those who cannot maintain the output levels however are likely to be disciplined or removed.

2. INCENTIVE SCHEMES FOR INDIRECT WORKERS

Workers and management who are not directly involved in the manufacturing process often have their own incentive schemes. These include:

      (i)   a bonus share or share ownership scheme;

      (ii) merit rating.

(i) A Bonus Share or Share Ownership Scheme

A bonus share paid from profits, or a system by which shares in the organisation and subsequent dividends are made available to the workforce has proved popular in some organisations. Such schemes hope to gain a long term commitment to efficiency from employees but have the problem that participants cannot readily see the benefit of their own contributions.

(ii) Merit Rating

Extra money paid for what is regarded as outstanding effort is called 'merit rating'. The payment of such awards is determined by management but the dubious objectivity of such payments may often cause disputes between management and trade unions.

It may be thought that only the poorer sections of the workforce would be interested in such cash rewards but this is not necessarily so. In the National Health Service even top consultants and physicians are paid 'merit awards'. The amounts that each consultant receives is partly based on the judgement of his performance by his peers. Thus the incentive is not only monetary reward but also becomes a symbol of status within the profession. In fact whatever level of remuneration employees receive it is preferable that they believe that the amount of their pay is fair and relates to their worth as an employee. An employee's worth is not easily determined and can often fluctuate with the market forces in the labour market. Thus at any given time an organisation may be keen to attract new employees and if necessary be willing to pay high salaries for the right people.

Thus fairness, the worth of an employee to an organisation and changing market forces can all be important in setting the level of wages or salaries. Of course it can be argued that as individuals have different characteristics, the wage incentives offered to individuals should be specifically tailored in the same way. Unfortunately an agreed scientific basis for this approach is difficult to implement.

MONEY AS A MOTIVATOR

A person's level of remuneration is not always the sole source of job satisfaction: nor is it necessarily the major motivator. Nevertheless dissatisfaction with pay can still result in employees leaving their present employer to seek better pay elsewhere. Furthermore it may also result in staff, who are dissatisfied with pay, taking collective industrial action. Take a job in which there is an annual pay rise in April and this is the normal pattern for pay settlements. Staff will be looking forward to the increase and may even have adjusted their standard of living in advance of the rise. When employees receive the rise on the due date they feel pleased, even elated. The short term result of the rise is likely to be an increase in motivation or an increased level of job satisfaction. However an important question is how long the beneficial effects of the increase will last. This may be no longer than a week or two. Clearly it would be unreasonable to expect a rise every month or so to regularly stimulate motivation. Consider however, the likely outcome if the pay increase was not given when it was expected. In such circumstances a major emotional response will be an increase in dissatisfaction. Thus while the annual increase in pay does not bring a prolonged increase in motivation to work, the rise is important to maintain the existing level of motivation.

LONG TERM EFFECTS OF FINANCIAL INCENTIVE SCHEMES

In our earlier examination of financial incentive schemes, we noted that they may have a short term effect in motivating people to work at a higher rate. However, in the long term, bonus schemes may prove to be less of an incentive to the achievement of greater productivity. Furthermore the administration costs involved in timing the work, running the scheme, collecting the work sheets, calculating the bonus and settling the minor arguments and grievances that are caused by the scheme may appear as disadvantages. Examples of minor problems which could be experienced include the difficulties involved in timing 'one-off' jobs so that the bonus rates can be determined or stoppages in work due to shortages of incoming materials and the consequent dissatisfaction this will cause when it prevents workers earning bonuses. The workforce may feel that such a problem was not their fault and that it would be unfair if they had to suffer financially. In such circumstances a new type of incentive scheme may be introduced such as measured day work or high day rate which will provide a new and more stable form of incentive to replace fluctuating bonus payments.

In the long term it is the attitude of the work force which may prove to be the most important determining factor in the choice of incentive scheme. For instance if a large proportion, say 40%, of a worker's pay is dependant on bonus payments and overtime, then in times of worsening financial conditions the worker may feel that this portion of his pay is insecure and depends on the whim of management. The same conditions may not exist for 'white collar' or monthly paid staff and so production workers regard the situation as being unfair. This could result in production workers adopting a 'them and us' approach and being less co-operative.

INDIVIDUAL BONUS SYSTEMS

Certain types of incentive schemes may even cause problems between the operatives themselves. Some types of bonus scheme are calculated and paid on the output of each individual worker so in effect each 'works for his own bonus'. Piece work schemes, where a bonus is paid for each extra item of production, are typical of individual bonus systems. However, the rates set differ from job to job. Some are regarded by the workers as 'slack' or easy to achieve and others are 'tight' or difficult to achieve. This can often lead to arguments and disagreements between workers over who shall be given the 'best' jobs. The following quote from a worker involved in such a scheme illustrates the point. "It was dog eat dog. If you wanted a crane for your next job you chained it to your bench to stop anyone else using it. Many of the older workers had secret methods, jigs and tools for completing jobs which they jealously guarded in their lockers."

Such bonus schemes can mean that management have to spend much of their time in the administration of the scheme. In fact achieving the bonus can often come to be the worker's number one priority. Employees may lose sight of the organisation's objectives and specific customer needs may be ignored if they prove difficult to fit within the bonus system. Sometimes accurate forecasting of the time to complete a job or an estimation of the cost proves difficult if each new job means a drawn out wrangle over rates of pay.

EXTRINSIC AND INTRINSIC REWARDS

It is possible to differentiate between the types of rewards that different people seek from their work. They can be catergorised as extrinsic (often monetary rewards) and intrinsic (psychological rewards to the individual). Examples of an extrinsic reward could be a bonus incentive payment while an intrinsic reward could be the satisfaction felt from a job well done. Clearly it is not always possible to achieve both extrinsic and intrinsic rewards from every job. Furthermore individuals may vary as to the rewards that they believe are important.

SATISFYING NEEDS

An organisation should aim to reward its workers in ways which most fit their needs. In so doing they should achieve the greatest level of efficiency. Yet management may not clearly understand the needs of an individual worker or even the general needs of all employees. One theorist, A. Maslow, believed that people's needs were in ascending order, with the basic needs at the bottom and increasing in order of complexity.

Ascending Needs

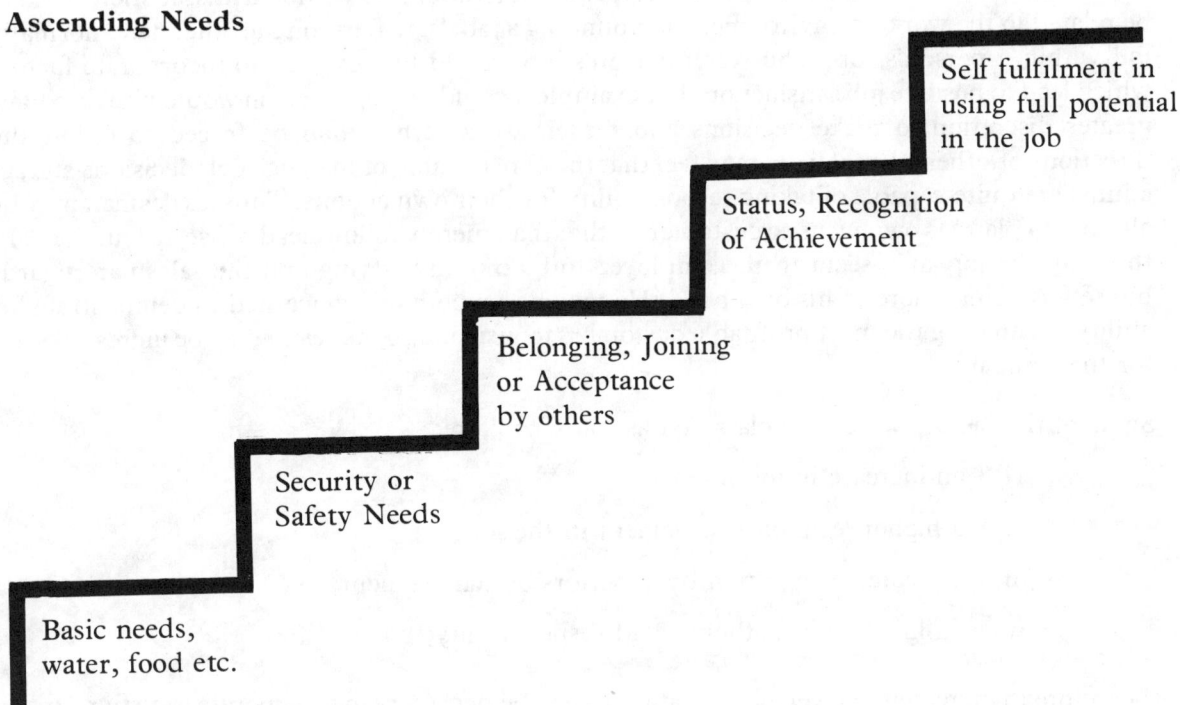

He believed that an individual was motivated by the needs of each level but once that need was fulfilled, motivation would come only from higher levels of need. So for example an individual who is hungry, will be motivated by money to enable him to buy food but once he has sufficient money to satisfy his physical needs, he may require other motivators such, as working with a good team, to stimulate further efforts.

Dissatisfiers and Satisfiers

Other writers such as Herzberg, suggest that there is not simply one set of factors affecting motivation but two distinct sets. These are referred to as:

      (i)   dissatisfiers; and

      (ii) satisfiers.

(i) Dissatisfiers or maintenance factors

These factors can prevent dissatisfaction and maintain the existing level of motivation. However in themselves they do not actually improve motivation to any great extent. An example could be the conditions of the work environment. If working conditions are overcrowded, badly ordered, noisy or poorly lit, then people may grumble and complain. This creates dissatisfaction and distracts from their work. If, however, the conditions are improved by a move to a better planned working environment, then the cause of dissatisfaction is removed. It would be a mistake, however, to believe that the change provided a great degree of motivation to work. It simply removed the dissatisfaction. As we explained earlier, money may be classified in the same way. The annual pay rise may prevent dissatisfaction but will provide little real incentive for increased motivation. Further examples could include an employees relationship with management or colleagues or the fact that, for many people, a constant source of dissatisfaction may be stifling, petty policies, procedures and rules that are used in an attempt to order the pattern of behaviour within an organisation. An unfair distribution of fringe benefits may also result in dissatisfaction. It is worth noting that many of these dissatisfiers exist in the environment surrounding a person's job rather than in the job itself.

(ii) Satisfiers

If the source of dissatisfaction has been removed, then people become more amenable and so management may then be able to seek to improve motivation. As we noted 'dissatisfiers' tend to be related to the working environment surrounding a job, 'satisfiers' on the other hand normally fall within a person's job. Thus each person's job should be designed to incorporate factors which lead to positive job satisfaction. For example it could be that a person would prefer to have greater discretion to make decisions about their work rather than be forced to follow the directions of others. Employees may feel that they are capable of making such decisions and, as adults, are quite capable of taking responsibility for their own actions. Thus a salesman may be allowed to plan his own visits to customers rather than merely follow head office instructions. In this way the job may seem to the employee to be more satisfying and the salesman regards himself as being 'more of his own boss'. He may be much more concerned to demonstrate his ability in choosing the most profitable customers to visit and so the result may be increased sales for the company.

Some of the factors which are classified as 'satisfiers' are:

     (i)   an increase in job interest;

     (ii) a higher level of achievement in the job;

     (iii) a greater recognition by superiors of achievement;

     (iv) an increase in authority and responsibility;

Therefore to increase the level of motivation it may be necessary to incorporate 'satisfiers' into a person's job. To achieve this some organisations will apply a technique known as 'Job Design'.

JOB DESIGN

Good working conditions and pay are important but in themselves they cannot create interest in a boring job. People wish to be treated as 'thinking adults' and not just as 'organic machines' without ideas or emotions. Thus an improvement in the 'design' of jobs could mean that people are employed more effectively and this could lead to higher productivity and better benefits and pay. The job design will have failed if the new 'efficient' methods of production mean the job has less variety, the worker is asked to perform fewer tasks and these require less skill or there is a reduction in the freedom to make decisions.

DECISION MAKING

People in their private lives make decisions and accept responsibilities and therefore we must ask why management does not allow them to do so at work. Mangement's reluctance to allow their workforce to take decisions concerned with their work is often counter productive. It discourages initiative and fails to use the full potential of the organisation's workforce. Of course workers cannot be given a completely free rein as it is management's responsibility to control and co-ordinate an organisation's operations. This will involve them in making policy decisions.

However as long as the decisions which the workforce take do not conflict with overall policy they should be allowed as much freedom as possible.

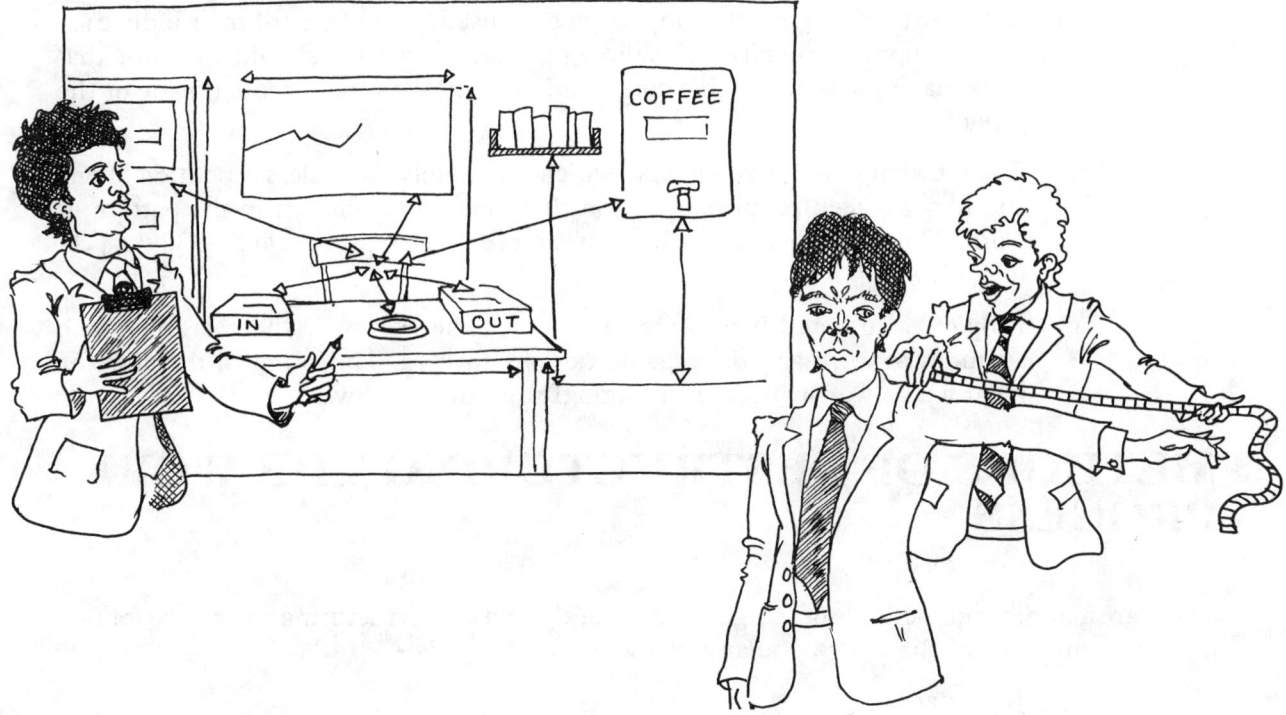

THE CONSEQUENCES OF POOR JOB DESIGN

If jobs are not designed to meet people's needs, as well as the needs of the task and the organisation, then it is possible that:

    (a)   The potential of the workforce is not being fully used and therefore the organisation's most important and expensive resource is being wasted;

    (b)   The individual worker gains little satisfaction from the job. Consequently the person is less likely to take pride in his job and so may be less concerned about the quality of output or the service given.

    (c)   Worker's expectations are not realised and this may lead to frustration and resentment. As individuals grow up they will normally expect to accept more responsibility for their actions and to rely more heavily on their own judgement. They may become disenchanted with work if they are then expected to simply follow instructions and endlessly repeat the same simple operations.

The possibility must therefore exist that such resentment and frustration may lead to poor motivation, non co-operation, absenteeism, poor quality work, industrial unrest and a high turnover of staff.

PRINCIPLES OF JOB DESIGN

A well designed job will have certain characteristics and may follow many of the principles listed below:

    (a)   The job will use as many as possible of the skills and abilities an individual possesses. This will involve both an individual's mental and physical skills.

    (b)   There should be aspects of the job in which the individual has both authority and responsibility allowing him to use discretion and make decisions.

    (c)   People enjoy working with others. Where possible, opportunities should be available for group work.

(d) The job should not be so simple that workers feel that it is below their level of competence. It should be reasonably demanding and present a suitable level of challenge.

(e) People often feel powerless in a large organisations and regard their individual contribution as insignificant. Where possible the worker should recognise that he is making an identifiable contribution to the eventual product made or the service given.

(f) The job should not involve tasks which are merely an endless repetition of one another. To keep people's attention there must be a change in the pattern of work. Therefore there must be provision for variety in the range of tasks performed.

(g) People's values and beliefs are important. These provide the basis on which attitudes to work and the organisation are formed. The job must therefore be regarded as worthwhile and meaningful by the employee.

METHODS OF RESTRUCTURING THE WORK PROCESS

There are a number of methods of reorganising, redesigning or restructuring work. The following represent some of the most popular and successful methods:-

1. Job rotation

2. Job enlargement

3. Group work and group technology

4. Autonomous group working

5. Job enrichment

1. JOB ROTATION

This is an attempt to alleviate the boredom of relatively simple and repetitive jobs. Workers are trained to be able to tackle a number of different jobs and they are moved from task to task to give them a variety of work. The rotation must not occur too often as work speeds have to be built up after each change. The best results may be obtained where the workforce decide themselves when to change jobs.

Critics of this approach suggest that there is a potential difficulty in that a worker will not be on any one job long enough to build up satisfactory skills or working speed. It is also suggested that swapping one inherently boring job for another does not bring a great deal of motivation. Some individuals do not like changing jobs on a regular basis and have a preference for certain types of work.

2. JOB ENLARGEMENT

Often a process or operation may be subdivided into a series of short, cyclical and repetitive tasks. An example is where one individual must check a small part of the information on a form before it is passed to another person to complete another part. It is almost a production line process where each person does only a few seconds work on each item before it is passed to the next worker in the chain.

A further example could involve the assembly of a lawn mower from its component parts. At each stage an individual employee receives their work on a conveyor. Each has a different task to do in a predetermined order. For example one worker could attach the cutting blades and tighten the holding nut in position before the part-assembled mower travels on. An alternative to this arrangement is to supply each employee with all the parts and allow them to complete the whole process. In this way more satisfaction is gained by a worker employing more skills and completing an easily identifiable part of the work output.

Critics suggest that in many cases this so called 'job enlargement' consists not of one short boring task but now just a collection of them! Many organisations have adopted an alternative approach to the problem of repetitive tasks. Instead of treating people like programmed human machines they have replaced them with real machines. The advantages being that real machines run tirelessly under a variety of unpleasant work conditions. This has the added advantage that people are now required to set, modify, maintain and programme the machines and this places a greater demand on their ingenuity, skills and flexibility. For this type of flexibility human beings are especially suited. However for relatively short production runs, where a wide variety of products are made, automated machinery would be too expensive as it may stand idle when it is not needed for that particular operation.

3. GROUP WORKING AND GROUP TECHNOLOGY

Some organisations, such as the Volvo car company in Sweden, have moved from the production line method of manufacturing. Groups of workers complete a whole task, such as building an engine, and the company has experienced an increase in employee morale and motivation by implementing this method. This beneficial result comes from the increased productivity of team work.

In a similar manner, some organisations have changed their production methods to take advantage of group technology. Instead of many different departments each filled with a particular variety of machine, they have grouped together machines that can produce a specified product by an individual group of workers. For example instead of turning, milling, drilling, polishing and plating departments each containing their own specific type of machinery, groups of workers are given the full range of machines they need to manufacture the complete product. The advantage of this approach is that it allows workers to identify with the organisation's product as a completed whole rather than viewing their own part as a separate entity. It can also often speed manufacture because it removes the problem that may have existed where an invididual departments in an integrated production process may have proved to be a bottleneck. in delay.

4. AUTONOMOUS GROUP WORKING

Here an experienced group of workers is given more control over the order, planning and timing of their own operations. Instead of following instructions from a supervisor, they have discretion in decision making and have to agree between themselves on the individual tasks. Take the example of a group of fork lift drivers in a brewery. When management decides that the group is sufficiently experienced they are given customer orders and allowed to decide between themselves how the transport should be loaded. The role of the supervisor is then seen primarily as a communications link and a problem solver for the group. A similar experiment has been used successfully at Volvo for some years with the groups voting for their own informal leader who acts as the link or co-ordinator for the group.

This method of working does mean however that the group have to be willing to accept the extra responsibility and the supervisor has to relinquish considerable authority to the group. It may be more difficult for the management to adjust to their new roles than the workforce!

5. JOB ENRICHMENT

Job enrichment is the name given to the redesigning of jobs to include some of the 'satisfiers' or motivating factors as decribed by Herzberg. It is claimed that job enrichment provides the opportunity for the employee's psychological development. The employee's full potential is realised by allowing him to tackle more complex tasks. The new tasks are designed to 'stretch' people or given them greater challenges in their daily work. They will have an opportunity to utilise previously unused skills and expand their capabilities. Management must recognise that people vary in the degree to which they are attracted to take up these challenges. Certainly they must not be forced to accept their new role otherwise they will resent the new tasks rather than be motivated by them. It is useful to present the changes in terms of opportunities rather than demands and it should be permissable for individuals to decline the new task opportunities and continue to do the jobs they have always done.

Job Enrichment Factors

The aim of job enrichment is to improve productivity and task efficiency while at the same time increasing worker satisfaction. This is done by:

(i)   building into people's jobs greater scope for personal achievement;

(ii)   recognising achievement;

(iii)   providing more responsible and challenging work; and

(iv)   creating opportunities to make decisions in their own sphere of work.

Measuring Successful Job Enrichment

In implementing a job enrichment programme and measuring the validity of its success it is important to distinguish between improvements which are the consequence of the programme and those which are the result of other factors. For example, an experiment was carried out to test methods of reducing high labour turnover in an organisation. Changes were made to company policy and procedures, pay levels, work supervision and working conditions. After several years it was noted that a lower percentage of people left the company each year and it was claimed that the new changes were successful. However unemployment rates had been steadily increasing over the same period and it was becoming increasingly more difficult for employees to change jobs. The question which arose was whether the improvement in labour turnover was due to the changes made inside the organisation or to the external changes in the job market? Perhaps the only way to have answered this question was to have had a 'control' group of workers who had experienced no improvements or internal changes. Their behaviour could then have been compared with the workers taking part in the trials and the effect of the external influences determined.

Trials and experiments in job enrichment have been out by Imperial Chemical Industries (I.C.I.). A number of different job categories were chosen and attempts were made to ensure that any changes that were noted were brought about solely by the job enrichment factors and not by some other external effect.

The Sales Representative Experiment

One of the successful trials carried out by I.C.I. involved some of their salesmen. Initially these individuals, working outside the company premises, had a number of restrictions placed on their work. They were expected to visit their customers according to plans specified for them by their superiors and they had to make written reports on each call. If a customer complained of faulty material the salesmen were not allowed to take any action on their own initiative. They were given price lists for all products and were not permitted to vary the prices offered to the customers. After determining the initial sales levels (which had been falling) and deciding on a 'control' group, a number of changes were made:

(i)   The representatives were allowed to decide when and what to write in reports about customers;

(ii)   Where customers had a complaint regarding product performance, the representatives had authority and could exercise their own judgement to make a small settlement;

(iii) In cases of customers having faulty or unwanted products the salesman had the right to make a decision on whether to take back material or make a settlement;

(iv) Representatives were given the discretion to offer up to 10% discount if they felt this was the only way to make a sale.

The result at the end of the year was that the representatives involved in the trials had achieved a sales increase of over 18%, while those who formed the 'control' group actually experienced a decrease in sales.

DIFFICULTIES IN ADOPTION OF JOB ENRICHMENT

The above example of successful job enrichment is only one example of the many which have been achieved. However, while it may be thought that such a successful technique would have become commonplace, an analysis of 125 industrial firms in the U.S.A. showed that only 5 had attempted to formally introduce job enrichment programmes. Three major problems exist:-

(i) The difficulty in measuring productivity benefits;

(ii) The difficulty in redesigning existing jobs;

(iii) The difficulty that all employees may not react in the same way to the job enrichment changes.

(i) Measuring Productivity Benefits

It is unlikely that management would be willing to introduce expensive and time consuming changes in job design if such changes did not result in improved productivity. Satisfying employees needs must be linked with reaching organisational goals if the management are to be interested.

It is reasonably simple to assess the effects of change to jobs which are directly related to production or sales (as in the previous example). Any alterations to the job can be related to the consequential changes in the output. Problems arise with jobs in which the improvements cannot be so easily and objectively measured over a short period of time. Suppose the changes result in improved employee attitudes towards the organisation. These could not easily be measured in the short term. The output of some jobs, especially those in the service or public sectors, is difficult to measure in a precise way. For example, an office administrator had responsibility for analysing problems and producing reports for the guidance of management. If the administrator's motivation was improved it would be difficult to monitor the expected outcome. Would there be an expectation that reports would be produced more quickly, with a greater degree of competence? The problem is that the reports may take longer to produce if the work is done in a more diligent fashion. Only a subjective appraisal of the schemes success is possible. Thus the employee's superior may express the opinion that the reports are now an improvement over the standard previously attained. There is no doubt that this form of appraisal, because it is not based on hard fact, has less impact when it comes to persuading managers to change long established work systems.

(ii) Difficulty in Resdesigning Existing Jobs

Many organisations, such as Volvo, find that radical changes may be readily achieved when introduced in a new factory or office with a mainly new workforce. In long established organisations, entrenched attitudes, customs and practices built up over a number of years are not easily discarded. The resistance to change may be partly due to fear of the unknown and to worries over potential loss of status.

Furthermore it is not easy to change job structures whilst trying to maintain output. Most successful organisations are busy, and reluctant to chance any possible breakdown in the supply of goods and services that could result from a major job designing exercise. Finally available technology may restrict the manner in which jobs are performed making it difficult, if not impossible, for them to be redesigned.

(iii) Employees Reaction

While some studies indicate that the majority of employees tend to react in a particular manner, this does not necessarily indicate that all are enthusiastic for change. Suppose a worker performed a repetitive and essentially boring task. He may become extremely skilled at this task and so be respected for being so adept. Consequently he receives a high wage. Such a worker may regard the job merely as a means of earning a good wage and so it is unlikely that this person will welcome any change.

It may also be true that many workers do not wish, or because of their age no longer wish, to increase their responsibilities. They may feel inadequately equipped to deal with the new challenge effectively. The demands of their private lives may deter them from accepting greater responsibilities.

ATTITUDES

Increasing the motivation of the individual is not achieved by one simple method or some infallible technique. Much depends on identifying the motivating needs or factors of an individual and being able to satisfy these needs and at the same time achieve organisational goals. The attitudes of the workforce are critical. Management have now to recognise the link between needs, goals and rewards. Workers have to believe that their efforts are worthwhile. Management attitudes are just as important, as any pressure for innovation or change must come from them. They must be willing to risk changes which involve some delegation of their authority over decision making to the workforce. They must also be able and willing to adopt a fresh approach to human relations rather than just pursue solutions to problems of output.

ASSIGNMENT — THE MAIL ORDER BLUES

The Office staff of J.H. Mail Order Co. were having a discussion during their lunch period. Jean said that the pay was 'alright' but what annoyed her most in the job was the rules and restrictions. One of her jobs was to write to customers when they had queries yet she was only allowed to send printed 'standard' letters even though they did not always fully answer the customer's questions. Anne, Joan and Bill said that their jobs were boring. They all dealt with customers orders but worked on a 'production-line' where each of them dealt with only part of the paper-work and passed the orders on for the others to complete their part. Anne said that they felt 'out-of-touch' with their customers. Jim said that he had worked there for ten years but was not allowed to make any decisions for himself. He often knew more about the job than his supervisor but was not allowed to place orders with the suppliers for materials, for example, even though he knew that some suppliers were slower than others. His supervisor was involved in too much work dealing with the rest of the section to give these orders his full attention. The typist, Carol, said that she had been trained to use the word-processor but the rest of the staff did not understand its capabilities for writing good financial reports and she was only asked to type what the senior staff had hand-written. Janet said it was a shame they never really got to know people or what they did in other departments. She often wondered why another department completed the paperwork in a particular way, as really it was a waste of effort since the new computer was brought in last month. Janet was discouraged from taking up this point as she was told it might look like 'interfering' and 'we do not want them interfering here'. She felt that the organisation was a series of 'water-tight' departments, where the staff never met inside or outside the building. Frank said that his section worked hard to complete the stockcheck over the weekend. None of the management seemed to be aware of this and there were never any 'pats on the back'. Tony said that the only time the manager spoke to him was to reprimand him for being late one morning.

TASKS

1. You are employed as a member of a Team of Management Consultants engaged by J.H. Mail Order to carry out a survey of organisational processes. Your specific task is to investigate staff motivation at the company and for this purpose you are expected to produce an informal report. Use the information in the case-study to assist you in producing the report which should:

    (a) highlight possible reasons for poor motivation of staff;

    (b) suggest how the jobs described in the case study might be redesigned to improve motivation.

DEVELOPMENTAL TASK

2. Working in groups identify specific jobs known to you and evaluate the extent to which factors in the job either help or hinder good motivation.

ASSIGNMENT — THE GATESFIELD BUS CO.

John Harris has just taken over the position of General Manager of the Gatesfield Bus Co and was reviewing reports on personnel, which he had asked each head of department to produce. The company has never had a Personnel Manager. Each individual manager was expected to deal with all matters concerning his own staff. Two years ago, in response to a severe cost reduction exercise, the Training Department was closed. This was expected as no trainees had been recruited for the past four years and the last apprentice had completed his four-year training in the Maintenance Depot. Any new recruitment was strictly limited and the company attempted to enlist qualified workshop staff by offering them higher pay than they were receiving with their original employer. This meant that staff in the workshops had a variety of pay rates, which often caused discontent. Lately there had been problems in recruiting experienced staff for the workshops. One Maintenance Manager said that sometimes he was forced to accept recruits that were not wholly suitable, just to meet the demands of the new maintenance and safety regulations. New buses were replacing the old fleet and, although more luxurious and appealing to the customers, their maintenance demanded a knowledge of more complex and sophisticated components that many of the staff did not possess. Company policy expects all managers to retire at 60 and with an expansion of the company in the early 1950's, 60% of the present senior managers are aged 55 or more, while with other levels of management the percentage of those aged 55 or over is 35%. At present management training varies from department to department but has little real planning behind it.

The Marketing Manager wishes to invest in new computerised booking systems but is unsure of the staff's ability to operate the equipment successfully. None of the administration staff are operating word-processors and reports and publicity brochures are behind schedule.

TASKS

1. As assistant to the General Manager you have been asked to prepare a report on the above situation. In the report you should:

   (a) analyse the personnel and manpower planning policy at Gatesfield Bus Co;

   (b) identify and describe the various personnel problems that exist;

   (c) suggest how improved manpower planning would benefit Gatesfield Bus Co.

DEVELOPMENTAL TASKS

2. Devise a questionnaire that will give information as to the extent of manpower planning in a given organisation.

3. Visit a work organisation in your locality and report on their manpower planning approach.

Chapter 9

GROUPS AT WORK

An organisation should be structured in such a way that it is able to achieve its objectives. To carry out the tasks necessary to achieve this, authority must be delegated to various levels of management. Such authority is necessary to allow managers to plan and take appropriate action. In this way the organisation's operations are broken down and divided between various departments and sections. This allows staff to specialise and develop expertise in particular jobs or functions. To complete any complex task it is usually necessary for a group of individuals to work together. There must also be co-ordination and co-operation between the various groups.

It is possible to identify the following characteristics which are common to most work groups.

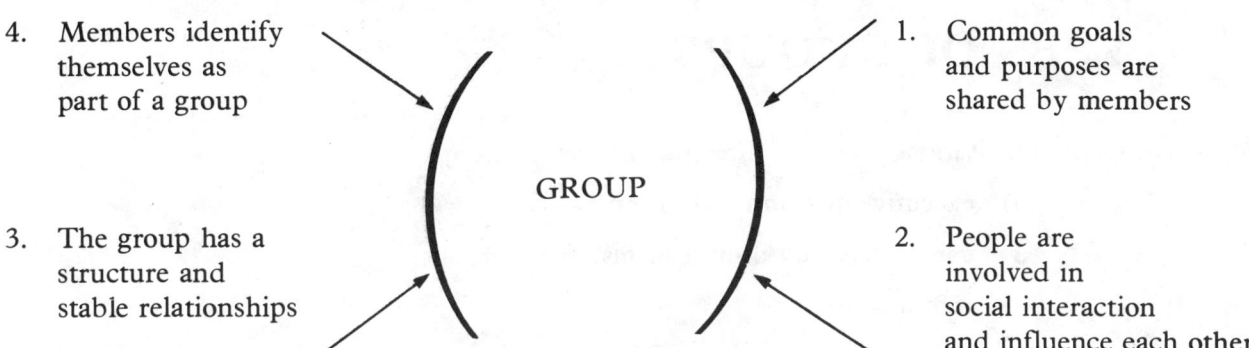

4. Members identify themselves as part of a group

1. Common goals and purposes are shared by members

GROUP

3. The group has a structure and stable relationships

2. People are involved in social interaction and influence each other

1. THE SHARING OF COMMON GOALS

All of the group's members wish to achieve a common purpose. They believe this can be most successfully done collectively. However, individuals may have a variety of goals and of course may be members of several groups. Thus they may work closely with their boss in an office while still being a member of a trade union. Sometimes the goals of unions and management groups are the same, such as creating a stable organisation with security of employment. Sometimes they may be in conflict, such as a disagreement over wage rises.

2. INFLUENCING EACH OTHER

Social interaction means that people in a group influence the values, ideas, beliefs or attitudes of other members. This influence may be a result of discussion between the various members, for example at a committee meeting where people may be encouraged to adopt the beliefs of the majority.

Non-verbal communication may also play a part in influencing a member of a group to conform to group thinking. For example the social rejection of a member by 'sending him to Coventry' often represents considerable pressure upon an individual to conform to the group will. A trade union may decide that some form of industrial action is necessary. A complete ban on overtime is called for. If one individual member defies the ban, the 'sending to Coventry' pressure may make him feel that the long term displeasure of his fellow workers is not worth the short term gain of overtime payment.

3. GROUP STRUCTURE

The group will normally have some form of structure or set of rules, however informal, so that members can relate more easily to one another. Group names, or the values that a group shares, may be stable and consistent over a long period and may well outlast the original group members.

Often an unofficial leader emerges as the person most likely to act as group spokesman on any issue.

4. RECOGNITION OF MEMBERS

Members of a group must recognise fellow members in some way and also know who is not a member of their group. Football teams and their fans, as well as the military, depend upon uniforms, slogans or songs. Some form of emotional tie between the group will exaggerate these outward signs. Work groups which are cohesive or closely bound together are generally more productive. Groups can also provide social status, security and social satisfaction particularly if the members are encouraged to participate in the decision making process and enjoy social events together.

TYPES OF GROUPS

In work organisations there are three main types of groups:-

> (i) executive or command groups;
>
> (ii) committees and project or task force groups;
>
> (iii) informal groups.

For each kind of organisation there may be variations of work groups under each of these main headings. Compare the work groups in a prison to those in a printers. The first two types of groups are formal in that it is for management to decide the makeup of the group and its assigned tasks. The third type of group is often seen as an alternative to formal groupings.

(i) Executive or Command Groups

Such groups are composed of managers and their staff and may have a wide variety of tasks including planning, organising, motivating and co-ordinating the different groupings within the organisation. Each of these groupings or departments will have their own specialism and must co-ordinate with other groups. Thus the manager of a group, for example a production planning manager, will be head of a group providing plans to guide the production of goods manufactured on the shop floor.

At the same time the production planning manager is part of a group headed by the production director and this group must meet regularly to discuss production problems relating to such matters as quality and quantity.

The manager of each group can thus be seen as the link between fellow members of the work group and the executive or command group. So, while each formal group has the responsibility to carry out specific tasks in the organisation such as work study, they must co-ordinate with other groups, such as production, to provide a service that will benefit the organisation as a whole rather than simply to perform their own tasks in isolation. The work study department should seek improvements in efficiency in areas of greatest priority to the organisation. Clearly it would not benefit the organisation if this department sought only to evaluate those areas which the department's members regard as being of greatest personal interest.

(ii) Committees or Project Groups

Such formal grouping could be either long term, such as a committee which meets every month to discuss a particular area of responsibility. An example is the safety committee. Alternatively they may be short term and established to perform a specific limited project. Such a project group could be asked to design a package for a particular product or have the task of surveying a specific piece of development land. The project group would be disbanded at the end of the project but could be reconvened for the next task. A long term committee, such as the housing committee of a local authority will have defined objectives and a structure that will endure beyond the participation of the original members.

The more formal the committee, the greater is the need for elected officers, such as a secretary and a chairman. Rules and procedures, such as standing orders will help to reinforce the status of the committee and enable individual members to define their roles more clearly. Project or task groups draw people from various departments and as such cut across the normal structure of the organisation. Such groupings may assist communications and co-operation throughout the organisation as well as achieve tasks.

(iii) Informal Groups

Informal groups will vary in the degree of 'informality' they possess. They can range from semi-formal groups such as casual meetings called by managers to discuss current problems to the informal group which congregates at the drinks machine during breaktimes and discusses a variety of subjects including the latest rumours, scandals and the shortcomings of the management.

Informal groups have certain advantages:-

(i) they provide security for there is 'strength in numbers'. People feel less worried when they know that there are others 'in the same boat' as themselves;

(ii) they allow people to establish their own identity or status which is more recognisable in a small group. In a large organisation individual workers may fell they are only 'a small cog in a large machine'.

(iii) they help to satisfy people's needs for friendship and support. Members can share jokes and grumbles with friends and so improve social relationships.

(iv) they provide the opportunity for people with similar ideas and values to meet together and reinforce their attitudes. This is common with people of similar political persuasion;

(v) they provide an informal communication network which supplements the formal channels. This is often called the "grapevine" by which one group can pass messages to another and so rumour can spread rapidly. It can sometimes be used by managers as an unofficial channel to pass on information.

(vi) they may provide solutions to problems for a group. For instance if a member is unwell the rest of the group may recognise this and so work harder to 'carry' the less productive member.

Unfortunately informal groups can produce certain disadvantages:-

(i) The group could show considerable resistance to change despite management's concern to improve group working. Such inflexibility may mean that managers will develop a reluctance to introduce innovations;

(ii) Members may be reluctant to 'step out of line' and so may supress their own feelings if these radically differ from the groups attitudes. Such conformity could lead to less innovation or creativity;

(iii) The 'grapevine' is often the source of rumour which may have no foundation in truth but nevertheless can cause serious disharmony in an organisation. The vacuum created by the lack of positive information from management will be quickly filled by rumours created by the mischievous or the ill-informed.

(iv) The group may test its strength against the rules laid down by management. For example members may finish work early or expand tea and lunch breaks. This could lead to conflict with a 'them and us' situation developing with management which will not improve industrial relations or efficiency.

PURPOSE OF GROUPS

Groups may evolve or be formed for various purposes. They can evolve out of a random collection of individuals who find themselves bonded together by some common interest, such as the threat of redundancy. If the reason for membership of a group becomes obsolete then members will lose interest.

An Individual's Need for Group Membership

Individuals join groups for the following reasons:-

(i) as a means of achieving goals or targets. Personal or organisational objectives may be more easily attained in a group. A singer joining a group of musicians is an example in which both an individual's personal ambitions and those of the group may be enhanced by providing a more versatile combination;

(ii) in order to satisfy their social needs. People are naturally sociable and need to be with others and share common ideas, values and pleasures. They may join clubs or societies simply to enjoy the company of others;

(iii) in order to share or help in a process that requires more than one person. This may be giving a service, producing goods or recreational purposes such as a football team;

(iv) as a method of establishing and displaying their own stance in society. A person may join a political party with the intention of becoming a future candidate for a local election or perhaps to help and encourage others to do so.

The Organisation's Need for Groups

An organisation uses groups for one or more purposes:-

(i) to carry out tasks which are not easily carried out by an individual alone. To have a successful racing car team needs skills and talents which are brought together in harmony. Each member of the team has his own duties and responsibilities and the work is distributed amongst the team;

(ii) to ensure that important aspects of the work are well managed and controlled. The group could have a specific responsibility within the organisation, such as work study measurement, and would be expected to ensure that this was carried out effectively and efficiently;

(iii) to make decisions and solve problems. Pooling the knowledge and experience of a number of people may result in better quality decisions. Local authorities make extensive use of committees to decide both policy and the priority of objectives. The operation of the organisation is then delegated to the full-time employees of the corresponding department;

(iv) for arbitration, conciliation and negotiation processes. Often a group provides a variety of personnel with a wide spread of values, ideas and beliefs which could give a more objective view in solving disputes of various kinds. There is also a legal requirement to have a wide representation on bodies such as industrial and administrative tribunals;

(v) to seek to involve workers in decision making and so encourage commitment which facilitates the effective implementation of the decision. If people are allowed to put forward their own ideas and these are adopted, then there is a stronger commitment to seek a successful outcome than if the decisions for change were made elsewhere and thrust upon them;

(vi) for gathering, processing and distributing information. A committee may be formed to undertake this role and so provide a vital co-ordinating link between departments. The role of the Safety Committee in an organisation, composed of members from each department, is an example of this;

(vii) to evaluate and analyse past decisions or events. A committee may be set up to evaluate past decisions and to initiate inquiries.

OVERLAP OR CONFLICT OF PURPOSES

Individual and organisational purposes may overlap. They may combine and confirm each other such as the ambitious executive's desire to be part of a successful company. In some cases, however, these purposes may conflict. Some of the social activities of informal work groups, such as a long chat during tea breaks, may well stand in the way of higher production and so conflict with organisational objectives. Work groups may informally agree to lower outputs per man than those expected by management. Sometimes an individual's needs are lost in conforming to group decisions. For example a group decision to ban overtime may reduce an individual's earning capacity and so conflict with his purpose of maximising earnings.

Individuals often belong to a number of different groups and so could adopt differing roles in each. Such membership of several groups will not pose problems as long as such roles are not in conflict. It would be awkward if the manager belonged to the same union as his staff and a conflict developed over pay and conditions of work between the management and staff levels in the organisation.

PRACTICAL STUDIES OF GROUP WORKING

One of the largest social studies ever carried out in industry was undertaken at the Hawthorne plant of Western Electrics in the U.S.A. during the 1920's and 1930's. Groups at work were studied and individual group members were interviewed. Over a period of two years 20,000 employees were interviewed. The findings confirmed earlier studies which identified the human problems facing management. The results showed that when the objectives of a group of workers and management coincided, the group could be motivated to produce a much higher output. If the objectives did not coincide it was evident that the group could hold down output regardless of the wishes of management. The following are the outlines of extracts from the Hawthorne studies which illustrate where group objectives coincide or conflict with those of management.

Objectives that Coincide

One of the most famous of the studies carried out at the Hawthorne plant was the lighting experiment. Here the researchers chose a group of workers employed on a large production line manufacturing components. The workers were reallocated to a small production line where the conditons of working could be easily altered and their individual output measured. The components were small and it was thought that by increasing the level of lighting the working conditions would be improved. Consequently the lighting was upgraded in stages and the group's reaction was measured at each stage. With every increase in lighting there was an increase in output. Eventually a researcher secretly reduced the lighting and was surprised to find another increase in output. With further reductions to comparatively low lighting levels the output remained high. Apparently the increase in output was due more to the presence of those carrying out the experiments than the lighting levels. The experiment had created unique conditions where, for once, the workers regarded themselves as a 'special' team and they discussed the work amongst themselves with great interest. This introduced new factors of motivation such as pride in the job, which were not present before. It could be said then that external physical conditions were less important than the new values of the team. The result was an increasing output became the common objective of the team and the management.

It would be wrong to suggest that the previous experiment showed that changes in physical conditions had no effect on output. However, in that particular case, the group was motivated by the very fact that it was an experiment. This shows the need for careful structuring of experiments and the necessity for control groups where conditions are not altered. It should be noted that under careful, controlled conditions it has been found that there are optimum levels of lighting for different tasks. Moderate levels of illumination are sufficient for reading tasks whereas high levels of illumination are needed on the hospital operating table.

Objectives that Conflict

A group of workers were secretly observed while they worked wiring components together into large installations for telephone exchanges. The workers were paid a bonus based on the efforts of the group as a whole. However it was soon clear that the workers, although they may have wished for a larger bonus, commonly agreed a restriction in output. This represented the group's ideas as to what it collectively regarded as was a 'fair day's pay for a fair days work'. Norms of 6000 units per day were set as the target for production, but this was less than the group could have produced at full capacity. Anyone who deviated from this target however risked abuse or social pressure from the rest of the group. It was thought that too high an output (and consequent bonus) would make management alter the bonus rates and to produce too low an output was unfair to the others in the group. Thus the group objectives were not to seek high levels of productivity, which the bonus set by management should have produced. The group preferred instead to set their own target and so brought social pressures to bear on individuals to conform to the group's values. Thus a group which is cohesive may not necessarily adopt the same objectives as management. Norms, values and customes of the group may be more important to an individual than the extra bonus.

MODERN VIEWS OF GROUPS

At present there are a number of interesting developments concerning work groups. These include 'think tanks', 'brainstorming', group technology, autonomous groups, quality circles and many others. Some details of these will be given later in this chapter. However it is as well to remember that many of the new developments have their basis in the ideas produced by earlier work. A brief summary of this earlier work reveals the following characteristics:-

    (i)   People are mainly social animals and prefer the company of others;

   (ii)   Work is often a group activity;

  (iii)   Small Primary, informal groups are important to an organisation to carry out particular tasks;

  (iv)   The social world of adults may centre around their work activity;

   (v)   For good morale and high productivity, the need for recognition, job satisfaction, security and a sense of belonging may be more important to the employee than physical conditions;

  (vi)   Social demands both inside and outside work may be powerful factors in forming an employee's attitude and effectiveness.

(vii)   A good team or cohesive group can have the potential for high productivity but must be planned for and developed.

THINK TANKS AND BRAIN-STORMING

In searching for new ideas regarding products or processes it has been found that a group of people, with a range of expertise, are capable of generating ideas amongst themselves. These methods are referred to as 'think tanks' and often use a 'brain storming' approach to generate ideas. Here the group is allowed to suggest possible answers to problems without immediate criticism being allowed. It is held that criticism makes others reluctant to put forward their ideas. Only when all ideas have been written down does the team rank them in order of usefulness. The team can then adopt an approach which is objective, rather than the subjective criticism that may arise in an ordinary meeting. A 'half-baked' idea from one member can be an inspiration for another and refined by yet another.

GROUP TECHNOLOGY AND AUTONOMOUS GROUP WORKING

Both these ideas have been mentioned in chapter 8 in relation to motivation. The basic reasoning behind these approaches is that the small group should work on an identifiable product or process and thus not feel like an insignificant cog in a large machine. Group Technology, as the name suggests, ensures that all machines required to make a product or range of products are located within a small area where a particular group works. Thus the product 'belongs' to that particular group. Previously the group may have worked in a department using only one type of machine, for example lathes, and completed only a small part of the work on a product as it passed through each department. Autonomous group working allows the group to take decisions, such as planning the work schedule and deciding who is to tackle a particular part of the overall task.

Turnover and absenteeism are said to be lower and job interest higher with this technique. There are a number of variations using this approach which move away from separating workers on the production line to a close-knit team approach.

QUALITY CIRCLES

This approach is said to originate in Japan. The basis of the technique is to allow a group of workers to make decisions regarding problems in their own work. Originally problems regarding the quality of a product were used, hence the name, but any problems connected with the groups work could be chosen. The groups normally meet outside their normal work hours and only volunteers need attend. The supervisor may propose problems for discussion and present the group's findings to management. Otherwise the supervisor is not expected to act as the 'boss' but only as a member of the team or perhaps as a chairman. No criticism of individual members is allowed and the team are expected to think objectively about the problem. Expert advice, can be called on, for example regarding costs. Any solutions are put to management and quick action, if agreed, is expected.

This method of solving work problems usually brings together the people most experienced with the job; the workers. If their ideas are put into practice then they are more likely to be committed to ensure success. Thus commitment and motivation may both be present. It may also be one way to tap the potential for ideas from a workforce who are normally never asked for their opinions and such involvement will make their work more satisfying.

INTER-GROUP RELATIONSHIPS

Competition may be used to promote team spirit within groups and thus improve productivity. This may take the form of a prize for the sales area team with the best monthly sales figures. This may work well, especially where the overall objectives are common, such as improved safety in all plants. However, where a common objective is forgotten, competition may turn to rivalry and even strong hositility. Making another department look foolish may become the real objective, rather than to improve the service to the customer.

CONFLICT

In the past, management attempted to squash all conflict in an organisation as it was regarded as being harmful. It is true that unresolved conflict between groups can undermine good industrial relations and inter group rivalry may lead to industrial action and strikes. Examples taken from the past include the rivalry between craft unions in shipyards where some workers believed that jobs that required the skills they possessed were being 'stolen' by other workers. Demarcation disputes were once common. Where aluminium was bonded to wood panelling, there was a dispute over who should bore the holes, the wood workers or the metal workers. A contemporary example is the rivalry between the traditional print unions such as SOGAT 82 and the electricians union, the EETPU, over the manning of plant at News International's Wapping print works. However not all conflict is necessarily harmful. For example if some people were not dissatisfied then perhaps no one would look for improved solutions. Allowing discussion and participation within an organisation will allow the management to be aware of the conflict and new approaches may be organised and conflict made productive.

PROMOTING COMMON GOALS

An organisation usually tries to promote common objectives between groups by a process of good communications thus stressing the interdependency of each and so promoting a sense of unity of purpose. Good co-ordination and co-operation between departments is valuable. Some organisations identify how each group has another group as a 'customer'. For example 'packing' may be a customer of 'final assembly'. The groups are then encouraged to see how best they can meet their 'customer' needs. Shared facilities, such as a canteen, may often promote co-operation. Organisations have changed since the 'Hawthorne Experiments' were first reported but the importance of groups are often under estimated with resulting under performance.

ASSIGNMENT — THE BITTER PILL

Health Products Ltd. are a producer of pharmaceutical pills, powders and other medicines for retailing and for prescription in Chemist's shops throughout the country and abroad. Many of the products it makes use the latest technology and the production management work closely with research and development. Although they rarely admitted it, many of the production managers enjoyed the technical challenge of manufacturing the products. In fact many could be said to manage products and processes better than people. Every Monday the management team met to discuss the priorities and problems of the job. This Monday the least technological part of the process was under discussion for the first time. The problem lay in the packing section, which had just been taken over by a new manager Mr Ray East, and it was he who raised the particular problem. The products were packed using production-line techniques, where operatives stood at 'stations' two metres apart. Here each operative had quantities of a few of the products which they placed into boxes that were slowly moving down the conveyor. Sometimes the order attached to the box required the products a particular individual handled and sometimes not. The problems that Mr East found on his appointment were recounted to the meeting. Absenteeism was the worst problem and it meant either high overtime bills or orders not being available to the customer at the promised time, or both. He said that discussions with the packers showed a lack of job interest or boredom which resulted in mistakes, accidents and suspected sabotage. One day the conveyor ground to a halt, with much cheering from the operatives who all sat down on the nearest box and all groaned when the repair was finished. The repair showed that the breakdown was caused by a bolt that had been dropped into the conveyor cogs, sabotage was suspected but impossible to prove. Statistics showed that accidents and mistakes were on the increase. There was a lack of team spirit and the operatives were unwilling to help each other when the occasion arose. The operatives were paid just the same as others doing the same type of job in the region.

Mr. East proposed that the production-line was scrapped and that the operatives worked in groups and sat at 'desks' which stocked all the company's products and then one packer could complete a whole order for a customer. Small groups may even deal with particular sets of customers which they may come to consider as 'theirs'. The 'desks' would be arranged so that they could see and talk to each other as they worked. The details were not worked out as Mr East wanted to consult the packers first and seek their active participation in making the change. Some of the managers welcomed the idea but others were unconvinced. Their criticisms were: "Asking the workforce for their ideas will only complicate the issue, explain the plan and sell it to them", "They only work for the money, give them a bonus for better work", "We tried participation ten years ago and it did not work" and other disheartening statements.

TASK

1. As Mr East's assistant you have been asked to prepare an informal report to help him sell his idea for improving the effectiveness of the packing section at the next meeting of the management team. In the report you should:

    (a) prepare arguments to answer the criticisms of Mr East's proposals;

    (b) stress the advantages of group working for the packers;

    (c) suggest the likely consequences of adopting the proposal.

DEVELOPMENTAL TASK

2. Undertake a role play exercise of a meeting between Mr East, his assistant and some of the packers where their active participation is sought for planning the proposed change.

ASSIGNMENT — THE TECHNICIANS

In 1986 Bill James graduated from University and gained employment with a large engineering company in the Midlands. Because of his technical knowledge he was put in charge of five technicians in the Production Quality Control Laboratory. The technicians tasks were to take random samples from components on the assembly line after they had been through the zinc, nickel, cadmium or chromium plating baths. These samples were then brought back to the laboratory to undergo a variety of tests. After testing and comparing the components with the original specifications, decisions had to be made as to whether the components were suitable for passing to the next stage in the manufacturing process. Decisions also had to be made on how much chemical should be added to the plating baths to ensure reliable performance.

Much of the work involved standard routines and Bill, as the supervisor, checked the results of the tests and signed for the additions of chemicals to any bath. He expected that as he had been formally appointed as the technicians' supervisor, that they would naturally come to him with any problem or queries. However, he soon found out that the technicians used a less formal system of their own for dealing with problems. One of the group, John, seemed to be the spokesman for the others when any criticism was levelled at any of them. They all protected each other in such a way that it was difficult to fix blame for careless work. The group appeared to organise the work between themselves in such a way that the same number of tests were performed each week. Bill had tried giving them 'pep talks' to increase output but to no avail. Although he was their supervisor, they often sought the advice of another, older technician in an adjacent section. During the lunch break, three of the technicians played football, while the other two played cards with a different group.

One day Bill had lunch as usual with some other supervisors, and confided in one, Jim, as to his situation and asked Jim's advice.

Jim has promised to give the matter some thought and meet Bill later in the week when he will attempt to advise him.

TASK

1. Assume the role of Jim in the above case. To enable you to effectively advise Jim you have decided to prepare a set of notes in which you

    (a)   Identify and analyse the informal relationships in the above case;

    (b)   Suggest the possible advantages and disadvantages of the various relationships;

    (c)   Suggest the action that Jim should take;

    (d)   Envisage the likely consequences of the action.

DEVELOPMENTAL TASK

2. Undertake a role play exercise in which the meeting between Bill and Jim is simulated.

Chapter 10

THE ORGANISATION AND CHANGE

THE ORGANISATION AS A SYSTEM

An organisation is a system which has its own purpose and objectives and must seek to satisfy customer needs and be responsive to its external environment. There are many possibilities for change in customer needs, and the external environment. The organisation's system must be sufficiently dynamic so that it can operate efficiently and yet still remain responsive to change. Some of the factors that may affect or be affected by change are shown in the following figure.

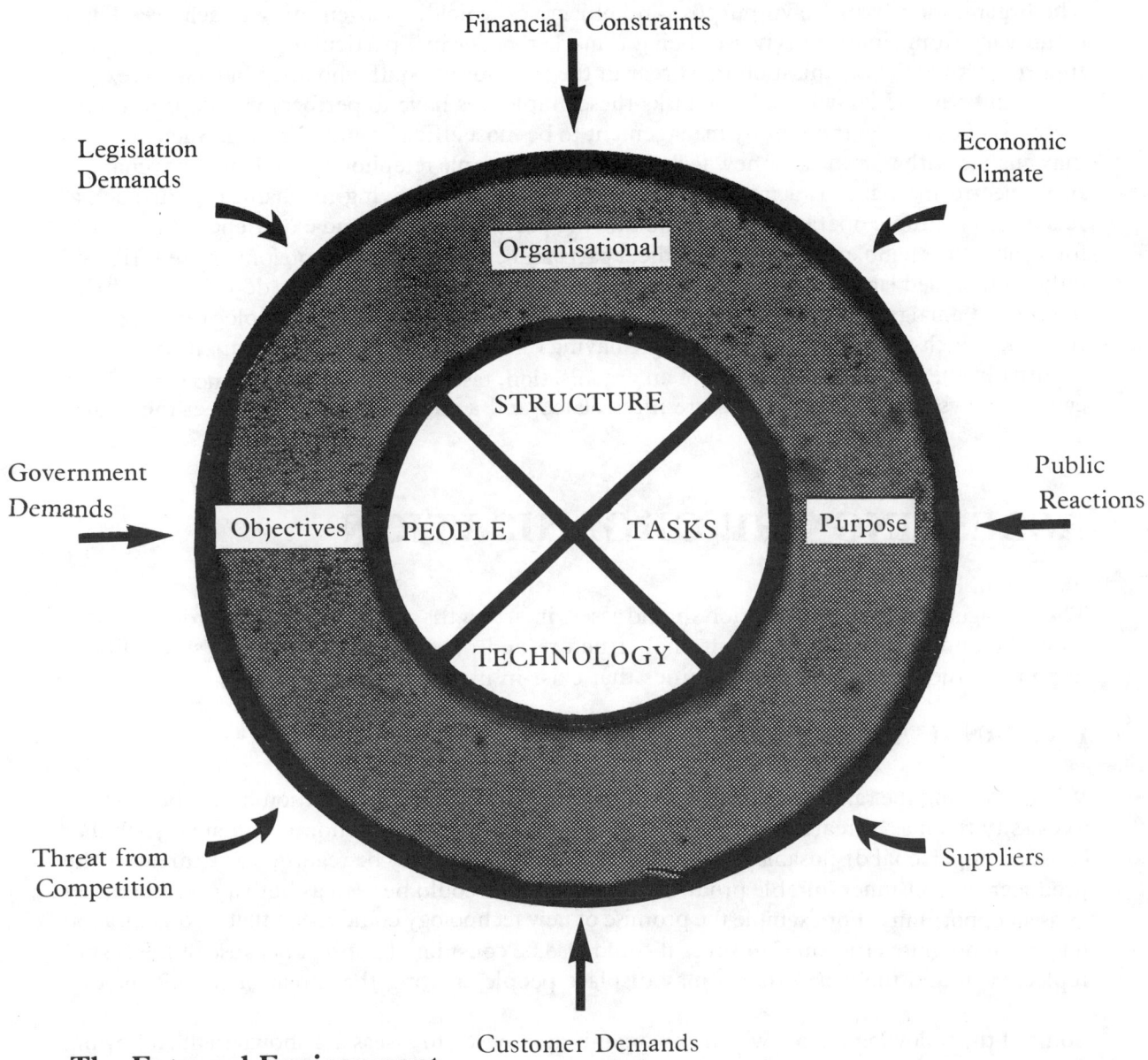

The External Environment

THE EXTERNAL ENVIRONMENT

The organisation and its members cannot readily modify the external environment but must react to changes caused by it even if this means modifying some of their own objectives. The organisation cannot produce and sell what it has traditionally produced if there are changing customer needs. An example is the demise of the British motor-cycle industry because of its unwillingness to adapt to changing customer needs. Changes in the law may enforce changes on an organisation. For instance a factory making lead products may not omit fumes that exceed the limits laid down in safety regulations. Enforcing the regulations may be so expensive for an old plant that it is forced to close. The Health & Safety at Work Act 1974 can bring about these and other changes which will be explored later in this chapter.

Government policies, such as those to restrict spending in the public sector can severely limit the growth of services. Changes in technology or other innovations may bring a threat from competiton which has gained a temporary advantage following the introduction of new methods within their organisation.

THE INTERNAL ORGANISATION ENVIRONMENT

The organisation has its own purpose and objectives which it is attempting to achieve. These could vary from simple survival to being a market leader in a particular field. To accomplish these objectives the organisation must recruit the appropriate staff who must have skills, experience, abilities and knowledge. The tasks these employees have to perform will depend on the methods of operation thought by management to be most efficient and effective. Such methods may change with new ideas or new technology. For example telephone switch gear has changed from electro-mechanical (a mixture of electrical parts and moving mechanical parts such as relays) to electronic operation (few or no moving parts). The skills and experience of the workforce, able to assemble complex mechanical parts and electric wiring, is no longer used. Instead only semi-skilled labour is needed to assemble fewer electronic parts. Large departments shrink in size and amalgamate with each other. Essentially the change in new technology has changed the task, which in turn needs fewer people having different skills. The organisation structure is eventually altered. Thus four facets of an organisation, tasks, people, structure and technology, can be analysed separately but all are interrelated and a change in one will affect the others.

ASSESSING THE ORGANISATION

The management of an organisation should assess its strengths and weaknesses in order to determine the appropriateness of its internal structure and sytems and evaluate its suitability to respond to the threats and opportunities that exist in its external environment.

EXTERNAL ASSESSMENT

When assessing the range of external factors which influence an organisation it may be possible to classify them as 'threats' or 'opportunities'. For example if the economic climate is such that consumers personal disposable income was falling then this may be regarded as a threat by the producers of consumer durable products. Some changes could be seen as both a possible threat or as an opportunity. For example the promise of new technology could mean that an organisation may become more efficient. However it could also be considered a threat because of the cost of replacement and the worry that it may displace people creating the threat of redundancies.

Some of the following factors which any organisation needs to assess are shown in the following figure.

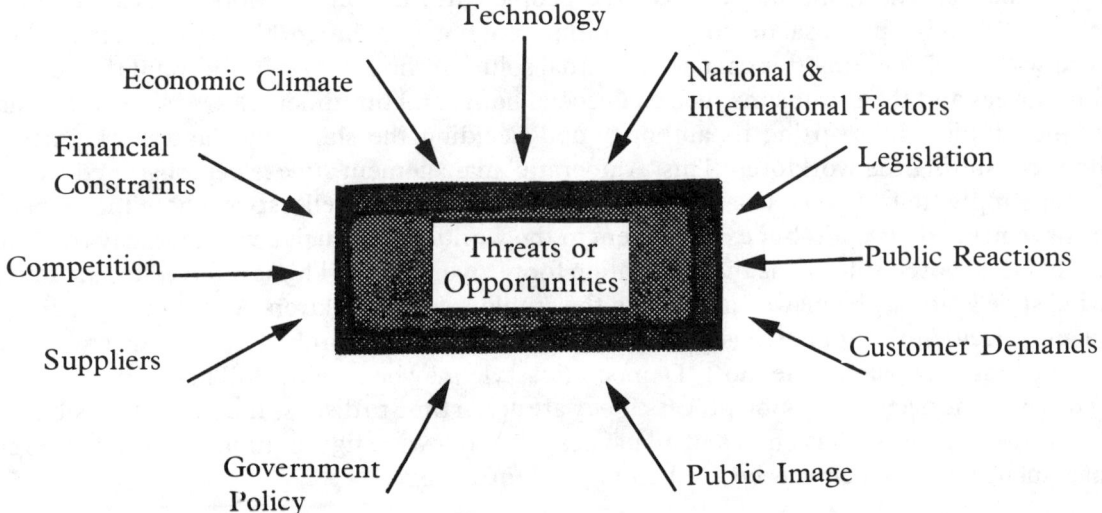

Many of these factors are discussed in detail elsewhere in this book. It is the case depending on the type of organisation, some factors will have a greater priority or importance than others. Government Policy may have the greatest impact on organisations in the Public Sector. However, competition and customer demands will probably present the greatest threats and opportunities to organisations in the Private Sector.

INTERNAL ASSESSMENT

A variety of factors could be used to assess the internal strengths or weaknesses of an organisation. In general the following factors could be analysed and assessed in relation to the internal threats and opportunities.

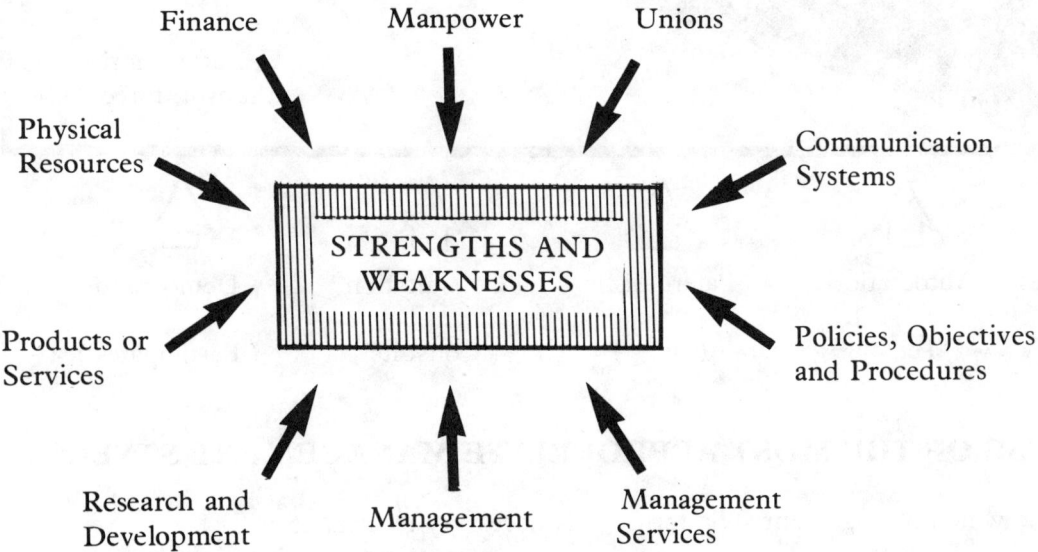

Many of these factors will have a great effect on the success of an organisation. However as we noted in chapter 8 one of the most critical factors is the capability and motivation of the organisation's workforce.

CHANGE AND MANAGEMENT STYLE

The style that management adopts for dealing with change is extremely important. Many of the problems concerned with change have no easy answer. They require an answer which best suits the particular situation, specific task and the people carrying out the work. An example of a specific problem is a proposal to reduce the number of hours in the working week. Management is faced with implementing this change. The final solution should take into account the needs of the employees and their problems such as unsocial hours and bus timetables. Management may solve the problem by exerting its authority and deciding the shift times and work patterns without consulting the workforce. This 'Autocratic' management style is demonstrated when a manager simply 'tells' people what to do. A variation could be a 'sells' style where the management have made their plans but explain them to the workforce in such a way that may convince them that the chosen solution is the best option for the work force. This is referred to as a 'Paternalistic' style as it may be viewed as treating the employees like children. Alternatively management may decide to adopt a 'Consultative' style and discuss the problems with the employees before making a decision. The most 'Democratic' style may be to allow full participation by all employees in the decision making process. They are given time to discuss the various possibilities and come to an agreed decision to suit all parties. The following figure summarises the different management styles which can be used to implement change:-

MANAGEMENT STYLE

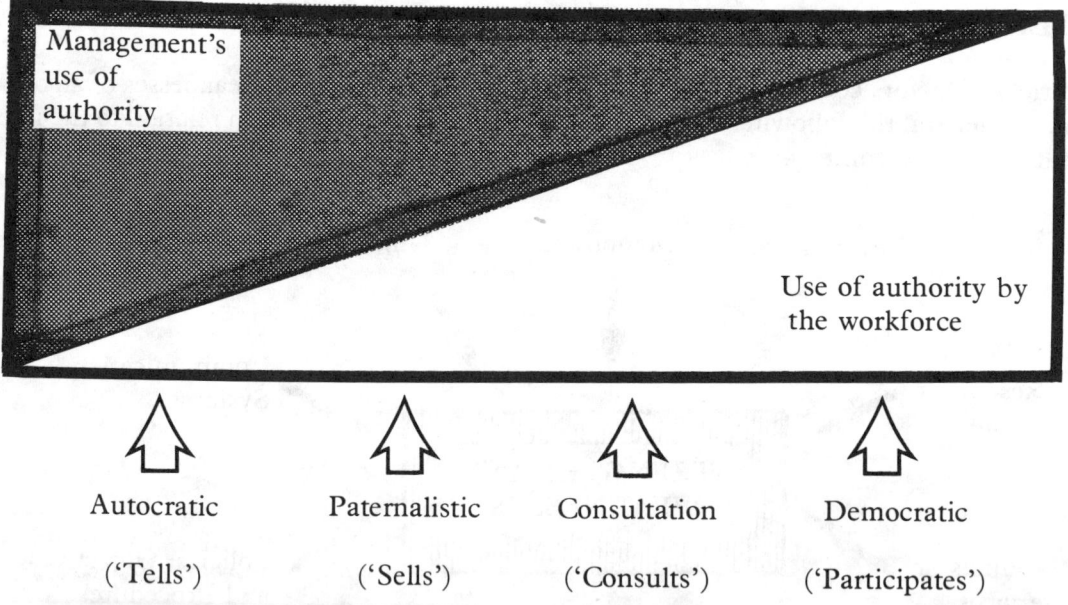

THE USE OF THE MOST APPROPRIATE MANAGEMENT STYLE

To decide which management style to use it is necessary to consider:

    (i)   personality, skill, experience and ability of the manager;

    (ii)   the situation;

    (iii)   the need for the workforce to participate in decision making.

(i) Personality

Every manager differs in his or her ability to adopt a particular style successfully. Clearly a manager should evaluate his or her own personality and talents before adopting a particular management style. Often a very inexperienced manager may find that democratic management may be difficult to handle.

(ii) The Situation

Sometimes the situation itself may dictate the style to use. For example in a crisis or an emergency the workforce may look to management for a strong lead in decision making. In fact the workers may expect an almost autocratic style. If there was a fire on the fifth floor you would not expect a debate and a show of hands to decide on which exit route to use! Rules and procedures which have been laid down by management are expected in such circumstances.

(iii) Participation

The workforce may not feel the need to participate in certain decisions. If the decision involves a problem that is not directly related to a person's task, then there may be little interest in active involvement. However, keeping people informed of decisions on changes may still be important and could be considered to be a lesser form of participation. Some organisations make an effort to keep all employees informed of top level decisions through the use of briefing meetings and in-house magazines and newspapers designed to give news, views and interests in the organisation as a whole.

Participation in decision making has the advantage of using more fully the untapped potential of all employees of the organisation. There is also the advantage that employees become more interested in the organisation and so want it to succeed and consequently work harder to achieve this. New processes are more likely to succeed where the people who have to make them work have a part to play in deciding the changes to be made. Let us examine the case of a new coating process which was to be introduced into a factory. To speed up the brush coating method, the management introduced a new spray coating process. This was done without consulting the supervisor or the workforce in the area. Very poor results were achieved and this part of the process became a bottleneck holding up production.

The engineering designers arranged a meeting with members of the workforce and their supervisor in this critical area. Ideas were shared and agreements made on changes. A new spraying method was instituted which proved a success. However the question arises whether this success was due to the good ideas of the workforce on work method or the fact that they were strongly committed to seeing their own ideas succeed. Many management experts believe that both factors are important.

PARTICIPATIVE METHODS

Many methods have been tried to gain the participation of employees. Group methods include: staff committees which may be both formal and informal; quality circles where groups meet to consider particular problems; autonomous work groups in which some work decisions are made by the group rather than their supervisor; and project teams where a group meets on a regular basis representing different departments in the organisation to tackle specific problems. These methods were examined in chapter 9.

Apart from these group methods many organisations try to stimulate individual approaches. Some people prefer to think and work on their own and are inhibited by speaking in front of a group. Suggestion schemes, often with financial or non-financial rewards, are used in a variety of forms to stimulate the employee to put forward ideas for change. The best schemes also force management to vet the ideas thoroughly and put the useful ones into action as soon as possible.

TYPES OF PROBLEMS

It would be wrong to think that all management's problems were best decided by committee. By its very nature participation is a relatively slow process and if time is short it may be better for a single individual to make the decision. Naturally if more participation is needed then management must try to plan further ahead to allow time for it to take place. Generally the problems best tackled by participative means are those which do not have 'one best answer' but have a variety of alternatives to choose from and the best in any particular situation is the one which best suits the organisation, structure, the situation, the customer and the staff needs.

There are of course many changes which need some correct technical decisions. These should be made by experts. Suppose that you are lying in a hospital bed and the doctor who was about to give you an injection held a debate and a show of hands among nurses, porters, administration and catering staff as to what quantity should be injected, then you may feel that you are not receiving the service you require. Technical problems need technical decisions by experts and should not be confused with the many general and human problems faced by management.

INTERPERSONAL SKILLS

The interpersonal skills needed by management to bring about change must include the ability to be a good listener as well as a good communicator. At meetings the manager may sometimes act as a leader in proposing new ideas, or counselling certain courses of action. However, often the manager should 'take a back seat' and have a chairman's role in encouraging debate and decision making by others. Everyone should be given the chance to contribute at the appropriate time and the meeting should not be dominated by a few strong personalities. Often a consensus decision is to be preferred. This is one where all agree to the decision without a vote. The process of voting may leave those who are against a motion which has been passed with a feeling of defeat, which is certainly something which should not be encouraged if the organisation is to work in harmony. Management are paid to make unpalatable decisions such as declaring redundancies or taking disciplinary action. Such actions cannot be readily delegated to others so a management approach should be adopted which recognises that good human relations are still important in such circumstances.

CONSULTATION

Consultation between management and workers requires skills of 'listening and asking' but may also involve management taking the initiative to 'inform' workers by using various techniques. Consultative committees are set up in many organisations with representatives of management and elected representatives of staff.

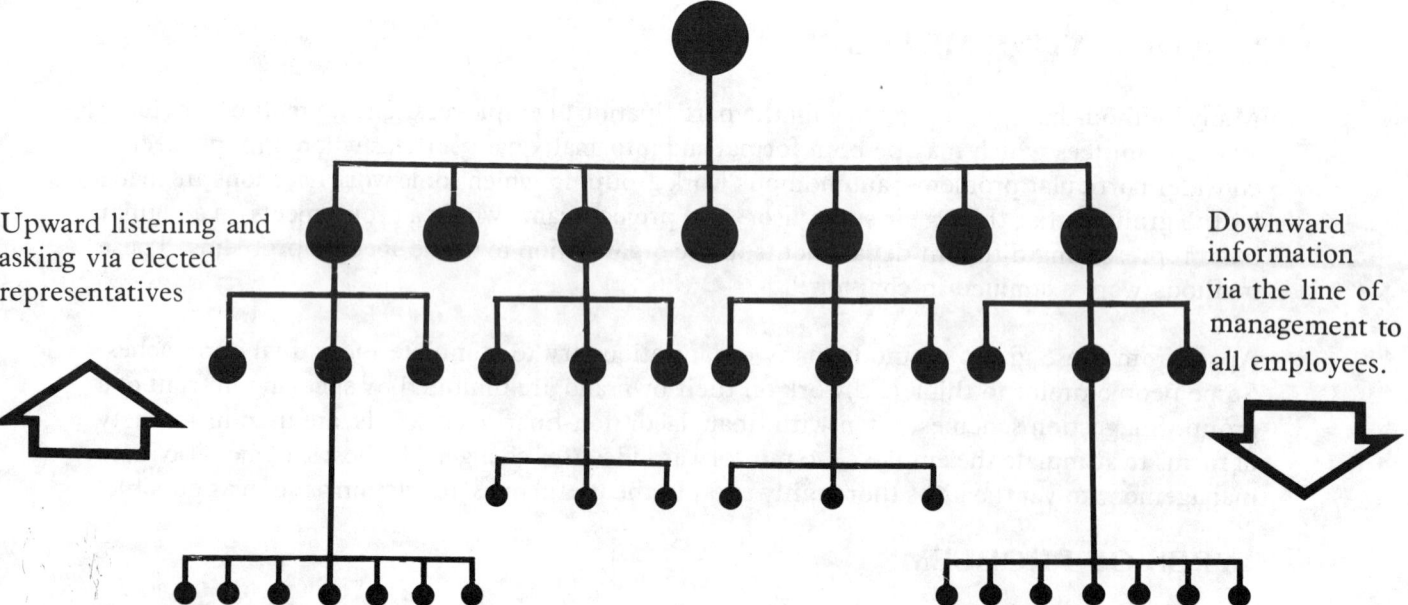

Upward listening and asking via elected representatives

Downward information via the line of management to all employees.

The consultative committees allow management to listen to the ideas and problems of staff through their representatives. Management should also be encouraged to include items on the agenda so that they can 'ask' for employees views. The downward communication process should be carried out by each team or group leader.

Face to face communication is effective if questions and discussion are also possible. It is usual to use written material at the same time, as many facts may be forgotten, especially numerical ones. It is often difficult for people to remember dates, times and quantities unless they are written down for later reference.

ITEMS FOR CONSULTATION

Policy and prime objectives are decisions made by the most senior management and not normally open to consultation, but how best these may be put into practice is often the matter for detailed discussion. While technical and urgent decisions are best made by the individual manager, consultation should be used where it does not slow decision making down or limit its flexibility. Long term decisions or those which will affect a large number of employees, their work practices or working conditions, are likely to be better discussed in advance of planning and action. Good consultation here should reap long term advantages.

CHANGE AND THE PROBLEM OF SAFETY

The change and rapid advance of industrial processes have brought dangers that were often not fully recognised or appreciated until some disaster occurred. The Factory Acts and Factory Inspectorate began as far back as 1833 but the legislation laid down to regulate and improve safety was usually outpaced by technological advance. Problems with the use of steam, electricity, internal combustion and now atomic power have usually occurred in advance of adequate safety measures. Recent problems with atomic power plants in U.S.A. and Russia are all to ready reminders.

To meet these changes and to have suitable regulations prepared as they were needed became a priority. The Health & Safety at Work Act 1974 laid down the foundation of new legislation to be made when required in the form of regulations. It also covers almost all people at the work place and attempts to protect those affected by health risks or dangers from places of work.

COPING WITH CHANGING CONDITIONS

In order to cope with changes at work the Health and Safety at Work Act provides the basis for:-

(a) A safety policy for all organisations to guide management;

(b) Management action to improve safety as a continuing exercise;

(c) An outline of the responsibilities of management and other employees;

(d) Safety Committees;

(e) Trade Union Safety Representatives;

(f) Provision for producing new regulations, Codes of Practice or guidance notes where required;

(g) An Inspectorate with strong powers of action against unsafe practices;

(h) General duties under the law for employees, suppliers, designers and manufacturers of plant and equipment.

SAFETY POLICY AND RESPONSIBILITIES

All but the smallest organisations must now prepare a safety policy, available to all employees, which outlines action expected from management and employees. It is a guideline for future action and usually the detailed procedures for complying with this policy are expected from the organisation. Examples are the setting up of safety advisors, fire drills and First Aid facilities. Management responsibilities also include the provision of training so that new employees are fully aware of the correct method of using any machinery and of dangers that must be avoided. Management must provide not only a safe place for working but safe working methods. There must be adequate supervision provided and this is especially important where trainees are using new machines or new processes. Any machinery that is improperly guarded must be corrected by the seller. It is no longer an excuse to say that it was imported as the importer has a clear responsibility for seeing that the machinery is safe for use. Designers must also ensure that full and adequate instructions are available relating to the correct use of their products. Appropriate research must be carried out to determine a product's safety.

In the final analysis the greatest source of danger is not machinery but the human element. This accounts for about 80% of all accidents. The Act lays down quite clearly that all employees have a responsibility to work in a manner which does not endanger themselves or anyone else.

Workers must be co-operative with manangement in ensuring that safety regulations are met and must not misuse any items of safety equipment. Management's duties do not end with providing safe places of work, safe methods and training. They must continually check to see that people have not slipped into dangerous practices such as not wearing safety headwear or eye shields simply because they can be uncomfortable.

THE HEALTH AND SAFETY INSPECTORATE

The Inspectorate and the Executive of the Health & Safety Commission are continually trying to improve safety measures and legislation in the light of changes in organisational practices. If the regulations are broken the Inspectorate can prosecute the organisation, or in certain cases the individual offender. This is a slow process and the Inspectorate has more immediate powers. Inspectors have wide powers of entry and can call people who have been witnesses to any accidents. They can order offending machines, processes or even people to change to safer methods. To do this they can serve an 'improvement notice' requiring changes to be made by a given date or an immediate 'prohibition notice' stopping an operation if there is a risk of immediate danger to workers or the general public. The Inspectorate is also able to give advice but expects organisations to be able to settle the majority of their own disputes.

SAFETY REPRESENTATIVES AND SAFETY COMMITTEES

Trade Union Safety Representatives have the right to Safety Training and, after consultation with management, to make arrangements to promote, develop and check safety measures. They will carry out the following functions:-

    (i)   Investigate potential hazards or dangerous occurrence at work and examine the causes of accidents;

    (ii)   Investigate employee complaints about health, safety and welfare at work;

    (iii)   Make representations to the employer about any matters arising from investigation;

    (iv)   Keep up to date with information from the Inspectorate;

    (v)   Attend Safety committee meetings as a Safety Representative.

SAFETY COMMITTEES

Legislation cannot cover every minute detail of work. Clearly the processes carried out in different organisations will differ greatly. What is 'safe' is not always clear cut. For instance what would be a reasonable weight to ask someone to lift? It may depend on the individual, the size, the shape and awkwardness of the situation. For example, a practised lift of 25 kilos in one unbroken motion with a straight spine is less hazardous than leaning over to pick up a 4 kilo container from the boot of a car.

Where detailed regulations do not exist specific safety provisions may have to be agreed. Discussion must take place to reach an acceptable, reasonable and practicable solution. The Safety Committee, made up of interested representatives of management and employees, can provide an excellent basis for consultative decision making on safety matters and a 'watchdog' on incidents caused by change. The chairman is usually a senior manager and the meeting usually takes place at regular intervals. One of the Committee's responsibilities is to study reports of accidents and recommend appropriate action which will help to avoid their reoccurence. The committee must also ensure that the maximum publicity is given to any measure designed to improve safety. Senior management should make a speedy reply to the Committee's recommendations and take the necessary action as soon as possible. The committee and its members should also encourage employees to take an interest in safety affairs.

The Safety Committee should be seen as a co-operative venture involving consultations between workers and management. It is important if the committee is to work effectively, that there is good communication between the management and the committee and between the committee and employees. There must be a genuine desire on the part of the management to gain ideas and commitment from employees with regard to safety matters. Employees must also genuinely wish to see better standards of health and safety at the work place. If either management or workforce pays only 'lip-service' to their obligations then the legislation and Inspectorate can only have limited success. Fines may have only limited effect on an organisation, but a commitment to safety by all members of the organisation will produce savings not only in pain and injury but also in the costs of operation and provide a real opportunity for co-operation and participation.

ASSIGNMENT — THE NURSES ROTA

A group of nurses met together for a reunion after not seeing each other for many years. They talked about 'the old days' and how their hospitals were managed. At one time the union had successfully fought for a reduction in the hours they had to work each week. Naturally, there still had to be a continuous nursing presence on the wards for patient care. With each nurse working less hours per week, there had to be changes in the shift and rota arrangements. For many nurses, changes in their start and finishing times caused social or transport problems.

One nurse, Joan, said that in her hospital there had been runours about how the problem would be solved until one day the matron pinned up on the staff notice-board a list of the new working arrangements. A number of nurses were upset at the new rotas and shift times but little could be done and there were some who applied to work in other hospitals.

Jill, another nurse, recalled that the ward sisters were called to a meeting organised by the matron. Afterwards each ward sister called their own staff together for a meeting. The sister explained what the new plans were for future working arrangements. The benefits of the new arrangements were stressed and questions were invited, although some said afterwards that queries seemed to do little good when the management's mind seemed to be made up as to what was best for them. June said that in her hospital the ward sisters were instructed to have discussions with their own nurses about the problems of change. The ward sisters then attended a meeting chaired by the matron where the various viewpoints put forward by the staff were discussed. Minutes were taken at the meeting where much discussion took place. Within a week of the meeting the matron sent a copy of the new arrangements to all staff and the new arrangements seemed to take account of many of the points raised at the previous meeting.

TASK

1. As assistant to the Regional Personnel Officer of the Area Health Authority you have been asked to write a report on management styles in the health service. Using the above information you should deal with the following:

    (a) identify the possible social and other problems that nurses of different ages and circumstances may have with changes in shift times and work rotas;

    (b) analyse the incidents described by Joan, Jill and June and describe the management styles that were exhibited;

    (c) suggest the management style that would be most effective, giving reasons for your choice;

    (d) suggest possible situations where the other two management styles may be appropriate.

DEVELOPMENTAL TASK

2. Question family, friends and fellow students and discover whether any major changes have been made to their work patterns and how management handled the change. Write short notes on any examples you identify and orally present the examples to small groups for discussion.

14/01/88

ASSIGNMENT — TELECOMMUNICATIONS CHANGE

Telco Ltd. is a divison of a large international organisation and for the last fifty years has had a good reputation as a supplier of products to the telecommunications industry. In the past the telephone operating equipment was mechanical or electro-mechanical in operation. There were a large number of moving parts, needing not only careful manufacturing but considerable skill in assembly, which required dexterity and experience. There had been some previous trials with electronic equipment, which required few moving parts, but the trials usually showed the limitations of the new technology and were unreliable in operation. Telco pressed ahead with its research and development as it knew that its competitors, at home and abroad, were doing the same and it wished to keep its name as a main supplier of the best equipment. If a new development was sufficiently attractive to the main users, then the replacement of the original installations would bring in good profits and new orders for at least the next ten years.

One day the company announced proudly that it had developed a reliable and versatile electronic product, which had shown in trials to be a valuable replacement for the present equipment. The company realised that some of its <u>competitors</u> had approval for similar equipment and production had to start as soon as possible and be of high quality. Although the new product meant new orders, less manpower was needed and few of the old skills with the mechanical components were needed. For example the relays, which could be seen to open and shut and required skilful precision adjustment, were replaced by the 'black-box' electronic devices bought from another supplier. The working of these devices were known to few employees and they needed no adjustment. Previously hundreds of components were finally connected together by skilled workers, who were able to decipher complex wiring diagrams and correctly wire and solder together the appropriate parts. Now the process was one of connecting together a much smaller number of sealed units and simple wiring diagrams and techniques were all that were needed. These skills were quickly taught but the skill and experience of the older workers now became of little value. Many of the older workers preferred early retirement rather than transfer to new work in the restructured departments. Some of the old sections were amalgamated and many of the managers were given new posts or offered early retirement or voluntary redundancy. The changing tasks of the trainers meant that new training staff were needed. Counselling sessions were necessary before any changes were made, in order to help the workforce to readjust. Supervisory staff had to learn new skills in personnel management and communication. The exercise was completed in planned and recognised stages and it took nearly two years before all the changes were all carried out and working satisfactorily and the company was operating profitably.

TASK

1. Assume the role of a Planning Department assistant from head office who has come to write a report on the changes so that lessons can be learned for future operations. Your report should contain the following:

    (a) an assessment of the external conditions that promoted the change and the internal strengths and weaknesses of the organisation;

    (b) an analysis of the problems for the employees caused by the changes;

    (c) a description of possible action which should be taken to help the employees overcome their problems.

DEVELOPMENTAL TASK

2. Undertake a role play exercise in which there is a meeting between management and a group of the workers (including their trade union represesentatives) in order to discuss an impending major change.

Finance

Chapter 11

PERSONAL FINANCE

One of the most important problems facing us all in our day-to-day lives is the management of our finances. As a young person you may not have the financial responsibilities of a family or a mortgage but doubtless from the moment you gained some degree of financial independence you will have encountered the problem of making ends meet. If you are a millionaire then this chapter is perhaps less relevant to you as many of the financial troubles which worry the average person will not be a concern. In fact you should turn to the section on investment on page 209 where you may gain some advice on the best means of keeping and adding to your wealth. However, let us assume that in common with the majority of people, the amount of money you have or can earn is insufficient to satisfy your every need. At some time in your life you will have financial difficulties. This chapter will offer some advice and guidance as to how best to manage your money and so minimise your financial problems.

YOUR PERSONAL BUDGET

Each individual is different. We all have different personal circumstances and varying wants and needs. As a college student it is likely you are single, living with your family, and share many of the tastes of your contemporaries. You will want to have nice clothes, enjoy holidays and have sufficient spending money left so that you can go out and relax at a disco or cinema. The total cost of these items taken over a year will represent a considerable part of your annual expenditure. It is possible to break this spending down into two categories:

      (i) current or revenue spending; and

      (ii) capital spending.

(i) Current or revenue spending

Unless you are a dedicated home-lover you will want to go out quite often. If you are working you may have to pay rent or board every week or month. And unless you buy very hard wearing clothes, you will need to replace shoes, coats and jeans as they become shabby or unfashionable. Every lunch time when you start to get hunger pangs you will go off to buy a meal or a snack. All of these items have one factor in common. They are bought on a regular basis. Such expenditure is described as current spending. Because of its regular nature you can anticipate how much you will spend on each category on a weekly basis, with a reasonable degree of accuracy. As we will see later in the chapter if this current spending is consistently greater than your regular income you will go deeper and deeper into debt. So it is worth assessing how much you spend in this way as it will give you some idea as to the extent to which you may have to trim your present life style, or the extra cash you have available for the second category of spending.

(ii) Capital spending

Have you ever stood in front of a shop window and gazed at the latest stereo system? If you can imagine it taking pride of place in your home probably it will be the price tag which will next attract your attention. You may own a car or a motor bike or wish to have one in the future. All these products fall into the category of capital expenditure. They are essentially one-off purchases which you will make only when you feel that you have sufficient spare cash to be able to afford them immediately, or you think that your future income will give you enough surplus to be able to pay the credit repayments. However there is a need for an element of caution. Your circumstances may change and your income may fall. You should not commit yourself to long term repayments which you are not confident of meeting. This is perhaps one of the first lessons of personal budgeting. Live within your current income where possible and do not be over optimistic about your future income. A repayment period may last for perhaps three years and how many of us can confidently predict our personal circumstances so far ahead?

We will be returning to these categories of spending when we examine the financial management of organisations so it is important to be clear about the distinction.

Taken together your current/revenue and capital expenditure make up your annual outgoings. As we have already stated there can be no set figure for this. It will depend on your own particular circumstances, personality and buying habits. However the major influence on your level of expenditure will be your current and anticipated level of income and your accumulated wealth. Let us now consider your income.

Personal income

In order to effectively manage your finances you should have a reasonable idea of your regular income If you are employed this will consist of your regular weekly wage. Alternatively if you receive a grant you should be aware of the amount the local authority will give you at the beginning of each term. Of course you may have neither of these sources of income and instead may have to rely on social security payments or a weekly allowance from your family. Whatever the source of their income most people have a specific sum on which they can regularly rely. Use this as the basis of your budget calculations. It is foolish to include irregular payments such as overtime which is occasionally offered at work or an extra few pounds from a doting grandparent who you see now and again. Worse still would be the inclusion of the £50,000 which you confidently expect to win on the pools. Such payments provide the surplus cash to allow you to finance additional capital spending but should not form part of the calculation on which you base your regular current expenditure, for they are erratic and unpredictable.

An important point to bear in mind when calculating your income is to base it on the net figure. By this we mean that you should subtract any deductions which are made at source such as PAYE or National Insurance contributions. We will consider these in some detail a little later in the chapter. Furthermore do not assume that your income will continue at the current level unless you can be sure that this will be so. A temporary part time shop job may only last through the store's busy periods.

When you have carried out these calculations you should be reasonably sure of your income. Adjust your spending patterns to this income level and try not to anticipate increases in your income of which you are not certain. A few useful guidelines may keep you within your personal budget:

1. Be realistic in your regular spending habits. It is perfectly acceptable to have the occasional extravagance but be wary of regularly spending money on unnecessary items.

2. If you have to economise then do it sensibly. You cannot survive without food and clothing and living in a cardboard box behind Waterloo station will not be fun, especially during the winter.

3. Try to budget in a way that will allow you at least some luxuries. Life can be very boring if you cannot afford at least the occasional extravagance.

4. Save some money for the unexpected 'rainy day'. It is impossible to try to run a

car if you have not anticipated the problem of a major repair bill. A few pounds saved in a bank or the building society will not only provide you with a sense of growing wealth but also give you some 'insurance' should a large bill suddenly appear.

Thus the key to successful budgeting is to be clear as to your income, be aware of your expenditure and save a little if at all possible. If you find that your level of spending does exceed your income then make appropriate cuts in spending immediately. Do not get depressed when you are short of money and take the attitude of some people that the only way to cheer yourself up is to go out and buy something! You will find that a sensible budget brings with it its own rewards. You will reduce your financial worries and improve your mental state. So the trick to budgeting successfully is, whenever possible, to maximise your income while keeping control of your outgoings. If you do find that you are facing financial difficulties then you should seek help from the possible sources of personal finance. This will form the next part of this chapter.

SOURCES OF PERSONAL FINANCE

Many people have the mistaken impression that borrowing money is in some way wrong. They feel that everyone should live within their budget and getting into debt is the first step on the road to financial ruin. This is a rather old fashioned attitude as credit has now become part of everyday life for most of us. We may find ourselves with a temporary cash shortage as bills pile up and money we are owed has not been paid. In such circumstances we may be able to gain the benefit of a short term loan to ease the immediate difficulty. Additionally many of us enter into much longer term credit agreements by taking out a mortgage to purchase our home or buying a piece of furniture or a car on hire purchase. As we stressed earlier when discussing personal budgets it is obviously foolish to take on financial commitments which you will never be able to meet. Nevertheless, it is possible, and in many respects sensible, to anticipate certain future income and use it as the basis for borrowing so that you may enjoy some of the better things in life now rather than later. You may also ease an immediate financial difficulty instead of allowing it to become a more pressing worry.

You may believe that anything worth having is worth saving for. Yet imagine trying to save money from your weekly income to buy a £30,000 house. You would be too old to enjoy it even before you moved in. Thus it is clearly a better proposition to borrow the money on a mortgage and so be able to enjoy a decent home while you are paying for it. What is more we shall see that the government positively encourages people to borrow money in this way by allowing them tax relief on mortgage interest payments while at the same time it penalises savers by taxing them on the investment income.

The post war period has seen a massive growth in personal borrowing. This has been the result of an increasing acceptance by many people of using credit as a means of finance. It is also due to a greater degree of sophistication in the financial system which has meant that more and more people can be regarded as being 'credit worthy' and so suitable for a loan from one of the financial instititutions. This development has occured as the number of people with bank accounts has risen. Once a bank has had a customer as a current account or savings account client for an appropriate period, it is able to assess the person's financial record and so may feel sufficiently confident to offer a loan. Similarly a building society or hire purchase company will make enquiries into a potential borrower's 'credit status' to try and find out whether or not they are likely to be able to repay the loan or whether they have ever defaulted on a loan in the past. Lenders will be particularly careful in the light of consumer credit legislation which increases the rights of borrowers in the event of a loan not being repaid in accordance with the initial agreement.

The type of security which was required in the past to back a loan was usually in the form of some sort of physical asset such as a house or other property, or some type of financial guarantee such as a life insurance policy. While such security may still be necessary for some loans, increasingly a secure job with a guaranteed income and settled personal circumstances is now sufficient to give the lender confidence that the borrower is likely to repay the loan.

It is vitally important at this point that we stress some of the pitfalls involved in borrowing. With the range of credit facilities so readily available in todays economy there is a great temptation for people to get into too much debt. It is a very simple matter to sign a hire purchase agreement once you are over the age of 18. Many companies will supply young people with credit cards. Most of the large department stores have their own credit facilities which allow the customer to run up substantial debts. The sources of temptation are many and those who are inexperienced or unskilled in money management can easily find themselves with not one but a series of debts. Remember these organisations are lending you money not for any altruistic reason but for commercial reasons. You have to pay interest on these debts and this will continue to build up as long as the debt remains unpaid. We shall see later that the level of interest charged is often highest on those forms of credit which are most easily obtained. This is because a greater number of people will default on such loans and so the lending organisation spreads the cost of such losses by increasing the interest to all who borrow in such a way. So do not overstretch yourself by borrowing, more people end up in court through being unable to pay their debts than for almost any other reason. So with that cautionary note let us lead you through the various sources of finance and advise both where and when not to borrow.

THE COMMERCIAL BANKS AS PROVIDERS OF PERSONAL FINANCE

For the majority of people the most common source of personal finance is a bank. To be more precise we refer to the high street banks as the 'commercial clearing banks' because they operate within a joint process known as the clearing system. This simply means that they exchange the cheques deposited in one bank against the account in another bank of the person who made out the cheque. Without an effective clearing system you would only be able to make out cheques to people or organisations who held an account in the same bank as yourself. Therefore the system allows major transactions to be carried out using cheques and so reduces our reliance on cash transactions. Most cheques can be 'cleared' within three working days although there may be some delay and you should be careful not to assume that a cheque has been cleared before about five working days have elapsed.

As well as providing the mechanism by which most money transfers can be made, the commercial banks are also vital to the economy in their role as sources of credit and as institutions which will accept savings and pay a level of interest in return. Thus they act as 'middle men' between the saver or investor who has money he wishes to lend and earn interest on, and the borrower who seeks funds and is willing to pay interest to borrow them. Because of this function the commercial banks are known as 'financial intermediaries'. They provide a sophisticated financial system without which many individuals and organisations could not survive. Other financial organisations which perform a similar function include the building societies and the finance houses. These are referred to as 'non bank financial intermediaries' or NBFI's. We will look at the NBFI's as a source of personal finance later in the chapter but first we will examine the different ways in which the commercial banks provide finance to the individual.

FORMS OF BANK LENDING

Overdrafts

An overdraft is the cheapest way to borrow money from a commercial bank. To obtain an overdraft you must have a current account with the bank. A current account is a normal cheque account which allows you to deposit cash and cheques into the account and withdraw money by using either cheques, standing orders or other forms of bank transfer. We will consider current accounts a little later when we look at forms of saving. In the context of seeking to borrow money from a bank you will need to have operated a current account with the bank for some time. The exact length of time the account has had to be running varies from bank to bank. If you have kept your account in credit, or 'in the black' as it is sometimes called, the bank will accept that you are managing your financial affairs in a sensible manner. Also your wage or salary may be paid directly into your account by your employer and the bank will see this regular deposit and be confident about your financial stability. However if you have allowed your current account to go into debit, or 'into the red' without the banks agreement, then they may regard you as being rather cavalier in your attitude to money management and so you will have a lower credit rating with the bank. Therefore if you are going to ask the bank for an overdraft you are in a much stronger position if you have previously stayed in credit.

The advantage of an overdraft, or overdraft facility as it is often called, is that you will only be required to pay interest on the amount owed on a daily basis. Thus the bank may have given you an overdraft facility of £200 but on a particular day you are only £50 overdrawn. Interest is due only on the £50 and not on the £200 which is the potential loan. Overdrafts are also a relatively cheap way to borrow. The rate you pay depends on two factors:

(i)   the current base rate of the bank. This is the interest rate the bank will charge to those borrowers who have extremely good security; and

(ii) your credit standing with your bank.

Together these two factors influence the overdraft rate you will be asked to pay. For instance if the base rate is 10% then the bank may ask 2% more for all overdrafts plus an extra percentage according to the status of the borrower. Therefore a person regarded as being a poor credit risk may be asked to pay 10% base rate plus 2% overdraft rate plus another 2% because of their credit standing. 14% in all.

Getting an overdraft is not always easy. The bank may ask questions about what the loan is for and may even advise the borrower as to his level of current spending if they regard this as being too high in relation to his income. They will set a time limit on the length of the overdraft and will normally keep to this unless an extension is negotiated. However most banks are usually sympathetic to a customer who they know and will normally provide reasonable overdraft facilities.

Perhaps at this point we should offer a word of warning. It is very unwise to ask the bank for an overdraft and mislead them about its purpose. An overdraft is not a means of living on credit for life. As we have already noted the overdraft will have a fixed time limit and the bank will wish to see it repaid promptly. If you abuse your overdraft facilities the bank will not look kindly on any future requests and a bad credit rating can be difficult to live down. The bank may also require a guarantor to agree to cover the loan should the actual borrower default on repayment. This person may be a parent or a friend who has assets sufficient to cover the loan. But remember that if you cannot repay the overdraft when it is due, the guarantor will be forced to do so. Many young people have found their relationship with friends or family deteriorate when the latter have acted as guarantors and been forced to pay up in the end.

Personal loans

A personal loan is a fixed term loan usually for a specific purpose such as the purchase of a car. They are normally more expensive than overdrafts as the interest is calculated on the total amount of the loan which is given at the time it is arranged. It is normally repaid on a regular monthly basis and the interest is then calculated on the reducing balance. They have the advantage of imposing a discipline on the borrower to repay regularly and the loan may be spread over a number of years. But as we have said they are usually more expensive than overdrafts and the bank will require you to keep your current account in credit while you have a personal loan with them. However they are a better way of borrowing than hire purchase to make large purchases if your credit rating is good, for the interest will be considerably less.

As with all borrowing on a relatively large scale, it is unwise to take on a large personal loan if you will be unable to meet the commitments. Thus the bank will want details of your present and

. . . found their relationship with friends or family deteriorate. . .

future income to reassure themselves that you are not going to overstretch yourself financially. In the same way as with an overdraft, you will have a much better chance of being given a personal loan if you have a reasonably good banking history.

Budget accounts

Most of the commercial banks offer this service but it is given different titles by some of the banks. It may be called a 'budget account' or a 'cashflow account' but whatever its name all budget accounts normally operate in the same way. The idea behind them is that they should allow you to manage your finances more effectively. It is probable that you will have different expenses occuring at different times of the year. So for instance major bills like gas, electricity, car tax and insurance come either quarterly, half yearly or annually. It is likely that you will spend quite a lot of money at Christmas when you generously buy presents or over-indulge yourself. Holidays are also expensive and their cost is concentrated in one part of the year. The difficulty is that you will normally be paid on a regular weekly or monthly basis throughout the year and the temptation is to spend your money as you get it so leaving yourself short of cash when the large bills drop through the letterbox.

A budget account therefore requires you to make a regular monthly payment which is taken directly from your current account and transferred into the budget account. The amount you choose to transfer each month then determines the credit limit the bank will allow you on your budget account. The limit varies from bank to bank but may range from 12 times your monthly transfer to 36 times the amount. Assume it to be 24 times. Thus if you were to transfer £20 per month you would then have £480 available credit to pay your bills.

Naturally if you draw more out of the account than the amount you have accumulated from your monthly transfers this will mean that you have to pay interest. But such an account does allow you to spread the cost of large bills evenly throughout the year. You will be given a separate cheque book to make withdrawals from the budget account and some banks now offer interest payable to you if the budget account is in credit. Unfortunately the rate of interest on money borrowed in this way is high in comparison to a normal overdraft facility or a personal loan, and you may be tempted to simply run the account up to its limit and be unable to get it back into credit with your monthly transfers. Therefore a budget account, like all forms of credit must be treated with caution.

OTHER FORMS OF PERSONAL BORROWING

As we noted at the beginning of this section there has been a rapid increase in personal credit in the post war period. This has been partly the result of changing attitudes to credit and a feeling that it is more socially acceptable, but also because of the growth of the financial institutions willing to provide credit. In this section we will look at borrowing from the Non Bank Financial Intermediaries (NFBI's) and in particular at the process of borrowing through hire purchase from the finance houses, by the use of credit cards and through a mortgage from a building society.

Hire Purchase

This form of credit is a very popular way of purchasing large consumer items such as cars, electrical goods and furniture. However it can be a rather expensive way of borrowing. Let us begin by considering the legal process of hire purchase. First we should make it clear that there are in fact two different types of legal agreement which you can enter into which many people wrongly describe under the general term 'hire purchase'. These are:

> (i)   hire purchase; and
>
> (ii) credit sales.

(i)   Hire Purchase

This is not a simple purchase of a product. What actually happens is that a finance company buys the car, refrigerator or stereo from the seller and then 'hires' them to the consumer, who agrees to make regular payments to the finance company until the full value of the goods plus interest is paid. The goods remain the property of the finance company until the final payment is made. Because the consumer does not own the goods until the end of the agreement there are important legal implications relating to default on payments, resale of the goods or damage to the goods prior to the final payment.

In the case of default on payments the law states that if less than one third of what is owed has not been paid before the payments fall into default the finance company has the right to repossess the goods without reference to the courts. If more than one third has been paid, the company must seek a court order to repossess and in such circumstances the court may review the agreement and order that lower repayments should be made over a longer period. Alternatively it may simply grant an order allowing the company to take back the goods. Of course the hire purchase company many not wish to take you to court as the value of repossessed goods will normally be low. It may therefore be willing to renegotiate repayments and the time period for those who face financial problems.

As the consumer is not the legal owner until all payments have been made he cannot resell the goods until the agreement ends. This can be a problem for those who run into financial difficulties while they still have hire purchase commitments. Finally as the goods are still the property of the finance company until they are paid for, the hirer will often be required to keep them in a good condition until the ownership passes at the end of the repayments.

(ii) Credit Sales

With a credit sale, ownership of the goods passes to the consumer immediately. However he will still have to repay the finance company the full amount for the goods plus interest by regular payments. There is an important legal difference between credit sales and hire purchase. In a credit sale if you default on payment the credit company may require the full amount immediately, even if one third of the amount owed has already been paid. If the full amount is not forthcoming the goods can be reclaimed. However as the purchaser is the legal owner he can treat the goods as he wishes and resell them as long as the finance company is paid what it is owed.

Some general points about both hire purchase agreements and credit purchases should be made. The first is that you will not be allowed to enter into either if you have a bad credit rating. This usually means that you have defaulted on some form of credit agreement in the past. Most of the large credit companies hold computer records of consumers' credit ratings and specialised agencies keep track of poor creditors. These records are available to all credit companies so it is no good being a bad payer with one company and hoping that you can get credit easily with another.

Another major disadvantage of gaining credit in this way is that the interest rates are usually very high. The reason for this is simple. Finance companies find that many of their borrowers default. They have to repossess goods which have fallen in value or the court orders repayments over a very long time which is clearly to the lender's disadvantage. Some people simply disappear with the goods without completing payment. Therefore the finance companies must take account of substantial bad debts. To cover themselves they charge very high rates of interest to all borrowers so that those of us who do repay on time are penalised by those who default. Occasionally you may find some credit companies which offer special low interest or even 'interest free' deals on certain products. If you find these they are usually well worth considering but these tend to be somewhat our of the ordinary. Therefore generally if you want to buy a large item on credit, you have a bank account and your credit standing with the bank is good, then borrow the money through a personal loan rather than through a hire purchase or credit sale agreement. It will work out much cheaper.

MORTGAGES

For many of us the largest expenditure in our lives will be the purchase of a house. It is likely to cost thousands of pounds and unless you are extremely wealthy you will have to borrow the money. The most common form of borrowing for house purchase is through a mortgage. It will normally come from a building society although the commercial banks are increasingly becoming involved in mortgage lending. The process is the same whichever source you choose. It is somewhat similar to a hire purchase agreement in that when you take out a mortgage to buy your house the building society or bank will hold the deeds of the property until the intitial sum advanced plus the interest is repaid. However they differ from hire purchase in that you are usually free to do most things with the property, except to sub-let it without the lender's permission. Also you can sell the house when you wish and then repay the outstanding mortgage from the proceeds of the sale. The annual rise in house prices in many parts of the country, especially London and the South East, exceeds the inflation rate, so house owning can be a valuable means of building up capital. As the value of your house increases so does your equity in it. The equity which you have in your house is that part of the market value which is left after deducting the remainder of the mortgage. A mortgage normally has a much longer term than a hire purchase agreement. Most mortgage periods are for 25 years although they may be longer or shorter depending on the age and circumstances of both the borrower and the property. There are a number of major advantages of buying a house through a mortgage. These include:

1. Tax relief is given on the mortgage interest up to a limit of £30,000. This means that the mortgage repayments will carry a much lower interest rate in real terms for anyone who is both a tax payer and holds a mortgage.

2. The monthly repayments are the same throughout the period of the mortgage subject to fluctuations in interest rates. This means that if inflation continues to

rise over the 25 year period the burden of the repayments gradually reduces in real terms as incomes rise.

3.   It is usually possible to take out life assurance to cover the mortgage so that if you die before it is cleared the insurance company will pay off the remaining amount and the property will pass to your heirs.

As we have said the commercial banks are increasing the number of mortgages that they wish to offer. This has meant greater competition for potential mortgage borrowers and so should mean lower interest rates. Unfortunately the mortgage rate is closely tied to overall interest rates and it is the fluctuations in interest rates as a whole which are most important in determining the mortgage rates offered by both the banks and the building societies.

Other types of mortgages include (i) endowment linked mortgages offered by the insurance companies which usually carry a higher rate of interest but also provide both life insurance cover and a lump sum payable to the borrower when the mortgage is completed; and (ii) fixed interest mortgage which, as their name suggests, have a mortgage rate which does not vary. These are fine if the interest rate is low when they are taken out but can be very expensive if the initial mortgage fixed is high and other rates begin to fall. For this reason they are not very common.

Getting a mortgage

There are normally two major factors determining whether or not a mortgage will be granted:

1.   The value, age and type of the property.

2.   The personal circumstances of the borrower.

1.   The property

The building society or bank which is lending the money will have to ensure that the property which is its security on the mortgage has a value which is at least equal to the size of the loan. Therefore it will have the property valued by a surveyor who will look at its location, condition and assess a market value. Some building societies are reluctant to advance money on certain types of property. So for instance it may be more difficult to find a lender for a mortgage on a flat which is part of a converted old house. The mortgage offer may also only be a percentage of the value of the property depending on the age of the property, (for example only 80% may be offered on old houses), or the status of the buyer, so a second time buyer is less likely to get a 100% mortgage than a first time buyer.

2.   The borrower

The building society or bank will wish to be sure that the borrower will be able to repay the mortgage. Despite the fact that it holds the security of the deeds to the property it will not want to have to take possession as this will involve the difficulties of eviction and resale. Therefore the borrower will have to show that he or she has a regular, relatively secure income and has other outgoings that will leave sufficient to pay the mortgage. In fact the building society will undertake a similar personal budgeting exercise to the one we discussed earlier in the chapter. It is difficult to generalise for all building societies and banks but it is usual to find that a mortgage will not be given which is greater than two and a half times the person's income. Some lender's may be a little more flexible. If a married couple seek a mortgage the general rule is two and a half times the husband's salary plus once times the wife's, doubtless a rather sexist approach.

Building societies and banks will also give mortgages for home improvements such as double glazing or central heating but they will often charge a higher rate for any such additional loans.

. . . depending on the age of the property . . . or the status of the buyer . . .

OTHER FORMS OF CREDIT — CREDIT CARDS

The most significant and widespread growth in credit in the last twenty years in this country has emerged through the introduction of credit cards. Today more than ten million people in the U.K. have some form of credit card. They provide immediately accessible credit and have revolutionised consumer purchasing. They are the first step to what is called the 'cashless' society where we need no longer carry cash or cheque book but instead use 'plastic money'. They allow the card holder to spread the cost of purchasing if necessary over a period of months or years. But one should remember they are in fact simply another way of borrowing money. There are basically three types of credit cards:

1. Bank credit cards

2. Charge cards

3. Commercial trading organisations charge account credit cards.

1. Bank credit cards

The most widely used bank credit cards are Visa and Access. Both cards are provided by groups of banks. Visa is the name of an international credit payments system which in this country includes Barclays, the Bank of Scotland, the Trustees Savings Bank, the Yorkshire Bank and the Cooperative Bank. Access was established by Lloyds, the Midland, the National Westminster, the Clydesdale Bank, the Royal Bank of Scotland, the Northern Ulster Bank and the Bank of Ireland. It is associated with the Mastercharge system which is similar to Visa in its world wide network.

Such credit cards have the advantage of being accepted not only throughout Britain but also throughout the world. They also provide a certain period of 'free' credit because the outstanding balance is not payable for about three weeks after the card holder receives the monthly statement. This means that you can purchase a product using your credit card early in your credit period and not have to pay for it for almost two months. This is very attractive if you are able to settle the credit card bill in full each month.

The interest rate charged on any amount which is left unpaid is rather high, and as only a minimum payment is necessary each month, there is a temptation to allow the debt to rise to the credit limit leaving a continuing debt which may be difficult to repay. In fact many people have been made bankrupt by such mis-management of credit cards. The credit card companies are in the business of making a profit by lending money so they will increase a card holder's limit which may lead to further debt. The banks nevertheless pursue a policy of encouraging their customers to apply for whichever credit card system the bank belongs to.

2.   Independent Charge Cards

A different type of credit card is the charge card. The two most widely known are Diners Club and American Express. Like Visa and Access they can be used world wide. The difference between them and normal credit cards is that the outstanding balance should be paid off immediately, although they do allow up to two months free credit. Thus they do not allow the long term debt spreading of Visa and Access but prevent a card holder building up extensive debts over a period, which cannot easily be paid off.

3.   Commercial Trading Organisations Charge Account Credit Cards

The large department stores recognised the widespread use of Visa and Access and many have now introduced their own credit cards. They are similar to other credit cards in that no interest is charged on bills which are settled immediately but the company will charge quite high interest on outstanding amounts. Like the other cards the holders will be given a specified credit limit or ceiling but the main disadvantage is that they can only be used in the store or chain of stores which issues them.

MONEY LENDERS

The final source of personal finance we shall consider in this section is the use of money lenders or credit brokers. This source has been left until last because that is what it is — a last resort. There are currently over 2,000 legitimate licensed money lenders in Britain, as well as many more whose activities are both unscrupulous and unlawful. They advertise in the newspapers offering immediate cash loans which may be secured or unsecured. Normally their interest rates are ridiculously high. This is because anyone who has an acceptable credit rating will borrow money elsewhere and so only those who are desperate and cannot get finance from a bank will turn to money lenders. Not only are their interest rates high, they are notorious for their pursuit of bad debts and will quite happily bankrupt those who cannot repay money they owe. It cannot be stressed too strongly that such sources of finance should be avoided if at all possible. Many people turn to them because they are frightened of banks and are able to find immediate offers of money from the money lenders. Despite the somewhat intimidating impression of banks they are in the long run a much better bet as a source of finance than the money lenders.

. . . unscrupulous and unlawful.

PERSONAL SAVINGS AND INVESTMENT

In the previous section we assumed that there are going to be times in your life when you will need to raise finance. Hopefully there will be other times when your personal budget is such that you will have money to spare. In this section we will examine the main forms of personal savings and investment. While these terms are often used to refer to the same sort of activity, there is a specific difference. Saving does not usually involve the risk of losing your initial sum. As a consequence of this lack of risk the interest rate that savings schemes offer will be lower. Investment involves an element of risk. Of course some investments are relatively safe and so will attract individuals who wish to be sure of a relatively guaranteed return on their investment. Other forms of investment may result in a fall in value or even a total loss of the money invested. Because of this they should also provide a higher rate of return. We will concentrate on investing in financial organisations so if you are interested in other forms of saving and investment such as saving stamps or old masters as a way of making money then you will need to consult another book.

There are three main methods of savings and investments. These are:

     a.   the commercial banks

     b.   other forms of personal savings

     c.   investment in stocks and shares.

a. SAVING WITH THE COMMERCIAL BANKS

The two most common forms of bank account are the current account and the deposit account.

The current account is sometimes referred to as a cheque account as you will receive a cheque book when you open the account. This allows you to withdraw cash or to make transactions by signing cheques. You can also instruct your bank to make regular payments, such as monthly mortgage or HP repayments, from your current account by issuing a standing order. A current account should not be regarded as a savings account for you will not be paid any interest if you are in credit and may well be asked to pay bank charges if you go into debit.

The commercial banks do however offer a variety of deposit acounts which have differing rates of interest. The rate offered is usually linked to the length of notice you are required to give prior to withdrawal. For this reason they are technically called 'time deposits'. An ordinary deposit account will normally require seven days notice of withdrawal although this may be waived if the depositor agrees to forgo the previous week's interest. Longer term deposit requirements range from months to years and as the notice required gets longer the interest rate increases. This is because in order to pay the depositor interest on the deposit the bank needs to lend this money out to borrowers. However it must cover itself against a possible withdrawal of a deposit by holding some of it in cash. Obviously it can confidently lend out money which has been placed on a five year deposit as it knows the depositor cannot withdraw it until the time has expired. The banks are willing to pay for this greater security by giving a higher interest rate. Of course money in a current account may be withdrawn at any time. It is technically called a 'sight deposit' as money can be withdrawn 'on sight'. Because of this the banks must hold a much higher percentage of current account deposits as cash in their tills and so will not offer an interest rate to those whose current account is in credit.

The rate of interest paid on all types of deposit account is governed by the bank's base rate. Deposit rates are always lower than the base rate and borrowing rates are always higher. This allows the banks to make a profit on the difference between the interest it charges to borrowers and the rate it pays to depositors. As the base rate goes up and down, the lending rates and deposit rates rise and fall correspondingly.

Despite the attractions of bank deposit accounts they can have some major disadvantages. Money can only be withdrawn at the branch where the deposit account is held and income tax on the interest is paid directly by the bank. This is a major disadvantage to those whose income is so low that they would not be required to pay tax on the interest on other forms of saving.

OTHER FORMS OF PERSONAL SAVING

The two other ways to save money are with either:

> (i)   the government; or
>
> (ii)   other financial bodies.

(i)   Saving with the government

The most important form of personal saving with the government is through National Savings. This is one of the only means of saving in which the interest income is not taxed at source. The government keeps this distinction because it needs to borrow money and this tax incentive attracts savers. We shall be considering borrowing as a source of income for the government in chapter 12.

Under the heading of National Saving there are a number of different means of saving:

> 1.   The National Savings Bank;
>
> 2.   National Savings Certificates and Index Linked Saving Certificates;
>
> 3.   Income and deposit bonds;
>
> 4.   Premium bonds.

1.   The National Savings Bank

The National Savings Bank uses as its outlets the branches of the Post Office and in fact was previously called the Post Office Savings Bank. It offers an ordinary account which is tax free for small amounts saved and an investment account for larger sums which carries a higher interest rate but which is liable for tax. However as we noted above the interest is not taxed at source and so will benefit those on low incomes who fall below the taxable limit. Both these accounts are essentially for relatively short term saving in which the money is readily accessible both in terms of the amount of notice required for withdrawal and their physical accessibility through any main Post Office.

2.   National Savings Certificates and Index Linked Certificates

These are specifically for medium and long term savings of say five years or more. A certificate is purchased by a saver when it is issued by the Department of National Savings (DNS) for a specified amount and then the initial payment plus interest is repaid when the certificate matures. With the normal issue savings certificates, the interest is determined when they are first purchased, however the DNS has also issued index linked certificates whose interest rate fluctuates with inflation. It is usually a few percentage points above the rate of inflation and such certificates are particularly attractive in times of high inflation.

3.   Income and deposit bonds

These are loans of fixed amounts such as £1000 to the government which provide a regular monthly income to the depositor rather than giving annual interest payment or only being cashable on maturity.

4.   Premium bonds

Unlike other forms of saving with the government, Premium bonds do not guarantee a rate of interest. In fact if you are unlucky and your number is not selected by the Electronic Random Number Indicator Equipment (called ERNIE) in the monthly draw then your initial investment will remain the same and actually fall in value in real terms if there is inflation. So premium bonds should not really be regarded as part of a savings plan but rather as a little 'flutter' instead of putting your money on the pools or horses and at least with ERNIE you may not win but you are always guaranteed your initial stake money back when you want to cash in the bonds.

(ii)   Saving with Building Societies

We have already discussed the role of the building societies in providing mortgages for home buyers. Of course in order to be able to provide these funds the societies have to attract savers who will deposit such funds. There are hundreds of building societies in this country ranging from the Halifax which claims to be the largest in the world to the small local society with only a few local branches. However the rates they offer to borrowers and lenders tend to be relatively similar. This is because they are mostly members of the Building Societies Association (BSA) which meets regularly to recommend a scale of interest rates which most societies adhere to. However there are some interest rate variations as some societies may find themselves short of funds and so offer higher deposit rates, or with surplus funds when they will drop their mortgage rate.

Saving with a building society is a very safe form of saving despite the occasional fraud scare because the BSA will guarantee to compensate any depositor whose money is lost with a member association. Interest rates offered are usually competitive with bank deposit accounts because the building societies are vying with the banks for the same savers. Similarly building society interest rates rise with the length of time of the deposit because the societies are more secure in making longer loans with long term funds. The interest rates offered by the societies however tend to fluctuate less than those offered by the banks as the societies prefer to see an overall change in the interest rate trend before making changes which are administratively expensive.

. . . . a little 'flutter'. . . .

INVESTMENT IN STOCKS AND SHARES

As we noted at the beginning of this section, investment involves some element of risk. Therefore it is not recommended for those who seek an absolutely safe form of saving. However it should not be regarded as the preserve of the rich. Investment in government stocks and bonds or in well established and regularly profitable public companies does not carry with it the dangers of total loss. Increasingly in this country as in many part of the western world there is a tendency for the small saver to look for higher rates of return and the added excitement of investing in stocks and shares.

Buying stocks and shares is a means of sharing in the ownership of a limited company. As a part owner of the business you benefit if it is profitable but alternatively if it is loss making you have to share some of the loss. Fortunately the nature of limited liability companies means that your liability as a share holder is limited to the amount of unpaid shares that you hold and so you are not personally responsible for all of the company's debts. The relationship between the shareholder and the limited liability company is discussed in some detail in chapter 18.

However let us assume that the company in which you buy shares is well managed and profitable. The shareholders benefit in two ways:

> (i)   the company will pay a dividend; and
>
> (ii)   the shares should rise in value.

(i)   The Share Dividend

If the company is profitable and the directors decide that the profit should be distributed to the shareholders they will declare a dividend. This is a payment per share held, for example 10p for each £1 share. It should be stressed that the dividend is based on the 'nominal' value of the share when it was initially issued and not on its current market value. So you may have bought a share for £1.75 on the stock exchange but its nominal value is only £1. If the dividend is 10p per £1 share you will only receive 10p, even though you paid more for the share.

Dividends are normally declared twice a year. The first corresponds to the first half year's trading of the company and is known as the 'interim dividend'. At the end of the company's financial year a 'final dividend' is declared which represents the distributed profit in the second half year's trading. Of course the directors are under no obligation to declare a dividend and will only do so if they judge that the company's profit position justifies the distribution of some of the profit to the shareholders.

(ii)   The Share Value

As each share represents a part ownership of the company's assets and its future profit potential, the value of the share will rise and fall with the company's trading performance. If other potential shareholders believe that a company is going to grow they will value a share more highly and so will be willing to pay a higher price for a share in its ownership. Thus the share's market value will rise. The opposite is the case if the belief is that the company is doing badly, the share value will fall. A further complication may be that some people are buying shares merely as a form of short term speculation and so may buy shares, wait until they rise in price and then sell them immediately so that they can gain the benefit of the short term profit. Thus a fall in a company's share value is not always a sign that the company is doing badly, merely that investors are turning their investment into cash. Investors who are taking a longer term view will hold onto their shares despite short term fluctuations in their value if they believe that the company's future is basically sound.

Taken together the dividend and the changes in the share value will provide the shareholder with a return on his investment. Therefore a shareholder in a company, which declares a small dividend because it wishes to reinvest its profit internally within the company, may be compensated by a large rise in the share value as the company's assets increase, and vice versa if a large dividend is declared but there is little company growth. Clearly the decision on whether or not to distribute profits as dividends is a complex one for the directors, who have to weigh up the objectives of the company for growth with the shareholders' desire for distributed profit. The decision depends on the interaction of objectives of the managers and owners of the company and is discussed in some detail in chapter 18.

THE METHOD OF BUYING STOCKS AND SHARES

First it is important to recognise that there are three different types of limited company:

> (i)   Listed Public Companies;
>
> (ii)   Unlisted Public Companies;
>
> (iii)   Private Companies

We look at the legal distinction between public limited companies and private limited companies in chapter 18 and the different classes of shares that can be issued in chapter 12; in this section we concentrate on the means by which an individual investor can buy shares in each type of company.

(i) Listed Public Limited Companies

Most of the country's largest companies have only been able to grow by selling shares to the general public and so increasing their capital. To allow the general public to buy the company's shares in the first place they need to be generally offered for sale. This is normally undertaken by inviting the public to apply for shares either at a set price or by bidding for them by tender. Advertisements are often placed in the quality press announcing a new share issue. Such advertisements will explain something of the company's trading activities, its recent and projected profitability and will offer a 'prospectus' which will give details of the share issue. There will be a set date by which offers should be received. The share issue may be 'underwritten' by a finance house or merchant bank which will have agreed to buy the shares at a price below that at which they are offered to the public. If all the shares are sold the underwriters will make a profit but if the shares are not all taken up by the public then they must bear the cost. Recent major examples of such share issues include the British Telecom share issue which attracted so many potential buyers that it was extremely oversubscribed leaving the underwriters with substantial profits.

A major attraction to a potential shareholder is the ability to resell a shareholding should he wish to turn his investment into cash or transfer his investment to another company. To be able to do this easily shareholders require a market in which they can buy and sell shares. In response the Stock Exchange has grown up. However it is not a market in the sense that any potential buyer can simply walk in and buy and sell shares. Instead share transactions are undertaken on the shareholders' behalf by firms of stockbrokers who act as agents for the investor. There are stockbrokers in most major cities in the country and you can instruct them yourself on any share transactions that you wish to make. Alternatively a bank will undertake the transactions for you by instructing their stockbroker. As shareholding has spread amongst the general public, some stockbrokers have tried to make the process more accessible by opening the equivalent of retail outlets or 'share shops' where an investor can go to buy and sell shares through the stockbroker. New regulations introduced in 1986 allow much wider dealing in shares and the commercial banks can act as stockbrokers and deal directly with the general public. If you are able to invest substantially on the stock exchange it is important to build up a relationship with your stockbroker as he will be able to advise on the wisdom of possible share dealings.

The other intermediary in the buying and selling of shares is the share 'jobber'. These are people who only work in the stock exchange and do not deal directly with the general public. They act as middle-men in that they buy and resell shares to and from stockbrokers. They tend to specialise in a particular industry or group of industries. They are willing to offer one price to buy a particular share and a higher price to sell it. The difference between the jobber's buying and selling price is his profit or 'margin'.

There is an increasing interest in share transactions and you can get some feel as to how the stock market is faring by following the Financial Times (FT) 30 Share Index which is quoted each evening on the news. This shows how the share prices of the thirty major companies in the UK have risen or fallen in the day's trading and gives some impression of the movements in the stock market as a whole.

(ii) Unlisted Public Companies

If you consult the stock exchange listings given daily in one of the better quality papers you will see that most of the major companies that are household names have a stock exchange listing. However there are thousands of other public companies which are not yet large enough or which have not been trading for a sufficiently long period to have their shares traded in the Stock Exchange. Yet as they are 'public' companies the general public is free to deal in their shares. To facilitate the buying and selling of such shares two other markets have grown up;

(a)   The Unlisted Securities Market; and

(b)   The Over the Counter Markets.

a. The Unlisted Securities Market (USM)

This market was established in the early 1980s to cater for the buying and selling of shares in some major companies which did not have stock exchange quotations. The rules for selling on the USM are much less strict than on the stock exchange and so dealings in such shares carry more risk. However the type of company whose shares are traded on the USM are often the rapid growth 'high tech' companies whose profits can be spectacular. Unfortunately such businesses can also easily face financial difficulties as the Acorn and Sinclair computer companies found in the middle of the 1980's. The Acorn company was rescued from financial collapse by a takeover by Olivetti the Italian typewriter and office machine company and the Sinclair company was taken over by one of its major rivals, Amstrad, in 1986. The extraordinary growth of Amstrad from a very small London based business to a major international supplier of computer equipment and other 'high tech' products in a very short time period proves a good example of the growth of a USM company.

b. Over the Counter Markets

This is the term used to describe the various dealings in the shares of unquoted public companies outside recognised markets which has grown up in recent years through a network of dealers. This involves agents who match potential buyers with potential sellers and charge a commission on the transaction. Other organisations act as independent 'jobbers' buying shares on their own account in the hope of finding potential buyers. This undefined market is relatively new and as yet it is not recommended as a major avenue for investment funds, however it is growing rapidly and could become of greater importance in the future.

(iii) Private Limited Companies

Because of their legal definition, dealing in the shares of private limited companies is not allowed between members of the general public. All sales of such shares have to be sanctioned by a majority of the existing shareholders and there are precise rules relating to such trading. Therefore this is only a possible avenue for investment for a person who is aware of the company and can agree a share transaction with a majority of the existing shareholders. This may appear to be an extremely limiting restriction, however it should be noted that the government has now introduced tax concessions which encourage investment in such companies. These are explained below.

GOVERNMENT ENCOURAGEMENT TO INVESTMENT IN LIMITED COMPANIES

In recent years the government has established two schemes which are aimed at encouraging investment in limited companies. These are: (i) The Business Expansion Scheme (BES); and (ii) the Personal Equity Plan (PEP).

(i) The Business Expansion Scheme

The BES is intended to channel investment funds from investors into small businesses. It was introduced in 1983 and extended in 1986. It allows individuals to invest up to £40,000 in small limited companies and claim back tax relief on their investment. The scheme is credited with creating over 4,000 jobs in its first year of operation by encouraging investors who would not normally have invested in such small companies had it not been for the tax advantages. The scheme particularly favours high risk companies in the manufacturing and service sectors.

(ii) The Personal Equity Plan

This scheme was introduced in 1986 to encourage small investors to put their money into public company shares. It allows an individual to invest up to £2,400 per year in shares and be exempt from tax on any capital gain, reinvested dividends or profit made from the share transaction if the shares are held for between one and two years. The shares must be bought through a stockbroker, bank or other financial institution and so it excludes personal share dealings in private limited companies. The scheme is seen as a further attempt by the government to encourage a wider shareholding amongst the general public.

INVESTMENT IN GOVERNMENT SECURITIES

As we will see in chapter 12 the government is the single largest borrower in the country. We have already seen that it attracts personal saving through its National Savings Scheme. However it also borrows money in a different way through the issue of government securities or stock. These are referred to as 'gilt edged' stock or simply 'gilts' as they were traditionally edged with gold.

Gilts are loans to the government for a specified length of time and carry a fixed rate of interest. So £100 worth of 12% 1998 treasury stock bought for £100 will provide the investor with £12 interest each year from the government until 1998 at which time the security 'matures' and the initial £100 paid will be returned to the investor. This may appear to be a very safe form of investment in that the initial sum invested will eventually be repaid to the lender. In that respect it is a form of saving. However the difference between this and other forms of saving with the government is that the stock is saleable on the stock market before it matures. We refer to it as the government's 'transferrable debt' as it is not owed to a specific individual.

Because the stock is a saleable commodity its value will rise and fall. Its current value is determined by the interest rates being offered by other forms of investment. As the government stock has a fixed interest return of say 12% this will mean that its resale value will increase if interest rates offered by other investments are less than 12% and will fall in value if the market interest rate for other investments is greater than 12%. For this reason each issue of government stock must be given an interest rate which is competitive with other market interest rates at the time the government stock is issued. Of course the interest rate is fixed until it matures and so its market value rises and falls conversely with other interest rates.

Gilt edged securities come in many different forms and have differing lengths of time until they mature. These can be as long as 30 years. Of course as they can be purchased on the stock market at any time until maturity, it is possible to buy short term government stock at any time prior to its redemption date. They can be bought and sold through a stockbroker in the same way as private company stocks and shares.

PERSONAL TAXATION

In the previous sections we have concentrated on the means by which an individual can borrow, save and invest his money. However one major factor which affects us all is the level of personal taxation. In chapter 12 we will consider the different types of taxes which we must all face and examine personal taxation in some detail. Therefore in this section we will briefly consider the method by which individuals must pay income tax and national insurance contributions.

INCOME TAX

For most individuals the major form of tax they pay is income tax. This is paid on all income, both earned and unearned, but is subject to certain allowances which are not taxed and are determined by the individual taxpayer's particular personal circumstances.

The PAYE Scheme

Most employed people pay their income tax through the Pay As You Earn (PAYE) scheme which means that your employer will deduct the appropriate amount of tax due from your wage or salary each week or month and pay it on your behalf to the Inland Revenue. If you are employed and you look at your wage slip you will see that you are not paying tax on everything that you earn. This is because you are allowed certain tax allowances. These depend on your personal position, for instance whether you are single or married, or if you have dependant relatives. (The full list of personal tax allowances are given in chapter 12.) The allowances you are given are shown by your tax code. This will be something like 233L. The figure (233) is the actual amount of allowance you have been allocated, in this example, £2335, and the letter which follows it indicates the taxpayer's status. So the L indicates a lower status, in other words a single person's allowance. If you were a married man the code will end with an H indicating a higher allowance while an E indicates emergency code. This is normally given to people whose tax allowances have not been finalised, for instance because they have recently changed employer and the Inland Revenue are in the process of adjusting the code. A single person will have the lowest tax allowance and so will pay tax on a higher proportion of their income than a person with other allowances such as a large mortgage or a dependant relative.

As we noted above income tax is payable on both earned and unearned income and so the interest you may receive on savings and investments discussed earlier in the chapter, will in most instances be liable for tax. You are also taxed on many state benefits such as a pension, supplementary benefit or a student grant. Exemptions from taxation include Family Income Supplement, maternity allowances and the death grant.

The rate at which an individual will pay tax increases with their income and as such is said to be progressive. In other words the proportion of income paid as tax increases as income rises. We will discuss the rates of taxation in more detail in chapter 12.

Self Employed Tax Payers

Self employed people are outside the PAYE system and pay tax on a twice yearly basis. Their tax bill is detemined by the Inspector of Taxes at the Inland Revenue who will examine their annual accounts and assess a tax liability on the basis of the income shown. While a self employed person has the same tax allowances as an employed person with similar personal circumstances, he is normally able to offset expenses genuinely incurred in the conduct of his business against his tax bill. This will often make self employment more attractive from the point of view of a person's tax liability.

The Annual Tax Return

To claim your tax allowances you must complete a tax return. This is an annual declaration to the Inland Revenue of all your income, including any perks or fringe benefits such as tips or a company car. The tax return also allows you to claim any deductable expenses such as union fees or special work clothes. In it you will also specify your personal circumstances and make a claim for any dependants. It is very important that you should complete your tax return for failure to do so will often result in the Inland Revenue setting your allowances at the lowest level and ignoring any claimable expenses.

National Insurance Contributions

In addition to your income tax deductions you are also required to pay national insurance contributions. These will also be deducted at source from your wages or salary if you are an employee, in the same way that PAYE is deducted. Additionally employers must also make a contribution to National Insurance for all their employees earning above the lowest wages. Such contributions by both employer and employee are on a sliding scale with the lowest paid workers exempt from payments and a gradual increase in the contributions up to 9% of income for employees and 10.45% of income for employers.

It is important that both you and your employer pay these National Insurance Contributions for they affect your entitlement to certain state benefits such as sick pay, unemployment benefit and the old age pension.

THE ROLE OF THE ACCOUNTANT

Most tax payers will never have the need to consult an accountant. Their tax liability is calculated and paid by their employer. Their only dealings with the Inland Revenue will be the requirement to complete the annual tax return which will detail their personal circumstances and indicate any income they have received other than their wages or salary. This will allow the Inland Revenue to determine their tax coding and so allocate the appropriate level of personal allowance. However filling in your tax return should not be too daunting a task and most people are able to complete it without the aid of an accountant.

An individual who is self employed may well use an accountant. In such circumstances the Inland Revenue prefer an accountant to prepare the individual's annual accounts and if necessary to verify their accuracy. If the business is a limited company there is a legal requirement for an auditor to report on the accounts to the company members or shareholders. It is also in the self employed tax payer's own interest to have the services of an accountant for he will advise on tax matters and ensure that all the allowances that are due are claimed. The accountant will also act as the intermediary between the tax payer and the Inland Revenue and should be able to handle any tax queries and problems that arise. This should reduce the administrative burden on the businessman. A further substantial advantage in consulting an accountant is that he should be able to offer advice on the management of the business, raising finance and suggest means of achieving greater financial efficiency and this aspect of the accountant's role is examined in chapter 13.

ASSIGNMENT — HELLO JOHN, GOT A NEW MOTOR?

Having worked hard for two years, John Gilmore has successfuly completed his BTEC National Certificate Course. In recognition of his efforts, his employers have given him a pay rise of 20% on his current wage of £75 per week. John has also recently passed his driving test and has decided to purchase a car. He immediately begins the search for a suitable vehicle.

In the local paper he sees an advertisement for a Ford Cortina 2.0 XL, priced at £1,499. This, John believes, is the car for him and he decides to visit the garage where the car is for sale the following morning.

That evening, in the pub, John tells his friends of his pay rise and the 'new motor' he intends to purchase. One of his friends, Peter Miller, tells John of an advert he has seen in the paper that morning. It was placed by a company called Fast Loans Ltd., who "offer loans to virtually anybody". Peter says it should suit John, as he has no security. This may well be true, as John still lives at home with his parents.

Another friend, Tony Dixon, is a little less enthusiastic about John's venture. He knows that John struggles to surive on his current wage, largely because of his active social life, and also due to the fact that he only infrequently pays 'board' to his parents. He believes that John is about to commit himself to repayments which he cannot manage. John, however, is convinced that he can easily afford the car with his increased income, and his only concern is to decide on the best way of purchasing the vehicle.

TASKS

1. Assume the rule of Tony in the above situation. Tony is adamant that John should not take on the loan and arranges to meet him to try and persuade him not to go ahead. To enable you to present a rational case prepare some notes in which you identify the arguments you would use.

2. If John is still convinced that he should proceed with the purchase, he must consider all possible sources of finance which are open to him. Draw up a comprehensive list of alternative forms of finance which are available to him and identify the advantages and drawbacks of each method.

DEVELOPMENTAL TASK

3. Research possible sources of finance in your own area for the purchase of a major consumer item such as a car or a stereo system. Compare the ease with which such credit may be obtained, the legal and commercial restrictions on each type of borrowing, such as age and status, and the interest rates which are being asked. Produce this in the form of an information brief for the student's union at your college. As the final page of the brief draw up a list of those questions which you would expect new borrowers to be asked when seeking credit. After each question leave space for an answer to be given by the prospective borrower.

ASSIGNMENT — 'SPEND, SPEND, SPEND?'

When she was born, Melanie Hodgson's parents bought her £10 worth of premium bonds. Last week, almost nineteen years later, Melanie was delighted to discover that E.R.N.I.E. had chosen one of her bonds as the winner of a £5,000 prize.

As often happens in such situations, Melanie was inundated with advice on what to do with her new found wealth. Her father suggested that the money should be placed in either more premium bonds or in National Savings Certificates. Mrs Hodgson, Melanie's mother, believed that the money should be used as the deposit for a flat. This would allow Melanie to establish her independence. "Never become totally dependant on a man" was her motherly advice.

Jenny, Melanie's sister works in a Building Society, and suggested that the most sensible decision would be to open a share account and gain interest on her money. Melanie's brother, Derek, has what he believes is the perfect solution. "Lend me half of the money for a week" he says, "and I will repay you twice as much". Derek is renowned for his none too successfu specuation on certain four-legged animals, and Melanie treats his suggestion with considerable suspicion.

Gordon Metcalfe is Melanie's boyfriend. He is not terribly popular with Mr and Mrs Hodgson, who see him as a "waster with no future". Since leaving school, he has drifted in and out of a variety of menial jobs, and is currently unemployed. On hearing of Melanie's good fortune, Gordon suggests that the two go into business together. He wants to set up a video rental shop, and says that Melanie's money could be used to buy the initial stock of tapes. Melanie could leave her present job with the local council and they could both work together full time in the business.

Melanie herself is totally undecided. She recently bought a new stereo system. The store offered her a 0% interest agreement and she has also acquired a sunbed on a similar 'interest free' scheme. She is considering paying off the balance on these items, which stands at a total of £825. A new car is another option. The local garage have Mini Metro's for only £4,100, and can arrange finance at 22% APR.

TASK

1. You are a good friend of Melanie and have worked for a firm of accountants for three years. She has told you of the suggestions which she has received, and asks for your advice. Examine all of the options which have been suggested to Melanie. You may wish to consider other possible uses for her £5,000 which have not been mentioned. Prepare some notes for Melanie in which you consider the advantages and disadvantages of each option and make suggestions as to the best alternative in Melanie's case.

DEVELOPMENTAL TASK

2. Imagine that you have been given £200 as an eighteenth birthday present. Examine the different forms of saving and investment which are available in your area. Prepare a table in which you list all these and compare their return, risk and accessibility.

Chapter 12

SOURCES OF FINANCE

RAISING FINANCE FOR ORGANISATIONS

In the previous chapter we were concerned with the financial affairs of individuals. We considered how they raise finance, save and invest and the way in which the government taxes individuals. However in chapter 18 we emphasise the point that individuals cannot live in isolation. We cannot exist in today's world without constantly interacting with organisations. We are educated by an organisation, may work for an organisation, buy from organisations and are governed by an organisation. Therefore the remaining part of this section of the book will be concerned with the financial management of such organisations.

In this chapter we will examine the means by which different organisations raise the finance which will allow them to establish and operate. To begin with we need to distinguish between those organisations operating in the public sector and those in the private sector. If you are unsure of the distinctions between each form of organisation you should refer to chapter 18. Such differences are crucially important. Private organisations must prove to those who will provide finance that they will be profitable and so can provide a return on any money lent to or invested in them. In contrast some public organisations, and in particular the central government, have the power to raise finance through taxation. Politically, governments need to justify the raising of such finance in terms of the services that they are able to provide to the tax payer, rather than simply in monetary terms.

Therefore this chapter will fall into two sections. The first will examine private sector organisations and consider how they are able to raise finance from financial bodies and also from the general public by issuing shares. The revenue which a private sector organisation gains from the sale of its product is considered in chapter 26. The second half of the chapter will consider the public sector and will evaluate its main sources of finance: taxation and public borrowing.

FINANCE FOR PRIVATE SECTOR ORGANISATIONS

Any new business will find that it is difficult to raise finance from outside sources and so anyone hoping to establish a new business may be forced to provide their own capital. A person starting in business as a sole trader, therefore, will normally provide at least part of the start up finance himself and similarly a partnership will rely heavily on the partners to make a contribution to the initial capital required. However many businesses will also need to borrow money from an outside source and this will normally mean from a commercial bank. The ease with which such a loan can be obtained will depend upon a number of economic factors. Any prudent banker making a loan will want an acceptable rate of interest, some guarantee of security on the loan and a reasonable prospect of financial success for the business. Therefore anyone who seeks to borrow money from a bank should approach the matter in a business like manner. If you want a loan to run a business the first step is to approach the bank manager in the way that a businessman would. This involves the preparation of a business plan.

Any new business will find that it is difficult to raise finance from outside sources and so anyone hoping to establish a new business may be forced to provide their own capital.

A person starting in business as a sole trader, therefore, will normally provide at least part of the start up finance himself and similarly a partnership will rely heavily on the partners to make a contribution to the initial capital required. However many businesses will also need to borrow money from an outside source and this will normally mean from a commercial bank. The ease with which such a loan can be obtained will depend upon a number of economic factors. Any prudent banker making a loan will want an acceptable rate of interest, some guarantee of security on the loan and a reasonable prospect of financial success for the business. Therefore anyone who seeks to borrow money from a bank should approach the matter in a business like manner. If you want a loan to run a business the first step is to approach the bank manager in the way that a business man would. This involves the preparation of a business plan.

PREPARING A CASE FOR A BUSINESS LOAN

As we have seen when a business seeks finance from a bank, the bank manager will want to be convinced that the business is sound and there is a good likelihood of the loan being repaid. If the business has been in operation for some time then the bank will wish to see sets of accounts for previous years. These will need to have been prepared by an accountant who will verify their accuracy. If the business is just beginning and requires a start-up loan from the bank then obviously there will be no accounts of previous years trading. Thus in order to allow the bank to judge the potential of the new business and the safety of its loan, the borrower needs to produce the following:

> (i)   a business plan; and

> (ii)   a cashflow forecast and a projected profit and loss account.

(i)   A Business Plan

A business plan is what it appears to be, a plan of operation for the business in the short and/or medium term. If the business idea is viable and the business plan is well prepared, it will help the case for the loan by impressing the bank of your competence in business. However if the idea is clearly not viable then no amount of good presentation will help. In a business plan you should include some brief background introduction to the business, setting out the products or service it is intended to supply and an indication of the scale of operation. The plan should specify those who will be directly involved in running the business, either the partners or the directors, and indicate the relevant experience they have. Clearly if the person starting the business has a number of years of useful experience in that particular trade or industry then it is likely that he will be more sure of what he is doing than some one who is completely fresh to the business. This does not mean that a total lack of experience will be a complete bar to a business start-up loan but it does mean that a borrower in such a situation will have to prove that he has done some extensive groundwork on the business project to show that he knows what he is doing.

The next part of the plan should discuss the product or service to be supplied and evaluate the need for it in the area in which the business will operate. This means that existing competition will have to be assessed and a reasonable estimate made of market potential. Other problems to be considered include the availability of skilled labour, supplies of raw materials and suitable premises.

The plan should indicate the proposed level of output over the coming period and the price which it should be possible to charge for the product or service. If the borrower has some experience of the problems involved in running a business this will help to convince the bank of the potential success of the business idea. A good business plan will also weigh up the strengths and weaknesses of the proposal. You should be honest with the bank manager. If you have already considered these and believe that the business idea is viable despite the possible draw-backs then hopefully you should also be able to convince a bank manager.

(ii) Cashflow forecast and a projected profit and loss account

The cashflow forecast is an attempt to show the anticipated inflow and outflow of money from the business in the coming year. Inflow is the revenue from sales of the product or service. Unless the proposed business is in retailing it is often common for a supplier to have to wait some considerable time for eventual payment after the goods have been delivered. Most business customers expect to be given some element of trade credit, others are simply slow payers. This is fine if it is you that owes the money but can be potentially disastrous when it is your business that is waiting to be paid.

If we consider the costs of operation that make up the outflows, the business will have to pay wages and other bills on a much more prompt and regular basis than some other payments. It may be fine to leave the bill for the supply of raw materials to be paid until the end of the month but try explaining to the workforce that they are not getting their wages for the next six weeks! Therefore at different times throughout the trading year the business will find that it will have varying levels of cash shortage when it must pay bills but is waiting to be paid itself. These circumstances need to be anticipated so that agreement can be made with the bank to provide sufficient funds at the times when they will be needed. In essence this is all that a cashflow fore-cast is — a monthly statement of cash spent and cash received leaving a balance which may be in surplus, which is fine, or in debit which will need financing by the bank. It should be borne in mind that severe cashflow problems that are not resolved by suitable borrowing can cause a business to collapse. Creditors may soon lose patience with the business debtor who regularly pleads that the debt will be paid as soon as its outstanding accounts are settled. The unsympathetic creditor may respond by bringing bankruptcy proceedings. Thus the cashflow forecast is not simply a means of impressing a bank manager sufficiently for him to grant the loan. It is in fact a very useful and often vital management tool and should be compared carefully with what actually happens once the business is operating. If the actual cash balances regularly appear less than those forecast then it is time to consult the bank manager again to ensure that additional finance can be arranged.

The second financial statement required is a projected profit and loss account. This will simply show the total projected sales from the business in the coming year and place against it a total for the projected costs of operation. This will allow a projected net profit to be estimated by subtracting costs from revenue. We will consider the structure and interpretation of the profit and loss account in more detail in chapter 14.

TYPES OF SHORT TERM FINANCE

In chapter 11 we have already made the distinction between an overdraft and a personal loan. Here we examine the issues associated with short term business borrowing arrangements.

By short term finance we normally mean an overdraft. This is generally the cheapest way of raising short term finance from outside the business. Many businesses will operate permanent overdraft facilities which will give them some flexibility in their cashflow management. The bank will agree an overdraft limit and the business should avoid exceeding this in the same way that an individual borrower should. The business should avoid using an overdraft to finance capital spending such as the purchase of new plant or machinery. This should be financed through medium or long term loans. In fact it is best to use an overdraft only to solve cash flow problems in circumstances where money is owed to the business but not yet received and debts now have to be paid.

Factoring

A further means of raising short term funds open to organisations facing a cash flow problem is factoring. This simply means that an organisation which has debts owed to it, sells the right to this money to a factor (an organisation willing to provide immediate cash in return for the right to collect and keep the monies owed from the organisation's debtors). The factors are often subsidiaries of clearing banks or major financial groups. The factor will usually pay the organisation less than the face value of the debts (3-10% less) and so if he can collect in full, this % is the factor's profit on the transaction. Thus a debt is an asset owned by the business, and like any other type of asset can be sold if a suitable buyer is available.

MEDIUM TERM FINANCE

Approximately 40% of all business loans are now taken for periods ranging from 3 to 10 years. Most of these loans are secured against the assets of the business or are guaranteed by the owners of the business. Borrowing money in such a way has major advantages for a business. It allows the liability to be spread over a longer period and the repayments can be made gradually on a regular monthly or quarterly basis. The period for which the loan is given is usually sufficient to allow the business to make profits from the investment in new plant or machinery for which the loan has been negotiated.

Such medium term loans are especially useful for the purchase of assets which have a particular life span. So for instance if a machine lasts five years before it needs replacing then it is sensible to take out a five year loan to finance it and spread its cost over its life cycle.

A medium term loan such as this may also be used to refinance an overdraft. In this way the cost of finance can be spread over a longer term avoiding financial difficulties should an overdraft facility come to an end.

Normally, then, a medium term loan is designed for a business which has established itself and solved the initial start up difficulties which most firms face. It will normally have some assets and it is quite common for the bank to require a fixed charge to be taken as security. What is meant by a 'charge' on the business assets is considered a little later.

LONG TERM FINANCE

Long term loans are usually provided to allow a business to buy plant or machinery which will have a considerable life span. By long term we normally mean 10 years or more, and as well as being used to buy plant it may also finance takeovers or other forms of expansion. However if the business is sound, as it must be if it is to contemplate such long term finance then it may be better advised to raise finance through a share issue rather than take on such long term debts. Banks may well be reluctant to make such long term loans to a small business if they lack confidence about its long term prospects for growth. Certainly no long term loan of this sort will be given by a bank without concrete guarantees and security. It is also likely that the bank will seek a higher rate of interest on such loans. You may argue that the business is wiser to seek shorter term and cheaper loans but this ignores the advantages that the business gains from not having to repay its debts quickly. It is able to schedule its debts repayment in line with its revenue growth and also will not have the problem of continually having to renegotiate its loan position.

Loan Gearing

In chapter 15 we will be considering a number of financial indicators which will allow judgements to be made as to the financial health and stability of an organisation. It is worth briefly introducing one of them now. This is the concept of loan gearing, which is simply a measurement of the degree to which a business is financed by loans rather than by equity. When a business seeks a loan from a financial institution such as a bank, the lender will often require the business to put up a proportion of its financial needs itself from its internal funds to demonstrate the ability of the business to be self-financing. So for instance the bank may specify that for every pound the bank loans the business, the owners must match it, pound for pound. This is referred to as a 1 : 1 gearing ratio. Many banks will now accept a much higher ratio of loan to internal financing but this will depend on their belief in the business and their confidence in its future. We will return to gearing later in chapter 15 but now we will consider the way in which the government seeks to help businesses who are seeking loans.

The Government's Loan Guarantee Scheme

We have already recognised that one of the difficulties any business will face when it seeks to raise money from a bank is that it may well have a lack of security. To try to help overcome such problems the government introduced its loan guarantee scheme in 1981. Under the scheme the government is willing to act as guarantor for 70% of a loan to small businesses up to a loan limit of £75,000. One major disadvantage to the small business borrower was the requirement to pay a premium of 5% on top of the interest rate to cover the costs of the guarantee. Of course this made any loan very expensive and despite considerable initial public enthusiasm the scheme did not prove as successful as the government had hoped. In an attempt to revive the scheme the premium was halved to 2.5% in the 1986 budget. This is still an expensive rate at which to borrow although it may be that it will result in a greater take up than the low level of borrowing which had existed prior to the change. Companies involved in retailing, construction and manufacturing are eligible for the scheme but not those involved in banking, education and some other services.

The Business Expansion Scheme

A further government attempt to encourage the provision of funds for private business is the Business Expansion Scheme. This allows private investors to put their money into new and growing companies by giving substantial tax concessions to the investor, who is able to offset against personal income tax any investment in non listed companies up to a value of £40,000. The investment must be held for a period of at least five years if it is to qualify for the tax relief.

The idea is to encourage investment in small or medium sized businesses which will provide the investor with a more attractive return because of the tax advantages.

Other sources of finance from public funds

There are a variety of sources of government funds available from both central and local government as well as other government backed agencies and the European Economic Community. As the majority of such aid is restricted to businesses which are located in the country's assisted areas it is part of the government's regional policy and is covered in some detail in chapter 25.

LEGAL RESTRICTIONS ON BORROWING BY BUSINESSES

As far as a sole trader is concerned, there is no limitation on his borrowing powers, but of course, he remains personally liable to the full extent of his personal wealth for any debts entered into. In a partnership, every partner is the agent of the firm and his partners, for the purposes of the partnership business. Therefore in a trading partnership, every partner has the power to borrow money for a purpose apparently connected with the partnership business. This rule has the effect of making every partner in a firm jointly liable with the other partners for all the debts incurred by the firm while he is a partner.

The law makes a distinction between the borrowing of non-corporate and corporate businesses. We shall examine each in turn.

a.   Non Corporate Bodies

If we are to consider the legal rights which a business lender such as a bank has when it lends money to a sole trader or a partnership we need to determine whether the loan is secured or unsecured. An unsecured loan means that the lender has no rights over the borrower's property in the event of the borrower's default in repayment. The lender's only option is to bring a court action to attempt to recover the debt. In the present economic climate, it is more usual for a lender such as a bank to require the added protection of a secured loan. One of the most common forms of secured loan is a 'commercial mortgage' which uses freehold or leasehold land or other business assets as security. Under a commercial mortgage, the borrower, known as the mortgagor, in return for a loan from the lender, referred to as the mortgagee, will transfer the ownership of the mortgaged property to the lender, with the stipulation that the property be transferred back to the borrower on repayment of the loan plus the agreed amount of interest. A mortgage may be entered into by drafting a mortgage deed. This is called a legal mortgage. Alternatively a mortgage can exist simply by depositing the title deeds of the property with the lender. This is known as an equitable mortgage. This method of raising capital is used by both sole traders and partnerships.

b.   Corporate Bodies.

Companies often borrow money by means of issuing debentures. These may be secured or unsecured. The definition of a "debenture" is very wide and includes all forms of securities, in other words undertakings to repay any money borrowed, which may or may not be secured by a charge on the company's assets. A charge simply means a legal right to take the asset. Debentures usually consist of a trust deed which will create a fixed charge over a specific piece of company property by mortgage, and/or a floating charge over the rest of the company assets. The difference between fixed and floating charges is basically that a company is not free to do what it wishes with assets which are subject to a fixed charge. In other words it is not free to sell or mortgage them. However a company is free to do what it likes with any of its assets covered by a floating charge. The floating charge will normally be created over a class of assets, such as the company's trading stock, which is of course a variable asset. However, a floating charge is said to 'crystalise' and becomes a fixed charge should money become repayable under a condition in the debenture, and is then not paid. This could happen for instance when repayment on part of the interest on the loan is due. The lender may then take steps to enforce his security because the interest due has not been paid by the borrower. The principal rights of a debenture holder are outlined in the debenture deed and will include:-

1. The date of repayment of the loan and the rate of interest;

2. a statement of the assets of the company which are subject to fixed or floating charges;

3. the rights of the company to redeem the whole or any part of the monies owing;

4. the circumstances in which the loan becomes immediately repayable, such as if the company defaults in payment of interest;

5. the powers of the debenture holder to appoint a receiver and manager of the assets charged.

All trading companies have an implied power to borrow money to finance their business activities. In the case of non-trading companies, there is no such power unless expressly provided for in the Memorandum of Association. Power to borrow money is usually conferred on the company directors in the Articles of Association. There is nothing to prevent a company limiting its own borrowing powers to a specific amount in the Memorandum of Association, for instance by including a limit on borrowing of not more than two-thirds of the value of its paid up capital. In effect the company will be introducing an almost self imposed loan gearing. Power to borrow will also carry with it an implied power to offer company property as security for a loan. As a general rule, if a company borrows beyond its powers, then the loan and any security given for it is void on the grounds of ultra vires. This is the legal term given to an act which is beyond the powers of the company. If this happens the lender cannot sue for the return of the loan. Provided, however, that the company has power to borrow money the lender is under no obligation to discover the purpose for which the money is to be used.

This position has been qualified somewhat by the European Communities Act 1972 and has now been included in the Companies Act 1985. This provides that in the case of a person dealing in good faith with the company, any transaction decided upon by the directors shall be held to be within the powers of the company. Therefore provided the lender did not know the loan was 'ultra vires' he may recover any debt owed.

As we noted in the section on long term finance a business which has become established may find that a more appropriate way of raising finance is not through borrowing but by issuing shares. The method of raising finance through share issue will now be considered.

THE ISSUE OF SHARES AS A MEANS OF RAISING FINANCE

If a business wishes to expand it may be faced with the problem that the funds needed to finance the expansion cannot be met either internally from business profits or through borrowing from financial institutions. One of the other options open to the business is to bring in new capital from outside sources. This means issuing shares and spreading the ownership of the business. Many small businessmen may resent this reduction in their direct control. However broadening the ownership need not always lead to a reduction in control. In chapter 18 we discuss this relationship between ownership and control and it is often found that new investors are not interested in the day to day management of the business and only seek a safe and profitable return on their investment. There are many professional investors who are looking for small businesses in which to invest funds and this can have a number of major commercial benefits.

The added capital introduced into the business by the sale of shares can give it a much sounder financial base and also open up other avenues for raising funds. The company's bankers will recognise that the new investors have endorsed the future potential of the business and so it may be easier to arrange overdrafts or other forms of short and medium term finance.

If the new share capital is sold to a professional investor such as a merchant bank then it is likely that they will want to appoint a representative to the board of the company. This may seem like an intrusion on the management and policy making of the business but often such appointees have wide business experience and as they seek to protect their investment they will want the business to succeed and so will usually offer sound advice.

It is unlikely that professional investors will want to share in the capital of small businesses or those which are just starting up but for a medium sized business in need of funds to expand it may prove to be a mutually profitable move. Small businesses will not be able to get professional investors to buy their shares and so must seek individuals who are willing to buy shares. As we have seen earlier in the chapter the government is seeking to encourage such involvement through its Business Expansion Scheme.

Before moving on to consider the mechanics of share issue and the restrictions involved in raising capital in this way we need to consider some of the distinctions between the expressions used. Unfortunately, the use of the term 'capital' when applied to companies can have many different meanings, so in order to try and minimise confusion, we shall begin this section by considering some of the more widely used expressions.

a.   **Authorised Capital.** This expression refers to the value of shares that a company is authorised to issue and is included in the capital clause of the Memorandum of Association of a company. This is discussed in some detail in chapter 18.

b.   **Issued Capital.** This is the value of the company's capital which has actually been issued to the shareholders in the form of shares.

c.   **Paid up Capital.** This is the amount of capital which has actually be paid to the company on the shares issued. It is possible to issue shares which are not paid for or which are partly paid. Under the European Communities Act, 1972, if a company makes a reference to share capital on its business stationery or order forms it must refer to its paid up share capital, that is the amount of capital the company has actually raised and received.

d.   **Unpaid Capital.** If shares which have been issued are not fully paid for then the amount outstanding is referred to as unpaid capital. For example if 10,000 shares issued, each have a nominal value of £1 and only 50p has been paid up on them, in other words paid to the company, then the issued share capital is £10,000, the paid up capital is £5,000 and the unpaid capital is £5,000. Shareholders may be required to pay up the unpaid amount on their shares by the company making a 'call' on them to do so. This may happen if the business begins to face financial difficulties and cannot meet its debts.

e.   **Reserve Capital.** A company, by special resolution which requires a 75% majority vote, may declare that any portion of its unpaid capital shall not be called up except if the company is being brought to an end (liquidated) by a winding up. This is called reserve capital and cannot be converted into ordinary capital use in the operation of the company without the court's permission.

Having dealt with the various types of capital which may exist in a company, it is now possible to show how this capital may be divided into different classes of shares. This is actually done in the Articles of Association, which also specify the rights attaching to each class of shares, and how the shareholders' rights can be varied. Again the Articles of Association of a company are discussed in more detail in chapter 18.

CLASSES OF SHARES

The majority of companies in the U.K. have one class of shares which are referred to as 'ordinary shares' or the 'equity share capital' of the company. However there is nothing to prevent a limited company from having more than one class of shares. If different classes of shares are issued they will have different rights, relating to such matters as voting rights, payment of dividend, in other words the sum distributed to shareholders out of any profit made, and the return of capital to shareholders should the company go into liquidation. The two main types of shares are preference shares and ordinary shares.

a.   Preference Shares. The main characteristic of a preference share is that it will grant its holder the right to a preferred fixed dividend. All this means is that the holder of a preference share is entitled to a fixed amount of dividend, for instance 6% on the value of his share, before the ordinary shareholders are paid any dividend. A preference share is therefore a safe investment with a fixed reward, no matter how small or how large is the company's profit. Some preference shares are non-cumulative while others are cumulative which means that, if in any year, the company's profits are not sufficient to declare a dividend, the shortfall must be made up out of profits of subsequent years. Often preference shares carry no voting rights.

b.   Ordinary Shares. Ordinary shares are often referred to as the "equity share capital" of a company. These are the shares which involve risk, for having declared a dividend and paid the preference shareholders, the company will now pay a dividend to the holders of ordinary shares out of the remainder of the profit. It follows therefore, that an ordinary shareholder in a well managed company which is making high profits will receive a good return on his investment and the nominal value of his share will rise, so for instance a £1 ordinary share could rise in its market value to £1.50. Unfortunately, the opposite is also true. If there is no profit then there is no dividend and the shares may fall in value. So inevitably ordinary shares involve a certain risk. This risk is reflected in the amount of control that an ordinary shareholder has over the company's business, for while voting rights are not normally attached to preference shares, they are to ordinary shares. The ordinary shareholder can therefore usually voice his opinion in the company's annual general meeting and vote on major issues involving the running of the company. Ordinary shares also carry the right to a share of any surplus assets once liabilities have been met should the company be wound up. While preference shares normally carry no such right, their capital is usually repaid in preference to the capital of ordinary shareholders.

Raising Share Capital

We have already seen that the basic classification of companies is between those which are public and those which are private companies. Under the Companies Act 1985 a public limited company is one which, by its Memorandum of Association, states that it is a public limited company and has a nominal share capital of at least £50,000, of which at least one-quarter is paid up capital. All other companies are private. Also, a private company has no right to invite public subscription for shares by issuing a prospectus. As we saw in chapter 11 a prospectus is an advertisement offering shares or debentures for sale to the general public.

This restriction effectively limits the ability of a private company to raise large amounts of capital, for it must rely totally on those individuals who are aware of its existence and who might be willing to subscribe for its shares. A public company, however, has never been limited in its membership size or the rights of shareholders to freely transfer their shares. However as we have already seen only certain public companies are quoted on the stock exchange and so shareholders in unlisted companies have greater difficulty in buying and selling shares. To raise initial capital or increase its issued capital, a public company will issue a prospectus to induce the public to subscribe for shares or debentures. The prospectus must, however, contain certain information including:-

    a.   Particulars of all material contracts entered into by the company in the last two years which are likely to influence prospective investors.

    b.   An auditor's report showing the company's assets and liabilities, profits, losses and dividends paid over the last five years.

    c.   If the proceeds of the share issue are to be used to acquire property or a business, a statement giving particulars of the prospective vendors and the purchase price.

The prospectus is often published in the quality newspapers and of course must be truthful. An investor who can show that he was induced to buy shares because of false statements of fact in the prospectus, may sue to reclaim any money paid, terminate the share issue, and possibly obtain damages from the persons responsible.

As we noted in chapter 11 it is usual practice, when a company makes an invitation to the public for share issue, to have the issue underwritten. In return for a commission, an underwriter, often a merchant bank will agree to subscribe for any shares which the public do not take.

SOURCES OF GOVERNMENT REVENUE

TAXATION OF PERSONAL INCOME

Personal income tax is the government's major source of revenue. As we have already noted in chapter 11 an individual is liable to pay tax on both earned income (wages and salaries) and unearned income (rent, dividends and interest). Each individual is entitled to certain allowances against tax which depend on his or her particular circumstances. So, for example, a married man is allowed to earn more before he is taxed than a single person. Other allowances include those for taxpayers with dependent relatives or those who are blind.

The table below shows the allowances as declared in the 1986 budget.

Tax Allowances — 1986 Budget

Single person	£2335
Married man	£3655
Wife's earned income	£2335
Age allowance — single person	£2690
married man	£4505
Additional personal	£1320
Housekeeper	£100
Dependent relative	£100
— if claimant is a single woman	£145
Son's or daughter's services	£55
Blind person	£360
Widow's bereavement	£1320

Once an individual's income exceeds the allowance granted, he then crosses the tax threshold and any additional income is taxed. The present system has a series of tax bands which are normally increased each year.

The table below shows the tax bands operative from the 1986 budget.

Bands of Taxable Income — 1986 Budget

£	Per Cent
0 - 17200	29
17201 - 20200	40
20201 - 25400	45
25401 - 33300	50
33301 - 41200	55
over - 41200	60

It may be helpful at this point to show how tax liability is assessed by looking at two examples relating to the tax position in 1986-87.

EXAMPLE 1

Assess the tax liability of a single person earning £6,000 per annum and who has no dependants

	Income	£6,000
less	Personal allowance	£2,335
	Taxable income	£3,665 (which falls into the 29% tax band)

Tax due

29% of £3,665 =   £1062.85 per annum

EXAMPLE 2

Assess the tax liability of a married man earning £25,000 per annum.

	Income	£25,000
less	Personal allowance	£ 3,655
	Taxable income	£21,345

(The first £17,200 is taxed at 29%
The next £3,000 is taxed at 40%
The final £1,145 is taxed at 45%.)

Tax due

29% of £17,200	£4,988.00
40% of £3,000	£1,200.00
45% of £1,145	£ 515.25
TOTAL	£6703.25 per annum

The important point to note is that the tax rate relates to marginal income, not all income. If, for example, a person earns £50,000, the top tax rate of 60% does not apply to all of it, but only to that part over £41,200 once their allowances have been subtracted. Thus income tax rises progressively on marginal income.

The PAYE System

One of the advantages of the UK's income tax system is that for most employed people there is a relatively convenient method of payment. The procedure involved is called the Pay As You Earn (PAYE) system. The scheme began in 1944 and involves weekly and monthly paid employees, and other employees paid on a regular basis, having their income tax deducted at source by their employer.

It is the employer's duty to deduct tax from the pay of employees whether or not directed to do so by the Inland Revenue. Failure to comply may result in the employer being required to pay over to the Inland Revenue the tax which should have been deducted and, additionally, may result in the imposition of penalties on the employer. To ensure compliance the Inland Revenue is empowered by law to make inspections of employers' records from time to time in order to satisfy itself that the correct amounts of tax and National Insurance contributions are being deducted and paid over. Employers are also required by law to keep all pay records and other documents relevant to the scheme for at least 3 years from the end of the year to which they relate.

Taxpayers who are self-employed are not covered by the PAYE scheme. Instead their tax liability is calculated over a whole year and is charged on a lump sum basis. Because of this, prudent individuals will make provision for their tax liability by setting aside regularly from their income the amount they will be required to pay.

To conclude, let us summarise the pros and cons of the PAYE system.

The advantages of the PAYE system are:
   (i)   tax is paid at the same time that income is received and so the person's ability to pay the tax, and any changes in that ability, are accounted for;

   (ii) income tax paid in this way is difficult to avoid;

   (iii) much of the cost of collection is borne not by the Inland Revenue but by the employer and so it is a very economical tax from the government's point of view.

The PAYE system is criticised on the following grounds:
   (i)   employers face considerable time, effort and cost in calculating and collecting their employees' tax payments but this is countered to some extent by the fact that PAYE and National Insurance is paid over to the Inland Revenue monthly while most employees are weekly paid. Thus the employer has the use of the money for this period;

   (ii) the system is sometimes inaccurate and the taxpayer may pay more tax than is due;

   (iii) the system is unfair when compared to a self employed person who would pay tax in two instalments, one every six months, whereas employees are required to pay the tax immediately the money is earned.

TAXES ON PROFITS

Corporation Tax

A second important form of direct taxation is corporation tax. This is levied on the profits of a company as distinct from partnerships or sole traders who pay income tax. The present system of corporation tax is levied on the profits of all public limited companies, private companies and State owned public corporations.

Profit is defined as the net income of the business resulting from its trading activities. The important phrase here is net income, for this means that all costs of production can be deducted from the business revenue in order to determine the overall profit or net income. Clearly, if the company's costs of production are greater than its revenue from sales then the business will be making a loss and so would not be liable for corporation tax.

Furthermore a business is permitted to include certain capital allowances against its tax liability. For example, the cost of investment in plant and machinery is allowed to be progressively deducted from revenue over a period of years to take account of depreciation as the initial value of these capital assets declines with use.

As in the case of income tax, the rates of corporation tax can vary from budget to budget. The rates of corporation tax for the financial year 1986-87 are 35% for medium and large companies and 29% for small companies. The classification of small, medium and large companies is made on the basis of profit earned rather than assets or turnover, so to some extent the terms are misleading.

The advantages of corporation tax are as follows:

(i) One of the major arguments in favour of corporation tax is that it is a popular form of taxation with the general public who would resent corporate bodies earning large untaxed incomes while they themselves faced the burden of income tax.

(ii) It appears to be a lucrative source of income to the government, although the amount it yields is much less attractive.

There are a number of distinct disadvantages:

(i) it may be argued that corporation tax deters investors from putting their money in businesses. They prefer instead to put their money into deposits involving less risk, such as government stocks and bonds and pay income tax alone, rather than have the company first pay corporation tax and then themselves have to pay income tax later on the distributed dividend; however the income tax on dividends is offset against corporation tax. The tax which is paid is the difference between the corporation tax and the shareholder's marginal tax rate;

(ii) corporation tax reduces a company's ability to finance its own investment from its own funds. Trading companies are conscious of the need to pay attractive dividends to keep shareholders happy;

(iii) as costs of production are deducted from revenue to determine the company's tax liability there is less incentive to hold down costs and so inefficiency and waste may result;

(iv) investment decisions may be made for tax reasons rather than the business requirements of the company.

(v) high levels of corporation tax discourage investment by overseas companies;

(vi) high corporate tax rates encourage companies to seek schemes to avoid paying tax;

(vii) corporation tax encourages multi-national companies to engage in transfer pricing. (This is discussed in detail in chapter 23).

Petroleum Revenue Tax

One of the government's most important sources of taxation has come from the development of the UK's North Sea oil reserves. This has added considerable revenue to the Exchequer without imposing an additional tax burden on traditional taxpayers. The tax levied is called Petroleum Revenue Tax (PRT).

One of the most significant aspects of PRT is that proceeds from each oil or gas field are taxed separately to prevent the oil companies off-setting the development costs of one field against the profitable proceeds of another. Furthermore PRT is now charged on a monthly instalment basis which helps the Exchequer's cashflow.

Despite the initial cries of dismay from the oil companies that PRT would make the North Sea economically unviable the North Sea oil fields continued to be an area of profitable development as well as a major source of revenue to the UK government until 1985. However the substantial fall in world oil prices in 1985-86 meant a dramatic reduction in revenue from PRT. The 1986 budget estimated a return from PRT of £2.4 billion in 1986-87. This was a dramatic fall from the previous year's forecast of £8.2 billion.

In addition to PRT the government also levies corporation tax on the profits made by oil companies in the North Sea and charges royalties based on the value of any oil produced in the North Sea for which the oil companies have been granted a licence to explore and extract.

To compensate the oil companies for the extremely high rates of taxation they are forced to pay on the oil from the North Sea, and also to encourage them to seek to develop some of the less profitable fields, they are allowed relief against tax based on the difficulty of exploration of the oil field they are drilling.

The benefit of the North Sea oil reserves to the UK cannot be underestimated. They have provided a dramatic injection to the government's revenue at a time when the economy as a whole was in decline. Clearly the growth of North Sea oil tax revenues has had an important bearing on the composition of the overall tax burden.

It is predicted that North Sea oil production will fall steadily and by 1993 will be little more than half its peak level of 1985. The general uncertainty in world oil prices makes it extremely difficult to predict future government revenue from this source.

Nonetheless we should not ignore the impact that the discovery of North Sea oil has had on the UK economy. As well as the extra revenue from PRT, which has benefitted the government's revenue, there has also been the impact of a multiplier effect on the UK economy.

During the period of its development, oil exploration created considerable new employment both in the construction of rigs and terminals and in the oil servicing industries. This addition to the workforce has produced obvious benefits, not only to those directly involved, but has also added to the tax yield of the government through additional income and corporation taxes.

One of the major criticisms of government policy in the last ten years has been its unwillingness to use the bonus of North Sea oil revenue to revitalise the economy.

The government was faced with a number of options regarding the use of this "windfall" revenue:

(i)   It could have reduced the overall burden of taxation.

(ii) It could have used the extra funds to enhance the provision of services.

(iii) It could have re-invested in British industry to provide a more sound base for economic rejuvenation in the post-North Sea oil world.

Unfortunately the economic policies pursued by the government during the North Sea oil bonanza and the decline in industrial activity in this period have meant that the majority of North Sea oil revenue has had to be used to finance the increased unemployment which has plagued the country.

The one major benefit from the oil discovery has been that the UK has become self-sufficient in the production of this fuel and, as such, many of the balance of payments difficulties which proved a major hindrance to economic self-determination in the 1970s has been eased. Britain is no longer faced with an oil deficit on its balance of trade but has instead become a net oil exporter. This fact has, however, masked to some extent the decline in our other industrial sectors.

TAXES ON CAPITAL

So far in this chapter we have examined the income of individuals and the profits and revenue of companies as sources of government revenue. We will now consider the extent to which the taxation of capital provides a further source of revenue.

At the present time there is no tax which is levied merely on the holding of capital or wealth. Rather the government levies tax when capital is transferred or it gains in value.

The government sees such taxes as

(a) a means of raising revenue, although admittedly a relatively small proportion of the total tax yield, and

(b) as a method of reducing the inequality in income and wealth distribution in the country through the taxation of the more affluent members of society.

It is also regarded as a popular tax by the majority of the populace who do not have to pay it.

Against this may be put the argument that taxation of this nature discourages capital accumulation and savings and so reduces the level of investment likely to be enjoyed by British industry.

We shall now consider the two main forms of capital taxation.

Capital Transfer Tax (CTT)/Inheritance Tax

The taxation of capital transfers has long been an established aspect of the UK tax system. It was previously levied in the form of death duties or estate duties paid when capital assets were passed on to heirs either at the time of death or in the seven years prior to it.

Then in the 1970's it was extended to include gifts made during a person's lifetime. The aim of this extension was to prevent the widespread practice of the wealthy taking the expedient measure of avoiding tax by transferring their assets to their heirs by gift prior to death.

This was abolished by the 1986 budget and only transfers on death are now taxable. In 1986-87 the CTT rate ranged from 30% to 60% of the transfer but no tax is levied on transfers of less than £71,000.

To a very limited extent the tax has had the effect of reducing the concentration of vast wealth in a few hands, but there are many loopholes in this form of taxation and the impact can be mitigated by the establishment of such devices as trust funds for a donor's children.

Capital Gains Tax (CGT)

This was introduced in the 1960's as a way of taking all short-term capital gains. It is levied on the increase in the value of assets between the time they are acquired and the time that they are sold. It is levied on the increase in real terms of the asset and it is index linked to allow for the effects of inflation.

This tax, in common with CTT, is intended to reduce the level of inequality in the country.

Certain assets, such as a person's principal dwelling house, are exempt and small capital gains (in 1986 up to a limit of £6,300) are also non-taxable. All other gains are charged at a fixed rate of 30%.

Difficulties can often arise in the actual market valuation of assets, both at the time of purchase and sale, and CGT has had only limited effect on either redistributing wealth, or as a source of income for the government.

INDIRECT TAXATION

Taxation on the consumption of goods and services is referred to as indirect tax. The tax is usually paid to the government by manufacturers, retailers or the providers of services, but its burden is ultimately borne by the consumer.

There are three main forms of indirect taxation currently in operation in the UK today:

> (a)   Value Added Tax;
>
> (b)   Customs and Excise Duties;
>
> (c)   Licences.

Value Added Tax

Value Added Tax (VAT) has been in operation since 1973 and superceded purchase or sales tax which the government had levied since 1940.

VAT is imposed on most goods or services produced or sold in this country. There are, however, a number of exceptions. Some goods are zero rated and as such bear no VAT. These are products or services regarded as necessities and include food, fuel, children's clothing and passenger transport. Other goods exempt from VAT in this category are education services, health services, insurance and postal services. Exemption enables suppliers to reclaim the VAT on inputs to the productive process.

Apart from these two special classifications, all other goods and services are currently taxed at 15%. This is levied at each stage of manufacture or sale.

The process of levying VAT has two aspects to it. At each stage of production, VAT is calculated at the input stage and the output stage.

(i)   the input stage

When a manufacturer buys raw materials, the supplier charges VAT and as such the manufacturer regards it as input tax.

(ii)   the output stage

Once the manufacturer has processed the raw materials and they are ready for resale as a finished product he then adds 15% VAT to the sale price. Here the tax becomes an output tax.

At the end of the tax period the manufacturer deducts the VAT he has paid as an input tax from that he has charged as an output tax and the residue is paid to the government and collected by the Customs and Excise Department.

The example below illustrates how this works in money terms.

EXAMPLE

Assess a manufacturer's VAT liability

Cost of raw material purchased by manufacturer	100,000
VAT charged at 15% by raw material supplier (*input tax*)	15,000
Sale price of manufactured product	150,000
VAT charged at 15% by manufacturer to customer (*output tax*)	22,500

The manufacturer has added

$$£150,000 \; less \; £100,000 = £50,000$$

of extra value to the raw materials by his manufacturing process

His VAT liability is assessed as

output tax   input tax

£22,500   *less*   £15,000 = £7,500

This is equivalent to 15% of the value he has added to the raw materials

15% of £50,000 = £7,500

The process of taxing only the added value clearly gives VAT its name.

If the manufacturer should sell his product for less than the cost of his raw materials, for instance, because of a fall in price, then he is entitled to a VAT rebate because the output tax he receives will be less than the input tax he has paid.

VAT is the single most important indirect tax in the UK and its introduction was seen as a first step towards a standardisation of the EEC's tax system. It is suggested that should European economic unification ever be achieved, VAT will be the EEC's central source of finance.

One of the major criticisms of VAT is that it is not a convenient tax to collect. It has very high administrative costs and places a considerable burden, particularly on small businesses, in its calculation and payment.

Customs and Excise Duties

There is a distinction between Customs and Excise Duties.

Customs are taxes levied on goods produced abroad and imported into this country while excise duties are taxes placed on certain domestically produced products.

Between them they have a number of objectives.

(a) to raise revenue, and to this end they are placed on certain items which have a high inelasticity of demand, such as alcohol and tobacco;

(b) to protect domestically produced products. For this purpose customs duties are placed on imports to ensure that they will not dramatically undercut home products;

(c) to deter consumption of products which the government may regard as harmful to society. Products such as alcohol and tobacco, as well as being ideal revenue raisers because they have inelastic demand, are also damaging to health and therefore the government places a high level of duty on them with the justification that it is protecting society.

Licences

The final form of indirect taxation on consumption is the imposition of licence fees on certain commodities. This involves the levy of a fee on:

(a)   the ownership of an article or animal such as a dog, or

(b)   the use of an asset such as a car, or television or CB radio, or

(c)   the provision of a service such as gaming or the sale of alcohol.

The fees, which in fact contribute a relatively small proportion of tax revenue, go either to central or local government.

Despite common belief, the licence fee is usually not allocated for a specific purpose. For example the 'road fund tax' which is actually called Vehicle Excise Duty is not used exclusively for road improvements but is merely another source of revenue for the central exchequer.

There are a number of advantages of indirect taxation:

(i)   One of the major arguments for indirect tax is that it is less evident or visible to the consumer, who is not aware of the extent of the tax being levied in most purchase transactions.

(ii)   VAT which is set as a percentage of the sale price is necessarily buoyant. This means that the government's revenue will rise as prices rise.

(iii) Indirect taxes may also be said to offer a choice to the taxpayer because he or she can choose whether or not to buy the taxed commodity.

However indirect taxation does have the following disadvantages:

(i)   Customs and Excise Duties are levied on quantities or volume, and as such must be increased regularly to keep pace with inflation. For example, if the price of cigarettes rose from £1.30 for 20 to £1.40 as a result of inflation and the duty was not raised, then the government's tax revenue would not rise in line with inflation. Unlike VAT, this tax is not buoyant. Therefore it is usual for such duties to be increased at each budget, bringing with it the cry that drinkers, smokers and drivers are hit again. In fact, the rise in duty is often no more than the rise in inflation.

(ii)   Perhaps the most damning criticism of indirect taxation is that it is not progressive and may therefore cause injustice. It is for this reason that the shift from direct to indirect taxation has been relatively slow in the period from 1940 until 1979. However, it has been an avowed aim of the Thatcher government to reduce income tax and this has only been made feasible by a corresponding increase in indirect taxation.

LOCAL GOVERNMENT TAXATION

In this section of the chapter we shall concentrate on local government taxation.

Local authorities receive their revenue from three sources:

(a)   grants from central government,

(b)   domestic and commercial rates,

(c)   charges for the services they provide.

Of these the largest single proportion of revenue is provided by central government grants. Here it is proposed however to concentrate on an examination of the rating system as the main form of local taxation.

The Rating System

Rates are levied on:

- (a) domestic dwellings,
- (b) non-agricultural land, and
- (c) commercial and industrial property.

As such, they can be seen as a tax on capital in the form of property and land ownership or as a tax on consumption on the use of the land and property.

Rate determination

Rates are determined by two factors:

- (a) the rateable value of the land or property,
- (b) the rate poundage charged by the local authority.

Rateable value

The rateable value is, in theory, based on the net annual value which could be achieved if the property were let. As most rated property is not rented however but consists rather of owner-occupied domestic dwellings, then this basis of rateable value has become rather unclear.

Instead a value is determined by the Inland Revenue.

This is based on:

- (a) the size of the land or property,
- (b) the location,
- (c) the potential market value.

It is a very unsatisfactory system which has been subject to much criticism, mainly on the grounds that it can produce injustice. Furthermore rateable value reviews occur very infrequently, currently about once every ten years, and so circumstances, and obviously rateable values, can change drastically during this period.

The rate poundage

The rate poundage determined by the local authority can be regarded as the 'tax rate' for rates.

It is given in pence per pound and is calculated by firstly, determining the local authority's revenue requirements, and secondly using the total rateable value of the authority's area to find out how much in the pound needs to be charged.

The Example below illustrates how this is done.

EXAMPLE

Assess the rate poundage to be charged by a local authority

Local authority's revenue requirements   =   £100m

Local authority's rateable value   =   £125m

Therefore rate in the pound

$$= \frac{100}{125} \; x \; \; 100$$

=   80p in the pound.

Like other forms of taxation, the rating system has its advantages and disadvantages. Once again we shall examine them both in turn.

The advantages of the Rating System:

(i)   The system is well-established, it is understood, and to a greater or lesser extent accepted by the taxpayer.

(ii)   Rates have a wide tax base in that most people pay them either directly or through their landlord.

(iii)   They provide a substantial yield, are relatively cheap to collect, and their yield is certain (i.e. the local authority is aware of the extra revenue it will raise by increasing the rate poundage).

(iv)   There is little scope for evasion or avoidance as people normally will not move from one rating area to another simply to achieve a lower rate bill.

(v)   Taxpayers are normally aware of their likely tax liability and so are able to make allowance either by putting money to one side at regular intervals or by paying in instalments.

(vi)   There is a direct relationship between the tax revenue raised and the expenditure it is used for. This is because the local authority is both the tax levier and the tax spender. Therefore if the taxpayer is not happy about how much tax is being levied or how it is being spent he has the power through the ballot box to make changes.

The disadvantages of the Rating System:

(i)   As already mentioned, the procedure for assessing rateable value is heavily criticised.

(ii)   There is not necessarily any correlation between an individual's rate bill and his or her ability to pay. It is often the case that older people, living in a large house with a high rateable value, find that their income falls dramatically as they reach pensionable age. However, their rate bill will not be correspondingly reduced and so they face paying a much higher proportion of their income in rates. It is not always true to suppose that those who live in larger houses have higher incomes. This problem has been reduced to some extent by the provision of rate rebates.

(iii)   It is a very evident tax as people are made well aware of their tax burden. The taxpayer is faced with a large tax bill twice a year which must be paid from disposable income. Many authorities have attempted to alleviate this burden by introducing instalment payments.

(iv) Rates also lack buoyancy as a tax. The yield from the rates will not rise automatically with the rate of inflation. Instead, each year councils must increase the rate poundage. This in turn tends to act as a continual focus of opposition to local authority finance.

(v) Industry pays rates and yet has no vote on local authority control.

(vi) If the rates are very high in a particular area this may encourage industry to move out with consequent job losses.

Because of criticisms such as these, the government has seriously considered a number of alternatives to the rating system including local income tax and local sales tax.

Currently the government is planning to replace the rating system with a new community tax which will involve a tax on all adults living in a local authority's area rather than a tax on individual property.

GOVERNMENT BORROWING

So far in this chapter we have discussed taxation as the major source of government revenue. However, the level of taxation is insufficient to meet total government expenditure. The government is faced with a short-fall.

In order to meet this it must turn to its second source of finance, borrowing. The amount of the short-fall between government expenditure and government revenue is called the Public Sector Borrowing Requirement (PSBR). This is the annual figure which the government must borrow to pay its way.

Because the government must borrow year after year this figure accumulates and the total amount owed by the government is the National Debt.

Fortunately this debt does not have to be repaid in one lump sum. If it did it would require more than one year's total tax revenue. In fact this debt is a rolling debt. This means that as one part of it is repaid, the government will borrow more, with repayment to be made sometime in the future.

Sources of Government Borrowing

There are four main sources of government borrowing:

(a) Marketable debt

Here the government borrows by using securities such as Treasury Bills (short-term loans for a period of 91 days) and gilt-edged securities (longer term loans ranging up to 25 or 35 years).

This is referred to as marketable debt because ownership can be sold on the stock exchange or financial markets in the same way as stocks and shares.

These loans come mainly from large institutional lenders such as:

(i) banks,

(ii) building societies,

(iii) finance houses and companies,

who regard such loans to the government as being very secure and also capable of being sold quickly to realise cash.

(b) Non-marketable debt

Non-marketable debt is mainly in the form of loans from individuals who hold:

       (i)   National Savings Certificates,

      (ii)   Premium bonds,

and other forms of individual securities.

Their ownership cannot be transferred but, if the individual wishes to cash them in, then the government will repay the loan (although some forms of savings may require that the money is left with the government for a specified period).

(c) Official holdings

The government actually borrows money from itself. Technically, certain government funds are held in separate accounts. For instance, National Insurance contributions are not paid directly into the Exchequer but to the National Insurance Fund. The government will borrow from these funds and pay a rate of interest as it would to non-government lenders.

(d) Overseas holdings

In the past the government has been forced to borrow from abroad to finance wars or financial crises. Thus the government still owes a little money to foreign banks and governments.

In recent years it has had to turn to organisations such as the International Monetary Fund as a source of loans, but this form of borrowing has declined of late.

The figure below illustrates the distribution of holdings of the National Debt.

The Distribution of Holdings of the National Debt

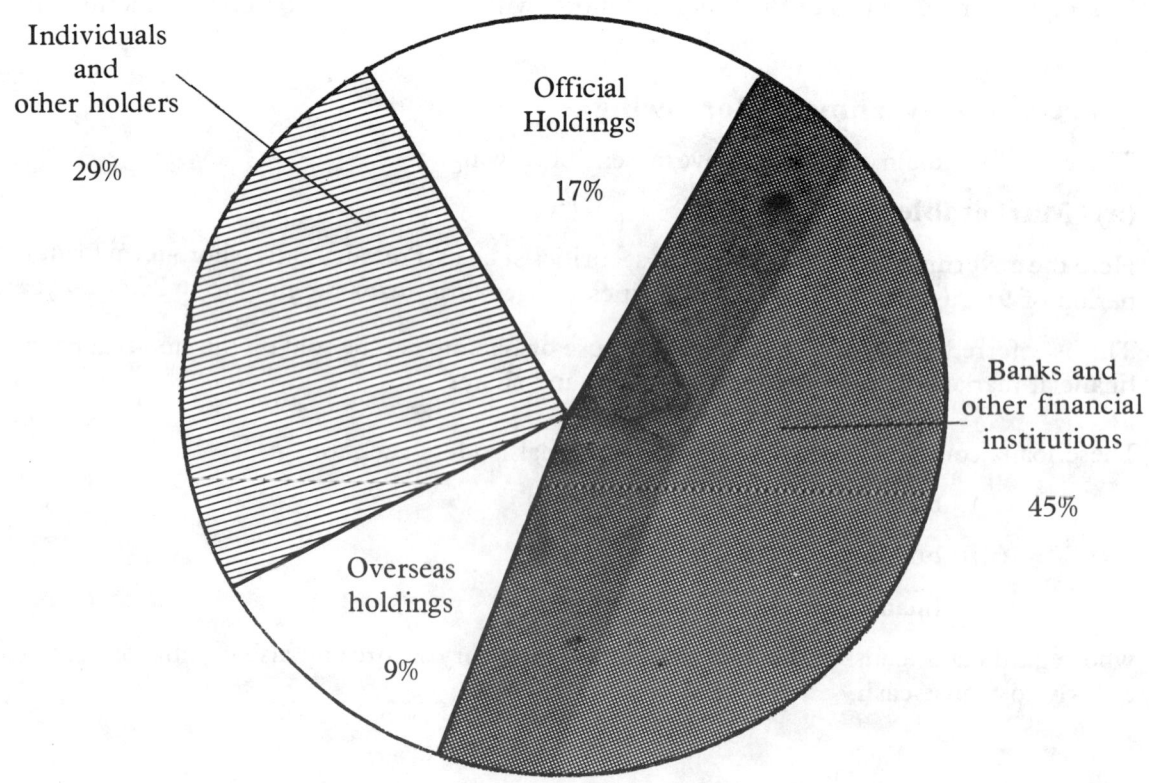

The National Debt should not be regarded as a reflection of the bad housekeeping of successive governments. This is not a fair reflection of the situation. The debt has accumulated for a number of justifiable reasons and its burden is not as serious as at first sight it may appear. The reasons for this are as follows.

(i) A considerable portion of the debt has been incurred as the State has increased its productive capacity. Thus the nationalised industries were purchased using borrowed money. In such cases the debt can in effect be offset by the increase in the State's productive assets.

(ii) Interest payments on the debt are only a burden on the economy if they are paid to overseas holders. Domestically held debt receives interest but this can be viewed merely as a transfer from one sector of the economy to another.

(iii) The National Debt has fallen dramatically in terms of its proportion of national income and the interest on the debt now only accounts for about $3^1/_2\%$ of Gross Domestic Product. The burden of the debt in real terms has continued to fall, particularly during periods of high inflation. This is because a large proportion of the debt is in the form of fixed interest securities and if inflation rises the 'real' rate of interest on these fall and in doing so reduce the government's repayments in real terms.

Clearly the size of the National Debt and its efficient management are of considerable importance to the government and the Treasury. For this reason the Bank of England must be careful to ensure that the government is able to fund the debt as cheaply as possible.

One particular consideration they must bear in mind is the effect such large-scale borrowing will have on interest rates and the rate of inflation. If the government seeks to borrow substantial funds from the money markets this can reduce the level of funds available to other borrowers and to push up interest rates. The government can also be accused of 'crowding out' private sector borrowers who may be seeking loans to finance business investment.

By borrowing from banks the government actually increases their ability to lend out more money to other customers. This may appear strange but it is because the banks are permitted to regard short-term loans to the government as part of their liquid reserve assets. In chapter 25 you will see the bank multiplier depends on the extent of these liquid reserves, and so any substantial increase resulting from government borrowing can lead to an increase in bank lending, pushing up the money supply and causing a rise in inflation.

ASSIGNMENT — RUSSELL-HOBAN

RUSSELL-HOBAN PLASTICS' FINANCIAL CRISIS

The Company

Russell-Hoban Plastics Ltd. is a small private company formed in 1968 engaged in the manufacture and supply of high grade plastic engineering materials.

The company share structure is as follows:-

> **CAPITAL**
> **Authorised Capital** — £100,000
> **Issued Capital** — £60,000 (comprising 60,000 £1 ordinary shares carrying one vote per share)
> **Paid Up** — £45,000 (comprising of 75% of the value of each ordinary share issued)

There are three directors of the company — Ben Russell, Jack Hoban (Managing Director) and Andy Russell (Ben's son). Ben and Jack are the company's founders and each holds 20,000 ordinary shares, while Andy holds 11,000 shares. All three directors are actively involved in managing the company business. The remaining 9,000 shares are divided equally between three other shareholders who are ex-employees of the company. The company's main assets are its industrial premises over which the company own the freehold and which have a present valuation of £60,000. These are currently mortgaged for £40,000 of which £15,000 is outstanding and is repayable over the remaining 4 years of the mortgage period. The company's main liability is a five-year loan of £40,000 which the company obtained two years ago from its bankers (Barclays) and has £28,500 (capital and interest) remaining to be repaid.

Although having a history of trading at a healthy profit, declaring high dividends and providing capital for re-investment until 1984, the company declared a net loss of £4,200 in 1985 and £6,750 in 1986. This has been the result of increased costs of production. The company has been reluctant to pass on increased costs to their consumers through higher prices and has had only two small price rises of 7% and 4% over the last two years. In the same period, sales, in quantity terms, have increased by 10% per annum. In an attempt to meet the rising demand for their product, the company decided in January 1984 to invest in new advanced machinery purchased from Orbit A.G., a West German manufacturer. The cost of the machinery, £86,000, was met by using the company's total reserve capital. The directors decided to make a cash purchase in return for a substantial 30% discount. Since the introduction of this machinery, production has increased dramatically and sales are rising. Nevertheless, although these signs are good for the future, the directors have calculated that in the present year, 1986-87, the company will continue to make a loss (projected at £4,800).

The Financial Crisis

Jack Hoban has called a directors' meeting for 22nd December 1986 to discuss what he describes in the agenda of the meeting as the company's "financial crisis". Jack is concerned by the news from the company's two major clients that they are both in short term financial difficulties and require an extension of credit facilities on debts owed to Russell-Hoban Ltd. for plastics supplied by the company to them. The amounts owing are £2,600 and £4,700, respectively, and had been earmarked as sufficient to pay the December wage bill of £7,000. This could not otherwise be met from cash in hand which amounts to £1,500.

Jack, who tends to over-react, has openly said that "this is the last straw" and feels that it is "time to call it a day and shut up shop". He is supported by all three minority shareholders (the ex-employees) who are unhappy at not receiving any return on their investment for the last two years and are aware of the projected loss for 1986-87. They feel that a dissolution of the company and a sale of its assets would provide the best opportunity for a return of their investment. Ben and his son, Andy, are adamant that the company has a future and are determined that it should survive.

TASKS

You are an administrative assistant employed by Russell-Hoban working for Ben Russell. Mr. Russell is anxious to be fully briefed in advance of the crucial meeting. He has asked you to prepare a confidential report in which you consider the following issues:

1. In the past board decisions have always been reached without the need for a formal vote. Anticipating that in this instance a vote will be demanded, Mr Russell needs to know which alternative combinations of voting shareholders exercise control for:

    a. the carrying on of normal company business;

    b. the authorisation of the company's dissolution?

2. What are the possible sources of short term finance necessary to meet the December wage bill?

3. In the event of a stalemate between Jack and the minority shareholders on one side and Ben and Andy on the other at the metting, what are the possible alternative courses of action which could be taken?

4. How could the company be put on a firm financial footing for the future bearing in mind possible alternative sources of finance?

DEVELOPMENTAL TASK

5. Undertake a role play exercise in which the board meeting is simulated.

ASSIGNMENT — TAXATION POLICY

At the next meeting of the NALGO branch of Northdownshire County Council there is an item on the agenda which involves a consideration of the government's taxation policy. This will include an examination of any changes it has made over the last few years and the effects this has had on individuals and the economy as a whole.

TASK

1. You are the chairperson of the branch. In order to speak on this item prepare notes which outline the following:

    (a) the reasons for government taxation;

    (b) the main forms of taxation;

    (c) the advantages and disadvantages of each of the different forms of taxation.

To help in the preparation of your notes you should refer to the table given below which gives a brief summary of the changes in amounts raised from different sources of revenue over the period from 1974-1984.

GOVERNMENT FINANCE

	1974	1979	1984
Public Sector Borrowing Requirement (PSBR)	£M 6434	£M 12671	£M 10212
as percentage of GDP:-			
PSBR	7.7	6.5	3.2
Taxes on Household Income	11.7	10.3	10.8
Taxes on Corporate Income	3.4	2.6	3.7
Taxes on Expenditure	13.6	15.2	16.4
Taxes on Capital	1.0	0.5	0.5
National Insurance	5.9	5.9	7.1
Total Taxes and National Insurance	35.7	34.4	38.5

DEVELOPMENTAL TASK

2. Undertake a role play exercise in which you simulate the union branch meeting. Some members of the branch should adopt a stance in which they favour cuts in direct personal taxation while others should argue in favour of a reduction in indirect taxes as an alternative to income tax cuts. Others should propose a general increase in taxation as a means of financing an increase in government expenditure.

Chapter 13

THE DEVELOPMENT AND PURPOSE OF ACCOUNTING

The development of a sophisticated economy relies on commercial activity. As we note in chapter 18 an individual is unable to produce all the goods and services that he needs. Inevitably therefore he will trade some of those goods which he has or which he can produce, for those owned by others which he requires. Trade existed from the earliest times but initially took the form of 'barter' in which a direct exchange of one person's goods for another's was made. Barter however has one major drawback. It requires a mutual coincidence of needs. By this we mean that if you require a particular product you must find someone who not only has what you want but also wants what you have to offer in return. To find such a person was not always an easy task and so markets developed to which people took their goods in the hope of finding a trading partner. Trade of this sort flourished and the first financial records we have are dated from such times. If a person was involved in only a small number of trading transactions then no doubt he could remember all the deals negotiated. However for an individual taking part in many transactions it became necessary to record them in some way. This was often merely in the form of a list of the number of sheep traded for horses or grain bartered for cloth. There was no structure to such records and each trader developed a system of recording transactions which suited them. As trading developed the purpose and functions of accounting developed. They evolved into:

    (i)   the recording of financial information;

    (ii)   the provision of management information;

    (iii)   the provision of information to assess the stewardship of organisations.

1. THE RECORDING OF FINANCIAL INFORMATION

The development of markets certainly made barter easier but it still did not completely solve the problem of mutual coincidence of needs. However man is a resourceful creature and gradually developed a system which used currency. This was acceptable to both trading partners and could also be held and used later to buy other goods. As trading increased there also arose a need for merchants or middlemen who bought and sold goods, not for their own use, but in order to make a profit. For them the actual goods traded were not of the utmost importance. Instead the important aspect was the money that such goods represented.

Credit trading was a further development. Here the payment for goods was not made immediately but an agreement was made to pay later. Therefore it became necessary to establish a system by which the amounts of money that were owed to and owed by the trader were recorded. Thus what evolved was an elementary system of book-keeping which we can trace back to the earliest times, but which came into being as a recognisable and acceptable system of accounting in Italy in the 13th and 14th centuries. Such Italian traders were the first people to develop the method of book-keeping which is now universally applied. It is called 'double entry book-keeping'. At this time the needs of such trading organisations were merely to keep track of their transactions and the amounts of money that were owed and were owing.

2.   THE PROVISION OF MANAGEMENT INFORMATION

As trade developed outside the confines of the Italian city states, merchants came together in joint trading partnerships to exploit the potential of the Far East and other sources of trading commodities. Such trading ventures were extremely costly to finance but could prove very profitable. It became important to assess the cost of such ventures, determine the revenue gained from them and finally to share the profit among the participating trading firms. At this point the recording of transactions assumed a more important role. There began to be the need for management accounts which allowed the partners to judge the success of the trading ventures and so plan further trips.

3.   THE PROVISION OF FINANCIAL INFORMATION TO ALLOW THE ASSESSMENT OF THE 'STEWARDSHIP' OF ORGANISATIONS.

As commerce expanded throughout the world it was matched by the progress of the industrial revolution. In the United Kingdom in particular, invention and technical change meant that larger and more sophisticated trading organisations were needed to exploit the breakthroughs in production and distribution. To be able to finance such organisations it was necessary to raise money from much wider sources.

This need led to the introduction of the limited liability company in the mid 19th century where shares in a business were sold to those outside the organisation.

This form of business organisation was formalised with the passing of the Joint Stock Companies Registration and Regulation Act 1844, which created the office of the Registrar of Companies. The Act required that companies who invited the public to subscribe for shares had to be registered and the company's audited accounts had to be filed with the Registrar for public inspection. This was extended by the Limited Liability Act 1855, which introduced the principle of limited liability for all registered companies, the Joint Stock Companies Act 1856, which introduced the requirement of a 'Memorandum of Association' and 'Articles of Association' as the documents regulating the company's affairs and the Companies Act 1907, which introduced the private limited company.

As we note in chapters 12 and 18 the distinctive feature of the limited company is that often the shareholders do not manage the business but instead appoint executives who manage it on their behalf. Clearly the shareholders have a right to be kept informed of the trading progress of the business of which they are part owners and so the third purpose of accounting evolved. This is to provide financial information to the owners of a business who are not directly involved in its operation. This is referred to as the 'stewardship' function of accounting.

Let us recap on the three functions of accounting which have developed:

(i)   The recording of financial information;

(ii)   The provision of management information;

(iii)   The provision of financial records and information to assess the 'stewardship' of an organisation.

It is necessary to examine the precise nature of each of these functions in some detail but first some developments which have affected accountancy as a profession will be considered.

DEVELOPMENT OF THE ACCOUNTANCY BODIES

As we have seen the most common form of business organisation in today's economy is the limited company and it has been the increasing complexity of such organisations which has necessitated further developments and refinements in accounting. These have mainly come about as accountancy has developed as a profession. The days of Bob Cratchett as Scrooge's book-keeper perched on his high table filling in ledgers with a quill pen have long since disappeared. By the turn of the century a number of professional accountancy bodies had been formed. Today the most important of these are the Institute of Chartered Accountants (ICA), the Association of Certified Accountants (ACA), the Institute of Cost and Management Accountants (ICMA) and the Chartered Institute of Public Finance and Accountancy (CIPFA). These organisations have contributed to improvements in the standards and practice of accountancy by ensuring that their members are suitably qualified and by developing accounting techniques and applications. In 1970 the leading accountancy bodies jointly formed the Accounting Standards Committee (ASC) which is responsible for promoting good accountancy practice. Its recommendations have been in the form of Statements of Standard Accounting Practice (SSAP's) which provide their members with guidelines on such matters as auditing and the presentation of financial statements.

. . . accounting has developed as a profession.

Each of the main accountancy bodies have their own rules and regulations for membership but all require the potential accountant to study for and pass examinations during a period of training. While it is not uncommon to find members of each of the professional bodies in all areas of financial management there is a tendency toward specialisation.

Such developments have meant than an accountant is no longer regarded merely as a book-keeper but instead he is an important part of a management team within an organisation or as a valuable financial advisor to a business. We will discuss the precise role of the accountant a little later in the chapter.

THE PURPOSE OF ACCOUNTING

In the section above we identified the three main functions of accounting as: (i) the recording of financal information; (ii) the provision of management information; and (iii) the 'stewardship' function. We will now examine each of these in some detail.

(i) THE RECORDING OF FINANCIAL INFORMATION

The accountancy function has developed from the need of the organisation to keep accurate records. This process is referred to quite simply as 'book-keeping'. Such records must be kept in a suitable format so that they can be interpreted and analysed. (It is this stage of the process which is referred to as 'accountancy'.) As we shall see in chapter 14 financial statements are the means by which we are able to assess the performance of an organisation, however it is important to recognise how these statements are compiled, what initial data is included in them and how this financial data is assembled and processed throughout the accounting period. It is a very un-wise manager who relies solely on the end of period financial statements to judge the progress of the organisation. Throughout the year the decision maker must have accurate financial inform-ation readily available on which to base day-to-day operational decisions.

Other people will also wish to see that accurate financial records have been kept. The Inland Revenue, Customs and Excise (who administer the VAT system), bank managers and other pro-viders of finance may require sight of the organisation's records. Thus it is essential that the system used to maintain the records of the organisation is comprehensive, accurate and can be interpreted not only by the organisation's own managers but also by outsiders. Therefore the organisation must employ a method of 'book-keeping' which adequately meets these require-ments.

THE PRINCIPLES OF BOOK-KEEPING

To be able to more fully understand the financial records of a business it is necessary to appreciate the basic principles of book-keeping. It is important to ensure that the type of books which are kept should be suitable to the form of organisation that is being operated. Clearly the larger the enterprise, the more complex and sophisticated should be the book-keeping system. However here we will concentrate on a relatively simple system to allow you to understand the basic principles.

The basic records to be kept.

There are some essential books that all businesses should keep. These are:

1. Cash Books
    (i)   A Bank Account Book;
    (ii) Petty Cash Book.

2. Wages Book.

3. Day Books (or Journals)
    (i)   A Sales Day Book;
    (ii) A Purchase Day Book.

4. Ledgers
    (i)   Sales Ledger;
    (ii)   Purchase Ledger;
    (iii) Nominal or General Ledger.

1. Cash Books

These should be kept to allow the organisation to keep control of its cash payments and receipts. There are normally two main records of cash transactions, the bank account book and the petty cash book.

(i) The bank account book

This will record all cash receipts into the organisation and their subsequent payment into the organisation's bank account. It will also record all withdrawals from the bank account whether they are made by cheque, direct debit or standing order. The business should also retain all the cheque stubs, paying in books and bank statements as a means of confirming the accuracy of the bank account book.

(ii) The petty cash book

Normally a business will carry a cash float as petty cash to cover the purchase of small items of expenditure. A record of this float should be kept in the petty cash book and a note made of all petty cash withdrawals. This should mention both the amount withdrawn and its purpose. This is an important area, for many organisations find that petty cash is one aspect of the business which can often be abused. It is always important to keep receipts for even the smallest transaction as it may be necessary to verify them later. The petty cash book should be checked on a regular basis, perhaps once a week or even daily if large sums of petty cash are involved. The book should agree with the receipts held and the cash in hand.

2. Wages Book

If the organisation employs staff it must, by law, keep a record of employees wages paid showing a breakdown of gross pay, deductions for tax and National Insurance Contributions. This record must be kept for all employees earning above the minimum level for National Insurance contributions, however it is wise to maintain records of all wage payments made to staff even if it is not required by law.

3. Day Books (or Journals)

If the organisation is a trading concern it should keep records of all transactions in which it is involved. These are normally of two kinds — selling and buying and the business should record each.

(i) A sales day book

This will record all sales made and invoices issued on a daily basis. It will identify different sorts of sales if the organisation is selling more than one type of product and it will show the VAT the organisation charged its customers. The business will later have to pay this over to the Customs and Excise as output tax.

(ii) A purchase day book

This will list, on a daily basis, all purchases and expenditure incurred by the organisation. It should be sufficiently detailed to analyse the different categories of expenditure that the organisation makes. Therefore it should classify transactions into groups such as purchases, rent, rates, energy, postage and telephones etc. This will provide useful information for the financial management of the organisation as it will then be possible to identify how much has been spent under different expenditure headings at regular intervals. It should also separate out the VAT which the business has had to pay on its expenditure so that this can be reclaimed as input tax.

4.   Ledgers

If the business deals in credit transactions then it is necessary to keep a sales and a purchase ledger. These are kept to identify transactions with individual suppliers. Therefore the organisation will normally keep:

(i)   A sales ledger

This contains the individual accounts of customers which are known as personal accounts. These will clearly indicate the amount of business the organisation is doing with individual customers and allow the control of unpaid invoices from customers who are slow payers. It is normal practice to record credit sales on the left hand side of the ledger and customer's payments on the right. At the end of each month it is possible to deduct the right hand column from the left to find out how much each customer still owes the organisation and so a statement can be drawn up.

(ii)   A purchases ledger

This will keep a record of the transactions with individual suppliers. Again this is a useful source of management information as it identifies important suppliers and may alert the management when the organisation is becoming too dependent on one supplier. The purchase ledger is kept in a similar manner to the sales ledger except that payments to a supplier are recorded on the left hand side while the value of items purchased are shown on the right. It is then possible to determine a monthly position showing the amount the organisation still has outstanding as debts to suppliers.

(iii)   A nominal or impressed ledger

This will be an overall record of expenditure and income and should classify each transaction according to its purpose. It brings together the information from the other ledgers (which are referred to as 'primary' ledgers).

> Basically the keeping of any ledger is a means of analysing transactions on a daily basis. The number of accounts contained in a ledger is determined by the degree of analysis required by the business. The nominal ledger will therefore contain accounts for Sales, Purchases, Heating, Wages, Rent, etc.

THE SYSTEM OF DOUBLE ENTRY BOOK-KEEPING

We noted earlier in the chapter that the system of double entry book-keeping began in Italy in the middle ages as a means of monitoring and controlling the transactions of merchants. It has evolved to become the most common method of book-keeping in the world. It is not our intention here to provide you with a training course in the method however, it is worth understanding the basic principles as it will allow you to interpret financial statements more easily in later chapters.

The basis of the system is that every transaction in which the organisation is involved must have a dual aspect. In other words if it buys goods the organisation is the buyer and money will leave the business. At the same time its supplier will provide goods or services which are adding to the organisation's stock of wealth. Conversely if it sells goods then its customer is the buyer and will provide payment while it will lose goods in making a sale.

Let us use some simple examples:

Example 1:   The business makes a sale to a customer, J. Jones, to the value of £1,000.

The entries in the books in respect of this will be to enter £1,000 on the left hand side of the account for J. Jones which is kept in the sales ledger, and to enter £1,000 in the right hand side of the account for Sales which is kept in the nominal ledger.

The entries tell us that J. Jones owes the business £1,000 and that the business has earned income from its selling activities amounting to £1,000. Note that it is at the point of sale that income is deemed to be earned, not later when the customer pays.

For convenience accountants call the left hand side of an account the Debit side and the right hand side is the Credit side.

Remember: LEFT-HAND   = DEBIT
           RIGHT-HAND = CREDIT

When J. Jones eventually pays the £1,000 he owes, the cash book will have a debit entry of £1,000 and J. Jones' account will have a credit entry of £1,000. J. Jones' account will now be clear showing that he does not owe the business any money.

Example 2:   The business makes a purchase for an amount of £3,000 from W. Gibson Ltd.

In this case there will be a credit entry of £3,000 against the supplier, W. Gibson Ltd, in the purchases ledger to signify the purchase of the goods. There would also be a debit entry for £3,000 in the purchases account of the general ledger. When the supplier is paid for the goods, these entries are closed by a credit entry in the cash book and a debit entry to W. Gibson Ltd's account in the purchases ledger.

At certain points in time the books are balanced, that is that each account is looked at and any balance left on it is listed under either a debit column or a credit column. If an account has more in terms of monetary amounts on the debit side than on the credit side then the balance on that account will be a debit balance for instance:

J. Jones Account						
		£				£
1st May	Sales	1,000	15th May	Cash		1,000
3rd May	Sales	1,500				
10th May	Sales	2,000				

The balance on the J. Jones account is a debit balance of £3,500.

When all the debit balances are listed and added and all the credit balances are listed and added, the totals of the two lists should be the same.

These lists are known as the Trial Balance and check the accuracy of the double entry book-keeping. The fact that the Trial Balance balances does not however guarantee that everything is correct, only that the mathematical aspect of the book-keeping is correct. There may have been other errors such as items in the wrong accounts or items missed out altogether. Since the books are balanced however, the final account can be produced in the manner we will discuss in chapter 14.

(ii) THE PROVISION OF MANAGEMENT INFORMATION

The second of the accounting functions is the provision of information for management. As a basic concept this is as true for the sole trader as it is for the multi-national corporation. Both must be managed and both require appropriate and accurate financial information which will guide them in their decision making. The information that they require must enable them to:

(a)   establish and monitor the financial targets of the organisation;

(b)   control income and expenditure within the organisation.

This type of accounting is usually known as cost and management accounting and is concerned with the preparation of budgets for each part of the organisation and the costing of its operations. We will be considering these aspects of financial management in some detail in chapter 16.

(iii) THE STEWARDSHIP FUNCTION OF ACCOUNTING

The final function of accounting is to allow an assessment of the 'stewardship' of an organisation. By this we mean that it should provide a method by which the owners of the organisation can assess how effectively and efficiently the managers of the business are performing their task. Clearly this role is most important in organisations in which ownership (the shareholders) is separated from control (the management) for in such circumstances the individual shareholder will not wish to be involved or informed of the day to day operations of the business. It will be sufficient for the managers to provide an honest and accurate picture of the performance of the organisation over a trading period such as six months or a year to satisfy the owners. This is provided in the form of the balance sheet, profit and loss account and the other financial statements. These will be examined in chapter 14. Obviously it will be necessary to have such statements verified and it is at this stage that the accountancy function takes on the role of audit. Here an outside independent auditor will confirm the accounts and so ensure their accuracy.

Other individuals and organisations outside the business will also wish to be made aware of the organisation's performance. Therefore the Inland Revenue and the Customs and Excise Department have the right to inspect an organisation's financial records. Furthermore all limited companies must also provide sets of their accounts to the Companies Registrar which may then be examined by any member of the general public.

ASSIGNMENT — THE CASE OF THE VANISHING CHEQUE

Marshall's Cash and Carry is a large food wholesaler based in Barnet in Hertfordshire. Below are reproduced extracts from a recent series of the company's business correspondence.

Letter from David Brown & Co Ltd to Marshall's dated 20th September 1986

Dear Sirs,

May we draw your attention to the overdue item of £4,700 on our May account. Could you please offer an explanation as to why the account has not been paid or please pay the outstanding balance by return.

Letter from Marshall's to David Brown and Co Ltd. dated 3rd October 1986

Dear Sirs,

Thank you for your letter of 30th Sept., 1986. We wish to inform you that a cheque for £5,200 was sent to you on 30th June 1986. This cheque covered the £4,700 which was outstanding and also included a payment in error of £500 for goods which had been returned to you for credit.

Letter from David Brown and Co Ltd to Marshall's dated 9th October 1986

Dear Sirs,

Thank you for your prompt reply to our letter of 30th September 1986. We have no record of receiving the cheque mentioned in your letter and therefore request an immediate settlement of our account.

Letter from Marshall's to David Brown and Co Ltd dated 14th October 1986

Dear Sirs,

With reference to your letter of the 9th October we find that the cheque for £5,200 has been cleared by our bankers. As this would indicate that the cheque has been received by your company, we would ask that you further investigate the matter. To determine if some fault lies with us we will make an additional examination of our records.

TASK

You are employed in the Accounts section of Marshall's Cash and Carry and the owner, Harry Marshall, has asked you to investigate the matter detailed in the above letters. You check the records for the transaction and find that there has clearly been a mix up between the accounts of David Brown and Co Ltd and D. Browne Ltd, another of Marshall's suppliers. The relevant accounts are shown below.

DAVID BROWN & CO LTD

		£			£
April 30	Cash	2,500	April 1	Balance b/f	2,500
May 31	Cash	10,200	April 3	Purchases	7,600
	Returns	500	April 19	Purchases	3,100
June 30	Cash	5,200	May 16	Purchases	4,700
July 31	Cash	3,800	June 10	Purchases	3,800
Aug 31	Cash	2,000	July 18	Purchases	2,500
	Returns	500	Aug 14	Purchases	5,300
Sept 30	Cash	5,300	Sept 19	Purchases	4,000
	Balance c/d	3,500			
		33,500			33,500
			Oct 1	Balance b/d	3,500

D. BROWNE LTD

		£			£
April 30	Cash	8,000	April 1	Balance b/d	8,000
May 30	Cash	2,100	April 19	Purchases	2,100
July 31	Cash	7,700	May 16	Purchases	3,600
Sept 30	Balance c/d	7,200	May 19	Purchases	1,600
			June 16	Purchases	4,000
			July 18	Purchases	3,700
			Sept 16	Purchases	2,000
		25,000			25,000
			Oct 1st	Balance b/d	7,200

1. From the accounts identify any errors which have occured. Explain the errors in a memorandum to Mr Marshall.

2. Prepare a letter to David Brown and Co Ltd in which you apologise for the mistake and enclose the appropriate cheque.

3. Correct the errors in the accounts.

Chapter 14

FINANCIAL STATEMENTS

UNDERSTANDING FINANCIAL STATEMENTS

One of the most important aspects of financial management is the need to have a good understanding of the financial statements which will be prepared by an organisation. If you are managing a business you will want to know if it is financially sound. You will wish to compare its trading performance in the current year with previous years and you will need to identify changes in its level of assets, liabilities, revenue and costs. Others too will be interested in the organisation's financial standing and trading performance. A bank or other provider of finance will need to be convinced that the organisation is sufficiently viable to justify a loan. The Inland Revenue will need to assess an organisation's financial position and determine the level of its profits and losses so that it can accurately levy the appropriate amount of taxation. Furthermore as an educated individual you should be aware of the manner in which the government manages the nation's finances and this means understanding how it raises revenue and allocates its expenditure.

To be able to do this effectively you need to be able to understand and interpret the most important financial statements prepared by private and public sector organisations. In this chapter it is proposed to examine and explain such statements. We will not be requiring you to prepare such financial statements at this stage, however by the end of this chapter you should be able to read such financial statements with a degree of understanding and be capable of interpreting an organisation's financial position from them. We will begin with the financial statements of private sector organisations.

THE FINANCIAL STATEMENTS OF PRIVATE SECTOR ORGANISATIONS

The financial statements issued by private sector trading organisations include:

1. The Balance Sheet

2. The Profit and Loss Account

3. The Statement of Source and Application of Funds

4. The Notes to the Financial Statements

5. The Directors Report

6. The Auditors Report

1. THE BALANCE SHEET

The balance sheet gives us an indication of an organisation's financial position at a particular point in time. It will show the worth to the owners of the organisation. To do this it will itemise the value of the organisation's assets. These are the things that the business owns. To give its net worth it must also show the organisation's external liabilities, in other words any debts which the business owes either in the short or long term. The assets of the business less its external liabilities must always equal the source of its funding. In this way the balance sheet will always balance. Hence its name. Let us examine in some detail each aspect of the balance sheet.

a.   The organisation's assets

The assets of an organisation can be divided into two categories:

> (i)   fixed assets; and
>
> (ii)   current assets.

Fixed assets are those assets held for use by the concern rather than for resale. Fixed assets can be tangible or intangible. Tangible fixed assets include machinery, buildings, cars and fixtures and fittings. Intangible fixed assets include copyrights, patents and trademarks.

The current assets on the other hand are the stock of the business including its raw materials, work in progress, finished goods which remain unsold, the debts owed to the business for work that has been completed or for goods that have been delivered, and the cash held by the business in the bank or elsewhere.

The total assets of the business are the sum of its fixed and current assets. When an organisation's assets are listed on a balance sheet it is normal to rank them in order of liquidity i.e. how easily they can be turned into cash. So it is normal to start at the top of the balance sheet with non-liquid assets such as buildings and fixtures and fittings which may be difficult to sell quickly. We then move down to more liquid assets such as vehicles which could be sold and their value turned into cash relatively easily. Finally at the bottom of the balance sheet there are debts from customers which are likely to be paid in the near future and cash in hand or in a bank account.

b.   The organisation's liabilities

In order to purchase assets in the first place or to fund work in progress, the business must have acquired capital. If the business is a sole trader then the owner may have put up the capital himself or borrowed money from a bank. As we saw in chapter 12 the loans that an organisation has may be short term, in the form of an overdraft, or longer term loans in the form of bank loans or a commercial mortgage. If the business is a limited company the shareholders will have bought shares and so introduced funds into the organisation. Of course if the business has been operating for some time and it has made profits then it may have used some of these to fund the purchase of fixed assets or finance current assets. In whichever way the business has raised the capital it will regard it as part of its liabilities.

A distinction is drawn between short term sources of finance (such as a bank overdraft or creditors to whom the business owes money) which are referred to as 'Current Liabilities' and long term finance (such as a long term loan or money introduced by the owners) which is called 'Capital Employed'. So a sole trader will regard the money he introduced as his own personal funds which the business owes him. The shareholders will regard their share capital as their own and the bank will eventually want its money repaid. Thus all these are liabilities which the business may eventually have to repay at some time in the future.

In the explanation above, current assets were defined as the debts owed to the business for work already completed, the value of work in progress and cash in hand or in bank accounts. Current liabilities were defined as money currently owed by the business and any short term loans such as an overdraft. In effect the current liabilities are financing the current assets. In other words the overdraft allows the business to be able to wait for payment for the goods already sold. Conversely if we did not take time to pay our creditors then the amount of cash in hand would fall. Therefore the difference between the two is described as 'Working Capital'.

As we have already noted the organisation's assets will be equal to its liabilities and so we can produce a balance sheet to illustrate this relationship.

AN EXAMPLE OF A BALANCE SHEET

In this chapter we will use the financial statements of a private limited company to illustrate the main points we shall make. The company chosen is Extra Time Sports Limited (ETS). It is in retailing and has a shop selling sports equipment. It is situated in a city centre site which it currently rents on a five year lease. It was established in September 1984 and the financial statements which are used relate to its second year of trading activity which ended on the 5th September 1986. To assess its current financial position we will first examine its balance sheet.

EXTRA TIME SPORTS LIMITED

**BALANCE SHEET
AS AT 5TH SEPTEMBER 1986**

	1986	**1985**
FIXED ASSETS	5438	6305
CURRENT ASSETS		
Stock	40684	22843
Debtors	4673	1481
Cash	48237	5781
	93594	30105
CURRENT LIABILITIES		
Creditors due within one year:		
Trade Creditors	26398	17544
Tax & Social Security Costs	7246	8582
Dividend Payable	12000	—
Corporation Tax	17953	—
Accruals	—	2185
Sundry Creditors	2535	4071
	66132	32382
NET CURRENT ASSETS (Liabilities)	27462	(2277)
	£32900	£4028
FINANCED BY:		
Share Capital	100	100
Revenue Reserves	32800	4153
	32900	4253
Deduct Formation Expenses	—	(225)
	£32900	£4028

You will note that the balance sheet for 5th September 1986 provides us with two sets of figures. Those relating to the current position in 1986 and those for a year earlier in 1985. The 1985 figures are given to the right of the 1986 figures to allow a direct comparison of the changes in the company's position over the last year to be made.

The Assets of Extra Time Sports Limited

Consider first the company's fixed assets. These are the shop fixtures and fittings and the cash register installed in its premises when it commenced trading. Their value in 1985 was £6305 but by 1986 this had fallen to £5438. This is because over the period they have depreciated in value. (We will examine the concept of depreciation later in the chapter.)

Now move down to the company's current assets. The first of these is stock, the sports equipment which the company has in the shop but which has not yet been sold. Stock has increased. This is because the company has increased the range of goods its sells, this has resulted in increased sales and in order to satisfy the increased demand the company must now hold more stock.

The second of these is its debtors, money owed to the business for goods which it has sold but which have not yet been paid for. These have risen from £1481 to £4673 over the period. This is because the company has increased the amount of sports equipment it is selling on credit.

Finally under current assets is cash. This may be cash in the shop till or more likely cash in the company's accounts at the bank. This has risen from £5781 to £48237 over the period of the year. This means that the company's immediate cash liquidity position has improved. However this is not necessarily a good thing as any cash held in a bank current account will not be earning interest. Cash holding is not always bad if part of the cash is held on short term deposit with the bank the company will receive some interest.

We can now calculate the sum of the company's total assets. At 5th September 1986 these stand at £99032 (made up of £5438 fixed assets plus £93594 current assets). This is a substantial increase on the position in the previous year when assets stood at £36410.

The Liabilities of Extra Time Sports Limited

Now examine the company's liabilities. You will see that under current liabilities, creditors due within one year are specified. Trade creditors are listed first. These are the company's suppliers, the manufacturers of the sports equipment it sells, such as Nike and Adidas. They have delivered their goods but have yet to be paid. Most suppliers will allow a period of trade credit, for instance twenty eight days from delivery. At the time the balance sheet was prepared these stand at £26398 and have increased from £17544 at the same date in the previous year.

Then we list tax and national insurance costs. These are the debts the company owes to the Inland Revenue and the DHSS for tax and national insurance contributions for its employees which it has deducted from their wages but has not yet paid over. This currently stands at £7246, a decrease from the previous year's figure of £8582.

Below that is the dividend payable of £12000 which the directors have chosen to distribute to the shareholders. You should note that no dividend was paid in the previous year as the directors considered the profits to be too small to justify it. Clearly if the business had continued to make very small profits year after year then the shareholders may feel that their investment in the company was not proving to be financially rewarding. Fortunately the dividend in the current year will go some way to providing them with a satisfactory return on their investment.

This year's healthy profit has not only meant a dividend for the shareholders but has also meant that the company is now liable for corporation tax of £17953. As you will note, the previous year's profits were insufficient to produce a corporation tax liability.

Next is listed accruals which in the current year is zero. In the previous year it was valued at £2185. Accruals are debts that the company owes for products or services which it has consumed in the current year but which it has yet to be billed for. For instance it may have incurred charges for telephone calls which will appear on its next telephone bill. (The accrual concept is considered later in the chapter.)

Finally we list sundry creditors of £2535. These are debts the company owes to suppliers such as printers, the newspapers for advertising or the repair firm who fixed the till when it went wrong. The company has received the product or service but has yet to pay the bills. As you can see these have fallen from £4071.

By adding together all the company's current liabilities, we find that they come to £66132, a substantial increase over the previous year's figure of £32382. Fortunately the assets of the company have also grown as we have seen above.

Net Current Assets (Liabilities) of Extra Time Sports Limited.

The next stage is to net the current assets and the current liabilities, in other words to take one from the other. This is known as the 'Working Capital' of the business. As we have noted the current assets totalled £93594 while current liabilities stood at £66132. Subtracting liabilities from assets shows a net surplus of current assets of £27462. This is a much healthier position than the previous year when the figures showed net current liabilities exceeding net current assets by £2277. Because it is a surplus of liabilities over assets, the figure is shown in brackets.

We can now add the company's fixed assets of £5438 to the net current assets of £27462 to give a total of £32900. This has increased from last year's figures of £4028 showing a substantial impovement in the company's position.

Source of Funding of Extra Time Sports Limited.

As we noted earlier in the chapter the balance sheet will always balance as the assets of the business must equal the source of its funding plus the extent of its debts. In this case it has been financed by share capital of £100 and revenue reserves of £32800. Reserves are profits which the company has earned for its owners but has not distributed to them. They are represented by a corresponding increase in net assets but they must never be confused with cash. As such they are a liability owing to the owners and thus represent part of the capital invested in the business. You will note that the company also had formation expenses in the previous year of £225. This was the cost of establishing Extra Time Sports as a limited company and as such is a 'one-off' expense.

SUMMARY OF THE BALANCE SHEET

We can sum up the balance sheet by noting that all assets and liabilities must fall into one of the following caterories.

1. Net Assets Employed

All the organisation's assets must be used as

      a.   fixed assets — plant, buildings, machinery, cars

      b.   working capital — stocks, debtors, cash

      c.   investments — in stocks and shares or government securities.

2. Financed by

All the organisation's assets are financed by

      a.   Owner's capital introduced — either cash introduced by sole trader or partnership or share capital of a company

      b.   profits — retained profits from the previous year's trading

      c.   loans — short, medium and long term loans, debentures and mortgages.

2.   THE PROFIT AND LOSS ACCOUNT

We noted that the balance sheet gave us a picture of the organisation's position at a single point in time. This is normally at the end of one period of trading for the organisation, in most cases one year. The profit and loss account is different. It shows how the business has performed throughout the entire period. In other words it normally covers a whole financial year in the life of the business. It is intended to present a list of all the income or revenue the business has earned in that year through sales or other forms of income and to compare it with all the expenses or costs the business has had to meet in the same period. By subtracting the total income from total expenses we are able to come up with the organisation's profit or loss position. Hence the name 'profit and loss account'. Clearly if the total income earned by the business in the year is greater than its total expenses then the business will have made a profit. If the total expenses exceed total income then it will have made a loss.

If total income is examined in more detail this will show that it is made up of the value of all sales made to customers and clients and also any other income such as returns on any investments the business may have, or rent earned from its premises which have been let to others. It is normal practice to include the full value of all sales made even if payment has not yet been received.

On the expenses side we will first find the costs of all the materials used to produce the organisation's products and all labour costs involved in the manufacture. If these are subtracted from the income received from sales income this will give us the gross profit. We will see later in chapter 15 that when the gross profit is expressed as a percentage of the sales figure it will provide a good measure of the organisation's trading efficiency.

However these will not be the only costs the business will incur. We must also include what are sometimes referred to as 'management expenses' and these would include rent and rates for the organisation's premises, heating and lighting, travelling expenses, petty cash costs and depreciation on the company's assets. (We will return to the question of depreciation later.) It is important to note that the value of all expenses are incurred when the goods or services are received and not at the time they are paid for. This parallels the point made earlier that sales should be included when they are made and not when they are paid for.

Thus the comparison of income and expenses should indicate whether or not the business has made a profit or a loss in the trading period. In order that it should accurately reflect the trading position of the business, all trading income and expenses of the organisation should be included. However it is important to make a few distinctions at this point. It is easy to get confused as to where certain business income or expenditure should be recorded. The rule is that if income or expenditure relates to the current year, for instance raw materials or goods which are immediately consumed in the production process, then they should go in the Profit and Loss account. If new assets have been acquired by the business during the year and they will continue to be of value and used by the business in future years, such as new machinery or a new vehicle, then these will go in the balance sheet as an additional asset of the business. Similarly all income from sales or other sources which relates solely to the organisation's operation in the current trading year goes into the Profit and Loss account. Other income such as an extra bank loan or new capital introduced into the business is shown in the balance sheet as a business liability.

AN EXAMPLE OF A PROFIT AND LOSS ACCOUNT

Bearing these points in mind we can now examine the Profit and Loss Account for Extra Time Sports Limited for the year ended the 5th September 1986.

EXTRA TIME SPORTS LIMITED

PROFIT AND LOSS ACCOUNT
FOR THE YEAR ENDED 5TH SEPTEMBER 1986

		1986		1985
Sales		376279		224097
Deduct Cost of Sales				
Stock at 6th September 1985	22843		—	
Purchases	255214		180625	
	278057		180625	
Less Stock at 5th September 1986	40684	237373	22843	157782
	(36.9%)	138906	(26.6%)	66315
Deduct Wages		9721		6207
		129185		60108
Deduct Expenses				
Advertising	3740		6582	
Audit and Accountancy Fees	900		540	
Bank Interest & Charges	1028		1628	
Heat, Light and Water	1440		1339	
Hire Purchase Charges	373		62	
Insurances	915		821	
Legal Expenses	—		917	
Motor Expenses	1922		1935	
Printing, Postage & Stationery	1030		393	
Rent & Rates	29821		17203	
Repairs & Renewals	2574		3598	
Sundries	684		1210	
Telephones	1273	45700	727	36955
		83485		23153
Deduct Depreciation		1647		2101
		81838		21052
Deduct Directors Remuneration		22413		16899
		59525		4153
Deduct Corporation Tax	18553		—	
Formation Expenses	225		—	
Dividend Payable	12000	30778	—	—
Retained Profit for the year		£28647		£4153

In the same way that they appeared in the balance sheet, the previous year's figures are also given to the right of the current year's to provide a comparison.

The Sales of Extra Time Sports Limited

The first figure shown on the Profit and Loss account is the sales figure for the year. As you can see the company increased its sales in its 1985/86 trading period to £376,279 from the previous year's sales of £224,097. This has occurred because there has been a substantial increase in demand for sports equipment as a result of the leisure boom. The directors of the company had anticipated this boom and that was the major reason for establishing the company in the first place.

The Cost of Sales for Extra Time Sports Limited

Under this heading we first find the value of the stock held at the beginning of the trading period. As you can see it was £22,843. This figure also appears as a current asset in the previous year's balance sheet. As the 1984/85 trading period was the company's first year of trading it had no comparable opening stock on the previous profit and loss account.

Next is shown the item relating to the goods the business has bought during the year. This is the purchase of the goods amounting to £255,214. Clearly as the business has prospered it has needed to buy in more goods to sell.

By adding together the purchase costs of the goods and the value of the opening stock we can find the cost of all the goods that were either already in the shop at the start of the year or which have been bought into the shop during the year. This comes to £278,057. However we must remember that there is still sports equipment on sale in the shop or in the store room at the back at the end of the trading period. It would be wrong to include this as a cost in the current year as it will not generate revenue until the coming year. Therefore we must do a stock take as close to the end of the trading period as possible and value the stock we have. ETS Ltd did this at the weekend preceeding the end of its financial year and found that it had stock valued at cost price worth £40,684. As this is a cost on next year's trading it must be deducted from the current year's direct costs leaving a total for the costs of the sports equipment of £237,373.

It is often useful to find the gross profit percentage for a business. This is the ratio between the company's sales revenue and its direct cost of sales. This will give an indication of the company's efficiency in buying cheaply and selling at the right price. To find this we subtract the cost of direct sales from the sales revenue. In other words £376,279 minus £237,373 leaving a gross profit of £138,906. We then divide the gross profit of £138,906 by the total sales of £376,279 and then multiply by 100. This gives a percentage figure of 36.9%. This is quite a high gross profit figure and the managers of ETS Ltd should be pleased with their performance, particularly when it is compared to the previous year's figure of 26.6%. (We will be examining the use of such ratios in more detail in chapter 15).

Next we deduct the wages of the shop assistants employed by ETS Ltd which came to £9,721. This was an increase from the previous year of £6,207 because the company had decided to hire extra staff on Saturdays to cope with the increased demand.

We can now find the profit left from sales after direct costs have been deducted. From the initial sales turnover of £376,279 is deducted the £237,373 costs of the sports equipment and then the £9,721 of the wages leaving a profit of £129,185. However from this must be deducted all the company's other expenses.

Operating and Management Expenses of Extra Time Sports Limited

Under this heading come a variety of expenses which the company has incurred in the last year. Most are self explanatory and are listed as expenses in the profit and loss account, however a few are worthy of a little more examination. The first is the advertising costs of £3,740 which have fallen almost by half from the previous year's figure of £6,582. This is because the company needed to advertise extensively when it was initially established. In fact it took a full page advertising feature in the local evening paper to announce the opening of the shop. However in this trading year it is now reasonably well established and so the directors feel that regular quarter page ads on the sports page of the paper are sufficient to allow them to stay in the customer's eye. A second major fall has been in the bank interest and charges. These have fallen from £1,628 to £1,028. This is due to the increased trade in the current year which has meant that the company has had less need to use its bank overdraft facility. Finally you might note that the charges for rent and rates have risen substantially. In fact the increase has not been on the rent, for this is fixed in the lease for the whole five year period. Rather there has been a rise in the rates which have been increased by the local authority as government grants from central government have been cut. The total of all the operating expenses is £45,721 and this is deducted from the gross profit of £129,185 to leave a trading profit of £83,464.

From the trading profit we must take the depreciation of the company's fixed assets. This is the reduction in the value of the fixtures and fittings over the year. It is intended to be a way of allocating the amount of wear and tear and the consequent fall in value to the trading period in which this fall in value occurred. (The concept of depreciation is examined in the next section).

The directors' remuneration is then deducted. This payment of £22,413 is the amount the directors receive for their work during the year. Finally we subtract the corporation tax and the dividend payable which we have already discussed in the section on the balance sheet. This leaves a retained net profit for the company of £28,647 which you can see is a considerable improvement over the previous year's profit of £4,153. On this basis the directors of Extra Time Sports Limited can be well pleased with the performance of the company in this year.

Depreciation

At this point we should consider how to deal in the accounts with assets which are purchased by the business in one trading year but which continue to be of value for a number of years in the future. Take for example a machine which costs the organisation £4,000. The machine has an expected life of 4 years. Therefore the cost of it to the organisation should be spread over four years. A simple way to do this would be to divide the cost of the asset by the anticipated life span and charge it as expenditure to the profit and loss account each year. As a by-product of this, the apparent value of the asset will be reduced by the amount charged for depreciation.

Of course we must also take account of the changing value of the machine in the balance sheet. When the machine is bought it has a value of £4,000. However by the end of the first trading period in which it was bought its value will have depreciated by £1,000. It is at the end of the period that the balance sheet is produced so that we must show the purchase price of the machine less the depreciation to that point as this is the estimated value of the machine as an asset of the business at that point. In other words we would first show the purchase price, then the depreciation, to give the net value which would be shown as £3,000. In the following year the machine begins the period being valued at £3,000, however by the time the balance sheet is drawn up its estimated value has depreciated by a further £1,000 and so we could now show its net value as £3,000 - £1,000 = £2,000. This process of depreciation will continue until the value of the machine has fallen to zero and it is 'written off'.

Opening and Closing Stock

If the business has been operating for some time it would be fair to assume that at the end of any trading year when its profit and loss account is drawn up there is likely to be stocks of goods which have been finished or produced but which have yet to be sold. As we will have included the costs incurred in buying or producing these products as part of the business expenses it is necessary to deduct the value of such stock from costs in order to ensure that only the actual costs of the goods sold during the year are included as an expense. Therefore at the end of each trading period it is necessary to do a 'stock-take' where all stocks held are valued at cost for inclusion in the accounts as closing stock. Of course this closing stock continues to be held over into the next trading year as it is then that it will be sold. Therefore in that year it should be entered into the expenses side of the Profit and Loss Account as opening stock as it is in effect a cost which the organisation has incurred. If you look back at the profit and loss account for Extra Time Sports Ltd you can see an example of how this principle is applied.

3.   STATEMENT OF SOURCE AND APPLICATION OF FUNDS

The Balance Sheet and the Profit and Loss account of a business show between them the position with regard to its assets and liabilities at the beginning and end of the year and the amount of profit and loss made between these two points. However, the profit and loss account deals with revenue items only and takes into consideration sales made for which the cash is still owing, and purchases and other expenses incurred for which the money has not yet been paid. Th Balance Sheet shows the position at two points only, and it may not be evident where money has come from or the areas in which it has been spent. The practice in recent years has been to provide an additional statement with the Balance Sheet and Profit and Loss account which summarises the movement of cash in and out of the business. This statement is called the Source and Application of Funds Statement, usually simply referred to as the 'funds statement'. It is not a substitute for the Balance Sheet and the Profit and Loss account but is supplementary to them.

The purpose of the funds statement is to show where the business has obtained money from during the year and in which areas it has been spent. Normally the statement illustrates this in two parts. The first of these is the change in working capital between the two balance sheet points; the reason for this is that cash is part of working capital, but any increase or decrease in working capital is not necessarily equal to the increase or decrease in cash, because of the change in debtors, stock, creditors, etc. The second shows the changes in the individual components of working capital and highlights specifically the change in the current liquidity position.

The sources of funds are:-

> Share capital contributed by the owners;
>
> Borrowed capital (Debentures, etc.);
>
> Net profit before tax and depreciation;
>
> Proceeds of the sale of fixed assets.

The application of funds are:-

> The purchase of fixed assets;
>
> The repayment of capital or loans (not dividends or interest);
>
> Net losses before tax and before depreciation;
>
> The payment of taxes;
>
> The payment of dividends.

Most of the above items are easily understood but the Net Profit before tax and depreciation needs clarification. Funds (Working Capital) are generated from sales but this is not necessarily in the form of cash as some sales are on credit and not all sales in a year will necessarily be paid for in that trading period, but cash receipts will include money received from outstanding debtors in respect of sales made in the previous year. Similarly funds (Working Capital) are expended on purchases and other expenses. Since sales less purchases (adjusted for stock changes) less expenses equal net profit, then it is true to say that net profit generates funds. However some of the expenses incurred in earning the net profit do not involve spending money (depreciation is a prime example) so we have to add it back to the net profit before that type of expense is shown as a basic source of funds. In the statement itself this is shown as being added back to the net profit before tax figure. A diagram showing how funds move in and out of the organisation is shown below.

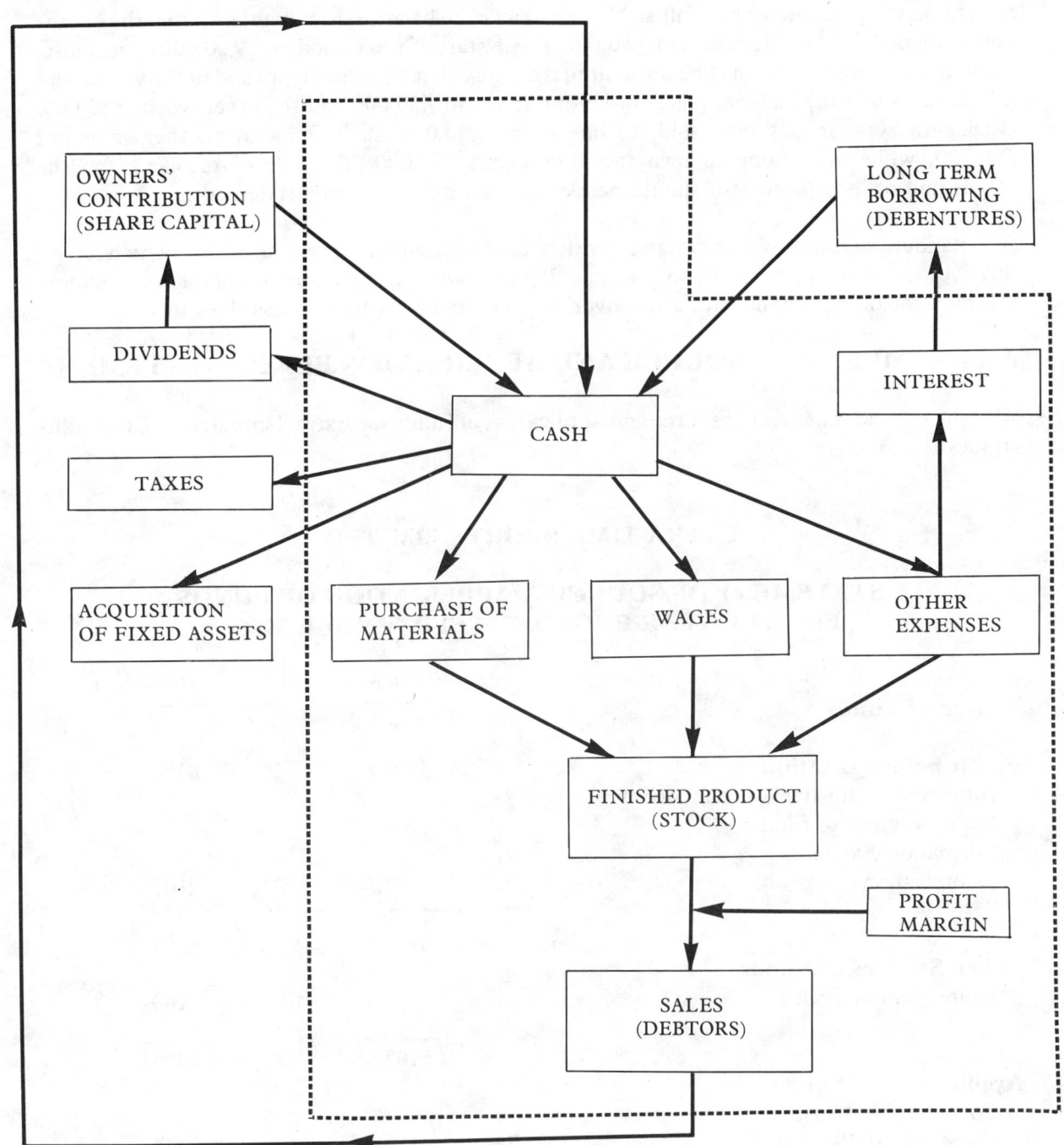

THE WORKING CAPITAL FLOW

All items inside the dotted boundary lines constitute movements within working capital. Items outside the dotted lines are contributions to and from working capital which are not self generated.

Profit before tax is taken as the starting point because the tax charge in the financial statements is normally an estimated provision (in addition the amount of tax a company pays is affected by factors which are not related to the profit it makes) and quite often the amount shown in the financial statements differs from that actually paid.

One of the major uses of the funds statement is that it will relate the balance sheet position at the beginning of a trading period, the profit and loss account and the balance sheet position at the end of the period. To enable this to be easily interpreted the statement should itemise major changes in the position of the company. For instance the balance sheet may show that the organisation owned freehold land worth £80,000 at the start of the period and £90,000 at its close. From the balance sheet it may be difficult to recognise that what has happened in the year is that the business initially had two pieces of land, one worth £50,000 and the other worth £30,000. During the year it may have sold the one worth £50,000 and purchased another valued at £60,000, while continuing to own the land worth £30,000. The sale of the land and the acquisition of its replacement should be clearly shown in the funds statement.

It is standard accounting practice to provide a funds statement for all businesses which have a turnover or gross income of more than £25,000 although they are becoming increasingly common for organisations with a turnover or gross income which is less than this.

AN EXAMPLE OF A SOURCE AND APPLICATION FUNDS STATEMENT

We now use the statement of source and application of funds for Extra Time Sports Ltd to illustrate these points.

EXTRA TIME SPORTS LIMITED

STATEMENT OF SOURCE & APPLICATION OF FUNDS
FOR THE YEAR ENDED 5TH SEPTEMBER 1986

		1986		1985
Source of Funds				
Profit before taxation		59200		4153
Adjustments for items not involving the movement of funds				
Formation Expenses	225		—	
Depreciation	1647	1872	2101	2101
		61072		6254
Other Sources of Funds				
Share Capital Issued		—		100
		61072		6354
Application of Funds				
Formation Expenses	—		225	
Fixed Assets Purchased	780		8406	
Corporation Tax Paid	600	1380	—	8631
		£59692		£(2277)
Movement in Working Capital				
Increase in Stock		17841		22843
Increase in Debtors		3192		1481
Increase in Creditors		(3797)		(32382)
		17236		8058
Movement in Net Liquid Funds				
Increase in cash		42456		5781
		£59692		£(2277)

Source of Funds for Extra Time Sports Limited

As you can see the profit before taxation was £59200 in 1985/86. First we show the depreciation of £1872 which does not involve the company in receiving or expending funds and so is added back to the profit as was explained above. Next we show other sources of funds for the company, in this case the issue of shares. As the company was formed in the previous year the £100 share capital is shown there and as no further shares have been issued in the current year there is nothing to add to the £61072 explained above.

Application of Funds for Extra Time Sports Limited

The company purchases fixed assets valued at £780. This was the new till which was installed. It then paid corporation tax of £600. The remaining corporation tax remains as a liability of £17953 and is shown in the balance sheet as such. You should note from the profit and loss account that the total corporation tax liability is £18553, made up of the £600 already paid and £17953 still to be paid.

Movement of Working Capital of Extra Time Sports Limited

The company's stock has increased by £17841. This figure can be verified by subtracting the opening stock of £22843 from the closing stock of £40684 shown in the balance sheet.

The company's debtors have risen by £3192. Again this can be checked by subtracting the debtors shown in the 1985 balance sheet of £1481 from the 1986 value of £4673.

Its creditors have increased by £3797 and this is shown in the balance sheet in the change from the current liabilities in 1985 of £32382 to the 1986 figure of £66132. This gives a change of £33750 from which must be deducted the company's liabilities for dividends of £12000 and unpaid corporation tax of £17953, leaving an increase in other creditors of £3797.

Movement in Net Liquid Funds

Finally we can see that the company has increased its holdings of cash by £42456. This can be seen in the balance sheet by comparing the 1985 cash holdings of £5781 with the 1986 holdings of £48237.

As you can see all aspects of the funds statement can be found from the profit and loss account and the balance sheet. However it is much easier to see the movements when they are presented in this way rather than having to extract each piece of information from the two other financial statements.

As you may have realised in order to fully explain the changes in the financial position of Extra Time Sports Ltd we have used information not included in the Balance Sheet, Profit and Loss Account or the Funds Statement. The majority of this additional information is found in the notes to the Financial Statement and the Directors report.

4. THE NOTES TO THE FINANCIAL STATEMENT

Certain items will always be found in the notes. These are:

(i) Details of the accounting policies used in the preparation of the Financial Statements. These are the specific methods chosen by the organisation to apply the fundamental accounting concepts, which we discuss later in the chapter;

(ii) Details of the Balance Sheet items, such as the types of fixed assets owned by the organisation. In the Extra Time Sports Ltd Balance Sheet only one figure appears for fixed assets, £5438. The notes show the specific assets held, such as motor vehicles, fixtures and fittings together with details of their cost and the amount by which they have depreciated.

(iii)   Details of the Profit and Loss Account items. For example it will show corporation tax and the notes will show how this charge has been estimated, when it is payable and any corrections due as a result of adjustments to the previous year's provision for corporation tax;

(iv)   Details of Post Balance Sheet events. Quite often events occur in the time between the date of the balance sheet and the point at which the Financial Statements are prepared. Such events could affect our understanding of the Financial Statements. For example there was a fire at the Extra Time Sports Ltd shop on the 13th September 1986 and part of the store was destroyed. Fortunately they were insured and so received the full value of all they lost. These events happened after the year end but would have been reported in the notes to the financial statements.

5.   THE DIRECTORS REPORT

The Directors Report is a statement issued by the Directors of the organisation to the shareholders. It normally contains:

(i)   a summary of the company's performance in the financial year and its expected performance in the coming year;

(ii)   details of the directors of the company and their shareholdings in the company;

(iii)   a statement of the principal activities of the company;

(iv)   details of the proposed dividend.

6.   THE AUDITOR'S REPORT

The shareholders of a company are often not the people who run the company. The directors are the people who run the company and it is their responsibility to prepare the financial statements and present them to the members. The shareholders need to know if the financial statements are a reasonably accurate reflection of the profit the company has made and of its financial position at the balance sheet date. In order to know this, the shareholders appoint an independent qualified person to examine the financial statements and to pass an opinion on them. The independent person is the auditor.

The Auditor's report is an expression of his opinion as to the 'truth and fairness' of the financial statements and of the profit of the company. This opinion is based upon his examination of the financial statements and various financial tests which have been carried out. Auditor's reports can be 'unqualified' where the auditor states the financial statements show a true and fair view, or they may be 'qualified'. Where the auditor's report is qualifed the auditor will explain those aspects with which he is not satisfied and what effect this has upon the financial statements.

Occasionally an auditor will issue a 'disclaimer of opinion'. This means that the results of his examination have been inconclusive and he cannot form an opinion whether or not the financial statements show a true and fair view. In all cases you should read the auditor's report before going on to interpret the financial statements.

PRESENTATION OF FINAL ACCOUNTS

The purpose of presenting final accounts is to make them understandable to those who need to read them. There are a number of ways of laying out balance sheets, profit and loss accounts and funds statements but in the previous examples we have given the most commonly used method. The layout is similar for all types of businesses with the main difference being in the way in which any profit (or loss) which is made in the trading period is shown. So, for example, a sole trader will receive all the trading profit made and will be liable for personal tax on the entire amount after any capital and personal allowances are made. In the same way a partnership will divide the profit according to the respective partnership shares and each partner will be taxed accordingly through personal income tax. In the Extra Time Sports Ltd examples given above, as the organisation is a limited company then the trading profit is taxed through corporation tax. The profit which remains after corporation tax has been paid may then be retained by the company and included in its reserves or could be shared out among shareholders as a dividend. Any dividend which the directors decide to declare is obviously distributed among the shareholders in accordance with the percentage of the company's shares that they hold.

THE FINANCIAL STATEMENTS OF THE PUBLIC SECTOR

1. THE CENTRAL GOVERNMENT

The most important financial statement produced by central government is the Financial Statement and Budget Report (known as the Budget) which is presented to the House of Commons by the Chancellor of the Exchequer each Spring. It has a similar purpose to a private sector organisation's report and accounts and includes a review of the government's financial performance in the past year, a statement of its policy objectives and its proposals for change in the coming year. The central aspect of the financial statement is the budget itself. This itemises the government's receipts and expenditure for the past and coming years. The budget for 1986 is given on the following page.

As you can see the receipts are broken down by source. Because of the uncertainty involved the receipts for the coming year are forecasts. For the previous year, 1985-86, both the budget forecasts and the latest estimates are included. These are then totalled to show the general government receipts. For 1986-87 these are forecast as £155.9 billion.

On the right hand side of the statement is shown the expenditure of the government. Again this is itemised but in this case by spending department. From the statement you will note that the Department of Health and Social Security is by far the largest spending ministry. It is also worth noting that proceeds from privatisation are listed. This shows that in 1986-87 the government expected to raise £4.7 billion from this source. Privatisation is discussed in detail in chapter 25.

The final element of the budget is the difference between expenditure and revenue which has to be financied by borrowing. This is the Public Sector Borrowing Requirement (PSBR) and for 1986-87 was estimated at £7.1 billion.

The central government will also prepare additional financial statements for each department and the nationalised industries which provide details of specific financing and expenditure.

2. LOCAL AUTHORITIES

Each local authority is required to produce an abstract of its account for inspection by the central government and by the general public. The Local Government Planning and Land Act 1980 now requires that they also produce an annual report which provides information on a wide variety of the authority's activities. The two statements are often combined to produce the authority's Report and Annual Accounts. Some authorities are conscious of the need to provide such information in a form which is accessible to the average ratepayer and so produce documents which are model examples of data presentation. Birmingham is a case in point and in chapter 5 there are extracts from its accounts reproduced in the section on the presentation of data. Also in that chapter there is included an assignment which uses the financial statement of a county council. If you refer to that section you will note that the council itemises its expenditure by service. For each service it shows the revenue it has raised and the net expenditure for the service. From its total net expenditure it can determine the amount of revenue it must raise from other sources. The two most important are the government block grant and the rates. Further consideration of these sources of revenue for local authorities is undertaken in chapter 12 and in chapter 25 where the central government's control of local authority financing is discussed.

The Budget

The finances of the public sector

RECEIPTS	£ billion 1985–86 1985 Budget[1]	1985–86 Latest estimate	1986–87 Forecasts	EXPENDITURE	£ billion 1985–86 1985 Budget[1]	1985–86 Latest estimate	1986–87 Forecasts
Income taxes	35·3	35·6	38·7	DHSS—Social security	40·0	41·3	42·9
Corporation tax excluding North Sea[2]	8·2	8·4	9·4	Defence	18·0	18·0	18·5
Capital taxes	1·9	2·5	2·8	DHSS—Health and personal social services	16·5	16·7	17·7
Expenditure taxes:				Scotland, Wales and Northern Ireland	14·2	14·5	15·0
Value added tax	18·3	19·3	20·7	Education and science	13·6	14·3	14·3
Local authority rates	13·6	13·7	15·6	Other departments	29·3	31·7	31·2
Petrol, derv, etc., duties	6·5	6·5	7·3	Privatisation proceeds	−2·5	−2·6	−4·7
Spirits, beer, wine, etc.	4·2	4·2	4·4	Reserve	5·0	—	4·5
Cigarettes and other tobacco	4·3	4·3	4·7	Adjustments	—	—	−0·4
Other	8·6	8·6	9·3	**Public expenditure planning total**	**134·2**	**133·9**	**139·1**
Total expenditure taxes	55·6	56·6	61·9				
North Sea revenues:							
North Sea corporation tax[3]	2·8	3·0	2·7				
Petroleum revenue tax	8·2	6·4	2·4				
Oil royalties	2·5	2·1	1·0				
Total North Sea	13·5	11·5	6·1	General government gross debt interest	17·8	17·7	18·2
Other[4]	−1·2	−1·4	−1·2	less public corporations' market and overseas borrowing	−2·3	−1·3	−0·4
Total taxes and royalties	**113·2**	**113·1**	**117·6**	Other national accounts adjustments	5·5	5·0	5·7
National insurance and other contributions	24·6	24·3	26·2				
Interest and dividend receipts	6·4	6·4	6·4				
Gross trading surpluses and rent	3·1	2·9	2·7				
Other	3·1	2·9	3·0				
General government receipts[5]	**150·4**	**149·6**	**155·9**	**General government expenditure[5]**	**159·8**	**157·7**	**163·4**

Difference between expenditure and revenue financed by borrowing:

	1985–86 1985 Budget	1985–86 Latest estimate	1986–87 Forecast
General government expenditure	159·8	157·7	163·4
General government receipts	150·4	149·6	155·9
General government borrowing requirement	9·4	8·1	7·5
Public corporations' market and overseas borrowing	−2·3	−1·3	−0·4
Public sector borrowing requirement	**7·1**	**6·8**	**7·1**

[1] On current definitions.
[2] Including advance corporation tax but excluding corporation tax on capital gains.
[3] Before advance corporation tax set off. See footnote [3] to Table 6 B.3.
[4] Adjustments for advance corporation tax set off against North Sea corporation tax plus accruals adjustments.
[5] In these and other tables, constituent items may not add up to totals because of rounding.

ACCOUNTING CONCEPTS

In the previous section we discussed the major financial statements used by organisations in both the private and public sectors. However it is important to recognise that the structure of these statements and the manner in which they are presented rely on the application of several accounting concepts. It is the use and limitations of such concepts which we shall be considering in this part of the chapter.

It is fair to say that accountancy is neither an art nor a science. It is a profession in which the practitioners present and interpret information in a particular way. As you might realise financial information could be presented and interpreted in any number of ways. Therefore to allow different people to understand how others are performing this task it is necessary to establish some rules and regulations which most people working with financial information will use and understand. These are the basic concepts and conventions of accountancy. In this book we will not be able to examine all of these. However we will attempt to introduce to you the main ideas so that you can interpret financial information consistently.

In accounting, terms such as accounting concepts, conventions, principles and rules are used almost interchangibly. Here we shall use the definitions as applied by the 'Statements of Standard Accounting Practice' produced by the Institute of Chartered Accountants in England and Wales. This describes fundamental accounting concepts as the broad assumptions which underlie the periodic accounts of business enterprises. The statements single out for special mention four of these in particular:

      (a)   the 'going conern' concept;

      (b)   the 'accruals' concept;

      (c)   the 'consistency' concept; and

      (d)   the 'prudence' concept.

These concepts are so widely used that it is not normal to explain them in published accounts and it is presumed that they are being observed unless the opposite is stated. Unlike the rules of natural science they are not fixed and are capable of modification and evolution. However we will begin by stating them as they are currently applied.

(a) THE 'GOING CONCERN' CONCEPT

In most normal circumstances when a balance sheet is prepared it is assumed that the business will continue to operate in the future, in other words that it is a 'going concern'. This is the concept of 'continuity'. For this reason the assets of the business are valued at their worth to the business and not at the price they would fetch if they were sold on the open market.

So for instance an engineering company may have a factory which has been specifically converted for their use with the installation of specific machinery such as overhead cranes. The initial cost of the factory, the conversion and the installation of the machinery is £100,000. Yet should the business close and the factory and its equipment be put up for sale, there may be little demand in that particular location for a fully equipped engineering factory. The sale would only generate £50,000 as the factory may be bought for an alternative use. However for the purpose of the accounts, the assets would be valued at cost less depreciation if the business was continuing to operate, for that is their true worth to the engineering company rather than the value they could fetch should they be sold. The same principle could be applied to stock or to debtors. They would be valued on the assumption that the business was a going concern although they may clearly be worth less should the business cease.

The valuation would be different of course should the business cease trading in which case the liquidator, the person appointed to sell off the business assets and settle its liabilities, would only be able to value the assets at their market value. As this will only occur on the winding up of the business, we should use the concept of continuity while the business is assumed to be a going concern.

(b) THE 'ACCRUALS' CONCEPT

We have already stressed that the profit and loss account should reflect the costs incurred in the trading period so they can accurately be compared against the income earned in the same period. However it is likely that many of the expenses incurred by the business are not charged over the same accounting period as the organisation has for its financial year. So the organistion's financial year may well be run from 1st May in one year to 30th April in the following year, yet it may pay the rent for its premises on a calendar year basis, in other words from 1st January to 31st December of the same year. If it pays the rent in advance then it would be wrong to allot the full calendar year's rent to a financial year which ended part way through the organisation's financial year. A simple example may illustrate the point.

An organisation is charged a rent of £1,200 for the calendar year 1985. However for the calendar year 1986 the landlord increases this rent to £1,500 with the agreement of the business as the tenant. The organisation's financial year runs from the beginning of May 1985 until the end of April 1986. Thus the amount of rent which should be included in that financial year's Profit and Loss Account will be calculated as follows:

> 8 months (May to December 1985) of the 1985 calendar year's rent which is 8/12 of £1,200 equal to £800

plus

> 4 months (January to April 1986) of the 1986 calendar year's rent which is 4/12 of £1,500 equal to £500

The total rent to be included in the Profit and Loss Account for 1st May 1985 until 30th April 1986 is £1,300.

Obviously some bills will be less easy to divide such as fuel or telephone bills and so an accurate estimate is included in the accounts. The principle of accrual will apply equally if the bill has been paid or has yet to be paid. So in the rent example above we assumed that the bill was paid in advance. Perhaps it may be paid in arrears. In either case the total rent owed by the business in its 1985-86 trading period is £1,300 and this is the amount which should appear in the Profit and Loss Account.

(c) THE 'CONSISTENCY' CONCEPT

We have already made the point that one of the main reasons for preparing financial statements is that they will allow a comparison of the performance of the business over a period of time. Therefore it would be misleading to regularly change the basis on which an organisation's accounts are prepared. Thus if the initial cost concept is applied in one year's accounts it would be wrong to change it every year without clearly noting the change.

Examples include the manner in which the business may value its stock. For instance if it based this on an average stock value in one accounting period it would cause difficulties in financial interpretation if in the next set of accounts it adopted a first in first out (FIFO) valuation approach.

Accepting this convention does not mean that the business cannot ever change the basis on which its accounts are prepared as major variations in circumstances, such as a period of high inflation, may mean that the value of the organisation's assets and liabilities are no longer accurately recorded in the balance sheet. However this would obviously be the exception rather than the rule.

(d) THE CONCEPT OF 'PRUDENCE'

It is always wisest to err on the side of prudence or conservatism rather than over expectation. Thus accountants will invariably accept the highest level of projected expenses and the lowest level of projected income. In this way the projected profit of a business will be the least that is probably expected. This may appear to be an over cautious approach to adopt, however it is reasonable to say that it is better to be pleasantly surprised if profit turns out to be higher than was anticipated than to be bitterly disappointed if a projected profit turns out to be much lower than was hoped.

Of course conservatism does have its drawbacks. Some risky business ventures may not be pursued because the projected level of profit is insufficient to make it seem worthwhile but nevertheless adopting this approach will inevitably save the over optimistic potential businessman from bankruptcy.

OTHER ACCOUNTING CONCEPTS OR CONVENTIONS

The four concepts discussed above are the major concepts defined by the Statement of Standard Accounting Practice. However there are several other concepts or conventions which are worth noting. These are:

(e)   Money Measurement;

(f)   Separate Business Entity;

(g)   The Dual Aspect of Financial Recording — Double Entry Book-keeping;

(h)   Stability — The Cost Concept;

(i)   The Realisation concept;

(j)   Materiality.

We shall now consider each of these in turn.

(e) MONEY MEASUREMENT

In financial management it is only reasonably feasible to measure transactions in terms of money. For example if one used car dealer stated that he had sold 200 cars while another said he had sold 300 cars we might assume that the second dealer had the larger turnover. However if the average price of the first dealer's sales was £2,000 per car and that for the second was £1,000 per car then we can see that the first has a turnover of £400,000 (200 cars at £2,000 each) while the second has only a turnover of £300,000 (300 cars at £1,000 each). Thus to allow us to accurately compare turnover between the two businesses we can only measure performance in money terms and not in terms of the quantity of actual goods and services bought and sold.

Other factors may be of vital importance to the success of the business. A well established shop may have built up considerable business goodwill. By this we mean that customers are used to trading with the business and have developed a degree of confidence in it. This is obviously a valuable asset of the business. A business which has an established customer base is clearly more viable than one which is merely starting and has to develop such a reputation from scratch. However it is not an easy task to value that goodwill when preparing a balance sheet for the business and because it cannot easily be measured in monetary terms it is omitted. Of course when an established business is sold it is normally the case that the seller and the buyer agree upon a value for the business goodwill and this is included in the selling price but this really depends on the buyer's assessment of its worth.

Similarly, an efficient workforce not only increases the profits of the business in the current trading year but is also a tremendous asset for the future. Should then 'efficient workforce' be included as an item in the balance sheet? As we cannot put a money value on it, it cannot be included although in the same manner as business goodwill it may well influence the price if the business is sold.

Therefore stating business information only in monetary terms provides an excellent way of objectively comparing business performance either from one year to another for an individual organisation or for the same trading period between different organisations.

However it is worth raising one point of caution when comparing monetary measures. The value of money changes over time as a result of inflation. So the fact that a business has a net profit in 1974 of £20,000 and a net profit of £30,000 in 1983 does not necessarily mean that it has become more profitable. In fact in this instance the reverse would be true. Over the period from 1974 to 1983 inflation rose by 230% and so the value of money fell proportionately. The business would need a profit of £67,000 in 1983 merely to have kept the same level of profitability in real terms. The causes of and possible solutions to inflation as a economic problem are examined in chapter 25.

Even within a single balance sheet, monetary values for different items may not accurately reflect their immediate true worth to the business. So if under the assets column in the balance sheet there is a value of £500 recorded as debtors, indicating money owed to the business, this is a less liquid asset than £500 shown as cash in hand. The business may have to wait some time for payment from its debtors while the cash in hand can be used at once and so it has, in effect, more immediate value. Nevertheless while bearing these limitations in mind, the use of money measurement is an important accounting concept and without it the interpretation of financial information would be much more difficult and fraught with error.

(f)   SEPARATE BUSINESS ENTITY

We should always regard a set of accounts from the viewpoint of the business. In other words the organisation, whether it is a sole trader, partnership or limited company should be seen as a separate business entity. If the business is non-corporate, either a sole trader or a partnership, then the owner's personal accounts should be separate from those of the business. So, for instance, if the owner introduces money into the business this should be recorded as capital introduced or as a loan under the liabilities of the business while it would be regarded as an asset in the owner's personal accounts. Of course there is a possibility of confusion as the business is not a separate legal entity and its assets and liabilities are regarded under the law as being those of the owner. However under this accountancy concept it is important to see the owner and the business as separate accounting entities even though they are not separate legal entities. The legal regulation of sole traders and partnerships is discussed in chapter 18.

The situation is obviously more clear in the case of a limited company for the business is both a separate legal entity and a separate business entity distinct from its owners, the shareholders.

(g)   THE DUAL ASPECT OF FINANCIAL RECORDING — DOUBLE ENTRY BOOK-KEEPING

If we wish to fully understand the financial transactions of a business we need to know both how money has come into the business and how it has been used. Therefore every transaction has two aspects and this gives its name to the concept of the 'dual aspect'. The method we use to record transactions in this way is known as 'double entry book-keeping'. To appreciate this process refer back to our examination of the balance sheet.

If for instance the owner of the business introduced an extra £5,000 into the business this would be recorded as an additional liability on the balance sheet. However the balance sheet now does not balance. This is because we do not know what has been done with the £5,000. It needs to be shown on the balance sheet under the appropriate entry. Here are some of the ways the money may possibly have been used.

(i)   The £5,000 may simply have been deposited in the business bank account. In which case the bank entry under assets will increase by £5,000.

(ii)   It may have been used to purchase a new car in which case the new purchase will be entered under the fixed assets heading.

(iii) Alternatively of course it may have been used to pay a bill and so reduce the organisation's creditors. In this case the £5,000 will be shown as an increase in liabilities as capital introduced while the creditors figure, also under the liabilities column, will be reduced by £5,000. The net result is to leave the liabilities figure the same and not to affect the assets.

Whichever way the money has been used, we have recorded it so as to keep the accounting balance by maintaining the relationship that Assets are equal to Liabilities plus Capital Employed.

(h) STABILITY — THE COST CONCEPT

When preparing a balance sheet it is usual to show the organisation's assets at their cost price. As we have already noted when considering the concept of continuity, this means that the value of the assets shown does not represent their true current market value. However it would be impossible to accurately assess the market value of every asset each time a balance sheet is prepared. Therefore in the interests of consistency and objectivity, we assume the current value of the asset by taking its initial cost and depreciating its worth as it is used. In this way we can allocate a part of the assets value to each trading period in which it is used. It is often the owners choice as to how quickly he will 'write down' an asset although the Inland Revenue specifies the length of time over which some business assets such as cars can be written off, but this is only for tax purposes — the choice is still the owners as to how it is depreciated in the balance sheet.

Assets such as buildings and freehold land which do not depreciate in the same way as machinery or other assets are not normally written down in this way. Instead they are normally re-valued from time to time so that the balance sheet will more truly reflect their worth to the organisation. However, such re-valuations will usually bear in mind the convention of prudence which was discussed earlier in the chapter.

Because of the high rates of inflation which were prevalent in the 1970's it became a common practice for financial statements to carry a note to the accounts in which the possible effects of inflation on particular assets or transactions are pointed out.

(i) THE REALISATION CONCEPT

This concept is similar in nature to the 'accruals' concept. As we have already noted when looking at the Profit and Loss Account it is important to record all transactions in the trading period in which they occur and not in the period in which money is received or paid. Thus it is normal practice for an organisation to send an invoice to a customer at the time the goods are despatched or the service is completed. In chapter 12 when we considered cash flow forecasting we noted that business customers often expect a period of trade credit or are simply slow payers. Because of this probable delay, which could obviously stretch from weeks to months, we record a sale in the accounts at the time the invoice is sent, in other words at time of delivery. If money is still owing at the end of the trading period for work done or goods delivered then this amount will be shown as trade debtors in the balance sheet and will not affect the Profit and Loss Account.

(j) MATERIALITY

This is a consideration of whether every transaction, every asset acquired and every liability incurred should be recorded. This will be determined by assessing the material needs of the organisation. So for example most businesses would not bother to list every item of office equipment as a fixed asset despite the fact that its working life may extend into a number of trading periods. It would be a time consuming and ultimately fruitless exercise to record a stapler in the assets column of the balance sheet at a cost of £3.50 and then to depreciate it over the following four years. Such minor items would be included as a current expense in the Profit and Loss Account and would, in effect, be 'written off' immediately.

Of course the level of 'materiality' depends on the size of the organisation. While an office photo-copier would be regarded as a major item of expenditure for a small one man business and would be included as a fixed asset, the same photocopier would not normally be itemised in the accounts of a multi-national corporation. Similarly while a company with a turnover of £100,000 would include a bad debt of £10,000 in its accounts, it may be that another company with a turn-over of £10m would not show the same bad debt of £10,000. As you will appreciate such decisions can be somewhat arbitrary and it is usually a question of experience to decide what should be regarded as a balance sheet item and what may be simply written off as a current expense.

It is important to bear these concepts and conventions in mind when you attempt to understand and interpret the Balance Sheet and Profit and Loss Accounts of both private and public sector organisations. It is always worth turning to the end of the accounts to see if the concepts or conventions under which they have been prepared have been specified and also to check if the accountants or auditors who have verified the accounts have qualified them in any way.

PROBLEMS IN APPLYING THE FUNDAMENTAL ACCOUNTING CONCEPTS

The major difficulty in applying these concepts is that for most business enterprises they will have some transactions which spread into different accounting periods. Therefore it is necessary to make decisions as to how expenditure in one period may produce revenue in future years, in other words should certain assets be classified under the Profit and Loss Account or under the Balance Sheet? Similarly in certain instances the business may be paid in advance for work that it has yet to complete. Again the difficulty lies in the extent to which this revenue should be carried forward into the future trading period. Other examples of this type of dilemma involve the valuation of work in progress or stock which has yet to be sold, the realistic profitable life of fixed assets such as plant and machinery and consequently the period over which it should be written down, and the extent to which other forms of investment such as that incurred in staff development or product research will produce revenue for the business in the future.

Thus the business is constantly dealing with events which have yet to happen and as such are uncertain. It is at this point that the commercial judgement of the financial manager must be used. Perhaps it would be a good idea to supply them with crystal balls to allow them to predict the future more accurately!

In the next chapter we will be looking at financial statements and using some of the information which is presented in them to interpret the financial position and the performance of an organisation.

ASSIGNMENT — HARTLEBOROUGH ROVERS

Hartleborough Rovers is a professional football club which is currently playing in the fourth division of the football league. At present it is an average middle of the table side with six or seven good young players and a number of ageing professionals. The club has a squad consisting of 17 full time professionals whose basic wage averages £250 per week.

There are bonuses for winning matches of £50 per match and for drawing matches of £20 for an away draw and £10 for a home draw. The bonuses are only payable to the twelve players selected for each match. There are also 5 apprentice professionals who are paid £100 per week plus match bonuses where applicable.

The playing record of the club suggests that out of the 46 league matches played in a season it will tend to win 16, lose 18 and draw 12 (6 at home and 6 away). In addition to this, the club can be expected on average to participate in 8 cup matches of which they will win 5 and lose 3. Appearance money of £100 per player irrespective of status, is paid for each cup match plus the usual bonuses. The club has a manager who is paid £30,000 p.a. and a qualified coach who is paid £20,000 p.a. Other salaries and wages of office staff, groundsmen, gatemen etc. amount to £40,000 per year. Policing of the ground costs £18,000 p.a. and other running costs amount to £22,000 p.a.

The average gate for home matches over the season excluding season ticket-holders is 2,600 at an average price of £3. There are also 400 season ticket holders who pay £85 each.

The only other income of the club is a contribution from the football pools of £55,000 p.a. and the net proceeds of programme sales and advertising of £40,000.

Hartleborough Rovers have a bank overdraft of £130,000 at present which is personally guaranteed by the club chairman who has also loaned £100,000 to the club free of interest.

TASKS

1. You have been appointed as financial consultant to investigate the affairs of Hartleborough F.C. In this capacity you are required to produce financial statements to show:

   a) the profit or loss the club can expect to make in the coming year;

   b) the projected bank balance or overdraft at the end of the year.

2. Produce a report in which you:

   a) include the financial information derived from Task 1;

   b) identify those areas in the financial statements where there may be cause for concern;

   c) make recommendations as to the ways in which the club could be made more financially stable.

DEVELOPMENTAL TASK

3. Undertake a role play exercise in which you present the report at a board meeting of the club.

ASSIGNMENT — THE AGM

Wingrove Village Cricket and Rugby Club is the sporting hub of the small village of Wingrove. It has a club house attached to the pavilion in which it has a members bar and lounge. The club has a team participating in the local cricket league in the summer and two rugby teams, the adult side and a colts team, which play regularly throughout the winter. In the past year the bar has been extended and modernised to provide a more convivial atmosphere for the post match celebrations or commiserations. Unfortunately a new pub has recently been built on the outskirts of the village and this is proving extremely popular with the locals. This has meant that the turnover at the club's bar has fallen by about 15% in the last year. Each summer the club has an Annual General Meeting at which the club's accounts are presented to the members. The accounts are prepared by Matterson and Ainley, a local firm of Chartered Accountants. These are shown below.

WINGROVE VILLAGE CRICKET AND RUGBY CLUB
BALANCE SHEET AS AT 31ST MAY 1986

	£	£
Fixed Assets		
Freehold Land, Buildings at cost	13,700	
Additions and Extension during the year	12,000	
	25,700	
Depreciation provided to date	8,600	
		17,100
Equipment at cost	4,000	
Depreciation provided to date	2,160	
		1,840
		18,940
Current Assets		
Stock	800	
Debtors and Payments in Advance	170	
Cash at Bank	330	
Cash in hand	110	
	1,410	
Less: Current Liabilities		
Creditors and Accruals	310	
		1,100
		20,040
Financed by:		
Capital Fund		
Balance at start of the year		11,740
Less: Deficit for the year		3,300
		8,440
Mortgage Loan from Brewery		11,600
		20,040

WINGROVE VILLAGE CRICKET AND RUGBY CLUB
INCOME & EXPENDITURE ACCOUNT FOR THE YEAR ENDED 31ST MAY 1986

	£	£
Bar Trading Account:		
Sales		12,500
Cost of Sales:		
Opening Stock	500	
Purchases	8,600	
	9,100	
Less: Closing Stock	800	
		8,300
Trading Profit on Bar Activities		4,200
Other Income:		
Subscriptions	300	
Season ticket sales	400	
Gate Receipts	3,800	
		4,500
Donations		3,000
		11,700
Expenditure:		
Honoraria — Groundstaff	2,000	
Players Expenses, Travel & Insurance ...	7,000	
Heating & Lighting	1,000	
Referees, Umpires & Linesmen	600	
General Rates and Insurance	750	
Depreciation — Property	1,900	
Equipment	460	
Telephone	200	
Secretary's Expenses	130	
Other miscellaneous expenditure	960	
		15,000
Net Deficit for the Year (excess of expenditure over income)		3,300

TASK

You have been elected Treasurer of the Club and in this position you must present the accounts at the Annual General Meeting. You have received a copy of the accounts from Tony Matterson, the accountant, prior to the meeting.

1. Prepare a set of notes which will help you to make your presentation. Remember that most of the club's members are unfamiliar with accounts and therefore you will have to explain each item in the accounts very carefully. You wish to anticipate potential questions on the accounts and so you should prepare answers to the following questions:

   (i)   What is depreciation?

   (ii) Why does the club have to borrow money?

   (iii) Why are the depreciation figures different in the Balance Sheet and the Income and Expenditure Account?

Chapter 15

INTERPRETING FINANCIAL INFORMATION

THE MEASUREMENT OF FINANCIAL PERFORMANCE

In the previous chapter we looked at the way in which financial statements are presented and examined their basic structure. However simply knowing what such statements are is not enough. To effectively manage an organisation or to assess its financial performance it is necessary to be able to interpret and analyse the information presented in financial statements. This involves three stages:

(i) you should know the information for which you are looking;

(ii) you should be capable of interpreting the information when you have found it; and

(iii) you should be able to compare it against some other measure of performance.

THE ORGANISATION'S OBJECTIVES

Before we begin to look at an organisation's performance we need to recognise that it can only be measured against its objectives. Different organisation's have different objectives. These are dependent on the type of organisation it is. These are discussed in some detail in chapter 18 where we consider a range of objectives for different organisations and examine the way in which these can be set externally or internally.

A trading company seeking to maximise its profit will have very different objectives to a government department serving the community. A nationalised industry may be seeking to achieve the dual objectives of being commercially profitable and providing as wide a service to its consumers as possible. We examine performance indicators used in the public service in chapter 7 so here we will restrict our study to measures of performance in commercial organisations. In saying that, we will be stressing the need for such businesses to provide a satisfactory return on investment, to be profitable and to use efficiently the resources at their disposal. Of course all of these are to some extent inter-linked but it is only by examining each individually that it is possible to begin to appreciate where the strengths and weaknesses of an organisation lie and how these can be improved to make financial management more effective.

THE USE OF PERFORMANCE RATIOS

Often on the evening news bulletin you will hear an item which mentions the trading performance of a large company like ICI or BP. The newsreader may say that it has earned profits of hundreds of millions of pounds. Is this a good, bad or indifferent performance for the company this year? It may sound impressive but what we do not know is how much is invested in the company in relation to its profit or whether it is so inefficient that its profits represent only a tiny percentage of its sales. To be able to judge such figures we use performance ratios. These are merely comparisons of one piece of financial data against another, expressed as a percentage, proportion or ratio. The following simple example may illustrate this.

You will understand that if you deposit £100 in a building society you may receive £8 interest at the end of the year. This can be expressed as a performance indicator on your savings in the following way:

$$\frac{\text{Interest paid}}{\text{Money saved}} = \frac{£8}{£100} \quad x \quad 100 \quad = \quad 8\%$$

Therefore we find that you are getting an extra 8% return on your savings. Is this a good return? The answer to that question depends on the rate of return you could get if you saved your money elsewhere and also on a number of other important considerations. With your money in the building society you know that it is safe and so you may be willing to accept a lower rate of return than you might receive on a more risky investment. A further consideration is that perhaps you were able to get 10% from the same building society last year before interest rates fell and so you are less satisfied with the 8% now. All of these factors and others will influence your feelings as to whether or not you are getting a good return but in each case you are using a performance ratio indicator to make a judgement. Commercial organisations use similar ratios to measure their performance and in this chapter we will examine some of these.

We will use the financial statements of Extra Time Sports Ltd to illustrate the points we are making. Therefore you should refer to the Balance Sheet and the Profit and Loss Account of ETS Ltd shown in chapter 15 to examine and calculate the ratios as they are explained.

1. THE RETURN ON CAPITAL

We have already noted that the capital invested in a business can come from a number of sources. For sole traders and partnerships, the money usually comes from the owners themselves. This will come either from their own savings or from borrowing, normally from a bank. In a company, the capital is share capital provided by the shareholders plus the organisation's reserves. In the case of a small private company there may be only a few shareholders, while in a large public company there may be hundreds or thousands of investors.

Wherever the initial capital comes from, the people who provide it all have a similar objective — they wish to see a return on the money they have invested in the business. This is assessed by determining the return on capital employed.

The Return on Capital Employed (ROCE)

By this is meant the profit that the business has made expressed as a percentage of the capital invested in it. It is not meant to measure the actual money received by an owner or part owner of a business as a percentage of the money invested in it, but rather to measure the amount earned by the business on the owners' behalf.

In the case of a sole trader or a partnership this return will consist of the net profit of the business expressed as a percentage of the owner(s) capital as follows:

$$\text{For a Sole Trader:} \quad \frac{\text{Net Profit}}{\text{Owners' Capital}} \quad x \quad 100 \quad = \quad \text{ROCE}$$

$$\text{For a Partnership:} \quad \frac{\text{Net Profit}}{\text{Partners' Capital}} \quad x \quad 100 \quad = \quad \text{ROCE}$$

Note that since sole traders and partners are responsible for their own taxes based on their own share of the business profits, these figures are expressed before tax is considered.

In the case of a limited company the return will consist of the net profit of the business expressed as a percentage of ordinary share capital plus undistributed profits (reserves); the latter being profit earned in previous years which have not been paid out as dividends, and therefore kept or reinvested in the business on behalf of the shareholders. The return is therefore expressed as:-

$$\frac{\text{Net profit before Tax}}{\text{Ordinary Share capital plus reserves}} \times 100 = \text{ROCE}$$

Although a limited company is responsible for its own taxes, the return is measured before tax, in order to be able to compare with other types of business (sole traders and partnerships). This having been said, there is no reason why a limited company should not go on to measure the ROCE based on net profit after tax if this is needed.

Note also that limited companies may be partially financed by preference shares and/or debentures, both of which carry fixed rates of dividends and/or interest. As such they have fixed ROCE. Because of this it is better to exclude these from your calculations at this stage.

An example of an ROCE can be seen if a small limited company has an ordinary share capital of £50,000 and accumulated reserves of £30,000 and made a profit of £20,000 for the year, its ROCE would be 25%. This is shown below:

$$\text{ROCE} = \frac{£20,000}{£50,000 + £30,000} = \frac{£20,000}{£80,000} = 25\%$$

Return on Capital Employed for ETS Ltd

In the case of ETS Ltd, there is only a very small share capital of £100. However part of the capital employed is the revenue reserves of £32,800 which gives a total capital employed of £32,900. Thus for ETS Ltd the ROCE for 1985/86 is:

$$\text{ROCE} = \frac{£59404}{£32900} \times 100 = 180.6\%$$

As you can see this is very high. This is because ETS Ltd has had a very profitable year. It also has a very small share capital. In fact it has only four shareholders, each of whom hold share capital of £25.

2.   PROFIT MARGINS

(i)   Net Profit Margin

The second major area in which performance ratios can be applied is in the assessment of profit margins. This compares the level of profit made from sales after all expenses have been deducted but before tax and dividends have been paid. As we discuss in chapter 21 the highest level of profit that a business can make does not always come from maximising sales output. In fact the business needs to have an 'optimum' output as the organisation may find that in order to increase its sales it may have to lower the price it can charge for its product or service, or it may find that its costs are beginning to rise disproportionately to its sales revenue. Bearing this in mind we can calculate a profit margin using the following example.

A business has a net profit of £30,000 before tax and dividends have been paid. Its sales revenue is £600,000.

$$\text{Net Profit Margin} = \frac{\text{net profit before tax and dividends}}{\text{sales revenue}}$$

$$= \frac{£30,000}{£600,000} \times 100 = 5\%$$

The business has a net profit margin of 5% on sales. It is impossible to say whether this is an acceptable profit margin without examining the same ratio in previous years and the profit margins of other businesses in the same and other industries. We will return to such comparisons later.

The Profit Margin for ETS Ltd

From the ETS Profit and Loss Account can be seen that for 1985/86 the company had a net profit before tax, interest and dividends of £59,404 and a sales revenue of £376,279. This produced a profit margin of:

$$= \frac{£59404}{£376279} \times 100 = 16\%$$

This is quite an acceptable profit margin for this type of business and compares favourably with the previous year's profit margin of 2%. It should be stressed however that the 2% margin was made in the first year of trading for ETS Ltd.

(ii) The Gross Profit Percentage

A further useful profit margin ratio is the gross profit percentage.

This ratio indicates the relationship between sales revenue and the direct cost of sales. So for example a greengrocer may sell £50,000 worth of fruit and vegetables in a year after having spent £30,000 on purchasing them from the wholesalers. Thus his gross profit margin is £20,000 or 40% of sales. This figure will indicate his efficiency in buying his products sufficiently cheaply at the market. Also from these figures we can calculate his 'mark-up', in other words the percentage he adds onto the cost price of his produce. If he buys for £30,000 and is then able to sell for £20,000 more (his gross profit) he has added 2/3rds to the cost price before he has sold them to his customers. His average mark-up across his range of fruit and vegetables is 66.6%. Of course this will only be an average and he may have a larger mark-up on pears which will compensate for a less than 66.6% mark-up on potatoes.

Gross Profit Margin for ETS Ltd

The gross profit margin for ETS Ltd for 1985/86 is 36.9% and is found by dividing the direct costs of the business of £138,906 by the sales revenue of £376,279 and multiplying by 100. As you will see this is a substantial improvement on the previous year's figure of 26.6%. This reflects the increasing awareness by the company's management of the right price both to pay for its goods and sell them for.

It is worth noting at this point that it is possible to express any expense item in the Profit and Loss Account as a percentage of sales revenue. For instance if we wished to find the sales revenue/advertising percentage we know that sales are £376279 and the advertising expenditure is £3740 the ratio would be:

$$\text{advertising/sales percentage} = \frac{£3740}{£376279} \times 100 = 1\%$$

Thus in this trading year every £1 spent on advertising generated £100 in sales.

We could use a similar calculation to show labour costs/sales ratio or rent/sales ratio or any other comparison we need to make to assess whether one element of our costs is excessive and requires monitoring.

3.   TURNOVER OF CAPITAL

This ratio measures the use that has been made of the organisation's capital in producing the level of sales. In other words has the capital employed which has financed the business assets been fully utilised in the period? It is normally expressed not as a percentage but as a turnover of capital. A very low turnover of capital would indicate that the organisation has not produced a great level of sales in comparison to the amount of capital it holds. This is often a charge which is levelled against some of the more capital intensive nationalised industries. It is calculated simply by comparing the sales revenue with the capital employed. So if an engineering company has a capital of £300,000 which is represented by plant and machinery and earns sales figures of £900,000 we can say that it has a turnover of capital of 3 times. Note that this is not given as a percentage but as a multiple of the capital employed.

$$\text{Turnover of capital} \quad = \quad \frac{\text{Sales revenue}}{\text{Capital employed}} \quad = \quad 3 \text{ times}$$

It is important to note that capital employed must include all capital employed except long term borrowed capital. So capital employed is equivalent to fixed assets plus current assets minus current liabilities and long term liabilities.

THE RELATIONSHIP BETWEEN THE THREE RATIOS

We have just examined three important ratios: (i) the return on capital employed; (ii) the profit margin; and (iii) the turnover of capital. They are all concerned with the profitability of the business and its rate of return on capital invested. In fact all three are inter-linked. The return on capital is determined by the relationship between the profit margin and the turnover of capital. Using the following example we can illustrate the relationship. Assume that a business has a profit of £100,000, sales of £1,600,000 and capital employed of £800,000.

return on capital employed	=	profit margin	x	turnover of capital
$\dfrac{\text{profit}}{\text{capital employed}}$	=	$\dfrac{\text{profit}}{\text{sales revenue}}$	x	$\dfrac{\text{sales revenue}}{\text{capital employed}}$
$\dfrac{£100,000}{£800,000}$	=	$\dfrac{£100,000}{£1,600,000}$	x	$\dfrac{£1,600,000}{£800,000}$
12.5%	=	6.25%	x	2

From the above example you can see the interdependency of the ratios. Clearly an increase or decrease of profit, capital employed or sales will influence the others. However it also means that we may find similar returns on capital employed in industries operating on very different profit margins. So for instance food retailing which has a rapid turnover and very competitive prices may have a profit margin of only 3 or 4%. However it has a high turnover of capital because of the high volume of trade so the low profit margin of 3% - 4% may be compensated by a turnover of capital employed of 5 times giving a return on capital of 15% - 20%. Alternatively a manufacturing industry might expect a profit margin of about 8% - 10% but, because of the relatively long time required to produce each individual product, may have a comparatively low capital turnover of 1.5 giving a return on capital employed of between 12% and 15%. As you can see a potential investor will wish to carefully scrutinise all of these ratios before determining where to place his investment.

THE POSITION OF ETS LTD.

As we have noted earlier from its balance sheet and profit and loss account ETS Ltd has a profit of £59,404, sales of £376,279 and capital employed of £32,900. Thus it has the following ratios:

$$
\text{return on capital employed} = \text{profit margin} \times \text{turnover of capital}
$$

$$
\frac{\text{profit}}{\text{capital employed}} = \frac{\text{profit}}{\text{sales revenue}} \times \frac{\text{sales revenue}}{\text{capital employed}}
$$

$$
\frac{£59,404}{£32,900} = \frac{£59,404}{£376,279} \times \frac{£376,279}{£32,900}
$$

$$
180.55\% = 15.78\% \times 11.44
$$

THE CONTROL OF WORKING CAPITAL AND LIQUIDITY

We have seen the organisation must attempt to maintain its profitability if it is to provide a satisfactory return to those who have provided capital. However in order to survive it must also keep a close watch on its short term liquidity position. By this we mean its ability to pay its immediate debts. As we discuss in chapter 19 a business can easily become bankrupt or be wound up if it becomes insolvent. Its employees will expect to be paid and certain creditors such as landlords or materials suppliers may be unwilling to give the business any degree of extended credit. So if the business cannot get credit from its suppliers then it may be unable to produce and so may be forced to close. Thus it is important that a business has some means of assessing its liquidity position and to do this it can use two ratios:

1. The Current Ratio
2. The Liquidity Ratio (Acid Test)

1. THE CURRENT RATIO

The current ratio compares all the organisation's current assets to its current liabilities. You will remember from our discussion of the balance sheet in chapter 14 that current assets are those which are liquid and can easily be turned into cash. Therefore they would include stocks of goods which are ready for sale, work in progress, debtors and cash in hand and at the bank. Current liabilities would include creditors who are seeking prompt payment and short term loans.

Current ratios are always expressed in ratio fashion, that is as 'something' to 1, for example 5 : 1. The current ratio is expressed as:

Current Assets : Current Liabilities

The current liabilities should always represent the '1'. They are calculated by dividing both sides of the equation by the current liabilities. So for example a business with current assets of £7,500 and current liabilities of £5,000 would have a current ratio of 7,500 : 5,000 or 1.5 : 1.

It is most difficult to generalise about what is an acceptable current ratio but most businesses would be very wary of having a ratio which was less than 1 : 1 for this would mean that current liabilities exceeded current assets and they could not pay their immediate debts. However it is almost as bad financial management to have a current ratio which is too high for this would mean that too much cash was being tied up in stocks or that the organisation's debtors were taking too long to pay. Most organisations would therefore be satisfied with a current ratio of between 1 : 1 and 2 : 1.

THE CURRENT RATIO FOR ETS LTD

ETS Ltd has current assets of £93594 and current liabilities of £66132 and so its current ratio is:

$$\frac{£93594}{£66132} = 1.4 : 1$$

What we are showing here is that ETS Ltd is able to cover its short term debts to others 1.4 times by its current assets, therefore it appears to be reasonably solvent.

2.   THE LIQUIDITY RATIO

This ratio is sometimes called the 'acid test' because occasionally it is all important. It refers to the relationship between those assets which are extremely liquid and current liabilities. In other words it is concerned with how much ready money you can lay your hands on when the creditors are queueing up at the door. This would include all available cash, short term investments such as government stock or shares which can be quickly cashed in, and debtors who can be pressed for payment. It would exclude stock which it may not be possible to sell quickly or work in progress which may be difficult to finish in a short period. It is expressed as follows:

$$\text{Liquidity ratio} = \frac{\text{Debtors plus Cash}}{\text{Current Liabilities}} \text{ or } \frac{\text{Current assets less stock}}{\text{Current Liabilities}}$$

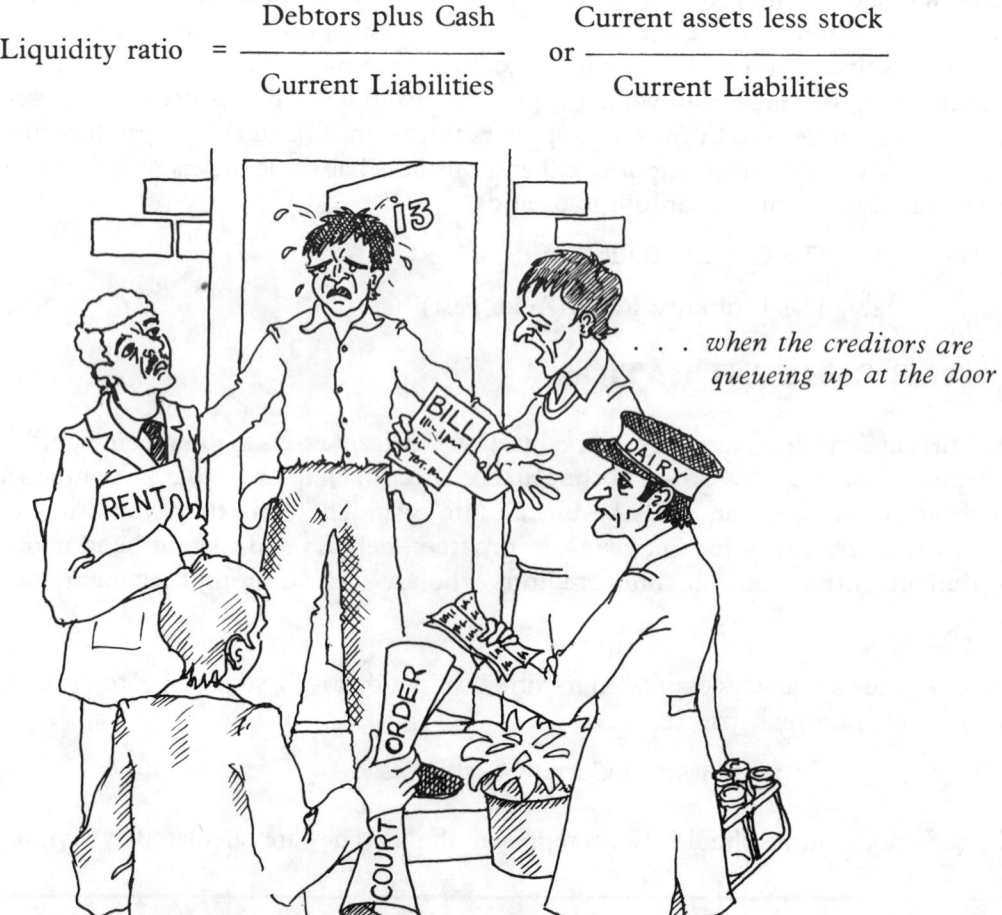

. . . when the creditors are queueing up at the door

Surprisingly many organisations can operate with a liquidity ratio of less than 1, in other words with current liabilities exceeding available liquid assets. This can happen if the business has a bank overdraft facility which is not at its limit and can be drawn on at short notice. It may also be possible to relieve a short term liquidity crisis by rescheduling the organisation's debt and paying off short term loans with more long term credit.

In the case of ETS Ltd its current liabilities stand at £66,132 while its current debtors of £4,673 and cash of £48,237 only total £52,910. Therefore its liquidity ratio is:

$$\frac{£4673 \text{ Debtors} + £48237 \text{ Cash}}{£66132 \text{ Current Liabilities}} = \frac{£52910}{£66132} = 0.8 : 1$$

Note that the ratio is still expressed in terms of 'something' to 1 (where 1 equals the current liabilities).

Fortunately the company does not expect its creditors to press for immediate payment, and even if they do it has an overdraft facility at the bank of £15000 which can be utilised if necessary.

When looking at liquidity ratios it is well to note that we are measuring the liquidity at a particular point in time (the date of the balance sheet from which the ratio is taken), but this gives us no idea of the time element involved in:

- a) turning stock and debtors into cash; and

- b) the company's creditors being paid.

We therefore use a further series of ratios which will indicate the time span of the cashflow. These are:

- i) Stock Turnover (cash in)

- ii) Debtors Turnover (cash in)

- iii) Creditors Turnover (cash out)

i)   Stock Turnover

This can be expressed in two ways which are inter-related:-

- a) The number of times the average stock is turned over in the trading period (usually 1 year);

- b) The length of time it takes (in days) to turn over (or 'move') the average stock once.

To determine the Stock Turnover ratio we need to know the average stock figure, which will usually be the opening stock plus the closing stock divided by two, and the cost of goods figure, which can be obtained from the Profit and Loss Account. The calculation for a) above is:

$$\frac{\text{Cost of Sales}}{\text{Average Stock}}$$

and for b) above it is:

$$\frac{365}{\text{the answer to a)}}$$

For example if a business has an opening stock of £40,000, a closing stock of £50,000 and purchases of £460,000 with sales of £600,000 then the cost of sales is £40,000 + £460,000 - £50,000 = £450,000. The stock turnover is therefore:

$$\frac{£450,000}{(£40,000 + £50,000) \div 2} = \frac{£450,000}{£45,000} = 10 \text{ times}$$

This means that the average stock is turned over (sold) 10 times in one year. This can then be expressed in days by dividing 365 by 10 to give 36.5 days. This means that in 36 or 37 days the money tied up in stocks will be released by the sale of that stock. This does not mean that there will be no stock left after 36 or 37 days as any stock sold will be replaced by new purchases, which will form part of the next cycle. Neither does it mean that the actual cash will be available for the payment of creditors, because if the sales are made on credit, there will be a further transfer before the cash is finally collected (see Debtors turnover).

Another way of calculating the timespan is by inverting the Average Stock/cost of sales figures and multiplying by 365. This is shown as:

$$\frac{£45,000}{£450,000} \times 365 = 36.5 \text{ days}$$

An increase in the stock turnover figure will produce a reduction in the timespan. For instance if stock turned over 12 times in the year this would give a figure of 30.5 days. Clearly a decrease in the stock turnover figure reduces the time span.

An increase in the stock turnover from one year to the next will indicate either:

    a)   increased sales with no corresponding increase in stockholding; or

    b)   decreased stock holding with no corresponding decrease in sales.

For example if sales were increased to £640,000 with the same gross margin of 25% the cost of sales should become £480,000. In this case the stock turnover will become:

$$\frac{£480,000}{£45,000} = 10.67 \text{ times}$$

If sales remained constant at £600,000 but the average stock fell to £40,000, the turnover will be:

$$\frac{£600,000}{£40,000} = 15 \text{ times}$$

Stock Turnover for ETS Ltd

In the case of ETS Ltd, the stock turnover is calculated as follows:

$$\frac{£237,373 \text{ (cost of sales)}}{(£22,843 \text{ opening stock} + £40,000 \text{ closing stock}) \div 2} = \frac{£237,373}{£31,763.5} = 7.47 \text{ times}$$

$$\text{or} \quad \frac{£31,763.5}{£237,373} \times 365 = 49 \text{ days}$$

It should be clear that the higher the stock turnover ratio, the sooner that profit is earned on the stock sold and that therefore a business with a high turnover can operate on lower profit margins. In essence the profit is determined by the speed of turnover. Therefore businesses with a 'quick' turnover such as petrol filling stations and fruit and vegetable businesses can still make acceptable profits but with low profit margins. On the other hand a slower stock turnover rate means that higher margins must be earned when stock is sold to compensate for the slower turnover. For example a jeweller's business, which must carry high stocks to attract customers, may have a low stock turnover rate but must rely on higher profit margins.

You should note that it is the cost of stock which is used in the stock turnover ratio and not the price at which it is sold. This is because the selling price would include the profit margin and any other costs incurred in the sale while this ratio is concerned about how often the stock is replaced at cost price.

ii) Debtors turnover

This is very similar to the stock turnover in the method of its calculation in as much as it expresses the relationship between sales on credit and the debtors arising from these sales. Like the stock turnover figure it can be expressed as a number of times the debtors are turned over in a year or as the number of days it will take to collect the average debt. The equations are:

a) $$\frac{\text{Credit Sales}}{\text{Average Debtors}} = \text{Debtors Turnover}$$

b) $$\frac{365}{\text{Debtors Turnover}} = \text{The Number of Days}$$

or $$\frac{\text{Average Debtors}}{\text{Credit Sales}} \times 365 = \text{The Number of Days}$$

Carrying on the example used for the stock turnover figures, if the debtors at the start of the year had been £90,000 and at the end of the year £110,000, the average for the year would be £100,000. If the whole of the sales of £600,000 had been on credit the debtors turnover figures would be:

a) $$\frac{£600,000}{£100,000} = 6 \text{ times}$$

b) $$\frac{365}{6} = 61 \text{ days}$$

or $$\frac{£100,000}{£600,000} \times 365 = 61 \text{ days}$$

This means that it will take an average 61 days to collect the average debts once. However it must be stressed that this does not mean that there will be nothing collected for 61 days, as all the debts will not have been collected on the last day.

When the stock turnover (36 days) is added to the debtors turnover (61 days) you can see that to convert stock into cash will take 97 days or just over three months. However because of the profit element in sales the cash when collected should be more than that which was first paid out to purchase the stock.

Since ETS Ltd. is a retail selling outlet it mainly deals in cash over the counter, it does not have many debtors and so in this case it is most probably not necessary to calculate a debtors turnover figure.

Today of course, even retail outlets such as ETS can have substantial debtors, particularly if they accept credit cards such as Access or Barclaycard from customers.

Although the debtors turnover figure is a very useful ratio, it may be distorted by old or long standing debts being included in the debtors figure, therefore an attempt should be made to analyse debts by age.

The 'age' of debtors

By the 'age' of a debt is meant the length of time that a debt has been outstanding. The organisation should list its outstanding debtors chronologically in the order of the time at which they incurred the debt. Thus those debtors who owe money for the longest period will be listed first and then other debtors ranked in order according to the length of time for which their debt has been outstanding. Such a schedule will highlight those debtors who have the longest standing debts and should indicate where to put on pressure to pay. In other words who should get the strongest letters demanding payment, when the business should instruct its solicitors to take legal action to seek payment and so on. This method should also point to those debtors who are particularly slow in paying and the organisation may then decide that it will not trade with such customers in the future without an improvement in their promptness of payment. Unfortunately it is often the largest companies who are most tardy in their payment of bills and for the small business these may be very important clients which it can ill afford to lose. Therefore it must bear the difficulties in slowness of payment rather than offend a major customer.

The 'age' of debtors

iii) **Creditors Turnover Ratio (Average Collection Period)**

In the above example we have considered the time taken for a business to be paid by its debtors. However, it is important to recognise that there are two sides to this picture and it is likely that the business is itself taking time to pay its creditors. The length of time that it is taking to pay debts can be calculated in the same way that the debtors turnover was found.

$$\text{Average Collection Period} \quad = \quad \frac{\text{Creditors}}{\text{Purchases}} \quad \times \quad 365$$

In the case of Extra Time Sports Limited, it has creditors of £26,398 and had purchases of £251,102 in the 1985/86 period. Thus its creditors turnover period for 1985/86 is:

$$\frac{\text{£26,398 Creditors}}{\text{£251,102 Purchases}} \quad \times \quad 365 \quad = \quad 38 \text{ days}$$

While for 1984/85 it was:

$$\frac{\text{£17544 Creditors}}{\text{£176377 Purchases}} \quad \times \quad 365 \quad = \quad 36 \text{ days}$$

This slight increase in the period reflects a greater confidence in the business by its creditors, such as Nike and Adidas. They have been dealing with the company for some time now and are reasonably confident that it is established in business and so will be less concerned about the safety of their money. It is not difficult to recognise that businesses which have only just been established are often the ones which are most quickly chased for payment by their creditors.

At this point it is worth making a comparison between the stock turnover figure and the creditors turnover figure for ETS Ltd. As we saw earlier the stock turnover for the business was 49 days. In other words, the average item of stock stays on the ETS shelves for 49 days. Yet as we have seen the creditors turnover ratio for 1985/86 is only 38 days. This means that the creditors are in effect being paid before the stock is sold to customers. This might appear to place an increased strain on the company's cashflow as the outflow to creditors is quicker than the inflow from customers. However it should be recognised that each sale should earn a profit for the company above the cost of the purchase. As such profits accumulate they allow the company to pay creditors and yet still build up stock.

CASH CONTROL

The final element of working capital is cash or an overdraft facility to provide liquidity to the business. Of course for most businesses there is a limit both to the cash it has available and the overdraft limit it is able to secure from a bank. Therefore it must control its debtors, creditors and stock levels with this in mind and manage its short term financial position accord-ingly.

CIRCULATION OF WORKING CAPITAL

As we have already noted earlier in the chapter the current ratio is usually regarded as the most important means of monitoring working capital of a business. However, financial managers will also be concerned to examine how efficiently this working capital is being used. This is measured by the circulation of working capital. This shows the speed at which the working capital circulated. The ratio for this is:

$$\text{Circulation of Working Capital} \quad = \quad \frac{\text{Sales}}{\text{Working Capital}}$$

For Extra Time Sports Ltd, its net current assets (or its working capital) for 1986 stood at £93,594 and its sales for the year were £376,269. Thus its circulation of working capital was:

$$\frac{£376,269}{£93,594} = 4X \text{ (times)}$$

This shows us that each £1 of working capital has produced £4 of sales.

INVESTMENT RATIOS

Having looked at the main accounting ratios for determining the performance and the position of a particular business, it will now be of benefit to look at some ratios which are used by investors with no particular interest in running the business, but who spread their money around and look for the best returns they can get. This type of investor seeks two elements:

  a)   a good return in terms of income from his investment; and

  b)   capital appreciation of his investment.

We shall now consider some of the ratios which may help him to make the correct decisions about where to invest his money. These are:

  (i)   Earnings per share

  (ii)   Earnings yield

  (iii)   Price/Earning ratio

  (iv)   Dividend yield.

(i)   EARNINGS PER SHARE

When a limited company finally determines its profit for a year, there are certain calls made on that profit. These are called appropriations of profit. The first of these is the Inland Revenue in respect of Corporation Tax. There may also be preference shareholders who need to have their return by way of a fixed percentage dividend. Dividends are based upon the issued nominal value of a share. The nominal value is the value which the company has decided its share capital will be split into. For instance a company may have issued 10,000 shares of nominal value £1. This gives a share capital of £10,000.

It could have divided this £10,000 share capital into 20,000 50p shares. However if we assume that there are 50,000 10% Preference shares of 50p each issued, the preference dividend will be £2,500 (10% of £25,000).

After tax and preference dividends are provided for, the remainder of the profit is available for the ordinary shareholders — the 'equity' shareholders. This amount is divided by the number of ordinary shares issued to give the earnings per share ratio.

$$\text{Earnings per share (E/S)} = \frac{\text{Net profit after tax and preference dividend}}{\text{Number of ordinary shares}}$$

This is the figure which tells an investor (shareholder) exactly how much that the company has earned for him after all other claims have been met.

Care must be taken when calculating this ratio since it is the number of shares which have been issued which is used and we have already seen that a company with an issued share capital of £50,000 may have 50,000 shares of £1 each, 100,000 shares of 50p each or 500,000 shares of 10p each.

Note that the key phrase is 'earned for him'. This means that the company has accumulated during the year out of its activities a sum of money for its shareholders. It does not mean that this amount is actually paid to the shareholders, because the company may wish to hold some of its profits for expansion or other purposes. The amount actually paid to the shareholders is known as the 'dividend' and is usually expressed as a percentage of the share capital issued; so a dividend of $12\frac{1}{2}\%$ on an issued share capital of £80,000 would give £10,000 to the shareholders or $12\frac{1}{2}$p per £1 share or 6.25p per 50p share.

(ii) EARNINGS YIELD

Often the nominal value of a share is not the same as its market value. The latter is the price at which the share will change hands if there is a buyer and a seller, and is determined by the level of the company's reserves, its performance, assets and other market forces. For instance if a company has an issued capital of £50,000 and reserves of £50,000 the company is showing a worth of £100,000 and if its share capital is in £1 shares, each share will be worth £2 on the market, in other words twice its nominal value.

A truer picture of the relationship between earnings and investment is therefore obtained by expressing the earnings per share as a percentage of the market value of the share. This is obtained by using the following formula:

$$\frac{\text{Earnings per share}}{\text{market value}} \times 100 = \text{Earnings yield percentage}$$

For example if a company has an issued share capital of £100,000 in £1 shares and reserves of £50,000, which gives a market value of £1.50 per share, and earned a profit of £30,000, then its earnings per share is:

$$\frac{£30,000}{100,000} = \text{30p per share}$$

Its earning yield is:

$$\frac{30p}{150p} \times 100 = 20\%$$

This means that if you were thinking of investing in that particular company you would receive a return in terms of earnings (not dividends) of 20% on your investment. To determine whether this is a good or bad investment, you would have to compare it with the earnings yield figures from other companies or the yields from that company in earlier years.

(iii) PRICE/EARNINGS RATIO

This measures the relationship between the market price of the share and its earnings and is really the earnings yield ratio inverted, the formula being:

$$\frac{\text{Market value of the share}}{\text{Earnings per share}} = \text{Price/Earnings Ratio}$$

In the example used above the P/E ratio will be calculated as follows:

$$\frac{150p}{30p} = \text{5 times}$$

This means that on current figures it would take 5 years to recover in earnings the price that would have to be paid for the share. Obviously there is a relationship between the P/E ratio and the earnings yield. In effect the higher the P/E ratio, the lower the yield and therefore not such a good prospect for an investor.

Generally speaking the lower the P/E ratio the better it is to invest in that particular share. It may mean however that the share is undervalued by the market and since other factors, not necessarily highlighted by the above ratios, may influence the share's valuation, then other enquiries should be made before making the decision to invest. Other examples of the relationship between theP/E ratio and the Earnings yield are:

P/E ratio 10   :   Earnings Yield   10%

P/E ratio 8   :   Earnings Yield $12\frac{1}{2}$%

P/E ratio 20   :   Earnings Yield   5%

(iv) DIVIDEND YIELD

This ratio for most investors is probably a more important ratio than earnings yield. It expresses the dividend declared as a percentage of the market value of the shares and measures the actual return on investment which the shareholder will receive in his pocket. For example let us suppose that the company mentioned above declared a dividend of 15%, that is 15p per share. The dividend yield will be:

$$\frac{15p}{150p} \times 100 = 10\%$$

In such a situation as an investor you will receive (in your pocket) 10% return on your investment.

One aspect of investment as well as income earned is capital growth, and anyone who is looking to invest in a company will wish to see how much of the company's profits after tax and preference dividend is retained by the company for expansion and growth. This can be done by calculating a divided cover, which is effectively the number of times the dividend is covered by the profit available out of which the dividend is to be paid. In the example we have used the available profit is £30,000, the dividend is £15,000, therefore the dividend cover is 2. This is another way of measuring the relationship between earnings per share and dividend per share. It means that out of every £1 profit earned, 50p is kept for expansion and 50p is distributed as dividend. If the dividend had been 10% the cover would have been 3. In other words out of every £1 earned $66\frac{2}{3}$p would have been retained and $33\frac{1}{3}$p distributed. This would indicate a fairly good retention (growth) policy on behalf of the company but may not appeal to investors as the dividend yield will only be:

$$\frac{10}{150} \times 100 = 6\frac{2}{3}\%$$

This is not as good as the average building society investment which of course carries no risk. As an investor you would be looking for a good balance between the two ratios.

Finally it must be said that the use of accounting ratios must be tempered with common sense. It is all too easy to come to incorrect conclusions, using accounting information without balancing it against other business information which may be available. Accounting ratios are a very useful tool for the measurement of performance, solvency and investment potential of any business, but care must be taken not to jump to the wrong conclusions without looking at other sources of information.

In this section of the chapter we have not used the example of Extra Time Sports Limited as this is a private limited company. As such its shares are not traded on the stock exchange and so it is difficult to determine their market value.

ASSIGNMENT — THE ASPEN TAKEOVER

Aspen Ale plc is a large public company which was originally founded as a brewery but which is now engaged in a wide range of activities. At a recent board meeting it was resolved to further diversify into food retailing. In the board's view the safest and most prudent way to do this would be to acquire an existing business already operating in this field. Two relatively small companies have been identified, Foodline Ltd and Handy Stores Ltd as possible candidates for takeover. Both are suitable for acquisition by Aspen Ale and the final decision as to which of the companies to takeover rests on the issue of their respective financial positions. The final accounts of Foodline and Handy Stores are given below.

BALANCE SHEET AS 31 JULY 1986

	Foodline Ltd.		Handy Stores Ltd	
	£'000	£'000	£'000	£'000
Fixed Assets		345		270
Current Assets				
Stock	160		135	
Debtors	260		219	
Balance at Bank	45		—	
	465		354	
Creditors: Amounts due within One Year	180		306	
Current Assets less Current Liabilities		285		48
Total Assets less Current Liabilities		630		318
Creditors: Amounts due after more than one year (10% Debentures)		—		90
		630		228
Share Capital and Reserves				
Issued Share Capital*		300		150
Reserves		330		78
		630		228
Market Value of an Ordinary Share at the Balance Sheet Date		£1.80		40p

* The Shares issued by Foodline Ltd are £1 shares and those issued by Handy Stores Ltd are 25p shares.

PROFIT AND LOSS ACCOUNTS
FOR THE YEAR ENDING 31ST JULY 1986

	Foodline Ltd		Handy Stores Ltd	
	£'000	£'000	£'000	£'000
Sales		1,080		1,290
Less: Cost of Sales				
Opening Stock	111		123	
Purchases	742		942	
	853		1065	
Less: Closing Stock	159		135	
	694		930	
Other Costs of Sales	116	810	102	1,032
Gross Profit		270		258
Selling and Distribution Costs	105		86	
Administration Expenses	90		103	
Interest on Debentures	—	195	9	198
Net Profit for the Year before Tax		75		60
Less Corporation Tax Provided		30		22
Net Profit for the Year after Tax		45		38
Less Dividend Proposed		15		18
Retained Profit for the Year		30		20

TASKS

1. You are employed as an assistant to the financial manager of Aspen Ale. You are required to advise on the possible takeover of Foodline Ltd or Handy Stores Ltd. For this purpose produce a report in which you:

    a) use suitable account ratios to draw a comparison between the two companies in relation to their profitability, solvency and investment potential;

    b) make recommendations on the basis of your findings.

DEVELOPMENTAL TASKS

2. Undertake a role play exercise in which you present the financial report to the senior management of Aspen Ale plc.

3. Obtain the annual reports of a number of major public limited companies. Compare their performance using appropriate accounting ratios.

Chapter 16

BUDGETING, PLANNING AND COST CONTROL

In the previous two chapters we have concerned ourselves with the structure and interpretation of financial statements. As we have seen the information contained in such statements is used by the senior management of an organisation, by providers of finance and by the tax authorities as a means of assessing the performance of an organisation. However, financial statements may not be of the utmost importance to financial managers who are concerned with the day-to-day operation of the business. Such managers require very detailed information about such matters as the costs involved in producing their product or service, potential changes in the market for their goods which may influence prices they can charge and other factors likely to influence the long term planning of the operation. In this chapter we will concentrate on an examination of the financial and accounting techniques which will allow a business to be most effectively managed.

This will be divided into three sections:

1. Budgeting and Planning;

2. The Costs of Production;

3. Capital Investment Decisions.

1. BUDGETING AND PLANNING

In chapter 11 we discussed the need for personal budgeting. Essentially we recognised that as individuals we must assess our current and potential future income and plan our spending accordingly. We must budget so that our spending does not outstrip our income and if it does, we must be clear of the reasons for such overspending, find additional sources of income such as an overdraft or other credit facilities to cover the excess expenditure and then adjust our life style so that we can live within our budget.

A business must undertake a very similar exercise if it wishes to expand and prosper. However, in an organisation, whether it is in the public or private sector, there is a need for such budgeting and planning to be much more professional and more thorough. The more accurate the budget forecast is and the more comprehensive is the level of planning that accompanies it then the lower will be the level of risk which the organisation faces.

This is not to say that it is possible to eliminate all commercial risk simply by efficient budgeting and planning. If that was so then once a financial manager had mastered these techniques the organisation would automatically be successful. This cannot be true, for budgets and plans are estimates for the future and as such can often be inaccurate. However if the budgeting and planning process is undertaken professionally this should reduce the degree of inaccuracy and so more effectively allow the organisation to manage its future.

BUDGETS AND PLANS FOR BUSINESS START-UP

The majority of business failures occur in the initial stages of operation. It is then that there is the greatest potential for unaccounted factors to occur and produce problems. We have already discussed in chapter 12 that it is normal practice to present a bank manager with a business plan when seeking initial finance and this is usually accompanied by the preparation of a cash flow forecast. Let us reiterate what is involved in such a business plan to stress its importance.

A business plan should include:

(i) information on the market for the product. This will include an assessment of the competition, the potential size of the market and the number of customers;

(ii) an appraisal of the prices which are currently being charged for the product or service and whether these tend to fluctuate;

(iii) the likely cost of production. This will include an evaluation of possible prices for labour, raw materials, machinery and equipment, premises and other overheads. It should also anticipate potential changes in the price or availability of the factors of production;

(iv) the projected level of profit which the business seeks to achieve and an assessment of whether or not this will prove to be a satisfactory return on the capital introduced into the business;

(v) proposals regarding the management of the business including such factors as the experience of those who will make the policy and management decisions and the manner in which such decisions will be implemented and administered;

(vi) a business strategy which will outline the future development of the organisation in both the short and medium term. This should include plans for expansion and growth. It may also outline contingency plans which could be implemented should the original ideas not come to fruition or events occur which prevent the organisation from achieving its aims and objectives.

As we noted in chapter 12 this business plan has a number of objectives. It allows the providers of finance such as the bank or other investors to assess the viability of their loan or investment. Clearly they will be much more confident in providing finance for an organisation which appears to be well managed and which seems to know where it is going. However it also has the major advantage of being an extremely useful management tool which can be used to plan the operation of the business and monitor its performance once it is running. If you are going to manage your own business you will want to be able to measure its performance and be able to gauge the level of reward you will receive from your labours and the risks you are taking.

THE TIME SCALE FOR PLANNING AND BUDGETING

At this point it is worth considering the time period for which an organisation should plan and budget. This is not a simple question to answer. Perhaps the easiest way to view this is to plan as far ahead as it is feasible to do. A number of factors will influence this.

(a) The requirement of providers of finance. Any bank which is making a loan available to a business will require it to plan for a period which is as least as long as the length of the loan. So if the business is only seeking a six month overdraft facility, then a plan for the forthcoming year may suffice. However a business which seeks longer term finance will have to plan accordingly. Often a period of three years is required. Any longer period may be unrealistic because of the uncertainty involved.

(b) The time period required to pay back the initial investment. This will be based on an assessment of the likely annual return from the business. It will examine the time period necessary to begin to make a profitable return on the initial capital introduced. Clearly it would be unwise for a person to invest his or her life savings in a business which is not likely to make returns for twenty or thirty years. Therefore a plan should be sufficiently far sighted to reasonably accurately predict when returns will be made.

(c) Change in the market. Some products by their very nature have a very short product life cycle. For instance the demand for certain products are very heavily dependent on fashion or taste which is notoriously fickle. A toy manufacturer who based long term investment plans on the success of a product which was tied to a particular film or TV programme would be gambling on the continued popularity of the programme. They may be lucky to have chosen 'Walt Disney' games or less lucky to have based their business planning on the production of 'Boy George' Dolls.

(d) Changes in the production process. As you know some industries are in a state of constant technological flux. The micro electronic industry is continually inventive and innovative. Thus a business which is in such an industry must be aware of the speed of such change and adjust its organisational planning accordingly. So it is foolish to plan to introduce a new product or productive process which may be obsolete even before it is fully installed.

THE DETAIL OF A BUSINESS PLAN

The detailed planning of any organisation decreases with time. Thus the planning for the forthcoming year should, whenever it is possible, be in quite specific detail. Thus it should specify the likely pattern of sales and income (remember that these will not necessarily coincide), the scheduling of production to meet anticipated sales, the costs which will be incurred throughout the year on current expenditure and plans and costings for the introduction of new capital expenditure. Thus a good business plan should be able to tell the financial manager reasonably accurately what the position the organisation is likely to be twelve months hence. Of course there is always the possibility of changes occurring which have been unaccounted for but the wise organisation should have available contingency funds either in the form of its own financial reserves or accessible loan facilities should they be necessary.

As the time period extends into the future the level of detail contained in the plan will reduce. This is for the obvious reason that there is a greater degree of uncertainty concerning both the internal operations of the business such as cost and efficiency levels and external factors such as market variations or changes in inflation or interest rates. Normally long term projections, such as those referring to more than three years in the future may be restricted to anticipated market trends, the planned market share of the business or potential changes in products or technology. We consider markets and market share in more detail in chapter 26.

In the section above we have examined the concept of planning as a means of managing the organisation's progress over a period of time. We should make the distinction between planning and budgetary control. In its widest sense planning is concerned with the overall aims and objectives of the organisation. For this reason it is sometimes referred to as strategic or corporate planning. It should assume a wide perspective and consider the broad aspects of the organisation's operation. Budgetary control on the other hand normally has a much narrower perspective and is concerned with the short term financial planning of the business to achieve its objectives in the coming year.

BUDGETARY CONTROL

Budgetary control is the process of setting and monitoring the short term objectives of different aspects of the organisation's operation. It involves the day-to-day financial management of each department of the business and therefore must be based on the individual objectives, targets and goals which each department must have. It is important to recognise that this precise management of the organisation's resources is an essential part of the achievement of the overall plan.

Any budget essentially has three distinct aims:

1. to allow the organisation to meet its objectives through the co-ordination of a range of activities;

2. to allow the allocation of the appropriate level of finance to facilitate the achievement of these objectives; and

3. to permit the efficient management of the organisation's financial resources and ensure that it is aware of the extent of and timing requirements for finance.

Without the detailed adherence to invidual budgets the organisation's wider objectives may be hindered. As an integral part of the overall plan it must progress through a number of stages and we will consider each of these in turn.

THE PREPARATION OF BUDGETS

It is a normal practice in most organisations for senior management to negotiate a budget for their own departments. This is the prelude to budgetary control. This will take place in the previous financial year and will obviously be constrained by the overall budget of the organisation.

If we were to look at this process in the largest organisation in the country, the government, we would find that in the autumn of each year there will be a cabinet meeting at which each departmental minister will be arguing for the budget for his own department. Prior to this meeting the ministers will have required their civil servants to prepare a programme of expenditure for their area of responsibility for the coming financial year. This proposed expenditure programme will be based on a survey of the needs and requirements of the department and will anticipate possible changes in the level of its spending. Of course this only forms the basis for the initial 'bids' which are made by cach minister.

Overseeing the spending of the government as a whole is the Treasury, with the Chancellor of the Exchequer at its head. It is his responsibility to set a target budget for the government as a whole which will be financed by the expected levels of taxation, revenue from services and government borrowing. Obviously the level of income must be realistic and acceptable to the citizens of the country. If all ministers were allowed to spend as they wished this would require a degree of taxation which would bring howls of dismay from the overburdened taxpayers. Thus it is within this constraint that the budget is decided. Through a process of negotiation the budget is allocated and then each ministry must divide its allotted expenditure according to its priorities. Obviously some projected expenditure will have to be forgone as the budget will not permit it. They must work within their own departmental budget.

A similar process is undertaken in most other large organisations both in the public and private sectors. In local authorities the budget will be allocated through a series of council meetings and negotiations between the senior officers responsible for each of the authority's services. In a private organisation it will be the Board of Directors who will meet to share out the organisation's spending according to their cost requirements. However we should note that budgeting should not be seen solely as the preserve of senior management. There should be a great deal of consultation with the workers of the organisation who are going to have to live with the budget once it is allocated. As we note in chapter 10 it is often the management style employed in the organisation which determines the extent of employee participation in decision making. Yet it is in this area of financial budgeting that many of the problems of worker dissatisfaction can emerge. Therefore a sensible management will avoid imposing a stringent budget on its workforce without participation or consultation beforehand.

In whichever type of organisation this takes place, this process must take account of the overall plan and objectives of the organisation. The budget must show a high degree of co-ordination so that one department is not under financed to the detriment of the whole. So, for instance, the marketing department must be given a sufficient level of expenditure to advertise and sell the organisation's products. It would be highly inefficient to have a production department manufacturing a high level of output which was not being sold.

This process can be shown more clearly in a diagrammatic form.

THE PREPARATION OF BUDGETS

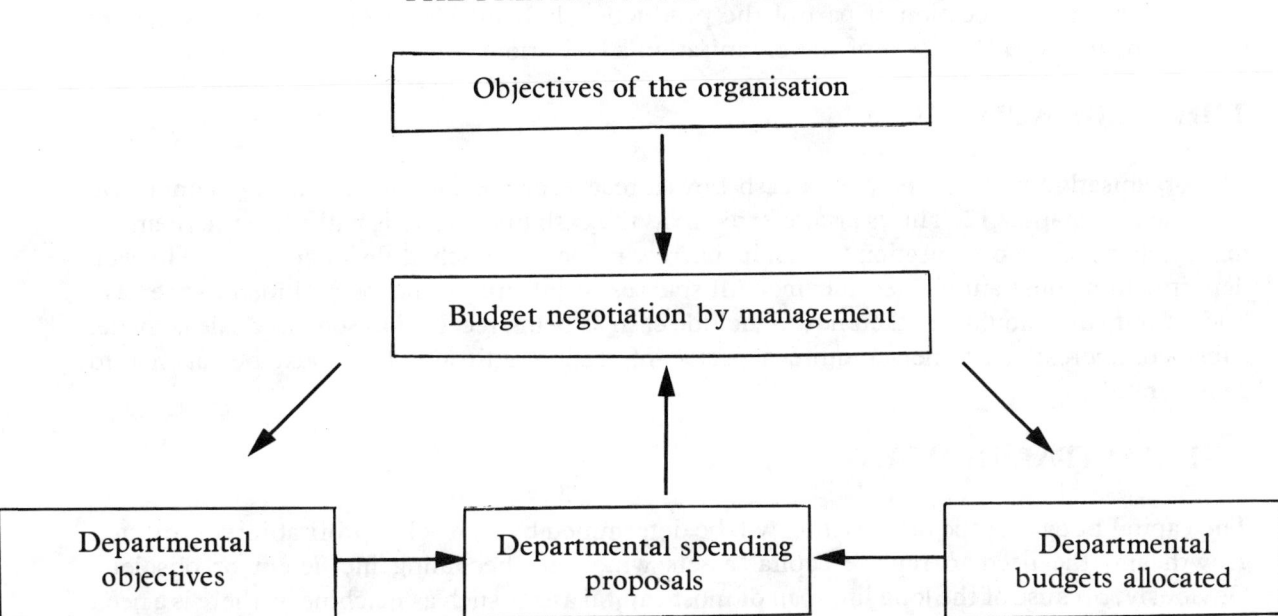

BUDGETING FOR CURRENT AND CAPITAL EXPENDITURE

It is important to make the distinction between budgets for current and capital expenditure. With the former a sufficient budget must be allocated which allows for the efficient operation of a department at its anticipated level of operation for the coming year. There is a tendency when proposing a departmental budget to take the amount that was spent in the present year and to increase it in line with inflation. This is a very negative attitude for it does not evaluate the changing needs or level of output of the department for the coming year. This is why departmental objectives are so important. The departmental managers should carefully cost out their spending requirements to meet the targets they have been set by the overall corporate plan. This requires foresight to avoid an over estimation of the costs involved which will mean that other departments may be left with insufficient finance to operate efficiently while conversely an under estimation can result in the departmental staff feeling that they have not been given enough finance to carry out their jobs adequately.

OPERATIONAL BUDGETS

There is often a distinction made between operational budgets and departmental overheads. Thus the production department should be able to identify the amount it will need to spend on materials and labour to meet a specified level of output. This may well involve the department in producing seperate purchasing and manpower budgets.

Thus the operational budget should include:

(i)   all costs incurred in the operation of the department for the time period of the budget irrespective of when payment is actually made;

(ii)   it would exclude the purchase of capital equipment even if it is purchased during that budgetary period;

(iii)   it would exclude the depreciation on capital assets used during the budgetary period.

In addition it should quantify the overhead costs such as rent or administrative support which are attributable to production. In this way each section should contribute its appropriate share to the overheads of the organisation as a whole. Of course this does not mean that the production director will have to pay the wages of one typist in the general office. Instead it will simply involve a notional allocation of part of the production budget. However it does allow a more precise costing of each aspect of the organisation's operations.

THE CASH BUDGET

The organisation will also prepare a cash flow forecast for the coming year in the manner we discussed in chapter 12. This is also referred to as the cash budget. This will allow the financial management of the organisation to plan its borrowing needs by scheduling expenditure in each department against anticipated income. All sources of income would be included in the cash budget but care should be taken not to include cash as being received as soon as a sale is made. Most commercial customers require a period of trade credit and this must be taken into consideration.

THE CAPITAL BUDGET

The capital budget of the organisation will be determined by its level of profitability, projected growth and the need to replace capital assets which are becoming inefficient or obsolete. Obviously, because of the long life span of most capital assets such as machinery, there is a need for considerable forward planning. Thus the capital expenditure budget must be interlinked with the corporate strategy to allow sufficient finance to be made available in the accounting year when the asset is to be purchased. This may entail each department planning its own capital expenditure over a period of years and submitting this to form part of the organisation's overall capital budget. As we noted earlier in chapter 12 capital expenditure often involves external financing and such loans or share issue must be co-ordinated to make them most cost effective.

MONITORING BUDGETS

It is normal practice to break the financial year into budgetary periods. These may be monthly, quarterly or half yearly depending on the nature and size of the business. This subdivision of the year allows the department manager to more effectively monitor the progress of budget expenditure in his own area and to adjust spending should it become necessary.

It is normal practice to compare the budgeted figure with the actual expenditure and assess whether there is any variance. A deviation from the budget in one month may not be of concern if the variance is in the other direction in other months. Thus usually a cumulative budget report is prepared which not only shows the current month's position but also the cumulative picture for the year. An example of a budget report is given overleaf.

PRODUCTION DEPARTMENT MONTHLY BUDGETARY REPORT

COST HEADING	Month			Cumulative (1st 10 months)		
	Budget	Actual	Variance	Budget	Actual	Variance
Raw Materials	145	149	+4	1580	1650	+70
Labour	289	272	-17	2975	2900	-70

These figures are usually then fed to the organisation's financial managers who are able to compile them into a 'rolling' budget for the organisation as a whole. This provides them with a regular check on both over and under spending and permits them to more effectively control the organisation's borrowing requirements. They will normally prepare a set of 'management accounts' at regular intervals which are, in effect, a profit and loss account for the part of the year up to date. Large organisation's will often prepare these monthly while smaller businesses may find that half yearly management accounts are sufficient for their needs.

BUDGETARY ADJUSTMENTS

Earlier in this chapter we made the point that budgets are estimates of expenditure needs and as such are prone to be inaccurate. The organisation must therefore have some mechanism which allows it to adjust budgets as the year progresses. The factors which will make such changes necessary are either over or under achievement of the department's targets or external changes such as an unexpected growth or decline in demand. This approach is often referred to as 'flexible budgeting' and is particularly important for organisations which are subject to constant fluctuations in costs and output. To allow such flexible budgetary control it is important to stress the need for constant monitoring of all department budgets. It would be very inefficient for a business to find that it cannot expand output to cope with an increase in demand because the production budget is exhausted while at the same time being unaware that it still has a considerable amount left in the transport budget.

If there is continuous need for major budgetary adjustments every year this will indicate that the organisation is not undertaking its budgetary process efficiently in the first place and so may require an examination of the manner in which budget allocation is made.

However, budgets have the major objective of requiring operational managers to control their expenditure. As such they need to be reasonably fixed. There is little incentive to a manager to insist on cost control if he knows that as soon as his budget is used up he can simply ask the board for an extra budgetary allocation. If the budget is prepared properly in the first place and no major changes have occurred which have been recognised by senior management then the budget should be adhered to wherever possible.

2 THE COST OF PRODUCTION

There are a number of ways that an organisation can assess what price to charge for its product or service. A simplistic approach may be to add up all the costs of producing it and add on a sufficient amount to provide some level of profit. Yet the costs of production may not be the only consideration in setting price. A business must decide what the customer is willing to pay. It must evaluate the demand for its product or service. It might produce a demand curve or demand schedule. It could use some form of market research to plan its marketing strategy. Such market research techniques are considered in chapter 26.

However, in this chapter we will concentrate on the way in which the business will determine the costs of production and show how these costs will be influential in determining at least the minimum price that the organisation is willing to set.

THE ORGANISATION'S COSTS

The costs of production which face an organisation depend on the level of output or provision it seeks to make. Costs will include payment for the factors of production that are required; its labour force, premises, machinery and other capital equipment. It is necessary to classify them according to how they can be varied to meet an organisation's needs. In order to do this we must look at the timescale of operation, for this is crucial in influencing how they can be varied and combined.

SHORT RUN AND LONG RUN COSTS

The timescale needed to produce anything may be divided into short run and long run. This is an imprecise and rather arbitrary distinction. The length of time that each of these periods encompasses will depend on the type of operation that the organisation is involved in.

a. The Short Run

The very short run is the period in which we define all organisational costs as being unable to be varied. In other words all costs of production are fixed. This simply means that the labour force cannot be increased or reduced, the organisation cannot change its premises or acquire new capital or equipment. For some businesses, this may be as short as a week or a month. For instance labour employed for a period of less than two years may be dismissed with only the minimum period of notice required. However, for staff employed for a longer period who are entitled to redundancy payments, more extensive notice is needed to inform them of their imminent redundancy. This entails 90 days notice for redundancies of more than 100 employees who are members of a recognised independent trade union. Thus the freedom of the organisation to vary its workforce may be limited by statute, in this case the Employment Protection (Consolidation) Act, 1978.

Time is obviously needed to recruit new staff if the organisation is trying to expand its workforce. Of course, this short run is much longer for factors of production such as buildings, for it will be unable to buy, build or rent new premises in a matter of weeks and the length of time needed to dispose of existing property will be dependent on the state of property market. For example, if demand is low in the property market it may be difficult to sell existing premises at an acceptable price. This may take months or even years. Therefore costs which are fixed cannot be changed if the business wishes to vary its level of output. For instance in the short run, if a business experiences a rapid decline in demand, it may be incapable of selling off machinery, moving to smaller premises or making staff redundant.

b. The Long Run.

If we take a longer timescale an organisation moves from the short run to the long run. Time allows the organisation to vary some of its costs. They become variable. Clearly, as the timescale increases even more the organisation is able to vary all its costs by hiring new staff, buying new equipment and finding more spacious accommodation. Of course, if it wishes, it could lower potential output by doing the opposite.

FIXED AND VARIABLE COSTS

By considering the timescale we are able to make the distinction between those costs which are fixed and those which are variable.

(i)   Fixed Costs

Once an organisation has established a certain scale of production it will have to pay rents, rates, interest on any loans, administration costs and certain other costs regardless of its output. These are fixed costs. Even if it produced nothing in a particular week, it will have to pay these costs. We can show fixed costs remaining constant as output increases in the first of the figures below. If the organisation wishes to increase the 'scale' of its operations, for instance by buying a new factory, this will mean that its fixed costs are 'stepped' up to a higher level. This increase is shown in the second of the figures below.

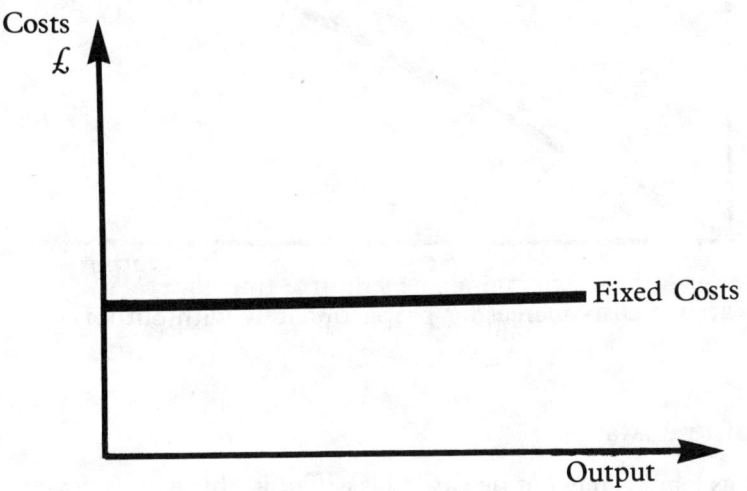

Fixed Costs are constant for the initial stage of operation

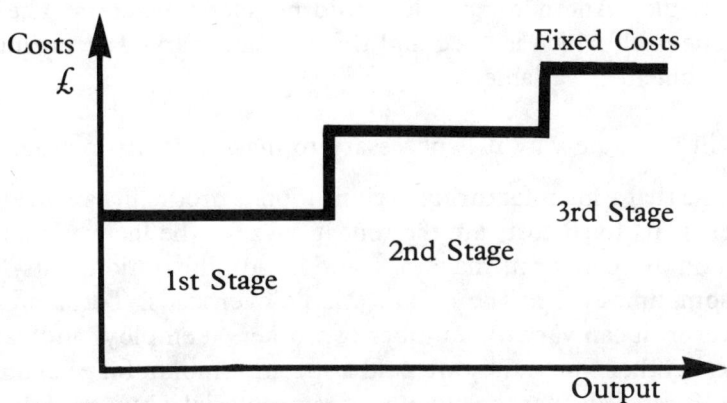

As output moves to higher stages (such as extra factories) fixed cost steps up.

(ii) Variable Costs

There are some factors of production that an organisation need not contract to purchase before it is aware of the level of production it will require to meet demand. For example, it may not have to purchase raw materials or electricity to power its machines if it has no production in a slack period. It will not have to spend money on motor fuel if it has nothing to transport. Because these costs can be increased or decreased to match the level of production the business requires in a particular period they are referred to as variable costs. These are shown increasing proportionately with output in the next figure.

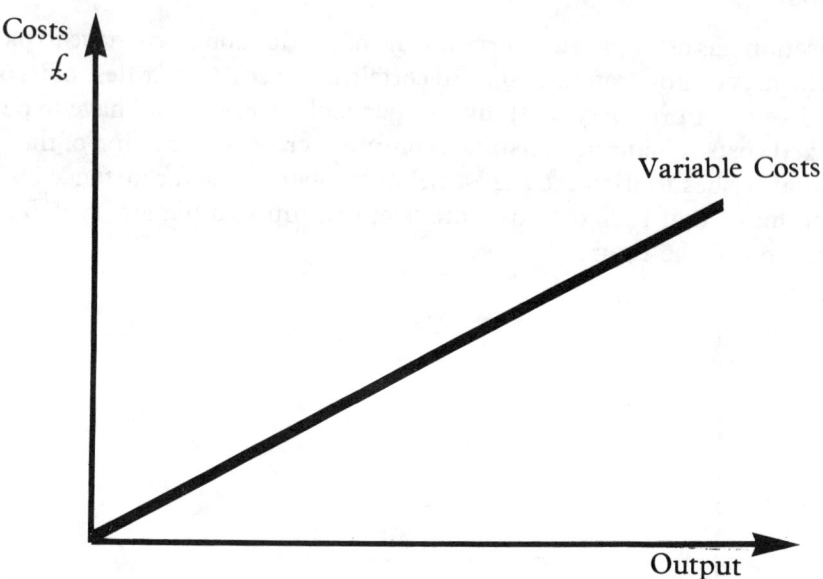

Variable costs increasing proportionately with output

(iii) Semi-variable costs

Certain costs such as labour may not be easily classified in this way. They are said to be semi-variable. For instance the organisation may have to pay the basic wage of its workers for a week but if it wishes to expand output it can ask them to do overtime. This would clearly mean that the organisation would not be able to vary part of the wage bill (the basic wage for the workers which would be fixed) but could vary the amount of overtime it asked the staff to undertake (this element would be variable). Another example would be telephone costs. There is a quarterly rental for the telephone itself which is fixed and the calls are charged according to the number that are made. This element is variable.

A simple example will illustrate why it is necessary to make this distinction.

> Assume that a manufacturing organisation is producing small engineering components. Its fixed costs are the rent it pays for the factory, its rates, the repayment on the loan for its machines, and its administration costs. The last of these are sometimes called the organisation's overheads. These are its fixed costs. However, it can vary the number of workers it employs and pay them on piece work, in other words they are paid a specific amount for each unit that they produce. It can also alter the amount of raw material it buys and the power it uses to work its machinery. These increase as the organisation makes more components. They are its variable costs. It is important to recognise that these variable costs do not always increase in direct proportion to the organisation's level of output. In some circumstances they will decrease proportionately as the organisation benefits from economies of scale, for instance it may benefit from bulk buying and consequent cheaper prices as its output increases. Or it may be able to install

more specialised and sophisticated machinery as its level of output increases and this may make it more efficient. However it may also face a situation where these variable costs increase proportionately as output rises. This may be due to the fact that it has employed all the most efficient workers and if it wished to produce more it must employ less skilled workers. It may have used up all the cheapest sources of raw materials and so it must search further afield, and at a higher cost, for additional supplies of its raw materials. The cost of each extra unit of production, the marginal cost, will rise. This is known as diseconomies of scale.

Let us examine a cost schedule to demonstrate the distinction between fixed and variable costs. Assume that the organisation has fixed costs of £500 per week and that its variable costs change with the level of output.

1	2	3	4	5	6
Output in units	Fixed (FC) Costs	Variable (VC) Costs	Total Cost	Average (AC) Cost of each unit	Marginal (MC) Cost of each extra unit
£	£	£	£	£	£
0	500	0	500	—	—
100	500	200	700	7	2
200	500	300	800	4	1
300	500	350	850	2.8	0.5
400	500	450	950	2.4	1
500	500	600	1,100	2.2	1.5
600	500	800	1,300	2.17	2
700	500	1,050	1,550	2.21	2.5
800	500	1,350	1,850	2.3	3
900	500	1,700	2,200	2.4	3.5
1,000	500	2,100	2,600	2.6	4

You can see from the above table that column 4 gives the total cost of production at various levels. Thus it costs £1,300 in total to produce 600 units. This total cost must rise as production increases. However you will note that fixed costs remain constant at all levels of production and it is variable costs which rise and so cause total costs to increase.

Total cost (column 4) is made up of:

a. Fixed Costs (column 2) as you can see, does not vary with output. In this example it is £500 whatever the level of production in the range given. It includes rent, rates, debt repayment, etc. We have illustrated a short run situation, for eventually if the organisation wishes to substantially increase its level of production it will have to find bigger premises, more machines and thus have to pay more in rent, rates, loan interest and repayments.

b. Variable Costs (column 3). These increase as the level of the organisation's output rises. In this case, it must pay its workforce more, buy extra raw materials and use more power.

The table also shows the average cost per unit (column 5). This is calculated by dividing total costs by the level of output. So for example:

$$AC = \frac{\text{Total Cost}}{\text{Quantity}} = \frac{£1,100}{500 \text{ units}} = £2.20 \text{ per unit.}$$

From the table you will note that AC decreases until 600 units are made and then rises. This is because at this point the extra variable cost (column 3) required to produce an extra 100 units also rises, in this case to £250 to produce the 100 units between 600 and 700.

Finally, we show marginal cost (column 6) which is the extra cost of producing an additional unit. This is found by dividing the addition by the extra units made. For example to produce 100 units more than 400 incurs £150 extra total cost. This is then divided by the extra units.

$$\text{MC} = \frac{\text{Extra Cost}}{\text{Extra Output}} = \frac{£150}{100 \text{ extra units}} = £1.50$$

Clearly, it is very difficult to evaluate marginal cost as precisely as this in most cases, but it is important to try. This is because marginal cost will indicate to the producer what each extra unit costs to produce and if he seeks to make a profit he must be able to sell that unit at a price which is greater than the marginal cost. You will see from the table that MC starts to rise after the production of 300 units. This is because the variable cost of producing the extra 100 units (300 - 400), that is £150, is greater than the cost of producing the previous 100 units (200 - 300), that is £100. These points can be illustrated graphically as follows:-

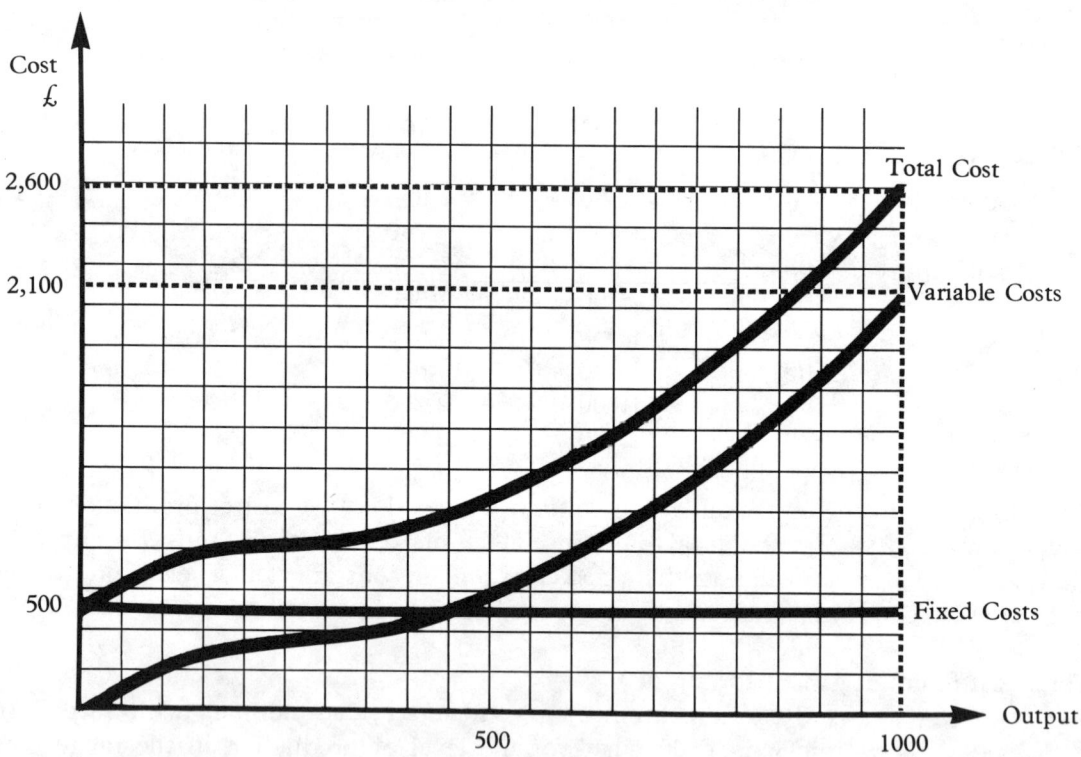

Total Cost, Fixed Costs and Variable Costs of an organisation

BREAK-EVEN POINT ANALYSIS

As you can see from the above diagram we are able to combine all the cost figures onto one diagram. However this diagram can also be used to calculate the amount of loss or profit the organisation will make at any particular level of output and specifically, the level of output which will allow it to 'break-even', in other words to completely cover all its costs of production. This is found by adding a line to show the total sales revenue that the organisation would receive from selling the goods or services that it produces. Assume that the organisation was able to sell every unit that it produced at the same price, for example at £3 each. This would produce a total revenue line which will rise proportionately from the origin of the graph. Therefore if no units were sold the total sales revenue would be 0; if 100 were sold it would be £300 and so on. This total revenue line is now shown on the graph. As you can see the break-even point is at 285 units for at that point total revenue equals total cost.

If the variable cost has been increasing proportionately there is a simple formula which will indicate the break-even point. This is:

$$\text{Break-Even Point} = \frac{\text{Fixed Costs}}{\text{Selling price per Unit} - \text{Variable Cost per Unit}}$$

If for example the variable cost per unit had been a constant £2, the fixed costs had been £500 and the selling price had been £3 then the organisation would have had to sell the following number of units to break even:

$$\text{BEP} = \frac{£500}{£3 - £2} = \frac{£500}{£1} = 500$$

Once the break-even point has been passed the organisation will be making profit. However if variable costs begin to rise then profits may fall and there may come a point when the business goes back to a loss making situation. This is illustrated in the figure below.

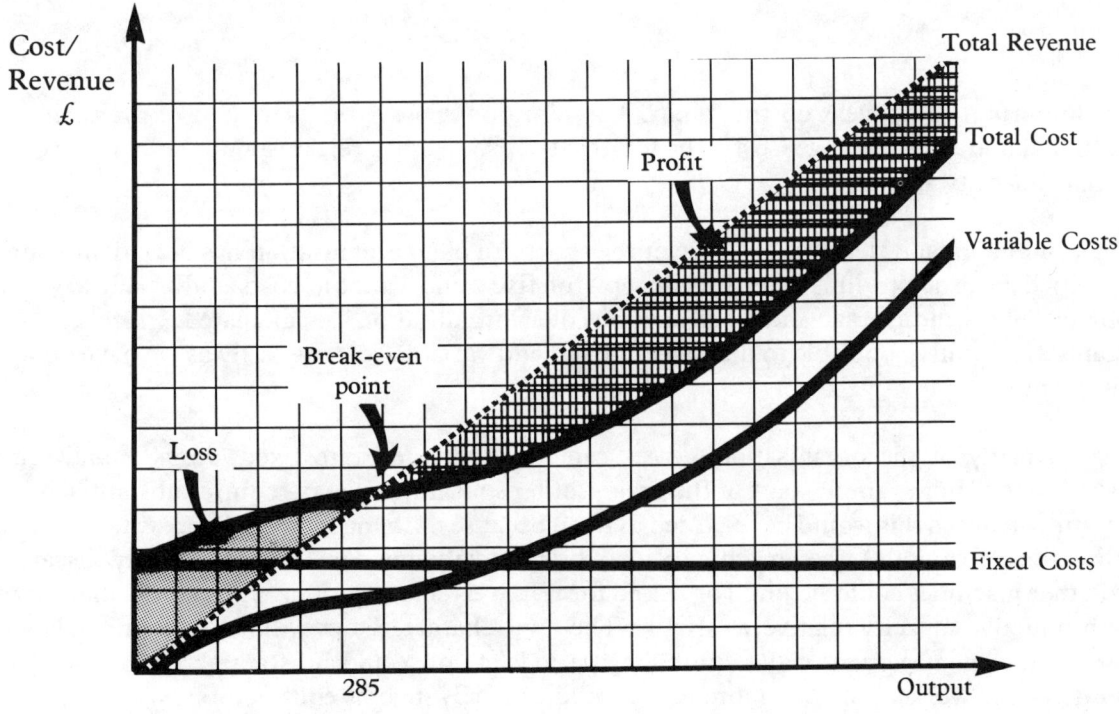

Break-even Analysis

AVERAGE AND MARGINAL COSTS

In the short run, the organisation's average cost curve is somewhat U-shaped and it is at the lowest point of the U that the organisation is at its optimum level of production, its most efficient size. If it produces more it will do so less efficiently and so average costs will rise. You can see from the diagram that MC cuts AC's lowest point. This is because if MC is less than AC then the additional cost (MC) of each unit will pull AC down. Once MC is greater than AC it will pull it up.

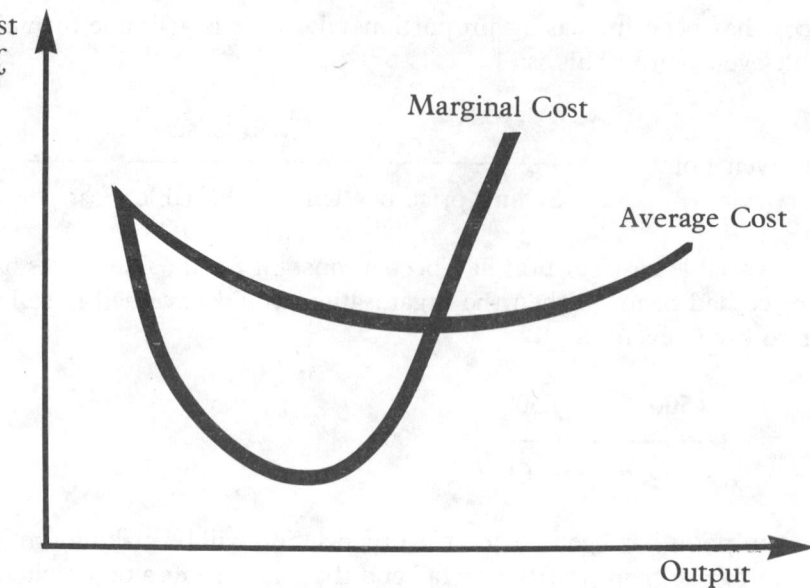

An Organisation's short run Marginal and Average Costs

It is important to be clear on this point. The Marginal Cost is the extra cost of producing an additional unit. The Average Cost is the total cost of producing a certain amount of units divided by that quantity made.

You will understand that this example of the short run of an organisation has been deliberately simplified in order to illustrate the concepts of fixed and variable costs and to allow you to appreciate how the average and marginal costs of an organisation are calculated. In reality, most organisations will not be able to distinguish fixed and variable costs as easily as we have done in this example.

Clearly, many of the organisation's costs can be subdivided into fixed, variable and semi-variable costs. For example, part of the organisation's machinery may require substantial initial investment and so this would be regarded as fixed because to change it would necessitate massive redirection of capital. Other machinery may be relatively inexpensive and so easily discarded and other machines could be hired or leased for relatively short periods and so make that part of the productive capacity relatively variable. The same characteristics will be found in the labour force. Senior management may require long periods of notice and substantial redundancy payments. Other workers may be more easily hired or fired, such as contractors. Of course as we have already noted, labour laws relating to the rights of employees in respect of unfair dismissal and redundancy payments contained in the Employment Protection (Consolidation) Act, 1978, as amended by the Employment Act, 1980, will mean that all labour costs are less readily variable. Temporary workers may be employed for relatively short periods to meet a particular expansion in demand for service but it is less simple to reduce the workforce for short periods, although short-time working or lay-offs are becoming increasingly common in industry during the present recession.

If an organisation is involved in providing a variety of different products or services that it may be possible to move factors of production from one part of the organisation to another if demand is varying between them. For instance, in a local authority, a reduction in the level of provision for recreation may allow clerical staff to be transferred to the Housing Department where, for instance, the council is implementing the government's policy of selling council houses to tenants. However, from this analysis of short term costs it is clear that fixed costs which are determined by the organisation's scale of production are spread over the average cost of providing the product or service.

LONG TERM COSTS

As we have already noted, it is impossible to set a specific time period as "the long run". This is dependent on the type of organisation, the product it provides and the factors of production it uses. However, we classify the long run or long term as the timescale required to be able to vary all the factors of production, in other words, sufficient time to acquire new machinery or equipment, new premises or more labour if the organisation is seeking to expand, or alternatively to shed these costs if it is contracting. In the long term, the organisation should be able to accurately assess the level of demand for the good/service it provides and so adjust the scale of the manufacture of the product or the provision of its service to achieve the optimum level of production. We have definded this as the point where average costs are at a minimum. However this does not mean that the organisation will always produce at the optimum level for this will be determined by the relationship between the costs of production and the extent of the demand. In the long run the organisation can increase its productive capacity by increasing the fixed factors of production. Thus, it could build additional factories, open extra offices, hire more premises. This will be reflected in the cost curves of the organisation by a series of individual short run cost curves reflecting each step in the extension of output.

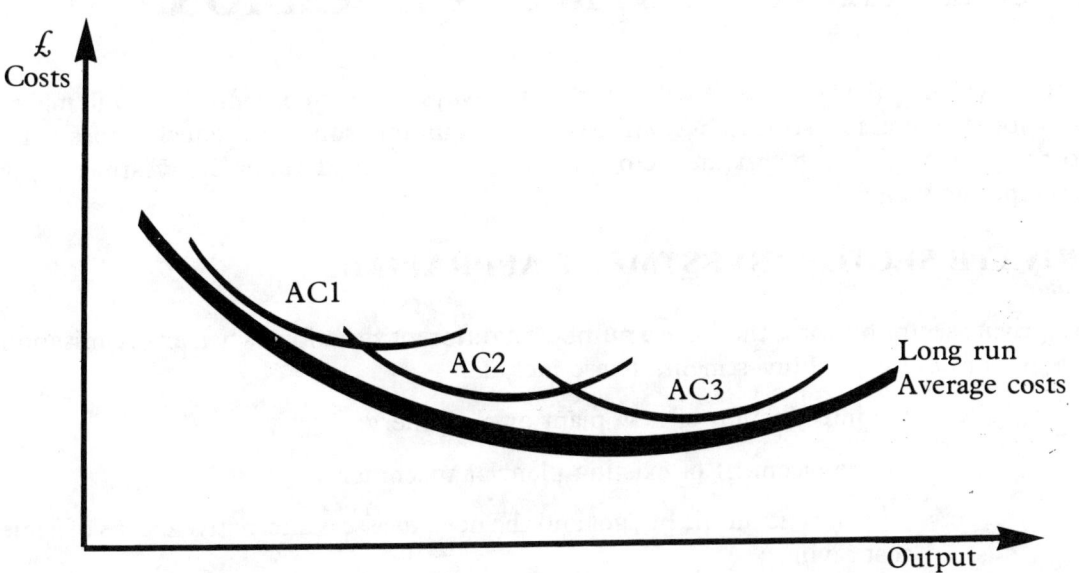

Long run average costs of an Organisation

The average cost curves AC1, AC2, AC3, etc. represent the costs at different scales of production. They show how costs would change in a situation with fixed factors of production which could not easily be varied. For instance, if the organisation operated one factory only, the average costs would be shown by AC1. The second factory would have costs represented on AC2 and so on. The first few AC curves tend to move downward because the organisation is able to spread some of its fixed costs over production at a few factories. The organisation will still only employ one managing director even if it has 2 or 3 factories and so the cost of his salary is spread over a greater level of output and so average costs come down. The organisation can gain increasing economies of scale as it moves from one level of production to the next. It will be able to purchase in bulk, employ specialist staff, cut average distribution costs by purchasing its own fleet of lorries and so on. These are only possible as it increases the level of its output by moving to a larger scale of production.

Eventually the organisation will reach its optimum level of long term production, that is it will have achieved the scale of production at which overall average costs are at their lowest. (In the diagram this is gained with scale of production 3). Following this, the organisation begins to suffer from diminishing returns to scale (or diseconomies of scale). This means that as output is raised average costs tend to rise. This can be the result of several different causes — the organisation may become too large to manage efficiently, sources of raw materials or labour may become more difficult to find and thus more expensive, labour unrest may develop due to the massive impersonal nature of the organisation and so increase costs as strikes or stoppages halt production. Whatever the causes, it is a characteristic of all organisations that eventually average costs will tend to increase as outputs rises. The scale of production at which this happens will depend upon the type of industry. Some industries such as the chemical industry may be able to continue to reduce average costs until a massive scale of production is achieved. These short run average costs curves are summated to give a long run average cost curve.

It is the extent of the output that an organisation can achieve before average costs begin to rise which will determine the structure of the industry. If one producer can continue to reduce average costs while meeting the total needs of the market it is possible that a monopoly will evolve. If it can only meet part of demand, this may result in imperfect competition or oligopoly. The costs of production of the organisation are therefore crucial in determining which part of the market it will supply or the extent of demand that it will meet. These different market forms and their effect on pricing, output and competition are also considered in chapters 21 and 26.

3. CAPITAL INVESTMENT DECISIONS

In this section of the chapter we will consider the ways in which organisations will make decisions about capital investment. We will begin by examining some of the techniques which are most popularly used in the private sector and finish with a consideration of investment appraisal in the public sector.

PRIVATE SECTOR INVESTMENT APPRAISAL

In a private sector business there are a number of different situations when an organisation may have to consider capital investment. These include:

    a. the introduction of new plant or machinery;

    b. the replacement of existing plant or machinery;

    c. possible cuts in the budget and the need to assess alternative means of achieving cost savings;

    d. the possible expansion of the organisation's operations and the feasibility of introducing new products or investing in research and development.

In each of the decision making situations listed above the financial manager is faced with the same issue: to decide whether the benefits which will be gained from the investment will outweigh its costs. To reach such a decision it is necessary to evaluate the flow of income which will be generated from the investment over a period of time and compare it with the immediate cash outlay. This involves a projection of the cash inflow for the expected lifetime of the investment. There are two possible problems here. Firstly, as with all projections, there is an element of uncertainty. This will be increased where the time period for which the projection is made is far into the future. Secondly, it is important to value the income generated in future years in real, present day terms, for this will be the only way that the benefits can be accurately compared with the costs. There are a number of alternative methods of investment appraisal but here it is proposed to concentrate on one method which has wide applicability. This is the Discounted Cash Flow technique.

DISCOUNTED CASH FLOW

This technique involves assessing the initial cost of the investment project. The future earnings from the project are then estimated on a yearly basis for the life of the investment and then each year's return is discounted to give its Net Present Value. This technique is concerned with evaluating an investment proposal in terms of the net cash flows generated by the capital expenditure over its estimated lifespan expressed in present day values, compared with the initial cost of the investment. It recognises the time value of money insofar as a £1 today is worth more than a £1 received five years' hence.

Essentially we may view an investment decision as involving the 'opportunity cost' of investing in a capital project compared with an alternative course of action, for example investing in a bank deposit account. Thus we must 'discount' future cash inflows in order that we may make a meaningful comparison with present day investment. We may consider discounting to be the reverse of compounding — £1 invested at a rate of 10% per annum will amount to £1.10 at the end of year 1 and eventually be worth £1.61 at the end of year 5. Conversely, £1 received at the end of year 5 is worth approximately £0.62 at todays value if we 'discount' using the same 10% interest rate.

An example may provide a more meaningful illustration.

Assume that a company decides to invest in new machinery. The capital outlay is £1,000. It is expected that the machine will operate for a period of 5 years and will generate a cash inflow of £300 annually. The projected cash flows are as follows:

	Cash Outflow £	Cash Inflow £
Year 1	(1,000)	300
Year 2		300
Year 3		300
Year 4		300
Year 5		300
Year 6		300
Total	(1,000)	1,500

From the information above it would appear that the project is clearly advantageous to the company, as the total cash inflow exceeds the total cash outflow by £500 (£1,500 - £1.000). However, this assumption ignores the time value of money, namely that £300 received in year 5 is worth considerably less than £300 received in year 1. In order to evaluate the cash inflows more correctly we must 'discount' the amounts using some suitable interest rate. If we assume a 10% interest rate as the cost of capital this may be used as the 'cut-off rate' for assessing the investment. Thus we now have to apply a discount rate of 10% over the relevant period (5 years in this case) to the cash inflows. Using the same information as above we proceed as follows:

	Cash Outflow £	Cash Inflow £	Discount Rate 10%	Discounted Cash Flow £
Year 1	(1,000)	300	.9091	272.73
Year 2		300	.8264	247.92
Year 3		300	.7513	225.39
Year 4		300	.6831	204.93
Year 5		300	.6208	186.24
	(1,000)	1,500		1,137.21 = NETT PRESENT VALUE

We can clearly see that the cash inflows expressed in terms of 'Net Present Value' (as the result of discounting) is now £1,137.21. Thus the project still produces a surplus, albeit somewhat reduced, of £137.21 (£1,137.21-£1,000) compared with the original £500 calculated without using DCF. As the Net Present Value is in surplus (a positive figure) after discounting at 10% the actual rate of return must be greater than 10%. If the Net Present Value has been negative then the project return would have been less than 10% and would not, in the present circumstances, be an acceptable investment.

The use of Discounted Cash Flow and Net Present Value can be applied to any investment appraisal but care must be taken not to use a discount rate which is unrealistically high for this will produce a Net Present Value which is below the true worth and so lead more marginal projects to be rejected. Similarly a discount rate which is too low will reflect a Net Present Value which is misleadingly high and thus lead to less potentially profitable investments being undertaken. These techniques are in common use in the private sector and as will be seen in the next part of the chapter, their processes are applied in other circumstances in the public sector in the use of Cost Benefit Analysis.

PUBLIC SECTOR INVESTMENT APPRAISAL

COST BENEFIT ANALYSIS

This part of the chapter examines one of the most important techniques used to evaluate investment projects both in the nationalised industries and in the public sector as a whole.

This is known as Cost Benefit Analysis (CBA) which is essentially an aid to the decision-maker in evaluating the cost of the project and weighing it against the potential benefit. What distinguishes CBA from many other forms of investment appraisal is that it attempts to introduce the social costs and benefits occurring and to give a monetary value to these. This is no easy task, for many of these social effects are difficult to quantify both in their extent and in money terms.

CBA has been used to help in a wide range of problems faced by public decision-makers. They include:

(a)   massive public investment projects such as the location of the third London airport, or

(b)   the economic viability of constructing the Victoria Line on the London Underground system.

CBA has also been used in more modest, though no less important, decisions on such problems as:

(a)   the continued existence of branch line railway services, or

(b)   the provision of kidney dialysis machines in the National Health Service.

Before undertaking a detailed examination of the technique involved in CBA, it is worth stressing that it is merely an aid to decision-making. Its merits are that it provides a sound, reasoned framework in which the final decision can be made, but it does not provide the definitive answer as to whether or not a project should go ahead. It simply gives the decision-maker additional information and data to help make the choice. As we will note later, the final decision often involves other considerations, many of which are political, and in several very extensive CBA appraisals the final decision has been contrary to that suggested by the CBA.

THE PROCEDURE FOR COST BENEFIT ANALYSIS

There are seven basic steps involved in a Cost Benefit Analysis evaluation. These are:

1. The establishment of objectives;

2. Establishing the extent of the effects of the project;

3. Valuing the effects;

4. Establishing a time scale;

5. Discounting the value of the effects;

6. Evaluation;

7. The final decision.

1. THE ESTABLISHMENT OF OBJECTIVES

The starting point for any project appraisal must be a statement of the objectives being pursued by the decision-maker. It is impossible to make a rational choice unless the decision-maker is clear about what he is trying to achieve.

This can take a number of forms:

(a) The decision may be about the overall viability of a new project, for instance should we build a new sports centre or not?

(b) It may seek to evaluate the best choice from a number of alternatives once the initial decision to proceed with the project has been made, e.g. we have decided to build a hospital so where is the best site to locate it?

(c) The choice may be between a number of different investment projects, for example should we build a new swimming pool, provide an extension to a school or build more old people's houses?

(d) The decision may be whether or not to continue to provide a service or maintain its provision, for instance should we continue to subsidise unprofitable coal mines or uneconomic railway lines?

CBA will tackle each of these objectives in a relatively similar way — by determining and listing the possible alternatives.

2. ESTABLISHING THE EXTENT OF THE EFFECTS OF THE PROJECT

The next stage of the Cost Benefit Analysis is to establish parameters (or limits) for the effects of the project. This means identifying everyone who is going to be affected either positively or negatively by the project. All the costs and benefits of the project must be listed and then those which have only a marginal effect may be eliminated.

One method of classifying costs and benefits for the project is as follows;

(a) Financial (or private) costs and benefits

Financial costs are usually the easiest to identify because they include the actual cost of the project in terms of:

(i) site,

(ii) construction,

(iii) labour,

(iv) materials, and

(v) maintenance costs.

This is merely a technical problem and would normally be dealt with by the project architect, engineer, or planner. They will have a positive value (although this may be subject to considerable error in the planning stage). Financial benefits from the project include any returns from the sale of goods or services produced throughout the economic life of the project, for instance admission charges to a swimming pool, rent from council housing or fares from a public transport project.

(b) Social costs and benefits

These are more difficult to identify and isolate. A new airport would cause noise, a new power station might create pollution, or a new road might mean the loss of countryside with outstanding beauty. These are all costs to society and must be taken into account. Conversely, a new road might reduce congestion in a city centre or a bridge may improve employment prospects in an area. These are clearly social benefits of the project and may counterbalance the social costs. The importance of social costs and benefits and the consequent justification for government intervention into the market are discussed in more detail in chapter 24.

3.   VALUING THE EFFECTS

The third step in the Cost Benefit Analysis involves establishing a value for all the costs and benefits identified. As we have just seen, this is relatively simple in respect of the financial costs and benefits but is much more complex for the social effects. This is because financial costs and benefits can be established using market values. Material costs, the price of land, and labour costs can be calculated by comparing them with similar existing projects.

For social costs and benefits, however, it is necessary to devise a method of evaluation in money terms. For example a decision-maker choosing a location for a hospital would want to:

(a)   take account of the relative convenience of alternative locations for patients and visitors, and

(b)   estimate the different times people would spend travelling to and from the alternative sites.

But although it is clear that people value savings in time, there is no obvious market in which travelling time is bought and sold. A further example is the social cost of noise. A new airport would considerably increase the noise levels in an area but how are we to place a monetary value on quiet?

The way that this valuation is normally undertaken is through the use of opportunity cost prices. The opportunity cost of anything is what a person must forgo in order to consume the service. The cost, then, of an extra hour's travelling time to the hospital is the loss of an hour's work or leisure time. As we are able to value an hour of work, we can put a similar cost on the travelling time. Using the noise example, a new airport built close to your home may reduce the market value as new buyers are deterred by the increase in noise. The cost of the extra noise, therefore, is the fall in the value of your house.

4.   ESTABLISHING A TIME SCALE

Once the various costs and benefits involved in the project have been established, it is then necessary to decide upon a time scale for the life of the project, not just in terms of how long it will take to build, but the length of time that benefits will be gained from it in the future. Initial costs of construction are immediate but benefits and running costs stretch for years into the future. The decision maker must decide on a viable life for the project. In some cases such as that of the third London airport, the life of the project was estimated at twenty-five years. In other smaller projects, a shorter life span is usually selected. So for instance the life span of new houses may be estimated at twenty years.

The decision on the time preference (the technical term for the choice of life span) is important, because an over-optimistic life span with the consequent additional benefits which will result may make the project appear more attractive than it really is. Conversely, a very short life span under-estimates the total benefits which will accrue in comparison with the initial costs. This could lead to the project being rejected unnecessarily.

A further difficulty with the determination of time preference is that the longer the period chosen, the more uncertain are the potential benefits and costs and the more difficult it is to place a satisfactory value on them. Because of this, most cost benefit analysis studies tend to err on the side of caution and choose a time preference which is perhaps shorter than the practical life of the project. In the example given above the life span of a house would probably be much longer than twenty years.

5. DISCOUNTING THE VALUE OF THE EFFECTS

Once all the costs and benefits of the project have been quantified and a time scale allotted, they must then be reduced to a Net Present Value. This means that the value of a benefit gained in, say, ten years time must be reflected in its current value. For instance, if you were offered £100 in a year's time or an equivalent sum today, how much would you be willing to accept immediately? Clearly it will depend on the rate of inflation (and the rate of interest) for the coming year.

So if the rate of inflation is 10%, then a sum of £90.91 today is equivalent to £100 in a year's time

$$£90.91 \quad x \quad \frac{110}{100} \quad = \quad £100.00$$

Thus all benefits and costs for subsequent years must be discounted backwards to determine their value in today's terms.

This is achieved by selecting a discount rate which will take into account the anticipated rate of inflation. The initial Treasury Test Discount Rate (TTDR) was 8% but this was later increased to 10%.

As we have already noted, the longer the time span of the project, the less certain the future inflation rate will be. The discount rate, therefore, is always something of an estimate as the decision-maker must project into the future.

6. EVALUATION

The next stage is to evaluate the project by comparing the benefits at net present value with the cost at net present value.

This should then indicate whether or not, on the basis of the study, the project provides a net surplus or net deficit. This stage is essentially a question of arithmetic in adding together the sum of the benefits and subtracting them from the sum of the costs. Therefore, if benefits exceed costs the project is worth considering while if costs exceed benefit it should be rejected.

7. THE FINAL DECISION

The point we made at the beginning of this section is important here. Cost Benefit Analysis is merely an aid to decision-making. The public sector decision-maker may have to weigh up many other factors such as political and social considerations as well as the economic data provided by the CBA study. Thus in many cases the result of the study is just one factor of the final decision.

Perhaps the most famous CBA of the last twenty years was that undertaken by the Roskill Commission in the late 1960s on the siting of the third London airport. It finally considered four possible sites and in its recommendations the least favourable site on economic grounds was that at Foulness on the Thames Estuary. Nevertheless, this was the site which was initially chosen by the government because of considerable pressure and lobbying against the other, more preferable, locations. Eventually, for a number of reasons, the government decided not to build a third airport at that time, and Roskill's report now merely stands as an example of a comprehensive, large scale CBA Study.

ASSIGNMENT — DAVE DAYBREAK AND THE SUNSETS

This year the city of Westhampton celebrates its 900th anniversary. As part of the festivities, the City Council resolves that it should hold a series of concerts reflecting the City's musical heritage. The Director of Leisure Services is given the task of promoting these concerts; and, although the Council has allocated a substantial budget for these events, it is clear that some will make considerable losses while others should prove profitable. The concerts will include early church music, medieval music, chamber music and rock and roll. One of the events which it is hoped will be profitable is a show given by Dave Daybreak and the Sunsets. Dave, an ageing rock star, is a "local boy made good" and should prove to be a crowd-puller. However, the Director is wary in case crowd trouble should break out and blemish the festival, so he insists that there must be a more than adequate number of bouncers to control the fans. The event is to be held in one of the Council's public halls in the city centre. The hall is quite old and not particularly safe, and so stringent conditions have to be laid down.

Under these conditions there must be at least 30 bouncers if 3,000 or fewer tickets are sold, one extra bouncer for each 20 tickets sold between 3,000 and 4,000, and one extra bouncer for each 10 extra tickets sold over 4,000. Each bouncer is paid £20 per night. The capacity of the hall is 5,000. The price of tickets is set at £3 each. The cost of heating, lighting and administrative staff for the event is £1,500, and this must be paid regardless of the number of tickets sold. Dave Daybreak and the Sunsets charge £1,000 performing fee, and £650 must be spent on hiring a PA System for the evening.

It is clear that, in order to sell tickets for the concert, it must be advertised, and this can be done in three ways: on posters at a cost of 20p each; in the local papers at £50 per advert; and on the local radio at £100 per spot. The Director estimates that to attract 3,000 customers it is necessary to spend £200 on posters and £500 on newspaper ads. If local radio is used, however, more tickets can be sold, as follows:

> 1st radio ad sells 1,000 more tickets;
>
> 2nd radio ad sells an extra 500 tickets;
>
> 3rd radio ad sells an extra 250 tickets;
>
> 4th radio ad sells an extra 50 tickets.

TASK

1. As an officer in the Leisure Services Department of the Council, advise the Director on the following points:

    a) What are the fixed costs of the concert and what are the variable costs?

    b) How many tickets must be sold to break-even?

    c) How many tickets should be sold to make the maximum profit?

    d) How much advertising should be carried out?

Explain your advice in words and in the form of a break-even chart.

DEVELOPMENTAL TASK

2. Contact any organisation which promotes social activities such as dances or concerts. This may be your students union, youth club or your employer's social and entertainments committee. Analyse any social event which they have or intend to promote. Prepare a break-even analysis to demonstrate its profitability.

ASSIGNMENT — HOWARD'S DILEMMA

"Why have we never got enough money to pay the bills?" thought Howard Ratcliffe as he arranged yet another meeting with his bank manager to extend the overdraft facility of his business. "We seem to be increasing our sales all the time and yet the bills seem to go up every month.

Howard is the founder and Managing Director of Ratcliffe Potteries, a small limited company based in Kidsgrove near Stoke on Trent. The company makes a wide variety of pottery and earthenware and has been established for six years. Howard's background has mainly been in sales and marketing and he has concentrated his efforts on the promotion and distribution of his company's products. He has generally left the internal management of the company's operations to the Works Manager, Sam Hazley and while output has continually increased and quality standards have been improved, the general financial control of the manufacturing aspect of the business has been rather slipshod and badly managed.

Howard is sufficiently concerned about the financial state of the business that he decides to introduce a system of strict budgetary control. He calls Sam to a meeting in his office in which he outlines his proposed financial controls. Sam is clearly suspicious of the changes as he feels that it is a means of monitoring how he and the other section heads are performing. He asks for time consider the proposals and Howard arranges a meeting of the management team to discuss the matter in two weeks time.

TASKS

1. You are employed by Ratcliffe Potteries as a personal assistant to Howard. He believes that he must have a sound and reasoned case for introducing the budgetary control measures into the company. Prepare briefing notes for Mr Ratcliffe in which you outline the advantages to be gained by the company from the introduction of budgetary control.

2. A second agenda item at the management meeting is a consideration of the purchase of a new kiln for the production of porcelain. The cost of the new kiln is £50,000 which must be paid immediately. Howard anticipates that the kiln will generate £12,000 p.a. extra revenue for the business for the next five years. He is concerned that this is an insufficient return to justify the purchase of the kiln. Using a discount rate of 12% prepare a Discounted Cash Flow schedule which will determine the financial viability of the new kiln. Prepare a memo to Mr Ratcliffe in which you inform him of your conclusion.

Chapter 17

THE FACTORS INFLUENCING FINANCIAL DECISION MAKING

We now have to look at the way in which information obtained from various accounting records is used to help the management of organisations to make decisions about their organisation. First of all let us consider some of the decisions that may face an organisation, in particular whether:

(i) To continue the production and marketing of an unprofitable product;

(ii) To close down an unprofitable branch;

(iii) To change the pattern of production, for instance alter the working week to 3 shifts per day from a working week of only 8 a.m. to 5 p.m. per day production or vice versa;

(iv) To buy another company;

(v) To invest money in capital equipment;

(vi) To supply goods on credit to particular customers;

(vii) To determine the selling price of a product or range of products.

A closer consideration of the issues detailed above will help us to appreciate the difficulties management face in making such decisions.

1. TO CONTINUE PRODUCTION AND MARKETING OF AN UNPROFITABLE PRODUCT

In order to enable decisions to be reached about this we must first have a sufficiently detailed management accounting system. This should analyse the direct costs of production (marginal cost) and give an indication of the contribution that the product is making to the profits of the organisation.

If the accounting system shows that a particular product is not making as much contribution to the profits as other products or indeed if the product is actually making a loss, then certain decisions will have to be made. These may be summarised as follows:

a) Stop production of the product;

b) Increase the selling price of the product;

c) Continue to produce in the hope that it is contributing something to the organisation.

Stopping the production of a product is not such an easy decision to make as it first appears. Stopping production entails possibly closing down plant. Such plant may not be capable of being sold, and consequently will remain in the factory doing nothing and taking up space which could be occupied by other plant. It may also mean that certain members of the workforce may have to be made redundant. Furthermore it may mean that the other products of the organisation become less viable by having to make a greater contribution to overheads. An example of this is as follows:

Product	A	B	C
	£	£	£
Selling Price per unit	15	25	30
Marginal cost per unit	8	15	25
Contribution per unit to gross profit	7	10	5

The organisation makes and sells 1000 units of each product in a particular time span and during the same time span has fixed overheads of £15,000. These are spread evenly over each of the products. The products will each show the results seen below:

Product	A	B	C
	£	£	£
Income from Sales	15,000	25,000	30,000
Marginal Cost	8,000	15,000	25,000
Contribution to gross profit ...	7,000	10,000	5,000
Overheads	5,000	5,000	5,000
Profit	2,000	5,000	nil

As we can see the total revenue produced from the three units is £70,000, the total expenditure is £63,000 (£48,000 marginal costs plus £15,000 overheads) and the total profit is £7,000. Clearly product C has not contributed anything to the profit.

If the manufacture of product C was stopped it is likely that the overheads would not necessarily be reduced by £5,000. Indeed they may not be reduced at all in which case the overheads will have to be spread over product A and B. The situation would be as follows:

Product	A	B
	£	£
Income from sales	15,000	25,000
Marginal Cost	8,000	15,000
Contribution to gross profit ...	7,000	10,000
Overheads	7,500	7,500
Profit (Loss)	(500)	2,500

Not only do the other products become less profitable (in fact product A now makes a loss), but also the business profit falls from £7,000 to £2,000. This is a result of the overheads which had previously been allocated to C now having to be absorbed by only A and B.

Clearly on the basis of these figures the correct decision is not to stop producing C. Rather the appropriate action would be to investigate ways of making C more profitable.

The answer may lie in actually taking on more salesmen to attempt to increase the company's share of the market, not only for C but for all three of the products. This will initially increase overheads, but in the long run may make the organisation more profitable by selling more. This in itself could lead to the organisation having to take on more labour and so making a contribution to the country's unemployment problem. It may be decided that the selling price of the product is not high enough, but care must always be taken to ensure that the products are not priced out of the market. One final item that may be examined is the company's internal costs; can the organisation make economies in the area of costs (direct and indirect)? This unfortunately may involve dismissing some of the labour force because of the inefficiency of some of the production methods and perhaps replacing them with a greater level of automation. Whatever the answer is, it is not an easy decision to make. Certainly if there were no system for obtaining the financial information required it would indeed be impossible.

2. TO CLOSE DOWN AN UNPROFITABLE BRANCH

To a certain extent the issues discussed in the previous section apply here, but in this instance the branch is substituted for the product. There is a difference however, in that all of the expenses incurred at branch level can be considered as direct costs which will disappear if the branch is closed. If there is an apportionment of head office overheads allocated to a branch, then consideration must be given to what will happen to these overheads should the branch be closed. If they are to be absorbed by other branches it may make one or more of them unprofitable, in which case it would be better to keep the branch open on the basis that it is contributing something to the general overheads of the business.

Finally in considering branch closure, a close analysis should be made of selling prices. The appropriate level of selling prices can only be ascertained by scrutinising the accounts prepared for the branch which will show the cost of sales and the overheads. Selling prices can then be adjusted to cover these items and leave a margin for profit. There is a consideration of selling prices later in the chapter. It should be borne in mind however that selling prices are often determined by the market and an increase which is too large may have the opposite effect to the one desired for sales may fall.

3. TO CHANGE THE PATTERN OF PRODUCTION

A business may often find that to maintain adequate production levels it may have to operate a shift system. Instead of working only from 8 a.m. to 5 p.m. Monday to Friday production is carried on constantly on the basis of three shifts. These shifts are usually 6 a.m. to 2 p.m., 2 p.m. to 10 p.m. and 10 p.m. to 6 a.m. including weekends.

There will inevitably be occasions when decisions have to be made whether to change from shift working to daily working and vice versa. This may be a consequence of demand for the product rising or falling. In order to help the management to make these decisions, detailed analysis of the costs involved in operating a shift system as opposed to a daily system can be obtained from properly prepared accounts. Management could pose the following questions. If a shift system is introduced how much extra can be produced? What are the extra direct costs involved? How much will overheads increase? In other words is it worth it and can we make the same level of profit?

It may well be that the reverse situation applies. The market for the product is falling, stockpiling is taking place and the company cannot sell as much as it is producing. This means that stocks of finished products are increasing the company's stock costs. This type of information may be obtained from an analysis of the accounts. The company should consider the savings to be made from a change from shift working to daily working. Again this information will be found in the analysed cost accounting records and budgets.

4. TO BUY ANOTHER COMPANY

This is often one of the most important decisions that will face a business. There are a number of reasons why a business may wish to buy another:

      a)   to eliminate a competitor;

    b)   to ensure that supplies of raw materials are available when needed. This can be done by buying the company which sells the required raw materials;

    c)   to ensure that there is a market for the company's own product. This can be achieved by buying a company which requires the product;

    d)   to diversify in terms of its product base and activities.

Whatever the reason it is important to ensure that the company to be bought is a sound one. We can determine this by scrutinising its financial accounts over a number of years. A judicious use of the correct ratio analysis enables us to reach conclusions about whether a particular business would be a sound investment or not.

5.   INVEST MONEY IN CAPITAL EQUIPMENT

A business may be operating with old plant and machinery and management may feel that it is desirable to replace it with new equipment. To determine this financial and management accounts will be used in different ways.

The management accounts (including budgets etc) will give information about how much the existing plant is costing to run, maintain, etc, and the level of production which is achieved from it. Budgets prepared for the projected new plant and machinery will give information about the same items in respect of such new plant. A comparison of the two will help management to decide if replacement of old machinery is desirable. This is not the end of the story however. The financial accounts will need to be examined to determine if money is available for such an investment. If it is not available, a decision will have to be made about financing. Forecast accounts will determine whether the cost of borrowing will exceed the benefits to be derived from the new machinery. With regard to this type of decision the discounting factor of cash flow will also have to be considered, especially if a decision involves comparing one project with another.

6.   TO SUPPLY GOODS ON CREDIT TO PARTICULAR CUSTOMERS

Selling its product is of paramount importance to any business. We have already seen that selling on credit provides the bulk of income for many businesses. Selling to companies that have a long standing business relationship does not often present a problem. Such companies will usually be in a position to pay within the terms laid down and moreover will probably do so.

When attempting to open up new markets however an organisation may have to sell goods on credit to customers of whom very little is known. One way of assessing the economic standing of a new customer is to examine its financial accounts. From them we can determine whether the potential customer is solvent. We can also determine by the use of relevant ratios how long, on average, a particular customer takes to settle debts. A manager of an organisation will have to make a decision based on the accounts of the potential customer and his organisation's own accounts. This decision involves comparing benefits to be derived from the increased sales with the disadvantages of having a new customer who is slow to settle his account.

It is an increased financial burden for the business if it has to wait three months for a customer to pay for goods supplied, while at the same time having to pay its own creditors within one month. This can and often does cause short term cash flow problems and can make it difficult for a business to plan its own activities.

7.   TO DETERMINE THE SELLING PRICE OF A PRODUCT OR A RANGE OF PRODUCTS

This is often the most important decision that has to be taken by a business, especially a business which manufactures goods. A business which merely buys and sells goods (a wholesaler or retailer) will often have pricing decisions taken from it. The product manufacturer will have recommended a maximum resale price for the goods. The trader however may have to decide the extent to which prices can be reduced in order to maintain competitiveness and at the same time make a profit.

A manufacturing business has however to determine its own pricing levels and this would be an impossible task without access to accounting and management accounting information.

If a company manufactures a particular product, it will have to have details of its production costs. This involves determining the cost of raw material used, the time taken for manufacture, the amount of labour involved, the costs of running, maintaining and depreciating plant used in production and the extent of overheads which can be allocated to it. Such details can only be found by having a fairly sophisticated cost accounting system.

Having determined from the costing records how much a product costs to make the next step is to decide how much profit the business requires from the product. Once this is determined the selling price can be fixed. It is worth restating that:

COST OF PRODUCTION + PROFIT REQUIRED = SELLING PRICE

When fixing selling prices however there are other factors to consider such as the competitors' prices for similar products and the extent of the market for the product. There would be no point in a business producing a product which could not be sold because the price was too high or because the market did not exist.

Major decisions illustrated above should be sufficient to indicate why the financial information contained in and gleaned from a company's accounts play an important role in management decision making. There are however probably many more examples which could be given to illustrate the usefulness of accounts to an organisation.

OTHER FACTORS INFLUENCING BUSINESS DECISION MAKING

Having looked at a number of examples where the information supplied by the financial or management accounts of an organisation is essential in the process of decision making, we shall now consider other factors which may influence the company in such a process. Taking the same general headings as above the following may give some indication of factors other than financial ones which may have to be considered.

1. TO CONTINUE PRODUCTION AND MARKETING OF AN UNPROFITABLE PRODUCT

If the accounts indicate that it may be better on balance to cease production of a product which is not making a profit this may have an effect in other areas.

It is likely to cause redundancies in the production and/or the marketing team, possibly causing a knock-on effect for the administrative staff. Redundancies themselves may be an additional cost to the company but it is the social impact on the community that will be most strongly felt. This will be potentially more disastrous in an area where there is little alternative employment available.

Redundancies may be followed by unemployment which in turn reduces the capability of the community to buy other products. This may have an effect on the profitability of other businesses in the area. Business which could be affected include retailers, garages and filling stations. This may itself lead to further redundancies and bankruptcies.

A further consequence of discontinuing a product is that it is likely to lead to parts of the business premises becoming redundant particularly if the machinery is fairly specialised and cannot be used in other forms of production or cannot be sold. This in turn may result in the property (or that part of it) becoming derelict and so becoming an unsightly part of the landscape. The converse of the situation is that the business may be able to relocate the machinery and perhaps allow the local community to take over the space available for other uses.

Another possibility is that the former employees form a co-operative to continue to run the business, using their redundancy money as capital. It may be that with their skill and expertise and without the huge overheads of a large organisation they can continue to produce and sell the product profitably.

2.   TO CLOSE DOWN AN UNPROFITABLE BRANCH

Once again there is the immediate problem of redundancies with all their adverse consequences but there may also be other factors to consider. Often, particularly in a rural community a branch store is the focal point of the village or small town. It often serves not only as a retailer of food, but as a newsagent, post office, cafe etc. Its closure may involve some difficulty for the local population in having to travel elsewhere to shop. If local transport is inadequate this will further increase the problem. A business faced with such a decision might consider the needs of the local community and should also bear in mind the loss of goodwill for the business as a whole.

3.   TO CHANGE THE PATTERN OF PRODUCTION

Here the problems are slightly different. Obviously to change from shift working to daily working will result in a reduction of the workforce, with the same disadvantages to the local community.

Alternatively to change from daily work to shift working may well bring other problems. Firstly will there be sufficient fully trained workers available to fill the new posts created by the change? If not then a training programme will have to be undertaken. This in turn could initially cost more money and may prove to be a burden but this should be outweighed by the advantages of increased production. Secondly, a change to shift working would necessitate the workforce in changing their habits. It is never easy to change from a pattern of working regularly from 8 a.m. to 5 p.m. Monday to Friday, to one of 5 shifts per week at varying hours and including weekends. A whole new pattern of social behaviour emerges which the current workforce may not be happy with.

Such a change therefore may mean long and protracted discussions with the trade unions. It will certainly mean the business having to pay higher wage rates (a shift allowance) for the inconvenience of shift working. This of course will have a beneficial effect with the increase in the community's spending power.

4.   TO BUY ANOTHER COMPANY

There are not many factors other than financial ones which a business must consider in this case, other than possible redundancies in the company bought, or possibly its eventual closure with production being transferred to the acquiring company. These problems have been discussed earlier with reference to other areas.

There is also of course the fact that the purchase of another company can reduce competition and therefore result in the creation of a monopoly with the possibility of price rises which members of the public have to endure, simply because there is no cheaper alternative product. This is discussed in some detail in chapter 27.

As far as the remaining three discussion points are concerned there are not many, other than financial factors that may influence the decision making process. Supplying goods on credit to particular customers should not affect the local community.

Investing in new capital equipment may cause a loss of jobs but it may also lead to a better working environment. People are often happier working with newer more efficient machinery than with old, obsolete machines. However this may require retraining with increased costs to the company.

Finally, other factors which may influence the fixing of selling prices of rival products, the maximum that the ultimate buyers are prepared to pay and the level of market saturation. These areas are discussed in chapter 26.

In this chapter we have discussed seven possible areas of decision making where financial accounting information is of paramount importance. But we have also seen that there are other factors involved in such a process, factors of a social, rather than an economic nature.

There are many more than seven areas where business organisations have to make decisions based on financial and social factors which have not been discussed in detail. Areas such as the effect that possible pollution from a factory will have on the surrounding area or the effect that quarrying or open cast mining will have on the landscape. Consider the problem of weighing up the advantages of cheap energy through nuclear power against the effects of pollution and injury if an accident occurs.

ASSIGNMENT — CLOSING THE RESTAURANT

Doggards Ltd is a private limited company which runs a department store in the small market town of Northallerton. The store sells the usual range of goods which are normally found in a department store such as ladies wear, men's wear, hardware, electrical goods, perfumeries, groceries and sports equipment. It also has a restaurant which serves morning coffee, lunch, afternoon teas and high tea. The restaurant occupies approximately half the area of the second floor of Doggard's building. The store has five floors altogether including the basement, but the top floor is given over entirely to staff accommodation, store rooms and offices. All the floors are of equal size.

The managing director of the company believes that the restaurant is not producing any of the profits of the store. Indeed he suspects that it is actually running at a loss. He has asked the company's accountant for a complete analysis of the store's activities, department by department and finds that whilst all departments involved in selling are making profits, the restaurant is in fact making a loss. In response he is considering closing down the restaurant and using the space that is released to expand the toy department which has proved to be one of the most profitable departments. Another director of the company is not convinced that this change is in the best interests of the business and wishes the restaurant to remain open.

TASKS

1. As a management trainee with the store you have been asked to investigate the situation and produce a report which will eventually be used as a basis for deciding whether the restaurant should be closed or remain open. Draw up checklist, prior to producing the report, in which you carefully identify for your own benefit, the various factors which you consider relevant in arriving at a decision about closing the restaurant.

2. Write the report to the Board of Directors on the proposed closure.

DEVELOPMENTAL TASK

3. Produce a simple questionnaire that could be completed by visitors to the store to provide you with data on customers' attitudes to a possible closure of the restaurant.

The Organisation
in its
Environment

Chapter 18

THE ORGANISATION

THE FORMATION OF ORGANISATIONS

THE REASONS WHY ORGANISATIONS ARE FORMED

The society in which we live is complex and sophisticated. As consumers we demand a variety of goods and services to enable us to maintain the quality of life we enjoy. In order to satisfy these demands suppliers must produce what the customer wants by combining the factors of production in the most efficient manner. By this we mean that they must hire workers, rent or buy premises, invest in plant and machinery and purchase raw materials, and then organise the manufacture of the final product in such a way that they will make a profit and society will gain the greatest benefit from the way in which these scarce resources are used to produce products. Suppliers under such a system are known as commercial organisations.

If we wish to see society ordered and governed in such a way that individuals are free to express their demands and producers are able to meet such wants then it becomes necessary to form organisations to control and regulate society through a variety of administrative structures. These are the bodies which make up the organisation of the state. In the UK, these are Parliament, the Government and its Executive, the Civil Service, the Local Authorities and the Courts and the justice system. These bodies are required to carry out legislative, administrative and judicial functions.

If you examine the nature and range of individual demands in an industrialised society you soon realise that most of them cannot be met other than by organisations. Individually we lack the knowledge, skills and physical resources to manufacture products that fulfil our needs, whether these are single or sophisticated. It would be as difficult for us to attempt to make a biro as a television, or a Floppy Disk as a computer.

Admittedly some goods or services can be supplied by an individual working alone. A farmer may be able to grow sufficient food to satisfy himself and his family without any help from others. But what if he requires other goods and services? It is unlikely that the farmer will also have the ability or resources to produce his own combine harvester or tractor. If he did not have such products which are manufactured by others then his life would be much simpler but no doubt harder. A similar situation applies to the provision of services. A strong and resourceful individual may try to protect himself and his property from the dangers posed by thieves or vandals. However, if he cannot, then he may turn to the state to demand protection. Recognising that a failure to respond to such demands from its citizens would lead to an anarchistic system the government must accept the responsibility and establish a legal system incorporating law enforcement agencies to provide the protection being sought.

. . . turn to the state . . . to provide the protection being sought.

How then are these goods and services produced? It is clear that the individuals working independently would be unable to meet our complex physical and social needs. Therefore society has developed a system where people join together to form organisations. These bodies are extraordinarily diverse. They manufacture products, which they distribute and sell. They also supply all services that we need. Thus the BBC is an organisation producing a product in the same way as the Ford Motor Company does.

Clearly then, if individuals within society are to have all their varied needs satisfied, there must be co-operation between workers. Each must specialise in a certain aspect of the supply process. These workers must be organised and allocated a role in which to perform specific co-ordinated tasks. In this way businesses are formed. These are normally organised with the purpose of producing and supplying a given product or service. In the private sector of the economy such businesses will usually have the objective of making a profit for the owners. Of course, this is just one example of an organisation. As we have already noted the state is another form or organisation which is clearly more complex than a business and it has a variety of objects such as increasing the wealth of citizens, improving their quality of life and protecting them if they are threatened. We are all members of organisations, some of which are formal while others are more informal. Your family is an example of an informal organisation, as is the group of friends you mix with. Other more formal organisations to which you belong or may have belonged are the school you attended as a child, the college you study at, the company which employs you or the youth club you support.

The tendency to form groupings is a characteristic feature of human behaviour. Human beings are highly socialised. They have a need to 'belong' and will generally find it uncomfortable and disturbing if they cannot find "acceptance" within a social group. An employee who is capable and confident in his or her job, and who is in turn regarded by the employer and the rest of the workforce as a professional gains a 'role' satisfaction through identifying as a vital part of the group. So organisations have an important role to fulfill in meeting the social needs of man. But perhaps more important in the context of this course of study is the function of organisations as providers of needs. They allow individual workers to develop specialist skills and as we shall see later this means that productive capacity increases.

As differing organisations concentrate on the supply of different products or services there must be a system established whereby products can be distributed to the consumers. Thus shops, wholesalers, transport companies, and so on must evolve. The fabric of the social and economic environment is based on a process involving individuals forming organisations which are dependant upon other organisations to survive. In just the same way that the needs of the individual cannot be met by the individual alone, so the same also hold true for organisations. They are interdependant. Organisational activity involves a perpetual interaction, one with another, as society steadily evolves in a direction that individually and collectively we try to guide. But as we shall see, even though the overall aim of society is the advancement of our physical wellbeing, the methods of achieving it are the subject of much disagreement.

CHARACTERISTICS COMMON TO ALL ORGANISATIONS

The specific reasons for the formation of organisations are many and varied and may not, of course, always be clearly defined. Some are the result of the need for individuals to find company for a social or leisure reason for example by forming a sporting or workingmen's club. Others are formed with a more precise economic objective in mind such as the desire to make a profit for the person who has established the business organisation. Some, such as the organisations which make up the state and the government evolve as particular needs within society become apparent and require government intervention. So for instance the Government established the National Health Service in 1946 to meet the needs of society for a high standard of free health care, available to all.

Nevertheless, most formal organisations have common characteristics. These may be simply stated as follows:

a. **The establishment of an organisation is usually for a specific purpose.** For example, the Automobile Association was founded with the precise objective of promoting the interests of motorists in this country. Other organisations may be launched with one prime aim but may later diversify in order to follow alternative causes or objectives. For instance, Guinness, the Brewery Company, was established to produce alcoholic drinks but now has subsidiaries making a variety of products including fishing tackle boxes and cassette cases. This illustrates how a business may try to evolve as the commercial environment changes and new commercial opportunities emerge.

b. **Organisations normally have a distinct identity.** People belonging to a specific organisation can identify themselves as being part of a group either because of their place of work or because of what they do. A Manchester United footballer wears a red shirt to show he is part of that organisation. A member of a trade union is given a union card to signify he belongs to the union. Manufacturing companies promote their brand name through advertising. You may wear a college sweat shirt to show that you are a part of the student body. This sense of identity, which we have already seen is an important need for most people, can produce extreme loyalty to the organisation.

c. **Most organisations require some form of leadership.** We have seen that the organisations are normally formed for a specific purpose. In order to achieve this purpose it is necessary to co-ordinate the efforts of the members of the organisation. This requires management or leadership. Formal organisations such as a company or a club have a specified management hierarchy which may be appointed by the owners of the organisation. For instance the shareholders of a company appoint the directors. Alternatively the leadership may be elected, as in the case of a club or society where the members vote to have a chairman, secretary and committee. However, once they are appointed this management team has the responsibility of ensuring that the organisation achieves its objectives.

d. **Organisation are accountable.** Such accountability applies both to those they deal with and those they employ. This concept of accountability is examined in some depth later in the chapter.

THE OBJECTIVES OF ORGANISATIONS

The objectives of an organisation are the targets it hopes to achieve. Clearly the objectives which are set will vary considerably with the type of organisation. However, for the purposes of this chapter let us begin by first concentrating on the objectives of commercial organisations (which we will refer to as businesses) and then look at the objectives of organisations within the public sector.

For business organisations it is possible to distinguish between a number of differing objectives.

Primary objectives — The prime objective of any business organisation is to survive. In order to achieve this it must make a profit. As we shall see later on in this chapter however, maximum profit may not always be the main goal of an organisation. The level of profit which it regards as satisfactory is often dependent on who is managing the business.

Secondary objectives — The Organisation may also make a profit through the achievement of what we may refer to as secondary objectives and these can be classified as:-

    (a)   economic; or

    (b)   social.

The diagram gives examples which are just a few of the economic and social objectives an organisation may have.

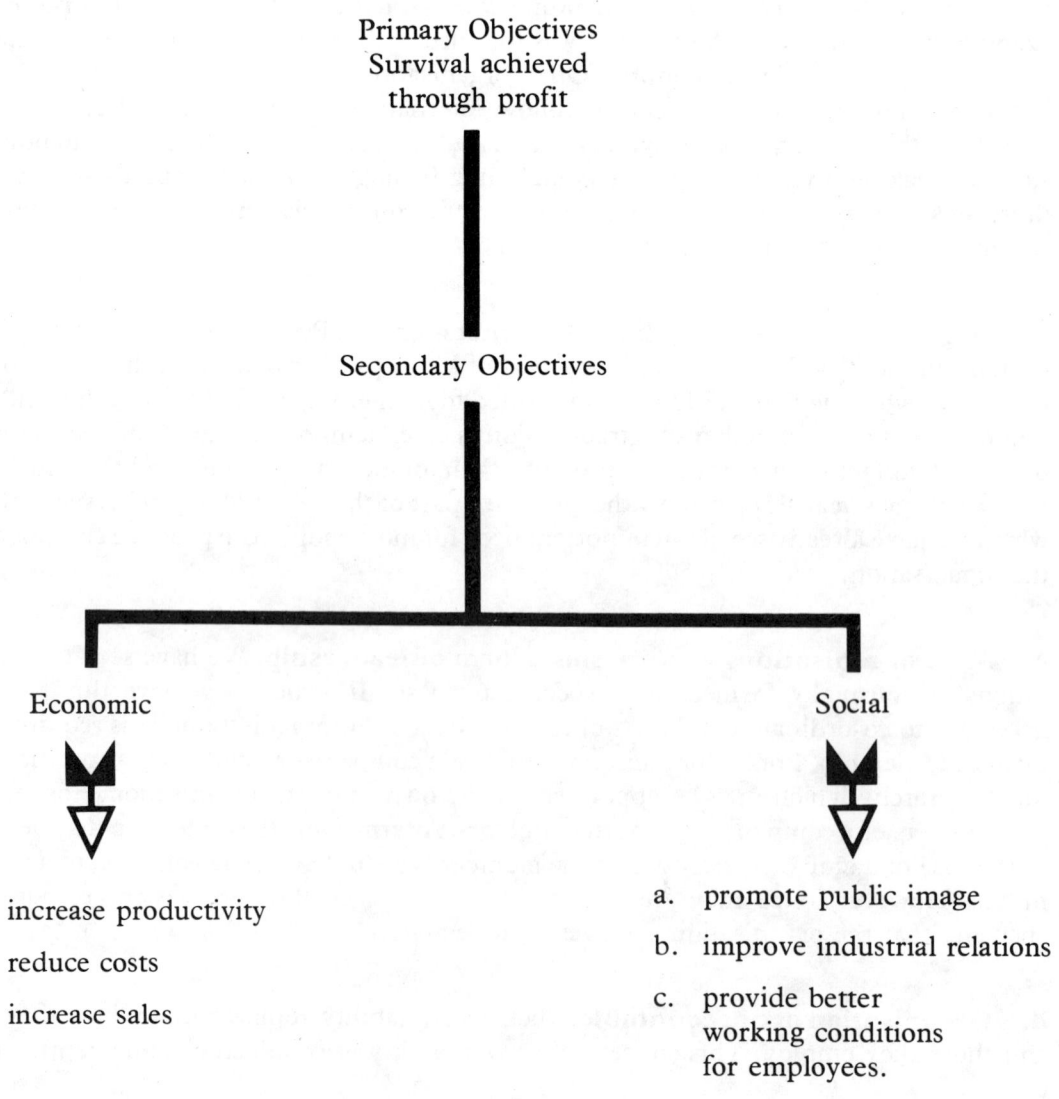

Primary Objectives
Survival achieved
through profit

Secondary Objectives

Economic

a.   increase productivity

b.   reduce costs

c.   increase sales

Social

a.   promote public image

b.   improve industrial relations

c.   provide better
working conditions
for employees.

Whilst we have made a functional distinction in the classification of secondary objectives above, they share a single underlying aim in any commercial organisation: the promotion of the primary objective of achieving profitability. For instance, a company may seek to enhance its public image by sponsoring a cultural or sporting event. However, the reason it wishes people to regard it as a generous benefactor is that as the public's opinion of the organisation improves it may increase their willingness to purchase its products. So be wary when you consider the motives behind the actions of business organisations, there is usually profit involved!

An important concern in the management of any organisation is that its objectives, whether economic or non-economic, should be clearly defined if at all possible. This is important because vague objectives cannot easily be achieved or quantified. The steps in setting an organisation's objectives should be as follows:

1. **Identify clearly objectives for the organisation.** For instance a manufacturing company may set itself the task of reducing production costs by 10% during the financial year;

2. **Ensure objectives do not conflict.** Using the same example a lowering of production costs may lead to a fall in quality and so an eventual decline in sales, when an increase in sales may be another important objective of the company;

3. **Determine the most appropriate means of achieving objectives.** Thus a reduction in production costs may be most efficiently achieved by ensuring a lower purchasing price for raw materials;

4. **Evaluate the success of the policy in achieving the objective within a given time period.** Check that production costs have fallen by 10% in the year;

5. **Reassess the objectives.** Examine again the objectives at regular intervals and decide whether or not they are still appropriate and achieveable. If they are not, set new objectives.

As you can see from the figure, an organisation may have a variety of objectives which will influence the way in which it determines its most crucial tasks. Because it may have a number of objectives the organisation must rank them in order of importance. So, for example, it may be faced with two problems, the need to increase revenue from sales and the legal requirement to improve the safety conditions within the production area. It might see little improvement in profitability from tightening safety procedures or spending money to fence its machines. Extra revenue from sales would help the organisation's financial situation much more. But when it is faced with the possibility of sanctions imposed by the Health and Safety Executive such as the closure of the dangerous production lines if it does not improve safety conditions, then clearly safety becomes the prime objective. We are being somewhat cynical here about the priorities of business organisations. It is fair to say that most good employers would always put the safety of their workers above a lust for increased profit, although the Health and Safety Executive itself noted a rise in industrial accidents during the recession which it has attributed to some employers spending less on safety measures and the increased use of outside contractors. This may have short term advantages to employers, but in the longer term such forms of cost cutting can prove more expensive through loss of production when vital staff are off sick, claims for compensation are made following accidents and higher insurance premiums.

1. Without defined objectives there is a possibility that individuals or departments may act in such a way that they contribute nothing to the overall performance of the organisation or might even act in ways which conflict with actual aims.

2. If objectives are set quantatively for instance by specifying a certain target for the growth in sales such as 20%, they can be measured reasonably accurately enabling performance to be judged against them.

3.   Objectives can only be set realistically by attempting to predict the future performance of the organisation and possible changes in the factors which may affect its performance. Therefore we need to have some idea of how an increase or decrease in demand for the organisation's product or service will affect sales. By attempting to forecast what is likely to happen, the company is in a better position to adapt to possible changes.

Non profit maximising Objectives

In the previous section we assumed that a business organisation would normally have profit maximisation as its main objective. However, this is not so in all organisations. Even an individual trader is not always seeking the greatest level of profit, but simply enough profit to satisfy his or her particular wants and needs. This is sometimes referred to as satisfactory profit. An example may be a small shopkeeper who chooses to close the shop at 5.30 p.m. in the evening instead of being "open all hours". This is because the shopkeeper will want to do other things such as spending the time with his or her family or enjoying a hobby or pastime. It is important to keep the running of a business in perspective. It is not a good idea to ruin your health or destroy your family life merely to gain greater and greater levels of profit.

We can also identify objectives other than profit maximisation in large organisations as well as in small ones. Consider a large company and how different groups involved in its operation may hold different objectives.

An important factor to recognise is that in the large organisations of today's business world there is a distinction between ownership and management and control. The owners are the shareholders who have bought a part of the company and their degree of ownership is in proportion to the percentage of the shares they hold. In many corporations the major shareholders are often large financial institutions such as insurance companies, pension funds and unit trust investment companies. Their objective is to earn the maximum return on their investment and to do this the investment managers of these institutions will buy and sell shares in companies according to their assessment of the potential profitability of each organisation. This means that a company must be sufficiently profitable to satisfy such institutional shareholders.

A second group who are involved in the company are the management and executives. In small companies the managers are the owners. In the larger corporate bodies, in which there is a substantial share capital, ownership and management will invariably be in different hands with the shareholders electing a board of directors as salaried, professional managers of the business. Whilst the owners have ultimate control over the managers, with the power to dismiss them the business could not be effectively carried on without permitting managers a broad degree of commercial freedom. Within this freedom they may pursue policies which are more personal than organisational. Some examples may illustrate this point.

A manager's salary or power is sometimes linked to the company's sales and so he may prefer sales maximisation to profit maximisation. Executives may also regard the size of the business as a reflection of their power and so might encourage the growth of the company even if this means a lower profit per share to the shareholders. Furthermore the executive may wish to see any profit that the business does make reinvested into the company to encourage further growth or new developments. This may be at odds with the shareholders who would rather see profits distributed to them in the form of dividends on their shares so giving them an immediate return on their investment.

Such conflicts are rarely seen in public. Instead the shareholders will put pressure on managers in more discreet ways, such as by threatening to vote them out of control at the shareholders' meeting if they do not follow the shareholders' line. The success of such pressure depends on whether or not the directors can command the confidence of a majority, 51%, of all shareholders, and therefore can afford to ignore the wishes of blocks of shareholders who remain the minority when it comes to the vote.

A final point to realise when looking at the objectives of managers is to consider what are known as behavioural objectives. These are distinct from economic objectives and refer to a manager's desire to influence his or her power, status or workload.

Behavioural objectives

As long as they are increasing the number of people working under them, many managers are happy. They feel that this increases their power. Conversely managers may simply seek an "easy life", resisting attempts to increase the size of their part of the company as it brings with it extra stress or strain. Clearly behavioural objectives depend on the individual manager concerned. You can probably identify within your own experience the type of person who is a 'go-getter' and others who are perhaps more 'laid back'. It is therefore not an easy task for shareholders to select management who are both competent and efficient and who will steer the fortunes of the business in a way which is compatible with the shareholders objectives.

ORGANISATIONAL STRUCTURE

The organisation of a business is concerned with the co-ordination and grouping of related activities to achieve its objectives. In order to do this it requires an organisational structure. An efficient business will have divided its activities into a logical sequence and will have allocated each sub division sufficient authority and autonomy to adequately perform its function. So to take an extreme example it would be absurd for the managing director of a large multi-national company to have to check and sign every small order for stationery sent out of the organisation. The talents of a hightly paid professional manager can be better utilised than this.

The responsibilities of each section of the business must be clearly defined. Again it would be inefficient if the maintenance department was also responsible for answering any incoming enquiries about potential sales. Each section must also be given sufficient authority to undertake its own responsibilities. Imagine the difficulty which would result if every time a telephone rang the receptionist had to ask permission from the managing director to answer it. Furthermore the overall organisation must ensure that there is co-ordination between the various aspects of the business and that clear lines of communication have been established. Chaos would occur if, when a sale is made, nobody remembers to inform the production department. However, the organisational structure must retain sufficient flexibility to allow it to adapt to change. For instance it must be able to expand as the business grows or extend into different functions if the organisation diversifies into other areas of business.

A formal organisational structure

The purpose of a formal organisational structure is to ensure that each individual is able to identify his or her position within the organisation. Each employee should be aware of their own responsibilities, to whom they are directly accountable and for whom they have a managerial or supervisory role. A further advantage of a formal structure is that it should allow management to develop areas of specialism and expertise within the organisation. If you work in an organisation you will probably be allocated specific duties. For instance if you are a sales clerk you may be responsible for processing the orders made by the sales department. You will be responsible to the sales manager or supervisor and eventually, as you are promoted, you may be given the task of supervising more junior sales clerks.

Almost certainly there will also exist some form of informal structure within the organisation. This will be the result of personal friendships, work patterns and practical expediency. Thus you may make friends with the people who work in your section or others that you come into contact with in the course of your job. Such informal structures are usually to be encouraged by the organisation as they improve the quality of the working environment and make people enjoy their job more. Only when such an informal structure conflicts with the efficient operation of the business should they be discouraged. No doubt we are all aware of some people who spend more time discussing their planned nights out than actually getting their work done.

Most organisations have a pyramid structure in which authority and responsibility extend downwards in a hierarchical pattern. In such a structure senior management will make the major executive and policy decisions. They have the overall responsibility for the success or failure of such policies and are given the authority to make such decisions by the owners of the business. As we move down the organisational pyramid, status, responsibility and authority normally decrease. So junior staff will not usually be required to make important decisions which affect the survival of the organisation. Not only are they paid lower salaries than senior managers, but they also lack the experience and expertise to make such decisions. It would clearly be inappropriate to give junior staff the authority to make important decisions for which they will not bear the responsibility, nor receive the financial rewards. So office juniors do not find themselves responsible for negotiating and signing the major contracts. In most businesses you will usually know when you are doing something that oversteps your authority. A senior will certainly inform you that you have acted out of line, and in any case your job description should indicate the limits of your responsibility.

The diagram below shows an organisation chart for a typical business. Organisation charts are an attempt to record the formal structure of the organisation showing most of the main relationships, the downward flow of authority and responsibility and the main lines of communication. Obviously it would be impossible to show on such a chart all the informal structures that can exist.

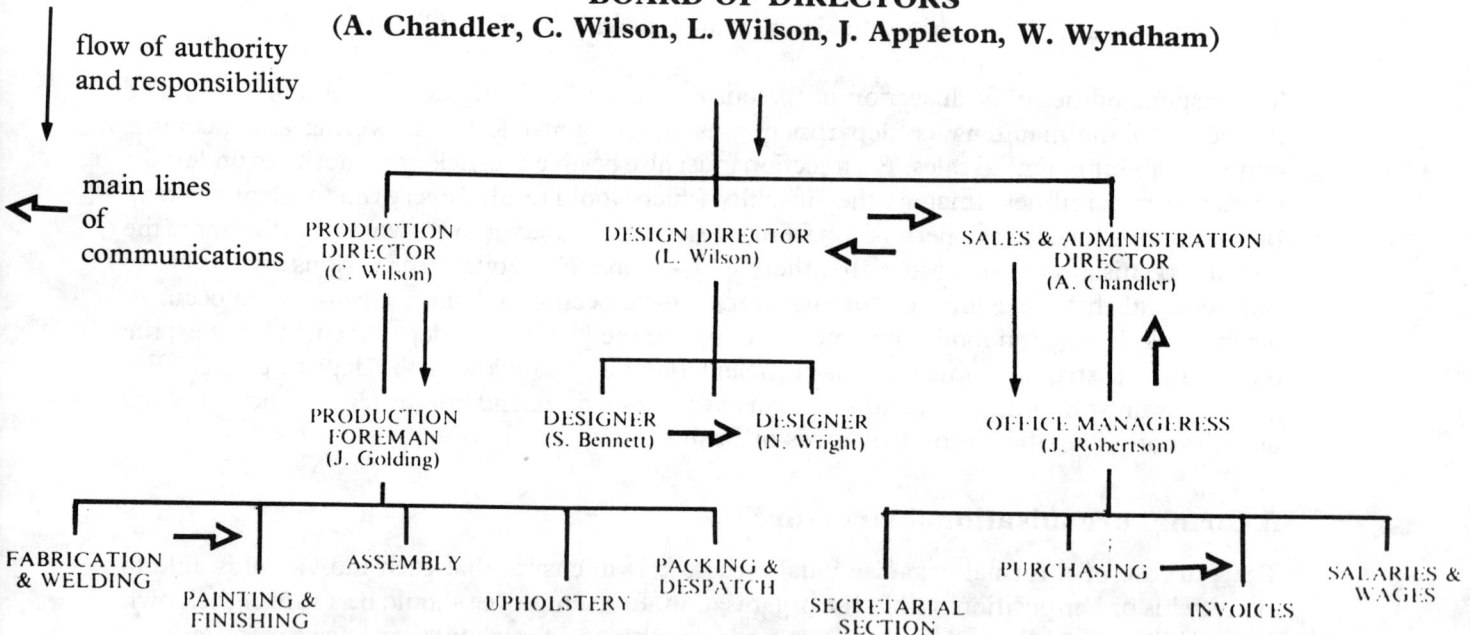

ORGANISATION CHART OF ABBOTSFIELD FURNITURE LIMITED

Imagine being faced with the task of drawing lines to show all the informal friendships in an organisation. Even if you managed to get it right you would have to change it every time two people had a quarrel and stopped talking to each other!

Organisation charts have the advantage of forcing senior management to clearly define organisational relationships. They are also a useful introduction to the organisation for outsiders and particularly for new starters. Additionally they can form the starting point from which management can initiate change or evaluate the strengths and weaknesses of the organisation. However they quickly become out of date as people change jobs and join or leave the organisation and they can introduce a degree of rigidity into the organisation as people feel constrained by the limits of their job defined by the organisational chart. This is why they must be continually reviewed and updated, and why an effective informal structure can be so beneficial.

TYPES OF ORGANISATIONS:

Within the economy it is possible to divide organisations into three sectors:-

        a.   primary

        b.   secondary

        c.   tertiary

a.   The Primary Sector. This sector of the economy encompasses all the production of all basic raw materials and therefore includes the coal industry, the steel industry, farming and fishing. Despite its importance in providing these necessary products, this sector has been declining as a major employer and now only about 4% of the working population are employed within it.

b.   The Secondary Sector. This is the manufacturing sector. It includes the car industry, engineering, the chemical industry, electronics, etc. The secondary sector converts the raw materials produced in the primary sector into the final products demanded by consumers. In common with most industrialised nations, the UK's secondary sector, while increasing its output, is employing less workers because of increasing technology and now about 40% of the national labour force work in manufacturing industries.

c.   The Tertiary Sector. This is the largest area of employment in the UK with about 56% of all workers. This area includes the service industries such as banks, insurance companies, retailing, distribution, the leisure industry and central and local government. It is increasing in size and this is characteristic of most developed nations, for as the population becomes richer it is able to devote a greater proportion of its income to services and luxuries. The UK, however, does have an exceptionally large public sector in comparison to most other Western European countries. About a quarter of all employees work for central and local government. The reason for the development of such a large public sector is discussed in chapter 24 on the State and its institutions.

THE OBJECTIVES OF PUBLIC SECTOR ORGANISATIONS

Let us now consider some of the objectives which are set for public sector organisations. Here we need to distinguish between organisations which have been established to provide a service such as health and education and those which are designed to produce a product for sale to the general public.

By defining public sector organisations in such terms we are, at the same time, identifying the objectives which they have been set. Let us examine each in turn.

Public Sector Service Organisations

One of the objectives of the state which has evolved over the last century has been that of improving the welfare of its citizens. Collectively the organisations which seek to achieve this are known as the 'welfare state'. They include the National Health Service, the Social Security system, the Education system and the Housing & Social Services departments of local authorities. Each of these have been given the responsibility by government to ensure that there is an acceptable level of provision of the services which they administer. When the National Health Service was established in 1946 its objective was "to secure improvement in the physical and mental health of the people of England and Wales and the prevention, diagnosis and treatment of illness". As you will realise this is a very broad objective. The Act of Parliament which established the National Health Service did not go into specific detail. It did not say that all people who require a kidney transplant should be given one or that all children should be innoculated against polio. The objective was phrased in such wide terms to allow the administrators of the Health Service to determine where priorities and needs lay. It is therefore the responsibility of the Department of Health and Social Security, the Regional Health

Authorities and ultimately individual hospitals and general practitioners to determine how best the health care of the nation should be provided. However this does not mean that such decisions can be made only with the needs of the patient in mind. Unfortunately the State has limited resources and the extent of the resources which are made available to the Health Service are determined by the overall evaluation of the competing demands of all aspects of the State by the central government. This involves a political judgement as to the amounts of taxation we are willing to pay. No doubt we would all welcome substantial improvements in the level of the health care, education and social services but we might not be willing to vote into power a government who proposed doubling income tax to finance such improvements. Obviously there are those who would accept higher taxation if this was accompanied by better services but politics does not operate in a way which presents the electorate with such straightforward choices. The political parties will only advocate that combination of taxes and services which they believe will gain them a parliamentary majority. Raising taxation is regarded by all of them as essentially unpopular.

In this context there is a yearly battle in cabinet, where the Chancellor of the Exchequer sets out the amount of revenue he thinks he can safely raise and then the competing government departments each argue their case for a large share of the resulting expenditure. Therefore it is possible to define the objectives of those departments which provide a service as being twofold:

> (i)   the provision of as wide reaching a service as possible in meeting the needs of the population;

> (ii)   the efficient and cost effective use of the budget which they have managed to receive.

Public Sector Producer Organisations

This group of organisations is sometimes collectively referred to as 'public enterprise'. In it we would include such bodies as British Coal, British Steel, the Electricity Generating Boards and British Rail. Each provides a marketable product. By this we mean that they sell what they produce to the general public. The objectives of these organisations have not remained constant over the years. Many were taken into public ownership in the late 1940's by the post-war labour government. At this time they were set the dual objectives of (i) providing as wide a level of service as possible and (ii) breaking even, taking one year with another. This meant that they were not intended to be profitable but should not overall be a burden on the taxpayer by continually making a loss. However over the last forty years the attitude of government to the nationalised industries has changed. By the mid 1960s it was decided that they should be run on 'commercial lines'. This meant that sectors of these industries which were continually making losses were closed. The result of this policy change was a widespread closure of many branch-lines on the railways and less viable coal mines. Nonetheless the need to provide an acceptable level of output of these products to the public was maintained.

With the coming to power of the Thatcher government in 1979, the attitude to the nationalised industries changed once again. They have been set objectives which are more closely in line with private sector businesses. They are required to be profitable wherever possible. This has meant a reduction in many of the services which had previously been subsidised from public funds. Prices have been increased to allow them to provide the government with a source of revenue and it is the objective of the government that once they are economically profitable they should be privatised. By this it is meant that they should be sold back to the private shareholders.

This has already happened with British Telecom and several other public corporations are scheduled for future privatisation. The issue of privatisation will be examined in more detail in chapter 25. Therefore it is possible to define the major objectives of the nationalised industries as the profitable provision of the goods and services demanded by the general public.

DECISION MAKING

So far we have not considered what is, in practice, a most important feature of organisational activity, namely the decision making process that goes on within it. A distinction needs to be made between the different levels at which the decisions on the operation of an organisation are made. We can classify decisions into three types:

(i) policy decisions;

(ii) management decisions; and

(iii) administrative decisions.

POLICY DECISIONS

These determine the overall policy direction of the organisation. So for instance in a private sector company a decision to expand into new markets, take over another company or reduce its workforce, is a major policy decision for the business which can have long term implications for the company's survival or failure. Such a policy decision is made by the board of directors acting in its role as the representative of the shareholders.

We can compare this type of decision in a private sector organisation with policy making in the public sector. The Prime Minister and the Cabinet are the ultimate policy making body in the country. They will make all the most crucial decisions relating to the government of the country. Therefore they decide whether taxation should be increased or decreased, if the country is to have nuclear weapons or whether we should be a member of the European Community. Of course most of these decisions must then be passed through both Houses of Parliament but as the government in power has the majority in the House of Commons it would be rare for the government not to have its policy approved. A similar situation exists in local government although here there is no such specific formal body as a local authority cabinet.

Instead the majority party will normally have a private party meeting (often referred to as a group meeting) where the party line on particular policy is decided in advance of council meetings. Such decisions are then debated at a meeting of the full council or one of its sub committees. Again as the ruling party will usually have a majority, its policy will normally be passed. Therefore we will find that policy decisions in most organisations are determined by the group holding power, whether this be a group of elected directors, shareholders or the government or majority party on a council elected by voters.

MANAGEMENT DECISIONS

Such decisions are often referred to as executive decisions. They determine the method by which policy is executed or implemented. The managers of a company are in many instances also the directors. In other words administrative and policy making is dealt with by the same people. They will attempt to ensure that a policy decision made by the board to expand the operations of the business will be achieved in the most efficient and commercially viable manner.

When we consider the public sector we find that it is in the process of management decision making that central and local government differ. In central government suitable Members of Parliament are selected by the Prime Minister to become Departmental Ministers. They are paid a substantial salary in addition to their normal MP's pay and are charged with responsibility for the management of a specific aspect of the government's affairs. For example the Minister of Education is not only a member of the Cabinet and so collectively responsible for its policy decisions, but is also required to make management decisions for the Department of Education and Science, such as the level of teachers' pay.

In local government, councillors are not paid a salary and so cannot be expected to devote the amount of time required to manage council business. Instead councils appoint paid officials, known as officers. Senior officers are required to manage the affairs of a department of the council, to make sure that policy decided by council is carried out and also to advise the council prior to its making such policy decisions. So, for example, the Director of Housing in a local authority will be responsible for the management of all aspects of the council's housing programme.

It is important at this point to again appreciate the difference between policy making and management. Policy making is carried out by elected representatives. Management is undertaken by paid employees whether they are paid directors or managers in a private business or paid ministers or officers in the public sector.

ADMINISTRATIVE DECISIONS

The day to day running of any organisation requires the implementation of a number of differing skills and talents. An able administrator must be aware of the overall policy objectives of the organisation and the direction set by the policy makers to achieve these. The administrator is responsible for a specific set of tasks. These may be routine and repetitive or may require the administrator to demonstrate his or her own initiative and intelligence. We would expect that the level of responsibility given to an administrator matches not only the ability and experience of the individual but is also reflected in their status and the salary they are paid.

Thus a section head in an organisation will be expected to be responsible for junior staff and also to ensure that the department's targets are met. A more junior administrator such as a clerical assistant in the civil service is responsible only for his own specific tasks and will be supervised by senior administrators. So in a private business the administration is delegated through a hierarchy comprising of section and department heads, clerks and juniors. In government departments it is the civil service who are required to administer the policy and management decisions made by cabinet and government ministers.

Local government has an administrative structure in which council employees carry out the council's policy as directed by the senior officers. In all cases without the efforts of a group of able administrators both policy and management decisions made by more senior members of the organisation cannot be carried out efficiently or successfully.

THE LEGAL CHARACTERISTICS OF ORGANISATIONS

So far the chapter has considered the reasons for forming organisations, and described their underlying structures. However, the picture is not complete until we examine the legal framework within which organisations are situated, the major impact of which is that it regulates their activities internally and externally, as well as governing their formation. Firstly we consider private business organisations, and then go on to look at public sector organisations.

PRIVATE SECTOR BUSINESS ORGANISATIONS

All business enterprises can be classified into two basic legal forms. They are either unincorporated bodies or corporate bodies. The fundamental distinction between the two is simply that an unincorporated body is either an individual, or more usually a group of individuals, who have joined together to pursue a common business purpose. The body, and the individuals who compose it, are not separate from each other under the law even though they may trade under a business name, not using their own names, thus superficially at least making it appear that the business is a separate entity. A corporate body, or corporation, is also made up of a group of individuals who have joined together for a common purpose, but by the process of legal incorporation they have created an artificial legal person which has a separate legal identity from the members who compose it.

The most common form of corporation is the registered company, or joint stock company as it is traditionally known, whilst the most common type of unincorporated bodies are the sole trader and the partnership. Below we examine these various organisations from the point of view of their legal status. As we shall see, the legal status of a business is a matter of considerable importance to its members, not least because it is largely responsible for describing what their rights and responsibilities are, and hence their relationship to the organisation and each other.

Sole Traders

The term 'sole trader' is an expression used to describe an individual who is self employed, operating a business alone and has sole responsibility for its management. In practice, of course, sole traders rarely work alone and will usually employ staff to assist them in the operation of the business. There are no specific legal formalities relating to the creation of such a business. However operating as a sole trader will necessarily involve the owner in buying and selling, employing staff and acquiring business premises. As an employer, a sole trader is subject to the law relating to employment contained in the common law, (that is law defined by the courts) and numerous statutes, (law determined by Parliament), the most important of which is the Employment Protection (Consolidation) Act 1978 (as amended). In addition, as a supplier of goods or services, a sole trader must comply with the law relating to consumer protection, for example the Sale of Goods Act 1979, the Trade Descriptions Act 1972 and the Supply of Goods and Services Act 1982. Some types of business enterprise must also acquire a licence to permit them to operate. For example a publican requires a licence to sell intoxicating drinks and a turf accountant a betting and gaming licence.

A sole trader's business will normally be financed by the owner himself, which means that the opportunities for raising business capital are necessarily limited. Whilst the sole owner is entitled to all the profits of the business, he has unlimited liability in relation to its losses and so must bear them personally. The sole trader form of business is therefore most suitable for an individual who wishes to retain absolute control of the sort of business enterprise which requires only a modest amount of financial investment. Obvious examples include retail shops and service trades such as plumbing, hairdressing and farming. Collectively, sole traders provide a valuable service to the community by making a wide range of goods and services available in a personal way, meeting needs which might otherwise be unfulfilled.

The responsibility for decision making in such a business rests with the owner, and there is no individual or group to which he is made directly accountable. This is very attractive to those who wish to 'be their own boss'. Of course there are groups who will be affected by the owner's actions such as the customers or clients, the creditors to whom the business owes money, and especially the employees of the business. Such groups have a valid interest in the decisions made by the sole trader and may ultimately seek to hold him accountable for his actions. For instance an employee may complain that employment rights have been infringed, or a customer that consumer rights have been abused. Accountability is perhaps at its most extreme level in the event of the sole trader becoming insolvent.

Over recent years there has been a substantial increase in the number of one-man businesses being established and this trend has been encouraged by the government by giving grants and tax advantages to small businesses. The present climate of unemployment has resulted in large numbers of skilled and unskilled workers losing their jobs and many receive lump sum payments as compensation. There is evidence that increasing numbers of such individuals have been willing to use their redundancy payments as initial capital to set up a business in which they will be their own employer.

Partnerships

The second form of unincorporated business organisation is a partnership. Partnerships are commonly referred to as 'firms'. There are no detailed legal formalities required when individuals agree to operate a business together and thus form a partnership. The agreement to form a partnership will, of course, be a contract but there is no legal requirement as to its specific form. It may be oral, in writing, contained in a deed, or even implied by the law from the surrounding circumstances. The Partnership Act 1890, which contains most of the legal rules relating to partnerships, defines a partnership simply as the "relation which subsists between persons carrying on business in common with a view of profit". All the partners in a firm will usually agree to put capital into it, work on its behalf and in return receive a share of the profits, often in proportion to the amount of capital they have contributed.

In addition to the numerous trading businesses which are run as partnerships, many professional people providing business services will operate as partnerships, normally because the rules relating to their professions prevent the partners forming limited companies, for instance partnerships of solicitors, chartered accountants and architects. Although there is a legal restriction upon the numbers of partners that may operate a firm, which is fixed at 20, professional firms are not subject to this limitation. In exceptional cases such firms may have more than one hundred partners, but a partnership of this size will be an unwieldy organisation.

The main risk in operating a business as a firm is that if the business should get into financial difficulties, the liability of the partners is not limited in any way. The individual members are liable to the extent of their personal wealth in order to pay off partnership debts.

The partners may choose any name they please for the firm provided it is not similar to an existing name and therefore not likely to mislead others. Also, there is a legal restriction that the last name must not be the word "limited" or any abbreviation of it, for this would indicate that the organisation is a company having limited liability. The words "and Co" at the end of the partnership name refer to the fact that there are partners in the firm whose names do not appear in the firm name. The obvious advantages of operating a business as a partnership include the increased sources of business capital available if more members are brought in and the possibility of obtaining greater credit. In addition, the opportunity of sharing management responsibility, the increased expertise that can be introduced and the minimal costs involved in the creation and dissolution of partnerships are of particular benefit to those in small organisations.

The Management of Partnerships

There are obvious problems inherent in attempting to reach the sort of joint decisions which are necessary to successfully manage a partnership and it is not uncommon for partners to disagree. There are also risks involved, both in having unlimited liability and in the fact that individual partners may be responsible for the acts and defaults of their co-partners. Each partner is an agent of the co-partners and as such has an agent's power to bind the partnership by his or her acts undertaken within the ordinary course of the business. It is crucial therefore that each partner has trust and confidence in his co-partners, the relationship being one of the utmost good faith. This is sometimes given its latin name and is known as a relationship of "uberrimae fidei". Each partner is therefore under a duty to make a full and frank disclosure to the firm of any matters affecting it that come to the partner's attention.

A fundamental feature of both the sole trader and the partnership is that the enterprise be carried on for the purpose of a 'business', Normally the expression 'business' presents no difficulty. It includes every occupation, profession or other commercial activity. It is an important expression as a number of Acts of Parliament, covering a range of matters such as taxation, consumer protection and the relationship between a landlord and tenant, have provisions relating only to those operating as a 'business'. Occasionally the courts have been called on to interpret the expression. Of course, sometimes the line between what may be regarded as a business and a mere hobby is very thin.

> In *Eiman v. London Borough of Waltham Forest 1982*, the issue was whether the defendant had been rightly convicted in the Crown Court of the offence of making a demand for unsolicited goods "in the course of a trade or business", contrary to the Unsolicited Goods and Services Act 1971. As

a full-time employee of the local authority the accused had, as a hobby, composed and published a book of verse. He had then sent out copies of the book to local libraries and made a demand for payment. The High Court held that the Crown Court was entitled to convict the defendant as what had started as a hobby, had become a 'business' as defined by the Act and therefore the Unsolicited Goods and Services Act did apply. The court found it possible to reach such a conclusion despite the fact that this was an isolated incident without any intention to make a profit.

A further example is provided by the decision in *Blakeman v. Bellamy 1983*. Here the question was whether the accused's spare time activity of buying and selling motor cars through advertisements, contravened the Fair Trading Act 1973, and the Business Advertisements (Disclosure) Order 1977. This is because in the course of a business it is an offence to "advertise goods for sale" without making it clear that the goods were sold in the course of a business. Offences under the Trade Descriptions Act, 1968 were also alleged which involved applying false trade descriptions to two of the vehicles "in the course of a business". Despite the number of transactions involved, eight in all, the High Court agreed with the Magistrates' finding that the defendant's activity was merely a hobby rather than a business. Accordingly the statutory provisions had not been infringed, for the sales were merely private bargains. This was despite the fact that the defendant's objective in making the sales was to achieve gain or reward and as the seller he had clearly demonstrated skill and expertise in the 'business' of buying and selling cars.

In the course of business, partnerships often enter into transactions with other organisations and individuals and inevitably such transactions are negotiated and executed for the partnership by individual partners, rather than by the firm as a whole. It has already been noted that each partner is an agent of his co-partners. A partner's ability to bind the firm as an agent extends to those contracts which come within the partners actual and apparent authority. Actual authority is the authority that the firm has agreed the partner shall hold. A firm, may for instance, expressly resolve in a partnership meeting, that each partner shall have the power to employ staff. Apparent authority is the authority the partner appears to others to hold. It therefore covers, 'carrying on in the usual way business of the kind carried on by the firm'.

In *Mercantile Credit Co Ltd v. Garrod 1962*, the court had to decide what could be considered as an act of a 'like kind' to the business of persons who ran a garage. It was held that the sale of a car to a third party by one of the partners, bound the other partners. This was despite an agreement between them that provided for the carrying out of repair work, and the letting of garages, but expressly excluded car sales.

Clearly a private exclusion of the powers of an agent is not an effective way to bring the restriction to the notice of an outsider dealing with the agent, and the law recognises this.

The following powers usually fall within the apparent authority of a partner:

a) in the case of all types of partnership the power to:

    (i)   sell the goods or personal property of the firm;

    (ii) purchase in the firm's name goods usually or necessarily used in the firm's business;

    (iii) receive payments due to the firm;

    (iv) employ staff to work for the firm.

b) in the case of a partnership whose business is the buying and selling of goods (i.e. a trading partnership), the following additional powers are within the partner's authority:

    (i) to borrow money for a purpose connected with the business of the firm;

    (ii) to deal with payments to and from the firm.

A partnership has no separate legal identity so that it is the individual partners who are ultimately accountable for all the firm's debts. Under the Partnership Act every partner is jointly liable with the other partners for all the debts and obligations of the firm incurred whilst being a partner. A legal action by a creditor seeking to recover money owed to him may be brought against any one or more of the firm's partners. However if the judgement obtained in the court does not satisfy the creditor he cannot then sue the remaining partners for, having sued one partner, he is precluded from suing the others for the same debt. Nevertheless the creditor, if he had chosen to do so, could have sued the firm in its own name rather than suing an individual partner of the firm. This has the effect of automatically joining all the partners in the action, and means that the judgement and the subsequent award of any payment to the creditor will be met out of the assets of the firm as a whole and, if necessary, out of the property of the individual partners.

The membership of a firm will normally alter from time to time. It may wish to expand its business by bringing in new partners to provide the benefit of additional capital or fresh expertise. Existing partners may leave the partnership to join a new business, or to retire. A changing membership poses the question of the extent to which incoming and outgoing partners are responsible for the debts and liabilities of the firm. Although partners are responsible for any matters arising during their membership of the firm, incoming partners are not liable for the debts incurred before they joined, nor outgoing partners for those incurred after they leave, provided the retiring partner advertises the fact that he is no longer a member of the firm. This involves sending notice to all customers of the firm while that person was a partner, and advertising the retirement in a publication known as the 'London Gazette'. If this is not done a person dealing with the firm after a change in its membership can treat all apparent members of the old firm as still being members of the firm. With regard to existing liabilities the partner may be discharged from them when he retires through the agreement of the new firm and the creditors.

Ideally the partnership relationship should be regulated by a comprehensive partnership agreement. Although the provisions of the Partnership Act will apply when the parties are in dispute as to the nature of their duties, and are unable to reach agreement amongst themselves in a business enterprise of this sort, where a member's entire wealth lies at stake, it is clearly of great value to execute a detailed agreement setting out in precise form the powers and responsibilities of the members. For instance it would be prudent for the agreement to provide grounds for the removal of partners, since the Act makes no such provision. Because the members of the firm have the freedom to make their own agreement, without the statutory controls imposed upon other forms of business organisation, such as the registered company, the partnership stands out as a most flexible form of organisation.

The duties that the Act sets out, are based upon a single foundation of fundamental importance to all partnerships, namely that the relationship between the parties is of the utmost good faith.

> This principle can be seen in *Law v. Law 1905*. A partner sold his share in the business to another partner for £21,000, but the purchasing partner failed to disclose to his co-partner certain facts about the partnership assets, of which he alone was aware. When the vendor realised that he had sold his share at below its true value he sought to have the sale set aside. The Court of Appeal held that in such circumstances the sale was voidable, and could be set aside.

A partner is under a duty to his co-partners to render true accounts and full information of all things affecting the partnership. Personal benefits can only be retained with the consent of the other partners.

> In *Bentley v. Craven (1853)*, one of the partners in a firm of sugar refiners, who acted as the firm's buyer, was able to purchase a large quantity of sugar at below market price. He resold it to the firm at the true market price. His co-partners were unaware that he was selling on his own account. When they discovered this they sued him for the profit he had made, and were held to be entitled to it.

Finally a partner is under a duty not to compete with his firm by carrying on another business of the same nature unless the other partners have consented. If a partner is in breach of this duty he must account to the firm for all the profits made and pay them over. If the partnership agreement prohibits the carrying on of a competing business, a court order, called an injunction, may be granted to stop a partner who disregards the limitation.

Further rights and duties set out in the Act state that, in the absence of a contrary agreement:-

(i)   all partners are entitled to take part in the management of the partnership business;

(ii)   differences arising regarding ordinary matters connected with the partnership business are to be decided by the majority of the partners, but no change can be made in the nature of the partnership business without the consent of all the partners and no person may be introduced as a partner without consent of all existing partners;

(iii)   all partners are entitled to an equal share of the business irrespective of the amount of time they have given to it, and must contribute equally toward any losses. Although statute does not require the firm to keep books of accounts, this will normally be provided for in the partnership agreement, together with specific reference to the profits each partner is entitled to. If there are partnership books, they have to be kept at the principal place of business, where every partner is entitled to have access to them for the purpose of inspection and copying;

(iv)   the firm must indemnify a partner in respect of payments made and personal liabilities incurred in the ordinary and proper conduct of the business of the firm;

(v)   a partner is not entitled to remuneration (i.e. a salary) for acting in the partnership business.

If any of the terms of the partnership agreement are broken, damages will be available as a remedy and where appropriate an injunction may be granted.

Corporate Bodies

Corporate bodies or 'corporations', as they are usually called, are artificial persons recognised under the law, which have a separate legal identity from the members who compose them. There are many types of corporation however in relation to business enterprises the most common type is the limited company. The members of such a company are its shareholders.

There are many thousands of registered limited companies in this country and between them they employ the majority of the nation's workforce and comprise about two thirds of the income made by the private sector. Companies can be formed which have only two members. They can also develop into the massive multi-national UK registered enterprises which have thousands of shareholders. Such is the diversity of these organisations that it is difficult to generalise on their structure and behaviour but most have been formed with the expectation of future expansion financed by the raising of capital through the issue of shares. As separate legal entities they also give the owners the protection of limited liability and it is this feature more than any other that has contributed to their popularity. Another appealing feature is that ownership can be divorced from management, thus an investor can stake capital in a company without having to be involved in the actual running of it and is at worst responsible only for debts equal to the nominal share value he holds.

Limited liability therefore means that in the event of the company facing financial difficulty the shareholders' legal liability to contribute to the payment of debts is limited to the amount, if any, unpaid on their shares. For instance, if an individual purchases 20 £1 shares in a company and pays 25p on each share (these are called partly paid shares) he is only liable to contribute the amount of the share value remaining unpaid, in this case 20 x 75p, a total of £15.

Companies can thus expand and diversify by raising additional capital when it is needed through the issue of more shares, and hence large scale commercial organisations have evolved with thousands of shareholders holding between them millions of shares. The growth of this form of business enterprise and the recognition of the company as a separate legal entity has however posed many problems and led to many abuses. The law has recognised these difficulties. Various Companies Acts, now consolidated in the Companies Act 1985, have attempted to regulate corporate behaviour, bearing in mind not only the interest of the shareholders themselves but also the interests of outsiders who trade with the companies.

As we have seen the limited company is an artificial legal person, and has some although not all the powers and responsibilities of a natural person. It is capable therefore of owning property, entering into contracts such as trading contracts and contracts of employment, and of suing or being sued in its own name. But its artificial nature imposes some obvious limitations upon its legal capacity. It cannot generally be held liable for criminal acts, since most crimes involve proving a mental element such as intention or recklessness and a corporation has as such no mind. Nevertheless there may occur circumstances in which the collective intention of the Board of Directors can be regarded as expressing the will of the corporation. Lord Denning has spoken of the company as having human body, the employees being the hands that carry out its work while "others are directors and managers who represent the directing mind and will of the company and control what it does". Of the various forms of company that can be created, the company limited by shares is the usual form adopted by commercial and industrial undertakings.

Under the Companies Act 1985, the two main categories of company are the public limited company and the private limited company. The main distinction between the two categories is that a public company has the authority to place advertisements which invite the public to subscribe for shares which can then be freely bought and sold whenever the shareholder wishes. A private company cannot advertise in this way and will also normally restrict the transfer of the shares by requiring the Directors' consent to be given before a sale to an outsider can take place, or a further offer of the sale of shares to existing shareholders can happen. To register as a public limited company, the corporation's public documents must state that it is a public limited company, the company must have a minimum share capital of £50,000 of which one quarter is fully paid up and the company name must end with the words "public limited company" or "p.l.c." It is possible for a private company to re-register as public and vice versa under the 1985 Act. We have seen that the membership of a company is distinct from the corporate body. All this means is that the company shareholders are separate from the company which has a legal personality of its own. Changes in its membership, including the death or bankruptcy of members will have no effect upon the company, which may have an almost perpetual life span if there remain investors willing to become members of it.

> The separation of a company from its members was confirmed in the famous case of *Salomon v. Salomon & Co. 1897.* The plaintiff sold his leather business to the defendant company which he had formed himself, and received in return the majority of the company's shares and a number of debentures. (These are a form of loan capital which entitle the holder to re-payment before other ordinary creditors in the event of a company being liquidated). Eventually the company went into liquidation owing £8,000 to ordinary creditors and having only £6,000 worth of assets. The plaintiff claimed that as a debenture holder with £10,000 worth of debentures he was a secured creditor and entitled to repayment before the ordin-

ary unsecured creditors. The unsecured creditors did not agree. The Court held that despite the fact that following the company's formation, Salomon had continued to run the business in the same manner and with the same control as he had done when it was unincorporated the company formed was a separate person from Salomon himself. When the company was liquidated, therefore, Salomon, like any other debenture holder, was a secured creditor and entitled to repayment before ordinary creditors. The court thus upheld the principle that a company has a separate legal existence from its membership even where one individual holds the majority of shares and effectively runs the company as his own.

A company is also the owner of its own property in which its members have no legal interest, although clearly they have a financial interest.

> In *Macaura v. Northern Assurance Co Ltd 1925* it was held that a majority shareholder has no insurable interest in the company's property. A fire insurance policy over the company's timber estate was therefore invalid as it has been issued in the plaintiff shareholder's name and not the company's name.

Both the Courts and Parliament have accepted that situations may arise in which it is right and proper to prevent the members from escaping liability by hiding behind the company, and so there are cases where the "corporate veil" as it is called can be lifted. The main thinking beind such exceptions has been to give effect to the economic reality of the particular case.

So for example if a company is wound up and the court is satisfied that the directors have carried on the business with an intention to defraud the creditors, they may be made personally liable for all the company's debts. This would cover trading and incurring debts, where they knew that there was no reasonable prospect that the creditors would be paid.

In rare cases, the courts will disregard the separate legal personality of a company because it was formed or used to facilitate the evasion of legal obligations.

> In *Gilford Motor Co Ltd v. Horne 1933*, the defendant had been employed by the plaintiff motor company and had entered into a valid agreement not to solicit the plaintiff's customers or to compete with it for a certain time after leaving the company's employment. Shortly after leaving the employment of the motor company, the defendant formed a new company to carry on a similar business to that of his former employers and sent out circulars to the customers he had previously dealt with while working for the motor company. In an action to enforce the restraint clause against the new company the Court held that as the defendant in fact controlled the new company, its formation was a mere 'cloak or sham' to enable him to break the restraint clause. Accordingly an injunction was granted against the defendant and against the company he had formed, to enforce the restraint clause.

> Similarly in *Jones v. Lipman 1962*, the defendant agreed to sell land to the plaintiff and then decided not to complete the sale. To avoid the possibility of an order of specific performance to enforce the sale the defendant bought a company, by purchasing a majority shareholding in an existing company to which he then sold the land. The plaintiff applied to the Court for an order against the defendant and the company to enforce the sale. It was held that the formation of the company was a mere sham to avoid a contract of sale, and specific performance was ordered against the vendor and company.

Formation of a Registered Company

A company is incorporated and so comes into being when the Registrar of Companies issues a document called the Certificate of Incorporation. This certificate is issued following an application by the persons who wish to form the company. Two of the main documents which must be included in the application are the memorandum of association and the articles of association.

The Memorandum of Association

The memorandum of association, which sets out the constitution of a registered company, is one of a group of documents to be sent to the Registrar of Companies prior to incorporation. A memorandum is required by the Companies Act 1985 which specifies that the memorandum must include the following matters:-

    (i)   the name of the company with "limited" as the last word in the case of a private company, or "public limited company" in the case of a public company;

    (ii)   the situation of the registered office identifying whether the company is situated in England or Scotland;

    (iii) the objects of the company;

    (iv) the liability of the members;

    (v)   the nominal capital of the company and its division into numbers of shares and denominations.

The Registrar of Companies maintains a file for all registered companies, which is open to public inspection on payment of a fee. The file for each company includes the company memorandum. The contents of the memorandum are of importance to the members of the company itself (the shareholders), and especially to those who deal with the company commercially. The indication that the company is a corporate body shown by the inclusion of the word "limited", serves as a warning to outsiders that in the event of the company being unable to meet its financial liabilities at any time, its shareholders, as we have previously seen, can only be called upon to make good any loss, up to the value which remains unpaid to the company on their shares. Once however the shares have been fully paid the shareholders' financial liability ceases.

Stating the country in which the company is situated determines whether it is an English or Scottish company. Usually a Notice of Situation of Registered Office, giving the company's full address is sent to the Registrar together with the Memorandum. It must be sent to him within fourteen days of incorporation of the company. The registered office is important since documents may be effectively served on the company by posting or delivering them to this address. Thus a writ (a document used to commence legal proceedings) served on the company will be effectively served if delivered to the registered office.

The objects clause sets the contractual limits within which the company can validly operate. Contracts falling outside the scope of the objects clause are not binding on the company, for they are beyond its powers (known as ultra vires). The need to state the company's objects may be seen as a protection to shareholders by giving them some reassurance as to the ways in which their capital may be spent. A company, can, however, resolve to alter its objects, and in any event it is usual to draft the objects clause very widely. Furthermore a transaction decided upon by all the directors can bind the company even though the transaction is ultra vires, provided the other party to the transaction is aware of this and is acting in good faith.

The liability clause is a formality which merely states the nature of the shareholders' liability.

The capital clause sets out the amount of capital the company is authorised to raise by the issue of shares, and the way in which the shares are to be divided. This amount can be raised by the agreement of the shareholders without difficulty, although a reduction in the share capital, whilst possible, is more of a problem to achieve.

The subscribers for the shares in the memorandum will often be appointed as directors. As the statutory minimum membership of a company is two, two subscribers to the memorandum will suffice to form the company.

The Articles of Association

The articles of association of a registered company must also be supplied to the Registrar of Companies prior to incorporation. Like the Memorandum of Association the Articles will then be included in the company's file kept at Companies House in Cardiff.

The articles are concerned with the internal administration of the company, and it is for those setting up the company (its promoters) to determine the rules they consider appropriate for inclusion within the articles. The Companies Act 1985 does however provide a set of model articles which a company can adopt in whole or in part if it wishes. Matters which are normally dealt with in the Articles include the appointment and powers of the board of directors, the rules in relation to members meetings and voting and the types of shares and rights attaching to the share categories and shareholders.

Once the company has been incorporated the articles may be altered or added to by means of a special resolution which requires a 75% majority of the members voting. Such alterations must however be made bona fide (in good faith) and for the benefit of the company as a whole. This is an important feature of the law regulating companies, for articles constitute a contract between the company and its members and identify members' rights, such as the right to vote. Clearly the ability of the company to change the terms of this contract at some future time may have the effect of placing individual members who might be harmed by such changes, in a disadvantageous position. Thus the courts reserve the power to refuse an alteration to the articles which has such an effect, unless there is a benefit to the company as a whole and the alteration has been made in good faith.

It is relevant to note in this context that a company has two principal sources of control over its affairs. These are the shareholders in general meeting, and the directors. The most important matters affecting the company, for example changes in its constitution, rest with the shareholders in general meeting. Decisions reached at such meetings are arrived at through the putting of resolutions, which are then voted on. Generally a simple majority vote is sufficient to carry them, although some matters of special significance require a 75% majority. Since voting power plays such an important role in company matters the type of shares the company has issued is of considerable significance. Some shares, for example ordinary shares, usually carry full voting rights, however other classes of share, such as preference shares, may carry no voting rights at all and therefore exclude shareholders of that class from effectively influencing the company.

Since all public companies and many private companies consist of numerous members it is impractical to operate the company on a daily basis by means of general meetings. The articles will therefore provide for directors to be responsible for the daily running of the company and usually grant them the right to exercise all the powers of the company. They will remain answerable to the members in a general meeting although acts carried out by the directors within the powers delegated to them under the articles cannot be affected by decisions of a general meeting. So, if the directors have acted contrary to the wishes of the members, the ultimate sanction is to dismiss them or to change the articles and so bring in provisions that restrict the powers of the directors. In small companies the directors will often be the principal or sole shareholders, so that such considerations will not be relevant.

We have seen that a partnership is subject to few statutory regulations and the partners are free to decide for themselves such matters as the conduct of meetings, the keeping of records and accounting methods.

Registered companies limited by shares however, are different. The fundamental principle of accountability of the directors to the members necessarily involves stricter regulation of the company's operation. The Companies Act provides therefore that every company must, in each year, hold an annual general meeting and that every member is entitled to notice of this meeting. In addition, the holders of one-tenth or more of paid-up shares with voting rights may at any time compel the directors to call an extra-ordinary general meeting. The articles usually regulate the procedures to be adopted at these meetings, but in any case the minutes of all meetings must be strictly recorded.

Decisions at general meetings are usually taken by ordinary resolution, that is a majority of voting members present. For some types of business usually related to the company's constitution, such as the alteration of the Articles or objects of the company, a special resolution is necessary which requires a three-quarter majority of voting members.

Each year a company must submit an annual return to the Registrar of Companies which has to include details of the company's share capital, share division, debts secured by mortgages, and a list of members and directors. Also company's legislation contains detailed provisions relating to the preparation of accounts, the information to be included in these accounts, and the need for submission of annual accounts to the general meeting and the Registrar of Companies. Generally the accounting records must be kept at the registered office of the company and must be available for inspection by shareholders. Company accounts must also be audited, and the auditor's report must be read before the company in general meeting, and must be open to inspection by any member. Other documents which a company is obliged to keep include a register of the interests of directors and their service contracts, a register of the company members and debenture holders, and a register of members who have substantial interests in the company, that is, of those who have one-tenth or more of the share capital of the company.

These requirements not only ensure the members are kept informed, but also assist outsiders in assessing the strength of the company prior to investing in it or doing business with it. Investments in a company can be undertaken in two distinct ways.

(a)   By lending money to the company in return for an issue of debentures. A debenture holder is a secured creditor of the company who is entitled to a fixed rate of interest on the investment.

(b)   By taking up shares and becoming a company member. The rights of a shareholder depend upon the type of shares involved but generally a shareholder has the right to receive a proportion of the profit of a company, vote in general meetings and share in the capital of the company if it is wound up.

Position of the Members

We have seen that a shareholder, unlike a partner, will often play no part in the day to day management of the company as this will be the responsibility of its directors. Nevertheless, ultimate control of the business is in the hands of the shareholders by the exercise of voting power in the general meeting.

In any vote which does not produce a unanimous outcome there will be two groups, the majority shareholders and the minority shareholders. In effect it is the majority that make the company decisions. If the minority have a grievance, legally there is little they can do to redress it.

> In *Pavlides v. Jenson and others 1956*, a company sold an asbestos mine for £182,000 when its real value was close to £1,000,000. A minority shareholder brought an action for damages against three directors who were responsible for the sale and against the company, alleging gross negligence. The Court held that the action could not be brought by a minority shareholder because it was the company itself which should decide whether to redress the wrong that had been committed.

The court would not interfere in the internal management of the company. In such circumstances perhaps the only remedy for the member is to sell his or her shares. But sometimes it would be quite inappropriate to deny the claims of minority shareholders and there are a number of situations in which their grievances can be heard and dealt with by the courts.

These include:

    (a) seeking an injunction to restrain the company from acting in an ultra vires manner or so as not to benefit the members;

    (b) preventing the infringement of personal rights (such as voting rights), and where fraud or oppression is being alleged.

An example of the latter can be seen in *Daniels v. Daniels 1978*. Here two company directors, in 1970, instructed the company to sell land to one of them for £4,250. In 1974 the land was resold for £120,000 and a minority shareholder brought an action claiming that damages should be payable to the company. The Court held that despite no allegation of fraud the action by the individual shareholders should be allowed to proceed.

In addition to the common law, the Companies Act confers certain statutory rights on minority shareholders.

An important example of this is the provision which gives a member the right to apply to the court for an order on the ground that the affairs of the company are being or have been conducted in a manner which is unfairly prejudicial to some members (including at least himself), or that any actual or proposed act or omission of the company is or would be prejudicial.

If the case is proved the court may issue a court order which could:

    (a) regulate the companys' affairs for the future;

    (b) require the company to act or refrain from acting in a particular way;

    (c) authorise civil proceedings in the name and on behalf of the company by a person; or

    (d) require the purchase of any member's shares by the company or by other members.

An example of a court order regulating a company's future affairs is seen in *Re: H R Harmer Limited 1959*. The company was run by an elderly father acting as chairman and his two sons as directors. The father had voting control. He largely ignored the wishes of the board of directors and ran the business as his own. On an application by the sons as minority shareholders, alleging oppression, the Court held that relief should be granted. The father was appointed life president of the company without rights, duties or powers and was ordered not to interfere in the company's affairs.

The Position of Directors

The management of a registered company is carried on by the directors who are responsible for policy making, contract making and supervising the company property. Company directors are normally appointed in a manner prescribed in the Articles of Association, for example by the company in general meeting or by the existing directors. The Companies Act 1985 specifically provides, however, that despite anything in the articles to the contrary, a director may be removed by an ordinary resolution. There is nothing to prevent the Articles conferring special voting rights on certain occasions.

In *Bushell v. Faith 1970*, the company had an issued share capital of £300 equally divided between three members. Each share carried one vote. The Articles provided, however, that on a resolution to remove a director, the directors' individual shares should carry three votes per share. Two of the members voted to remove the third from his position as director but were defeated because their 200 votes were cancelled by the individual directors 300 votes. The court held this to be in order.

Directors' Powers

The specific powers of directors are stated in the Articles but in addition to this actual authority to carry out functions, the directors will also have an authority to act which is implied under the law. This is because the director is an agent of the company and can bind it whether he acts within his actual or apparent authority.

Of course if a director enters into an ultra vires transaction on the company's behalf, then whatever his agency powers are the transaction is invalid. This is because it is beyond the company's power to complete the transaction, and the director gains his powers from the company. But if the director merely fails to comply with the internal rules of the company when making a transaction this does not amount to an ultra vires act and the company will be bound.

This principle can be seen in the leading case of *Royal British Bank v. Turquand 1856*. Here a company conferred power on the directors to borrow such sums as were authorised by an ordinary resolution of the general meeting. The directors borrowed money without such a resolution being passed. The court held that the company was bound by the loan and laid down the following basic principles:-

a.   An outsider who is dealing with a company is not bound to inquire whether the internal regulations of the company have been complied with, such as passing resolutions to authorise specific acts. Basically, therefore, an outsider is entitled to assume that the directors have acted properly.

b.   An outsider is not entitled to rely on this presumption if he is aware of the irregularity or ought in the circumstances to have made inquiries.

This aspect of the principle can be seen operating in the two following cases.

In *Howard v. Patent Ivory Manufacturing Co. 1888*, the directors of the company had power to borrow up to £1,000, with larger amounts having to be authorised by the general meeting. The company borrowed £3,500 from the directors without a resolution being passed. The court held that as the directors were aware of the procedural irregularity the borrowing was only valid up to £1,000.

In *Underwood Ltd. v. Bank of Liverpool 1924*, the director of a company paid cheques, made payable to the company, into his personal account. An action was brought against the bank to recover the sums paid. The court held that the bank was not entitled to assume that the director was acting properly, as the circumstances were so unusual that the bank ought to have been suspicious.

Even if an individual has not been actually appointed as director or managing director, should the company, through the directors, expressly or impliedly represent him as such, then as far as the outsider is concerned the individual will have all the apparent authority of a director.

In *Freeman Locyer v. Buckhurst Properties 1964*, an individual director, with the consent of his fellow directors, employed the plaintiff architects to do some work. The director had been held out as managing director although he had not been appointed to this post, and the contract of employment was held to be binding. To enter into such a contract was within the apparent scope of a managing director's power.

Finally, some mention must be made of the effect of s.35 of the Companies Act 1985. The section has the effect of regarding a contract which has been decided on by the directors to be intra vires (within the powers) the company, when dealing with an outsider who is acting in good faith. It seems, therefore, that provided the transaction is decided on by the directors collectively, and the person dealing with the company is acting in good faith, then even if the transaction is ultra vires the directors, it will be binding on the company.

Legal Position of Directors

The position of directors under the law is difficult to define but they have been described as merely commercial men, managing a trading concern, for the benefit of themselves and all other shareholders in it. A director enjoys a fiduciary relationship with the company which means that he is in a position of trust. In his capacity as a director he must act in good faith and for the company as a whole. So if it can be shown that the directors have acted out of their own self interest, then their action may be declared void.

In *Piercy v. S. Mills & Co. Ltd. 1920*, the directors used their powers to issue new voting shares to themselves, solely to acquire majority voting power. The court held that the directors had abused their powers and the allotment was declared void.

To act for the benefit of the company as a whole places a duty on the directors to ensure that any action they take is in the best interests of their organisation rather than improperly favouring one section or sectional interest within the organisation, such as the directors, the employees, or the ordinary shareholders. In carrying out their functions, directors are under a duty to exercise reasonable care by performing their duties to the best of their own abilities and acting with total honesty. They must also ensure that they do not place themselves in such a position that their personal interests and the interests of the company might conflict. In particular a director must not use his position to make a secret profit for himself, for if he does, he will be in breach of his contract of employment, and may also be made to hand over such profit to the company.

In *Boston Deep Sea Fishing & Ice co. v. Ansell 1888*, the managing director of a trawling business received a secret commission on placing an order for the construction of fishing boats. The court held that the company was entitled to the commission.

PUBLIC SECTOR ORGANISATIONS

It has already been seen that the term public sector is very broad embracing a variety of politically and economically important organisations, many of them non-commercial but all of them playing a vital role in the United Kingdom. Here we examine some of them.

GOVERNMENT DEPARTMENTS

It is the Prime Minister's prerogative to determine the administrative organisation of the government which he or she heads. The system which is operated in the United Kingdom involves a division of the administrative workload on functional lines. Each government department, of which there are at present nineteen, is responsible for a specific aspect of state activity. Some of these activities are essentially economic, whilst others are social. Since the war the trend has been towards amalgamating smaller departments into larger ones, often referred to as 'super ministries'. An example was the creation in 1978 of the Department of the Environment.

The role of each department is as an agency for administrating the legislation generated both by Parliament and by the subordinate bodies and individuals granted delegated law making powers by Parliament, for example Secretaries of State.

The personnel of a government department can be categorised into the political office holders, who in theory at least are responsible for formulating policy, and the political civil servants who administer it. In fact there is considerable overlap.

A large department, such as the Department of Employment is headed by a Secretary of State, who is a member of the Cabinet. He or she is assisted by a Minister of State and Under Secretaries of State. The Secretary of State must ultimately account to Parliament for his or her actions and the activities of civil servants within the department.

The consequences of this accountability can be very significant, as evidenced by the resignation of the then Secretary for Trade and Industry, Leon Brittan, over the Westland affair in 1986. The Secretary of State is also accountable before the courts for the actions of civil servants employed within the department. In 1931 the Report of the Royal Commission on the Civil Service defined a civil servant as,

> "a servant of the Crown (not being a holder of a political or judicial office) who is employed in a civil capacity and whose remuneration is found wholly and directly out of money voted by Parliament".

The major characteristics of the Civil Service are that it is permanent, in that is its membership does not alter with changes in government following an election, and that is politically neutral. Obviously the latter element goes a long way towards explaining the former.

It has been argued that the Civil Service is too powerful, often resisting government policies and presenting Ministers with biased information. Conversely it is said that for a politician to become a Minister he or she will be in most cases a powerful personality unlikely to be easily dissuaded from pursuing an identified policy. Whatever the merits of these arguments Mrs. Thatcher had endeavoured to reduce the role of the civil service during her Premiership.

Of the various government departments the most important is the Treasury. Its concern is the implementation of the overall economic strategy being followed by the government, which involves controlling the level of public expenditure, dealing with financial and monetary policy, and economic forecasting.

The Treasury is central to the government's control of finance. Without its approval other departments are unable to increase their expenditure. The effects of its actions are thus felt throughout the public sector, including the public corporations and especially in the local authorities for whom a major source of income derives from central government grants, notably the block grant introduced under the Local Government Planning and Land (No. 2) Act 1980.

LOCAL GOVERNMENT

Government at the local level is carried out by means of local authorities, which are corporate bodies, whose structure, composition and responsibilities are regulated by statute, principally the Local Government Act 1972. As corporate bodies local authorities are subject to the ultra vires principle.

Councillors

All local authorities, whether they be district or county councils or London boroughs consist of two distinct groups of individuals who operate them. These are the elected members, the Councillors, who like their political counterparts in control of government departments, are responsible for determining, within the scope of the functions of the authority, the policies it is to pursue, and there are the officers of the authority who administer its functions. Local authority councillors are elected to office every three years. For the most part they are members of a political party. Their work is unpaid, although they are entitled to certain allowances and expenses, such as attendance allowance for time spent on council business. Councillors are, like M.P's, answerable ultimately to the electorate, and they hold 'surgeries' like M.P's to enable the people they represent to present problems and grievances. A councillor can be disqualified from office for non attendance at council meetings.

. . . to present problems and grievances . . .

Since the range of work for which an authority is responsible is very wide it is not possible for the full council to supervise it effectively, and so the bulk of its work is discharged through the use of a system of committees and sub-committees, on which councillors sit. Typical examples of such committees are housing, education, social services, highways, and planning. Most authorities will also include a policy and resources committee which will oversee the work of the other departments in order to ensure that the corporate plan of the council is being fulfilled. This committee will be directly accountable to the full council. The existence of a corporate plan will have involved an attempt at identifying the aims and objectives of the organisation and a recognition of the need for a form of corporate management. The same process occurs within business organisations operating in the private sector, as we have seen earlier in the chapter.

Since a local authority is a corporate body it is distinct from the members (the Councillors) who make it up. It follows that councillors, like shareholders, are not legally liable for the wrongs committed by their organisation. However, if the wrong in question was clearly authorised by the authority, an award of damages against it may have to be made good by the members who authorised it. In some circumstances members who are responsible for incurring expenditure that is ultra vires the authority can be surcharged; that is legally obliged to repay the amout out of their own pockets.

Officers

Local authorities are granted the power under the Local Government Act 1972 to appoint, "such officers as they think necessary", for the discharge of the authority's functions. An officer of an authority is a paid employee, like the civil servant working within central government departments, and enjoys the rights granted to employees under the Employment Protection (Consolidation) Act 1978.

The most senior officer of an authority is the Chief Executive, who is responsible to the Council for the co-ordination of the work carried out by the Chief Officers, the individuals responsible for administering the individual departments, for example the Director of Housing. Within such departments there are sections, and staff working in the department are employed on a graded career structure.

Although officers act under the supervision of the council and its committees it is a common practice to delegate powers to them, the effect of which is to grant them express authority to bind the council by acts carried out within the powers granted. Indeed this is not the only circumstance in which an officer can act as an agent on behalf of his or her employing authority. There may be circumstances in which an officer can bind the authority by acts that come within his apparent authority (i.e. the authority that to an outsider it would be reasonable to assume he or she holds). This parallels the position within the private sector. Thus when a member of the public makes enquiries of the Highways Department about a proposed road widening scheme, and is negligently advised by an officer that it is not taking place and suffers loss as a result, the negligence of the officer will be treated as the negligence of the authority. This is an example of the doctrine of vicarious liability, under which an employer can be held responsible for the acts of employees committed within the course of their employment.

One circumstance in which it is not possible for an authority to be bound in this way is where the council, or its committee, have a statutory discretion in exercising its functions. An example is the discretion granted to planning committees in determining planning applications. Were a planning officer to be able to bind his authority by comments made about planning matters to a member of the public it could have the effect of preventing the committee from exercising the function Parliament demands of it, by binding it in advance.

> An example can be seen in *Western Fish Products v. Penwith District Council 1978* where the council's chief planning officer indicated to the Company that the use to which it was putting its factory did not require it to seek planning consent. Subsequently the council did require a planning application to be made, which it then turned down, thus preventing the company from legitimately continuing with its business operations. The company claimed that the council was bound by the planning officer's original assertion, but the court took the view that to allow this would be to prevent the council from fulfilling its statutory planning duties, by tying the hands of the planning committee.

THE ACCOUNTABILITY OF ORGANISATIONS

At the beginning of the Chapter we saw that one of the characteristics common to all organisations is accountability. In the conclusion to the Chapter we examine some of the features of accountability as it affects organisational activity.

THE MEANING OF ACCOUNTABILITY

When we talk about accountability we are concerned about two things — how to determine the nature af an organisation's responsibilities and to whom it is responsible. Probably it is appropriate to add additional components. What consequences follow from an organisation's failure to fulfil its responsibilities? Are there measures that can be taken against it, and if so what are they, who can institute them, and how will they affect the organisation?

The idea of accountability is very basic to human nature. Throughout one's life occasions arise when it is necessary to answer for one's actions. This is as true for the business executive whose handling of an important agreement is being challenged by his Board of Directors as it is for a child who fails to present his or her homework when it is required. Usually the nature of accountability rests firmly upon a belief that we have a personal responsibility for our individual actions, which derives from a freedom of choice of action. The business executive had options available to him in the negotiation of the agreement but failed to secure the account because he followed the wrong one; the child could have used the time devoted to playing with friends to complete the homework instead. If there was no real choice available then it would be wrong to hold an individual responsible for what was in fact the only course of action that could be taken. But where alternatives present themselves, then it is in order to judge people retrospectively in accordance with the choice that they made.

But we need some criteria by which to make the judgement. Thus we may say of the business executive that he should be responsible for making the wrong decision because he is employed to make the right decisions, it is his job to do so. The problem with this is that terms such as right and wrong are value judgements. They will vary from person to person according to what one regards as being right and wrong. Hence what we need in order to establish an efficient system of accountability is a predetermined set of quantifiable statements which we can use as a yardstick against which to measure a person's, or organisation's behaviour. Put another way accountability only makes sense if there are clearly defined ground rules which regulate the activity. This may be as simple as the teacher telling the children that the only acceptable ground for failing to complete homework is evidence that an unsuccessful attempt has been made at it, or as complex as the Board of Directors telling the business executive that they feel his experience and competence has entitled him to represent the company in its negotiations and that the successful negotiations will maintain the financial viability of the organisation for the next year.

It may be helpful to consider your own role within the organisation you work for or the college at which you are studying and recognise the rules of the game that are being applied in terms of your accountability. Are you able to identify clearly what is expected of you and therefore when it might be that you should have to answer for not meeting those expectations. If you can do so how far are the expectations realistic, and who imposes them? They will usually be external controls, but of course we all operate self assessment mechanisms by which we act as judges of our own conduct and hold ourselves accountable even when others would not, setting standards quite distinct from those operated by the organisation employing us. In this way it may be that a person is held accountable for conduct which he or she believes is quite appropriate to the situation, but which the employer does not. If we finally return to our business executive he may be of the opinion that the lost contract occurred in spite of his best endeavours to prevent its loss, but the Board of Directors may not share his perception and attach responsibility to him either out of belief that he was genuinely at fault, or perhaps for more subtle reasons, for instance to use him as an example to others or to sacrifice him as a scapegoat.

METHODS OF CLASSIFYING ACCOUNTABILITY

It has been seen so far that accountability may operate at both an internal (self evaluating) or external level. If we look more closely at the external level it becomes clear that there are a variety of forms of accountability which have a functional foundation to them. It is useful to examine the functional aspect through a comparison between the public and private sectors. If we take the example of a manufacturing industry operated by a public limited company we can identify at least five distinct groups for whom the operations of the company give rise to issues of accountability. They are:

(i)   the capital contributors, in other words the shareholders or members, who are looking for a management of their organisation which will enhance the value of their interests and provide them with a satisfactory return on their investment;

(ii)   the managers themselves, the directors, formulating company policy, implementing management decisions and keeping under review the operations of the company;

(iii)   the employees of the company, following the directions given by the management and executing the work of their organisation;

(iv)   the clients and customers of the company, supplying it with goods and services, and consuming its products; and

(v)   the creditors of the company, ranging from suppliers owed money for contracts fulfilled to financial institutions that have provided capital on a secured basis (e.g. through debenture arrangements). Into this final group can be added the Inland Revenue with its legitimate claims for tax on profits, and the local authority in respect of rates on company premises.

Between each of these quite separate groups, a complex relationship of functional accountability emerges. The directors are answerable to the shareholders for the decisions they make, employees are answerable ultimately to the Board if they fail to fulfil their job specifications. The company as a whole is answerable to its creditors and its customers in the event of it failing to meet their legitimate demands and requirements. In each case the function being fulfilled by the group tells us something about the nature of its accountability. Its function is what it exists to achieve and if it fails to achieve it then measures are needed to overcome the failure. If the Board do not capably manage then a general meeting may seek to censure them or even dismiss them. If an employee is incompetent at his or her job a dismissal may be appropriate. If a payment due to a creditor is not forthcoming the creditor may seek to realise the security to which the loan is attached, or alternatively take legal action against the company, a remedy also available to customers who purchase faulty products from the company. Likewise accountability for local and national taxes is ultimately determinable before the courts.

In the public sector functional accountability is equally apparent, although by its nature the public sector pursues aims and objectives which do not always parallel the private sector, hence the nature and forms of its responsibilities are not always identical. Many public sector organisations pursue social rather than economic objectives, and because they are controlled directly or indirectly by political masters they demonstrate characteristics quite distinct from those of organisations controlled by investors.

In the same way that a system of accountability operates within private sector organisations, similar systems operate within the public sector. In a limited company we have seen how the organisation is ultimately controlled by its owners, the shareholders, to whom the managers of business, the directors, have to account when called upon to do so. The underlying feature of such accountability is the desire of the owners to see the assets of their business being managed in a manner appropriate with their investment aims. These of course may vary considerably. A large institutional investor such as a pension fund will look for a safe investment with an average return, whilst some smaller investor may be prepared to risk their capital in entrepreneurial ventures which could greatly increase the value of their holdings if the venture is successful, or lose them everything if it fails. Whatever the specific aim may be in investing there is an inescapable economic truth which operates throughout the private sector; investors are using money to try and make more money. Capital is being directed into ways to increase itself.

The public sector does not always reflect this approach, but before considering the system of accountability in the public sector, we first need to identify the types of organisation that occupy it. Probably the most striking feature of this sector is its diversity. In it we find manufacturing and service industries, some of them operating as monopolists such as British Rail, others competing in a free market such as British Airways. We also find the departments of central government, the local authorities, the health authorities, the police force, and a variety of other centrally created national organisations known as quangos (quasi-autonomous national government organisations). An example of a quango is the Manpower Services Commission (MSC). With such diversity it is not easy to place each organisation within a slot that tells us precisely what the organisation does, who controls it, who funds it and to whom it is accountable. But presumably since all these organisations are referred to as 'public' they share some common characteristic.

The expression 'public' is in fact somewhat misleading. It is really used in two senses. It may indicate the type of interest the organisation is in existence to serve, thus we speak of a local authority as an organisation providing a public service since its functions include operating an education system to which all children between 5 and 16 years are statutorily entitled, a housing function with an obligation to accommodate certain categories of homeless person, and a variety of other functions imposing responsibilities upon it toward all the inhabitants of its area, such as providing library and sports facilities, refuse collection, and highways repair and maintenance. The local authority's role is to meet the specified needs of all who reside within the district for which it has responsibility.

Moreover, the obligation to meet these needs is imposed by statutes, most of which are public statutes and statutory instruments (laws created by government departments and Ministers) dealing with health, housing, education, planning, highways, social services and other matters.

Central government departments may also be said to be 'public' bodies in this sense, and while they do not generally become involved in physically implementing the functions that are listed above, they are nevertheless responsible for ensuring that these functions are carried out in a manner in keeping with the policy of the department in question. The relationship between central and local government is sometimes described as a partnership. Since central government provides a substantial contribution to the finances of local government, and is thus able to exercise a degree of control over its activities, central government may be regarded as the senior partner in the relationship.

Each individual government department, unlike a local authority, has a responsibility to the United Kingdom as a whole. Thus whilst individual local authorities deal with planning applications in respect of their areas which are dealt with by planning committees, the Department of the Environment is responsible for an overall planning policy. It will for example issue departmental circulars to all local authorities advising them of such matters as planning procedures to be followed, and requiring statistical information from them, such as the length of time taken to process planning applications.

The other sense in which public may be used is by reference to ownership. British Rail is a public, as opposed to a private body, since it is said to be in public ownership. What this means in practice is that its assets are not owned by private individuals but by the State. It would appear to follow that each of us should therefore have some control over the way in which it is managed, as shareholders have, but this is not so. Apart from other considerations, such a system would be unworkable. In fact it is Parliament that manages state owned industries, as the representative of the public. Again, in practice, this means the government of the day. The government must account to Parliament for the management of nationalised industries, almost like a board of directors to its shareholders, but with the difference that since the government holds the majority of votes in Parliament it should normally be able to manage as it sees fit, without the fear of censure. Some industries that operate through registered companies, such as British Petroleum, straddle the divide between the public and private sectors. BP is a public limited company with a large percentage of its shares owned by the state. The rest are privately owned. As in any shareholding arrangement the larger the shareholding the greater the control the owner has over the operations of the organisation.

Many company decisions can be achieved by a simple majority therefore a stake of over 50% gives a controlling interest to the shareholder. The government's control of partially state owned industries is often considerable.

To conclude therefore you should recognise that an examination of an organisation by looking at its accountability not only tells us about the nature of the organisation's responsibilities but also a great deal about its objectives and structure.

ASSIGNMENT — THE ADVISORY UNIT

Hansborough suffers from a high level of unemployment, and the council is anxious to promote industrial and commercial activity in the area. At a full meeting of the Council two months ago it was resolved to set up a small advisory unit in premises in the city centre to provide information and assistance to people interested in establishing new businesses. You have been seconded to the unit from your post in the Administrative and Legal Department of the Council, for a period of six months. Including yourself, the unit has a staff of three.

During its first month of operation the unit has had to deal with a wide range of questions and has given assistance to a large number of individuals. To assist in the advisory process it has been decided to produce a 'Business Start up' booklet in which a number of the more obvious matters of concern could be included. It is thought that a question and answer format would be most appropriate for the booklet. You have been given the responsibility for the production of the booklet.

TASKS

1. Draft the questions and answers to be included in the booklet. Examples of matters you should cover include the meaning of the expression 'business', the various legal forms of business, the formalities involved in business formation and the difference between corporate and non-corporate bodies.

2. As a section of the booklet you should identify the sources of finance available to a new business and the problems involved in raising finance from such sources.

3. The final part of the booklet should explain the importance of a business plan and outline the contents of such a plan.

DEVELOPMENTAL TASKS

4. Decide upon the information that you feel should be included on the front, back and inside covers of the booklet and draft the layout of the cover. Bear in mind that the size of the cover must not exceed 5 inches wide by 6 inches deep.

5. City Printers, a local printing company has contracted with the council to produce the booklet. You are required to meet with Chris Beardsley, the company's graphic artist to decide on the booklet's final format. Prior to this meeting produce a set of notes which set out your ideas on the total layout of the booklet so that you can clearly communicate your thoughts to Mr Beardsley.

ASSIGNMENT — THE SUMMER FESTIVAL

Northchester City Council organises an annual Summer Festival in the City. This year, as part of the festival, the council organised and provided sponsorship for a rock concert. The concert was held three weeks ago and it has given rise to certain issues which the Administration and Legal Department of the Council has to deal with. The nature of these issues can be appreciated by reading the following documents.

L.A. Rich ACCA **Chartered Accountant**	**Breams Buildings** **West End** **Denton Grove** **Manchester**

The Director of Administrative and Legal Services
Northchester City Council
City Hall
Northchester   *9th June 1986*

Dear Sir,

I have been appointed as Liquidator of Jumping Jack Records Ltd. I understand that you are owed the sum of £600 by the company for a licence you granted to it to operate a small sales unit at the Northchester Rock Concert, from which it sold tee shirts, badges and similar items.

It is my view that the company lacked the authority to enter into this licence agreement. Its objects clause provides that:

"The objects for which the company is established are: to carry on and undertake the business of phonographic materials retailers: and to carry on any trade, business or mercantile operation which in the opinion of the directors may be incident, auxilliary or conducive to the above objects."

In the circumstances I must reject all liability for the licence fees due.

Yours faithfully,

L.A.Rich

L.A. Rich
Liquidator

CITY COUNCIL
ADMINISTRATIVE & LEGAL SERVICES DEPT.

MEMORANDUM

From: Senior Solicitor   Date: 11 June 1986

To: Clerical Officer   Ref: Rock Concert

You may recall that the Council engaged the firm of O'Brien & Co. to provide special lighting effects at the rock concert, but that at the last minute the firm failed to provide us with its services. A letter claiming financial compensation was sent by the Council to the firm last week. We have received a reply by telephone from Mr Johnson, one of the partners. He indicates that his firm disclaims any liability. His reason is that the agreement was negotiated by his co-partner, Mr O'Brien, who had no authority to enter into it, and did so whilst Mr Johnson was away on holiday. Can you follow this up, as I have no time to deal with it.

Telephone Message

Taken by: Janet Middleton, Telephonist

To: Legal Section: Date: 13 June 1986

A Mr Lorenzo has telephoned. He is the owner of the Pizzaria Bonavista, opposite the City Hall. He says that a senior official of the Council indicated to him prior to the rock concert that it would be in order for him to sell alcoholic drinks on the day of the concert, without an 'on-licence'. He has now been told by the police that they are intending to prosecute him for this licencing offence. He is very angry and holds the Council responsible.

TASKS

In your capacity as a clerical officer in the Administration and Legal Services Department you are required by the Senior Solicitor in the Department, to examine each of these issues with a view to him taking further action.

1. Draft a letter in reply to the liquidator's letter in which you set out the council's reason for rejecting the liquidator's argument.

2. Draft a written response to Mr Johnson's telephone communication with the Council refuting his disclaimer of liability.

3. Provide the Senior Solicitor with a memorandum outlining Mr Lorenzo's complaint, and setting out your view on whether the Council is responsible in any way.

Chapter 19

THE RESOURCES OF AN ORGANISATION

To be able to effectively operate, all organisations require resources. These include its workforce, the organisation's premises, any materials or equipment used and of course, finance. Each of these has its own particular characteristics in terms of the way in which it will be managed. For example the meticulous financial manager may prove to be rather less successful in his management of people yet each is characterised by the fact that it will cost the organisation money to acquire. Because of this the able manager must be competent in the processes of acquiring resources, managing their operation and disposing of them once they have served the organisation's purpose. Therefore this chapter is concerned with a classification of the resources an organisation could need; an examination of the legal processes involved in the acquisition of such resources; an analysis of the different styles which could be adopted in the managing of resources and some of the issues and problems which arise from resource management; and finally a consideration of the disposal of resources and the termination of a business organisation. As chapters 11 to 17 are concerned with the acquisition, management and control of the organisation's finances, this chapter will be restricted to a consideration of the organisation's other resources.

THE CLASSIFICATION OF RESOURCES

The traditional economic classification of the resources that are available to an organisation to produce goods and services are land, labour and capital. Land is the economic term used to describe all natural resources so that water, airspace and raw materials used in manufacturing such as iron ore, copper and oil come within the classification. Furthermore all producers need sites from which their work can be done. A farmer requires agricultural land, a local authority requires offices, and an industrialist needs an industrial site. Even a fisherman needs a stretch of ocean in which to cast his nets. The raw materials used by man in his productive processes and the land from which they come, have all been provided by nature. Natural non-human resources may, however, be improved and developed by man and may have a number of alternative uses.

Capital is the term used by economists to describe all the non-human and non-natural resources of an organisation. Within this classification are the assets of an organisation. These include money and debts but also a wide range of items such as machinery, tools, vehicles, goodwill, typewriters and even the factory buildings and offices from which an organisation operates.

The third and, some would say, the most important economic resource of an organisation is its human resources. Human resources are classified as 'labour'. The mental and manual skills of an organisation's workforce can also be improved and developed and may have a number of alternative uses.

The processes by which these factors of production are acquired and the consequences arising from their use is the subject matter of this chapter, but before each item is considered in turn it is helpful to be aware of how resources are classified under the law.

Anything capable of ownership under English law is classified as 'property', for example, land, buildings, cars, debts etc. Human resources are necessarily excluded from the classification. Many European countries have adopted the most obvious means of classifying property by distinguishing between moveable property such as goods, shares, cheques, etc, and immoveable property for instance, land and buildings. Unfortunately the English classification of property is not so simple due mainly to the historical development of English land law which has continued over 900 years. Under the English principles the basic division is between Real and Personal property. The diagram below illustrates this classification.

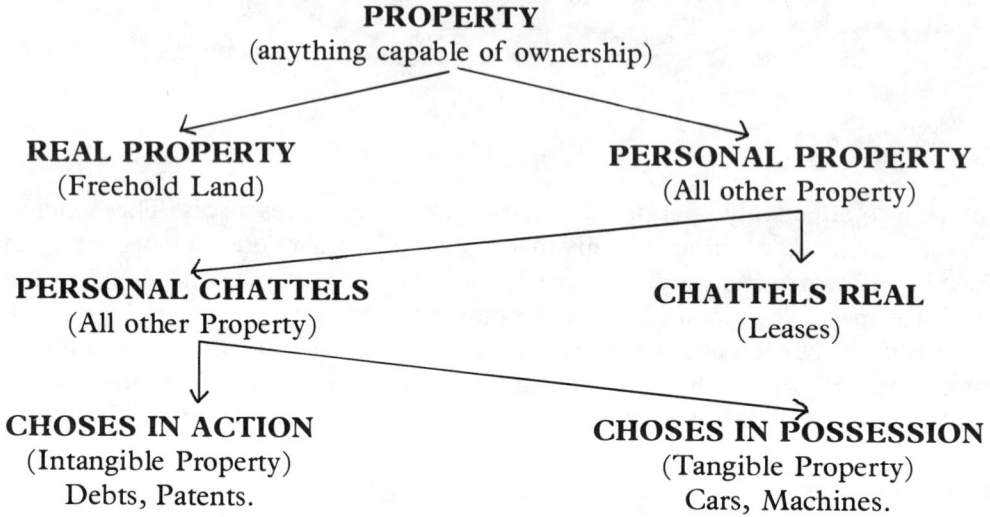

PROPERTY
(anything capable of ownership)

REAL PROPERTY
(Freehold Land)

PERSONAL PROPERTY
(All other Property)

PERSONAL CHATTELS
(All other Property)

CHATTELS REAL
(Leases)

CHOSES IN ACTION
(Intangible Property)
Debts, Patents.

CHOSES IN POSSESSION
(Tangible Property)
Cars, Machines.

The Classification of Property

The only category of real property is Freehold land (considered later) because originally it was the only type of property which was protected by a Real action in court. This meant that if a freehold owner was wrongfully dispossessed of his land, he could bring court action to recover the land itself rather than compensation for its loss. For all other types of property, personal property, originally if an owner was wrongfully dispossessed, he could only rely on a court action which gave him no right to recover the property lost and had to be content with compensation. As early as the 15th century however, the courts began to recognise exceptions to this rule, so that today, an owner wrongfully dispossessed of personal property can normally recover the thing lost. The classification of real and personal property however remains the same! Real property then is freehold land, and any form of property which is not freehold land is classified as personal property.

Personal Property

Personal property (technically known as chattels) is further sub-divided into chattels real (leases) and chattels personal (all other personal property). We shall consider the main characteristics of leases later in this chapter when we compare freehold estates and leasehold estates in land. As far as chattels personal are concerned, there is one further sub-division into Choses in Action (intangible property, e.g. cheques, debts, patents, copyright, goodwill) and Choses in Possession (tangible property, e.g. cars, typewriters, radios, etc.). The word "chose" comes from the French for "thing" and a chose in action is simply a thing which may be owned but has no physical existence. Choses in action may form a major part of the assets of an organisation and may be of great value to it, but being non tangible they can only be enforced by court action if the owner's rights are infringed.

a. Choses in Action

1. **Debts.** Debts owed to an organisation will form part of its current assets and the payment of a debt can be enforced by court action. In addition, debts can be transferred for value to someone else by assignment (this is simply a form of transfer).

2. **Shares.** A share represents the interests of a shareholder in a company and, in public companies, they are freely transferable for value whereas, in private companies, there may be some restriction on their transfer.

3. **Patents.** A patent has the effect of granting to the patent-holder (inventor) a legal monopoly over the production of the patented product. The holder's rights are contained in the Patent Act 1977.

4. **Copyrights.** A copyright has the effect of granting to the owner a legal monopoly over the reproduction of the subject matter to prevent copying, e.g. books, songs, films. Copyright is dealt with by the Copyright Act 1956.

5. **Goodwill.** Goodwill may be described as the value of an organisation's trade custom and trade connection. It will normally be valued on the sale of a business and included as a purchased asset.

b. Choses in Possession

These are things that have tangible existence and, therefore, can be transferred by physical delivery. An owner wrongfully dispossessed of a chose in possession could therefore recover the thing without the need for court action, e.g. repossess a car where the hirer, in a contract for hire purchase, defaults on payment. This class of property includes all types of tangible property such as goods, vehicles, animals, and furniture.

The legal classification of property therefore draws no distinction between national and man-made resources. While an economist would classify offices or a factory as capital goods, as they are non natural resources, the law regards buildings on land as part of the land. For the purpose of this chapter we shall adopt the economic classification of resources and consider the acquisition and use of human, natural and non natural resources.

THE ACQUISITION OF RESOURCES

The legal mechanism by which the resources of land, labour and capital are acquired is the contract. Here it is proposed to devote our attention to contracts concerning land and contracts of employment. The means by which an organisation can acquire finance is dealt with in chapter 12.

As far as land is concerned it should be stressed that while the term 'land' to an economist signifies only natural resources, for the purposes of acquisition, structures on land, while man made, are regarded as part of the land itself. Furthermore, as a general rule, the air above and everything beneath the surface is also part of land, subject to certain limitations. A distinction may also be drawn between the use of land for housing or as a base from which to operate a business and the use of land as a consumable natural resource, for instance, for the extraction of minerals.

FORMS OF LAND OWNERSHIP

Technically, all land is owned by the Crown, so when an organisation or individual purchases land, it is acquiring a legal estate. An estate is the measure of a person's interest in land from the point of view of time. Basically, there are two main types of estate under English law, freehold estates and leasehold estates.

a.   The Freehold

The main characteristic of this estate is that it is of uncertain duration. The two categories of freehold estate are:

1.   the life estate, which will last for the life of the owner; and

2.   the 'fee simple' estate, which is the freehold estate which we normally associate with absolute ownership of land. The term 'fee simple' means that the estate is inheritable and not subject to any conditions. Holders of a fee simple have the right to sell or leave their estate to anyone they wish.

b.   The Leasehold

The main characteristic of this estate is that it is of certain duration or capable of being made certain, thus a lease for ten years will expire after ten years and a monthly tenancy by giving a month's notice. Leasehold is held under the terms (covenants) of a lease, the effect of which is to give the tenant the right to occupy the land to the exclusion of all others, including the landlord. When the period of the lease expires or in the case of a periodic tenancy, one party gives notice (e.g. a monthly tenant gives one month's notice), the landlord has the right to re-occupy the land subject to the rights of a tenant to security of tenure (i.e. the tenant remains in possession). The rights of a private residential tenant to security of tenure after the contractual lease has expired are contained in the Rent Act 1977. Under the Housing Act 1980, the council tenant of a local authority has equivalent security of tenure. As far as a business tenant is concerned, his rights to security are contained in the Landlord and Tenant Act 1954, Part II, which we shall examine later.

Leases impose on the parties to them contractual obligations, some of which are expressly agreed in the lease and some implied under the common law and by statute. In the case of a business lease, the express terms usually relate to such matters as the payment of rent and rent review, the right to transfer the lease or sublet, the obligations to repair, and a restrictive covenant relating to the particular use to which the premises may be put.

In addition to express terms, except in so far as the lease provides otherwise, certain terms are implied under the common law. It is implied that the landlord will:

1.   not interfere with the tenant's enjoyment of the land by harrassing in any way;

2.   not derogate from his grant (i.e. detract from the value of the premises) by commiting an act which makes the premises less fit for the purpose for which they were let;

3.   ensure that furnished premises are fit for human habitation on the commencement of the lease.

As far as the tenant is concerned, it is implied that he will:

1.   pay those rates and taxes that the landlord is not obliged to pay;

2.   treat the property in a 'tenant-like manner' which involves doing the repairs to the premises you would expect a reasonable tenant with the same lease to carry out.

Failure to comply with the express or implied covenants in a lease may entitle the party who has suffered to bring an action for damages or in some cases to terminate the lease.

Anyone wishing to acquire a freehold or leasehold estate has to enter into a contract for its purchase. Contracts for the sale of land, to be legally binding, require written evidence under the Law of Property Act 1925.

The usual procedure is that an oral agreement for the sale of land is entered into and the formal contract is drawn up at a later stage after certain matters have been investigated by the purchaser's solicitor. Prior to the formal contract, the land is "sold subject to contract". The rule relating to the requirement of written evidence is subject to one major exception — it is called the 'rule of part-performance'. All this means is that if one party to the contract has performed an act which clearly demonstrates his intention to sell or purchase, this act may be sufficient to persuade a court to enforce the contract by ordering specific performance of it, in other words require the party to fulfil his obligations under the contract. Such an act could be spending money on the land, or moving in.

In *Rawlinson v. Ames 1925*, the prospective tenant of property required the landlord to carry out conversion work which the tenant supervised. On completion of the work, the prospective tenant backed out. The court held that the act of the landlord, in paying for the conversion for the prospective tenant's benefit, was a sufficient act of part-performance to require the tenant to enter into the lease, and awarded specific performance.

In *Wakeham v. McKenzie 1968*, the court awarded specific performance in the following circumstances. A widower of 72 asked his neighbour, a widow of 67, to come and look after him with the promise that he would leave his property to her when he died. The widow left her council flat and moved in agreeing to pay "her own board and her share of the coal". The widower died but there was no provision in his will leaving the property to the unfortunate old lady. The court ordered that the property should be transferred to her because of her act of part-performance in leaving her council flat and looking after the old man in return for his promise.

The decision in *Patel v. Ali 1984*, raised the general question as to the court's discretion to refuse an order of specific performance. The defendant agreed to sell her dwelling-house to the plaintiff. Four years after the contracts were exchanged however, there was still no completion and so the plaintiffs applied for an order of specific performance of the contract. The reasons for the delay were numerous including the bankruptcy of the defendant's husband, her serious illness, the fact that she had given birth to two children and her inability to communicate in English. The grant of an order of specific performance was reversed on appeal, the court deciding that there would be extraordinary hardship on the defendant if the order were upheld. The appeal court confirmed that hardship subsequent to entering into the contract could be taken into account in determining whether to grant the order.

As we have seen the contract is only the first stage in the purchase of a legal estate for it is simply the agreement to buy and sell. To transfer a legal estate, a deed of conveyance is necessary. This is a detailed description of the property transfer and has the effect of transferring the ownership. In contrast, a leasehold for a term of less than three years may be transferred without the need for a deed of conveyance.

FREEHOLD LAND (RIGHTS AND RESTRICTIONS)

As previously mentioned the holder of a fee simple freehold estate is for all practical purposes regarded as the absolute owner of a piece of land having the right to possession of the surface of the land, the air space above and the earth below. Nevertheless, the freehold owner is subject to many restrictions, particularly in relation to the use to which he may put the land.

The following rights are recognised:

a.   the right to minerals underneath the surface.

This right is restricted by the Crown's claim to gold, silver or petroleum and the rights of the State to coal.

b.   the right to possession of the air space above the surface.

This right is limited by the Civil Avaiation Act 1949 which provides that aircraft have a statutory authority to fly over the land at a reasonable height.

c.   the right to water.

The owner of land which adjoins a river enjoys certain rights with other owners called riparian rights. Generally a riparian owner may take water from a river in unrestricted quantities if it is used for ordinary purposes connected with the land. There is no right however for a riparian owner to take water for purposes not connected with the land.

d.   the right to treasure trove.

The Crown has a claim to all treasure trove found in the land, including gold or silver in any manufactured form which has been deliberately hidden and where the owner is unknown. If coins or objects have been lost however they are not regarded as treasure trove.

e.   the right to develop the land.

A freeholder is subject to the control of the local planning authority under the Town and Country Planning Act 1971 in relation to any proposed development of the land. Planning permission is required for any material alterations of buildings on land or the use to which they are put. If an individual is considering acquiring a piece of land, there is a means by which he can obtain outline planning permission for any proposed development to ascertain whether full planning permission is likely to be granted. The local authority will ensure minimum building standards by requiring that building regulations are complied with.

f.   the right to ownership.

Wide powers are conferred on local authorities with regard to the compulsory purchase of land. A freeholder can be required to sell his interests in the land to a local authority exercising compulsory purchase powers, usually in order to facilitate some development scheme. An owner can, of course, object to a compulsory purchase order and then a Public Local Inquiry will have to be held to consider the views of those affected. Such inquiries are conducted by an inspector who will recommend a course of action to the appropriate Minister (the Secretary of State for the Environment) and his decision is final.

g.   the right to use the land for his own purposes.

When a freehold estate in land is sold the parties may enter into covenants which bind the land, often for the benefit of land retained by the seller, for instance to use the land only for the purposes of a private dwelling house. Generally, if such restrictive covenants are registered at the Central Land Registry (this is known as a land charge) a subsequent purchaser of the freehold estate is taken to be aware of them and is bound by them. They remain enforceable by the holder of the land which benefits from then ((e.g. one piece of land may benefit from a restriction on building on another piece of land). Usually when land is developed, e.g. a housing estate is built the developer requires each purchaser to enter into restrictive covenants designed to maintain the general character of the estate and the value of the property on it. These covenants often prevent owners from keeping boats and caravans in their front drives and require the grass to be cut regularly. Every holder of a freehold property on the housing estate can enforce such covenants against every other holder. There are, however, statutory provisions which ensure that in some cases, restrictive covenants can be modified or discharged with or without the payment of compensation. The matter is dealt with by the Lands Tribunal which takes into account the changes in the character of the neighbourhood or the fact that the covenant impedes some reasonable user of the land.

Easements are rights which may exist over land normally as part of a land transaction or special agreement, but in some cases by implication if the easement has been in existence for more than twenty years. An easement can confer the right to use the land of another in a particular way, a positive easement, like a right of way, or the right to prevent another from using his land in a particular way, a negative easement, such as a right of light to prevent building on an adjacent property. Easements, like restrictive covenants, may bind successive owners of the land but in all cases, to be valid, there must be one piece of land which enjoys the benefit of the easement and one piece of land which bears the burden.

Finally the law recognises that a balance has to be struck between the rights of an owner to use his land for his own purposes and the rights of adjoining occupiers and the public. Possible legal liability arising from the use of land is considered later in the chapter.

Many of the above restrictions also apply to the leasehold estate whether as a periodic tenancy or a long fixed term lease. As previously stated the lease or tenancy agreement will expressly impose obligations and restrictions on the tenant or lessee. A residential tenant will normally be restricted to using the premises for residential purposes only. A business lessee will be required to operate a particular form of business on the premises and only adopt a change of use with the landlord's permission. In relation to improvements or alterations to the structure, the lessee has much less discretion than the freeholder and generally must seek the landlord's permission before any work is carried out. Also a tenant may not only incur liability in relation to adjoining occupiers for nuisance and annoyance but will also be in breach of the lease or tenancy for which the landlord may be entitled to evict.

HUMAN RESOURCES (LABOUR AS A FACTOR OF PRODUCTION)

Of all the factors of production which an organisation requires to produce goods or services, usually the most important is its workforce. Any organisation needs a workforce willing to contribute its skill, expertise and work in return for a wage or salary. Obviously, some forms of production may be capital intensive, that is require substantially more plant or machinery than labour. However even in these cases there is still a need for managers to ensure the smooth running of the process. Most organisations have a varied workforce ranging from managerial staff and administrators to blue collar workers manning or maintaining the production lines. The problem facing all organisations is how much labout to employ.

The Demand for Labour

Labour is not demanded for its own sake but because it can help to produce goods and services which consumers and society needs. The demand for labour is a derived demand and it will depend on the level of demand for the product or service which it helps to supply. As this increases or decreases so does the demand for labour. As the demands of UK industry for steel have decreased so has the demand for labour in the steel industry. Factors which will influence the demand of an organisation for labour include a worker's potential productivity, specialist skills, wage rates and the availability of alternative factor of production. The supply of labour throughout the country will also depend on a number of factors such as population size, age distribution, relative sex distribution and the willingness of people to seek employment. It is possible to consider the supply of labour in relation to the economy as a whole, to a particular industry or occupation, or to a specific region.

The Supply of Labour

This will depend upon the number of workers and their activity rate. The number of workers is determined by the size of the population who are of employment age (usually 16-65) and this will depend upon changes in the birth rate, death rate and immigration and emigration from the UK. Of course not all the population can work. People are restricted by law from working full-time under the age of 16 and workers may be required to retire at 65. Other people such as students, those engaged in bringing up families may not wish to find employment and some cannot work because they cannot find a job or are physically unfit. These people are economically inactive, however if wages rose sufficiently they could be attracted to a job. They are normally regarded as a secondary source of workers.

The Determination of Wage Rates

It is the interaction of the demand and supply for labour which is the most important determining factor in establishing rates of pay in specific occupations, particular areas and in the economy as a whole.

Certain types of work require highly specialised skills. These may have to be acquired through a process of study, training or apprenticeship. Because of the difficulties involved in acquiring such skills, the supply of suitably qualifed workers will be limited. If society continues to demand such workers they are able to ask for high rates of pay. Examples of this include computer staff, doctors or lawyers.

Conversely the demand for labour in a specific region may be faling as the traditional employers are closed or require fewer workers. This can result in certain areas such as Scotland or the North East of England having wage rates which are below the national average. Clearly the level of unemployment in a region will have a significant effect on the prevailing wage rate. This problem of regional unemployment is discussed in detail in chapter 25.

A further important factor in determining wage rates in a particular industry is the power of the trade unions. In industries which have a high proportion of their workers in trade unions, wage rates are often high. The printing industry is a good example of such an industry. In other industries the relatively low unionisation of the workforce means that workers are unable to collectively demand higher rates of pay. The catering and retailing industries are prime examples where there are low paid workers and relatively low union membership.

The government has traditionally played a part in determining minimum wage rates in certain industries. This has involved the establishment of wages councils which have the responsibility for establishing fair rates of pay. The Thatcher government however, believes that market forces should be permitted to determine rates of pay and so has reduced the level of government intervention in this area. The government believes that the setting of a minimum wage discourages some employers from increasing their workforce and so hopes that the unemployment problem, particularly among young people, may be helped by the relaxation of wage controls.

It is now proposed to turn to the mechanism by which an organisation employs its workforce, the contract of employment.

EMPLOYMENT RELATIONSHIPS

In all employment relationships a worker will offer skill and labour to an employer in return for a wage or salary. The parties may intend that the employment relationship should be only for a short term or, alternatively, an indefinite period of employment might be envisaged. The worker could be engaged to use a previously acquired skill or, alternatively, the employer could intend to provide on the job training to enable the worker to acquire a new skill. Whatever the parties intentions the employment relationships adopted will be one of two types recognised under the law.

> a) The contract of service (referred to as 'the contract of employment') which applies to all employed persons and governs the relationship between the employer and the employee.

b) The contract for services (referred to as 'self employment') which applies to self employed persons and governs the relationship between the employer and the contractor.

Under the contract of service the employer will wish to exercise a large degree of control over his employees on a long term basis, whereas under the contract for services the employer is primarily concerned with the carrying out of a specific task for a limited period or intermittently and so does not require a large degree of control over its performance. The classification of the two types of contract is crucial since there are a mass of legal and financial responsibilities which apply to any employment relationship but differ depending on whether the contract is one of service or for services. A comparison of some of the main rights and responsibilities under the two types of contract can be seen below.

CONTRACTS OF SERVICE (EMPLOYED PERSONS)

CONTRACTS FOR SERVICES (SELF EMPLOYED PERSONS)

EMPLOYER'S LIABILITY

1. An employer may be made liable under the law for TORTS committed by his employees during the course of their employment.

2. The law imposes a high standard of care on an employer with regard to the health and safety of his employees both under Statute and common law.

1. As a general rule an employer is not liable for TORTS committed by independent contractors during the course of their employment.

2. Generally a lesser standard of care is owed by an employer towards his contractors with regard to health and safety both under the common law and Statute.

ECONOMIC IMPLICATIONS

3. An employee's income tax is deducted by his employer from his wages under the pay as you earn scheme, i.e. PAYE (Schedule E).

4. Under the Social Security Act, 1975, both employer and employee must contribute to the payment of Class 1 National Insurance contributions.

5. As a result of making Class 1 contributions an employee is entitled to claim all the available welfare benefits, e.g. unemployment, sickness, industrial injuries benefit.

3. A self employed person is responsible for his own tax liability and pays tax under Schedule D on a preceding year basis. This can prove to be a more advantageous method for the taxpayer.

4. Under the Social Security Act, 1975, a self employed person is individually responsible for the payment of lower Class 2 National Insurance contributions.

5. A self employed person who makes Class 2 contributions has no entitlement to certain welfare benefits, e.g. unemployment, industrial injuries but may claim others, e.g. sickness benefit.

OTHER STATUTORY RIGHTS

6. Employment legislation, (Employment Protection (Consolidation) Act, 1978) as amended has conferred a number of rights and benefits on employed persons e.g.

   a. the right to a written notice of the details of employment within the first 13 weeks of employment;

   b. the right to receive certain minimum periods of notice on dismissal;

   c. the right to a redundancy payment in appropriate circumstances;

   d. the right to protection against unfair dismissal;

   e. the right to be a member of a Trade Union and engage in Trade Union activities;

   f. the right of protection against the employer's insolvency.

6. The majority of statutory rights under the Employment Protection (Consolidation) Act, 1978, are not available for self employed persons.

By comparing the major characteristics of the two types of contract shown above it can be seen that the status enjoyed by both the employed and self employed has benefits and detriments for employer and worker. The major advantage of self employed status is an economic one for both the contractor, in tax advantages and less national insurance contributions, and the employer, in reduced costs of administration. This benefit of course must be weighed against the detriment to the worker of less job security and the employer, of less control. Certainly an organisation which requires the performance of a specialist task either once, or only intermittently, could be advised to employ a contractor rather than engage a full-time employee. It should be stressed however that it is not possible to create a particular employment relationship by pinning a label upon it. Thus an employer could not rid himself of the numerous statutory duties he has in relation to his employees by simply renaming them contractors. It is the substance of any employment relationship which will determine its status.

DISTINGUISHING BETWEEN EMPLOYED AND SELF-EMPLOYED STATUS

The task of distinguishing between a contract of service and a contract for services has been left to the courts. Over the years various tests have been formulated to determine the worker's status. Originally, the courts would only consider the level of control over a worker by an employer. In *Performing Rights Society Ltd. v. Mitchell and Booker 1924,* McArdie J, said that "the test to be generally applied, lies in the nature and degree of detailed control over the person alleged to be an employee". Therefore, if an employer could tell his workers not only what to do, but also how and when to do it, then the worker was regarded as an employee, employed under a contract of service. Today, the courts adopt a much wider approach and, while conceding that the degree of control is an important factor, they also take into account all other circumstances to determine a worker's status.

> In *Ready Mixed Concrete Ltd., v. Ministry of Pensions 1968* the court had to decide the status of a driver for the plaintiff company. His written contract of employment (30 pages long) stated that he was not an employee but this, the court said, was not decisive, it was merely a factor to be taken into account. All aspects of his job were considered, e.g. he purchased the lorry from the company, he had to maintain it himself, his pay was calculated on the basis of concrete carried, he could in some circumstances delegate the driving. These factors pointed to him being a contractor, while others pointed to his status as an employee e.g. he had to paint the lorry in the company colours, he had to use it exclusively on company business, he was required to obey reasonable orders. Here, the court held that the majority of the provisions were consistent with their being a contract for services. McKenna J. stated that there is a contract of service if an individual agrees to provide his own work, submits to his employer's control and the majority of the contractual provisions are consistent with it being a contract of service. Certainly the power to delegate work was regarded as indicative of the contract for services.

The status of self employed cannot be achieved simply by including an express provision in a contract for the courts will look to the substance of an employment relationship to decide a worker's status.

> In *Ferguson v. John Dawson Ltd., 1976,* a builder's labourer agreed to work on what was known as 'the lump' and was described as a 'self employed labour only sub-contractor'. Having suffered injuries as a result of the employer's breach of a statutory duty, the labourer could only succeed in an action for damages if he could show that he was an 'employee' and therefore protected by Statute. The court held that the 'lump' was no more

than a device to attempt to gain tax advantages and in reality taking all the circumstances into account, the relationship is one of employer and employee and a contract of service.

. . . the lump . . .

A difficult case to reconcile with the decision in *Ferguson 1976* is *Massey v. Crown Life Insurance Co. 1978*. Here a branch manager of an insurance company, who also acted as a general agent, elected to become 'self employed' on his accountant's advice, despite the fact that his duties remained unchanged. The Court of Appeal concluded that this change of status had taken place. Ld. Denning M.R. stated that if there is ambiguity in the relationship then this can be resolved with a declaration one way or another.

While there was a degree of ambiguity in his original position as branch manager/general agent, there is no doubt that of great significance was the fact that here there was a professional man, having considered independent advice, making a declaration which he believed would be to his benefit. This is in contrast to the labourer in *Ferguson 1976* who was unadvised and could not be said to have consciously chosen to be a contractor.

Increasingly in this type of case the courts ask the question whether the worker is 'in business on his own account' or under the control of an employer in a continuing employment relationship.

Applying such a test the Employment Appeals Tribunal found it possible to conclude in *Airfix Footwear Ltd. v. Cope 1978* that homeworkers, employed to assemble shoe parts for a company using equipment supplied by them, were not contractors but employees. While the work was provided on a regular basis the employer argued that there was no obligation to provide work and the worker could also refuse it. The employment relationship in question had continued over a seven year period. In reality the employer decided the things to be done, the manner, means, and the time and place of performance. The homeworker was therefore held to be an employee.

The perennial problem of determining employment status where there is uncertainty as to the true relationship arose again in *O'Kelly and Others v. Trusthouse Forte plc 1983.* Here a banqueting department ran by the employer was staffed in part by full time employees but mainly by so called 'casuals'. In addition the casuals composed of 'regulars' who were given preference where there was work available, and were expected to work long hours and consequently had no other employment. The applicants who were 'regulars' and Trade Union stewards who were told by the employers that their services would no longer be required and so they complained of unfair dismissal. In determining their employment status the Tribunal acknowledged that its role was to "consider all aspects of the relationship". Applying this mixed or multiple test the Tribunal isolated factors consistent with a contract of service, factors inconsistent, and factors not inconsistent. Among the factors inconsistent was the lack of a mutuality of obligation to provide work and offer services and the custom and practice of the industry. These factors swayed the Tribunal to find that the applicants were not employees. The EAT allowed the applicants appeal deciding that the question of status was one of law which the Tribunal had applied incorrectly. On further appeal to the Court of Appeal however it was held that the Tribunal had not misdirected itself in law and had come to a conclusion which a reasonable tribunal could have reached. Its original finding had to stand and the applicant's action failed.

Unfortunately the Tribunal's decision in *O'Kelly 1983* does seem to ignore the economic reality of the 'regulars' employment, for a failure to work when required had the drastic impact of removal from the regular casual list. A rational application of the 'business account' test would reveal no capital equipment, no share in the profits, no multiple employment, no delegation of work and substantial control. Certainly it is difficult to reconcile O'Kelly with the decision of the Court of Appeal in Ferguson 1976 where clearly expressed intentions were overturned to find employment status for a worker who was badly injured. In O'Kelly the Court of Appeal was reluctant to find employment status for casual workers attempting to assert trade union rights.

The lack of a binding obligation to accept work highlighted in O'Kelly was also apparent in *Wickens v. Champion Employment 1984.* Here the EAT examined the employment status of 'agency temporaries'. These are individuals who are employed to provide secretarial services to clients of their agent. On a claim for unfair dismissal the question arose as to the status of the relationship between the agency and the client and the EAT found it to be one of self-employment. This was despite the large degree of control over the 'temps', the fact that the documentation referred to them as employees and the growing practice of agencies of giving employment status to temporaries.

FORMATION OF THE CONTRACT OF EMPLOYMENT

The general contractual rules governing offer and acceptance considered in chapter 21 are relevant to determine when a contract of employment has been entered into, thus:

  a.   an advertisement of a job is a mere invitation to treat;

b. an employer will make an express offer of a job to the successful applicant on specific terms which may differ with the advertisement;

c. a counter offer by the applicant will extinguish the original offer; and

d. the contract is concluded on the communication of the applicant's acceptance and, if the postal rules of acceptance apply, the acceptance is complete on posting.

Of course, this whole process may take place over a period of time involving conversations, exchange of letters and interviews.

There is no requirement that a contract of employment be in a written form, however it is usual pratice in many industries, for the employer to provide the employee with a formal written contract that the employee signs to show his agreement. Also the Employment Protection (Consolidation) Act 1978 (EPCA 1978) which contains most of the employee's statutory rights requires an employer to provide his full time employees with written particulars of employment within thirteen weeks of starting work. These written particulars should include reference to the main terms of the contract including:-

a. reference to the parties and the date on which the period of continuous employment began (stating whether a previous period of employment is included as part of continuous employment);

b. the scale of remuneration and the method of calculation;

c. the intervals at which remuneration is paid;

d. the terms and conditions relating to the hours of work;

e. the terms and conditions relating to holidays and holiday pay;

f. the terms and conditions relating to sickness and sickness pay;

g. the terms and conditions relating to pension and pension scheme;

h. the length of notice which the employee is obliged to give and be entitled to receive;

i. the title of the job which the employee is employed to do;

j. a specification of any disciplinary rules or reference to an accessible document containing such rules.

Instead of setting out the details of all the above matters in the statement it is sufficient if the statement refers to other documents available for inspection and containing the relevant information.

This requirement of a statutory statement is one of the numerous statutory provisions relating to employee's rights enforceable by means of a complaint to an industrial tribunal.

CONTENTS OF THE CONTRACT OF EMPLOYMENT

A contract of employment is, like any other contract, composed of terms which confer rights and impose obligations on the parties to it. Such terms may be expressly agreed by the parties or incorporated into the contract from another source. As far as contracts of employment are concerned, terms may be incorporated by collective agreements made between the employer (or employer's association) and a Trade Union (or Trade Unions). Employment terms may also be implied into a contract of employment by work rules, custom or the law.

Express Terms

These are the terms expressly agreed by the employer and employee and may be in writing or may be purely oral. The EPCA 1978 requires express terms to satisfy the test of reasonableness so that if a term is seen to be oppressive it may be regarded as void. Such would be the case if the employer reserved the right to dismiss the employee for a trivial breach of contract. The express terms of the contract usually relate to matters such as wages, hours, holidays, sick pay, job description and restraints. Contracts of employment are often in a standard form dependent on the type of employment e.g. office or manual worker. Of course, what has expressly been agreed by the parties may often require interpretation in the courts and industrial tribunals. The majority of employment disputes are first heard in industrial tribunals with the possibility of appeal to the Employment Appeal Tribunal and from there in certain circumstances to the ordinary courts.

> In *Cole v. Midland Display Ltd. 1973* the tribunal was faced with the problem of determining the meaning of the term "employed on a staff basis" when it was applied to a manager. The Tribunal held that the phrase meant that the employee was entitled to wages during periods of sickness or no work, but in return the employee could be required to work overtime without pay.

As a general rule the express terms cannot be varied by either party without the other's consent unless an express term confers this right on one of the parties. Any attempt by the employer to impose an unreasonable variation of the contractual terms on the employee will amount to a breach, e.g. require the employee to attend a place of work outside travelling distance from home. Of course a requirement to move may be expressly included or even implied from the contract of employment in which case there would be no breach.

> In *Jones v. Associated Tunnelling Co. Ltd., 1981* the EAT held that in the absence of express terms to the contrary there is an implied term in a contract of employment that the employer has the right to transfer the employee to a different place of work within reasonable daily commuting distance of his home.

To constitute an agreed variation of the contract of employment the courts must be satisfied that the employee gives a clear indication that he voluntarily accepts the new terms of his employment.

> In *Marriott v. Oxford District Co-op Soc. Ltd. 1970* the Court of Appeal was required to determine whether there had been an agreed variation in the contractual terms in the following case. A foreman supervisor was told by his employer that the position of foreman was no longer required and that his wages were to be reduced by £1 to reflect his loss of status. The employee continued to work under protest for three weeks before terminating his employment by notice, claiming redundancy. The Court of Appeal held, reversing the Divisional Court's decision, that there had been no free consent to the contractual variation and the change in terms amounted to a repudiation of the contract of employment.

Problems surrounding contractual variation are often associated with the interpretation of the content of the contract of employment and usually arise during, or are the cause of industrial action.

> An example is *Royal v. Trafford BC 1984*. Here a school teacher's pay had been withheld for refusing to work in accordance with the instructions of the head teacher in pursuance of an industrial dispute. In an action for breach of contract it was held that by refusing to take on more pupils (by

increasing the class size from 31 to 36) the teacher was indeed in breach of contract. However by allowing the teacher to render an imperfect performance of the contract the employer had affirmed the contract despite withholding salary. Accordingly the teacher was awarded his unpaid salary less 5/36ths for his breach of contract over the relevant period.

To determine whether action by an employer could amount to a breach of the contract of employment it is possible to apply to the High Court for a declaration.

In *Cresswell v. Board of Inland Revenue 1984* employees sought a declaration that their employer had broken the terms of their contracts of employment by introducing new technology and expecting them to adapt to it. The High Court declared however, that provided they received adequate training employees were expected to adapt to new methods and new techniques. There is a general contractual duty on employees to adapt to changing working methods. There was also a right for the employer to withhold pay from those employees who refused to conform to the new methods.

Implied Terms

Terms may be incorporated into a contract of employment from various sources including the law (Common law and statute) work rules, custom and collective agreements. The legal status of collective agreements is considered later in the chapter in the section on the role of trade unions.

Work Rules and Custom.

It is common practice in many spheres of employment for the employer to issue work rules by printing notices or handing out booklets. Such work rules often contain instructions as to time-keeping, meal breaks, disciplinary offences and grievance procedure, sickness and pension rights, and the employer's safety policy. Although there is still doubt as to their legal significance, it seems at present such documents are unlikely to contain contractual terms.

In *The Secretary of State for Employment v. Associated Society of Loco-motive Engineers and Firemen 1972* Ld. Denning stated that the rule book issued to railwaymen by their employer did not contain contractual terms but rather instructions to an employee on how he was to do his work.

At the present time, it is unlikely that a custom or practice will be incorporated into a contract of employment by implication. Certainly a custom would have to satisfy the tests of being certain, reasonable and well known before it would be regarded as legally enforceable. This was the case in *Sagar v. Ridehalgh 1931* where a custom that deductions could be made from the wages of a weaver for bad work was held to be legally binding.

Terms Implied by the Law.

In every contract of employment, certain terms are implied by the operation of the common law. These terms are the source of many of the rights and duties of both the employer and employee and are an integral part of the contract of employment. In addition to these well established common law duties there is an increased willingness by courts and tribunals to imply terms into individual contracts of employment. Furthermore by statutory intervention numerous individual employment rights attach to the contract of employment, in some cases arising after a period of continuous employment e.g. the right not to be unfairly dismissed. One statutory implied term which is considered later is the 'equality clause' implied into contracts of employment by the Equal Pay Act 1970. Statutory rights are examined in detail throughout this chapter and relate to redundancy payments, payment of wages, health and safety, trade union activities, action short of dismissal and unfair dismissal. An employee's remedy for infringement of these rights is by way of complaint to an industrial tribunal.

Terms are implied into a contract of employment by the common law imposing duties on both the employer and employee. Duties are imposed on the employer to pay wages, to provide the opportunity to earn the expected wage, to indemnify, and to provide a safe system of work. Duties of the employee include to act in good faith, to account for money received, to respect trade secrets and to obey lawful instructions.

Employer's Duties

To pay wages. The common law implies a term into a contract of employment imposing a duty on the employer to pay a reasonable wage for the work done. In the majority of cases, of course, the parties to the contract of employment will have expressly agreed a rate of pay or referred to a rate of pay contained in a collective agreement. However, in the unlikely event that no wage is expressly agreed, in the case of a dispute the courts will value the service provided and imply a reasonable wage. In addition to the common law, there are a number of statutory provisions surrounding the payment of wages. Under the EPCA 1978 every employee is entitled to receive a written itemised statement of his pay including deductions. This statement should include the gross amount, deductions and their purpose, the net amount and if the net amount is paid in different ways, the amount and methods of payment.

Since the mid-nineteenth century statute has regulated how wages may be paid in order to prevent abuse by employers. The Truck Act 1831 provided that wages of manual workers must be paid in current coin of the realm. This was to prevent the employers paying wages in kind (goods) or tokens. The Act also provides that deductions can be made from a workers wage only for certain purposes acknowledged in a signed agreement.

> In *Daley v. Radnor 1973* an oral agreement between an employer and employee provided that the employer would let premises to the employee at £10 per week rent, such a sum to be deducted from the employee's weekly wage. The employee claimed £1570 which had been deducted from his wages for this purpose. The court held that the sum was recoverable on the ground that the deduction was unlawful.

In order to permit the payment of wages in forms other than cash, the Payment of Wages Act 1960 was passed. This Act provides that by written agreement employees may be paid by cheque, bank giro, direct bank account debit, etc. There are proposals to remove the rights of manual workers to be paid in cash. Also to prevent discrimination in the remuneration paid to both sexes engaged in similar work, the Equal Pay Act 1970 was passed to attempt to ensure equal treatment. The requirement of equal treatment only applies where the sexes are engaged in similar work referred to as 'like work' or work of 'equal value'. Higher rates of pay can of course be justified where greater skill or responsibility is demanded. Any differences based on physical strength however and the time when work is to be done are to be disregarded.

> In *Electrolux v. Hutchinson 1977* female workers engaged in broadly similar work to their male counterparts where held to be entitled to equal pay, despite the condition that the men could exclusively be required to work overtime, at weekends, or at night. The fact that the men were rarely called on to do this was a major consideration.

The decision as to whether similar work is being carried on demands a comparison not between the contractual obligations of the parties, but rather a consideration of the things actually done and the frequency with which they are done.

In *Coombes (Holdings) Ltd. v. Shield 1978* the female counter clerks in bookmaker shops were paid a lesser rate of pay than their male clerks. The employers sought to justify the differences on the grounds that the male employees had extra duties including acting as a deterrent to unruly customers and transporting cash between branches. The Court of Appeal held that in deciding the question as to 'like work' it was necessary to consider the differences between the things the men and women were required to do. Furthermore it was necessary to consider the frequency with which such differences occur in practice. Finally the court must consider whether the differences are of any practical importance. This approach should enable the court to place a value on each job in terms of demands placed upon the worker and if the value of the man's job is higher he should be paid an increased rate for the job. In the present case the differences were not of sufficient importance to justify a different rate of pay.

One of the main effects of the Sex Discrimination Act 1975 in amending the Equal Pay Act 1970 was to provide that every contract of employment is deemed to include an equality clause. This clause automatically modifies a term of a woman's contract which is less favourable than a term of a similar kind in a man's contract where he is employed on similar work. The clause also has the effect of including in a woman's contract any term benefiting a man employed on like work. The equality clause will not operate however if the employer can show that the differences between the contracts is 'genuinely due to a material difference' other than one of sex. In cases where there are differences involving benefits and detriments the disadvantages of one term may be complemented by the advantages of another.

To provide work, indemnify and provide a reference. Generally there is no duty on an employer to provide work for his employees as long as their contractual remuneration is paid. If however an employee's pay depends upon the performance of work (piece-work) the employer is under an obligation to provide sufficient work to enable a reasonable wage to be earned. A further exception is where the employee's occupation is such that the opportunity to work is an essential part of the contract because of the possibility of loss of reputation, e.g. an actor, entertainer or journalist.

Under the common law, an employee is entitled to be indemnified for loss or expense incurred in the course of employment. In most cases, of course, expenses are provided for expressly in the contract of employment.

There is however, no legal duty to provide employees with a reference on the termination of their employment. If a reference is given however, the tort of defamation will provide a remedy for an employee if the employer has maliciously included false statements which damage the employee's character. Also an employer could be sued under the tort of deceit or negligent mis-statement by another employer who suffers loss as a result of employing someone following an unwarrantable good reference.

To provide a safe system of work. The present law relating to an employer's duties in relation to the safety of his workforce is embodied within the common law and statute. The common law duty arises under the tort of negligence and involves providing employees with a safe system of work. Statutory duties are imposed under various Acts, e.g. the Factories Act 1961, the Office Shops and Railway Premises Act 1963 (the contents of which are being incorporated by regulation into the Health and Safety at Work Act 1974).

An employer must under the common law exercise reasonable care with regard to the safety of employees by providing a safe system of work. It should be emphasised therefore that the duty imposed on an employer is not a strict one and may be fulfilled by the exercise of reasonable care. The basic elements of the tort of negligence are relevant to determine liability.

> In *Latimer v. AEC 1953* after a factory was flooded the employer asked his workforce to return, warning them of the dangerous state of the factory floor. Sawdust had been used to cover most of the damp areas but not enough was available and the plaintiff slipped and was injured. To determine whether the employer had broken the common law duty of care he owed to his employees the court weighed the cost of avoiding the injury against the extra risk of injury and held that the employer had acted reasonably in the circumstances.

The common law duty includes an obligation to provide safe fellow workers. An employer is vicariously responsible under the law for actions of his employees during the course of their employment. If these actions turn out to be negligent and a fellow employee or a third party suffers harm as a result, then the employer may be sued and be made liable in damages. An employer must therefore take reasonable care to ensure that he provides his workers with safe fellow workers. If the employer is aware of an employee who may create a dangerous situation at work by incompetence or practical jokes, he should discipline the employee, and if the practice continues, if necessary dismiss him. Such a dismissal may be regarded as justifiable in the circumstances.

> In *Coddington v. International Harvester Co. 1969* an employee negligently pushed a tin of burning paint towards a fellow employee and injury resulted. The court held that the employer was not liable as he could not have foreseen the danger. There was no record of the employee in question being guilty of dangerous behaviour in the past.

The common law duty also encompasses an obligation to provide safe plant and appliances. If an employer is aware that machinery or tools are not reasonably safe, and an employee is injured as a result, the employer will be in breach of his duty.

> In *Bradford v. Robinson Rentals 1967* the employer provided an unheated van for the employee to make a 400 mile journey during the winter. The court held that the employer was liable for the employee's frost bite which was reasonably forseeable.

In the past an employer could satisfy this duty by showing that he purchased equipment from a reputable supplier and had no knowledge of any defect. Now, however, following the Employer's Liability (Defective Equipment) Act 1969 injury occuring to an employee under those circumstances may be attributed to the deemed negligence of the employer. If damages are awarded against the employer, then it is up to him to seek a remedy from the supplier of the defective equipment. Since the Employer's Liability (Compulsory Insurance) Act 1969 requires all employers to insure against the risk of causing personal injury through fault to their employees an injured employee can be generally confident that damages awarded to him will be met.

The employers duty also imposes an obligation to provide safe working methods and safe working premises. To determine whether an employer is providing safe working methods, it is necessary to consider a number of factors including the layout of the work place, training and supervision, warnings and whether protective equipment is provided. It should be stressed that the common law duty on an employer is to take reasonable care, and if he gives proper instructions which the employee fails to observe then the employer will not be liable if the employee is then injured.

> In *Charlton v. Forrest Printing Ink. Co. Ltd. 1978* the employer gave proper instructions to an employee who was given the job of collecting the firm's wages. The instructions required the employee to vary his collecting arrangements to prevent robbery. The employee failed to do this and suffered severe injury when he was robbed. The Court of Appeal held that the employer was not liable as he had taken reasonable steps to cut down the risk.

As far as safety equipemnt is concerned, the common law requires an employer to provide it where necessary, and make it available for use. In some cases, particularly where there is a serious risk of injury, the employer's duty extends to ensuring that workers make use of the safety equipment provided.

> In *Nolan v. Dental Manufacturing Co. 1958* it was held that an employer
> was liable in negligence when he failed to ensure that safety goggles were
> worn by a tool setter who was injured while working on a grinding wheel.

In addition, the standard of care owed by an employer will vary with regard to each individual employee. A young apprentice should be provided with effective supervision while this may not be required for an experienced employee.

> In *Paris v. Stepney BC 1951* the plaintiff, a one-eyed motor mechanic, lost
> the sight of his good eye while working at chipping rust from under a bus.
> Despite their being no usual practice to provide mechanics with safety
> goggles, the court decided that they should have been provided to the
> plaintiff. The defendants were liable as they could foresee serious
> consequences for the plaintiff if he suffered eye injury.

Statutory duties imposed on employers in relation to health and safety are dealt with later in this chapter in the section on trade unions.

Employee's Duties

The duty of good faith. This duty is the most fundamental obligation of an employee and involves serving his employer faithfully. Faithful service involves working competently, respecting the employer's property, and not taking industrial action such as strikes, go-slows, work to rule etc., which would disrupt the employer's business.

> In *The Secretary of State for Employment v. ASLEF 1972* the Court of
> Appeal held that wilful disruption of the employer's undertaking would
> amount to a breach of this implied duty of good faith. Here the railwaymen
> were disrupting railway services by working to the letter of the British Rail
> rule book, but nevertheless held to be in breach of contract.

The relationship of trust and confidence which is said to exist between employer and employee may also demand that an employee reports matters of interest to his employer.

> In *Sybros Corporation and Another v. Rochem Ltd. and others 1983* the
> Court of Appeal held that while there is no general duty to report a fellow
> employee's misconduct or breach of contract an employee might be so
> placed in the hierarchy of an organisation so as to have a duty to report
> either his 'superiors' or 'inferiors' misconduct.

To account for money received. There is an implied duty on an employee not to accept any bribes, commissions or fees in respect of his work other than from his employer.

> In *Boston Deep-Sea Fishing & Ice Co. v. Ansell 1888* an employee who
> received a secret commission from other companies for placing orders with
> them, was treated as being in breach of his duty and his dismissal was
> justified.

To respect trade secrets. An employer would be in breach of this duty by working for a competitor in his spare time.

In *Hivac v. Park Royal Scientific Instruments Co. 1946* an employee was restrained from working for a competitor engaged in work of a similar nature.

There would be a flagrant breach of contract if an employee were to disclose trade secrets or other confidential information during the course of his employment. Even an ex-employee may be restrained.

In *Printer & Finishers Ltd. v. Holloway 1965* an ex-employee was restrained from showing secret documents to a competitor and disclosing confidential information he had obtained during his employment.

To obey reasonable orders. This duty could be included with the general obligation to render faithful service. To be reasonable an order must be lawful for there is no duty to obey an unlawful order, for instance to falsify some records. In determining the reasonableness of an order, all the circumstances must be considered including a close examination of the contract of employment.

In *U.K. Atomic Energy Authority v. Claydon 1974* the defendant's contract of employment required him to work anywhere in the U.K. Accordingly it was held to be a reasonable order to require him to transfer to another base within the U.K.

Also, in *Pepper v. Webb 1969* a head gardener, asked to plant some flowers replied "I couldn't care less about your bloody greenhouse or your sodding garden" and walked away. The court held that the refusal to obey the instruction rather than that language which accompanied it, amounted to a breach of contract.

The contract of employment, is of course, a purely legal mechanism for determining the rights and obligations of the organisation and its workforce.

In fulfilling the task of managing the workforce, managers must be aware of this legal framework, but should only be relying upon it as a last resort when difficulties and disputes arise.

An organisation is not functioning effectively if its managers are incapable of recognising that the workforce is made up of individuals whose performance is likely to be affected by the character of the orders, instructions and other mechanisms used to regulate their output. The quality of social relationships within the organisational structure of a business may be more important to the employees than the physical climate in which they work. In the following section we examine some of the aspects of managing people in terms of the differing managerial approaches that can be taken.

THE MANAGEMENT OF RESOURCES

APPROACHES TO MANAGEMENT

The operation of any organisation requires an effective form of management. This means that the various components used in the output process must be combined in such a way that the overall objectives of the organisation are achieved. However it has already been noted in chapter 18 that there are many differing objectives in any organisation. There are the objectives of the owners of the organisation whether they are the shareholders of a private company or the citizens of the community which owns the public sector organisation which is seeking to provide for their needs. It was also stressed that the managers of an organisation may also hold objectives of their own which could differ from those of the owners and may result in the organisation assuming a different orientation. In this section it is necessary to consider how the objectives of a part of the organisation which is crucial to its operation, the workers, may be in line with those of the organisation as a whole or may conflict with its objectives. It is therefore proposed to examine the alternative means of managing the organisation in the light of these problems.

To begin it is necessary to try to understand the basis of the relationship between those who manage and those who are to be managed. Earlier in the chapter it was noted that there is a relatively precise legal relationship, namely the contract of employment. However there are a more fundamental set of relationships which determine how in practice the organisation operates. Essentially these relationships evolve from the attitudes of both the managers and the workforce. They will be determined by the willingness or otherwise of the workforce to accept the 'right' of management to manage. They will also be influenced by management's view of the workforce. It may be that the managers regard the workers as merely 'cogs' in the productive process whose hopes and aspirations, quality and standard of living are of no real concern to them. Alternatively management may equate the well-being of the workforce with the efficient operation of the organisation. Such attitudes are of the utmost importance in establishing an organisation in which all those involved believe that their own objectives can be achieved.

There are two basic approaches to this fundamental question. The first approach is based on the belief that the managers, the workforce and the organisation all hold essentially the same objective, that the organisation should prosper and achieve its overall aims. In this way the owners of the organisation will receive what they desire, whether it is a greater profit or a better level of service. Management also benefits in that they will receive promotion and higher salaries in return for their efficient management and workers will gain security of employment and greater wage levels in return for their labours. This approach is called the consensus approach in that it assumes a consensus or agreement between the three different groups that we have mentioned, owners, managers and workers.

An alternative view is that each of the groups is seeking to pursue its own objectives and that these objectives are not necessarily in agreement. The owners may seek profit, the managers may look for power and status and the workers a greater share of the final profit gained by the company or a larger share of the budget of the public sector organisation. Because each group seeks to achieve its own objectives there will be inevitable disagreements with regard to the way in which the organisation is structured and operated. Thus this view is referred to as the conflict approach to management. Within each of these two basic approaches we can identify a number of differing ways of defining the management style that an organisation adopts and it is under these two broad headings that we shall examine some of these styles.

THE CONSENSUS APPROACH

1. The pluralistic viewpoint

This view of management assumes that, while workers and management do not hold exactly the same aims and opinions on every issue, basically they are in line on most major points and that both workers and management wish to see the organisation succeed. So in order to ensure the most efficient implementation of its decisions, management will accept the existence of trade unions as the legitimate representatives of the workforce and attempt to negotiate with them and to meet some of their demands. However trade unions are seen in essence as a necessary evil and the framework of the relationship is one in which the managers have the right to make major decisions independently and only then agree with the workforce the means by which such decisions will be carried out. To achieve this agreement or consensus there is often a formal negotiating procedure established which both sides agree to adhere to, and all contact between managers and workers on such issues as wages and conditions is made through this formal negotiating channel. The workforce is not consulted before policy decisions are made but it is clearly in the interests of management to bear in mind the likely reaction of the trade union to any management decision which will be put before them. This type of management style is typical of many organisations in the public sector.

2.　The consultative style

This form of management style also believes in the consensus approach and that both workers and management have similar objectives. However it takes the process one stage further that the pluralistic approach in that it believes in involving the workforce in the decision making process. We should use the term 'involving' carefully as the consultative approach is what it says — a process of consultation. Management seeks to gain the workers views before a decision is made but nevertheless still retains the right to take the final decision itself. Clearly this improves the workers input into the decision making process and will allow the workforce to feel that their opinions count. But its success as a management style really depends on how far the views of the workers are heeded. Some consultative procedures may appear to the workers to be a mere sham or facade if their opinions are continually ignored following consultations. An example of this happening has been the British Coal's Consultative machinery for deciding whether or not uneconomic coal mines should close. Unfortunately because some mines have been closed despite the unions opposition during consultation the unions now feel that their views count for nothing and that the consultation is meaningless. Other organisations use this consultative process much more effectively by giving due weight to the employees view in the final decision making.

3.　Worker participation

This approach involves the workforce having a full and equal say in the decision making process of the organisation. Such participation may operate at a number of levels. The most common would be in shop floor or section committees where workers and management regularly meet to decide on the practical operation of the organisation. Workers not only make suggestions as to changes in work methods or work rules but also have a vote in whether or not their ideas or those of management should be implemented. This democratic approach can be extended upwards through the organisation with middle managers and representatives of the workers such as shop stewards deciding on more major decisions. It is popular in American and Japanese companies. Finally an organisation may involve workers in policy making by having worker directors. In this way the workforce is not only informed immediately of any policy changes which are to be made but can also influence the decisions as they are being taken. The college at which you study will have a policy making body. In most colleges it is called the academic board. Many colleges now have representatives of the student union on the academic board as well as members of the college management, the academic staff and the non-teaching staff. However you will find in most organisations which have worker (or student) participation policy making bodies that they are usually in a minority and so must gain the agreement of the board as a whole to any proposal they wish to see adopted.

4.　Worker Control

The most extreme form of the consensus approach involves complete worker control of the operation of the organisation. The work force appoint some of their members to manage and administer the business while others are involved in the productive process. Such organisations are sometimes called 'worker co-operatives' and are becoming increasingly common as the recession has encouraged redundant workers who have been traditionally employees of other organisations to come together and establish their own businesses. There are occasionally problems in such organisations as sections of the workforce may resent some of their members appearing to hold and wield the decision making power. However if such problems can be overcome the co-operative organisation can prove very successful as not only do the workers feel they have a part in the decision making but they also normally receive a share of any profits made. A more limited form of worker control comes where employees are given or can purchase part of the company's share capital. The idea behind this is similar to a more complete worker participation in that it encourages the workers to identify with the business as they will have a feeling of ownership. They should therefore be more committed in their attitude to work and so the company should have less industrial relations problems.

THE CONFLICT APPROACH

1. The traditional management view

In more traditional organisations the view held by management tends to be that it is their job to manage without interference from the workforce. Management will have the objective of making the organisation as efficient and profitable as possible. They will use their employees only as a means of achieving this end. This does not mean that the employees will always be treated badly. Often the complete opposite is the case. The workers must be kept happy if the organisation is to function smoothly and so conditions and pay must be good. But ultimately all decision making must lie exclusively with management.

Trade unions and their supporters are seen as being outside the organisation's structure and therefore should be positively discouraged and whenever possible banned. They are seen as an alternative focus of loyalty for the worker and as such challenge the organisation's aims. Often management may allow a 'tame' company union which will share the management's view of the organisation. In such circumstances if differences should occur they can be readily overcome because of goodwill and the mutual aim of organisational success.

A recent example of this type of management approach which has gained considerable publicity has been the government's decision to ban trade unions from the Cheltenham GCHQ monitoring unit because it believes that trade union activity may be detrimental to its efficient operation. The civil service unions have strongly resisted such measures arguing that their members are equally loyal employees as their non-union colleagues. A further example of this type of approach has occured in the Fleet Street newspaper publishing business where employers like Rupert Murdoch and Eddie Shah have sought to have no unions in their organisations or only those unions who will continually accept management decisions. Such arrangements have been aided by 'single union' agreements, where the organisation has refused to allow more than one union to operate within it. In doing so it avoids inter-union disputes, and will be likely to accept as the single union the one which it regards as the most amenable. An example of a single union agreement is that in force at the Nissan Car factory in Sunderland. No other car manufacturer in the United Kingdom has a workforce exclusively belonging to a single union.

2. The trade union view of industrial conflict

It is sometimes argued that all trade unions are extremely militant in their views towards employers. This is not so. A trade union will normally only react with some form of industrial action in response to management attitudes which are directly opposed to the best interests of the union's members. Nevertheless most trade unions rightly see their role as protecting their members interests and improving their pay and conditions. In most instances this will mean ensuring the continued success of the employer organisation as in this way the trade unionists' jobs can be made more secure and their future prosperity enhanced. However the trade union will normally seek to gain for their members a larger share of the organisation's profits or budget. In this way they will often find themselves involved in conflict with the employer. Of course the vast majority of wage negotiations undertaken through collective bargaining will be resolved peacefully but when an impasse is reached the trade union may have no alternative other than recommending to its members that they should pursue their claims through some form of collective action. It is unfortunate that it is normally these disruptive instances which receive adverse publicity. The trade unionists are often blamed by the press for their selfishness. Yet many such claims are rightful and industrial action is the only course of action open to the workers.

Thus the way in which an organisation is managed is often a consequence of the attitudes and objectives which are held by both the management and the work force. It has been a criticism of British industry in the post war period that there have been too many instances of industrial strife which have seriously damaged our productive capacity and our reputation in the world, and that entrenched and intransigent attitudes on both sides have been the root cause. Such criticisms do have some basis in truth but they do not fully explain our poor industrial performance. In fact in recent years there has been, with some notable exceptions such as the miners strike, a much lower incidence of industrial unrest in this country than there has been in many of our competitors' economies. Therefore what is required for the future is a positive attitude on the part of both workers and management towards the work relationship. This requires an acceptance that the worker must be given a fair reward for his labours and has the right to some greater degree of participation in the running of the organisation. It would be a desolate future for the British economy if we were to return to the class ridden industrial relations picture of the pre-war years. In the next section we shall examine in more detail the legal position and role of the trade unions.

TRADE UNIONS

The development of trade unionism had its origins in the early nineteenth century mainly as a reaction against oppresive treatment by employers. Wage earners, mainly in the skilled trades, saw the benefit of organising into unions to protect their interests. After a bitter struggle, by the end of the nineteenth century trade unions were finally recognised under the law and legal protection in relation to industrial action was conferred by the Trades Disputes Act 1906. Today, it is only an 'independent trade union' which enjoys those legal benefits that remain and so it is necessary to consider their definition as contained in the Trade Union and Labour Relations Act 1974.

Under the Act a trade union is an organisation which either:-

    a.   consists wholly or mainly of workers of one or more descriptions and is an organisation whose principle purposes include the regulation of relations between workers of that description and employers or employers' associations; or which

    b.   consists wholly or mainly of constituent or affiliated organisations which fulfil (a) above or their representatives.

The principal purpose of such organisations must include the regulation of relations between workers and employers or its constituent organisations. Trade unions then are workers' organisations which are designed to regulate industrial relations but to qualify as 'independent' they must also not be under the control of an employer or employers' association or be liable to interference by any such group. The 1974 Act provides machinery under which a trade union may apply to a Certification Officer to establish itself as independent.

While independence carries with it a degree of legal protection for trade union officials, further rights and privileges can be achieved when a trade union is recognised. These rights include disclosure of information, consultation concerning redundancies and appointment of safety committees. Recognition involves either formal recognition by the employer, or a clear and unequivocal act which demonstrates that both parties intend particular conduct to constitute recognition. The entire recognition procedures formerly regulated by the Advisory, Conciliation and Arbitration Service and the Central Arbitration Committee were repealed by the Employment Act 1980. An employer can no longer be required to recognise a trade union following the recommendation of ACAS and the CAC.

COLLECTIVE AGREEMENTS

As we have seen the principal objectives of trade unions is simply to maintain and improve the position of their members. This is achieved mainly through the process of collective bargaining under which a union or association of unions negotiates with an employer or employers federation the terms and conditions of employment of its members. The product of such negotiations is included within a collective agreement and in the UK over 14 million workers are covered by them. Under the 1974 Act such agreements are conclusively presumed not to be legally enforceable unless in writing and expressed to be so. While the majority of such agreements are not legally enforceable and both employer and unions see the benefits of such a voluntary arrangement, there has been a recent trend for a minority of trade unions to negotiate legally binding agreements. In return for single union status some trade unions have been willing to agree to no strike clauses contained within such agreements. Nevertheless the vast majority of collective agreements are not legally binding but they do contain terms and conditions of employment which have an impact on individual employment relationships. Such terms have significance for the individual contract of employment and so may be legally enforceable by becoming part of it.

To be part of an individual's contract of employment, the general rule is that express reference must be made to the agreement, e.g. 'Union Conditions', 'subject to National Agreement'. Often, the statutory statement of the particulars of employment which the employer must serve, will make express reference to a collective agreement and therefore incorporate it into the individual's contract of employment. Unfortunately it is a difficult question to determine which parts of a collective agreement are capable of incorporation into an individual's contract of employment. Certainly if terms and conditions of employment are collectively agreed to the extent that they have significance for individual employees they will become part of individual contracts. Less certain would be the status of a redundancy scheme negotiated between the employer and a Trade Union.

> In *British Leyland (UK) Ltd. v. McQuilken 1978* a collectively agreed scheme of redundancy was negotiated to deal with a reorganisation involving the employees in retraining and transfers to other locations. When the employer failed to implement the agreed scheme in relation to the applicant, he resigned due to uncertainty as to his future. To succeed in an action for unfair dismissal it was necessary for the applicant to show that he had been constructively dismissed. For constructive dismissal it must be proved that the employer has been guilty of a breach of the employment contract. The EAT held that there was no constructive dismissal as there was no breach of contract. The redundancy scheme was a long term plan dealing with policy rather than individual employment right and was not capable therefore of incorporation into an individual contract.

The rights of individuals in relation to membership are contained in the Employment Protection (Consolidation) Act 1978. There it specifically states that an employee has the right to be a member of a trade union and take part in trade union activities. In addition an employer must permit an employee who is an official of an independent trade union, recognised by that employer, to take time off during working hours to carry out official duties or undergo relevant training or carry out public duties.

HEALTH AND SAFETY

In pursuing their principle objective of maintaining and improving the position of their members, trade unions have an important role to play in monitoring and encouraging a constructive attitude to health and safety at work in employers and in their members. Parliament has recognised that stringent safeguards are necessary in particular working environments and for this reason has introduced the criminal code into health and safety at work. Having a safety policy and setting up a safety committee are now statutory requirements for some employers and it is through the medium of safety committees that trade unions can make an effective contribution in maintaining health and safety requirements. Health and Safety at work and the role of safety committees are also considered in chapter 10.

In 1974 Parliament passed the Health and Safety at Work Act which is designed to provide a comprehensive system of law to govern health and safety at work. The Act lays down general duties on employers, employees, suppliers of plant and equipment, those who control work premises, etc. The principal general duty is that an employer must ensure, in so far as is reasonably practicable, the health and safety of his workers. This general duty involves:-

    a.   providing and maintaining safe plant and a safe work system;

    b.   making arrangements for the use, handling, storage and transport of articles and substances;

    c.   providing any necessary information, instruction, training and supervision;

    d.   maintaining a safe place of work and a safe access to an exit from it;

    e.   maintaining a safe working environment.

The scope of the general duty qualified by the words "reasonably practicable" is difficult to determine. It would be wrong to assume that it imposes a standard of care comparable with that required under the common law. The statutory duty is a much wider one and requires positive action to ensure health and safety unless on the facts this is impracticable.

Some guidance has been provided by the courts. In *Associated Dairies v. Hartley 1979* the employer supplied his workers with safety shoes which they could pay for at a £1 per week. An employee who had not purchased the shoes suffered a fractured toe when the wheel of a roller truck ran over it. There was an obvious risk to workers from roller trucks in the employer's warehouse. Accordingly an improvement notice was served on the employer requiring him to provide his employees with safety shoes free of charge (estimated cost £20,000 and £10,000 per annum thereafter). The Court of Appeal held that while such a requirement was 'practicable' in all the circumstances of the case it was not 'reasonably so' bearing in mind the cost in relation to the risk. The improvement notice was therefore cancelled the court confirming that in relation to the general duty the term 'reasonable' qualified 'practicability'.

The issue of the practicability and its scope in relation to an employer with a large workforce working with contractors was raised in *R. v. Swan Hunter Shipbuilders Ltd. and Telemeter Installations Ltd. 1981*. Here eight men had been tragically killed by a fire which broke out on a ship under construction on the river Tyne. The fire had been fueled by an oxygen enriched atmosphere caused by the failure of an employee of a sub-contractor (Telemeter) to turn off the oxygen supply over night. Both the employer and the sub-contractor were convicted of offences under the Act in the Crown Court and subsequently appealed to the Court of Appeal. The employer argued that the duty to provide a safe system of work to persons other than their own employees imposed an intolerable burden where there was a large workforce with many different direct employers. The court however having examined the wording of the Act decided that providing employees with a safe system of work may involve a duty to an employer to provide instruction and information to persons other than their own employees about potential dangers. Such instructions need not be given if the employer can show on the balance of probabilities that it was not reasonably practicable in the circumstances. Here the employer was aware of the dangers and by sub-contracting the work they were under a duty to 'inform and instruct'.

Whether evidence that the method of working adopted by the employers was a universal practice within an industry and ipso facto discharges the duty imposed by the Act was considered by the High Court in *Martin v. Boulton and Paul (Steel Construction) Ltd. 1982*. The court held that a universal practice whilst of great weight is not conclusive evidence that it was not reasonably practicable to use some other and safer method.

Under the 1974 Act a body called the Health and Safety Commission was created, which has been given the function of providing detailed regulations on health and safety applying to the various industries. In this way, the previous legislation on health and safety will gradually be replaced. The Commission also produced codes of practice which although not regarded as law, give guidance as to how the regulations may be fulfilled. Enforcement of the Act is in the hands of the Health and Safety Executive and for some purposes local authorities. The enforcement bodies have a number of powers at their disposal. It should be stressed that an employer or employee who infringes The Health and Safety at Work Act is in breach of the criminal law and may be prosecuted in a criminal court and fined or even imprisoned for a serious offence. Of course, the inspectors employed by the Executive will normally only prosecute after warnings have not been taken account of. One of the major innovations of the Act was the introduction of constructive sanctions which can be used by the Executive. If an inspector believes that a person is contravening one of the statutory provisions the inspector may serve on that person an improvement notice requiring that the contravention be remedied within a specific period. In cases where the contravention involves a risk of serious injury the inspector may serve a prohibition notice which will direct that the particular activity is terminated until the contravention is rectified.

INDUSTRIAL ACTION

By far the majority of trade union members belong to trade unions which are affiliated to the Trades Union Congress (TUC) and the majority of trade unions retain a political fund from which contributions are made to the Labour party. The recent statutory requirement under the Trade Union Act 1984 to ballot trade union members to determine whether they feel such a political fund should be retained has produced an overwhelming vote in favour. Under the Trade Union Act 1984 unions are required to comply with stringent balloting provisions in relation to the election of officers and the taking of industrial action. Furthermore under the Employment Act 1982 many of the immunities originally conferred on trade unions under the Trades Disputes Act 1906 have been removed. This means that individuals or organisations who suffer loss as a result of industrial action have now the opportunity of recovering damages from a trade union which authorises the action. A trade union may now be made vicariously liable for the torts or other unlawful acts of its members. In *Thomas v. NUM (South Wales Area) 1985,* the South Wales Area of the NUM was held liable for the tortious picketing of pits conducted by its branches.

In relation to industrial action, which would include strikes, blacking, go-slows, work to rule and overtime bans, trade union members have a limited immunity from legal proceedings in respect of their actions. Also the right to peacefully picket still remains although recent industrial action by the N.U.M. and N.G.A. has demonstrated the limited degree that it can be exercised in practice. Certainly there is no right to strike under English law and so a withdrawal of labour and most other forms of industrial action will amount to a breach of employment contracts and render employees liable to dismissal. Under s.62 of the Employment Protection (Consolidation) Act 1978 (as amended by the Employment Act 1982) if at the time of dismissal, the employee was taking part in a strike or other industrial action an industrial tribunal has no jurisdiction to hear a complaint of unfair dismissal. The only exception to the rule is if it can be shown that one or more of the employees of the same employer who took part in the strike have not been dismissed. This exception is contained in the EPCA 1978 and effectively means that if all those who take part in the industrial action are dismissed, then rights in relation to unfair dismissal are extinguished. While it is rare for an employer to dismiss his workforce in these circumstances a recent example is the dismissal of print workers by Rupert Murdoch's News International when they had taken industrial action. Furthermore it can be a difficult question to determine whether an employee is taking part in a strike or industrial action.

In *Coates v. Modern Methods and Materials 1982* the Court of Appeal held that for the purposes of the section an employee who stops work when a strike is called, and does not openly disagree with it, while he may be an unwilling participant, he is nevertheless taking part in the industrial action. Here the employee's fear of crossing the picket line and subsequent certified illness during the period of the strike were insufficient reasons to rebut the presumption that she was taking part in industrial action.

The extent to which s.62 can be used to remove statutory rights was demonstrated by the Court of Appeal in *Power Packing Casemakers Ltd. v. Faust and Others 1983*. Here the employees had been operating a voluntary overtime ban in pursuance of wage negotiations. When threatened with dismissal, all except three employees agreed to work overtime. The three were promptly dismissed and their complaint of unfair dismissal was upheld by an industrial tribunal. This was despite the fact that they were taking industrial action, for the tribunal felt that s.62 was inapplicable as the men were not in breach of their employment contracts. The EAT disagreed however, stating that the tribunal had no jurisdiction to hear the complaint as the men were taking part in 'other industrial action' within the meaning of s.62. The Court of Appeal held on further appeal, that industrial action whether in breach of contract or not, if it has the object of applying pressure or disrupting the employers business, must in accordance with s.62 remove the jurisdiction of the tribunal, unless the employees could show that they had been subjected to discriminatory treatment.

By pursuing a form of industrial action which does not constitute a breach of employment contracts the employees in the above case were nevertheless effectively stripped of statutory rights. Furthermore, s.62 was subsequently amended by the Employment Act 1982 which further weakens the position of the employee dismissed while taking part in industrial action. As a result of the amendment if an employer offers a dismissed employee re-engagement more than three months from that employee's date of dismissal, then the tribunal's jurisdiction in relation to unfair dismissal is still removed in relation to employees who are dismissed and not re-employed. This enables an employer to dismiss all those taking part in industrial action and then, after three months, selectively re-employ those employees he chooses.

THE CLOSED SHOP

It would be wrong to leave the subject of trade unions without making some mention of the 'closed shop' or 'union membership agreement'. Such agreements entered into by employers and trade unions provide that only members of an appropriate trade union or unions, will be employed as employees of a particular class at the work place. If the agreement provides that new employees must be members of a particular trade union then it is a 'pre-entry' closed shop. A 'post-entry' closed shop exists where the agreement is that every employee of the particular class must be a member of a particular trade union. The Employment Acts 1980 and 1982 have introduced stringent balloting provisions which must be complied with before closed shop agreements are legally effective. The closed shop is of course a peculiar British institution which has proved to be particularly durable and over five million people are covered by them. The main difficulty faced by those who object to their existence is that they are often informal agreements which have grown out of customary practice. Consequently they are therefore difficult to legislate against. Both employers and trade unions often see the closed shop as a valuable institution which reduces friction, ensures total representation of the workforce, and supports solidarity of action. In addition closed shops reduce the possibility of the formation of breakaway trade unions and deal with the problem of the 'free rider'. Obvious arguments against closed shops include the fact that access to jobs should be free and those who have objections to trade union membership should not be prejudiced.

At present union membership agreements (closed shops) are still recognised as lawful and subject to many exceptions may still be put forward as a defence to an action which would otherwise be an unlawful action short of dismissal or unfair dismissal. Union membership agreements are defined in the Trade Union and Labour Relations Act 1974 as an agreement which:-

a. is made by or on behalf of or otherwise exists between one or more independent trade unions or one or more employer's or employee's associations; and

b. relates to employee's of an indentifiable class; and

c. has the effect in practice of requiring the employees for the time being of the class to which it relates (whether or not there is a condition to that effect in their contract of employment) to be or become a member of the trade union or one of the unions which is or are parties to the agreement or arrangement or of another specified independent trade union.

The practical effect of the closed shop is therefore that employees of the affected class are required to join the union or one of the specified unions.

In *Sarvant v. CEGB 1976* the tribunal held that an agreement which was operated loosely so that a number of dissenters had not been compelled to join the union was therefore unenforceable. Recently however, in *Taylor v. Co-operative Retail Services Ltd. 1982* the Court of Appeal held that despite the fact that approximately ten per cent of the relevant employees were not members, a practice of adherence to the closed shop had been established and it was enforceable.

Given the existence of a valid closed shop agreement, a dismissal for non-compliance with it may be protected by the present legislation.

The relevant legislation provisions are contained in s.58 of the EPCA 1978 which deals with inadmissable reasons for dismissal. Under s.58(1) a dismissal is to be regarded as unfair if the reason for it is that the employee:-

a) was or proposed to become a member of an independent trade union; or

b) had taken part or proposed to take part in the activities of an independent trade union at an appropriate time; or

c) was not a member of a trade union or a particular trade union or had refused to become or remain a member.

Therefore non membership of a trade union is made an inadmissable reason for dismissal. This is subject to s.58(3) however which states that a dismissal is to be regarded as fair if:-

a) it is the practice, in accordance with a union membership agreement, for employees of the employer who are of the same class as the dismissed employee to belong to a specified independent trade union, or to one of a number of specified independent trade union; and

b) the reason for the dismissal was that the employee was not, or had refused or proposed to refuse to become or remain, a member of a trade union in accordance with the agreement; and

c) the union membership agreement had been approved in relation to employees of that class through a ballot held within the period of five years ending with the time of the dismissal.

The dismissal of an employee out of compliance with a closed shop is statutorily fair therefore if the reason for the dismissal is non-compliance, and the closed shop has been approved in accordance with the balloting provisions introduced by the Employment Act 1982. The validity of any such ballot is governed by s.58A which requires a majority of either not less than 80% of those entitled to vote or not less than 85% of those who voted, to vote in favour of the agreement. Even where s.58(3) has been complied with there are a large number of exceptions to it, introduced in earlier legislation and subsequently amended by the Employment Act 1982. The main exception is contained in s.58(4) and applies if the employee genuinely objects on grounds of conscience or other deeply-held personal conviction to be a member of any trade union whatsoever or of a particular trade union.

> Some guidance as to the meaning of "conscience or other deeply held personal conviction" was provided by the EAT in *Home Delivery Services Ltd. v. Shackcloth 1984*. Here the employee was a member of USDAW which had entered into a closed shop agreement with his employer in 1977. The employee left the trade union in 1983 because he objected to certain of its decisions and was then dismissed by his employer. This was despite the fact that he claimed to come under the closed shop agreement's escape clause allowing a non member in some cases to make donations to charity. On appeal the EAT held that the tribunal's construction of the escape clause was wrong and the employee could not come within it. The dismissal was fair under s.58(3) unless the provisions of s.58(4) made the dismissal unfair and the complainant could show that he came within one or the other of the statutory exceptions. Objections on the grounds of 'conviction' do not have to be of a moral or conscientious nature. The subsection was intended to enlarge the field and there is no reason why a deeply held conviction that a trade union has let an employee down should not come within the subsection.

Compensation available for dismissals relying on unadmissable reasons under s.58 was substantially increased by the Employment Act 1982. The minimum basic award is £2,000. A further 'special award' is available amounting to 104 times a weeks pay up to a maximum of £20,000 or £10,000 whichever is greater where the claimant applies for reinstatement or re-engagement. A further important development is the right of an employer or the complainant to join a party to the action or person or trade union who has induced the dismissal. In this way a trade union may be ordered to pay a substantial portion of the compensation awarded to a successful complainant.

DISCRIMINATION

One major area of responsibility that all those involved in the management of human resources should be aware of is the need to provide equal opportunities to their workers or potential workers. Numerous studies have shown that discriminatory practices are still widespread in Britain and this has resulted in the passing of legislation with the aim of introducing protection against discrimination and in so doing possibly re-educating those who are guilty of it.

The principal features of the legislation relating to discrimination are set out below. Both the Race Relations Act 1976 and the Sex Discrimination Act 1975 identify similar categories of unlawful acts of discrimination. It is convenient therefore to set out these unlawful acts in tabular form as a means of comparison.

Race Relations Act, 1976   **Sex Discrimination Act, 1975**

Direct Discrimination

This occurs where one person: Treats another less favourably on racial grounds such as by segregating workers.

This occurs when one person: Treats another less favourably on the grounds of sex or marital status such as by providing women with different working conditions or selecting married women first for redundancy.

Indirect Discrimination

This occurs where one person: Requires another to meet a condition which as a member of a racial group is less easily satisfied because:-

a) the proportion of that group who can comply with it is smaller; and

b) the condition is to the complainant's detriment and is not justified. There would therefore be indirect discrimination if an employer required young job applicants to have been educated only in Britian.

This occurs where one person: Requires another to meet a condition which as a member of a particular sex or as a married person is less easily satisfied because:-

a) the proportion of that sex or married persons who can comply with it is smaller; and

b) the condition is to the complainant's detriment and is not justified. There would therefore be indirect discrimination if an employer advertised for a clerk who is at least six feet tall.

Victimisation

This occurs where one person: Treats another less favourably because the other has given evidence or information in connection with, brought proceedings under, or made allegations under the Act against the discriminator.

This occurs where one person: Treats another less favourably because the other has given evidence or information in connection with, brought proceedings under, or made allegations under the Act or the Equal Pay Act, 1970, against the discriminator.

Sex and Race Discrimination in Employment

The Sex Discrimination Act 1975 is concerned with discrimination on grounds of sex either by males against females, or vice versa, and on grounds of marital status by treating a married person less favourably than an unmarried person either directly or indirectly.

> In *Nemes v. Allen 1977* an employer in an attempt to cope with a redundancy situation dismissed female workers when they married. This was held to be unlawful direct discrimination on the grounds of sex and marital status.

The Race Relations Act 1976 is concerned with discrimination on racial grounds which is based upon colour, race, nationality, or ethnic or national origin.

> In *Race Relations Board v. Mecca 1976* an individual telephoned to apply for a job but when the employer discovered the applicant was black, he put the phone down. This was held to be unlawful direct discrimination as the applicant had been denied the opportunity to apply for a job on racial grounds.

In relation to employment any discriminatory practice which comes within the three categories (direct, indirect or victimisation) is unlawful. It is therefore unlawful for a person in relation to employment by him to discriminate in the arrangements he makes for the purposes of deciding who should be offered employment, the terms on which it is offered or by refusing to offer employment. Also where there is a subsisting employment relationship it is unlawful for an employer to discriminate in the way he gives access to opportunities for promotion, transfer, training or any other benefits, or refuses to afford such access. Furthermore it is unlawful to discriminate by dismissing the complainant or subjecting her to any other detriment. It should be noted however that unlawful discrimination practices in employment do not apply to employment for the purposes of a private household or where the number of employees does not exceed five. The anti-discrimination legislation provides redress for those who "contract personally to execute any work or labour". In *Daley v. Allied Supplier Ltd. 1983* an allegation of racial discrimination could not be entertained because it was felt that working as a Y.O.P. trainee created relationships which were neither ones of employment or of personally executing work. Now however trainees under the Youth Training Scheme (Y.T.S.) have been brought within the discrimination legislation by departmental order.

Direct Discrimination

In an allegation of direct discrimination in relation to race, sex or marital status the burden of proof is on the complainant. The difficulty is of course often direct evidence of discrimination is not available and consequently it is sufficient if the complainant can provide evidence that points to discrimination.

> In *Humphreys v. St. Georges School 1978* a complainant woman teacher established the following facts. As an experienced teacher along with two less experienced and less well qualified male applicants, she had applied for two vacant posts within a school. These facts, along with the fact that both male applicants were appointed, were sufficient to raise a prima facie case of sex discrimination.

In the case of job applications it will normally be sufficient for the complainant to show that she possessed the minimum requirements for the job, that she was rejected, and yet later the employer continued to seek applicants or appointed one of the opposite sex. The employer may be called upon to justify his action with a clear and creditable explanation. If the employer puts forward a number of reasons for his conduct, some valid and some discriminatory, then provided the discriminatory reason was an important factor then there is unlawful discrimination.

> In *Owen & Briggs v. James 1982* a case involving race discrimination, the complainant was a young black girl who had applied for a job as a shorthand typist with a firm of solicitors. She was interviewed for the job but rejected. When the post was readvertised some months later she reapplied but when she arrived for her interview the employer refused to see her. The same day a young white girl was appointed to the post despite the fact that her shorthand speed (35 words per minute) was far inferior to the complainant's (80 words per minute). It was also established that one of the partners of the firm had said to the successful candidate "why take on a coloured girl when English girls were available". The applicant's unlawful direct discrimination on the grounds of race was upheld in the Industrial Tribunal and on appeal in the Employment Appeals Tribunal. On further appeal to the Court of Appeal by the employer it was argued that there could be no unlawful discrimination unless the sole reason for the conduct was the racial factor. This argument was rejected, the court deciding that it is sufficient if race is an important factor in the employers decision and accordingly the appeal was unsuccessful.

One major difficulty facing a complainant is that proving discrimination may be impossible without access to documents which the employers hold. Since they may be confidential the applicant cannot have access to them unless the Industrial Tribunal chairman believes that they are relevant.

The words 'on the grounds of' sex, race or marital status in the statutes would cover the situation where the reason for discrimination was a generalised assumption that men, women, married persons, or persons of a particular race, possess or lack certain characteristics.

> In *Skyrail Oceanic Ltd. v. Coleman 1981* two rival firms employed a man and woman who were subsequently married and for reasons of confidentiality, the woman was dismissed. The Court of Appeal held by a majority that, as the reason for dismissing the woman rather than the man was based on a general assumption that the man in a marriage is the breadwinner, and this is an assumption based on sex, this amounted to unlawful discrimination.

A useful tool to attack the credibility of the employers denial of discrimination is statistical evidence. This is particularly so when the management decisions on matters such as promotion or access to benefits are based upon subjective criteria such as 'excellence', 'potential' or 'efficiency'.

The types of questions asked in interviews may be of relevance to determine whether there has been discrimination.

> In *Saunders v. Richmond on Thames LBC 1978* the EAT confirmed that it is not in itself unlawful to ask a question of a woman which would not be asked of a man. Here in an interview for a job as a golf professional, the female applicant was asked whether there were any other female golf professionals and whether she thought that men would respond as well to a woman golf professional as to a man. Her claims of unlawful discrimination when she was not appointed did not succeed. The existence of direct discrimination depended upon whether she was treated less favourably on the grounds of sex than a man. Here, while the questions demonstrated an out of date attitude, the industrial tribunal was entitled to find that they were not asked with the intention of discriminating.

It is also unlawful to show an intention to commit an act of discrimination in relation to employment. Therefore the publication of an advertisement which invites applicants for the post of salesman or barmaids would constitute unlawful discrimination.

> Less favourable treatment on racial grounds was argued in *Showboat Centre v. Owens 1984*. The basis of the complaint was that the applicant had been dismissed for refusing to obey an instruction to exclude all black customers. The EAT upheld the complaint stating that less favourable treatment on racial grounds included circumstances where the race of a third party was the effective cause of detriment suffered by the complainant.

Finally it should be mentioned that a claim of unlawful discrimination will succeed if the arrangements made for the purposes of determining who should be offered a job operate to discriminate even though they were not made with that purpose.

> In *Brennan v. J.H. Dewhurst 1984* the EAT held that if the tribunal finds that in a job interview a shop manager shows that by his questions and manner that he has no desire to employ a woman then there is unlawful discrimination under the Act.

Indirect Discrimination

Indirect discrimination is a more subtle form of discrimination than direct discrimination and occurs where a person requires another to meet a requirement or condition which as a member of a particular sex, race or marital status is less easily satisfied. This is because the proportion of those of that type who can comply with the condition is smaller, and it is to the complainants a detriment and not justifiable. In an allegation of indirect discrimination it is necessary to show that the requirement of a condition is mandatory rather than one of a number of criteria which the employer would take into account. Also for the purposes of showing that the proportion of the complainants type who can comply with the condition is smaller there is no need to produce elaborate statistical evidence, but rather a common sense approach is to be encouraged.

> In *Price v. Civil Service Commission 1978* the complainant alleged indirect discrimination on the grounds of sex because far fewer women than men could comply with the age limits of $17^1/_2$ to 28 to qualify as an eligible candidate for the executive officer grade. By comparing the proportion of qualified women with the proportion of qualified men, it is obvious that as a larger number of women of that age group will be likely to be having or bringing up children, then the proportion who can comply with the age requirement is less. The EAT held that as the proportion who can comply in practice is less and the requirement was not justifiable, there was unlawful indirect discrimination.

It should be stressed that even if the complainant could comply with the requirement or condition, it is whether this is possible in practice that is important.

> In *Mandla v. Dowell Lee 1983* even though the Sikh child could comply with the school rule by cutting his hair and removing his turban, he could not comply in practice as this would contravene the rules of his racial group, defined by the House of Lords by reference to ethnic origins. As the no turban rule was thought not justifiable the allegation of indirect discrimination had been proved.

> A different result was reached in *Singh v. Rowntree Mackintosh 1979*. This time the complaint related to a 'no beard rule' operated by confectioners, which was alleged to be indirectly discriminatory against Sikhs. Here the EAT held that while the rule was discriminatory, it was a justifiable requirement on the grounds of hygiene, supported by medical advice, and therefore not unlawful. The burden of proof was on the employer to justify the requirement or condition and here the tribunal recognised that in adopting standards the employer must be allowed some independence of judgment as to what he believes is a common expedient in the conduct of his business.

> In *Bayoomi v. British Railways Board 1981* the requirement complained of was that the applicant for the post of telex operator should within six months, without formal training, become competent in using and operating a particular machine. Such a requirement it was alleged was indirectly discriminatory of the applicant's racial group, for as an immigrant, mastery of the procedures was more difficult, bearing in mind alien environmental factors. As the employer failed to justify the requirement of proficiency without formal training, the requirement was held to be unlawful.

Genuine Occupational Requirement

Both the Sex Discrimination Act 1975 and the Race Relations Act 1976 identify circumstances where discrimination in employment is lawful. They are referred to as instances of genuine occupational qualification (GOQ).

The categories of genuine occupational requirements are:

1. Where the job requires a man or woman for physiological reasons other than physical strength, or in dramatic performances or other entertainment for reasons of authenticity, e.g. female stripper or male model.

2. Where there are considerations of decency or privacy because the job is likely to involve physical contact with men in circumstances where they might reasonably object to it being carried out by a woman e.g. male toilet attendant.

3. Where there are statutory restrictions, e.g. women may not work underground in coal mines.

4. Where the work location makes it impracticable to live elsehwere than the employer's premises and it is unreasonable to expect the employer to provide separate facilities for sleeping or sanitation, e.g. an oil rig.

5. Where the personal service is most effectively provided by a man or woman, e.g. a female social worker dealing with unmarried mothers.

6. Where the nature of the establishment within which the work is done requires the job to be held by a man because it is a hospital, prison or other establishments for males requiring special care and it is reasonable that the job should not be held by a woman.

7. Where the job needs to be held by a man because it is likely to involve the performance of duties outside the United Kingdom in a country whose law and customs are such that the duties could not be effectively performed by a woman, e.g. Saudi Arabia.

8. Where the job is one of two to be held by a married couple.

The Race Relations Act 1976 also identifies instances where membership of a particular racial group is a genuine occupational requirement.

1. Drama and entertainment, where the person of that racial group is required for reasons of authenticity e.g. employing only a black actor to play the part of 'Martin Luther King'.

2. Artist's or photographic models in order to achieve authenticity, e.g. a photograph depicting a national scene.

3. Bar or restaurant work where the setting requires an employee from a particular race, again for reasons of authenticity e.g. Chinese Restaurant.

4. The holder of the job provides persons of that racial group with personal services promoting their welfare and those services can most effectively be provided by a person of that racial group e.g. a Bangladeshi social worker.

Enforcement and Remedies

In the employment field an individual may make a complaint of sex or race discrimination to an industrial tribunal. Such a complaint must be presented within three months of the act of discrimination as the last date of a continuing discrimination. Claims out of time may be permitted if it just and equitable and generally the tribunals are more lenient in applying this rule to discrimination rather than to unfair dismissal. A copy of the complaint must be sent to an ACAS concilliation officer who is duty bound to attempt to achieve a settlement if requested to by the parties or if he feels he has a reasonable prospect of success. The remedies available to the tribunal if the complaint is made out are:-

(a)   an order declaring the rights of the parties;

(b)   an order requiring the respondent to pay the complainant damages subject to the upper limit for unlawful dismissal claims;

(c)   a recommendation of action to be taken by the respondent to reduce the adverse affect of discrimination.

A failure by the respondent without reasonable justification to comply with a recommendation may lead to an award of increased compensation.

Enforcement of the legislation is also the role of the Commissions who can institute a formal investigation and being satisfied that unlawful discriminatory acts or practices have taken place, may issue a non discrimination notice on any person. Such a notice will require the person on whom it is served not to commit the acts complained of and also comply with any required changes in conduct. The Commissions may seek an injunction to prevent repeated discrimination within five years of the non discrimination notice becoming final.

The Role of the Commissions

The Commission for Racial Equality was established under the 1976 Act and is charged with the following duties:-

(a)   to work towards the elimination of discrimination;

(b)   to promote equality of opportunity and good relations between persons of different racial groups generally; and

(c)   to help keep under review the working of the Act and when required to do so by the Secretary of State, draw up and submit proposals for amendments.

Power is also conferred on the Commission to grant financial assistance to organisations which appear to be concerned with the promotion of racial harmony, and also undertake or assist in research on educational activities for this purpose. Every year the Commission must submit an annual report to the Secretary of State to be laid before Parliament.

A major role of the Commission is to review the working of the legislation, report and make recommendations. In 1983 the Commission produced a consultative paper called "The Race Relations Act 1976 — Time for a Change?" and also its Code of Practice for the elimination of racial discrimination and the promotion of equal opportunity in employment. Recommendations of the consultative paper included amendments to the definition of discrimination, the creation of a duty on employers to submit records to the CRE on request and the creation of a more flexible and shorter investigatory process. The Code's most important recommendation is that employers should monitor the effects of selection decisions and personal practices. This involves analysing the ethnic composition of the workforce and the selection decisions for recruitment, promotion, transfer and training in accordance with racial groups. The legal status of the Code is that it is admissable in evidence in tribunal proceedings and "if any provision of such a code appears to be relevant to any question arising in the proceedings it shall be taken into account on determining that question".

Only the Commission may bring proceedings before the county court in respect of certain unlawful acts namely discriminatory advertising, unlawful instructions to discriminate (s.30) and unlawful inducements to discriminate (s.31).

> The meaning of ss.30 and 31 were considered by the EAT in *C.R.E. v. Imperial Society of Teachers of Dancing 1983*. Here there had been a request by an employer to a school's head of careers that no coloured students should be sent to fill a job. The EAT held that there had been no instruction to discriminate under s.30 because the instructor had no 'authority' over the instructed. Nevertheless there had been a contravention of s.31, for the request was an attempt to induce an infringement of the Race Relations Act.

Where the unlawful act is committed by an employee in the course of his employment the principles of vicarious liability apply and the employer is also made liable for the act whether or not it is done with his approval. It is a defence for an employer to prove that he took such steps as were reasonably practicable to prevent the employees from doing that act or from doing, in the course of his employment, acts of that description. Furthermore a person who knowingly aids another to commit an unlawful act of discrimination will be treated as doing the unlawful act himself.

In relation to sex discrimination the 1975 Act established the Equal Opportunities Commission charging it with similar duties to those imposed on the Commission for Racial Equality. Such duties include an obligation to produce and submit an annual report to be laid before Parliament by the Secretary of State. Similiar powers are also conferred on the EOC to finance research and educational activities and issue codes of practice. The EOC is empowered to conduct formal investigations in which persons may be required to furnish information or give evidence. The EOC must then report and make recommendations in the light of any of their findings. If in the course of an investigation the EOC is satisfied that discriminatory acts or practices have occurred then it may issue a non-discrimination notice. Proceedings in respect of discriminatory advertising, discriminatory instructions or inducements can only be brought by the EOC. Both the CRA and the EOC have a role to play in assisting an individual who is an actual or prospective complainant. This assistance may be granted if the case in question raises an issue of principle or because of its complexity, it is unreasonable to expect the complainant to deal with it unaided or by reason of any other special considerations. The assistance which both Commissions may offer extends to giving advice, procuring a settlement of the dispute, arranging for legal advice and/or representation and any other appropriate assistance.

LIABILITY IN RELATION TO LAND USE

All managers must be aware of the potential liability that may arise as a result of the organisation's use of land. An organisation in possession of land may be made liable to adjoining occupiers, visitors or the public in relation to the use to which the land is put. To appreciate the various forms of liability it is necessary to examine the concept of a nuisance, the responsibilities of an occupier in relation to the safety of entrants and the legal position in relation to the use of land for high risk activities.

OCCUPIERS LIABILITY

All occupiers of land and buildings have a responsibility under the law for the safety of those who come into their buildings and onto their land. As far as lawful entrants are concerned they are given protection by virtue of the Occupiers Liability Act 1957. This Act imposes a duty on all occupiers in relation to the safety of visitors who come onto their premises. If the occupier fails to fulfil this duty and a visitor suffers personal injury as a result then prima facie he will have a right of action in tort to recover damages for the harm caused. All other entrants are classified as trespassers and any duty that is imposed on the occupier in relation to their safety was contained in the common law tort of negligence and is now ebodied in the Occupiers Liability Act 1984.

Under the Occupiers Liability Act 1957 the common duty of care is owed by an occupier of premises to all his lawful visitors. Notice that the duty is owed by the occupier and he is regarded as a person in control of the premises. He would certainly include the owner in possession or a tenant or licensee.

The common duty of care is expressed in the 1957 Act as a duty to take such care as in all the circumstances of the cases is reasonable to see that the visitor will be reasonably safe in using the premises for the purposes for which he is invited or permitted to be there. The term 'premises' is referred to in the Act as including not only land and buildings but also fixed or movable structures such as caravans, vehicles, houseboats or even aircraft. In addition to this general standard of exercising reasonable care towards visitors, the Act specifies that in relation to child visitors an occupier must be prepared for them to be less careful than adults. This suggests that a high standard of care is owed in relation to children and a warning sign that may be sufficient to protect an adult may not be so for a child.

The requirement of parental control however is a significant factor in establishing liability for injury caused to child visitors.

> In *Phipps v. Rochester Corporation 1955* two young children aged five and seven walked across a large open space which was part of a housing development. The younger child suffered injury when he fell into a long deep trench which had been dug up in order to lay a sewer. Both children were regarded as licensees, but in measuring the extent of the duty owed to them by the occupier, the court decided that the habits of prudent parents in relation to young children should be taken into account. Accordingly it was held that the occupier was entitled to assume that prudent parents would have ensured there was no dangers on the land or would have prevented the children from entering. There was therefore held to be no breach of duty.

The concept of the reasonably prudent parent is of particular importance when measuring the duty required of a local authority landlord in relation to a tenant's young children.

> In *Ryan v. London Borough of Camden 1982* a young child was injured when she leant against exposed heating pipes in the council flat rented by her parents. In deciding that the local authority landlord had fulfilled the duty of care owed to the child the court had taken account of the safety record of the heating system, its widespread use and additionally the precautions which one would expect to be taken by a prudent parent.

The role of the prudent parent was also emphasised by the Court of Appeal when child visitors were injured on local authority waste land.

> In *Simkiss v. Rhondda B.C. 1983* a seven year old suffered injury when she fell 30 or 40 feet after sliding on a blanket down a steep slope owned by the council. The High Court found the council liable for breach of the common duty of care in failing to either ensure that the mountainside was safe for children to play on or alternatively fencing it off. The Court of Appeal took a different view of the matter however and pointing out that adults would have realised that the mountainside must have been an obvious danger, the council was entitled to assume that parents would have warned their children of the danger. In reversing the decision of the High Court, the Court of Appeal stressed that the council's duty of care was not broken by failing to fence the mountain. To require a local authority to fence every natural hazard under its control would impose too onerous a burden.

Not only children but independent contractors are also singled out for mention in the Act. Such persons engaged to carry out specialist work should be aware of the risks inherent in their own trades.

> This is reflected in *Roles v. Nathan 1963* where, despite being warned of the danger, two chimney sweeps carried on working on a boiler and were killed by carbon monoxide poisoning entering from the ventilation system. The employer/occupier was held in the circumstances not to be liable. Ld. Denning M.R. stated that "when a householder calls in a specialist to deal with a defective installation on his premises he can reasonably expect the specialist to appreciate and guard against the dangers arising from the defect".

An occupier may satisfy the duty of care imposed upon him in one of two ways. He may either ensure that his premises are reasonably safe and free from dangers or give effective warning of the danger which is sufficient to enable the visitor to be reasonably safe. The latter course could be achieved by the prominent display of a warning notice. Prior to 1971, all occupiers of premises had a further option open to them. They could simply exclude or restrict the duty owed to their visitors.

This right to exclude liability has been modified to a large extent by the Unfair Contract Terms Act 1977 This Act applies to duties which arise for occupiers of business premises and states that liability for negligence including breach of the common duty of care under the 1957 Act causing death or physical injury cannot be excluded or restricted. This means that as far as business property is concerned neither owner occupiers, landlords or tenants can exclude or restrict liability for physical injury resulting from a failure to fulfil their respective obligations. The Act also provides that liability for other loss or damage can be excluded or restricted but only to the extent that such provision satisfies the test of reasonableness laid down in the Act.

Where injury is caused to a visitor because of the negligent workmanship of a contractor then the liability of the occupier will depend on whether he acted reasonably in entrusting the work to the contractor in the first place. Certainly the occupier will have acted reasonably if he selected a reputable organisation to do the work rather than a local handyman.

> In *O'Connor v. Swan & Edgar 1963* the plaintiff was injured by a fall of plaster when she worked as a demonstrator on the first defendant's premises. The fall of plaster was due to the faulty workmanship of the second defendants who had been engaged as contractors to work on the premises. The court held that as the first defendants had acted reasonably in entrusting the work to a reputable contractor then as an occupier he had satisfied the duty of care which was owed. The second defendants however were held liable in the tort of negligence for faulty workmanship.

Trespassers

A trespasser is not a lawful visitor so therefore the 1957 Act has no relevance in determining any liability that may be imposed if he suffers injury. The duty owed towards trespassers was found by referring to the common law, and the traditional attitude of the courts was that, so long as an occupier did not set out to injure trespasses intentionally, then he would not be made liable for their injuries.

> This approach is illustrated in *Addie v. Dumbreck 1929* where the defendant occupier of a colliery was held by the House of Lords to owe no duty of care under the common law towards a child trespasser who was crushed in the wheel of the defendant's haulage system.

The harshness of this attitude was mitigated to some extent by the doctrine that if the children habitually trespassed and an occupier took no steps to warn them off his land, the child trespasser could be regarded as a lawful visitor and was thus owed a duty of care. The contemporary approach is reflected in the following decision of the House of Lords which effectively overules the precedent of *Addie v. Dumbreck*.

> In *British Railways Board v. Herrington 1972*, British Rail had negligently failed to maintain fencing which ran between their railway track and a park frequently used by children. A six-year old climbed through the fence, wandered onto the track, and suffered severe injury on the electrified rail. The House of Lords held the Board liable in negligence to the child trespasser. The Court stated that, ". . . if the presence of the trespasser is known or ought reasonably to be anticipated by the occupier then the occupier has . . . a duty to treat the trespasser with ordinary humanity". Among the factors to be taken into account in such cases are the degree of potential harm faced by the trespassers, the financial resources of the occupier and, in the case of children, whether the premises act as an allurement. In this case the Board were aware of a known and potentially lethal danger particularly to children. The standard of care required of an occupier in these circumstances was to "act as a conscientious humane man, with his knowledge, skill and resources, could reasonably be expected to act". British Rail had not fulfilled this duty and were liable for damages.

It should be noted that the duty owed to a trespasser is a restricted duty and much less than the standard of care owed to a lawful visitor. In addition, the court pointed to the economic resources of the occupier as a factor to determine whether he had acted reasonably.

An important factor to determine whether child trespassers are forseeable is whether or not the occupier has things on his land which might attract a child, e.g. building site, water, fire.

> In *Harris v. Wirral BC 1976* the defendant local authority, who failed to board up an empty house under their control, were held liable to a child trespasser who wandered inside and was injured. The presence of the child, the court decided, was forseeable as he was attracted to the derelict property and the failure to prevent his entry was not the conduct to be expected of a conscientious humane local authority.

The High Court has recently imposed liability on an occupier for injuries caused to an adult trespasser.

> In *Umek v. London Transport Executive 1984* a canteen assistant employed by the defendants was killed when she crossed the railway tracks and was struck down by a train. The station subway was out of action due to flooding and the staff foreman had roped it off and put up a notice stating that staff should use the footbridge rather than cross the tracks. The plaintiff ignored the notice to her cost and her personal representatives subsequently brought on an action in negligence against the LTE. The claim alleged that train drivers should have been warned of the potential hazard of staff walking across the line. The High Court agreed that failing to warn was indeed negligent, given the fact that the LTE were aware that staff were crossing the tracks. The plaintiff as a trespasser was owed the common duty of humanity which had been broken by the defendants. As the plaintiff was 75% to blame for the accident however, damages would be reduced by that amount to reflect the contributory fault.

In an attempt to clarify the rules relating to the liability of an occupier towards trespassers the Occupiers Liability Act 1984 was passed. The Act replaces the common law, which includes the rules laid down by the House of Lords in Herrington's case, 1972.

Under the 1984 Act the occupier will owe a duty to trespassers if:-

    a.   he is aware or ought to be of danger; and

    b.   knows or has reasonable grounds to believe that the trespasser is or may be in the vicinity of danger; and

    c.   may reasonably be expected in all the circumstances to offer some protection to the trespasser against the danger.

Having established the existence of a duty the Act goes on to provide that the duty extends to taking such care as in all the circumstances is reasonable to see that the trespasser does not suffer injury by reason of the danger concerned. It is also provided that the duty may in an appropriate case be discharged by warning.

Whether the objective of clarification has been furthered by converting the law into a statutory form is to be doubted for the existence of a duty of care will still demand a consideration of "all the circumstances" to determine whether the trespasser deserves protection. This may well involve a consideration of the circumstances identified in Herrington's case such as the resources of the occupier, the extent of likely harm, the frequency of trespass etc. In addition the new Act has confined itself to personal injury and so the common law is still relevant if the claim involves damage to the property of the trespasser.

NUISANCE

The concept of a 'nuisance' covers a wide range of legal situations having both common law and statutory origins, and involving both the criminal and civil law. Under the common law a nuisance was originally confined to an interference with another's use of land. If the interference constituted the tort of private nuisance it was redressable by an action for damages and/or an injunction. The common law crime of public nuisance was a later development encompassing a wide range of petty offences redressable by prosecutions leading to fines and abatement orders. A further complication arose when the courts recognised that an individual who suffered special damage as a result of a public nuisance could maintain an action for damages based on private nuisance. Finally a nuisance has also been created in a statutory form, in particular by means of the Public Health Act 1936. Enforcement in respect of statutory nuisances created under various Acts of Parliament is in the hands of public bodies such as Local Authorities. Such nuisances are crimes.

Public Nuisance

The common law crime of public nuisance has been defined as comprising of an act or omission which materially affects the reasonable comfort and convenience of a class of Her Majesty's subjects. Such a wide definition would encompass many types of conduct harmful to others and although not restricted to the use of the land it has been held to include various ways in which land may be unlawfully used, e.g. selling or serving food from premises in unhygienic conditions or causing an obstruction of the highway.

In *Fabbri v. Morris 1947* a trader committed a public nuisance by selling ice cream through his shop window causing queues to form which blocked the highway.

Public nuisances have also been held to cover such activities as keeping a disorderly house or carrying on a dangerous activity near the public highway.

In *Castle v. St. Augustine's Links Ltd. 1922* the court held that the proximity of a hole on a golf course to the public highway amounted to a public nuisance, and the plaintiff taxi driver who lost an eye as a result of a golf ball striking the windscreen of his cab, succeeded in a tort action against the defendants.

It is a requirement of public nuisance that a number of persons must be affected by the act or ommission. In the above case these were the persons using the highway. If however an individual can show that as a result of a public nuisance he has suffered some special damage beyond the discomfort of the public at large then he can succeed in a tort action for damages against the creator of it.

The person responsible for a public nuisance is prima facie the creator of it so that if the nuisance eminates from premises, the occupier in possession will usually be made responsible for it. If the premises are let however, and the nuisance arises out of the landlord's failure to fulfil an express or implied repair obligation, then the landlord may be prosecuted for it. Finally it should be mentioned that acts which constitute a public nuisance may also amount to offences under statute, e.g. the Highways Act 1959 (obstructing the highways), the Sexual Offences Act 1956 (keeping a disorderly house), and the Public Health Act 1936 (emitting noxious substances into the atmosphere).

The Tort of Private Nuisance

An individual in possession of land who suffers harm as a result of interference by an adjoining occupier can have recourse to the law of tort to provide a remedy. To succeed in such an action the plaintiff would have to establish the tort of private nuisance. Private nuisance has been defined as an unlawful interference with the person's use or enjoyment of land or of some right over or in connection with it. As a general rule the creator of a nuisance remains responsible for it. Thus if a landlord lets property in such a state that it constititutes a private nuisance, he may be made liable in tort to an adjoining occupier who suffers an unreasonable interference with the enjoyment of his land as a result. Alternatively if the tenant creates the nuisance then he will be solely responsible unless the creation of the nuisance was the inevitable consequence of the purpose of the letting, e.g. carrying on a noxious trade.

Private nuisance exists to protect those in possession or occupation of land. Where the damage caused is of a continuing nature however the fact that it originally arose prior to the plaintiff's occupation will not prevent an action to recover the loss.

> In *Master v. Brent LBC 1978* the roots of the defendant's lime tree encroached and caused damage to the foundations of the plaintiff's house. The fact that the damage first began to occur before the plaintiff acquired possession of the house did not prevent the plaintiff recovering the cost of repair. The interference was of a permanent nature and some damage continued to occur when the plaintiff took possession.

> The responsibility of a public body to take action to prevent a nuisance caused by trespassers on its land was highlighted by the decision of the Court of Appeal in *Page Motors v. Epsom and Ewell Borough Council 1982* Here the plaintiffs were lessees of premises owned by the defendants and complained of gypsy trespassers encamped nearby who were causing a considerable nuisance by interfering with the plaintiff's business. Following repeated complaints about their conduct, causing smoke, smells and rubbish, the defendants obtained a possession order against the gypsies in 1974 but it was not until September 1978 that the site was finally cleared. The Court of Appeal agreed that once the local authority were aware of the nuisance caused to adjoining occupiers they were under a duty to take reasonable steps to remove the cause within a reasonable time. As a reasonable time would in the circumstances be the period up to January 1 1975 the local authority were liable for the nuisance inference from that date until it was abated in 1978.

For an action to succeed in the tort of private nuisance the plaintiff must establish the existence of three essential elements.

1.　That there has been an indirect interference with the enjoyment of land.

This could be evidenced by matters such as excessive noise, smoke, smells, heat, vibrations and encroaching roots or branches of trees. This is in contrast to a direct interference such as trespass to land.

2.　That the interference has caused some sort of damage.

Damage may occur in the form of physical harm to the land or discomfort or inconvenience to the occupier.

> The case of *Halsey v. Esso Petroleum 1961* provides an example of actual physical harm. Here smuts from the defendant's chimneys caused damage to the plaintiff's clothes which had been hung out to dry.

> The case of *Kennaway v. Thompson and Another 1980* provides an example of damage in the form of discomfort and inconvenience. Here the plaintiff

occupied a house adjacent to a lake where the defendants carried on motor boat racing during the summer months. Claiming grave discomfort, caused by the excessive noise, the plaintiff sued under the tort of nuisance for damages and an injunction to restrain the activity. The Court of Appeal awarded an injunction to restrain the defendants' racing to such an extent that it could not be said to constitute an unreasonable interference with the plaintiff's use of her land.

3.   That the interference is an unlawful one.

The determination of this question is a crucial one involving an examination of all the circumstances of the particular case. The words of Ld. Wright in *Sedleigh – Denfield v. O'Callaghan 1940* should be taken account of. "A balance has to be maintained between the right of the occupier to do what he likes with his own and the right of his neighbour not to be interfered with". Relevant considerations would include the following:-

a.   The sensitivity of the plaintiff

Generally under the law the standard that an individual has to adhere to is that of the reasonable man. An occupier of the land is only entitled to reasonable comfort in the the enjoyment of his land and can hardly complain if he is peculiarly sensitive to his neighbours' conduct. An occupier therefore who merely suffers harm because he is overly sensitive to the interference cannot complain of it.

> In *Robinson v. Kilvert 1889* the plaintiff tenant occupied the ground floor of his landlord's premises which he used for the purposes of storing brown paper. The paper became badly damaged as a result of heat rising from a boiler in the defendant landlord's cellar. In an action based on private nuisance the court held that as the level of heat rising would be harmful to most goods there could be no nuisance for damage caused to sensitive brown paper.

b.   The reason for the interference

The fact that the defendant shows that his activities which constitute the alleged nuisance are in the public interest is of no bearing in determining whether or not they are unlawful.

> In *Adams v. Ursell 1913* the defendant's claim that his fried fish shop in the East End of London performed a public service in providing cheap food for the working classes was held to be irrelevant in determining whether it constituted a private nuisance.

On the other hand the fact that the defendant is acting from a malicious motive has been held to be a relevant consideration.

> In *Hollywood Silver Fox Farm v. Emmett 1936* there was a dispute between the defendant who had a farm adjacent to the plaintiff's silver fox farm. In an attempt to interfere with the foxes breeding the defendant asked his son to fire guns as near as possible to the plaintiff's land. The court held that the malicious intention was sufficient to make the interference an unlawful one and damages and an injunction were awarded for private nuisance.

c.   The locality of the nuisance

The location of the interference is an important factor in determining whether it is unlawful. The words of Thesiger L.J. in *Sturges v. Bridgman 1879* "What would be a nuisance in Belgrave Square would not necessarily be so in Bermondsey" still have relevance. It would be unreasonable therefore for an occupier of property in a heavy industrial area to complain of smoke from his neighbour's fire if the atmosphere is already to a large extent polluted.

d. Duration of the nuisance

Although the act complained of must usually be of a continuous nature such as constant emissions of smoke from a factory, nevertheless a single serious act could constitute a nuisance if it is evidence of a dangerous situation. Thus an explosion may be evidence of a dangerous state of affairs.

> In *Spicer v. Smee 1946* defective wiring in the defendant's bungalow caused a fire which spread to the plaintiff's property and liability in nuisance was imposed.

> Also in *British Celanese Ltd. v. A.H. Hunt Ltd. 1969* light strips of metal foil stored over a period of time on the defendant's land blew onto the plaintiff's land and caused damage. The defendant's were held liable in the tort of private nuisance.

> However in *S.C.M. (U.K.) Ltd. v. W.J. Whittall & Son Ltd. 1970* a workman negligently severed a cable and cut off the electricity supply to the plaintiff's factory and the defendants could not be made liable in nuisance as there was no state of affairs to point to.

> Finally in *Miller v. Jackson 1977* the regular hitting of cricket balls from a cricket ground onto adjacent property was held to be a sufficient course of conduct for the purpose of nuisance.

Defences

The defences to an action in nuisance include:-

1. 'Volenti non fit injuria' i.e. consent of the plaintiff to the interference.

2. That the nuisance was caused by the act of a stranger of whom the defendant was unaware.

3. That the nuisance has been in existence for 20 years or more and falls within the Prescription Act 1832. Of course it is the nuisance rather than the interference which must have been in existence for the 20 year period.

> In *Sturges v. Bridgman 1879* a confectioner caused noise and vibrations in the course of his trade which affected the adjoining garden of a physician. The interference had been in existence for more than 20 years but no damage was caused until the physician built a consulting room in his garden. The court held that as the nuisance was not created until the damage was caused, the Prescription Act 1832 provided no defence.

4. That the act which constitutes the nuisance is authorised by statute.

> In *Allen v. Gulf Oil Refining Ltd. 1979* the Gulf Oil Refining Act 1965 authorised the defendants to acquire land for the construction of a refinery. The oil refinery was built and began operations, but following complaints by adjoining occupiers of noxious odours, vibrations and unreasonable noise, an action in nuisance was finally brought. The House of Lords held that the defendants could rely on the Gulf Oil Act as a defence to an action in nuisance resulting from the operation of the refinery, but only to the extent that the nuisance was the inevitable result of such operation.

Remedies

The various remedies for the victim of a private nuisance include an action for damages, abatement of the nuisance (e.g. cutting off offending roots or branches of a tree that cross the boundary), or an injunction to prevent the defendant continuing the nuisance. It should be noted that an injunction is a discretionary remedy and need not be granted if the court feels that the circumstances of the case do not merit its grant.

In *Miller v. Jackson 1977* it was held that the cricket club was liable in nuisance but the Court refused to grant an injunction to prevent the playing of cricket after weighing the loss of the club to the community against the risk of injury to adjoining occupiers. This decision may be contrasted with the approach of the Court of Appeal in the later case of *Kennaway v. Thompson and Another 1980* where an injunction was granted but only to the extent that the interference was unreasonable.

. . . regular hitting of cricket balls . . .

Statutory Nuisance

In addition to the common law crime of public nuisance and the tort of private nuisance there is the concept of the statutory nuisance. This is simply a nuisance which is covered by a statutory provision, the most important of which is the Public Health Act 1936. This Act defines a statutory nuisance as including matters such as:

a.   premises in such a state as to be prejudicial to health or a nuisance;

b.   accumulation, deposit or animals kept in a similar state;

c.   dust or effluvia (ejected steam) caused by any trade business, manufacture or process and being prejudicial to the health of, or a nuisance to, the inhabitants of the neighbourhood;

d.   a workplace which is not provided with sufficient means of ventilation, or which is not kept clean, or which is so overcrowded while work is carried on as to be prejudicial to the health of those employed.

Local authorities are under a statutory duty to inspect their areas for statutory nuisances, the task of which falls on the Environmental Health Departments. In many cases, complaints of statutory nuisance (often by a tenant of property in disrepair) are made direct to the local authority which, if it feels a statutory nuisance exists, must serve a notice on the person responsible to require it to be abated (ended). If the person responsible (usually the owner) takes no action then the local authority can do the work itself and recover the cost from him or obtain a court order to require him to act. In cases where the local authority fails to take action, a victim of a statutory nuisance can bring a case before the Magistrates Court on his own initiative. If he is successful, the court has power to fine the person responsible and order the abatement of the nuisance. The inclusion, as a statutory nuisance, of noise and vibrations under the Noise Abatement Act 1960, and the emission of dark smoke under the Clean Air Acts has led to a large number of prosecutions against trading organisations. The ultimate aim of this legislation is, of course, to ensure minimum standards for occupiers of property, workers at their place of work and people generally in the environment in which we live. One of the latest examples is the Control of Pollution Act 1974, which places responsibility on local authorities for the control of waste, noise, atmospheric pollution, and the pollution of waterways. Failure by an organisation to comply with the statutory requirements will constitute a criminal offence.

THE TORT OF RYLANDS v. FLETCHER

A further tort, which this time imposes a strict duty on the occupier of land is, the tort of *Rylands v. Fletcher* which obtains its name from the famous case of 1868. Strict liability means that an organisation or individual who occupies land could be made liable under this tort without being at fault. The justification for imposing strict or absolute liabilty for certain use of land is that there are some high risk activities which, while it is in the public interest that they are carried on, nevertheless are likely to cause harm. It is also in the public interest that the innocent victims of these activities are able to recover recompense if they suffer harm, without the need to prove any fault.

> *Rylands v. Fletcher, 1868.* The case concerned a mill owner who had employed a contractor to build a reservoir on his land. The owner was not aware that an old mine shaft was underneath the land and when the reservoir was filled flooding caused damage to the neighbour's mine. Despite the absence of negligence on his behalf the court held the mill owner strictly liable for the escape of water by creating a new principle of law, now known as the rule in *Rylands v. Fletcher*. The grounds for the decision were stated by Blackburn, J. and they have now given status as a separate tort. "We think that the true rule of law is, that the person who for his own purposes brings on his lands and collects and keeps there anything likely to do mischief if it escapes, must keep it at his peril, and if he does not do so is prima facie answerable for all the damages which is the natural consequence of its escape."

It is possible to appreciate the width of this tort by examining its various elements.

a. Brings and collects the thing on his land.

The occupier must have brought something, non-natural to the land which could include water in a reservoir, gas, electricity, oil in a refinery, rather than something which accumulated naturally.

> In *Pontardawe R.D.C. v. Moore-Glwyn, 1929* it was held that there could be no liability, under the tort, for an outcrop of overhanging rock which had not been brought onto the land.

b.   The thing is likely to cause mischief if it escapes.

Despite the limitation of non natural use there are many things which have given rise to liability and these include filth, petrol, fire, explosives and vibrations. These by their very nature must also be regarded as mischievous.

> In *Attorney-General v. Corke, 1933* it was held that a group of caravan dwellers could be included when they caused damage on neighbouring land. Moreover in *Hale v. Jennings Bros. 1938* the Court of Appeal held that the rule in *Ryland v. Fletcher* applied when a chair from a fairground 'chair-o-plane' broke free from the roundabout and, complete with its occupant, flew off and caused injury to a nearby stallholder.

c.   There must have been an escape.

It is fundamental to impose liability that there has been an escape of the mischievious thing in question.

> In *Read v. J. Lyons & Co. Ltd. 1947* the plaintiff, a munitions inspector, was injured by an explosion in the defendant's munitions factory while performing her duties. In the absence of any negligence the plaintiff alleged strict liability under *Rylands v. Fletcher* for the defendants had brought the dangerous thing (the shells) onto the land and she has suffered harm as a result. The House of Lords held however that as there had been no escape for the purposes of the tort there could be no liability.

d.   The proper plaintiff and recoverable damage.

There still remains doubts as to whether the tort extends to personal injuries and also as to whether the plaintiff must necessarily have an interest in land to sue. Certainly in *Hale v. Jennings 1938* personal injuries were regarded as a proper head of damage by the Court of Appeal. Also in *Perry v. Kendricks Transport Ltd. 1956* Parker L.J. did not believe that the tort only applied to damage to adjoining land or to a proprietary interest in land and not to personal injuries. The contemporary view seems to be that it is possible to maintain an action in the tort without the need to show interference with a proprietary interest. As far as the defendant is concerned there is no requirement that the person who for his own purposes collects and keeps the mischievious thing is a freehold owner in possession. The rule has been held to apply to a local authority which is statutorily bound to receive sewage into its sewers, a utility company which has a statutory right to lay pipes on land, a tenant in possession and even a licensee who brings the mischievious thing onto the land.

Defences

A number of defences to the tort have been recognised including:-

a.   The consent of the plaintiff to the thing.

The general defence of volenti non fit injuria applies but while a tenant in a block of flats may impliedly consent to the supply of water on the premises he does not consent in the case of a defective dangerous or unusual supply. Similar to the defence of consenting is the idea that the defendant is not liable for the escape of a mischievious thing which was maintained for the common benefit of the plaintiff and the defendant.

b.   An escape due to the act of a stranger.

In *Rickards v. Lothian, 1913,* the defendant was held not liable for the escape of water from his premises when he showed that the escape was due to the act of a stranger, who had blocked up the waste pipe and turned on a tap.

It is up to the defendant to show that the escape was due to the unforseeable act of a stranger without any negligence on his part. A stranger in this context would most probably be limited to a trespasser and unless the actions of the trespasser could have been reasonably forseen and its consequences prevented the defendant will escape liability.

c. Statutory authority to collect the dangerous thing.

In *Pearson v. North-Western Gas Board, 1968*, the plaintiff's house was destroyed by a gas explosion caused by the fracture of a pipe. As the defendants were under a statutory duty to supply the gas, there was no liability under the tort.

d. An act of God.

This defence relates to an escape due to natural causes without human intervention. It should be stressed however that the defence is only applicable where the event causing the escape e.g. high tide, high wind, heavy rainfall, lightening, could not with human foresight and prudence have been anticipated.

e. An act of the plaintiff

If the escape is due to the act or default of the plaintiff himself he can have no remedy.

THE DISPOSAL OF RESOURCES

When running a business or indeed operating any organisation it may be necessary at some point to dispose of and often renew the business resources. The place of operation may change or new premises acquired, capital equipment may be renewed or supplemented and manpower may be replaced or new workers taken on. Usually such activities present no difficulties and the organisation is free to dispose of its existing resources as it chooses. There has however been some statutory intervention to regulate the rights of the parties in particular in relation to the termination and renewal of a business lease and also the termination of employment. It is proposed in this section therefore to deal with these issues from the point of view of an organisation as a business tenant and an employer.

THE TERMINATION AND RENEWAL OF BUSINESS TENANCIES

We have already seen that many organisations will carry on their activities in premises they hold as tenants or leaseholders, either on a fixed term basis such as a ten year lease or on a periodic basis, such as a tenancy from year to year.

For such organisations a major issue is the ability to be able to renew the business lease. If this is not possible new premises will have to be sought, which can be a costly time consuming inconvenience both to the business itself and its customers. Since the mid 1950's it has been recognised that a measure of security should be available to the business tenant to help overcome the hardship of possibly being obliged to move premises on the termination of the lease. The statutory provisions to deal with the position are contained in the Landlord and Tenant Act 1954, Part II.

Procedure for determination

The most fundamental right conferred on the business tenant by the Act is security of tenure. This is provided for in the provision of the Act relating to continuation and renewal of the business tenancy. Under s.24 a relevant tenancy will not come to an end on the expiration of its contractual terms but will continue automatically as a contractual tenancy unless terminated in accordance with the Act.

Action by the Landlord under Section 25

If the landlord wishes to bring the contractual tenancy to an end he must do so in accordance with the Act's provisions. Under s.25 the landlord may serve a statutory notice on the tenant, in writing, and in the prescribed form. This notice must be served not earlier than six nor more than twelve months before the date of termination specified within it.

If the post is used as the medium to serve the notice, and this is usually the case, then it is critical that sufficient time is allowed for the notice to reach the tenant to comply with the time limits.

The following matters must be included in the section 25 notice:-

    a.   The date of termination of the current tenancy; (this date must not be earlier than the date the term expires in the case of a fixed term tenancy or the earliest date of termination by notice in the case of a periodic tenancy).

    b.   A statement which requires the tenant to notify the landlord by counter-notice within two months as to whether he intends to give up possession of the premises on the date of termination;

    c.   A statement that the landlord is not willing to grant the tenant a new tenancy and, on an application by the tenant for a new tenancy, a statement of the statutory grounds on which the landlard intends to rely.

Following the receipt of a s.25 notice if the tenant wishes to oppose the landlord's termination of the contractual tenancy he must serve a counter-notice on the landlord within the two month period informing him of his opposition to delivering up possession and his intention to apply for a new tenancy.

> In *Chiswell v. Griffon Land and Estates Ltd. 1975* such a counter-notice was sent within the two month period by the tenant's solicitors but was apparently lost in the post. Despite proof of posting, the court held that as the tenant had failed to reply to the landlord's notice within two months from its service the court had no power to entertain his application for a new tenancy.

Having served a counter-notice, and in the event of the parties failing to reach agreement the next stage is for the tenant to apply to the court for a new tenancy. This is achieved by the tenant filing an application to the county court or the High Court not less than two and no more than four months after the s.25 notice has been served.

> Once again it is a strict requirement that the action is taken within the time period prescribed as was demonstrated by the House of Lord's decision in *Dodds v. Walker 1981*. Here a s.25 notice was served by the landlord on September 30th 1978 and the tenant applied to the county court for a new tenancy on January 31st 1979. The House of Lords held that the relevant period for such an application was between two and four months ending on the corresponding date of the appropriate subsequent month, and accordingly the tenant's application should be dismissed as out of time.

Action by the Tenant under Section 26

In the absence of agreement between the landlord and tenant as to the grant of a new tenancy the Act provides a means by which the tenant can take action. Under s.26 the tenant can terminate the current tenancy by making a request for a new tenancy to the landlord. The request must be served on the competent landlord, be in writing and in the prescribed form. It must be stressed that the s.26 request cannot be served if the landlord has already served a s.25 notice and vice-versa.

The following matters must be included in the s.26 request:-

    a.   The date of commencement of the new tenancy; (this date must be at least six but not more than twelve months after the request has been made).

    b.   A statement of the terms of the proposed new tenancy including such matters as the property to be comprised, the rent payable and its duration.

Notice that the tenant can specify a renewal date which is up to twelve months ahead even if the contractual term will expire sooner. This means that a s.26 notice served six months prior to the expiration of the term and providing for renewal in twelve months time prolongs the contractual tenancy for a further six months.

A landlord wishing to oppose the tenant's request for a new tenancy is obliged, within two months, to serve a counter-notice which must include a statement of the statutory ground upon which the landlord intends to rely. Failure to serve such a notice effectively means that the landlord loses all rights to oppose the tenant's application for a new tenancy.

Landlord's grounds for opposition

The alternative grounds upon which a landlord can rely to oppose a tenant's application to the court for a new tenancy are set out in section 30 of the Act.

S.30(1)(a)   Breach of a repairing obligation

Relying on this ground the landlord must prove that in view of the state of repair of the premises resulting from the tenant's failure to observe a repairing obligation under the current tenancy, a new tenancy ought not to be granted.

S.30(1)(b)   Persistant delay in paying rent. Here the landlord must prove that in view of the tenant's persistant delay in paying rent due under the current tenancy, a new tenancy ought not to be granted. Here again the court must be satisfied that the delay is a serious one either over an extended time period or consist of a number of separate delays.

S.30(1)(c)   Other substantial breaches. In this case the landlord must prove that the tenant ought not to be granted a new tenancy in view of other substantial breaches of obligations under the current tenancy or for any other reason connected with the tenant's use or management of the holding.

Again the important question for the court to determine is the seriousness of the breach and whether the tenant has any proposals for its remedy. In relation to "any other reason connected with the tenant's use or management of the holding" an illegal use of the premises would certainly amount to such a reason.

    In *Turner & Bell v. Searles (Stanford-le-Hope) Ltd. 1977* the tenants were found to be using the premises unlawfully by parking coaches in breach of planning law, having had an enforcement notice served upon them. As it was clear that the tenants intended to continue the illegal use under a new tenancy, the landlord was held to be entitled to possession under s.30(1)(c).

S.30(1)(d)   Provision of suitable alternative accommodation.

Relying on this ground the landlord must prove that the tenant ought not to be granted a new tenancy as the landlord is willing to provide him with suitable alternative accommodation.

S.30(1)(e)   Letting or disposing of the property as a whole.

Here the landlord may object to the granting of a new tenancy in a case were the current tenancy was created by a sub-letting of only part of the premises let under a superior tenancy, and the interest of the tenant's immediate landlord is to terminate in the near future.

S.30(1)(f)   Demolishing or reconstructing the premises.

The objection of the landlord in this case is that the tenant ought not to be granted possession because the landlord intends, on the termination of the tenancy to demolish or reconstruct the premises, or a substantial part of them, or to carry out substantial work of construction on them and he could not reasonably do this work without obtaining possession of the premises.

S.30(1)(g)   The Landlord intends to occupy for his own purposes.

Here the ground is that the tenant ought not to be granted a new tenancy because the landlord intends to occupy the premises for the purpose of a business to be carried on by him therein or as his residence.

Proof of any of the seven alternative statutory grounds may be sufficient to enable the landlord to recover possession of the busiess premises and successfully oppose the tenant's application for a new tenancy. It should be stressed however that grounds 30(1)(d), (f) and (g) are absolute in that if they are proved by the landlord then the court must grant him possession. The remaining grounds 30(1)(a), (b), (c) and (e) are discretionary and even if proved by the landlord the court nevertheless has a final discretion to determine whether a new tenancy is granted.

The Court Application and the New Tenancy

It should be stressed that in the majority of cases and usually as the result of a compromise, agreement is reached as to the grant and/or terms of the new tenancy without the need for court intervention. In the event of failure to reach agreement however, a court application will proceed. If the rateable value of the property does not exceed £5,000 the relevant court is the county court, otherwise it is the High Court. In either case the court must determine two distinct issues. Firstly, whether the tenant is to be granted a new tenancy and if this is so, then to determine its content. The first issue, of course is determined by the court deciding whether the landlord has satisfied the s.30 ground relied on.

Having decided that a new tenancy is to be ordered, the court is faced with the second issue, as to its content. In the absence of an agreement the Act confers a wide discretion on the courts in this matter. The subject matter of the new tenancy, the demised premises, is generally that part of the premises occupied by the tenant for the purpose of the business under the original tenancy. This is the case unless the tenant has expressly agreed to accept a new tenancy as only part of the property to enable works to be carried out on the remainder. The landlord may require the whole of the property to be included in the new lease including any property which has been subject to subleases. So far as the length of the new tenancy is concerned, its duration is to be such, up to a maximum of 14 years, as the court considers reasonable in all the circumstances.

The rent payable under the new tenancy is that amount, having regard to the terms of the tenancy, that a willing lessor might reasonably expect to let the property at on the open market. Certain matters are to be disregarded under the Act including:-

1. the fact that there is a sitting tenant;

2. the fact that goodwill is attached to the property by reason of the tenant's or his predecessors business;

3. the fact that the tenant or his predecessor has carried out voluntary improvements to the property;

4. the fact that the tenant holds a licence to sell intoxicating liquor from the property, the benefit of which belongs to the tenant.

Obviously the open market rent could be affected by the profitability of the tenant's business and subject to restrictions in the lease if a more profitable use could be adopted. Evidence of this may be considered by the court.

Of course the question as to the rent payable can only be determined once the court is satisfied as to the remaining terms of the tenancy. In the absence of agreement the court will have regard to the content of the original tenancy to determine such matters as restrictive covenants in relation to use, service charges, repairs, etc. Certainly if the landlord seeks to grant a new tenancy with terms that differ from the original tenancy he will have to justify the changes. If a new tenancy proves to be onerous on the tenant, even in an indirect way, the court may not accept it.

The courts are concerned to ensure that if there is a variation in the lease there is a sufficient reason for it. Also there is a concern that a change in rent will adequately compensate the tenant for any variation in the lease. The objective is simply to achieve a fair and reasonable balance between the parties.

Compensation for Improvements

During the term of a business tenancy it is likely that the tenant, or his predecessors in title will carry out improvements to the property. These improvements will ultimately benefit the landlord, since they will increase the potential letting value of the property when the letting under which they were carried out comes to an end. The Landlord and Tenant Act 1927 provides for compensation, to be paid to the tenant by the landlord in such circumstances, subject to certain requirements being satisfied, and certain conditions being fulfilled.

Before considering these requirements and conditions, some general observations need to be made. At common law a tenant is entitled to carry out alterations and improvements to the property as he wishes. Since a landlord may wish to exercise some control over such activities it is common to find inserted into business tenancies a covenant that absolutely prohibits such work, or which is qualified by requiring the landlord's consent to the work. Although such consent cannot be unreasonably withheld, the landlord may lawfully impose conditions upon the granting of consent. He can require payment of any costs connected with granting of the consent such as surveyors fees, or the payment of a sum to cover the reduction in the value of the property caused by the work. Alternatively he may require reinstatement of the property if the work carried out has not increased its letting value. The parties cannot exclude by agreement the requirement that consent shall not be unreasonably withheld:

The right to compensation is contained in s.1 Landlord and Tenant Act 1927, which provides that . . . a tenant shall be entitled, at the termination of the tenancy, to be paid by his landlord, compensation in respect of any improvements. The improvements can only be compensated if they increase the letting value and not all improvements need have this effect. They may for instance be beneficial only to that particular tenant. Trade fixtures, such as shop fittings, which can lawfully be removed by a tenant before the end of the tenancy do not qualify for compensation as improvements. An improvement provides a benefit to a landlord when the tenancy comes to an end. If sub-tenancies have been granted, then an improvement carried out as a sub-tenant must be compensated by his immediate landlord who in turn must seek compensation from his own landlord.

The Conditions for Compensation

In order to obtain compensation it is not enough that the tenant has simply carried out the improvements. He must in addition have followed the statutory procedure laid down in the 1927 Act. Under this procedure the tenant must first have served notice on the landlord of his intention to carry out improvements, accompanied by a specification and plan of the works to be carried out. The landlord then has 3 months to serve a notice of objection. If he fails to do so then the improvement is regarded as being authorised.

The Claim for Compensation

This must be made by the tenant in the prescribed form and include the date the work was carried out, its costs, details of the work and the amount now being claimed by the tenant. The claim must be served on the landlord within the strict time limits set out under the Act.

It should be noted that compensation is only payable when the tenancy comes to an end, and of course, generally a tenant will be entitled to a new tenancy under the 1954 Act. It is nevertheless prudent for the tenant to ensure that he qualifies for the right to compensation, for should the tenancy end he would not be entitled to compensation if he did not originally qualify.

TERMINATION OF EMPLOYMENT

A contract of employment must inevitably terminate at some time either by the death or retirement of the employee, or death, dissolution or winding up of the employer. Also, as a general rule, contracts of employment for a fixed term will terminate when the contractual period expires, and contracts to do a specific job are automatically terminated on the completion of the project. Otherwise, under the common law, either side to a contract of employment may lawfully terminate it by giving reasonable notice or summarily (without notice) in some cases where the other party has committed a serious breach of contract. Since the Industrial Relations Act 1971 employees are given statutory protection against arbitrary dismissal by an employer, the provisions relating to which are included in the Employment Protection (Consolidation) Act 1978 as amended. Under the common law either party to a contract of employment may terminate it by notice, the period of which will depend on seniority and length of service.

> In *Hill v. Parsons 1972* the Court of Appeal thought that a chartered engineer who has been employed continuously for 35 years was entitled to at least six months notice.

Of course, the express terms of a contract of employment will often stipulate the required periods of notice. Also, the EPCA 1978 provides for minimum periods of notice but these may be increased by the contract.

Minimum periods of notice

After continuous employment for:	Minimum notice required:
4 weeks up to 2 years	1 week
2 years up to 12 years	1 week for each year
12 years or more	12 weeks

Wrongful Dismissal

The expression 'wrongful dismissal' refers to a dismissal in breach of contract in a wrongful manner. An example is where the employer does not give the dismissed employee the correct period of notice or payment in lieu of notice. The remedy for wrongful dismissal is an action for damages in the ordinary courts, the county court or the High Court. Of course under the common law summary (instant) dismissal without notice may be justified on certain grounds. These include gross misconduct by reason of disobedience, neglect, dishonesty or misbehaviour. Whether the conduct complained of is sufficient to justify summary dismissal without adhering to disciplinary procedures[87] is a question of fact for each case.

> In *Pepper v. Webb 1969,* which was considered previously, the action of the head gardener in wilfully disobeying a reasonable order was sufficient to amount to gross misconduct and give grounds for summary dismissal despite the contract of employment providing for three months notice. It should be stressed however that the reaction of the gardener in this case was the culmination of a long period of insolence and the isolated use of choice obscenities by an employee to an employer may not amount to gross misconduct if there is provocation.

In *Wilson v. Racher 1974* a gardener who proved to have an even wider knowledge of bad language, for which he was dismissed instantly was held to be wrongfully dismissed in the circumstances. The employer had provoked the outburst by his own conduct.

In *Laws v. London Chronicle 1959* an employee who disobeyed an express order of her managing director was nevertheless held to be wrongfully dismissed in the circumstances. The employee had acted out of loyalty to her immediate superior.

The action of a betting shop manager in *Sinclair v. Neighbour 1967* of borrowing £15 from the till, and leaving an IOU, was regarded as a sufficient ground to justify summary dismissal.

In relation to breaches of discipline it is sometimes the practice that express agreement will be reached between the employer and the trade union/workforce to identify types of misconduct and classify it as 'gross misconduct' which will warrant instant dismissal.

This was the position in *W. Brooks & Son v. Skinner 1984* where the employer had agreed with the trade union that anyone who became drunk at the firm's Christmas party so that he was absent from work the next day would be instantly dismissed. In accordance with the agreement the applicant was instantly dismissed and the court held that such action was unreasonable in the circumstances.

Unfair Dismissal

The law relating to unfair dismissal is contained in the EPCA 1978 as amended and the Act's interpretation in many reported cases. A dispute relating to dismissal is first dealt with by an industrial tribunal, with the possibility of an appeal to the Employment Appeals tribunal and from there in certain circumstances to the ordinary courts. Every employee to whom the EPCA 1978 applies has the right not to be unfairly dismissed. The basic qualifying period of continuous employment was raised by Order in 1979 to 52 weeks for an employee to obtain protection except in cases where the dismissal was for refusing to join a trade union or on grounds of sex or race discrimination. Under the Employment Act 1980 the period was raised to two years for employees of small firms (less than 20). The qualifying period for all employees whose period of employment begins after 1st June 1985 has been extended to 2 years. For those whose continuous employment began before the 1st June 1985 the previous periods apply.

The compensation payable in a successful claim of unfair dismissal may be composed of a number of awards. Firstly there is a basic award payable in all cases of unfair dismissal irrespective of loss and based upon continuous employment. The award is calculated in the same way as a redundancy payment and is based on a maximum week's pay of £152 and can amount to £4650. It should be noted however that if the tribunal finds that the claimant contributed to the dismissal by his own fault the basic award can be reduced by a just and equitable proportion. Secondly there is a compensatory award related to the loss sustained by the complainant in consequence of the dismissal and based upon present and future net income, the loss of job security and pension rights. The present limit of the compensatory award is £8000. Thirdly if the employer refuses to obey an order of reinstatement or re-engagement then a further additional award is available up to a maximum of £7804 making the total maximum sum recoverable over £20,000 excluding any special award. The special award is payable if the dismissal is in connection with membership or non-membership of a trade union under the EPCA 1978. The amount of a special award is one weeks pay multiplied by 104 or £10,000 which ever is the greater up to a maximum of £20,000.

Despite the reluctance of the common law to recognise the remedy of specific performance of a contract of employment nevertheless statutory remedies for unfair dismissal include power for the tribunal to order reinstatement or re-engagement. If the employee is reinstated the employer must treat the complainant as if he had not been dismissed. The complainant is entitled to be treated as if he had benefited from an improvement in conditions which would have applied to him had he not been dismissed. Alternatively an order of re-engagement requires the employer to employ the complainant in comparable work or other suitable employment. The practicability of reinstatement must first be considered in the light of the complainant's wishes, then re-engagement. It should be stressed however that these remedies are rarely granted and additional awards payable for a failure to comply with an order for reinstatement or re-engagement are rarer still. Such additional compensation is not payable if the employer shows that it is impracticable for him to comply with an order.

An employee who wishes to bring a complaint of unfair dismissal against the employer must submit an I.T.1 form to the Central Office of Industrial Tribunals within three months of dismissal. A conciliation officer will then visit both parties in an attempt to resolve the conflict and reach a settlement. It should be stressed that in many cases an amicable agreement is reached at this stage because of the conciliation officer's intervention. If the employee wishes to proceed with the claim before a tribunal however, then prior to the full hearing there is a pre-trial review at which details of the claim are heard. At this stage the applicant may be warned that full costs may be payable if he proceeds with the complaint. At the full hearing it is the complainant who must show that he has been dismissed. There is no dismissal if the employee:-

a. **Resigns.** This may occur by the employee expressly terminating the contract by notice or constructively where the employee by his conduct is taken to have brought the contract to an end, e.g. refused to work.

b. **Is a party to a frustrated contract.** This would occur when performance of the contract has become impossible because of some event, e.g. illness where the employee is unlikely to return to work for a long period.

c. **Completes a particular project.** If the employee is employed to carry out a particular project and the work is completed.

d. **Agrees to terminate.** If it can be shown that the employer and employee have expressly agreed that the contract should terminate on the happening or non happening of a specified event then the contract will terminate on its occurence.

In *British Leyland v. Ashraf 1978* the employee was given five weeks unpaid leave to return to Pakistan and he expressly agreed that if he failed to work on a particular date his employment would terminate. The failure of the employee to return to work amounted to a mutual termination of the contract of employment.

The extent to which the courts will accept a mutual termination in these circumstances must now be assessed in the light of *Tracey v. Zest Equipment 1982.* Here the applicant was given three weeks leave to return to Jamaica to visit his father who was dying. Having previously overstayed on a visit, the employer required the employee to sign a document stating that if he did not return on the 3/4/81 the employer would assume that the contract of employment was mutually terminated. When the applicant attempted to return to work late on 8/4/81 he was informed that his employment was so terminated. While the industrial tribunal applying Ashraf agreed the EAT held that the IT had erred in law in concluding that the contract of employment had come to an end by mutual consent. The EAT stressed that very clear words are required to constitute an agreement, that in the event of a failure to comply, there is a mutual consent to terminate the contract of employment. Here the words used were not sufficiently clear to establish a mutual agreement.

        e.   **Enters into a fixed term contract of twelve months or more and agrees in writing to exclude his statutory rights on unfair dismissal.** This is the only case where statutory rights on unfair dismissal may be excluded by agreement.

Having identified situations which could not be regarded as a dismissal it is necessary to identify those that would. A dismissal will be taken to have occurred if there is either an express termination by the employer, a fixed term contract is not renewed, or there is a constructive dismissal. If an employer expressly informs an employee that the contract is at an end by saying "you're dismissed", "collect your cards" or "you're fired" the dismissal is clear and explicit. Unfortunately in practice tribunals are often faced with placing an interpretation on the language used.

In *Tanner v. D.T. Kean 1978* the complainant was told that he could not use the company van outside working hours. When the employer discovered that he was doing so he said "that's it you're finished with me". The EAT held that in deciding whether the words or actions of an employer amounted to a dismissal the IT should consider all the circumstances. Here the words used indicated a reprimand rather than a dismissal.

A fixed term contract has been defined as a contract which must run for a fixed term and one which cannot be terminated by either party except for a gross breach of a contractual term. The possibility of the employee giving up his statutory rights relating to unfair dismissal in a fixed term contract over one year has already been mentioned. Quite simply therefore the expiration of a fixed term contract which does not come within this category will result in a dismissal if it is not renewed.

A constructive dismissal occurs where the employee terminates the contract of employment in circumstances where he is entitled to do so because of the employer's conduct. It now seems therefore that an employee has to show that his employer was in some way in breach of the contract of employment to demonstrate that the employee walking out amounted to a constructive dismissal. This would occur if the employer attempted to change employment terms unilaterally without the employee's consent, e.g. less pay, change of work place, etc. The breach of course is not limited to the express terms of the contract which would also cover breach of the implied common law terms. Also for this purpose tribunals are willing to imply terms into contracts of employment.

> In *British Aircraft Corporation v. Austin 1978* the employer was held to be in breach of his implied duty of safety when he failed to investigate a complaint relating to the suitability of protective glasses. This conduct was held to be a sufficient ground to entitle the employee to terminate the contract of employment, regard himself as constructively dismissed and seek a remedy for unfair dismissal.

In relation to discipline at the work place the EAT in *BBC v. Beckett 1983* held that the imposition of a punishment which is 'grossly out of proportion to the offence' can amount to repudiation by the employer of a contract of service and entitle the employee to terminate the relationship and claim that he has been constructively dismissed.

Often an employee who walks out is aggrieved not at the employer's conduct but at the conduct of a fellow employee for whom the employer is responsible.

> In *Isle of Wight Tourist Board v. Coombes 1976* the applicant secretary walked out following a remark by her superior "She is an intolerable bitch on a Monday morning". This was held to be a fundamental breach of the contract of employment and a constructive dismissal when she walked out.

Having established that a dismissal has taken place it is then necessary to determine whether or not it is unfair. This is achieved by identifying and examining the reason or reasons for dismissal and considering the reasonableness of the employer's conduct.

Reasons for Dismissal

To assist the applicant in a claim of unfair dismissal the EPCA 1978 provides that an employee with six months continuous employment who has been expressly dismissed is entitled, on request, to be supplied by his employer within fourteen days with a written statement giving particulars of the reasons for dismissal. An employer will be bound by the reasons given in the statutory statement. Furthermore the reasons relied on by the employer will give the employee an opportunity to scrutinise them in advance of the tribunal proceedings, and so prepare a claim that they are insufficient. If the employer unreasonably refuses to provide such a statement then the employee's remedy is by way of complaint to the tribunal who may make a declaration as to what it finds the employer's reasons for dismissal to be and also make an award that the employer pay the employee a sum equal to two weeks pay.

One of the most fundamental features of the law of unfair dismissal is that whether or not a dismissal is justified is determined by considering the reasons for the dismissal and ignoring facts which come to light after the dismissal. The statute therefore fixes a point when the fairness of the employer's action is to be assessed. Consequently the idea that unfair dismissal is to be assessed by considering all the circumstances of a given case and then concluding by applying a broad notion of justice the merits of the employee's action is illusory.

The concept of statutory unfair dismissal said Philip J. in *Devis & Sons v. Atkins 1977* may be described as "dismissal contrary to statute". Nevertheless while facts which come to light after the dismissal which give support or otherwise to the employer's action are not to be taken into account to decide the reasonableness of his action, they can be presented to support a claim of contributory fault leading to an award of reduced compensation.

The employer is required by statute to show the reason (or if there is more than one the principal reason) for dismissal. He must further show that it is a reason listed in the Act or some other substantial reason of a kind such as to justify the dismissal of an employee holding the position which the employee held. In practice a tribunal will consider all the reasons advanced by the employer and satisfy itself that they come within the broad heads listed in the Act.

Statutory Reasons

The statutory reasons upon which the employer may rely are contained in s.57 of the EPCA 1978 and include:-

A reason related to the employee's capabilities or qualifications for performing the work he is employed to do: the Act defines 'capability' as meaning skill, aptitude, health, physical or mental quality of the job, and 'qualification' means any degree, diploma or other academic, technical or professional qualification relevant to the job.

> In *Blackman v. The Post Office 1974* the employee was recruited for a particular job on an unestablished basis. A collective agreement provided that such employee's employment should only be continued if the employee passed a written aptitude test. Despite showing aptitude for the job, the employee failed the test three times. The Tribunal held that either capability or qualifications could be a ground relied on for dismissal.

A reason which relates to the employee's conduct; misconduct of the employee may occur in numerous forms and may cover such matters as lateness, absenteeism, incompetence, insubordination, breach of safety rules, immorality, etc. Of course, the gravity of the misconduct and its regularity are key factors in determining whether the employer has acted reasonably in treating it as a ground for dismissal.

In *Trust House Forte Hotels Ltd. v. Murphy 1977* a night porter who admitted stealing liquor from his employer was held to be justifiably dismissed for misconduct at work.

. . . justifiably dismissed . . .

Examples of misconduct at work sufficient to justify dismissal also include:-

> *Boychuk v. Symons Holdings Ltd. 1977* where the applicant was carrying on sexual relations during working hours; *Wilcox v. Humphries and Glasgow Ltd. 1975* where the applicant was in breach of safety instructions; *Atkin v. Enfield Group Hospital Management Committee 1975* where the applicant was justifiably dismissed for wearing provocative badges after having had repeated warnings.

> Misconduct outside work may be sufficient. In *Singh v. London County Bus Services Ltd. 1976*, the applicant who drove a one-man operated bus, was convicted of dishonesty committed outside his employment. The EAT held that misconduct does not have to occur in the course of employment to justify dismissal so long as it could affect the employee when he is doing his work. Here the employee's conduct justified dismissal.

> The ground of misconduct was relied on in *Bradshaw v. Rugby Portland Cement Co. Ltd. 1972*, the applicant being dismissed following a conviction for incest with his own daughter for which he was on probation. The Tribunal held that the dismissal was unfair as the offence had no bearing on his work as a quarryman, and the relationship that he had with his fellow employees had not deteriorated to any grave extent.

The redundancy of the employee: a redundancy situation will exist if the employer closes down his business or part of his business and no longer requires the services of the particular employee. It does not follow however that a redundancy situation will automatically produce a fair dismissal. The employer must have had consultation with his work force, observed proper selection procedures and considered the possible alternatives. He must have acted in good faith and consistently. Also it may be that a redundancy situation could be dealt with otherwise than by dismissing employees, such as by reducing overtime, short-time working or restricting recruitment.

This point was argued in *Allwood v. William Hill Ltd. 1974* where the employer closed down betting shops and declared the managers redundant without warning or offering alternative employment. The Tribunal held that a redundancy situation existed, but the employees did not have to be made redundant and more effort should have been taken to find them alternative work.

Because the employee could not continue to work in the position which he held without contravention of a restriction or a duty imposed by Statute; this means simply that an employer could not be expected to employ a worker if the employment was in contravention of the law for example a bus driver who is disqualified from driving.

In *Gill v. Wallis Meat Co. Ltd. 1971* to have continued to employ the applicant who worked on an open meat counter would have infringed Food Regulations for he had grown a beard. Having refused alternative employment his dismissal was held to be fair.

Some other substantial reason such as to justify the dismissal of an employee holding the position which he held; this reason provides a ground upon which an employer could rely if the reason relied on is not one of the previous categories.

It was relied on successfully in *Wilson v. Underhill School Ltd. 1977* where the applicant schoolteacher refused to accept less than a full pay award, as her colleagues had done, recognising the school was in financial difficulties.

The onus on the employer then is to establish as a fact the reason for the dismissal that it is within the Act. He must also show that he believed in the existence of the reason and that belief was supported by reasonable grounds such as a thorough investigation. If the employer has carried out a reasonable inquiry to establish the facts then it will be easier for him to show that at the time of the dismissal there existed in his mind a genuine belief in the reasons relied on. So, if an employer alleges misconduct and the facts show that this is not the true reason relied on, then obviously it will not be a sufficient reason.

In *Timex v. Thomson 1981* the applicant, a long serving manager, was selected for redundancy and his employer maintained that the selection was largely due to his incompetence and poor job performance. The tribunal concluded that the real reason for dismissal was not redundancy, as put forward by the employer, but incompetence and held the dismissal to be unfair. The EAT confirmed that the tribunal was entitled to find that the employer had not put forward the reason which was in his mind at the time of the dismissal and was using the redundancy situation as a pretext for dismissal.

Fairness

Having fulfilled the requirements of the Act and shown a valid reason for dismissal, the Act further provides in s.57(3) that the determination of the question whether the dismissal was fair or unfair, having regard to the reason shown, shall depend upon whether the employer acted reasonably in treating it as a sufficient reason for dismissal. This question must be determined in accordance with equity and the merits of the case, in particular the size and administrative resources of the employer. The determination of reasonableness then is one for the industrial tribunal acting as an industrial jury and provided the correct approach is adopted then the conclusion reached cannot be interfered with. The tribunal is not an arbitrator and has no jurisdiction to substitute its own views of reasonableness but rather must adjudicate upon what a reasonable employer would have done in the circumstances. This process involves a consideration of the reason for dismissal relied upon and also the procedure adopted. In considering the reason relied on the Tribunal is entitled to take account of good industrial practice.

In *Williams v. Compair Maxim Ltd. 1982* the complainants were dismissed for redundancy, the employer failing to consult with the Trade Union. Nevertheless the tribunal held that the dismissals were fair as the employer had selected to retain those employees he believed were best for the company. The EAT however felt entitled to reverse the decision on the grounds of its perversity. Measuring the conduct of the employer with that of a reasonable employer a tribunal, aware of fair industrial practice, could not have reached the decision that the dismissals were fair. In a redundancy situation a reasonable employer would warn the Trade Union, consult, identify objective criteria for selection, make a fair selection and consider the possibility of alternative employment. As the dismissals here were carried out in blatant contravention of standards of fair treatment, they were therefore unfair.

In addition to examining the reason relied on, the process of determining reasonableness also involves a consideration of the procedure adopted by the employer. There exists a Code of Practice on Disciplinary Practice and Procedures drawn up by the Advisory and Arbitration Service. This provides amongst other things that employees should be given fair warning before dismissal. For minor infringements an informal oral warning should be given first, then possibly a formal oral warning and if necessary a final oral warning and if necessary final written warning. If the misconduct continues a final step could be disciplinary suspension without pay before dismissal. Of course the graver the conduct the less need there would be for a long drawn out procedure. Whether the employer had adopted the Code, or something similar and also complied with it, is of assistance in assessing whether he has acted reasonably. Certainly in the early cases of unfair dismissal the requirement of compliance with procedure was rigidly insisted upon. Cases where a sufficient reason for dismissal was relied on were nevertheless upheld to be unfair where the procedure requirements were not strictly adhered to.

In *Earl v. Slater and Wheeler Ltd. 1972* the fact that the employee was not given the opportunity to state his case was sufficient to render his dismissal unfair. Had a proper procedure been adopted the employee's conduct would have justified a finding of a fair dismissal.

From late 1970's however there seems to be a change in attitude in relation to procedural fairness and a number of decisions have held that in some circumstances procedural defects can be overlooked. The justification for non-compliance with procedure is that the result would have been the same had there been strict compliance.

In *Gray Dunn & Co. Ltd., v. Edwards 1980* the employee was dismissed for working under the influence of alcohol in breach of disciplinary rules. The employer however failed to comply with the disciplinary procedure and refused to hear witnesses as to the employee's fitness for work. It was held that the test for determining the effect of non-compliance with procedure was whether on the balance of probabilities the same course would have been taken had a proper procedure been adopted. Also whether dismissal would have been considered reasonable whatever the evidence might have revealed.

MATERNITY RIGHTS

To complete the picture in relation to security in employment some mention should be made of maternity rights. The right to maternity leave and pay was introduced by the Employment Protection Act 1975. Unfortunately legislative provisions in relation to maternity leave and notice are difficult to interpret and have been described as being of "inordinate complexity".

The qualifying period for leave and pay is two years employment as at the beginning of the eleventh week before the date of her expected confinement. It is also necessary to notify the employer of her intention to return to work where reasonably practicable, not less than three weeks before her departure. Failure to do this may result in a loss of security of employment rights. It should also be stressed that reinstatement rights relate to the actual job which has been left or one that is substantially the same. The conditions for a valid claim for maternity benefits are that the employee should inform her employer, in writing, at least 21 days before her absence begins or as soon as is reasonably practicable that she will be, or is absent from work, wholly or partly because, of pregnancy or confinement and in the case of the right to return to work that she intends to return to work with her employer. In addition she must produce a certificate from a registered medical practitioner or a certified midwife indicating the expected week or her confinement if requested by her employer.

The first of the two statutory maternity entitlements is to pay for a period not exceeding in aggregate six weeks during which the employee is absent from work wholly or partly because of pregnancy or confinement. The amount of maternity pay is nine-tenths of a week's pay reduced by the amount of any maternity allowance payable for the week under the Social Security Act 1975. The second right is to return to work with her original employer or his successor at any time before the end of the period of 29 weeks beginning with the week in which the date of confinement falls. This right is to return to her original job and on terms and conditions which are not less favourable than those which would have been applicable to her had she not been absent. There are now a number of significant limitations to the right to return to work. An employer of less than five employees is relieved of the obligation if he can show that it is not reasonably practicable to reinstate the employee. An employer of more than five employees is relieved of the obligation if he can show that it is not reasonably practicable by reason of redundancy to reinstate the employee and there is no other suitable alternative employment. Such an employer is also relieved if he can show that it is not reasonably practicable for a reason other than redundancy to reinstate the employee provided he does offer a suitable alternative job which is unreasonably rejected. Finally all employers are relieved of the obligation to reinstate if the employee fails within 14 days of receipt of her intermediate enquiry to indicate her continuing intention to return to work. This intermediate enquiry in writing can be made by the employer at any time later than 49 days from the expected date of confinement to ask whether the employee still intends to return to work. The enquiry must notify the employee of her obligation to reply within 14 days. In addition the employee must exercise her right to return to work by written notification to her original employer or his successor at least 21 days before the date on which she proposes to return. The employer may postpone such a return for not more than 4 weeks from that notified date of return provided he informs the employee before that notified date and gives specified reasons for the postponement.

REDUNDANCY PAYMENTS

Redundancy is one of the specified reasons for dismissal which was considered earlier in this chapter. If the selection of those who are to be made redundant is in breach of agreed procedures, and there are no special reasons to justify such a departure then the dismissal will be unfair. Similarly if the real reason for the selection is an individual's trade union activities or membership then the dismissal is statutorily unfair. In a claim for unfair dismissal in a redundancy situation a tribunal may be called on to consider whether a dismissal for redundancy is unfair on the general test of reasonableness.

The right to redundancy payments for qualified workers, dismissed because there is no longer a demand for their services, was first introduced in 1965. The present provisions are now contained in the Employment Protection (Consolidation) Act 1978. This Act provides that an individual dismissed for redundancy is entitled to compensation calculated by a fixed formula of weighted years of service.

Redundancy occurs when an employee is dismissed because his employer has discontinued or intends to discontinue the business for which he was employed, or because the need for his particular services has diminished. Of course, the right to payment is lost if the employee unreasonably refuses to accept an offer of suitable alternative employment. The object of redundancy payment is to encourage mobility of labour while at the same time providing security for employees. Under the present scheme every employer makes contributions to the Redundancy Fund and will receive a rebate from the Fund for any payments he makes as long as notice is given to the Department of the Environment.

To fall within the scheme it is necessary to have worked as an employee for the same employer for at least sixteen hours a week for an unbroken period of two years after the age of eighteen. Excluded categories include: Workers at retirement age; where a more suitable scheme, contained in a collective agreement, has been approved by the Secretary of State; Registered Dock Workers and Share Fishermen; Civil Servants and National Health employees; Independent Contractors.

Dismissal due to Redundancy

To qualify for a payment the employee must have been dismissed[17] for reason of redundancy. Alternatively the employee may be entitled to a payment if he is laid off or kept on short time for the period specified in s.88(1) and complies with the requirements of the section.

There is a dismissal if the employer expressly terminates the contract, or a fixed term contract expires or there is a constructive dismissal as a result of the employer's death or dissolution. Failure to establish a dismissal may result in a loss of entitlement to a redundancy payment.

> In *Morton Sundour Fabrics v. Shaw 1966* the employee in question, having been warned of the possibility of redundancy left to take other employment. The court held that as he had not been dismissed, he was therefore not entitled to a redundancy payment.

It should be stressed that the right to redundancy compensation depends upon a redundancy dismissal, a unilateral act of the employer. Even a voluntary redundancy can still be interpreted as a dismissal if the employee does no more than place himself on a list of those who may be declared redundant.

There is a presumption in the 1978 Act that if an employee is dismissed it is for the reason of redundancy unless the contrary is proved. However the Act also provides that the right to redundancy compensation may be lost as a result of the employee's misconduct. There is no entitlement to a payment if the employer is entitled to terminate the employment by reason of the employee's misconduct and does so even if the reason given is redundancy. Where the misconduct relied on by the employer is industrial action in the form of a strike, then the above section has no application to an employee who is working out his notice for redundancy. Under s.92 in such a situation an application may be made to an industrial tribunal which has power to award part or the whole of normal redundancy compensation.

Certain reasons for dismissal will constitute redundancy under the Act. These are that dismissal is attributable wholly or mainly to:-

    a) the fact that the employer has ceased or intends to cease to carry on the business for the purpose of which the employee was employed by him, or has ceased or intends to cease, to carry on that business in the place where the employee was so employed; or

    b) that the requirements of that business for employees to carry out work of a particular kind in the place where he was so employed, have ceased or have diminished or are expected to cease or diminish.

The approach to be adopted in determining whether redundancy has occurred is to analyse the requirements of the existing contract of employment. It is only by assessing the contractual position of the employee rather than the job he actually does, that it is possible to determine whether the employer's requirements for the employee have ceased or diminished. Consequently there is less likely to be a redundancy situation in relation to an employee who is employed under a contract which provides that the employee can be required to perform many duties.

> In *Haden Carrier Ltd. v. Cowen 1982,* the Court of Appeal considered the position of Mr. Cowen who had been employed as a Divisional Contracts Surveyor to assist the Divisional Manager. When work fell off he was declared redundant on the grounds that the requirements of the business for work of the kind carried on by Mr. Cowen had ceased or diminished. In a claim for unfair dismissal, the applicant contended that he was not redundant, for an express term in his contract provided that he could be "required to undertake, at the direction of the Company, any and all duties which reasonably fall within the scope of his responsibilities". As there was not a reduction in the requirements of the Company for employees to carry out any and all the duties of which Mr. Cowen was capable, the Court of Appeal agreed with the EAT and held him not to be redundant.

If the employer attempts to unilaterally vary the contract of employment, for example by requiring the employee to change his job function or place of employment, then it may be that the employee can be classified as redundant. Of course if there is an express or implied term in the contract of employment which confers this right, there will be no redundancy.

> In *O'Brien v. Associated Fire Alarms Ltd. 1968,* the Court of Appeal held that men who had homes in Liverpool and were employed there could be impliedly required to work anywhere in the Liverpool area. An attempt to require them to work outside that area, for instance in Barrow-in-Furness, was not sanctioned by their contracts. Redundancy had occurred for there was a reduction in the requirements at their place of employment, in this case the Liverpool area.

In situations where an employee's skills have become outdated because of new working methods and he is dismissed, the question is whether there is a redundancy situation or a dismissal on the grounds of incapability.

> In *Cannon v. William King 1966* a french polisher who refused to do painting, was held to be redundant, whilst in *Smith v. AEK Purdy Trawlers Ltd 1966* a seaman who could not operate a new diesel driven trawler was similarly held to be redundant.

There can be no redundancy if the employer makes an offer of suitable alternative employment which the employee unreasonably rejects. The offer will be suitable if:-

1. the provisions of the new contract are similar to the previous contract; or

2. the provisions of the new contract do differ but the offer constitutes an offer of suitable alternative employment.

Whether the offer is suitable or not will depend on examining the circumstances of the particular case, e.g. work, pay, hours, conditions, travelling, fringe benefits, accommodation, social and family links, children's education.

> In *Devonald v. J.D. Insultating Co. Ltd. 1972* the applicant was required to move from a factory in Bootle to another in Blackburn. He refused, and on

his claim for redundancy the tribunal held that suitable alternative employment had been offered as he was already required under his present employment to do outside contract work.

However in *Fuller v. Stephanie Bowman Ltd. 1977* the applicant typist refused to move from Mayfair to a new office in Soho. She found the move distasteful particularly as the new office was above a sex shop. The tribunal found that the refusal to move was unreasonable in the circumstances as it was based on undue sensitivity and consequently the claim for redundancy must fail.

The recent decision of the EAT in *Gloucestershire County Council v. Spencer 1985* supports the view that it is for management to set the appropriate standard of work to be achieved. Here the number of cleaners at a school had been reduced from five to four and the hours of work of the remaining employees cut by 45 minutes. The employer recognised that standards would drop but maintained nevertheless that the new terms constituted an offer of suitable alternative employment. This offer was rejected by the remaining cleaners on the grounds that they felt they could not continue to do a satisfactory job. The Industrial Tribunal agreed and found that while the alternative jobs were "suitable", the employees refusal to accept the new terms was not unreasonable as they could not do the new jobs adequately. The EAT on the other hand held that the Tribunal was in error, for the standard of work set by the management cannot be reasonably objected to by employees as a ground for refusing work. Accordingly the offer of suitable alternative employment had been unreasonably rejected and the applicants were not entitled to redundancy payements.

Procedure and Calculation

The 1978 Act lays down the procedure to be followed in a redundancy situation particularly where an independent trade union is involved. It involves consultation, advance warnings, written notice to the Secretary of State, the Trade Union being given certain details surrounding the redundancy and individual employees being given time off to seek new employment. Certain details must be disclosed by the employer to trade union representatives and these include the reasons for redundancies, numbers involved and how they are selected. The duty to consult the authorised bargaining representatives of a recognised Trade Union is contained in the Employment Protection Act 1975. Such consultation should begin at the earliest opportunity. This must be at least 90 days before the first dismissal if 100 or more are to be dismissed at one establishment and 30 days before the first dismissal if the redundancy involves between 10 and 100 dismissals. Certain information must be given to the representatives including the reasons for the proposals, numbers and descriptions of employees who are to be dismissed, the method of selection and the method of dismissal. If the employer fails to comply with the consultation process then a complaint may be made to an industrial tribunal which has power to make an award of up to 90 days wages depending on the circumstances.

To calculate the amount of a redundancy payment it is necessary to establish the following:-

    i.   'the relevant date', i.e. the date that the contract of employment terminated;

    ii.   'week's pay', i.e. the minimum remuneration to which the employee is entitled in the week preceding the relevant date (maximum of £152);

    iii.   'years of continuous employment', i.e. the number of years of employment calculated in weeks in which the employee works 16 hours minimum. Certain matters will break the continuity such as long absence through illness and certain periods, although not breaking continuity, will not count, e.g. periods of absence due to strikes or lock outs after July 1964.

Having established the above matters, the calculation of redundancy payment is as follows:-

For each year employed between the ages of:	Amount of Redundancy Payment:
18-21	Half Week's Pay x No. of Years Worked
22-40	One Week's Pay x No. of Years Worked
Men 41-65 Women 41-60	One and a Half Week's Pay x No. of Years Worked.

The maximum length of reckonable service is 20 years and the maximum week's pay is £152, e.g. maximum payment under the scheme is for a man over 60, with 20 years continuous service, on a wage of £152 per week:-

$$20 \times 1.5 \times 152 = £4,560.$$

When making the payment the employer should give the employee a written statement of how it had been calculated and details of any lump sum given to a redundant employee. Failure to provide such a statement could lead to the payment being regarded as voluntary rather than a redundancy payment. It should be noted however that much larger sums are payable under private schemes for redundancy payments entered into by employers and Trade Unions.

THE TERMINATION OF BUSINESS ORGANISATIONS

In the final section of the chapter it is proposed to consider some of the rules in relation to the termination of a business. It is necessary therefore to distinguish between the position of unincorporated bodies and corporate bodies either of which could be dissolved without choice because of insolvency or because it is the wish of the owners that the business is terminated.

Termination of Unincorporated Bodies

An individual trader may terminate his business at any time subject to the limitation that all debts of the business must be repaid. The death of a sole trader does not automatically dissolve his business, for it can pass by his will or if there is no will under the intestacy rules to his successors in title such as his wife or children. Similarly, a partnership may be dissolved by express agreement of all the partners. However, the death or bankruptcy of an individual partner will automatically terminate it. Partnerships are sometimes entered into for a fixed term or to achieve a particular object and so when the fixed term expires or the object is achieved the partnership will terminate.

a.   Insolvency.

Insolvency occurs when an individual or organisation is unable to meet its current liabilities, that is pay money due to its creditors. If the insolvency is merely a temporary situation then the creditors may be willing to wait for payment. If, however, recovery is unlikely, the creditors may decide to sue for payment of their debts, enforcing any security they hold. This may eventually lead to the termination of the business. For an individual or firm this will mean bankruptcy.

b.   Bankruptcy.

If an individual or organisation is unable to pay its debts and it commits an "act of bankruptcy", in other words either:-

    1.   performs an act with the intention of defeating or delaying creditors; or

> 2. fails to comply with a bankruptcy notice which is a notice served by a credtor to pay a debt ordered to be paid by the courts (a judgement debt)

then its assets are transferred to a trustee in bankruptcy for distribution amongst its creditors.

Following an 'act of bankruptcy' any creditor who is owed at least £200 may present a bankruptcy petition in the County Court or the High Court. If the petition is accepted by the court, it will make a "receiving order" appointing an official receiver to control the affairs of the individual or organisation. Following the submission of a written statement of affairs, there is usually a court examination of the individual or organisation, in which the creditors are given the opportunity to pose questions to the debtor. The creditors will then decide whether to make the business bankrupt or accept what is called a "composition", an agreement to accept so much in the pound of the debts owed (e.g. 50p for every £1 owed). If the creditors opt for bankruptcy, a trustee is appointed to sell off the business property and distribute the money received amongst the creditors in proportion to their debts. A bankrupt individual, however, is allowed to keep tools of his trade, clothes and bedding for himself and his family and sufficient money to maintain them. The distribution of money is subject to the priority claims of creditors, some of which are preferred debts — rates and taxes, wages and redundancy payments. The bankruptcy of an individual partner in a partnership will operate to automatically dissolve the partnership from date of the commencement of the bankruptcy.

c. Additional Grounds for Termination.

Any partner of a firm may apply to the courts to dissolve the partnership on one of the following grounds:-

> 1. a partner suffering from a mental disorder;
>
> 2. a partner has been guilty of misconduct in his business or private life likely to be harmful to the carrying on of the business;
>
> 3. a partner has been guilty of wilful or persistent breaches of the partnership agreement such as erroneous accounts, refusing to meet, or constant disputes;
>
> 4. where circumstances have arisen which in the opinion of the court, makes it just and equitable that the partnership be dissolved. An example could be in the case of constant hostility between the partners.

When a firm is wound up, the assets must be used to pay off debts and liabilities, the individual loans to partners and the repayment of the partners' capital contributions. Finally the residue is divided among the partners in the proportion that the profits were divided.

TERMINATION OF CORPORATE BODIES

The process by which a registered company is brought to an end is known as winding up, or liquidation. Since certain technical expressions are used in liquidations it is helpful to identify them first. A petition is an application to the court requesting the court to exercise its jurisdiction in company liquidations. A contributory is a person liable to contribute to the assets of a company if it is wound up, i.e. present members of the company and a person who has been a member within the year preceding the commencement of the winding-up. A liquidator is a person appointed to take control of the company, collects its assets, pay its debts, and distribute any surplus to members according to their rights a shareholders. The Official Receiver is an office of the Department of Trade who may act in the capacity of liquidator in the case of compulsory liquidations. A committee of inspection is a group of creditors and/or members who assist and, to an extent, control the job of the liquidator. The London Gazette is a government publication.

When the process of winding up has been completed the company will be struck off the register of companies and will cease to exist, and of course no further claims can then be brought against it. Consequently for anyone who is connected with the company whether as an investor, creditor or employee, winding-up is of great significance.

The rules regulating winding-up are contained in the Companies Act 1985. There are in excess of one hundred sections in the 1985 Act which are devoted to aspects of winding up.

Although statutory winding up provisions are detailed and sometimes complex there are basically three aspects to a liquidation. Firstly, who has the ability to institute and control the winding up, and on what grounds. Secondly, what are the legal provisions to be fulfilled during the procedure, and finally, in what order are claims against the company for payment met. There are three methods of winding-up, of which the two principal methods are considered here. They are compulsory winding-up, and voluntary winding-up.

A compulsory winding-up is carried out by the court. This is either the High Court or, if the company's paid-up share capital does not exceed £120,000 the County Court in whose district the company has its registered office. Not all county courts however have the necessary bankruptcy jurisdiction. Proceedings are commenced by a person presenting a petition to the appropriate court. There are six grounds upon which this petition may be based. The fifth ground is probably the most commonly relied on; it is that the company is unable to pay its debts. Statute and case-law define the meaning of this important expression. A company is deemed unable to pay its debts if a creditor who is owed over £200 by the company has left a written demand at the company's registered office and the demand has remained unpaid for a period of three clear weeks. Amongst those entitled to present a petition are the company's creditors, its contributories, and the company itself (by resolution). If the company is in trading difficulties and cannot meet its debts as they fall due then it is usually a creditor who petitions the court. Since secured creditors can always realise their securities if the company is in difficulties, by taking possession of property charged and selling it, such a petition is likely to be brought by an unsecured creditor.

The petition is presented to the Registrar of the court who fixes a time and place for the hearing. The petition must be advertised in the London Gazette at least seven clear days (excluding Saturday and Sunday) before the hearing. Rules of Court set out the form in which this advertised information must be provided; if they are not complied with the petitioner may have to meet all the court costs. The aim of the advertisement is to invite interested parties, the company's creditors and contributories, to oppose or support the petition. A person intending to appear at the hearing must give notice of this to the petitioner. After presentation of the petition a provisional liquidator may be appointed who is generally the Official Receiver. In any event when the hearing takes place, and the court makes a winding-up order, the Official Receiver becomes provisional liquidator by statute, and continues as liquidator unless the meeting of the creditors and contributories agree to the appointment of some other liquidator. This person must be acceptable to the court and the importance placed upon the liquidator's role is illustrated by the court's practice of refusing to appoint anyone who is not an accountant of at least five years standing. The 1985 Act sets out the liquidator's powers. Essentially his or her task it to collect and realise the company's assets, including unpaid sums due to the company from contributories for their shares, to settle the lists of creditors and contributories, pay the company's debts in a fixed order, and finally to adjust the rights of the contributories distributing any surplus assets amongst them. At meetings of creditors and contributories it may be decided to apply to the court to form a committee of inspection. Having fulfilled these responsibilities the liquidator applies to the court for an order that the company be dissolved, and is then released from his or her role. The court, it should be noted, has a complete and unfettered discretion as to whether to make an order for winding-up. It may as an alternative conditionally or unconditionally adjourn the hearing, make an interim order, or dismiss the petition altogether.

A voluntary winding-up is the most common form of liquidation. It has the advantage of being less formal than a compulsory winding-up and therefore cheaper. It is initiated by the passing of a resolution that the company be wound up. Notice of the resolution must be advertised in the London Gazette within fourteen days of it being passed. If a majority of the directors within five weeks of the passing of the resolution make a statutory declaration that the company is solvent, then the company members manage the winding-up. This includes the appointment of their own liquidator. This is a valuable power for the person appointed will be under their control, rather than the control of the creditors or the court. The court can nevertheless remove a liquidator on the basis of unfitness for office. The declaration of solvency states that the directors have examined the company's affairs and formed the opinion that within a stated period (up to a maximum of twelve months) the company will be able to pay its debts in full. If a declaration of solvency is not made the winding-up is a creditors winding-up. A creditors meeting must be summonsed by the company to be held on the day of the resolution or the following day. Details of this meeting must be posted to creditors and members giving them at least seven days notice, and be advertised in the London Gazette and two local newspapers.

The business of the creditors' meeting is to receive from the directors a full statement of the company's affairs, to draw up a list of creditors with estimates of their claims, to appoint a liquidator who will insert a notice in the London Gazette notifying other creditors to send in claims and if considered necessary to appoint a committee of inspection.

When a company is in liquidation the usual consequences are that the business of the company ends, shares cannot be transferred without the liquidator's consent, and the powers of the directors cease. When the liquidator has realised all the assets, he discharges the company's liabilities in the following order of priorities:-

a) **payment of the costs connected with the winding-up:** expenses and fees incurred in collecting and disposing of the company's assets; including the liquidator's fees and expenses;

b) **payment of preferential debts:** into this group fall rates and taxes, national insurance contributions, wages and salaries of any "clerk or servant" and wages of any "workman or labourer" for services rendered preceding the date of the order to wind-up (or appointment of provisional liquidator if one was appointed) in a compulsory liquidation, or the date of the passing of the resolution to wind-up in the case of a voluntary winding-up. Such payments cannot exceed £800 per claimant. A director may rank as a clerk or servant if he is employed by the company on a salary by virtue of a power in the articles;

c) **payment of debts owed by debenture holders which are secured by means of floating charges;** the debts under (a) and (b) may be met out of property, subject to the charge. Debts secured by a fixed charge may be met by realising the asset(s) subject to the charge. If an amount then remains unpaid the creditor must prove this in the winding-up;

d) **payment of unsecured creditors;** such ordinary debts rank equally;

e) **payment of a share of any surplus to the members according to their individual rights:** articles of association normally entitle preference shareholdes to a return of capital in priority to ordinary shareholders.

The order of priorities listed above is important if the company is insolvent. If it is solvent however the debts may be discharged without following this order.

ASSIGNMENT — THE HOTEL UNION

The Hotel, Catering and Allied Workers Union (H.C.A.W.) is an independent Trade Union with a membership of approximately three hundred thousand. Its members are mainly classified as unskilled and semi-skilled ancilliary staff working within the Hotel and Catering Industry, including cleaners, bar staff, reception staff and waiters/waitresses. While other trade unions do recruit membership from these occupations, in the majority of large hotel chains in England and Wales the H.C.A.W. is the recognised trade union for the purposes of collective bargaining. This is the case with Oliver Kingston PLC, a large hotelier operating in major cities throughout the north of England.

In practice the terms and conditions of employment of ancilliary hotel workers are determined by national collective agreements negotiated between the H.C.A.W. and the National Federation of Hotel Employers, on which Oliver Kingston PLC is represented.

For a number of years Oliver Kingston PLC has operated the practice of employing ancilliary staff as either 'full-time employees', 'regular casuals' or 'casuals'. The casual workers are regarded by the company as having self-employed status and are responsible for paying their own tax and National Insurance contributions. The distinction between 'regular casuals' and 'casuals' is that the 'regulars' are given the first opportunity to work when required but if they refuse to work, which they are entitled to do at any time, then they become mere 'casuals'. Mrs. Ruby Marshall has worked as a regular casual in the banqueting suite of an Oliver Kingston hotel for the past five years as a waitress. She has worked on average 45 hours per week, 50 weeks per year, which is well in excess of the hours worked by full-time waiters. Having been accepted as a member of the H.C.A.W. Mrs. Marshall is informed by the management of Oliver Kingston that they no longer require her services and her contract is instantly terminated. When Mrs. Marshall made an oral representation to the management asking why her contract was terminated, she was given a written statement which identified 'general imcompetence' and 'sloppy work' as the reasons for dismissal.

The Union's national headquarters is located in a seventy year old office block in Central London. The Union has occupied the premises continuously since the second world war on short-term five year business leases. The choice of Central London was originally made because at that time most of the union membership lived and worked in Southern England. It was also thought that a London address carried prestige, and because London was highly accessible by road and rail. The membership of the Union is now more geographically spread. The current lease of the premises is due for renewal in eight months time. It was agreed for five years at an annual rent of £120,000. The landlord has indicated by notice that he wishes to raise the annual rent to £240,000 and is only willing to offer a two year lease. The Union surveyor had indicated that property values have risen by 70% in this area of London in the last five years.

For some time senior union officials have been considering a move to alternative premises and a location outside London has been mentioned. An office block which appears to be suitable has been found in Newcastle upon Tyne. One of the attractions of this location is that it is in one of the government's Development Areas. The accommodation is modern, but is more extensive than the union needs. The annual rent is £50,000, subject to rent reviews every five years and a fifteen year lease is available. Preliminary negotiations have indicated that the owner may be prepared to sell the freehold, and a figure of £800,000 has been mentioned.

TASKS

1. You are an officer of the H.C.A.W. employed at the union's national headquarters. As part of a training exercise for regional officials of the H.C.A.W. you are required to attend a day seminar in which the role of the union is the topic for discussion. Specific intems for discussion include:

a) the relationship between collective agreements and the employee's individual contracts of employment; 390 - 91 - 93

b. the relationship between common law and statutory health and safety as work obligations. 383 - 85

Prepare a set of notes which will enable you to participate in the discussion.

2. The National Executive of the Union is concerned about the large number of so called 'casual workers' employed in the hotel and catering industry. You have been asked to prepare an informal report in which you identify arguments which support the view that the employment status of 'regular casuals' at Oliver Kingston PLC is in reality the same as that of full time employees. 374 – 378

3. You are required to write a letter to the local union officials at Oliver Kingston's hotel setting out your view of the legal position of Ruby Marshall in relation to her dismissal. 396 - 602

4. Finally you have been asked to prepare a report for the National Executive of the union in which you set out the rights of the union in relation to the renewal of the business lease of their London headquarters. Identify the relevant economic implications of the proposed move to Newcastle and set out the pros and cons of acquiring the new premises on a fifteen year lease or purchasing the freehold outright. 415 - 620

370 - 373

DEVELOPMENTAL TASKS

5. Arrange to visit an industrial tribunal with the aim of acquiring material to enact a role play exercise of the unfair dismissal claim brought by Mrs. Marshall.

6. Obtain a copy of a contract of employment. If you are employed this may be your own. If you are not employed ask to see the contract of employment of a friend or a member of your family. Find out if it expressly contains a disciplinary procedure, or alternatively whether this is incorporated into the contract from some other source.

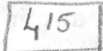 415

ASSIGNMENT — FOWLERS ENGINEERING LTD

Kirtley New Town on Merseyside has been trying to attract new industry by offering five-year fixed term leases at low rents for advanced factories on their industrial estate. Kirtley has a very high unemployment rate but is well served by easy access to road and rail transport. It is also in one of the government's development areas and so organisations who move there are allowed to claim substantial government grants and loans.

Fowler's Engineering Ltd,, a small private company engaged in the manufacture of light engineering components are attracted to Kirtley and decide to move from their existing location in East London. They secure a five-year lease on one of the new advance factories and commence operations in Kirtley on 1st February 1986. They employ 126 people, 78 of whom are female machine operatives. Fowler's factory is situated on the edge of the industrial estate immediately adjacent to a new residential housing development.

In their manufacturing process, Fowler's make use of an acid based cleaning fluid to scour the metalic components produced. Scrap metal trimmings coated with the residue of the cleaning fluid are stored in open skips at the rear of the factory. These skips are emptied once a fortnight and the trimmings are collected and taken away by Jackson and Cook, Scrap Metal Dealers. During the collection of the scrap on the 12th May, Andy Jackson, one of the partners of the scrap metal firm, despite being given a verbal warning of the danger of physical contact with the metal, fails to wear protective gloves when handling it. As a result, he suffers third degree burns on both hands and so sends a formal letter of complaint to Fowlers in which he alleges that the company have broken the Health and Safety at Work Act 1974.

Three weeks later on the 1st June, the company has made no change in its waste storate arrangements and the skips remain uncovered. Two brothers, Gavin Selby, aged 7, and Jason, aged 9, climb through a hole in the security fence at the rear of the factory in an attempt to retrieve their cricket ball which they have accidentally hit over the fence and into one of the skips. Jason helps Gavin to climb over the side of the skip. Gavin recovers the ball but, in so doing, comes into contact with the metal trimmings. The boy is burnt by the cleaning fluid residue. His father, Mr. John Selby, writes a letter of complaint to Fowler's Engineering Ltd. threatening legal action because of his son's injury. He also raises the matter at the next meeting of the local resident's association, where a number of other residents complain that in addition to this dangerous hazard, they are also unhappy about the excessive noise level which the factory makes during the night shift. One resident, Mr. Charles Turner, claims that he is particularly disturbed by the noise as it is interfering with his late night study which he is undertaking for the Open University. The meeting votes to take action on both the dangerous method of storage and the high noise level in an attempt to force the company to remedy the situation.

TASKS

1. You are employed by Fowler's Engineering and one of your duties is to be responsible for public relations. Prepare a set of notes for this purpose of discussing the various issues in a meeting of the Fowler's management team. In the notes you should set out your views on the legal position of Andy Jackson and Gavin Selby and the responsibility of the company for the level of noise from the factory in the evenings. You should also be prepared to advise on the best method of responding to the various complaints, any change in practice you would recommend and whether an offer of compensation is appropriate. You hope to obtain the meeting's approval to communicate the views of the company by letter to Andy Jackson in relation to his complaint, and by means of a meeting in relation to the complaints of the local residents association.

2. Draft a letter in which you respond to Andy Jackson's complaint. In the letter you should clearly state the legal position of the company in relation to liability to contractors on their

premises. You might also decide that it is wise to point out any proposed change in waste storage arrangements and hint at the possible economic consequences for Jackson and Cook if they pursue legal action against the company.

3. As public relations officer for the company you are requested to arrange a meeting with the representatives of the local residents association to discuss the company's waste storage arrangements, the possible legal claim on behalf of the Selby child and the level of noise from night time working. For the purposes of the meeting prepare a statement to be formally read out at its commencement setting out the company's views of the various issues.

DEVELOPMENTAL TASK

4. Undertake a role play exercise in which either the meeting of the management team is simulated or the meeting with representatives of the local residents association is simulated.

Chapter 20

NEW TECHNOLOGY

THE INTRODUCTION OF NEW TECHNOLOGY

New Technology has introduced a new industrial revolution. In the 18th and 19th centuries, the evolution of the machine age was to revolutionise the products that consumers were able to purchase and the means of producing them. In particular during the latter half of the 19th century, the widespread introduction of electricity and oil as forms of power meant that industry could make substantial improvements in its productive efficiency and provide an ever widening range of goods and services which would improve the quality and standard of life. Whether people are aware of it or not we are currently living in another equally significant era of change. The invention of the micro processor has resulted in the development of new and improved products and manufacturing techniques. It is an exciting time for us all. It is heralding a future in which much of the basic drudgery of life will be eased, when new products will test the inventiveness of man in recognising and applying the new technology and will provide the potential for vast improvements in the scope of man's ability to determine and influence his own environment.

You are no doubt aware of many of the current uses of micro technology. The watch you wear on your wrist may well have a micro processor inside it. The calculator that is a vital aid in your numerical work has been developed only since the evolution of the new technology. The television that you watch at home and the video games you perhaps play to pass some of your leisure time will be controlled by a small micro chip. You may have your own home computer which has cost only a few hundred pounds. Such technological innovation has had a tremendous impact. In fact this book was written using a word processor and printed using technologically advanced typesetting and printing techniques speeding up the production process and in so doing reducing costs. It would be difficult to identify an area of industry or commerce that is not already using new technology, or which will implement it and gain its benefits in the not too distant future. Just as the machine age had an impact on the lives of all who have lived from that time to the present, so too the new technology will leave its indelible mark upon us now and in the future.

But these technological changes are all relatively recent. In the 1960's and 70's the real benefits of new technology were only beginning to be recognised. The computer was used almost exclusively by large organisations. The pocket calculator that it is now possible to buy for less than £20 would have cost many times that amount. The breakthrough came in two ways. Firstly the components necessary to implement the new technology were reduced in size. We began to see the advent of micro technology. Secondly as the production and use of the new micro processors became more widespread they fell in price making them available for a much wider range of applications and to a considerably wider consumer market.

In this chapter we will attempt to give an overview of the uses to which this micro technology can be put. It would be impossible within the confines of this book to examine every conceivable application so we will concentrate on an analysis of the broad areas in which technology is applied. In so doing we will attempt to recognise that it is those organisations and countries which take advantage of the opportunities which micro electronic technology offers which will gain the productive and price advantages over their less technologically advanced competitors.

Before we look at the areas of application in some detail let us first recap on some of the advantages that micro technology can provide to the economy. These include:

    (i)   a wider range of goods and services for the consumer;

    (ii)   greater productivity while still using the same level of productive resources;

    (iii)   a more comprehensive application of information which can be used to aid management decision making;

    (iv)   relatively cheap computer systems which can be installed by even the smallest businesses and have the capability to be expanded to cope with business growth;

    (v)   a growth industry in its own right, providing employment and a potential for increasing the wealth producing capacity of the United Kingdom's diminishing manufacturing base, in particular through the development of overseas markets.

THE GROWTH AND DEVELOPMENT OF MICRO ELECTRONICS

The birth of the new micro electronic technology can be said to date from 1948 when the first transistor was invented by William Shockley. The transistor provided the basis for all future development in electronics. This led to the manufacture of the first computers, initially in the USA and later in Europe. These machines were massive pieces of hardware which filled a room. In comparison to the computers of the 1980's the early machines were incredibly slow and could only perform relatively simple numerical tasks. They were simply elaborate 'number crunchers' which could add, subtract, multiply and divide in a pre-programmed sequence. In the centuries to come these early machines will be regarded with as much curiosity and perhaps amusement as we perceive early flying machines.

However, through these initial developments man's inventiveness was awakened and in a relatively few years the early monolithic computers had been reduced in size and had increased in performance so dramatically that the capacity of the prototypes can now be contained on a single micro chip smaller than your finger nail. These micro chips or integrated circuits can be produced incredibly cheaply. In themselves they are capable of little. They must be combined with other electronic and mechanical components: keyboards, switches, disk drives and so on, to produce a system which is able to perform useful tasks. They also, as yet at least, cannot think for themselves. They must be programmed, that is given instructions. The programs which direct machines are called software, whilst the machines themselves and their peripherals such as video monitors are referred to as hardware.

THE DISTINCTION BETWEEN HARDWARE AND SOFTWARE

a.   Hardware

As we have already noted the term 'hardware' is used to describe the physical components of any micro electronic system. The heart of any hardware system is the Central Processing Unit (CPU). It is here that data and program instructions are held and processed. Attached to the CPU are the input and output devices. These are the means by which you can communicate with the computer and tell it what to do. This will enable it to reply once it has processed the information you have fed it. Input/output devices come in a number of forms but the most common input methods are using a keyboard terminal, a disk drive which can use either hard disks or floppy disks or magnetic tape input using a tape player. The output of the computer will come back through the same pieces of equipment, or it may feed onto a printer to give 'hard copy' in other words to print out the information. There are many other forms of hardware which may be attached to a computer system such as auxiliary second processors which can expand the capacity of the CPU, speech synthesisers which can simulate the voice or musical instruments, and joysticks which can be used to control the machine and which are especially popular in games playing. These are but a few of the peripherals which can enhance the capability of a machine and increase the user's means of controlling it.

b.   Software

The programe which the computer uses are known as its software. They are the set of instructions indicating to the computer the exact sequence of steps it must take in processing the data. The programs are written in a language which the computer is able to understand. There are numerous computer languages ranging from the most simple such as BASIC, which is very similar in structure to English, to more specialised and sophisticated languages which have their own particular applications and are difficult for the lay-man to understand. Unfortunately there is no single universally transferable system as there is with, say, gramophone records. Each computer uses a language or set of languages which may or may not be compatible with other machines. This has been a major drawback in the development of software as each programme may have to be re-written in a number of languages before it can be easily transferred from computer system to computer system. Software programs can be bought ready written from a commercial 'software house', specifically written for an individual's or organisation's particular needs or customised from existing programs. We shall see later that the organisation must decide how it wishes to utilise its micro processor and then determine whether or not suitable software has already been written.

APPLICATIONS FOR THE MICRO PROCESSOR

We have already noted there are many possible applications for micro technology. In fact the potential is almost as large as man's inventiveness. The important area of information technology is further developed in chapter 4. However here we will concentrate on examining three main categories of application:

1.   Consumer products;

2.   Information systems;

3.   Industrial process control systems.

1.   CONSUMER PRODUCTS

If you have a video tape recorder at home it will be controlled by a micro processor. Therefore when you press the button to record or playback, the machine will input this signal through the micro chip and activate the mechanical and electrical operation which you have selected. In fact the chip is acting merely as a switching device passing electrical currents into the appropriate circuit to activate the machine. Your video may be more sophisticated and may allow you to 'program' it so that it will record while you are out and the television is switched off. Again the processor is merely activating a time switch to correspond with your instructions.

The applications in this field are increasing rapidly. These range from alarm clocks which wake you, to stereos which entertain you, to micro wave ovens which cook your meals. Each performs a different function but the micro processors which control them are all basically similar. They are relatively simple to operate and normally do not require complex progamming expertise to use. In fact they are intentionally restricted in their programability to ensure that they are more reliable and less liable to go wrong. Other products which are in every day use include photocopiers controlled by micro processors which adjust the number of copies required and the quality of the reproduction, and the control instruments on some cars which monitor speed, performance or fuel consumption.

2. INFORMATION SYSTEMS

One of the main benefits of the computer is its ability to store and manipulate large quantities of data, whether in the form of words or numbers. In an office or other administrative situation which handles data the computer is the ideal alternative to traditional manual systems which require vast amounts of files and paper to hold the information. What is an even greater advantage of the computerised system over the manual system is that not only will it store material and allow it to be accessed when required (known as data handling and retrieval) it will also perform repetitive tasks using the data such as sorting, calculating and selecting (known as data processing).

In recent years computer systems have been designed for almost every commercial data processing application, including mundane clerical tasks such as stock control, wages calculations and time recording as well as more complex operations such as accounting and financial control. However, computers are being increasingly used by organisations to provide them with decision models which allow them to analyse data related to past events and introduce mathematical probabilities and so predict future events. Such applications can be used to predict the future market share for the organisation's product or to estimate changes in market demand should certain events occur. These are called computer models as they mirror likely outcomes. They can be incredibly comprehensive and include even relatively minor factors. For instance a large European brewing company which produces 'probably the best lager in the world' has a demand model which not only includes factors such as the levels of its competitors' advertising but also the long range weather forecast, (in hot weather people tend to drink more lager). In this way it is able to make accurate predictions of the amount of lager it is likely to sell in the coming three month period and so adjust its brewing capacity accordingly.

THE METHOD OF INFORMATION PROCESSING

In such information systems the usual method of data input is the computer terminal. This consists of a typewriter keyboard and a monitor. Using this method, the operator is able to type in the information and check that it is correct before transferring it, at the touch of a key, to the micro processing unit. This will have a certain amount of memory which holds the program which manipulates the data. The memory is normally of two sorts. (i) Random-Access Memory (RAM) which will hold only that data or program which has been input into the machine by the operator. Once the machine is switched off the RAM will clear; (ii) Read-only memory (ROM) which is included within the machine and contains its basic sub-programs. This ROM will not clear when the power is turned off.

As we have already mentioned other means of input for data include magnetic tape and disk. Using magnetic tape is usually a much cheaper alternative since the hardware required is less complex, but it is considerably slower than using disks. The processed data can then be returned to tape or disk, merely shown on the terminal monitor, or produced as hard copy on the printer.

Word processing

One of the most significant uses of information technology is word processing. This allows text such as letters, reports or even books to be produced. The material is input through the terminal keyboard with the operator able to see what has been typed on the visual display unit or monitor and to adjust, correct and rearrange the text before it is finalised and transferred by the computer to tape or disk. It can then be printed in total or in part as many times as are required. The major advantages of word processing over more conventional typing methods are that the text is permanently stored and can be retrieved at will; the text can be edited to eliminate mistakes or revise its content; material from different sources can be combined into a single document; multiple copies can be produced and can be personalised by deleting one name and replacing it with another, so allowing the preparation of standard documents which can be customised as required. The use of the word processor or the computer with word processing facilities has revolutionised office practice. It eliminates errors and can increase typing output considerably once the operator has mastered the technique.

The control of records

An important use of the micro computer is as a data base, in other words as a means of storing and manipulating records. A business can hold an individual record for each customer, client or component. The record might include particular details such as name, address and any transactions that have been undertaken. The system will then be able to sort through the file and seek to select a particular characteristic from the records such as slow payers or clients in a particular area. As new information is received the file can be updated immediately and comparisons of categories or totals of data can be produced easily. The major benefits of computer record file handling is that vast amounts of information can be held in a relatively small space on tape or disk, analysis of data can be undertaken quickly and efficiently and the information record can be kept up to date in a simple manner.

Information transfer and communication

As computers hold data in the form of electrical impulses there is enormous potential for the transfer of information using such media as the telephone network and television and radio signals. Therefore within an organisation information can be transfered from computer to computer using wires. This eliminates the need for the movement of paper. While on a wider scale information can be transmitted using the standard telephone system with the transmitting computer and the receiving computer both being fitted with a device called a modem to link them to the telephone system. In this way computers can indeed talk to each other without the need for human operators. As you will appreciate this technique will improve dramatically the speed by which an organisation can communicate. Thus orders can be placed and acknowledged almost simultaneously, directions and information can be passed to staff who are operating outside the organisation's base and information can be received and acted upon without the time delays associated with the mail system. Such techniques are a vast improvement on the conventional telephone system as they avoid error and misunderstanding and provide hard copy which may be important, for instance if contracts are being agreed.

Small business applications

The 1980's have seen the micro computer fall in price so much that it is now feasible for even the smallest business concern to take advantage of its benefits. Commercially produced software packages are available at modest cost and much of the drudgery facing the small businessman can be reduced. It allows a much closer control of finances and of trading transactions and permits the concern to demonstrate a professional and go ahead image to its customers and clients.

3.   INDUSTRIAL PROCESS CONTROL SYSTEMS

In the previous category we examined how the computer can be used in the management and administration of an organisation. Another major application is in the control of industrial processes. Many of you will be aware of the development of robotics as a means of industrial production. By this we mean the use of machines which are controlled by micro processors to carry out a specific manufacturing function. They can be used as measuring devices to test product quality or production quantities. They can be made to monitor environmental conditions within a manufacturing situation such as heat, light and humidity. For repetitive tasks such as component assembly, process production or stock handling they reduce the need for human effort to be used on boring work. What is more, if the equipment is reliable and efficient it can work 'around the clock' and so allow a more cost effective use of plant.

Nevertheless the machines cannot program themselves. It requires a precise understanding by a human programmer of the task that is to be performed so that the correct instructions can be programmed into the machine. Furthermore robot operation (known as "robotics") also necessitate close monitoring of the process to ensure that they continue to carry out the task as required. A micro processor cannot tell when it has made a mistake and a systems malfunction could result in disruption in the productive process. You may have seen the Walt Disney film

'Fantasia' in which in one sequence Mickey Mouse is cast as the Sorcerer's Apprentice. Mickey is left alone by the Sorcerer with strict instructions to clean and tidy the workshop. Somewhat anticipating the introduction of robotics the idle Mickey casts a rather inept spell and sets the brush and the broom to work on their own. Of course as in all such circumstances the situation gets out of control as the cleaning implements begin to run riot throughout the room operating uncontrollably. Mickey is only saved from disaster by the timely return of the highly annoyed Sorcerer who quickly reverses the spell and restores order and calm. This film extract could be shown to all production managers who believe that their robots can confidently be left to operate without any form of human control.

INSTALLING A COMPUTER SYSTEM

The decision to install a computer system requires a great deal of detailed consideration by an organisation. This is as true for a small trader who is debating whether or not to update his record keeping system with a £500 micro computer as it is for a multinational intending to replace its £5 million main frame system. For each of these two organisations it is crucial that they carefully plan the implementation. It is true that many a computer system has failed to be implemented successfully because the management decision to install it was not sufficiently well informed. Thus, for the implementation of any system, the following steps provide suitable guidance:

(i) **Undertake a preliminary survey.** This will determine whether there is a need for a computer system and the possible applications it may have.

(ii) **Prepare a feasibility study.** This will look in detail at the areas of operation of the organisation which are to be computerised and produce a general idea of the system which will be implemented. It should include an estimate of the potential cost of the system, the alternative hardware and software that could be used and the length of time which will be required to install the new system before it is fully operational. It should also list the savings in money, time and manpower that the new system will bring.

(iii) **The decision to proceed in principle.** Management should evaluate the potential costs and benefits of the new system and assess whether or not it will prove cost effective. It is important that management are not swayed in their decision simply by the novelty and attractiveness of new technology. The system must be cost effective. Many computer systems have been installed at considerable cost to an organisation to replace more traditional manual systems which later prove to have been cheaper to run and more effective to operate.

(iv) **Produce a detailed design of the system.** Once the decision has been made to implement a computerised system a detailed specification of the procedures which will be used and a flow chart showing each individual step in the system should be drawn up. This should indicate whether existing commercially produced software packages are available to perform the required tasks or whether new custom designed programs have to be written.

(v) **Choose the appropriate hardware.** There are likely to be a number of possible machines on the market which could meet the organisation's requirements. Thus it is necessary to weigh up their relative merits and disadvantages and to select the most appropriate system. Considerations include such factors as initial cost, available software, the language that the machine operates in, the cost and availability of peripherals, reliability of local dealer service and maintenance and potential for system development. One of the dangers involved in investing considerable sums in new technology is that developments in micro electronics are occurring so quickly that the hardware rapidly becomes outdated and obsolete. Thus it is a major advantage if the hardware chosen can be updated as new systems are developed or new hardware is introduced.

(vi) Staff training and development. We have already stressed the fact that computers do not work on their own. They require skilled staff who understand the system they are operating and can recognise the opportunities the computer offers to improve their jobs and increase organisational efficiency. Thus it is crucial that any organisation introducing a computer system does so with the full support and co-operation of its workforce. This obviously requires discussion with staff representatives at an early stage, and more progressive organisations might involve staff in the decision making process on whether or not a computerised system should be installed. If the advantages of new technology can be accepted and welcomed by the staff this will ease the transition to the new system. Once agreement has been reached and the system is scheduled to be introduced staff should be trained in the use of the new system and encouraged to develop their understanding of micro technology and the skills associated with it.

Some disadvantages of introducing a computerised system

Up to this point we have tended to stress the many advantages of installing a computerised system. However it is worth noting that there can be a number of drawbacks. These include the following:

(i)   Too great a degree of dependence on the system. There is a tendency to rely too heavily on a computerised system and this may result in the organisation's procedures becoming de-personalised. Any and all mistakes tend to be blamed on the 'computer' and the constraints imposed by the system can produce inefficiency. Complaints that a certain circumstance does not fit the computer system can result in resentment towards the system and, by implication, towards the organisation and its management which introduced it.

(ii)   Initial failure of a new system. All too often the initial enthusiasm for a new computer system can be severely dampened by initial hiccups in its operation. An organisation which abandons its manual systems and manual records as soon as the new computer system is installed is taking a considerable risk. Many organisations have found themselves left with no workable system or no records when the computer or its system malfunctions during the settling in period. A wise organisation will continue to operate its tried and tested systems in parallel with the computer system for a short while until it is confident that the new system is reliable.

(iii) Duplication of systems. We have just recommended in the paragraph above that the organisation should continue to operate its existing manual system until the new computerised system is fully proven. However there is a tendency in some organisations to continue to operate both systems even when the computer has shown it can do the job alone. This will be particularly true with older and more long serving staff who have come to accept the old system and see any new techniques as an unnecessary and unwelcome intrusion into their work pattern. They feel confident and safe operating the old system and so continue to do so in parallel with the new. This can result in an increase in administrative costs rather than the saving that the new system was intended to introduce.

(iv) Lack of backup. Any system can go wrong. Even the most sophisticated and advanced micro processor will occasionally fail. Thus it is vital to have a backup of records, data and programs. This will normally require that two or more copies of disks and tapes are held separately. Clearly the amount of backup that is required depends on the level of importance of the data or the system to the organisation. Imagine a company with 1,000 weekly paid employees which finds that its payroll program has 'gone down' the day before pay day. It needs some backup or it will find itself facing some very irate workers.

Lack of backup

THE IMPACT OF NEW TECHNOLOGY

This chapter has tried to provide an overview of the uses and applications of new technology in organisations in both the business and commercial world and in the public sector. It is by no means intended to be a comprehensive examination of this complex subject. That would require a book in itself. However we have attempted to show how micro technology can revolutionise management and administrative practices. As we have already noted we are just at the beginning of this new era. The developments are endless and it will, whether we like it or not, change our lives both in the work environment and in our daily existence. The concerns of those who resist such changes are essentially twofold. Firstly they do not understand the new technology and so will not be able to cope and adjust to its impact. This is an understandable worry. For many the terminology used is alien to them. When they overhear computer buffs discussing their interests it can almost be as though they were talking in a different language. Jargon such as RAM, ROM and CPU can convey little to those unversed in their meaning. For such people there can be the consolation that the technical data need never effect them. You may not understand the technical process by which television is transmitted and received but you can nevertheless still enjoy watching the screen.

A second major worry is that the introduction of new technology will severely reduce the number of jobs that are available. Traditional office jobs become less necessary as the more routine tasks are carried out more efficiently by machines. Production line workers fear the introduction of robotics as it will reduce the need for manual labour. These fears are to some extent justified. There will be considerable restructuring in many industries as new systems and technology are brought in. It is nevertheless very difficult to resist the tide of change. If a new process is available it will eventually be implemented. However the trade unions do have a justifiable case when they argue that the transition should be carried out with as much consideration for the workforce as possible. Employers should re-train whenever they can rather than simply re-staff. For most of us the challenge of learning and developing new skills is an important and encouraging part of life. The impact of new technology should result in an improvement in the welfare and productive capacity of the nation as a whole rather than benefitting only those who are willing to embrace it while costing others their livelihood. A further consideration of the impacts and effects of the introduction of new technology is included in chapter 22 where we examine its impact on the economy as a whole and on the industrial structure. We may finally note a highly significant feature of the government's response to new technology. Mindful of the need to educate the nation in the uses of this technology it has pursued a policy which has resulted in every school throughout the country possessing a micro-computer. For the next generations the use of these machines will be as commonplace as the use of the telephone was to their parents.

ASSIGNMENT — PRACTICE MAKES PERFECT

McGibbon, Richardson and Tate is a firm of Chartered Accountants based in Southend on Sea in Essex. It is a long established practice, having been founded in 1907 by John McGibbon, and has developed a reputation as being efficient, although rather staid in its approach. It deals with a wide range of clients, concentrating on audit and tax work but also provides a comprehensive book-keeping, VAT and wages service to its clients. The firm has four partners and has recently opened a branch office in Basildon, a few miles from Southend. The organisation chart for the professional partnership is shown on page 29 in chapter 1.

One of the major problems is the amount of paperwork which is generated by the work of the practice. Dorothy Robson, who is in charge of the secretarial side of the business, has complained to Stan Tate, the senior partner. Dorothy maintains that the typists and office junior cannot keep up with the number of accounts that have to be typed, amended, agreed with clients and then possibly retyped again. Stan tends to be rather old fashioned in his outlook but is willing to listen to new ideas. Dorothy suggests that the practice should scrap its old typewriters and antiquated filing system and instal a new computerised system.

TASK

1. You are employed as a trainee office manager/ess by the practice. Mr Tate calls you into his office and instructs you to prepare a special report in which you identify the possible uses for a computer system, the steps the practice should take were it to instal such a system and the problems that may be encountered.

    In your report you should include recommendations on the manner in which Mr Tate should introduce staff to the computer system.

DEVELOPMENTAL TASK

2. Research a range of computers that could be used in this situation. Identify their relative cost, capabilities and drawbacks. Make proposals as to the specific computers to buy and the cost involved in the transfer to such a system.

Chapter 21

THE WORKINGS OF THE MARKET MECHANISM

The market mechanism is a deceptively simple system of resource allocation. It accepts the existing distribution of income and wealth in that there are rich and there are poor, and argues that individual consumers will seek to maximise their personal satisfaction by demanding that combination of products and services which will give them the greatest level of satisfaction for the money they have.

The market system is based on the following ideas:-

i. that each consumer is free to spend as he wishes and, if the consumer is rational, the products bought should give him most satisfaction possible within his budget.

ii. that the movement of prices will indicate to the producers what they should supply in the future. If a product or service is in demand and not enough is being produced, then consumers will compete amongst themselves for the scarce commodity and as a consequence bid the price up. The higher price will then encourage producers to make more and this will solve the problem of the shortage and reduce the excess demand. The reverse is true if demand is lower than supply. Producers will find themselves with stocks left on their hands. They lower the price to get rid of them and produce less in the future. This reduces supply until it equals demand.

iii. that competition for customers between producers means they must keep their prices as low as possible. To keep prices low and still make a profit they must reduce their costs of production. In fact, they must be as efficient as possible. If they are efficient in producing and selling their products, they will make a profit. This will allow them to pay the highest wages to attract the best labour, pay high rents to have their business located in a prime site and pay high prices to get the best machinery and finest quality raw materials. They should therefore be able to produce the best products.

iv. that, as an alternative to (iii) above, an inefficient organisation will have high costs and so must either charge a high price and sell less, or keep prices down to sell more but make little profit. This will mean that the least efficient producers go out of business.

So when the market mechanism is working efficiently it will:-

1. provide freedom to the individual consumer to spend his money as he wishes;

2. indicate the demands and needs of the consumer to the producers and so ensure production of what is actually wanted;

3. encourage competition between producers and so promote efficiency;

4. adequately reward the most efficient organisations through high profits, and the best workers through high wages.

THE MECHANICS OF SUPPLY AND DEMAND

The market system is based upon the interaction of the forces of demand and supply.

By demand is meant the willingness and ability of consumers to purchase the goods and services they want. Supply is the willingness and ability of producers to meet these demands. When suppliers and consumers transact they do so by entering into legally enforceable agreements — called contracts. The importance of contracts in business transactions is examined in detail later in this chapter.

a.   DEMAND.

The demand for a product is the amount of it that consumers will buy at different prices. Market demand for a product means the total amount of it that will be bought in a specific market such as the UK, in a certain time period, for instance one year. With most products and services, it is usual to find that the higher the price the less of it will be demanded by consumers and, conversely, as price falls more will be bought as either existing buyers demand more, or new customers are attracted to the product.

If the product or service is free or relatively inexpensive then obviously more people will consume it than if it is very expensive. However, demand is not infinite even for 'free' products or services. Visits to the doctor do not cost anything directly to the patient and yet most people do not visit their doctor every week or every month. They only go when they need to. So demand is determined not only by price but also by need. If cigarettes were free many people would still not smoke because they believe the product to be harmful. Therefore the need and consequently the demand for a product is influenced by each individual's own tastes or preferences. Different individuals desire different products and services and obviously have varying abilities to pay for them. (Most of us may desire a holiday in Barbados but how many of us can afford to pay for it?)

It is clear that as our income increases, either individually or as a nation, we can demand more and more products. No doubt we may choose different products if we have more money (for instance the Barbados trip instead of two weeks at Butlins) but overall our demand will increase as we get richer.

Also, within a particular market the number of consumers will influence overall demand. If the consumer population goes up then demand increases. An example is the demand for social services for the elderly, which is increasing dramatically as a greater proportion of the population reach retirement age.

A final factor which will influence the level of demand for a product is not just its own price but also the price of other products and services. For instance, if the price of Mini Metros rose then motorists may buy an alternative car, say a Ford Fiesta, because it is a substitute. The demand for Fiestas would increase even though they have remained at the same price.

Alternatively, if the price of petrol rose this may effect the demand for both Fiestas and Metros. The reason for this would be that if petrol rose in price sufficiently, people would travel less and so demand fewer cars causing a decrease in demand. This is because petrol is a complementary product to cars. To use one you must have the other. If the price of the complement rises, then demand for the first product is likely to decrease. Another example to illustrate this principle is provided by energy prices. It is easy to recognise what would happen to the demand for electric cookers if the Electricity Board doubled its supply rates, whilst gas prices remained at an unchanged level.

Finally, the price of other purchases in the consumer's budget will influence demand. So if a person's rent rises, then he will have less money to spend on other things and so he will be unable to go to perhaps as many rock concerts, or buy as many records. In particular if the price of a necessity goes up, the consumer is faced with no alternative but to switch spending from less necessary purchases to pay the higher price. Items such as rent, food and clothing are clear examples of necessities, and even though as consumers we can adjust our spending on them, there are minimum levels of expenditure which we cannot avoid without finding ourselves homeless, starving and unclothed.

So the factors which determine the level of demand for a product or service are as follows:-

1. the price of the product or service;

2. the tastes or preferences of consumers, is it a necessity, enjoyable, fashionable, etc;

3. the level of income of consumers;

4. the number (or population) of consumers;

5. the price of other goods/services which are:-

    (i) substitutes, i.e. suitable alternatives;

    (ii) complementary products, which are jointly consumed;

    (iii) necessities also bought by the consumer.

But one fact is certain. A product will not be bought unless the consumer believes it will give him some level of satisfaction (or as it is called utility) when he enters into a contract to purchase it.

Expressing demand visually

Sometimes it is easier to express ideas in a visual form. In this book there are many examples of different forms of visual representation being used to demonstrate ideas and concepts. The demand curve, which is included below, is such an example.

If a car producer such as Ford found that it could sell varying amounts of its products (Escorts) in relation to varying price levels over a certain period (a month) the company could show this either numerically in a table; or by means of a graph (see below). You may find that the graph provides a more immediate impression of the relationships between the price asked and the quantity demanded, than can be obtained from the demand schedule table. The use of visual designs as a means of communicating information (whether or not it is numerical) is a valuable tool for all organisations.

Price	Quantity of Escorts Demanded
£5,000	4,000
£4,500	10,000
£4,000	15,000
£3,500	20,000
£3,000	25,000
£2,500	35,000

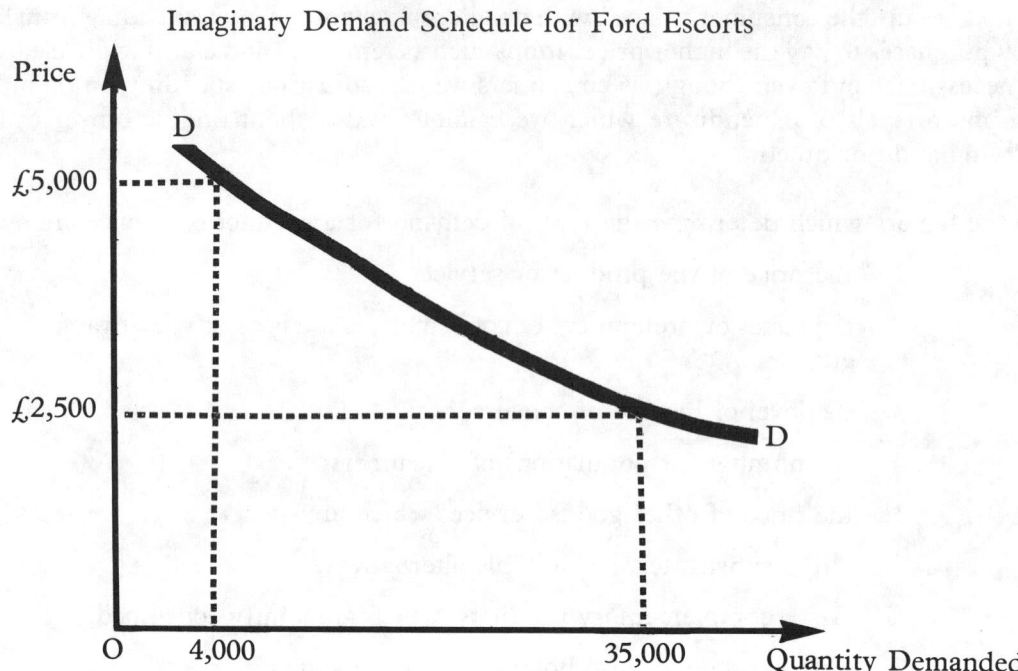

Demand Curve for Ford Escorts

As you can see from the graph, the demand curve slopes from top left to bottom right and this is characteristic of most demand curves. It is merely a graphical way of expressing the relationship between the quantity of a product consumers are willing to purchase and the price of the product over a range of different prices.

Changes in price

If Ford decided to set a price of £3,500, they would find that they could sell 20,000 cars. If they moved the price up to £4,000, they would sell less — only 15,000 Escorts. Changes in price of the product cause movements up and down the demand curve — or, more precisely, along the demand curve. A change in price does not move the demand curve itself, it merely changes the quantity bought because the price has changed. This is an important principle to grasp. Changes in the price of a product do not shift the demand curve but merely move the quantity demanded along it.

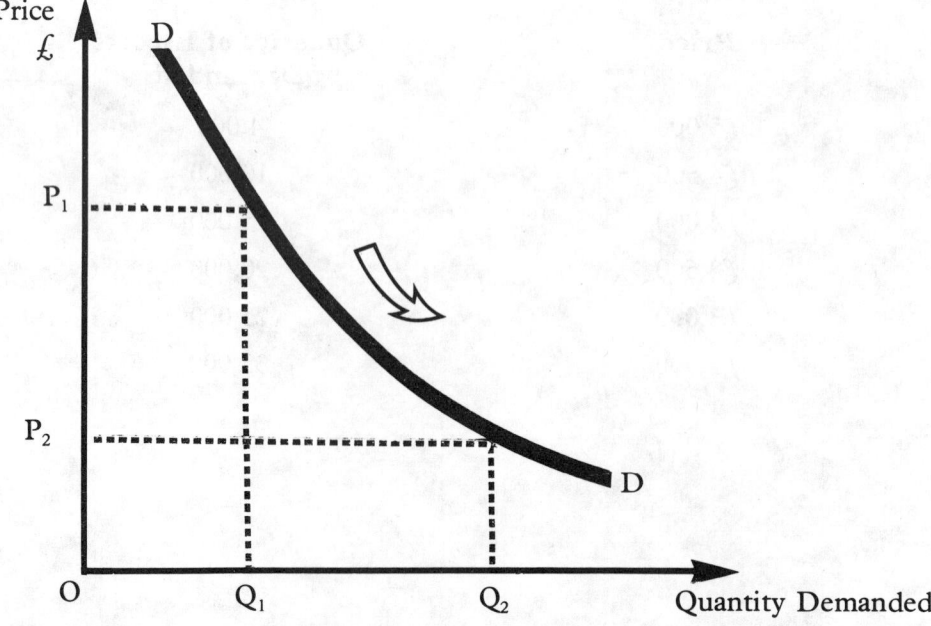

A Change in Price Moving Demand along the Existing Demand Curve

Does this then mean that the demand curve cannot move? It does not, for the other factors we mentioned earlier as influencing demand (as points (2), (3), (4) and (5)) will shift the demand curve if they change.

Changes in preference or taste

The figure below shows the demand curve for records for a top artist such as Phil Collins. He is fashionable. The public like him and buy his records. Let us say that they sell for £5 per album. If the records were cheaper, more would be sold. If they were more expensive, less would be sold. But consider what would happen if people's tastes changed and Mr. Collins became no longer popular. If the price had been higher, (say £7.50) proportionately less records would have been bought initially. Now as tastes have changed demand falls even though price remains the same. This fall in demand would occur whatever the initial price. So at £5 the demand shifts from D_1 to D_2. We can refer to this shift by marking the two curves as D_1 and D_2. Thus we can say there has been a shift from D_1 to D_2. The reverse (in other words a shift to the right) would obviously be the case if he became even more popular and larger numbers of people then bought his records.

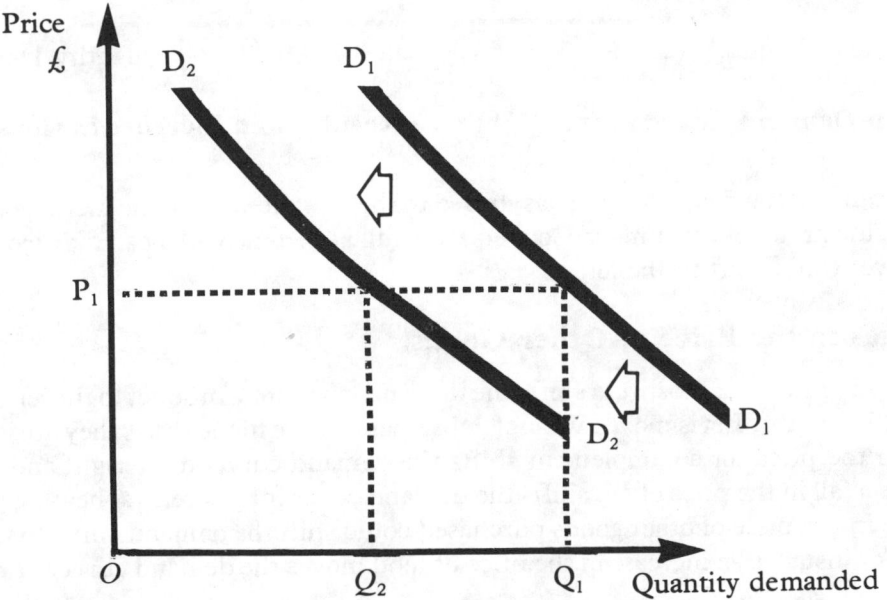

Shift in Demand Curve to the Left as a result of a Change in Preference

A Change in the Income of Consumers.

Now consider what would be the result of an increase in consumers' income on a product's demand curve. Let us explore an example to illustrate this. Over the past fifteen years, the income level of female school leavers obtaining employment has gradually increased. This has been due to a number of factors, including the impact of the Equal Pay Act 1970, and a general increase in the demand for female labour. Has the change had any effect upon the demand for necessities associated with female preferences such as clothes? The effect is described in the demand curve graph.

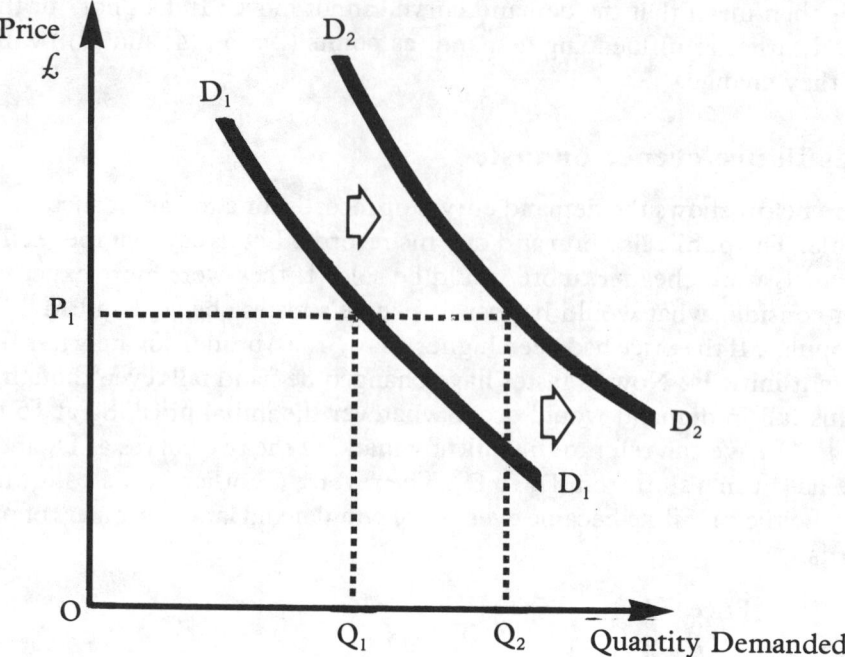

Shift in Demand Curve to the Right as a Result of an Increase in Consumer Income

As you can see, the demand curve has shifted to the right because of the increase in the income of our specific group of consumers. Conversely, a fall in income will mean they would buy less and the curve would shift to the left.

Changes in the Price of Other Goods.

A fall in the price of a substitute shifts the demand curve for a product to the left, and vice versa. So a fall in price of Levis moves Wranglers' demand curve to the left as they are jean substitutes. A fall in the price for a complement shifts the demand curve to the right and vice versa. For example a fall in the price of gas shifts the demand curve for gas central heating to the right. An increase in the price of other goods purchased could shift the demand curve to the left and vice versa. For instance an increase in the price of food moves the demand curve for cinema visits to the left.

All of these changes are illustrated in the following diagrams:-

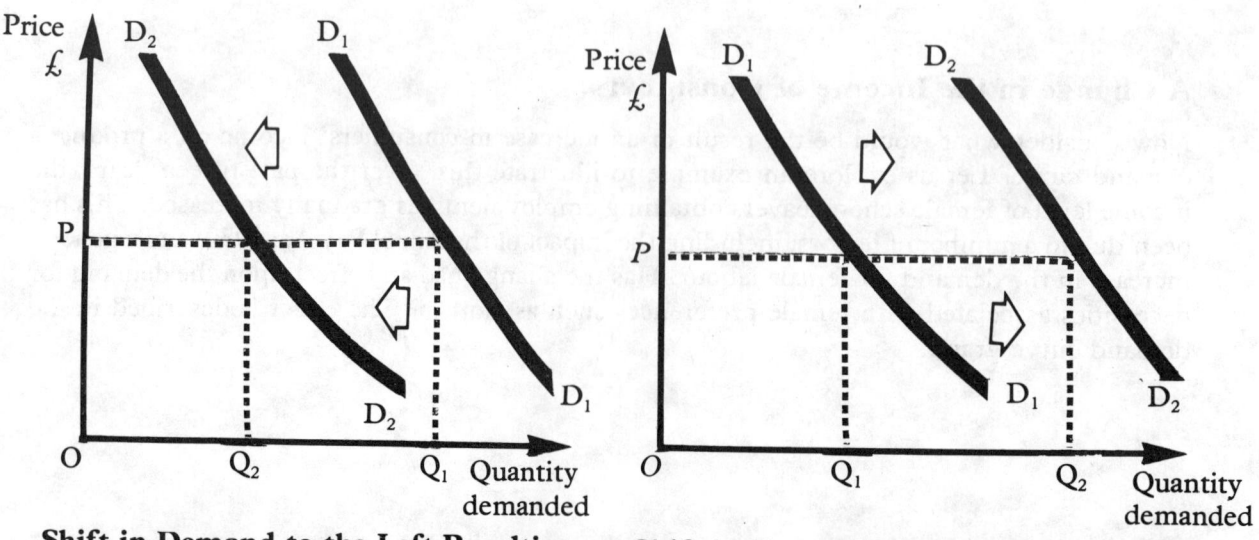

Shift in Demand to the Left Resulting from a Fall in the Price of a Substitute

Shift in Demand to the Right Resulting from a fall in the Price of a Complement

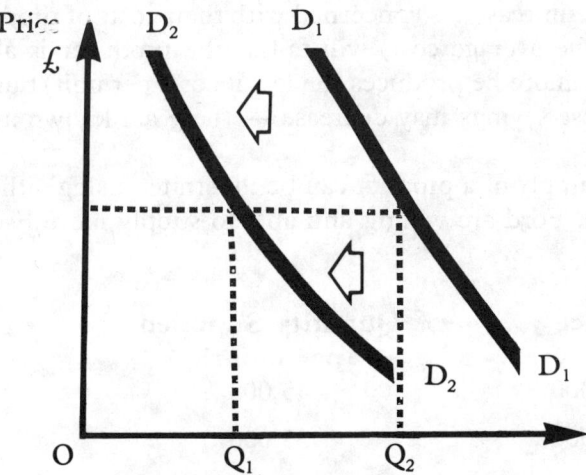

**Shift in Demand to the Left
as a result of an increase in the
price of other goods purchased by the consumer.**

SUPPLY.

The supply of a product or service is determined by the willingness and ability of producers and suppliers to meet the demands of consumers at a variety of prices. If the price offered by consumers is relatively high then producers are willing to provide more if they can. As price falls, suppliers are less inclined to produce as much. This is for two main reasons:-

1. efficient producers will make less profit per unit supplied;

2. inefficient suppliers will not be able to make any profit at all and so will go out of business.

The pattern of the supply curve is shown below.

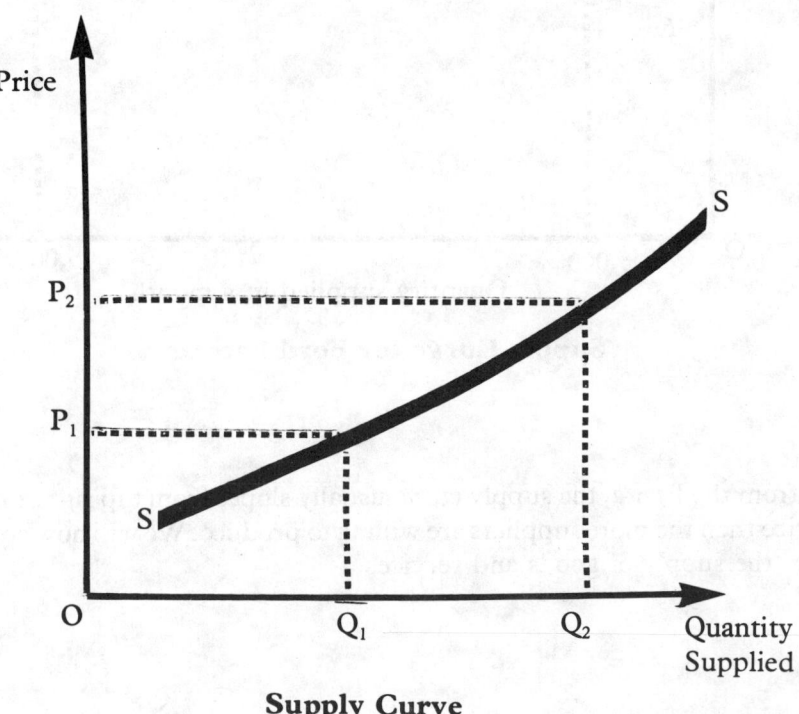

Supply Curve

There are many reasons why a producer is able to supply a certain quantity of a product at a certain price but the main reason is concerned with their costs of production. Initially, costs of production per unit (the average cost) will fall as the producer is able to take advantage of economies of scale (the more he produces the less it costs per unit) but as production increases past a certain level these savings may decrease — these are known as diseconomies of scale.

As with demand, the supply of a product can be illustrated using either a schedule or a graph. Use the same example. Ford are willing and able to supply more Escorts as price increases:-

Price	Quantity Supplied per month
£5,000	45,000
£4,500	35,000
£4,000	28,000
£3,500	20,000
£3,000	13,000
£2,500	5,000

Supply Schedule for Ford Escorts

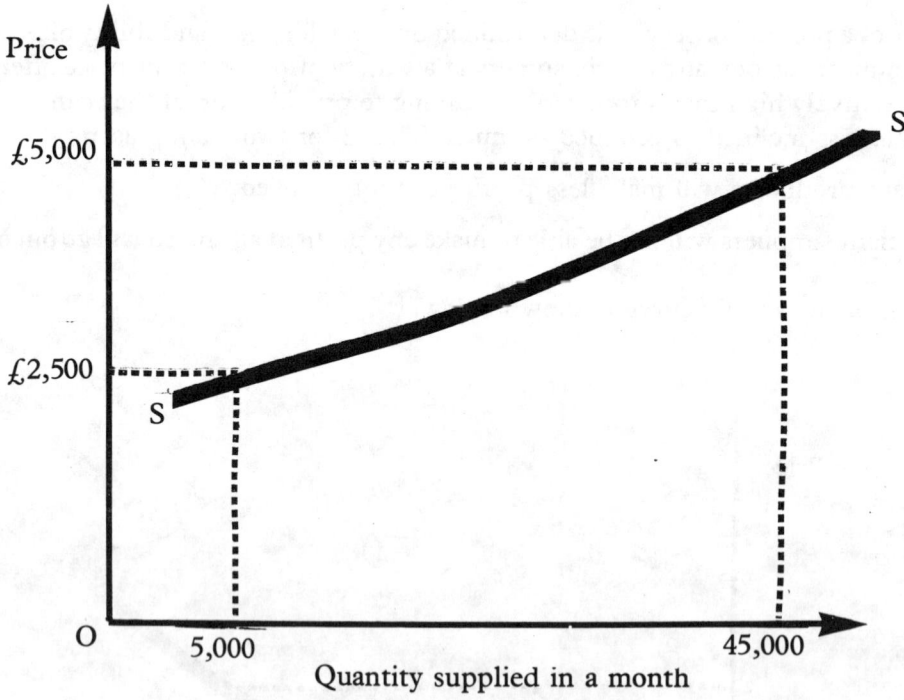

Supply Curve for Ford Escorts

As you note from the figure, the supply curve usually slopes from top right to bottom left. The higher the price then the more suppliers are willing to produce. We will now consider the factors that influence the supply of goods and services.

Determinants of Supply.

The price consumers are willing to pay is obviously the most important factor affecting the level of supply. Changes in the price that the producer can get for his products will move supply along an existing supply curve. This is shown in the diagram below.

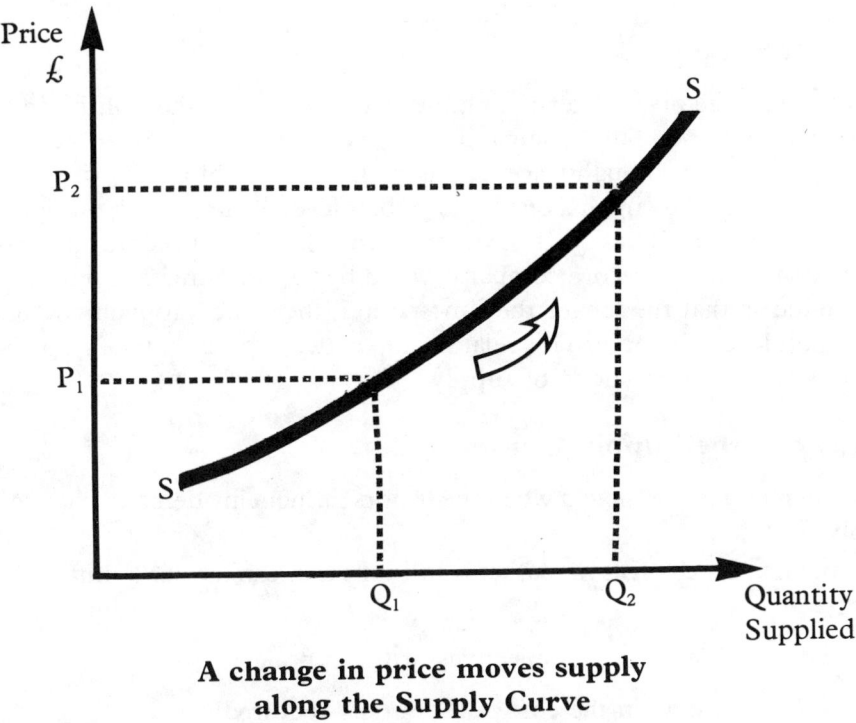

A change in price moves supply along the Supply Curve

However, there are other important determinants of supply:-

1. As we noted in chapter 18 many producers are not, surprisingly enough, interested in making the maximum profit. They may prefer to make a satisfactory profit, that is sufficient profit to give a reasonable return on their money invested and provide them with a decent living without incurring the risks of expanding their business, so that even a price rise might not be sufficient to encourage them to expand production.

2. One factor affecting all production is the cost of inputs required to manufacture the product such as labour, raw materials and power. If these inputs increase in price, the level of profitability of the organisation will change and the amount it is willing to provide may reduce at a particular price. For example, if miners' wages rise then British Coal may close certain coal mines and so reduce the supply of coal.

3. For some organisations their choice is between producing one product instead of another. For instance, a company producing plastic ashtrays could, if it wished, produce plastic toys. If the price of toys rises and that of ashtrays does not, then the organisation may simply transfer productive capacity from ashtrays to toys.

4. The level of available technology will obviously influence the level of supply. We discussed the importance of technology in chapter 20 and noted that if a new process is introduced or new machinery for production is developed, then the organisation may be willing to increase its level of production even though the price it can charge has remained the same. This type of change could also be the result of the introduction of new raw materials into the manufacturing process which are cheaper and so reduce costs. For instance, the introduction of man-made fibre has increased the willingness of shirt manufacturers to produce at a relatively low price.

5.   The Government may be influential in promoting or discouraging the production of certain goods/services. An increase in the tax on cigarettes will result in a decreased demand leading potentially to a reduction in the number of employees in the tobacco industry. The government may, of course, encourage the production of some products through tax concessions or subsidies. Exporters tend to be favoured in this way.

Changes in Supply.

One of the crucial factors in determining the level of supply is the ability of producers to change in response to a rise or fall in demand and price. The supply of some products cannot be increased quickly even though price has risen. If the price of apples rises in October, farmers must wait until the following harvest to raise their level of supply. The supply of other products can be changed relatively easily. If the demand for Phil Collins records increased substantially, there is no doubt that his record company would be able to increase supply almost immediately. What is found is that the longer the time period, the more suppliers are able to respond by changing their level of supply. This relationship between price and the responsiveness of supply to change is called the elasticity of supply.

Movement of the Supply Curve.

Just as the demand curve moved when the factors influencing demand changed, the same is true for supply.

If we summarise the changes in market conditions that can induce a shift in the supply curve we can note;-

1.   a change in the objectives of the supplier;

2.   a change in the cost of the inputs required;

3.   a change in the price of other products that the supplier can produce;

4.   a change in technology or the production process;

5.   changes in government policy.

Consider a few possible shifts in the supply curve:-

i.   if the supply process is revolutionised (for example, the introduction of robot welding machines in the production of cars), this will mean that producers are willing to produce more cars at the existing price. This would result in a shift in the supply curve to the right.

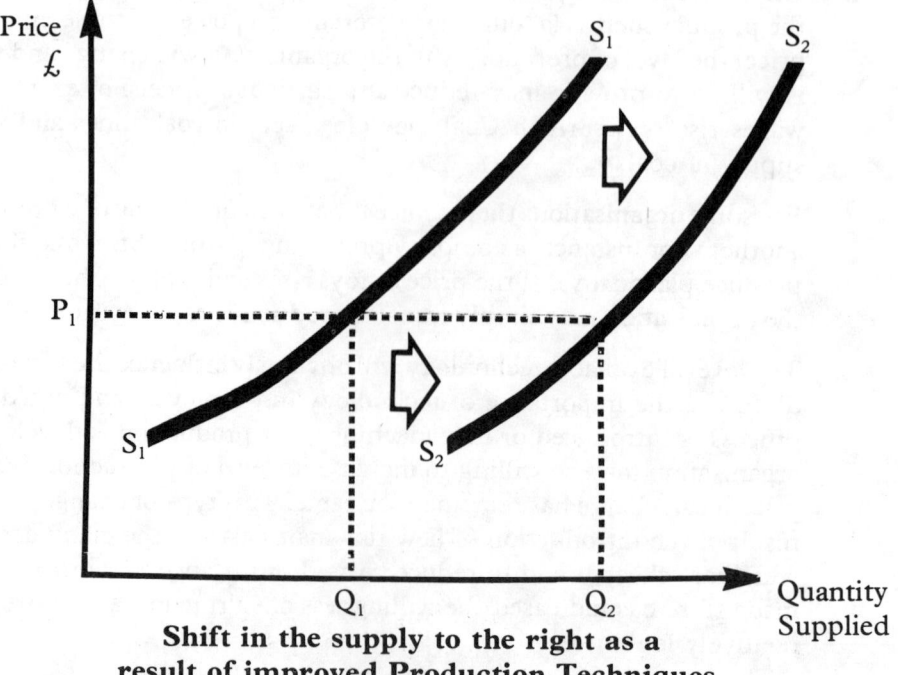

**Shift in the supply to the right as a
result of improved Production Techniques**

ii.   Conversely, an increase in the price of an alternative product may encourage a supplier to switch production and so result in a shift in supply to the left. (For instance, the level of profit to be made from bingo encouraged many cinema owners to stop showing films and switch to bingo which resulted in a reduction in the supply of cinemas).

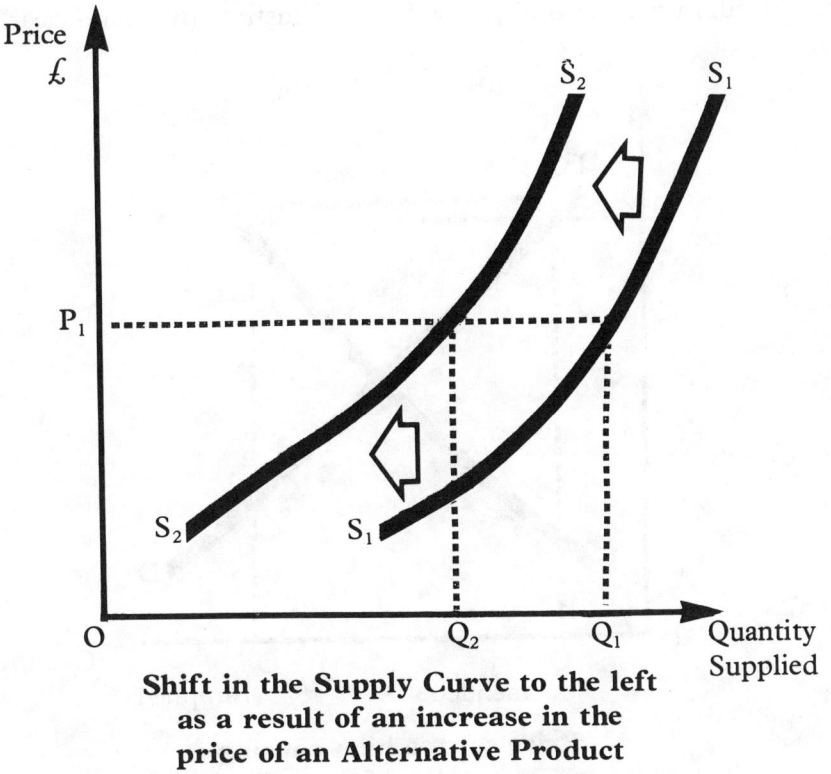

Shift in the Supply Curve to the left as a result of an increase in the price of an Alternative Product

Clearly, many other examples could be used to illustrate shifts in the supply curve but you should consider yourself how changes in the factors influencing supply could shift the supply curve.

THE INTERACTION OF SUPPLY AND DEMAND

A market for a product or service is merely the combination of the supply and demand for it. All that the market does is fix a price at which a certain quantity which consumers are willing to buy is equal to the amount that suppliers are willing to produce.

Using the example of Ford Escort cars it is possible to combine the Supply and Demand curves already illustrated:-

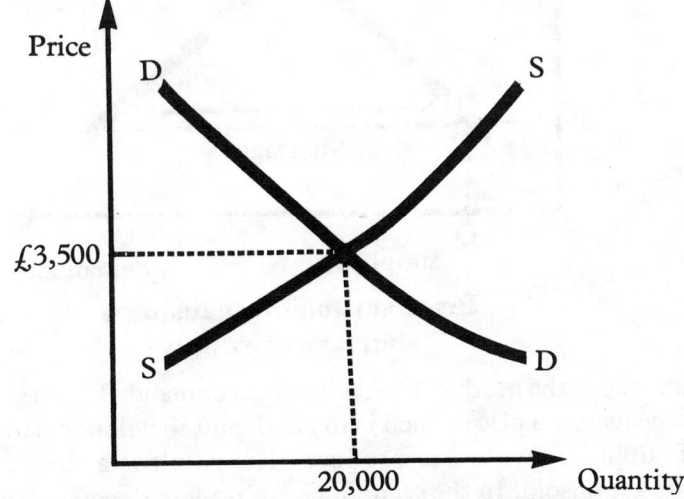

Demand and Supply Curves for Ford Escorts showing market equilibrium

As you can see, the point at which the price of £3,500 attracts 20,000 buyers is also the price at which Ford are willing to supply 20,000 cars. The market is said to be in equilibrium. Both consumers and suppliers are satisfied.

This situation is fine in theory, but in practice what often happens is that there is an excess of demand over supply or vice versa. This is because the price which is set (usually by the producer) is not the equilibrium price. Two diagrams help to illustrate this more clearly.

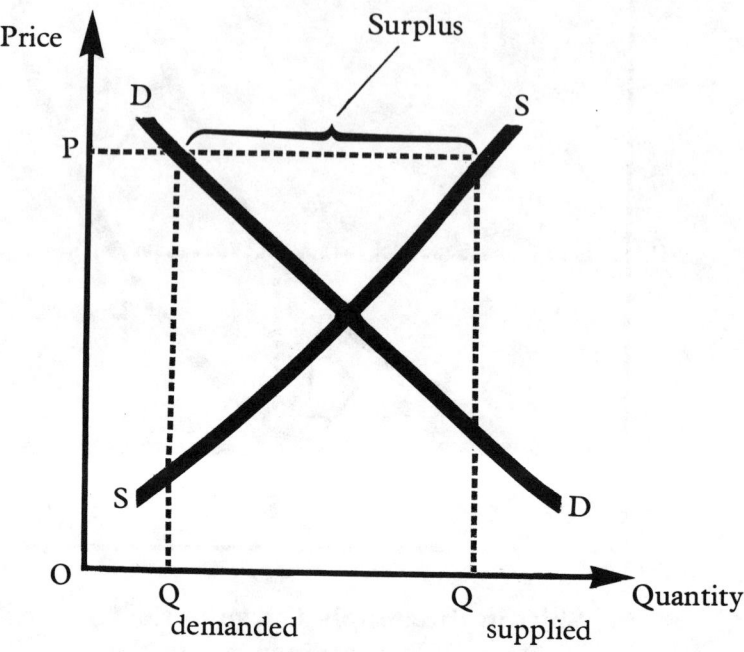

**Price set too high causing a
surplus of supply**

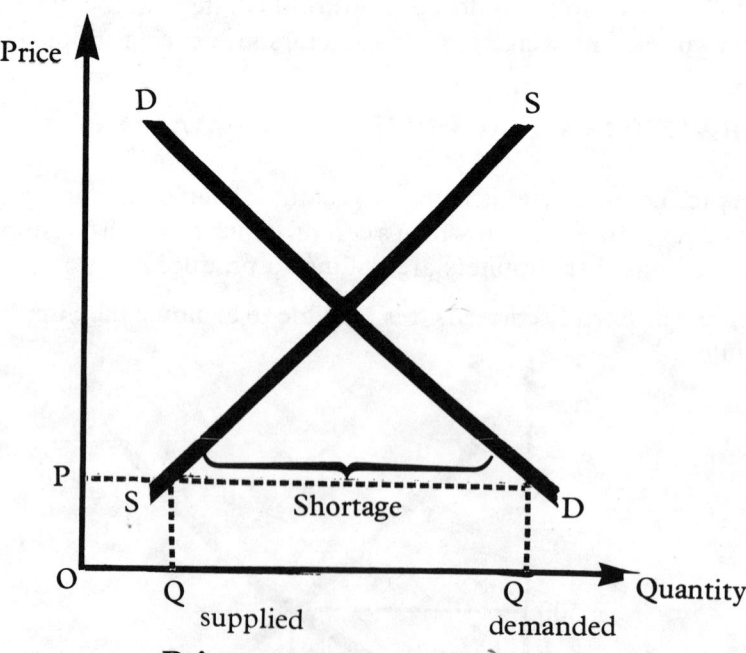

**Price set too low causing a
shortage of supply**

In the two diagrams above the producer has misjudged demand. The first diagram illustrates ths situation in which he has set a price which is too high and so will not attract sufficient buyers to meet the level of supply he wishes to produce. The result is a surplus of products and the producer has goods left unsold. In the second, he has underestimated demand and the result is a shortage. He has more customers than he is willing to supply at that price thus resulting in disappointed customers.

In situations like this, what usually happens is that the supplier readjusts his price — either up or down — towards the equilibrium position — or he changes the level of supply. In a surplus position he reduces supply shifting the supply curve to the left to find a new equilibrium at B instead of A.

In the case of a shortage, he increases supply and the new equilibrium is at C.

It should be clear from the section on Demand that the demand curve can also shift and the equilibrium position can change because of this.

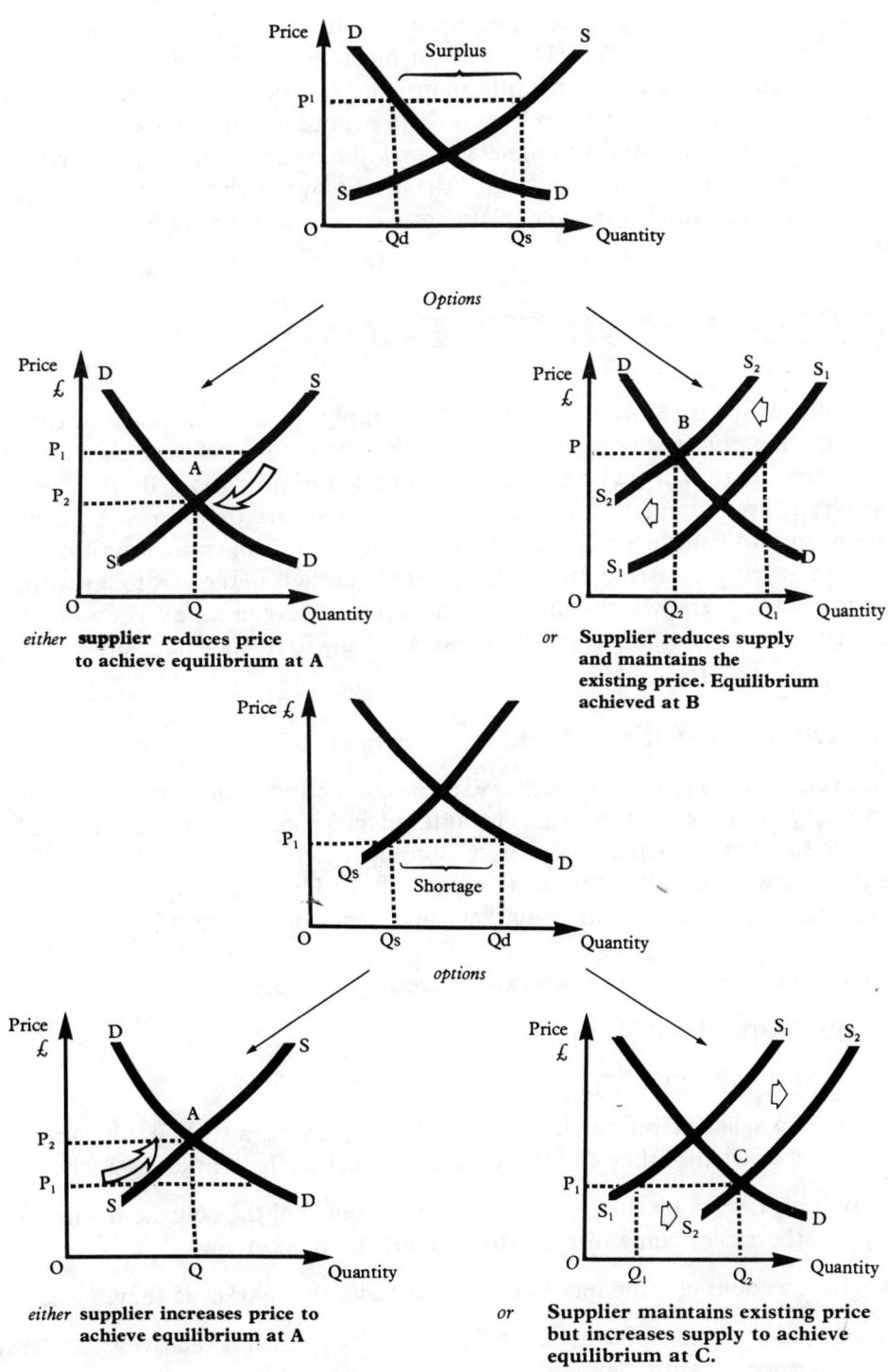

Eventually the market should, in theory, achieve a position of balance where supply meets demand at a price which satisfies both customer and producer, in other words at the equilibrium position. At that point there are no sellers who do not find a buyer and no buyers who cannot find a seller. A more detailed examination of pricing is considered in chapter 26.

But in the real world most markets are not in equilibrium. We constantly see "cut price offers" (indicating excess supply) or queues (indicating excess demand) or stock-piling (what does this indicate?). There is no unique market price at any one time. For instance where a house has been sold, the seller may have been willing to take less for the house than the final agreed price and the buyer may have been willing to pay more. But there is a certain price below which the seller is not willing to drop and another price beyond which the buyer is not willing to exceed. The actual selling price falls somewhere between the two and is the result of negotiation and bargaining between the buyer and the seller. Therefore in most situations there is no "fixed price". A shopkeeper will advertise a product in his shop window at a certain price but he is probably willing to lower his price if he gets no buyers. The negotiation in this case is non-verbal and is demonstrated by the customers' willingness or unwillingness to buy at the advertised price. A little later in the chapter we will be looking at the means by which the law regulates transactions such as these and we will also try to explain demand and supply in terms of the formation of contracts.

DIFFERENT MARKET FORMS

In the previous section we looked at the process of supply and demand and how their interaction detemines a market price for a product. However we have somewhat over-simplified the process by assuming that there is always a perfectly free market in operation. By this we mean that to achieve perfectly free interaction between buyers and sellers there must be many buyers all competing to buy the producers goods and also many sellers all competing for the consumers custom. This is rarely the case. In most of the product markets in the UK today we normally find only a few major suppliers who dominate the market and this can have serious disadvantages for the consumer. Before looking at such markets let us first consider some of the different contemporary market structures.

a.   Perfectly Competitive Market.

If a situation existed where there were many sellers competing against each other for products of a similar quality, and the contractual terms offered and accepted were all relatively the same, then we could say that the market was perfectly competitive. In reality, there are few situations in which there is what is called "perfect competition". However this concept can be used to measure the competitiveness of other markets, and hence does have at least a theoretical value.

For a perfectly competitive market to exist there needs to be:-

> i.   many sellers;
>
> ii.   many buyers;
>
> iii.   no seller or buyer either producing or buying a sufficiently large share of the market that they can individually influence the market as a whole or its price;
>
> iv.   awareness on the part of all parties involved of the contractual terms (including the price) being offered throughout the market;
>
> v.   freedom of suppliers to enter and leave the market if they wish;
>
> vi.   all producers offering a product or service which is relatively similar in terms of price, quality, delivery, etc;
>
> viii.   freedom to put workers, land and money to their most efficient and profitable use.

If these circumstances exist, then there will be competition between suppliers for potential customers and price will be kept as low as possible. The most efficient suppliers, who are able to keep costs of production down, will consequently make the most profit and so be able to pay the highest wages and attract the best labour; be able to pay the highest rents, so securing the prime locations. Thus they will be able to produce the best products — and of course make the most profit! Other less efficient producers will be less cost effective and so make less profit. The least efficient will make no profit and so go out of business.

Thus perfect competition encourages efficiency and keeps prices down for consumers. As we have already stated, perfect competition rarely exists in the real world. However, it is a useful concept for explaining the behaviour of markets. It is the actions of the market as a whole, total demand interacting with total supply, which determines price. Each individual supplier must accept the market price. In fact this type of market is sometimes referred to as a price takers market. If they try to charge a higher price, they will receive no offers to purchase their products. If they try to charge a price below that offered in the market, they act irrationally for they will not make as much profit per unit as they possibly could.

Why then does the efficient producer not reduce his price, sell more and so extend his market share? This can be because of the type of production with which he is involved. If he tries to grow much bigger his costs start to rise, so he should always seek to produce at his optimum level of production. This is shown graphically in the figure below.

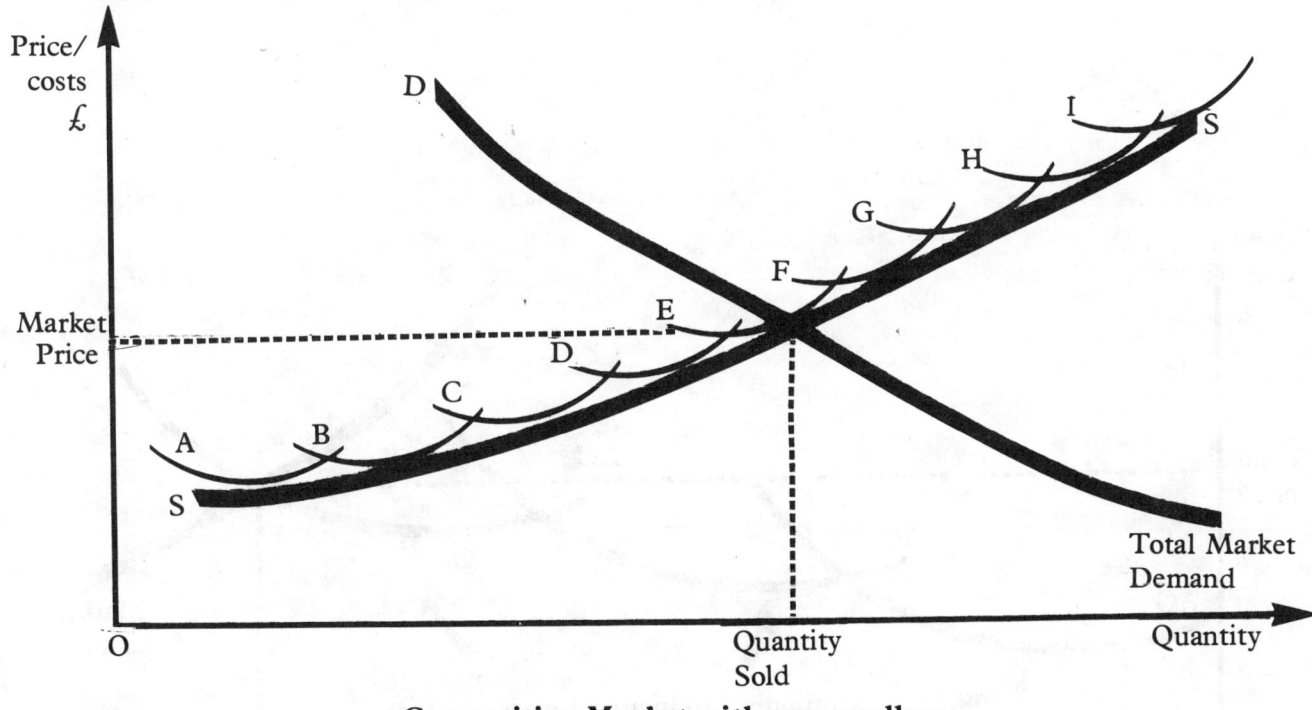

Competitive Market with many sellers

From this you can see that producer A is the most efficient, with lowest costs and producer I is the least efficient. With market demand at the level shown, only producers A to E remain in business. F to I cannot produce at a cost below market price because they are too inefficient.

b. Imperfectly Competitive Markets.

The concept of the optimum production level is important in determining how many producers will exist in the market and by implication how competitive it is. If the optimum level of production in an industry is such that one producer can meet total market demand then it is likely that only one producer will exist. This is referred to as a monopoly. If one supplier's optimum production can only supply a proportion of market demand then what could evolve is an oligopoly, where a few suppliers share the market. Let us illustrate these two situations graphically.

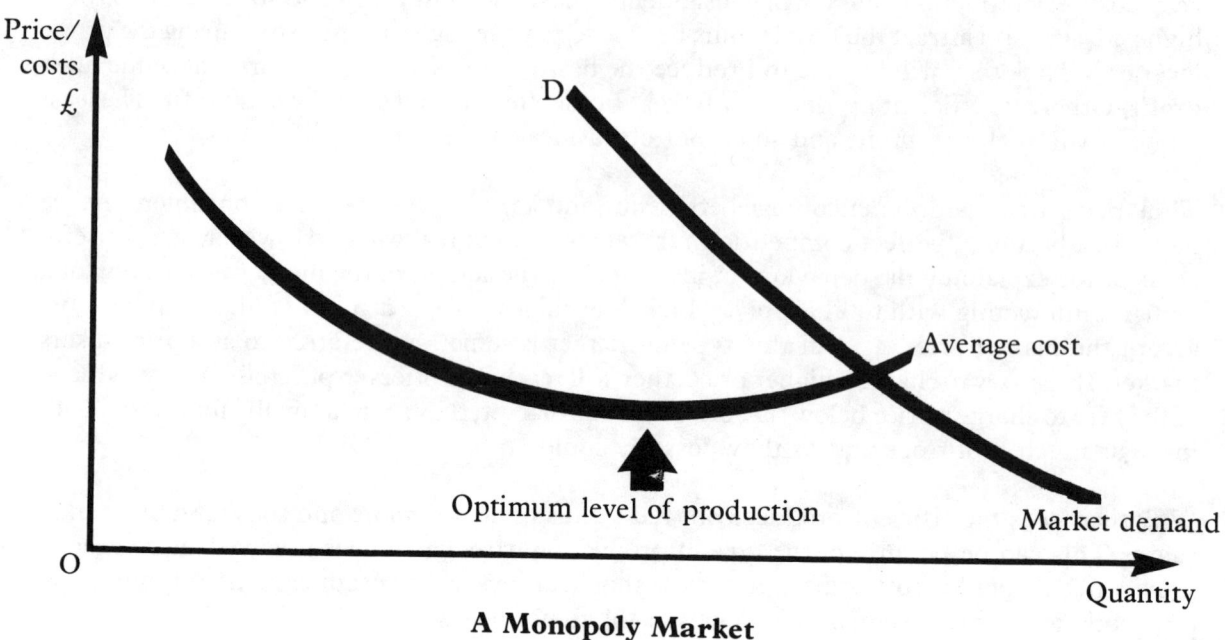

A Monopoly Market

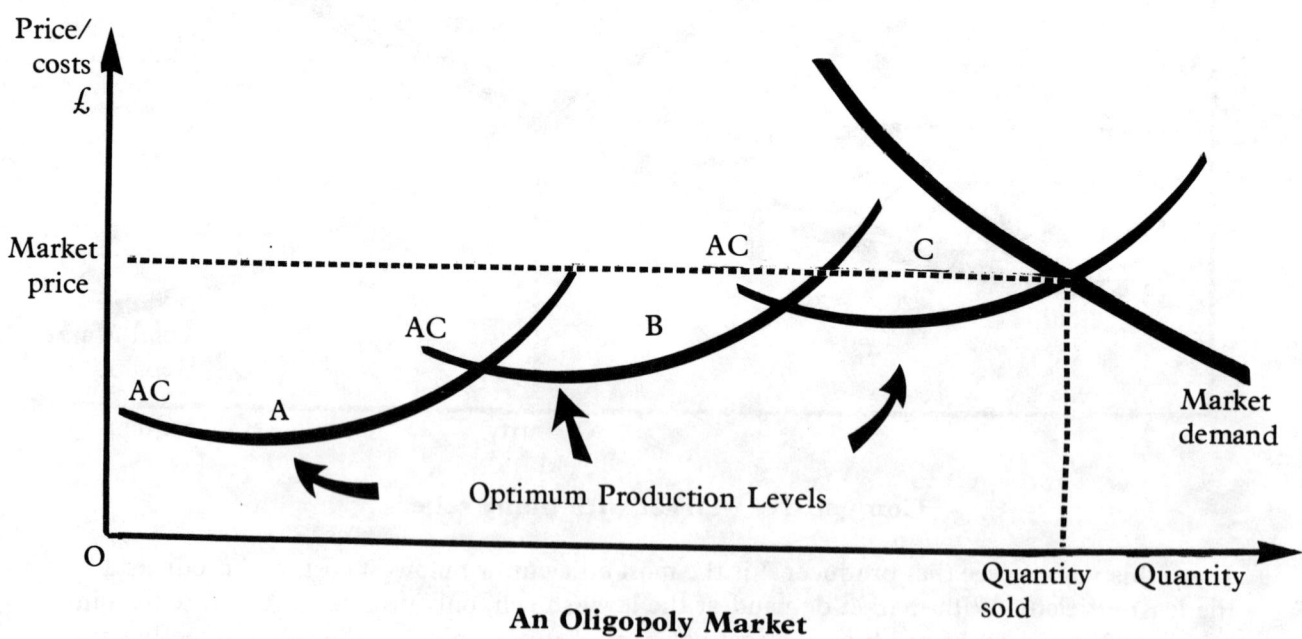

An Oligopoly Market

In the UK economy most markets for manufactured products are oligopolies. Here dominant suppliers are in a powerful bargaining position and can therefore dictate contractual terms to their buyers. Because of this both the government and the courts have sought to redress the balance between the unequal bargaining position of the parties.

Now let us recap on the different types of market that exist and their respective structures. They can be categorised as follows:-

Market Form	Nature
a. Perfect Competition (Price Takers Market)	Many producers with similar products. Many consumers, therefore high level of competition with prices determined by the market.
b. Imperfect Competition	
i. Imperfectly Competitive Market	Many producers but with different products
ii. Oligopoly (Price Searchers Market)	Few producers with relatively similar products. Normally many consumers but producers are in the dominant position particularly if they work together. Price often determined by major price leader with other firms following suit.
c. Monopoly (Price Makers Market)	One producer with individual product different from others. If product is in high level of demand then single producer is able to charge what the market will bear

Theoretically, all these market forms can exist and, to an extent, are found in the UK. However, the most important form of market in this country is oligopoly. It has been estimated that about 20 of the 22 main industrial and service sectors of the UK economy are oligopolies. Thus, for most of the goods and services you purchase, choice is limited to those supplied by a few major companies. This may not always appear to be true, because oligopolists often produce a range of brands of the same type of product. They try to create brand differentiation. The consumer sees a wide variety of brands on the supermarket shelf and believes he is purchasing from a different manufacturer if he chooses a "rival" product. In fact both brands may be made by the same company.

This does not always mean that the consumer does not have a choice. He is able to choose between a number of retail outlets. At this stage, that is prior to entering into a contract for goods or services, he may be able to buy from a numerous range of shops or supermarkets. However it is at the production stage where oligopoly is most evident. Most consumer durables, such as fridges, TV's, cookers, etc. are produced by a relatively small number of companies. Most of the processed food you eat is canned, if not actually grown, by big companies such as Heinz or Cavenham.

THE FORMATION OF OLIGOPOLY MARKETS

Oligopoly markets have come about through the evolution of massive companies. These organisations dominate the market. Their growth has been the result of economies of scale gained from large scale production. As output increases, the average cost of production falls as organisations are able to use more specialised methods of manufacture, mass production or increased mechanisation. Essentially, this means that a plant or factory may be much more efficient in terms of cost per individual item made it if produces on a very large scale than if it only makes a few units of production. The cost of the factory, rent, rates and other overheads must be paid whatever the level of production, and so, if more is produced, this initial or fixed cost is shared out over more products. It is very much the size at which the plant or factory will be most efficient — its optimum size — which determines how large it is likely to become and how much of the market it can supply. If costs (or, more precisely, the average cost of each unit made), continue to fall as production increases then the company will continue to expand. When average costs start to rise, the organisation will be forced to charge a higher price for its product, and so will be open to competition from lower priced competitors who may enter the market and take some of its sales. It is a combination of this idea of optimum company size and the level of demand which determines how a market structure evolves.

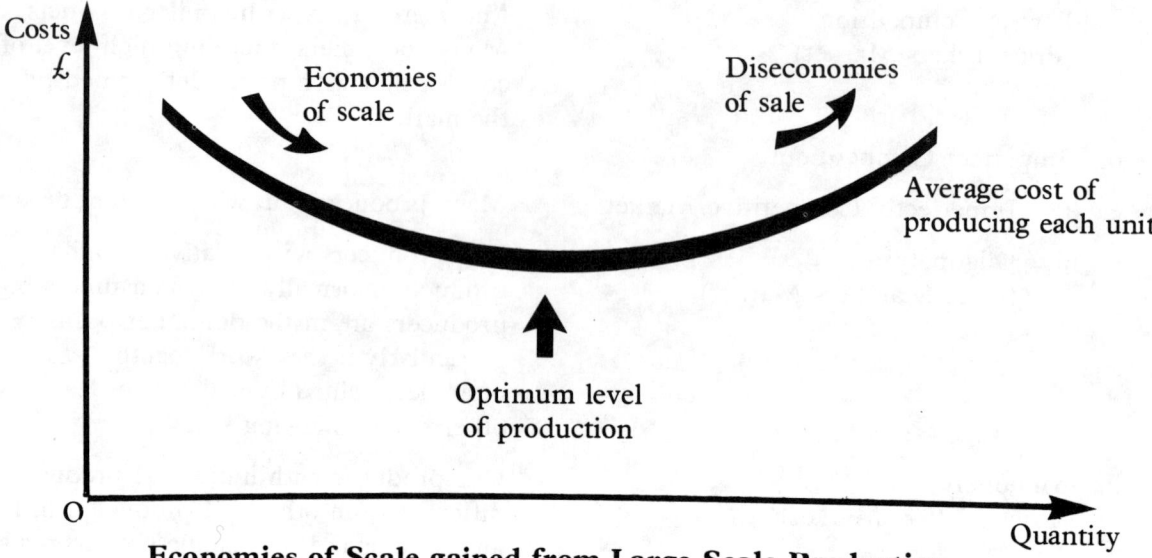

Economies of Scale gained from Large Scale Production

If a producer's optimum size of output (the output at which he stops gaining economies of scale) is equal to the extent of the demand for the product, then one company will dominate the market and it will become a monopoly. However, in most industries, the optimal company production level is only sufficient to cater for a part of the market.

As output increases, if the supplier is able to gain economies of scale, his average cost of production will tend to fall towards a bottom level. Once optimum production capacity has been achieved, average costs tend to rise. The extent of economies of scale which can be achieved will depend on such factors as the type of product, the productivity of labour, the ability to introduce machinery and managerial skill.

In the situation shown, none of the three producers can raise their level of manufacture without facing rising costs, and so each is satisfied with his share of the market. If overall market demand was to increase then it might encourage either an increase in the production levels of existing suppliers or persuade another producer to enter the market.

This diagram shows an oligopoly market shared between three suppliers — none is willing to supply total market demand because of rising average costs.

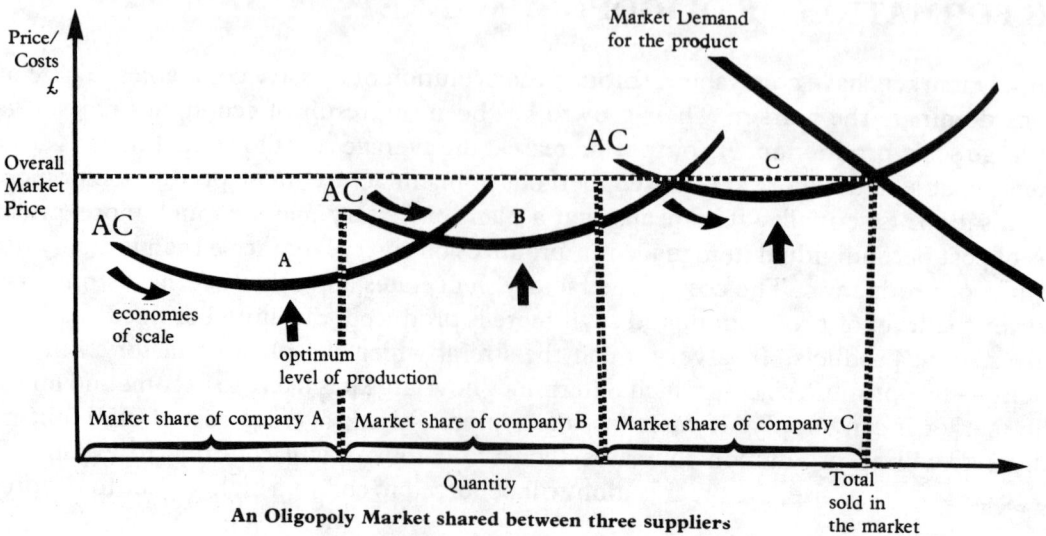

An Oligopoly Market shared between three suppliers

The Level of Market Concentration

We have already commented that the growth of oligopolies has been very pronounced in the UK economy. This is measurable by the level of concentration in individual markets, which indicate how many producers supply a large percentage of the total market demand. A high degree of concentration with only a few producers supplying most of the market, indicates an oligopoly. A low level of concentration suggests production is shared among many suppliers, and therefore presumably competition is greater.

Examples of highly concentrated industries are detergents (essentially only Unilever and Proctor and Gamble), confectionery (Rowntree Mackintosh and Cadbury Schweppes) and national newspapers (Associated Newspapers, the Mirror Group and News International). There are many other examples.

Does an oligopoly market mean that there will be a lack of competition? Obviously, from the examples which have been mentioned, you will realise that there is competition between oligopolists. There are continuous advertising campaigns by which the market leaders attempt to maintain or extend their market share. The aim is to try to tie consumers to the producer's particular brand. Often such brand names are considerably more expensive than those products which are not extensively marketed. For example, in the washing powder market, it is estimated that 40% of the total selling price is accounted for by advertising costs. This also means that Proctor and Gamble, the detergent manufacturer, and its main rival, Unilever, are always among the top twenty largest spenders on advertising in the UK. Manufacturers use sales gimmicks, such as competitions and free gifts, to attract and hold customers. We will examine the extent and objectives of such advertising in more depth in chapter 26.

Does the consumer really benefit from this type of competition? The main advantage to the consumer of fierce competition is that prices will tend to be kept as low as possible. Suppliers will be forced to reduce profit margins in order to attract new custom through low prices. If this is true in oligopoly markets there would be little cause for concern. However, as we have seen, the oligopolist's main concern is maintaining a market share which allows him to produce at his optimum level. If he has reached this level then he will have no incentive to lower his price. Competition through advertising is an attempt to maintain market share (and output at optimum size) rather than to increase it. It is only when a new competitor tries to enter the market and establish himself that a price-war can develop.

Supplier Dominance

It is the consumer who may lose out in an oligopoly situation because of the power of dominant suppliers. The consumer is in an unequal bargaining position because of two main factors:-

    a. **lack of choice** — he is restricted to a limited number of suppliers;

    b. **lack of competition** — there is no effective competitive drive between the dominant suppliers.

The Continued Growth of Oligopoly Markets

The UK as we have already seen, has the highest degree of market concentration (i.e. the greatest number of oligopolistic industries) in the world, and this trend is continuing. It will not be reversed unless either:-

    a. new producers enter the market and so reduce concentration; or

    b. the government takes steps to prevent the extension of oligopolies.

New Suppliers Entering the Market

New suppliers may find it difficult to enter an industry because of the massive capital investment required to break into existing markets. Eddie Shah's attempt to enter the highly capital intensive national daily newspaper market with his publication, Today, in February 1986 required him to make large scale investment on the new technology which would allow him to print the paper more cheaply, but he also had to institute a large scale advertising campaign on TV and radio to try and attract readers away from the existing national dailies. Entry into an industry which already has established and recognised suppliers is a risk, and often a costly risk.

One of the main forms of new competition is the entry into the market of a foreign competitor. The company may already have a firm foundation in its own country and so extra sales in this country may only require an increase in existing production rather than the initial cost of building new factories. An example of this has been in the car industry, where the market dominance of Ford, BL, Rover, Vauxhall and Chrysler has been seriously challenged by the "market penetration" of Japanese and Continental car manufacturers.

Government Intervention in the Market

We have noted that there are considerable disadvantages to the consumer resulting from the growth of oligopoly markets. For this reason the government will sometimes attempt to prevent the growth of dominant firms by restricting merger and takeover activity through its competition policy. This important area of government intervention into the market will be examined in some detail in chapter 27 therefore at this point we will simply make some general comments.

The State is usually reluctant to interfere in the free workings of the economy and the evolution of a particular market. It will normally only intervene if it can see clear disadvantages arising out of the increased concentration in a market or the behaviour of market suppliers. The government steps in to protect the individual (or the State itself) if the behaviour of such dominant organisations is seen to be detrimental to the public interest. However, as we will see later there is often considerable difficulty in determining what exactly is meant by the public interest.

BUSINESS TRANSACTIONS WITHIN THE MARKET

In this section we will examine the legal mechanism by which business transactions are carried out in the market. You will recognise that in the commercial world goods or services are normally purchased for consumption or resale. First the buyer and seller will negotiate the terms of the purchase and then they must enter into a transaction which will result in the sale. The parties to such transactions include commercial undertakings, public corporations, local authorities and private individuals but the legal mechanism by which they transact is always the same, they enter into a contract.

Freedom to contract for a wide range of goods and services is fundamental to the market economy. A market is created by trading and wherever buying and selling takes place and goods and services are exchanged, demands are created and fulfilled. Trading inevitably, of course, involves financial risk so that it is in the mutual interest of all the parties involved to have a recognisable set of rules by which they agree to abide.

If trading is to flourish it is reasonable for the participants to expect that in the event of conflict there is some formal means by which such conflict may be resolved, if other informal means have failed. The formal means available to resolve a dispute in relation to a transaction is to bring proceedings in a civil court. This is called litigation. Such a legal action will be founded on the law of contract. The civil courts which have initial authority over disputes in relation to the law of contract are the county courts and the High Court. Cases heard before them are said to be 'tried'. When an action in contract is brought before a civil court, after hearing both sides to the dispute the court has the authority to make a judgement in favour of one of the parties. Such a judgement will normally provide the successful party with some form of redress. Usually this will require the guilty party to provide the other with a remedy. Where there is a finding that one party has broken the terms of a contract, the party in breach will usually be required to pay the innocent party a sum in compensation. This is called damages. In the case of a serious breach the innocent party will also have the opportunity of treating the contract as terminated.

From the simplest to the most complex transaction, contracts involve parties entering into mutual undertakings which involve personal obligations. In a straight forward contract for the sale of goods a seller agrees to sell specific goods to a purchaser for a stated agreed sum. Such a contract basically involves an obligation on the seller to transfer the ownership of the goods in return for an obligation on the buyer's part to make payment. Obviously in complex transactions such as international trade deals and large scale civil engineering contracts then detailed and multiple groups of promises are exchanged.

One of the tasks often faced by the courts in a dispute involving a contract is to determine whether the parties have fulfilled the contractual obligations imposed upon them. Before determining this the court may face a more fundamental issue, namely whether the agreement imposing the obligations constitutes a contract and is therefore legally binding. This issue can only be determined by examining whether the elements of a simple contract are present in the agreement; in effect whether or not certain ground rules have been followed. Most trading is effected by means of a simple contract, but for certain purposes, notably to transfer certain interests in land, the more formal specialty contract (also known as a contract under seal or deed) is used. Thus in the sale and purchase of a house contracts first have to be signed and exchanged, but to complete the transaction, a deed called a conveyance, must be executed to pass ownership from the vendor (seller) to the purchaser.

Simple contracts then are agreements intended by the parties to have legal consequences and to be legally enforceable. They do not have any special formalities attached to them. Everyday examples of their use would include when:-

> a retailer agrees to sell goods to a customer;
>
> a builder agrees to repair a roof for a householder;
>
> an investor agrees to lend money to a company;
>
> a hairdresser agrees to cut a customer's hair;
>
> a garage owner agrees to sell a car on hire purchase to a hirer;
>
> an employee agrees to work for wages for an organisation;
>
> a taxi driver agrees to take a hirer to the station;
>
> a landlord agrees to let property to a tenant.

The above are all everyday examples where the parties to an agreement achieve their objectives by virtue of a contract. The fact that the parties have respective rights and duties which are contractual in nature simply means that if one party to the contract fails to perform his obligations, or performs his obligations in a defective manner, then the other party may sue for breach of contract and obtain a court remedy such as damages (compensation) and for serious breaches, termination of contract — known technically as repudiation.

Millions of these events are carried out every day and nearly all of them are performed to the satisfaction of the parties making them. As a general rule simple contracts need not be in any particular form. They may be oral or written, or a mixture of both. Sometimes the contract itself or evidence of the contract must be written. This is the case for transactions involving land. To protect the hirer, consumer credit transactions must be in writing. Examples of consumer credit transactions include hire purchase agreements and credit sale agreements.

The elements which must be present to constitute a legally binding simple contract are that:

1. the parties intend to contract;

2. they have reached a precise agreement through the process of offer and acceptance;

3. they have provided consideration to support the contract; and

4. they have legal capacity to contract.

Each element is now considered in turn to determine its nature and extent.

1.   Intention to create legal relations

To create a contractual relationship the parties must intend their agreement to have legal consequences. In cases where the parties to an agreement have not expressed their intentions clearly then it will be left to the courts to determine from the available evidence whether the parties intended to enter into a contract. The approach adopted by the courts is to classify the relationship of the parties as either social/domestic or business/commercial.

a.   Social or domestic agreements.

Having classified an agreement as a social or domestic one it is presumed that the parties to such an agreement do not intend legal consequences unless there is clear evidence to the contrary.

> In *Balfour v. Balfour 1919*, a family agreement where the husband agreed to pay his wife an allowance of £30 per month without any terms and conditions was not held to be intended to be legally binding and did not give rise to a contract.

> Alternatively, in *Parker v. Clark 1960*, the defendants, an elderly couple, invited their niece and her husband (the plaintiffs), to come and live with them. In return for domestic help the defendants promised to leave the plaintiffs their property in their will. The plaintiffs accepted the offer, sold their home, and moved in with the defendants. Unfortunately, differences between the parties arose and after much unpleasantness, the plaintiffs were asked to leave. In an action to recover damages for breach of contract, the court held that the evidence was sufficient to show that the parties intended the agreement to have legal consequences, particularly when considering that the plaintiffs had sold their home. Accordingly, a contract had been concluded and damages were payable for its breach.

b.   Business Agreements.

As far as business or commercial agreements are concerned, the courts apply the presumption that the parties intend to create legal consequences unless there is clear evidence to the contrary.

> The inclusion of the phrase 'binding in honour only' on a football coupon was held by the court in *Jones v. Vernons Pools Ltd. 1938*, to amount to clear evidence that there was no intention to create a contract.

. . . 'binding in honour only' . . .

Similarly, in *Rose and Frank Co. v. Crompton Bros. 1925*, a written agreement entered into by two commercial organisations included the following clause: "This arrangement is not entered into, nor is this memorandum written, as a formal or legal agreement . . . but . . . is only a definite expression and record of the purpose and intention of the . . . parties concerned, to which they each honourably pledge themselves". This clause, the court held, was sufficient evidence to overturn the presumption that commercial agreements are intended to be legally binding.

An everyday example of the use of such an exclusion is the common practice in the sale of property to agree to contract in the future by selling 'subject to contract'. Such an agreement is not legally binding and at this stage both parties are still free to withdraw from the sale. Collective agreements negotiated between employers and Trade Unions are considered in chapter 19. Under the Trade Union and Labour Relations Act 1974 they are presumed not to be intended to be legally binding unless they are stated to be so.

2. Offer and Acceptance

An agreement is said to come into existence when one party, the offeror, declares he is willing to be bound by certain terms and makes an offer and the other party, the offeree, declares he is willing to be bound by the same terms and accepts the offer. For instance where X offers to sell his car to Y for £1000 and Y agrees to pay £1000 for the car. The agreement may arise in many ways and sometimes it is possible to interpret an agreement that is created without words at all but merely by the conduct of the parties involved.

Often, it is necessary to analyse all the stages in the contractual negotiations to determine whether a valid offer has been made and also if there is a valid acceptance. Only then is it possible to discover whether a contractual agreement has come into existence.

THE CONTRACTUAL OFFER

In relation to a valid contractual offer the following points may be made:-

a.   An Offer must be Certain.

The details of the offer must be certain or capable of being made certain otherwise the offer is not capable of acceptance.

> In *Scammel v. Ouston 1941*, an agreement was reached for the sale of a van in which the balance of the purchase price was expressed to be payable "on hire purchase terms over a period of two years". In deciding whether a valid contract had been entered into, the court held that the words "on hire purchase terms" in the offer were too vague and therefore not capable of acceptance. The court would have been prepared to enforce the contract had there been a previous course of dealing between the parties from which it was possible to interpret the vague parts of the agreement, such as previous hire purchase dealings between the parties. But in the absence of such dealings, and since hire purchase forms are not standardised but vary from transaction to transaction, the court could not enforce the transaction.

Obviously, a vague term may be included in a binding contract if the parties agree the machinery to make such a term certain.

> In *Sykes (Wessex) v. Fine Fare 1966*, a producer of chickens agreed to supply between 30,000 and 80,000 chickens a week to certain retailers for one year and for a further four years, "such other figures as might be agreed". The contract provided that any differences should be referred to arbitration. In deciding a claim that the agreement was void for uncertainty, the Court of Appeal held that as the parties had laid down an agreed procedure of arbitration to settle disagreements, the agreement was certain and legally binding.

b.   A contractual offer may be made to an individual, a specific group, or in some cases to the world at large.

> The famous case of *Carlill v. Carbolic Smokeball Co. 1893*, laid down the principle that a contractual offer could be made to the world at large. The defendant company had inserted an advertisement in various newspapers offering to pay £100 to any person who, having used their medicinal product, the carbolic smokeball, for a specified period, then contracted influenza. It was also claimed in the advertisement that £1,000 had been placed on bank deposit "to show our sincerity in the matter". The plaintiff used the ball as advertised, contracted 'flu, and claimed the reward. Having been refused payment, the plaintiff sued the company alleging that a contract had been entered into. The court agreed, deciding that by placing such an advertisement, the company had communicated an offer of reward to the whole world. Such an offer was capable of acceptance by any person who complied with its terms by using the smokeball in the prescribed manner.

. . . used the ball as advertised . . .

c. The distinction between an offer and an invitation to treat.

It is important to distinguish a contractual offer from various situations which have been identified by the courts as constituting invitations to treat, in other words invitations to make an offer.

(i) Advertisements.

Apart from the exception 'offer of reward', advertisements of goods or services for sale contained in newspapers and magazines or trade catalogues are merely invitations to the reader to make a contractual offer. The individual or organisation who placed the advertisement is therefore in a position to reject an offer made for the goods or services.

> This principle was upheld in *Partridge v. Crittenden 1968*, where an advertisement had been placed in a magazine stating "Bramblefinch cocks and hens, 25 shillings each". The party who placed the advertisement was prosecuted under the criminal law for unlawfully 'offering for sale' a wild bird contrary to the Protection of Birds Act 1954. The court held that no offence had been committed as the advertisement did not constitute an 'offer for sale' but merely an invitation to treat.

(ii) Display of Goods

The same principle applies to the display of goods for sale by a shopkeeper.

> In *Fisher v. Bell 1961*, the display by a shopkeeper of a flick knife for sale did not constitute the offence of offering for sale an offensive weapon contrary to the Restriction of Offensive Weapons Act 1959.

As far as self-service stores are concerned, the court in *Pharmaceutical Society of Great Britain v. Boots Cash Chemists (Southern) Ltd. 1953*, confirmed the principle that the display of goods on shelves is merely an invitation to treat and the contractual offer is not made until the shopper presents the goods at the cash till and communicates his intention to purchase.

(iii) Invitation to Tender.

The tendering process is a means by which a prospective purchaser or seller of goods or services is able to invite offers. Local authorities are statutorily required to contract by such means for certain purposes. A tender then is the offer, but an invitation to tender is a mere invitation to treat. It is simply an invitation by an individual or organisation wishing to purchase goods or services to request suppliers to submit a contractual offer in the form of a tender.

If the invitation to tender stipulates expressly or impliedly that the goods or services will be required, then an acceptance of the tender will create a binding contract. Alternatively, the invitation may stipulate that the goods or services may be required, in which case an acceptance of the tender results in a standing offer to supply as and when required. A failure to order by the buyer in those circumstances will not result in a breach of contract.

(iv) Auction Sales.

As far as auction sales are concerned, the law is largely settled. The bidder at an auction makes an offer, the acceptance of which is signalled by the fall of the auctioneer's hammer. As we shall see later an offer may be withdrawn at any time prior to acceptance so, not surprisingly, it is possible for a bidder at an auction sale to withdraw his bid prior to the fall of the hammer.

> Reluctantly upholding the principle that an auctioneer makes an invitation to treat, the court in *British Car Auctions v. Wright 1972*, held that an auctioneer could not be convicted of 'offering for sale' a motor vehicle in an unroadworthy condition contrary to the Road Traffic Act 1972.

> The Court of Appeal decision in *Gibson v. Manchester City Council, 1978*, has cast some doubt on the traditional legal approach of distinguishing between an offer and an invitation to treat where protracted correspondence takes place. The case involved the prospective sale of a council house. The plaintiff council tenant, having completed a request for information, received a letter from the council saying it might be prepared to sell the house to him for £2,180 freehold and that if he wished to make a formal application to purchase he should return the application form. This the tenant did. Unfortunately he left the purchase price blank whilst at the same time inquiring whether the price took into account defects in the path of the property. A further letter from the council stated that the defects in the path had been taken into account in fixing the price. In interpreting the above correspondence a majority of the Court of Appeal held that a contract of sale had indeed been entered into. Lord Denning, M.R. put forward the view that in such circumstances there was no need to look for a strict offer and acceptance rather, "you should look at the correspondence as a whole and at the conduct of the parties and see therefrom whether the parties have come to an agreement on everything that was material". This decision was later reversed following a further appeal to the House of Lords in 1979. The Law Lords adopted the more traditional approach by analysing each piece of correspondence and held that no firm offer had been made or accepted by the council. The words the council "may be prepared to sell" only amounted to an invitation to treat and thus no contract of sale had resulted.

d. An offer will terminate or may be terminated in the following circumstances:-

(i) By Rejection.

A contractual offer will terminate if it is expressly rejected, by the offeree communicating his rejection. It can be impliedly rejected, by the offeree ignoring the offer. In addition, if the offeree makes a 'counter offer' this will have the effect of terminating the original offer.

> In *Hyde v. Wrench 1840*, an offer to sell land for £1,000 was met by a counter offer to purchase the land for £950. The court held that the counter offer destroyed the original offer which could not then be accepted unless revived by the original offeror.

It is important however, to distinguish a counter offer from a mere request for further information which will not destroy the original offer.

> In *Stevenson v. McLean 1880*, having received an offer to purchase iron at 40 shillings a ton the plaintiffs asked the offeror whether payment could be made over two months. Receiving no reply the plaintiffs nevertheless communicated their acceptance. The court held that a binding contract had been entered into as the enquiry relating to payment was a mere request for further information and not a counter offer which would have extinguished the original offer.

(ii) By Lapse.

A contractual offer that is expressed to be open for a stated period will lapse when that period has expired. Alternatively if no time period is expressed, the offer will lapse after a reasonable length of time.

For this purpose, what amounts to a reasonable length of time will depend upon the circumstances of the case, in particular the subject-matter. Obviously, an offer to purchase perishable goods or goods subject to fluctuating market value must be taken up reasonably promptly.

> In *Ramsgate Victoria Hotel v. Montefiore 1866*, the court held that an offer to purchase shares had lapsed prior to acceptance six months later. Such a period was regarded as unreasonable, particularly when you consider that the value of the shares was fluctuating daily.

(iii) By Withdrawal of the Offer.

An offer may be revoked at any time prior to acceptance provided that the offeror communicates his revocation to the offeree. For example, a bidder at an auction may withdraw his bid prior to acceptance or a shopper in a supermarket having offered to buy goods at the cash till may revoke the offer by replacing the goods chosen before they are purchased.

> In *Routledge v. Grant 1828*, the defendant, having offered to purchase the plaintiff's house and given the plaintiff six weeks to think it over, decided to withdraw the offer before the six weeks expired. In determining whether the revocation was effective, the court held that an offer can be withdrawn at any time before acceptance and there was no obligation on the offeror to keep the offer open.

Such an obligation would of course be imposed on an offeror who contracted to keep an offer open for a specific period.

Having stated that a revocation must be communicated, there is no requirement that it must be communicated by the offeror.

> In *Dickinson v. Dodds 1876*, the plaintiff having received an offer to purchase some property, discovered from a third party that the offeror had then sold the property to someone else. The court held that once the offeree was aware that the property had been sold to someone else the offer was impliedly revoked and not capable of acceptance.

THE ACCEPTANCE OF AN OFFER

An unconditional acceptance of the terms of the offer by the offeree will result in a contract and thus terminate the offer. As previously stated, a conditional acceptance is no acceptance. Acceptance must be unequivocal.

> Therefore in *Northland Airlines Ltd. v. Kerranti Meters Ltd. 1970*, an offer for sale of an aircraft to an offeree was held not to have been accepted when the offeree agreed to the offer subject to different terms relating to delivery and payment.

Of course an offer must be communicated and it is not possible to accept an offer of which you are unaware. Therefore if a person finds and returns a lost dog without being aware that the owner had offered a reward for its return, he has no right to claim the reward. Similarly an acceptance must be communicated to the offeror and it is not possible for the offeror to require that silence is the mode of acceptance.

> In *Felthouse v. Bindley 1862*, the plaintiff wrote to the defendant offering to buy a horse stating, "If I hear no more about him, I consider the horse mine at £30.15 shillings. The defendant made no reply and the plaintiff later claimed a contract. The court held that no contract had been concluded as it is not possible to stipulate that silence of the offeree will constitute acceptance.

The practice of suppliers sending goods to consumers who had not ordered them in the hope of inducing a sale has been largely overcome by the operation of the Unsolicited Goods and Services Act 1971 (as amended). This Act allows the consumer who receives such goods to treat the goods as an unconditional gift, after a certain time period has elapsed. It is considered in more depth in chapter 27.

At this point, some mention may be made of the rules that apply when the offeree relies on the post to make an acceptance. The general rule is that if the use of the post as a means of acceptance is expected by the parties because either:- the offer was made by post, or the offeror indicates that post may be used to accept, then the acceptance and therefore the contract, is complete, on the posting of a properly addressed and stamped letter of acceptance.

> The consequences of this curious exception to the general principle of actual communication is seen in *Household Fire Insurance Co. v. Grant 1897*. Here the defendant offered to buy shares in the plaintiff company and a letter of acceptance was subsequently posted to him. Despite the defendant never receiving the letter of acceptance, the court concluded that the contract had been entered into when it was posted. He was bound to pay for the shares.

> An illustration of this rule and the rule relating to revocation of offer can be seen in the case *Byrne v. Van Tienhoven 1880*. The defendants offered by post on 1st October to sell goods to the plaintiffs. Having received the offer on 11th October, the plaintiffs accepted by telegraph the same day. Three

days earlier the defendants had posted a letter revoking the offer and this letter was not received until 20th October. In deciding that a contract had been entered into the court confirmed the basic rules that:

    i.   the revocation of an offer is not effective until actually communicated to the offeree; and

    ii.   following an offer by post, an acceptance is complete at the time and place of posting.

The rule relating to postal acceptance can be expressly excluded by agreement and the commercial organisation may be well advised to take advantage of the opportunity.

> In *Holwell Securities Ltd. v. Hughes 1974*, an option (offer) provided that it should be exercisable "by notice in writing". The court held that this requirement effectively excluded the postal rule and that actual receipt of the letter of acceptance was necessary to conclude a contract.

3. There must be consideration exchanged

Under English Law a further requirement for the formation of a simple contract is that the parties must have provided 'consideration'. Consideration may be described as the value that is transferred by the parties and has been defined as "Some right, interest, profit or benefit accruing to one party, or some forebearance, detriment, loss or responsibility given, suffered or undertaken by the other". Consideration is really the 'buying' of a promise. It is most easily recognisable in a contract for the sale of goods where the consideration takes a tangible form of the price paid in return for the goods, for example 50p for a packet of biscuits.

However, commercial sales of goods or services are often agreements to sell, and the performance of the contractual obligations is delayed until some future date, for instance an agreement to sell on credit a consignment of flooring tiles for £1,000. Here the consideration transferred under the contract is said to be 'executory', the parties having exchanged promises to act in the future. Alternatively, if a promise is given in return for the performance of an act, such as £10 reward for the discovery and return of a lost watch, the consideration is said to be 'executed' since in order to accept the offer the offeree is required to perform an act, specifically to find and return the watch.

Essentially contract-making is seen as entering into a bargain and the courts have consequently been unwilling to enforce a promise made by A to B where B has not earned or bought the promise in some way, for there can be no bargain in such circumstances for A.

The following points may be made relating to the consideration necessary to support a simple contract:-

a. Consideration must be valuable but need not be adequate.

This means that the consideration transferred must have some value but it need not be adequate, that is economically equal to the promise it is supporting, for example £50 in exchange for a new car. Generally, the courts leave the parties free to make their own bargains and provided there is no fraud, misrepresentation, duress or undue influence the courts will not grant a remedy to a party who has simply made a 'bad deal'. Were they to do so they would in effect be determining market prices outside the normal market mechanisms.

b. Consideration must be sufficient.

Consideration is said to be insufficient when a party attempts to use an existing contractual or public duty as consideration to support a contract.

In *Stilk v. Myrick 1809*, the existing contractual duty was to sail a ship on a round trip from London to the Baltic. When two sailors deserted, the captain promised to divide their wages between the rest of the crew if they would work short-handed. The court held that such a promise was unenforceable as it was not supported by sufficient consideration as the sailors were under an existing contractual duty.

Of course, if the promise of additional payment is given in exchange for something extra in return, such as performing more hazardous work, then it will be legally binding.

An example of existing public duty imposed under the law is the case of *Collins v. Godefroy 1831*. Here the plaintiff had received a subpoena (a court order) to give evidence in court. He then agreed with the defendant to give the evidence in return for payment of his expenses. The court held that there was no contract for the payment of expenses, as the promise of payment was not supported by sufficient consideration. The plaintiff was under an existing duty to give his evidence.

c.   Consideration must not be past.

All that is meant here is that a party to a contract cannot use a past act as a basis for consideration. Therefore, if one party performs an act for another, and only receives a promise of reward after the act is complete, the past act would be past consideration.

The rule is illustrated by the decision in *Re: McArdle, 1951*. Here an individual carried out certain improvements to property without being asked. The persons who would ultimately benefit from this work then promised in writing to pay £488 for the work done. In deciding the validity of this promise, the court held that it was a clear case of past consideration, the work having been completed before the promise was made. Accordingly, no binding contract had been entered into.

4.   The Parties must have the Capacity to Contract

An unconditional agreement that is intended to have legal consequences and is supported by consideration will constitute a binding contract provided that the parties to it have legal capacity. By the term 'legal capacity' is simply meant the legal authority to enter into the contract in question. Adults, being persons of at least 18 years of age, are said to have complete contractual capacity and can enter into contracts of any nature. There are however two main categories of legal persons with restricted contractual capacity. Firstly, minors (persons under the age of 18) and secondly corporate bodies (artificial persons, including local authorities and registered companies).

THE CONTRACTUAL CAPACITY OF MINORS

The significance of the law relating to the contractual capacity of minors was greatly diminished following the lowering of the age of majority from 21 to 18 from January 1970. Unfortunately the legal position of minors is still overly complex, vague and certainly in need of reform. Here it is proposed to examine in outline only the various categories of contract that a minor may enter into which include binding, void, voidable and unenforceable contracts.

Firstly there are valid contracts which are legally binding on the parties to them and fully enforceable. The two types of contract entered into by infants which are binding on them are contracts for necessaries and beneficial contracts of service.

1.   Contracts for Necessaries

The term 'necessaries' refers to goods and services suitable to the minor's economic and social status and to his actual requirements at the time of sale and delivery. The law does not therefore provide for a categorisation of goods and services into necessaries and non-necessaries; the question of determining necessaries is subjective rather than objective.

> In *Nash v. Inman 1908*, the defendant, a Cambridge undergraduate who was still a minor, purchased a number of clothes from the plaintiff tailor including eleven fancy waistcoats. The plaintiff's action to recover the price of the goods failed, the court deciding that there was no binding contract as the goods supplied could not be regarded as necessaries. Apparently the purchaser was already sufficiently supplied with clothes at the time of the sale.

2.   Beneficial Contracts of Employment.

A contract of service entered into by a minor is regarded as valid and binding but only if it is substantially for the minor's benefit.

> Therefore in *De Francecso v. Barnum 1890*, a minor's apprenticeship contract for stage dancing provided that she was to be totally at her principal's disposal and there was no requirement that she should be paid. After examining its provisions the court decided that the contract was generally harsh and onerous in nature and therefore not legally binding on the minor.

Generally, to be regarded as beneficial a minor's contract of employment must provide for some element of education or training. The term education however is used in its widest sense and has been held to include professional boxing and professional billiard playing.

Secondly there are voidable contracts. A voidable contract is one which is binding but can be avoided (set aside) at the option of one of the parties to it. If a minor enters into a contract which is voidable in his favour he remains bound by its provisions but has the option of avoiding it prior to or within a reasonable time of attaining the age of majority. Within this category are long term contracts, or contracts where the minor obtains an interest in something of a permanent nature. They include contracts for a lease, the creation of a partnership and for the acquisition of shares.

A void contract is one which has no legal effect. Under the Infants Relief Act 1874 certain contracts entered into by minors are absolutely void. These include contracts for the repayment of money lent or to be lent and for non-necessary goods supplied or to be supplied.

It does seem from the case-law authorities that a void contract under the Infants Relief Act 1874 may have some legal effect for the courts have allowed an infant to sue on such a contract, and certainly money and goods transferred are not automatically recoverable, as they should be if the contract is truly void.

An unenforceable contract is one which is valid in all respects but unenforceable in a court of law. Under the Infants Relief Act 1874 an individual cannot sue on a promise by a person now of full age to repay debt incurred while a minor.

The Law Commission has recently indicated its general view that while minors require protection from certain contracts the present law does not suitably provide it. A balance has to be struck between the objectives of protecting minors against their own inexperience, and preventing undue hardship to suppliers contracting with them.

One proposal for reform of the law is that minors should be divided into two age groups, 16 and 17 year olds who are fully bound and those under 16 whose legal position should remain as it is now. The second proposal is to retain the existing rules but to substantially amend them.

The lack of contractual capacity possessed by minors explains why suppliers invariably require that agreements made between themselves and persons under 18 should contain the signature of a parent or guardian. This device renders the signatory liable to the contract.

THE CONTRACTUAL CAPACITY OF CORPORATE BODIES

A corporate body or corporation is simply an artificial person created under the law, either by statute or following a registration procedure, which has a distinct legal identity separate from the members who compose it. As a separate legal person therefore, having perpetual succession, a corporate body has the capacity to own land, enter into contracts, sue and be sued.

As a general principle registered companies are limited in their activities to achieving the objects as defined in the Memorandum of Association (the registered document containing a company's constitution). This rule is designed to protect the interests of the members and to some extent the company creditors who would not wish to see company funds dissipated on unauthorised activities. An activity which is ultra vires (beyond the powers) of the company may therefore be declared void and of no legal effect.

> The famous case of *Ashbury Rail Co. v. Riche 1875*, confirms this basic principle of law. Here the company entered into a contract for the construction of a railway in Belgium despite its objects being defined as to make or sell or lend or hire railway carriages and rail rolling stock. The court held that as the contract was clearly beyond the activities of the company as expressed in the objects clauses of the Memorandum, it was void on the grounds of ultra vires.

This rule has been modified to a large extent by the effect of European Communities Act 1972, (now included in the Companies Act 1985). As a result of this Act outsiders who deal in good faith with the proper agents of a company are given a measure of protection, for in such circumstances the activity engaged upon is presumed to be "intra vires" (within the powers of the company) as far as the outsider is concerned.

In relation to the corporate status of local authorities the same basic principles apply. They are statutory bodies created under the Local Government Act 1972 and as such the objects which such corporations may legitimately pursue must be ascertained from the Act itself. Over the years however, the ultra vires doctrine has not been applied rigidly to local authorities and the courts have consistently held that local authorities may not only do things for which there is express or implied authority, but also whatever is reasonably incidental to the doing of those things.

> Thus in *Attorney General v. Smethwick Corporation 1932*, a resolution was passed by the corporation for the establishment of a printing and stationery works for the purpose of fulfilling the printing requirements with the authority. An action was brought by the Attorney General on behalf of a ratepayer on the grounds that the proposal was ultra vires. The court held that the formation of this department was reasonably incidental or consequential upon the carrying out of the corporation's statutory duties and was not therefore ultra vires.

This common law approach is reflected in the general power to contract conferred on local authorties by virtue of s.111 Local Government Act 1972. This section provides that authorities are empowered to do anything (whether or not involving the expenditure, borrowing or lending of money or the acquisition or disposal of any property or rights) which is calculated to facilitate, or is conducive or incidental to, the discharge of any of their functions. Provided therefore that the activity carried on is related to the particular functions of the council in question it seems that it can be justified.

This general power to contract conferred on local authorities is of course supplemented by a multiplicity of specific powers from various statutes. For instance, the Local Authority (Goods and Services) Act 1970 enables an authority to contract with other public bodies for the supply of goods and services. However a local authority by its own conduct cannot extend its statutory powers.

> Thus in *Rhyl Urban District Council v. Rhyl Amusements Ltd. 1959*, the authority granted a lease relying on powers contained in private legislation. Realising that these powers did not authorise the grant of the lease the council purported to rely on a general leasing power conferred by the Public Health Act 1875. Such general power required the consent of the Local Government Board to the leasing and this was never obtained. The court held that the lease was void on the grounds of ultra vires as the council had not obtained the required consent to it. A further important point was that the plea of estoppel was rejected (estoppel is a rule of evidence which prevents a person from later denying the truth of some assertion previously made). The court confirmed that a statutory body could not be estopped (prevented) from later denying the validity of the lease and so indirectly enlarge its own powers.

In relation to contractual formalities, since the Corporate Bodies Act 1960 there is no longer a requirement that a corporation need always contract under seal. In local government however, it is usual practice to provide in standing orders that contracts entered into over a particular sum should be entered into by deed. A corporation is therefore in the same position as an individual in relation to contractual formalities and if a contract is required to be by deed or in writing for an individual, it is similarly so required for a local authority.

Local authority standing orders represent the internal rules that regulate the organisation, much like the Articles of Association of a limited company. In the same way that an outsider is not deemed to have knowledge of a company's articles, so an outsider is not treated in law as being aware of the contents of a local authority standing orders. Therefore it is of no value to an authority to claim that a contract with an outsider is void because standing orders have not been complied with.

As you will have realised, the formation of the contract is the single most important formal act in the commercial world. In the absence of the legal regulation of commercial transactions economic activity would rapidly decline. No buyer or seller could run the risk of the promises given or received not being met and there being no legal remedy to redress such a breach.

In theory the parties to a contract are acting on equal terms. The consumer would only buy if he wishes and the seller would only sell if he so desires. But in reality as we shall see later the world is not so simple. There are few products or services which have a market establishing the consumer and the seller on an equal footing. Most market practices tend to favour the supplier, as the dominant party, and suppliers often exploit their bargaining strength by trading on the basis of standard term agreements that are non-negotiable. Contracts entered into in this way are known as 'contracts of adhesion'. The law realises this and in various ways seeks to protect the party in the weaker trading position. In most cases this is the consumer and this is examined under the heading of the consumer in chapter 27.

ASSIGNMENT — THE MACRO

Parry and Lewis Ltd., a car dealer in Blackburn, has an exclusive dealership agreement with the Rover Group, for whom it is their main dealer in the area. The Rover Group has decided to make available a limited number of "Macro" family saloon cars at 5% below the standard Macro list price for a limited period. Parry and Lewis Ltd. have been allocated 100 of the new models which will be delivered to them on 1st September 1986. The Rover Group informs them that advance reviews of the car will appear in the press from the beginning of May.

In the 13th May edition of their local paper, the Blackburn Echo, Parry and Lewis Ltd. place an advert stating the following:-

---

PARRY AND LEWIS LTD.

are proud to announce

a limited number of Macros available for sale. The cars are on offer at **5% below standard** Macro list price and cost £6,375.50 (inclusive of number plates and seat belts) and will be available for delivery in **September.**

Applications in person or by letter must be made to **Parry and Lewis Ltd., Main Offices** by **30th May** and must include a 10% deposit, the remainder of the price payable on delivery of the car.

John Hall, a married man with two children, writes the following letter to Parry and Lewis Ltd. on 20th May:-

---

25, Goldstone Avenue,
Blackburn.

20/5/86

Dear Sirs,

   With reference to your advert in the Blackburn Echo of 13th May, 1986, I would like to purchase one of the special edition Macros for delivery in September 1986.

   Please find enclosed a cheque for £637.55 as 10% deposit on the car.

   I shall look forward to hearing from you.

Yours sincerely,

J. Hall

On 25th May 1986, Parry and Lewis Ltd. are notified by the Rover Group that, because of an industrial dispute, delivery of their 100 special edition Macros will be delayed until November 1986.

Parry and Lewis Ltd. then write the following letter:-

Parry & Lewis Ltd.
Rover Group Main Dealers
High Street
Blackburn

Tel. 0254 122684

25, Goldstone Avenue
Blackburn
Lancs.

26th May 1986

Dear Sir,

With reference to your letter of the 20th of this month, we are pleased to confirm that we are able to allocate one of the special edition Macros to you. However, due to an industrial problem beyond our control, delivery of the car will be made on 13th November 1986.

Yours sincerely,

J.R. Lewis.

J.R. LEWIS
(Managing Director)

At the beginning of June, Fiat announced a special offer on their family saloons including better trade-in prices and low interest rates on borrowing for new car purchase. John Hall is attracted by this offer especially as his wife has recently been made redundant, and also due to the fact that the Fiat is £573 cheaper than the Macro and is substantially lower on fuel consumption. This is particularly attractive as the government have recently increased the price of petrol by 20p a gallon.

Mr. Hall telephones Parry and Lewis Ltd. on 6th June and attempts to cancel his order and request a refund of the £637.55 deposit. The manager at Parry and Lewis Ltd. informs him that as the industrial dispute has now been solved, he is able to ensure delivery of the Macro in early September as originally agreed.

Despite this, Mr. Hall, having now decided to purchase a Fiat, continues to insist on the return of his deposit. The manager however maintains that Mr. Hall has contracted to buy the car and he is therefore obliged to accept delivery of it.

TASKS

1. Mr. Hall is a friend of yours and has asked your advice on the matter. Examine the newspaper advertisement and the correspondence between Mr. Hall and Parry and Lewis and then prepare some notes to enable you to give a reasoned opinion. In your notes you should consider the following issues:-

   a) the legal status of the advertisement;

   b) the legal status of the letter written by Mr. Hall to Parry and Lewis on the 20th May 1986;

    c)   whether or not the letter written by Parry and Lewis to John Hall on the 26th May 1986 gives rise to a legally binding contract; and

    d)   whether Mr. Hall is legally entitled to reclaim the deposit paid to Parry and Lewis.

2.   While looking at the problem Mr. Hall has asked you to explain the following points. Again prepare some notes to enable you to give a reasoned opinion.

    a)   Why have the Rover Group introduced a special cut price offer on the Macro?;

    b)   What will be the effect of the price cut on the demand for Macros?; and

    c)   What is the effect on the supply of Macros as a result of the industrial action?

DEVELOPMENTAL TASK

3.   Assume the role of press officer for the Rover Group. Prepare two press releases. The first should announe the nationwide introduction of the cut price deal on the Macro and the second should explain the circumstances of the industrial dispute which has reduced the production of the car.

ASSIGNMENT — BUSINESS BOOKS

Business Books Ltd. is a book publisher with a relatively small list of titles. Book-publishing involves the company in the following forms of commercial activity:- negotiating with and commissioning authors to write books; appraising and editing draft manuscripts; arranging the typesetting; printing and binding of books with outside printers; marketing and distributing books to wholesalers and retailers and acquiring and managing finance and staff. The book-publishing trade is highly competitive particulary in the market for student textbooks for business studies courses. Financial returns on successful titles are high but such profits can often be offset by the losses incurred with poor sellers. Businesses which make up the industry tend to be secretive about their activities for fear of attracting competitors into profitable areas. The company has recognised that a potential gap exists in the market for a business problems text-book for BTEC students. Currently there is only one textbook available which the company believes to be overpriced, poorly written and printed on inferior paper. However being the only book available it enjoys massive sales and makes substantial profits for its publisher, Hammond Ltd.

In an attempt to break into this lucrative market, Business Books approached two separate authors, Bernie Blake and Charles Quinn and asked each to provide a specimen chapter for a Business Problems book. These were then considered by the Editorial Board of Business Books. One of the chapters was well written but somewhat unorthodox in its approach while the other was considered too academic in nature. The Board decided in favour of offering the contract to Bernie with the proviso that they would reserve the right to substantially edit the final manuscript.

Following the decision of the Editorial Board, the Publications Manager, Mr. Richards, verbally instructs one of his staff to telephone Charles Quinn and tactfully explain that, for the time being, they had decided not to proceed with his book. In the ensuing telephone call between the member of staff and Mr. Quinn, a misunderstanding of the position leads Mr. Quinn to believe that the Board has in fact approved his specimen chapter. Four months later the company receives a complete manuscript from him whereupon Mr. Richards immediately writes to him explaining he was mistaken in believing that he had been given the 'go ahead' for the book. Mr. Quinn has written to the company claiming that he has a contract with the company for the book.

The company must decide on the quantity of books to print and the appropriate price to sell the book and undertake a small scale survey of all Colleges teaching BTEC courses in Business Studies. From the results of their questionnaire they estimate likely sales at a range of possible prices. These are shown in the schedule below:

Possible Price £	Estimated Sales of Books
15	300
14	500
13	1,000
12	1,500
11	2,000
10	2,500
9	3,000
8	4,000
7	5,000
6	6,000
5	7,000
4	8,000
3	9,000
2	10,000
1	12,000

The company has now decided to publish another book to cover the Accounting element of BTEC courses and you have been assigned the task of overseeing its publication. You have the following information about the publication costs of the book:

Typing costs	£150
Typesetting	£4,800

These costs must be paid before any books can be printed.

Printing costs vary with the number of the print run and are as follows:-

Print run (books)	Costs £
2,000	5,800
3,000	6,600
4,000	8,200
5,000	8,600
6,000	8,800
7,000	9,000

In order to sell the books the company will have to advertise and from past experience, they estimate that the advertising budget required to achieve certain sales is as follows:

Potential Book Sales	Advertising Costs Required £
2,000	1,500
3,000	2,200
4,000	3,000
5,000	4,500
6,000	10,500
7,000	16,500

The company will also have to pay author's royalties of 10% of the price of each book sold. The company has decided to set a price of £6 per book.

TASKS

Assume the role of a publications assistant employed by Business Books and directly responsible to Mr. Richards.

1. You are required to write a tactful reply to Mr. Quinn on behalf of the company in which you clearly and logically set out the company's reasons for claiming that no contract has been entered into.

2. Write a short memorandum to the Editorial Board in which you briefly state your opinion as to the view a court might take in relation to the company's dispute with Mr. Quinn.

3. Mr. Richards has asked you to prepare an informal report in which you advise on the number of 'Business Problems' textbooks to print and the price to charge to ensure the maximum revenue.

4. Prepare a second informal report for Mr. Richards on the company's publication of the Accounting Textbook. In your report include a recommendation on the amount of books to

print and the amount to spend on advertising which will produce the maximum profit for the company. Your report should include a clear statement of your calculations and a break even chart.

DEVELOPMENTAL TASK

5. Produce a questionnaire which would be circulated to all colleges teaching BTEC business studies courses which attempts to determine the level of demand for Accounting textbooks and the price which would achieve the maximum number of sales.

Chapter 22

THE CHANGING ENVIRONMENT

The last forty years has witnessed a period of significant change in this country. This is readily apparent if the social conditions of the early post war period are compared with those of today. Living standards for the majority of the UK's citizens have risen dramatically. This has been achieved as a result of the expansion of the UK's productive capacity and impressive increases in productivity and technology. The average individual, living in the nineteen eighties, is clearly more materially affluent than his counterpart in the nineteen forties.

Despite this we are currently facing one of the most severe economic crises this country has known. There are currently more than 3 million people who are unemployed. A major survey on living standards, Breadline Britain, undertaken in 1983 indicated that approximately 3 million people in Britain today cannot afford to adequately heat the living areas of their homes. Furthermore around 6 million go without some essential aspect of clothing, such as a warm waterproof coat, because of a lack of money. Findings such as these indicate a growing divide in this country between the 'haves' and the 'have nots'. In this chapter we shall outline some of the causes and the effects of the changing environment in which we live.

The society in which we live is, by its very nature, dynamic and complex. It consists of a series of inter-related environments which combine and interact. It is possible to identify a number of significant pieces within society's jigsaw. These include: social conditions and attitudes; the political environment; Britain's position within the world; the domestic and international environment; the legal and criminal justice systems; and technological development. In a book of this nature it is impossible to critically analyse and evaluate the changes which have occurred in each of these areas in the post war period and so we must restrict our study to certain specific examples of change which have had an important impact on individuals and organisations within our society.

THE CHANGING ROLE OF THE STATE

The most pronounced change in the role of the state in the last forty years has been in its provision of welfare services to its citizens. Under this broad heading is included the State's provision of the National Health Service, education, pensions, unemployment and social security benefits. The growth of the welfare state is a reflection of the attitude of successive governments who have increasingly recognised the responsibility of the State to provide for the greater welfare of its citizens. But what is meant by the 'Welfare State'? Although it is not possible to give a precise date to the establishment of the Welfare State, it is usually acknowledged that the Beveridge Report of 1942 laid the framework for the post-war development of the State's social services. This report proposed many significant reforms including:

    (a)   the introduction of a free national health service;

    (b)   pensions;

    (c)   maternity benefits; and

    (d)   comprehensive unemployment insurance.

It stressed the need to establish these services as a right without the implementation of a means test.

While the nineteenth century was a period when the State saw its role as 'filling the gaps' left by the personal and voluntary provision of these services, in the twentieth century and particularly in the post war era, there has been a growing acceptance that many of these services are demanded by the populace as "of right". The progressive nature of a civilised society requires the State to ensure that the standard of living of its citizens both in material terms and in social and cultural terms continues to rise. Thus the State's spending in these areas has grown dramatically. We should, however, be wary of assuming that a growth in this sector of state activity is always indicative of an increase in the welfare of all of its citizens. In many instances the reverse is true. One of the most disturbing features of the economy in the last fifteen years has been a massive growth in unemployment. (The causes of this economic problem are discussed in chapter 25). This has resulted in the State having to increase spending on unemployment and social security benefits and on various urban aid schemes. This has not been done with the intention of improving the welfare of its citizens but merely to ensure that they can maintain an acceptable standard of living. Thus it is the decline in the living standards of some of its citizens which has forced more State provision rather than the desire to improve their welfare in line with the growing prosperity of the country as a whole.

It is clear that in recent years there has been a significant shift in the role of the State as the provider of welfare. This trend is likely to continue because:

(a) if unemployment remains at its present level, or, as some predict, rises as this century proceeds, the need to provide a greater percentage of State expenditure in the form of unemployment and social security payments will increase;

(b) technological transitions will alter the structure of British industry requiring greater help for ailing industries;

(c) demographic factors will impose a greater burden on the Welfare State.

THE GROWTH OF PUBLIC ADMINISTRATION

The three main functions of government (executive, legislative and judicial) are considered later in chapter 24 on the State. The executive function consists primarily of initiating, formulating and directing government policy. While the legislative (law making) and the judicial (conflict resolving) functions have grown in importance since the second world war the most dramatic change has occurred in the role of the Executive, particularly in relation to public administration. 'Public Administration' is simply the machinery or agencies by which government policy is implemented, for instance the civil service, tribunals, local authorities and public corporations.

The fact that the functions of modern government have dramatically increased has led to a corresponding growth in public administration. In addition to the traditional functions of the state in ensuring stability and providing defence, many areas are now regarded as being among the proper purpose of modern government. These include the welfare state, town and country planning, public health, immigration, the control of pollution, education and training, legal aid, health and safety at work, industrial relations, discrimination, broadcasting, transport, the use of natural resources and many other spheres. Accordingly the administrative processes required to carry out these complicated responsibilities have grown in terms of their size and their degree of sophistication. There are a vast number of government agencies and institutions whose role is to operate these administrative responsibilities.

These processes include:

a) exercising discretionary powers within existing government policy and taking decisions such as compulsorily purchasing land or extending public sector housing;

b)   fulfilling statutory duties for instance providing adequate education and sanitation;

c)   inspecting various activities including education, the police force, prisons, safety standards at work, the sale and preparation of food, and the provision of housing;

d)   holding inquiries into various events and proposals, for example objections to compulsory purchase orders, the siting of nuclear power plants or airports and major accidents;

e)   licensing specific activities such as the carrying on of certain businesses (betting shops, public houses, credit brokers, public transport, the sale of milk); and the holding of certain information (the use of computer files holding personal data).

It is inevitable that both individuals and organisations will at some time come into contact with one or more of these administrative processes. It may be that administrators will impose demands on organisations which necessitate changes in organisational operation such as improvements in working practices, methods of waste disposal and building methods. Without such regulatory processes many of the changes, which necessarily involve the organisation in extensive expenditure, would be ignored. The validity of such demands may of course be challenged in the courts. Their lawfulness may be tested by having recourse to that growing body of rules which relate to and regulate the administration of government, administrative law. There is no doubt however that in the main, organisations must accept the increasing constraints and controls imposed by public administration reflecting the growth of state intervention in our daily lives.

Yet the Thatcher Government of the 1980s has consistently stated its intention to reverse the trend towards State intervention and provision. Such an attitude reflects the changing face of the political environment and it is that which we will consider next.

THE CHANGING POLITICAL ENVIRONMENT

The political complexion of the United Kingdom is significantly different today from what it was in the 1940s and 1950s. Not only does the country now have a three party system, the attitudes and policies of the parties have become increasingly polarised. A brief reflection on these developments will illustrate these changes.

1945-51 Labour Government in Power

The post war Labour Government was intent on pursuing a policy of nationalisation and state ownership. It also embarked on the establishment of the Welfare State. While the Conservative opposition did not agree with nationalisation, there was a clear consensus on overall economic management methods and on the need for greater welfare provision. This was illustrated by both party's support for the introduction of the National Health Service.

1951-64 Conservative Government in Power

A Conservative party in power during a period of relative economic affluence characterised by Tory Prime Minister Macmillan's phrase in 1957 "You've never had it so good". While the Labour party opposed some Tory policies, there was a gradual shift of both parties towards the 'middle ground' of politics. Both parties adopted policies which would allow them to shed their traditional class based images. The Conservatives attempted to be seen less as a party of the ruling classes and Labour tried to lose its 'cloth cap' image.

1964-70 Labour Government in Power

A time of industrial transition. The Labour Government attempted to alter the UK's industrial base. It was to be "forged in the white-heat of the technological revolution". However the difficulties involved in such a change produced a growing disillusionment with consensus politics and led to a period of considerable industrial relations unrest.

1970-74 Conservative Party in Power

The first seeds of significant economic and political change were sown. The Conservative Government's attempts to introduce industrial relations reform and pay restraint were regarded as extremely radical at the time. They produced a period of political uncertainty which led to a rethink by both politicians and economists.

1974-79 Labour Government in Power

A Labour government which was faced with growing economic problems attempted to pursue a consensus approach in seeking agreement with industry and the trade unions in an attempt to improve the country's economic position. A policy which failed and resulted in significant splits within the Labour party and the election of a radical Tory Government.

1979 onwards. Conservative Government in Power

Mrs Thatcher's election in 1979 has proved to be an extremely significant political event. The Thatcher Government's policies have been the most extreme in the post war period. Traditional economic thinking based on the Keynesian approach to government control of the economy (discussed later in chapter 25) has been replaced by monetarism. This has led to a widening of the political spectrum in which the void left by the polarisation of Labour and Conservatives has been filled by the establishment of the Liberal/SDP Alliance. By 1986 the electoral potential of each of the three parties is still unclear. In fact the UK's 'first past the post' electoral system makes the continuation of a three party position less likely. But what is significant is their wide differences on many policies such as the overriding need to maintain full employment. The period of consensus politics has been replaced by a era of conflict politics.

It is difficult to simply categorise the reasons for the changes in the political structure in the UK. The swing of the electoral pendulum has brought with it governments with differing political ideologies and alternative solutions to the UK's economic problems. A very simplistic analysis might indicate that the electorate tends to give 'the other side' an opportunity to show what it can do when one political party appears to have failed. The true cause is much more complex than this and is certainly related to changes in economic conditions and economic thinking.

THE CHANGING ECONOMIC ENVIRONMENT

The UK's economic problems in the post war period have been significant. In chapter 25 we examine the achievements of successive governments in attempting to simultaneously meet the objectives of stable prices, full employment, economic growth and balance of payments equilibrium. This task has been by no means easy. The 1970s and early 1980s were characterised by growing unemployment and high levels of inflation. This led to a change in economic philosophy and a switch from policies of Keynesian Demand Management to Monetarism. The details of these are also examined in chapter 25. Here it is sufficient to note that the rise of monetarism has introduced a government which publicly supports the belief that the role of government intervention in the economy should be modified and reduced and the importance of the self reliance of both individuals and organisations should be emphasised. Some of the effects of the changing economic environment can be seen in the last area we select to examine.

THE CHANGING PATTERN OF EMPLOYMENT

One element of change which may directly affect us all is the changing pattern of employment. The rapid growth in new technology in the 1970s and 80s and the continued growth of unemployment have made traditional work patterns less certain. There will be many beneficial effects from a fall in the demand for human labour. The amount of time one must spend at work may fall, there will be greater opportunities for education and training prior to entering the job market and a higher likelihood of early retirement. It will, however, also mean continued unacceptable levels of unemployment, particularly among the young, the less skilled and those living in the less economically affluent regions of the UK. For such people there will be a need to adjust to a life in which work is not a central focus. They will have a much poorer standard of living than those in work and when they do find jobs they may have to change them at regular intervals. This demands a change in attitude not just on the part of those who are unemployed but also on the part of society to those who are unable to obtain work. As we have already noted it is the government, as the elected representative of the people, which will play the major role in determining how such changes ultimately affect society.

ASSIGNMENT — THE CHANGING ROLE OF GOVERNMENT

"First, if our objective is to have a prosperous, expanding economy, we must recognise that high public spending, as a proportion of gross national product, very quickly kills growth . . . We have to remember that governments have no money at all. Every penny they take is taken from the productive sector of the economy in order to transfer it to the unproductive part of it. This is one of the great causes of our problems, because this government has increased the unproductive sector, and diminished the productive sector, so that during the lifetime of this government we have virtually no growth at all."

(Mrs Thatcher, quoted in Hansard, 25th July 1978.)

The extract given above is from a speech given by Margaret Thatcher while leader of the Opposition. In it she expresses her belief in the need to reduce government intervention in the economy.

TASK

1.   Assume the role of a member of a trade union. At your next union branch meeting an item for discussion is the changing role of the Government and the State in society. You wish to speak in this discusion. To enable you to do this effectively prepare a set of notes in which you consider the major significant changes in the role of the Government and the State in recent years and particularly the changing attitude of the Thatcher Government to this issue.

DEVELOPMENTAL TASK

2.   Undertake some research using government statistics such as the 'Blue Book' (obtainable from your college or public library) on the level of a range of government services such as social security, education, defence etc over the last fifteen years. Prepare a report on the changes which are apparent from your research. Illustrate your report using charts and diagrams similar to those shown in chapter 5.

Chapter 23

THE INTERNATIONAL ENVIRONMENT

INTERNATIONAL TRADE

The fundamental feature of any type of trade is that both parties to the transaction, whether they are individuals or nations, must gain some benefit from it. It is also important to recognise that the possibility of trade arises where one party has a surplus of a product or service that another party needs. If it were not for surpluses there would be no trade of any sort and it is only when countries have a surplus in a particular product that there can be international trade. In this chapter we will be concentrating on why there is international trade and what is its effect on the UK economy.

IMPORTS AND EXPORTS

Visible Trade

When we think of imports and exports, most of us tend to visualise tangible products being taken in and out of the country such as Japanese cars shipped into the UK and British machinery being sold abroad. These imports and exports are called "visible" trade for the obvious reason that they are tangible and can be seen. This part of trade is vital for the survival of all of us living in the UK.

This is because this country is not self-sufficient in many of the products we need. About half the food eaten in the UK is produced in other countries. Also despite the fact that this country is a major manufacturing nation, it has a scarcity of raw materials and so must import such commodities as copper, zinc, iron ore, and rubber. In fact, the UK spends about one third of its national income on imports. This proportion has increased as the country has grown richer, a characteristic which is common in most developed nations. The UK is in the same position as any other trading nation, in that it cannot continue to purchase goods from abroad unless it is capable of earning foreign currency by selling products and services to foreigners.

Fortunately, the UK is able to sell a variety of products and services abroad and this has, to a greater or lesser extent, meant that it has been able to pay its way in the world.

To illustrate the types of visible trade see the table below.

Visible Trade of the UK

Exports	%
Food, beverages and tobacco	6.6
Basic Materials	2.9
Fuels	21.8
Manufactures	66.2
Others	2.5
Total	**100.00**

Imports	%
Food, beverages and tobacco	11.0
Basic Materials	6.5
Fuels	13.1
Manufactures	67.6
Others	1.8
Total	**100.00**

Source: United Kingdom Balance of Payments August 1985 (HMSO)

It is interesting to note that the UK still accounts for 10% of world trade, but that this is a declining percentage as our influence in the world diminishes. For the period since the end of the second world war, in most years we imported more goods than we exported. This has meant a balance of visible trade deficit. By this we mean that more money is going out of the country to pay for visible imports than we receive as payment for visible exports. However since the discovery of North Sea Oil in the late 1970's, the country has not found it necessary to import as much oil and in fact we have become a net exporter of oil. This has meant that exports have improved relative to imports and the UK has now shown a visible trade surplus in several of the last years. Unfortunately the rest of our visible exports have not fared well and the improvement in the oil trade position has been countered by a decline in the relative import/export balance for other goods such as manufactured products.

See how this situation has changed over the years by refering to the table below.

Visible Trade Balance   £ million

	1974	1975	1976	1977	1978
Visible Exports	16394	19330	25191	31728	35063
Visible Imports	-21745	-22663	-29120	-34012	-36605
Visible Balance	-5351	-3333	-3929	-2284	-1542

	1979	1980	1981	1982	1983	1984
Visible Exports	40687	47422	50977	55565	60776	70409
Visible Imports	-44136	-46061	-47617	-53234	-61611	-74510
Visible Balance	-3449	1361	3360	2331	-835	-4101

Source: United Kingdom Balance of Payments August 1985 (HMSO)

Invisible Trade

As the table shows the UK had a massive visible trade deficit for many years. If this was the only type of trade in which countries were involved, then the UK would have gone deeper and deeper into debt. However another important aspect of international trade is the import and export of services. As these are not physical products and cannot be seen, this is known as "invisible trade". Examples of invisible exports are the UK's provision of banking, shipping and insurance services to the world. For these the UK receives payments from abroad and although it may at times have to pay out large sums, for instance on an insurance claim for a sunken oil tanker owned by a Greek shipping company, its receipts for these services outweigh the costs which it might have to bear.

Another important form of invisible trade is tourism. The position of tourism in the balance of payments can produce confusion. For example an American tourist coming on holiday to London is in fact part of our invisible exports. Although the tourist is coming into this country he is bringing in money to spend in Britain which is the equivalent of selling a British product abroad. Conversely, when a British tourist goes on holiday in Spain, that is part of our invisible imports for the money spent abroad is the equivalent of staying in the UK and importing a foreign product.

. . . invisible exports . . .

The following table shows the balance in invisible trade for the UK for recent years.

Invisible Trade Balance							**£ million**
		1974	1975	1976	1977	1978	
Invisible Balance	...	2034	1751	3016	2156	2514	
		1979	1980	1981	1982	1983	1984
Invisible Balance	...	2713	1739	3168	2332	4003	5036

Source: United Kingdom Balance of Payments August 1985 (HMSO)

The sum of visible and invisible trade is called the Current Account of the Balance of Payments and may be seen as the country's ability to pay its way in the world for goods and services without having to borrow.

Current Account of the Balance of Payments 1974-1984

	1974	1975	1976	1977	1978	
Visible Balance	-5351	-3333	-3929	-2284	-1542	
Invisible Balance ...	2034	1751	3016	2156	2514	
Current Account Total	-3317	-1582	-913	-128	972	

	1979	1980	1981	1982	1983	1984
Visible Balance	-3449	1361	3360	2331	-835	-4101
Invisible Balance ...	2713	1739	3168	2332	4003	5036
Current Account Total ..	-736	3100	6528	4663	3168	935

Source: United Kingdom Balance of Payments August 1985 (HMSO)

A little help on interpretation

If the figures shown have a minus sign (-) in front, this means that more money has left the country than has come into it, in other words a trade deficit. If there is a no sign or a positive sign (+) then this means that more money has come into the country than has gone out and so there is a trade surplus. Thus, on its current account the UK had a trade deficit for these years: 1973-1977 and 1979; and a trade surplus for 1969-72, 1978 and 1980-85.

Before going on to look at the Balance of Payments in detail let us first consider why Britain should trade and how important trade is to this country.

IMPORTANCE OF TRADE

Every economy has a certain combination of resources. These resources may then be combined to produce goods and services. Each country has a different mix of resources, so for example Canada has millions of acres of arable land suitable for wheat farming while Saudia Arabia may have limited arable land but has the advantage of massive oil deposits. The UK has a workforce capable of producing highly sophisticated technological products but has a shortage of many of the raw materials required to manufacture them. If every country in the world were to attempt to produce all its needs domestically and no international trade took place, then the world and its population would be much poorer, for each country would have to divert some of its resources from producing those products which they are capable of making most efficiently twoards less productive but necessary goods and services. If, for instance, the UK wished to produce all its own food, then capital resources would need to be taken from manufacturing industries and used to produce bananas or oranges under glass or in heated greenhouses. Therefore in each country it is often better for the workers to concentrate on developing a particular skill or expertise. It may be that the Canadian farmer should concentrate on producing wheat as cheaply as possible and the London banker on becoming as efficient as possible in the handling of finance. This will allow each to specialise in those trades which they can perform most effectively and the scarce resources of each country can be used in the most efficient manner. The problem is which goods and services should each country produce?

Countries tend to try to produce some of the basic necessities they need domestically so as not to be totally dependent on others. So for example the UK decides to produce some food in this country which could be produced more cheaply abroad. However, a country should specialise in the production of those goods and services for which it has a comparative advantage over other nations. Therefore, Brazil can produce coffee more cheaply than the UK and the UK can produce chemicals more cheaply than Brazil. So Brazil concentrates on coffee production and the UK on chemicals. This is of course just one simple example. More coffee and more chemicals are produced than if both countries had to make both products. Trade encourages specialisation and also makes it feasible.

Comparative Advantage in trade

Some countries are in an even more favourable position in that they can produce many products more cheaply and effectively than the rest of the world. Does this mean that the less efficient countries should produce nothing and buy from the cheaper country? Not necessarily. It simply means that they should produce those products in which they have the comparative advantage and the country which could produce most cheaply should specialise in those goods and services in which it has the greatest comparative advantage. A simple example may illustrate this point.

Assume there are two countries, one of which has an agricultural economy while the other is an industrialised nation with a highly trained manufacturing workforce. If both countries specialised in the production of those goods which they can make most efficiently then the overall output of both agricultural produce and manufactured goods will be maximised. They can then trade with each other so that both end up with sufficient food and manufactured products to meet their needs.

Least comparative disadvantage in trade

What if one of the countries is more efficient in the production of both types of output. Clearly it would be unrealistic for the less productive nation to sit back and produce nothing. If it did, it would have nothing to trade and so could not survive. Therefore it is most sensible for the less efficient country to produce those products for which it has the least comparative disadvantage. In other words if it is an agricultural economy it should concentrate on producing food. Throughout the underdeveloped world there are examples of agricultural economies which have diverted resources away from those products which they can produce best in order to try to establish an industrial base by building major capital projects such as steel plants or oil refineries. The outcome has often been that the final output from such ventures has been a costly product which could in fact be imported from abroad much more cheaply. The country's domestic agricultural economy has suffered as it has not received the capital investment that it requires to make it agriculturally efficient.

REALITY OF WORLD TRADE

Of course, the situation we have outlined above is a simplified illustration of what would be in the best interests of international trade. In many countries industries have grown and developed prior to the establishment of an effective system of international trade and transport. The capital investment which has already been made has created an industrial structure which cannot easily be changed. A country's labour force may well have developed certain specific trades or skills and so there would be considerable social and economic upheaval if the type of production or employment in which it traditionally concentrated had to be changed as other nations evolved their industrial base and particular productive strengths.

For example, the UK established manufacturing industries such as textiles or motor cars in the 19th and early 20th centuries. It is now evident that these products can be made more cheaply and effectively overseas. But to completely abandon their production in the UK would result in massive unemployment and consequent social disruption. Consequently we persist with their manufacture despite our comparative disadvantage relative to other countries such as Egypt in the case of textiles and Japan in the case of motor car manufacture.

Political factors are also crucial. Some countries may be unwilling to trade with others who hold a different political ideology even though, economically, it would be mutually advantageous. Thus, trade between East and West may be influenced by world politics. For instance, trade with China has only recently begun to develop as political attitudes have softened. Many countries will not trade with South Africa because of their repugnance for the Apartheid system and many Arab states refuse to deal with Israel because of their political differences.

NEED FOR INTERNATIONAL CURRENCY COMPARISON

Despite these factors which we have identified as restrictions on international trade it is nevertheless crucial to the world's economy. Therefore we must now go on to examine some of the financial aspects of world trade.

Any trading transaction, whether it is between individuals living in different countries or between the nations themselves, needs to be paid for. In some circumstances such payment may be undertaken in the form of barter. This is particularly true of East-West trade agreements. For example, the USA builds power stations in China in return for textiles and Abba, the Swedish pop group, were paid in oil instead of cash for the royalties on their record sales in Rumania. Such barter is not always possible or preferable as it requires a mutual coincidence of needs. In other words a nation must find a trading partner which not only wants what it has but also has something that the nation needs. Therefore most trade is paid for using currency which can then be used to buy other products in the world. However a problem lies in the fact that trading partners have their own individual currencies. An American manufacturer cannot pay his workers in pounds sterling and so, if he exports to the UK, he will require payment in US dollars. Alternatively if he does receive payment in pounds he will want some way of exchanging these pounds for dollars.

Consequently, either the English buyer must exchange the pounds which he wishes to spend for dollars prior to the purchase or the American seller must exchange the pounds he is given after the sale. In each case an international currency exchange must take place and there must therefore be a rate of exchange by which it is possible to achieve a comparative value. For instance £1 sterling may be equivalent to 10 French francs or $1.50 US. Each currency will then have a value not only domestically, but also in relation to the amount of other currencies which can be exchanged for it. The means by which this exchange value is determined will be considered later in this chapter.

BALANCE OF PAYMENTS

In the first part of the chapter we considered the nature of international trade and benefits countries may gain by trading with each other. We also looked at the Current Account of the Balance of Payments and saw how it is made up of visible and invisible trade. Now it is proposed to examine how Britain assesses the value of its trade and the importance of the balance of payments on the economy as a whole.

A country's balance of payments statement is simply an assessment of the value of a country's trade and other financial transactions with the rest of the world. It is a comprehensive summation of all the individual trading activities in which both the private and public sector of the economy take part. The Balance of Payments statement covers a specific period and although it is reported in the press and on television every three months, the most important time period over which it is measured is one year. At this time, the government uses figures to determine how much the country has bought or sold, in the previous twelve months and whether this trade has resulted in a surplus or a deficit.

THE MECHANICS OF THE BALANCE OF PAYMENTS

The system used to analyse the balance of payments is known as double entry book-keeping. All that this means is that every trading transaction is entered into the account twice. For instance, if ICI sell £1m worth of chemicals to France, the value of the chemicals (£1m) is entered into a trade account as a credit. The French company buying the chemicals must also pay for the goods either in Francs or by transferring the payment into pounds sterling. This is entered into a second account as an increase in the country's currency holdings. This increase, whether in francs or pounds, is shown in sterling. If the payment has been made in francs this entry is made by converting the value of the francs at the prevailing exchange rate.

THE CURRENT ACCOUNT

The Balance of Payments is made up of several accounts, the first of which is the Current Account. This itemises the transactions in goods and services which have already been described as visible exports and imports. This makes up the largest item on the debit side of this account. Fortunately the rest of the world buys many of our products to compensate for our visible imports and also the UK often acts as a middleman for the rest of the world's trade. So many of the imports seen on the debit side of the account as visible imports are then re-exported following manufacture into some finished product or simply after being re-packaged. For example, most of the tea drunk in Europe and America is grown in India then transported to London. It is thus shown as an import on the UK's Balance of Payments. It is then auctioned, re-packaged and shipped to Europe or the USA and so becomes an export on the UK's Balance of Payments.

Despite these exports and re-exports, the Visible Account has often been in deficit and such a deficit has come to be known as the "Trade Gap". As we have already noted the exploitation of North Sea oil has had a considerable impact on visible trade and in recent years we have seen some periods when this account has managed to reach a surplus position. The visible trade account is sometimes called the "Balance of Trade".

The second part of the trade account is the invisible trade account. This covers all the non-physical services which the UK provides and buys. The UK is the second most important country in the world with regard to invisible trade while the USA is the most important. In fact the City of London is the major financial centre in the world and its provision of banking, insurance and shipping services is a major foreign currency earner for the UK. Furthermore the growth of foreign tourism to the UK has been such that in terms of foreign currency earnings, spending by foreign tourists in the UK more than compensates for British tourism abroad. The invisible trade balance is normally in surplus and this helps to offset any visible trade deficit.

INVESTMENT AND OTHER CAPITAL TRANSACTIONS

The second part of the Balance of Payments is sometimes called the Capital Account but is correctly titled the Investment and Other Capital Transactions Account. This covers all transfers of capital into and out of the country. These occur as a result of investments, government lending or borrowing and the transfer of money through bank accounts. It is sub-divided into —

> a. official capital flows;
>
> b. private capital flows.

a.   Official Capital Flows. The UK lends money to other countries, such as the less developed countries, known as the LDC's. Most of this money will be repaid with interest and so represents a future credit to the Balance of Payments but its immediate effect on being loaned is to be classified as a deficit.

b.   Private Capital Flows. UK individuals and companies invest money abroad in the hope of earning profits. Prior to 1979, this type of transaction was controlled by the government, who sought to restrict the outflow of funds from the UK. However, these capital transfer controls were lifted and this freedom, combined with the low potential earning from UK domestic investment, has resulted in a substantial increase in UK investment abroad. This investment has come from large British companies and financial bodies such as insurance companies, pension funds and unit trust investment companies. Of course, these investments, should they prove profitable, will mean an influx of earnings in the future. However, the loss of investment in the UK clearly reduces our domestic growth rate. To some extent this is compensated by foreign investment in the UK, but the decline in UK economic demand has had a somewhat negative effect on the earning potential of investment in this country so it has fallen in real terms.

It would clearly be to the advantage of the UK if investment in this country was always greater than UK investment abroad as this would improve domestic employment and the demand for capital goods. However it is not always possible to create an economic environment which is sufficiently attractive to foreign investors. This problem is obviously of concern to the government and it encourages foreign investment by offering grants and incentives to foreign companies who establish plants here. An example is the way in which central and local government have persuaded the Japanese car company, Nissan, to build a factory in the North East of England.

This part of the balance of payments is further complicated by the inflow and outflow of money which is not being used for trade or investment purposes. This process is known as currency speculation and takes the form of the transfer of bank deposits held by governments, private organisations and individuals into and out of UK banks. These deposits can be easily transferred abroad. Such speculative capital is known as "hot money" and it is moved from country to country by its owners who hope to make maximum profit. This profit level depends on two factors:-

1.   the rate of interest offered in different countries;

2.   the changing value of the currency in which it is held.

The interest rates offered to depositors of capital vary from country to country and are influenced by each country's government. If interest rates are high in the UK relative to the rest of the world, this will encourage foreign speculators to deposit their money in this country because it will provide them with a high rate of return. Such inflows of money will be shown as a credit in the investment and capital flows account. If these speculators then choose to withdraw their deposits and move them to another country which has now increased its interest rates above those offered in the UK, this will then be shown as a debit in the account.

A further factor influencing foreign currency speculation is the relative strength of specific currencies. For instance if a speculator decides to deposit some money in a UK bank because of the high rate of interest offered here his money will be converted into pounds. Therefore if the pound were to fall in value he could lose out when he exchanges his money out of sterling again, despite having a high rate of interest paid.

This can be illustrated using a simple example. A German speculator deposits 4m deutchmarks in a London bank. At the time of the original deposit the exchange rate stands at 4Dm = £1. Thus, his account is credited with £1m. If the London interest rate is 10%, and he keeps the money in the London bank on deposit for 1 year his account now shows a value of £1.1m. But let us suppose that during the year in which the money is held in London the value of the pound has fallen to 3.5Dm = £1. Now when he transfers his assets back to Germany and back into marks, he will only receive the prevailing exchange rate. At the new prevailing exchange rate his £1.1m is now only worth 3.85m Dm. (£1.1 x 3.5Dm), and so his assets (in German currency) have fallen from 4m Dm to 3.85m Dm.

The importance of this hot money speculation on the value of the pound will be explained later when we consider floating exchange rates.

THE BALANCING ITEM

A final item must be included in the balance of payments to allow for any errors or omissions which can quite easily result as the statistics are collected and collated. These can be caused either by mistakes on the part of the traders who may incorrectly record prices or exchange rates for their transactions or as a result of a statistical error on the part of the government statistical office which collates the figures.

To counteract this discrepancy an extra entry is included into the accounts and this is called "the balancing item". When this adjustment is added the accounts should give a reasonable indication of the state of the country's position with regard to trade, capital movements and currency transactions.

OFFICIAL FINANCING

If the overall balance of payments has resulted in a deficit, this means that the country has spent more abroad than it has received. As with any case of overspending, this has to be financed in some way either through borrowing or from its foreign currency reserves which have been accumulated in previous good years in which there have been surpluses. The government will borrow foreign currency, either from the International Monetary Fund (IMF) or, occasionally from foreign banks. Of course if the overall balance of payments is in surplus then the government can use the spare surplus money to add to its foreign reserves or to repay its debts it has incurred in deficit years.

THE INTERNATIONAL MONETARY FUND

Let us digress slightly at this point to consider the role of the International Monetary Fund. The IMF acts as banker to 143 countries, including most western nations as well as China, Hungary, Rumania and Yugoslavia. It accepts annual deposits from each country in a combination of its own currency, foreign currencies and gold. This is referred to as the country's quota. The member countries then have the right to draw on these deposits. They are also allowed to borrow in excess of their deposits to help finance a temporary balance of payments deficit. The loan is then repaid in better years. If a country wishes to borrow very substantial sums, the IMF will ask that certain conditions are met by the borrowing country. As the size of the loan increases the stringency of the conditions which the debtor country has to meet also increase. The UK has used these facilities in the past particularly in 1976 and the restrictions imposed by the IMF at this time were a strong influence on domestic economic freedom forcing the then Labour government to implement very tight monetary control and substantially reduce public spending. The policies of the IMF are determined by an executive board of governors made up of 22 member nations. The board is made up of seven permanent members (the USA, West Germany, France, the UK, Japan, Saudi Arabia and China) and fifteen other members elected on a regular basis from each of the geographical areas in which the other members are located. While the traditional policy of the IMF has been to finance only short term loans to help solve temporary balance of payments problems, it has in recent years been increasing its longer term loans to the developing nations to help them develop their economies. The IMF has its own type of 'currency' which is known as Special Drawing Rights (SDRs). It was introduced in 1970 and is used in trade and as part of a country's reserves. It is a composite currency made up of a basket of currencies. These are the currencies of the USA, UK, France, Germany and Japan weighted with regard to their relative importance in world trade.

Of course, instead of borrowing, the government has the option of dipping into its reserves of foreign currency which it has built up over the years. Naturally enough, these tend to be most heavily depleted during times of war and so the government is reluctant to leave itself without any reserves in time of peace. We shall see in the next part of this chapter that the government must also use these foreign currency assets to maintain the value of its currency at certain times when it comes under speculative pressure. We finish this section by giving a full balance of payments account and means of financing for 1984.

Summary Balance of Payments 1984	£ million
Current Account	
Visible balance	- 4101
Invisibles	
Services	3985
Interest, profits and dividends	3304
Other transfers	- 2253
Invisible balance	5036
CURRENT BALANCE	935
INVESTMENT AND OTHER CAPITAL TRANSACTIONS	- 3291
OVERALL BALANCE OF PAYMENTS	- 2356
OFFICIAL FINANCING	- 1316
Balancing Item	- 1040
	- 2356

Source: United Kingdom Balance of Payments, August 1985 (HMSO)

THE VALUE OF THE POUND

Sterling as a Reserve Currency

In the earlier part of this chapter, we simplified the description of the currency transactions used in international trade by suggesting that most trade is carried out in the respective currencies of the trading partners. In fact, much of the world's trade is carried on in US dollars and to a lesser extent in other major currencies such as pounds sterling and deutchmarks. These are known as reserve currencies because not only is much of the world's trade transacted in these currencies but also because most countries in the world tend to hold their foreign currency reserves in these three currencies or in gold. This means that the value of these currencies can be influenced not only by the actions of their own countries' government and by trade transactions but also by that of other countries, organisations or individuals. This has placed a strain on the pound in recent years and the UK government has expressed the wish to see the pound no longer regarded as an international means of exchange. This problem is heightened by speculation in sterling which influences its value. However, until a more suitable system is established then it is likely that the pound will remain as a reserve currency.

FIXED EXCHANGE RATES

Before 1971, the pound's value in relation to other currencies was fixed by agreement until the government decided to change it. From 1948-1967 it was valued at £1 to $2.80 and then from 1967 until 1971 it was fixed at $2.40c to the pound. This system of fixed exchange rates, known as the Bretton Woods System, caused difficulties in international trade for it meant that a country which had a rate of inflation higher than the rest of the world would tend to lose exports, as they became more expensive for foreigners to buy, and buy more imports, as the rest of the world's products became relatively cheaper. A simple example will explain.

A UK manufacturer produces a product which he wishes to sell for £1. The exchange rate currently prevailing is $2.40 to the £1. Therefore, he asks $2.40 for the product in USA. However UK inflation rate is 10% and so his production costs rise and he must increase his prices. The product is now priced at £1.10. If they exchange rate remains the same, the American buyer must now pay $2.40 plus 10%. In other words, $2.64. But if the US inflation rate is comparatively low, say 2%, then this is an effective price rise as the price of a similar US manufactured product would have risen from $2.40 by only 2% to $2.45c. Thus the British product becomes less attractive and so discourages the purchase by the Americans. This is despite the fact that the British manufacturer is still only receiving what he regards as the same real value for his product as the £1.10 is only worth £1 in real terms to him beause of UK inflation.

Because the UK has tended to have a greater level of inflation than its industrial competitors in the rest of the world, the balance of payments was continually in deficit for most of the period from 1945 until 1971. The situation was reversed in countries such as Germany and Japan who had continuous large trade surpluses because of their relatively low inflation and the attractiveness of their exports. Because of this there developed a series of international liquidity crises when certain countries continually could not pay their way. So in 1971, a system of floating exchange rates was introduced.

FLOATING EXCHANGE RATES

In theory, this was based on the value of a currency being determined by its supply and demand. If the UK does not sell much abroad, then foreigners do not have a high demand for pounds as they do not need as many to pay British exporters. As the demand for UK exports falls there is a corresponding fall in the demand for pounds. In the same way that a fall in demand for any commodity will reduce its price, this fall in demand for sterling will reduce its price. In this case the price of the pound is the value it holds against other currencies. If the exchange rate falls, UK exports become relatively cheaper on world markets as foreign buyers do not have to pay as much in their own currency to purchase British goods. So the goods become more attractive and foreigners now buy more British goods and, in order to pay for them, they must have more pounds. Demand for pounds goes up and eventually the value of the currency will stabilise at a point where the balance of payments is in equilibrium.

Conversely, if the UK is selling more abroad than it is importing, the demand for pounds in relation to other countries is high and so the exchange rate goes up. This results in exports becoming less competitive and so fewer are bought abroad and imports becoming cheaper and so increasing in sales in the UK. In this case the fall in demand for pounds will push its exchange rate down until it stabilises at the point where the Balance of Payments is in equilibrium and imports and exports compete on relatively equal terms.

The price of the pound, the exchange rate, will therefore rise or fall according to demand for and supply of the currency until demand equals supply at the point where imports and exports match and the balance of payments actually balances. In other words the floating pound should at least in theory produce a system in which any surplus or deficit is self adjusting as the currency rises or falls.

The table below shows the changes in the value of the pound against the US dollar over the last few years.

Value of Sterling exchange rate against the dollar.

1977	1978	1979	1980	1981	1982	1983	1984	1985
$1.74	$1.92	$2.12	$2.33	$2.03	$1.75	$1.52	$1.34	$1.30

Source: Economic Trends, January 1986 (HMSO)

COMPLICATIONS FOR FLOATING THE POUND

There are two main problems which arise when the pound is allowed to float freely.

a.   The influence of speculation. The idea behind floating the pound was that the demand for currency for use in trade purposes would be the main determining factor in setting the exchange rate. However, as we have already noted, there is considerable speculation in world currencies using them not as a means of financing trade but as commodities which can be traded in themselves to make a profit. Thus speculators will transfer their capital to a currency whose exchange rate they believe is about to rise and out of a currency they believe is about to fall in value.

There are vast sums of money involved in such speculative capital movements. For instance it is estimated that there is approximately $175 billion owned by the Arab oil countries in circulation as speculative money in the foreign exchange markets of the world in 1986. A recent estimate suggests that 95% of all currency transactions undertaken in foreign exchange markets are undertaken for the purpose of speculation rather than as a means of financing foreign trade. These massive transactions can influence the value of sterling irrespective of the UK's balance of payments situation. If speculators decide that sterling is about to fall in value they will transfer all their money from sterling to dollars. This will cause a massive growth in demand for dollars and a similar drop in demand (and an increase in supply) of pounds. The result will be that the pound falls in value against the dollar. This manipulation of the value of sterling, whether intentional or not, by foreign speculators is obviously not a satisfactory state of affairs.

During 1984 and early 1985 the pound fell to its lowest ever level of £1 to $1.04c. This was because foreign speculators were worried that oil prices would fall and that the pound as a so called 'petro-currency', (because of the importance of oil as a part of the UK economy) would fall. As they lost confidence in sterling and transferred money to other currencies this had the precise effect they had anticipated. The demand for pounds fell and as it did so the value of sterling also fell. However by the middle of 1986 the pound had recovered substantially despite the predicted collapse in world oil prices. This was not as a result of any improvement in the UK's Balance of Payments position but merely because the speculators had regained some confidence in sterling and lost their previous faith in the strength of the dollar. It is therefore of some considerable concern to the British government that the value of our currency can be influenced by the whim of speculators' confidence and it is because of such problems of speculation that the floating exchange rate system has not been the success that many had hoped when it was introduced in the early 1970's.

b.   The effect of the exchange rate on domestic inflation. The exchange rate also has a significant effect on the rate of domestic inflation in the UK. As we have already noted the UK is dependent on imports for food, raw materials and many other necessities. These products will continue to be brought even if their price goes up. We say that they have an inelastic demand. So a fall in the value of the pound which causes import prices to rise will not result in a significant fall in imports but merely an increase in their price. It will be inflationary. As a rough estimate we can say that if the exchange rate falls 5%, this will cause a 1% increase in domestic inflation. Let us illustrate this with a simple example.

If the value of the exchange rate is $1.50 to the pound and it falls to $1.00 to the pound this is a fall of 50c or a 33.33%. This will result in an increase in domestic inflation of 6.5%.

So if a government is seeking to minimise inflation, it should attempt to keep the value of the pound as high as possible. However, if it does, this can result in less exports (as they are more expensive abroad) and more imports (because they are cheaper in the UK) and so can lead to a worsening of the balance of payments. This is clearly a dilemma which faces the government and it must decide what it regards as its most urgent priority, inflation or a balance of payments deficit.

DIRTY FLOATING

If the government were to allow the free operation of the forces of supply and demand for sterling, this could result in the pound becoming too strong in relation to other currencies and so causing a Balance of Payments deficit, or too weak with the resulting inflationary consequences. Therefore the government will sometimes intervene in the foreign exchange markets and influence the floating of the pound. This is known colloquially as "dirty floating". The government intervenes by manipulating the supply or demand for the currency. For instance, if the pound is too high then the Bank of England can sell pounds and so, by increasing its supply, reduce the exchange rate. Or conversely if the pound is falling too far or too fast, the Bank of England uses its foreign currency reserves and buys pounds on the foreign exchange markets, thus causing an artificial increase in demand for pounds and forcing the exchange rate up.

However, government intervention of this sort to "support the pound" can be expensive as it places a drain on our limited foreign currency reserves which must be used to buy pounds and so increase their demand. It is only really feasible if at other times the pound is strong enough to allow the Bank of England to sell pounds and use the foreign currency purchased to restore the strength of its reserves. Certainly no country in the world has sufficient foreign currency reserves to allow it to support its currency against a declining trend for any long period of time.

FUTURE PROSPECTS FOR THE UK BALANCE OF PAYMENTS

As we have already noted, the UK has been in Balance of Payments deficit for most of the last 30 years. However, recently the discovery of North Sea Oil has meant that the large deficits created by oil imports have no longer been necessary. The UK has become a net exporter of oil, thus adding to the credit side of the balance of payments. However, this favourable Balance of Payments surplus is somewhat misleading as UK exports in products or commodities, other than oil, have actually fallen over the same period in relation to imports. Thus, the Balance of Payments surplus shows something of a false picture with regard to UK industrial competitiveness with the rest of the world.

MEANS OF CONTROLLING THE BALANCE OF PAYMENTS

If this situation continues what are the possible alternative solutions open to the UK government?

Many people in this country believe that we should try to protect some of our infant industries. By infant industries we mean those industries which are only beginning to be established. For example the French government places import restrictions on certain electrical products. This is to allow the domestic French economy to develop their production. Also traditional industries may require protection from competition from abroad. Unemployment in industries such as textiles, motor cars, steel and coal is said to be the result of cheap imports and this has led to calls for a "seige economy". This is a colloquial phrase meaning that imports should be restricted by the use of:-

       a.   tariffs; or

       b.   quotas.

a.   Tariffs

Tariffs are taxes which can be levied on all imports or only on specific commodities. The effect of a tariff will depend on the demand for the product. If there is relatively inelastic demand and the domestic industry is unable to produce the product at a price which is less than the import price plus the tariff then the tax will be relatively ineffective. If demand for the import continues then it is in effect a tax on the domestic consumer. It will only be a successful means of curbing imports if the product has an elastic demand or home producers can step in to meet the demand, which has been diverted to domestic products because of the import tariff.

b.   Quotas

The use of quotas refers to restrictions being placed on the quantity of certain commodities which are allowed to be imported into the UK. Such quotas may be statutory (imposed by the government) or alternatively a voluntary agreement with the importers. For example there are voluntary agreement restricting the import of Japanese cars into the British market. This has been reached with the car importers who know that if they exceed their quota the government could then impose statutory limits.

There are several problems associated within the introduction of tariffs and quotas. Firstly, the UK is party to a general world agreement which discourages tariffs. This is called GATT (The General Agreement on Tariffs and Trade). This agreement is signed by 170 countries and has led to a general reduction in tariffs and quotas throughout the world. It is based on four principles: (i) that there should be no 'favoured nation status'. In other words all GATT member nations should receive the same treatment in respect of import controls; (ii) when import controls are imposed these should be in the form of tariffs and not statutory quotas; (iii) that there should be consultation between members wherever possible on matters relating to trade restrictions; and (iv) GATT members should work to reduce tariffs between members. GATT has proved very successful in reducing the imposition of tariffs and quotas and has led to a significant increase in world trade.

Secondly, the UK is a member of the European Economic Community (EEC) and this restricts our freedom to influence trade not only to and from fellow member countries but also in relation to trade from outside the EEC. The EEC has two functions: (i) it is a customs union and as such does not, at least in theory, allow the imposition of any trade restrictions such as tariffs and quotas between its member states; (ii) it imposes a common external tariff. By this is meant that imports to any country in the EEC are subject to the same level of tariff taxation. In this way the EEC increases the import price of those goods which are also produced within the EEC and so allows Community produce to compete on equal terms with imports which are produced more cheaply abroad. The structure and functions of the EEC are more fully discussed in chapter 24.

Thirdly, there is the possibility that such trade restrictions could actually be disadvantageous if levied on specific countries. It is suggested that these countries could retaliate in turn and impose similar restrictions on our exports to their countries. However, it has been pointed out that Japan, whose imports are often suggested as a possible target for such import controls, does not import on any major scale from the UK and so any retaliation on their part would be relatively ineffective.

Import controls have been suggested by some as a possible short term solution to any future Balance of Payments problem as they would allow a gradual realignment of Britain's industries without the shock of rapid upheaval in our industrial base caused by massive unemployment. Those who hold the opposite view have argued that such measures are merely "featherbedding" inefficient British industry. In other words tariffs and quotas would not allow such industries to face the harsh realities of economic life in the world today. If they are inefficient then they should go under and their productive resources used in more cost effective and competitive industries.

Perhaps the reality of the world economic situation is such that if we look at declining industries in most of the western world's nations we find that they are being subsidised to a much greater extent than those in the UK. Therefore the UK government could recognise that it must try and combine a realistic economic approach to international trade with the need for an understanding and compassionate approach to those workers faced with long term unemployment. Such job losses are partly a consequence of the decline in our traditional industries and so the imposition of trade controls should not always be seen as the abandonment of free market ideals but instead a recognition that we should protect the jobs of such workers.

c.   The government can stimulate investment by UK exporters.

A further alternative which has been suggested and tried in the past is the encouragement of UK industry to invest and in so doing to become more internationally competitive. Such a policy may involve the government in persuading the banks to give loans at cheaper rates to exporters. The government can also give exporters specific tax relief on investment or guarantee that exporters will be paid for their products sold in certain countries.

This can prove difficult in practice as was found in the early 1970's by the Heath Government who sought to encourage British industry to re-invest prior to the UK's entry into the EEC. The cheap loans which were given were often not used for investment in exporting industry but instead were used for property speculation and domestic consumption so helping to fuel inflation.

d.   The government could allow the pound to fall in value.

An further alternative to a long term trade deficit could be to allow or even force the value of the pound down so that exports will become cheaper and imports increasingly prohibitively priced. As we mentioned earlier, this may solve an immediate pressing balance of payments problem but may in itself cause domestic inflation.

e.   Deflation of the economy.

Finally, if the balance of payments deficit is sufficiently large, as it was in 1974, 1975 and 1976, the government may be faced with the need to deflate the overall economy and in so doing reduce the demand for imports. Unfortunately, this will have the side effect of also making it more difficult for exporters to produce as interest rates may increase and can also lead to higher domestic unemployment.

The United Kingdom is extremely lucky to have the cushion of North Sea Oil which will hopefully mean that the Balance of Payments is not a serious problem for the next fifteen years or so. However when the oil runs out, the country could well be faced with a repetition of the difficulties it had in the 1950's, '60's and '70's. Therefore during the next few years, it should attempt to revitalise its export industries and ensure that the products we make are capable of competing with those of the rest of the world.

THE ROLE OF MULTI-NATIONAL COMPANIES IN THE INTERNATIONAL ENVIRONMENT

One of the more significant factors affecting international trade both within the UK and throughout the world is the influence of multi-national companies. By the term 'multi-national' we mean a company which owns and controls a business operation outside the country in which it is based. In this country there are many such multi-nationals. Some have their headquarters in the USA such as Ford, General Motors and IBM, others are based in Europe such as Philips and Nestlé. Britain itself is the base for multi-national organisations such as British Petroleum, ICI and Lonrho, all of which have operations in many countries of the world. In most cases multinationals establish domestic subsiduaries to carry out their business in other countries and this will, to some extent, isolate the parent company from the government control of the countries in which they operate. So in this country Vauxhall is owned by General Motors of the USA and Nissan (UK) is a wholly owned subsidiary of the Japanese parent company.

THE GROWTH OF THE MULTI-NATIONALS

One of the most striking characteristics of multi-nationals is their size. The largest multi-national company in the world is Exxon. This may be a name with which you are not familiar. In fact in Britain it trades under the brand name of Esso and you will certainly recognise that particular brand of petrol. Exxon has a turnover throughout the world that matches the Gross National Product of all but the largest manufacturing nations. This is also true of General Motors and Ford who are the second and third largest companies in the world. It is a somewhat daunting fact to realise that the company president of Ford, elected by the shareholders, has control over a greater level of expenditure than the presidents of most of the nations of Europe. What is more his corporate objectives are merely to increase the wealth of his shareholders irrespective of the effect his decisions could have on the people who work for Ford throughout the world or the citizens of the countries in which his organisation has business interests.

Another significant factor to note is that the multi-nationals are growing at a rate which is almost twice that of the developed nations of the world and so in the not too distant future they could be as economically important as the major industrial nations. It would be impossible in a book of this nature to consider all aspects of the operations of multi-national companies but here we will make some comment as to their investment and pricing policies.

THE INVESTMENT POLICIES OF MULTI-NATIONAL COMPANIES

The multi-national companies are the most significant source of industrial investment for any country in the world. They invest in two ways: either through direct investment by building plant or facilities for their subsidiaries in a country or by investing in the share capital of domestic companies. Because of the financial size of this investment and the impact it can have on a particular country, the multi-nationals have considerable power. In the first place, they can decide where and how to invest in a country and secondly they can hold over a government the threat to withdraw their investment. So for example, Ford, a major American multi-national, has been able to influence the UK government's domestic incomes policy by indicating that it might place a major investment in a new engine works in Europe rather than in the UK and a Japanese multi-national such as Nissan can persuade the British government to offer it very attractive terms to establish a base in this country rather than on the continent.

Furthermore it is interesting to note that the strength of the multi-national has changed to some extent. In the post war period the major multi-nationals were American companies who tended to place their investments in countries where they felt confident of political and economic stability. Therefore there was major US investment in Europe, Canada and Australia. However the multi-national companies which have been most prolific in their growth in the last ten years have been Japanese and their investment has often been in areas which are close to their home base. So in this case it has been in Singapore, Taiwan and Hong Kong rather than in Europe or Canada. In this country we have seen a noticeable dis-investment or reduction in investment by many of the multi-nationals since the late 1970's. This has resulted in considerable job losses. The reason for this has been that the UK has become less attractive as an industrial base and other countries have become more attractive. As the multi-nationals are such large employers their policy of closing factories can produce major job losses and it is often beyond the power of our government to prevent such damaging action by the multi-nationals.

THE PRICING POLICY OF THE MULTI-NATIONAL COMPANIES

The multi-nationals have the ability to set prices for their products which will take the greatest advantage of the tax systems of the countries in which they operate. This involves making as little profit as possible in countries with high taxation and transferring it to countries with low levels of taxation. This is known as 'transfer pricing'. A simple example may help to illustrate the process.

A multi-national car manufacturer may build cars in Spain for eventual sale in the UK. Spain has a much lower tax on company profits than that in the UK. So the company wishes to make the profit for its Spanish subsidiary rather than its UK subsidiary and so consequently pay less tax. Consider two possible alternative pricing structures. In both the figures are all given in pounds and the tax rates simplified to allow the concept to be more easily understood.

Alternative 1

Car is manufactured in Spain at a cost of	£3000
Car is sold by the Spanish subsidiary of the multi-national to the UK subsidiary of the multi-national for	£3500
Profit to the Spanish subsidiary of	£500
Tax in Spain on Profits of 10%	
Tax Paid	£50
UK subsidiary have bought the car for	£3500
It is sold to a British customer for	£5500
Profit to the UK subsidiary of	£2000
Tax in UK on profits of 30%	
Tax Paid	£600
Total Tax paid to the Spanish and British governments by the multi-national's two subsidiaries	£650

Alternative 2

Car is manufactured in Spain at a cost of	£3000
Car is sold by the Spanish subsidiary to the UK subsidiary for	£5400
Profit to the Spanish subsidiary of	£2400
Tax in Spain on profits of 10%	
Tax Paid	£240
UK subsidiary have bought the car for	£5400
It is sold to a British customer for	£5500
Profit to the UK subsidiary of	£100
Tax in UK on profits of 30%	
Tax Paid	£30
Total tax paid to the Spanish and British Governments by the multi-national's two subsidiaries	£270

It is clear that the second alternative substantially reduces the multi-national company's overall tax bill. It is now free to withdraw the profit made from its Spanish subsidiary and either distribute it in dividends to its shareholders or reinvest it elsewhere. The problem here is that the UK government provides the service which the company may need to operate in Britian and yet gains little tax revenue from the company's activities. It could even be offering substantial incentives to the company to invest in Britain. The investment capital could have come from the profit made from the sale of the car we have just considered.

It is almost impossible for a single government acting on its own to curtail this practice of transfer pricing. If the UK government attempted to impose any restrictions on the freedom of the mulit-nationals to act in this way, it is likely that there would be considerable dis-investment in this country by the multi-nationals with consequent job losses. Therefore the power of the multi-nationals to set their own prices is considerable. Further analysis of the pricing policy of such companies acting in an oligopoly market is undertaken in chapter 26.

ASSIGNMENT — THE TWO CITIES HOTEL

The Two Cities Hotel is located in Shipston-on-Stour, approximately 35 miles from both Birmingham and Oxford. The main advantage of this location however, is its proximity to Stratford-upon-Avon. The hotel is extremely popular with foreign tourists, particularly Americans, who appreciate the luxurious surroundings afforded to them by its five-star accommodation.

One of the major attractions offered by the hotel is its cuisine. The restaurant is highly recommended in most 'Good Food Guides', and attracts custom from a wide area. A very popular feature of the restaurant programme is the twice-weekly 'International Evening'. These 'theme' evenings are based around food and entertainment from countries throughout the world. All dishes on the evening's menu are prepared with ingredients especially imported from the country concerned, and this has proved so successful with the customers that the hotel owners have been able to hire traditional 'native' cabaret entertainment. For example, a Flamenco guitarist appears at the Spanish Evening, whilst a Barbadian Steel Band accompanies the diners at the Carribean Evening.

Recently, however, certain events have taken place which could have far reaching effects on the hotel. The most important single event has been the dramatic fall in the value of the pound against most other major currencies, due to a rapid drop in the price of oil. This will inevitably have an effect on both the hotel and the restaurant, and the directors and management of the hotel have called an emergency meeting to discuss the implications of this change in the exchange rate.

TASKS

1. You are employed at the Two Cities Hotel as a trainee manager. Your immediate boss, Gary Rowell, has been invited to the management meeting to discuss the position of the restaurant in light of the falling exchange rate. Unfortunately, Mr Rowell will be away on vacation until the day before the meeting and so will not have time to produce a report. He has therefore asked you to prepare a brief report, and suggests that you include the implications of the exchange rate changes in terms of costs, and also proposals for future action.

2. In the bar after work, you are approached by Annette Earl, a barmaid at the hotel, who tells you that staff are worried about their jobs. She says that she has "heard on the news that oil prices or something had changed and that no Americans would be coming this summer because tourism would fall". A staff meeting has been arranged, and she asks you to speak to the workforce in order to try to clarify the position. Prepare a short speech outlining how oil prices may affect the exchange rate and the likely effect of the change on the American tourist trade. Bear in mind that not all of the staff are as well-educated as you!

3. Following the Executive Meeting, Gary Rowell confesses to you that he was rather confused at some of the discussion. He says that at one point, the Managing Director emphasised the importance of elasticity. Not having had a business education, Gary admits that he was "totally lost" at this stage, and asks if you could explain the concept of elasticity as it applies to this situation. Prepare some notes to help in this explanation.

DEVELOPMENTAL TASK

4. Research the importance of tourism to the UK economy in terms of the number of tourists visiting the country each year, the amount of income they produce for the country and the number of jobs they create. This information can be obtained from Government publications available in the library and also from data published by the British Tourist Authority.

ASSIGNMENT — THE TRADE DEALS

Mills and Casson International are an import/export company based in the East End of London. In 1986 the company negotiated two important trading contracts. The first was for the import of cotton shirts from Singapore. The initial contract agreement was made in January and a price of S$6.60 per shirt was agreed. (The currency for Singapore is the Singapore dollar, represented by S$). The contract was for 20,000 shirts which were to be delivered in July. Payment was to be made on delivery and in Singapore dollars. In January the exchange rate was £1 = S$3.30 but by July it had changed to £1 = S$3.20.

The second contract involved the export of £100,000 worth of Harris Tweed Cloth to the USA. The initial agreement was reached in May and the American buyer promised to pay US$150,000 for the goods on delivery. (The exchange rate in May was £1 = US$1.50). Delivery was not made until late August. The US $150,000 were paid although by then the exchange rate had changed to £1 = US $1.45.

TASKS

You are employed as a trainee in the finance department of Mills and Casson International. Your section head, Gerard Dominic, has asked you to examine the financial implications of each of the contracts.

1. Prepare a memorandum to Mr Dominic in which you explain the cost of the shirts in sterling to the company in the light of the change in the exchange rate.

2. Prepare a second memorandum relating to the American deal. Explain whether Mills and Casson have benefitted or not from the change in the exchange rate between the pound and the dollar.

3. Write a report to Mr Dominic in which you examine the advantages and disadvantages of the company negotiating its import and export deals in sterling or in some other currency.

DEVELOPMENTAL TASK

4. From the financial pages of a quality newspaper obtain the value of sterling against the US dollar, the French Franc, the West German Deutchmark, the Swiss Franc and the Italian Lira. Plot the changes of the pound against each of these currencies for a month on a chart and produce an explanation of any major fluctuations.

Chapter 24

THE STATE

This chapter examines two important aspects of the State. The first section is concerned with the economic rationale for the State's intervention in the workings of economy. In some countries the State plays a very limited role in the economic activity of the country, restricting itself to the provision of law and order and defence. Such countries are referred to as 'free market' economies. Conversely in the communist bloc countries, the State assumes the central economic focus for the industrial and commercial activity of the nation. The State determines the level and nature of economic activity which is undertaken. In this country as we noted in chapter 22, the role of the State has been changing with an increasing emphasis on State provision and control. It is the nature of the State itself and the economic philosphy of the governments which guide it which determine the extent of such State influence.

The second part of the chapter will examine the role of the State in its legislative, executive and judicial roles. It will note the specific nature of these roles in the United Kingdom and analyse the processes and institutions which have been established to carry them out. Finally we will consider the role and importance of the European Community of which the UK is now a member.

STATE INTERVENTION INTO THE MARKET SYSTEM

As we saw in chapter 21 the market system is, at least in theory, a very efficient mechanism for allowing individual consumers the freedom of choice to spend their income and wealth as they wish. It also acts as a means of indicating to producers which goods and services are in demand, and benefits society in general by ensuring that scarce resources are not wasted. The problem of how products are allocated to competing consumers is solved through the power of the purse, those that have sufficient income can purchase what they desire, those with less money are left wanting. There are, however, several major deficiencies in this system and these have prompted governments over the years into a policy of market intervention. These deficiencies in the market system are known as market failures. As a simple means of classification, market failures can be divided into the following three categories:

1. failings caused by the type of good or service demanded;

2. failings resulting from the development of the economy;

3. failings which are inherent in the market system.

1. FAILINGS CAUSED BY THE TYPE OF GOOD OR SERVICE DEMANDED

The market system is able to provide private goods, but private goods alone cannot meet all the demands and needs of society. Society needs to be supplied with two further types of goods or service:

      (a) public goods, and

      (b) merit goods.

(a) PUBLIC GOODS

A public good is a good or service whose benefit is indiscriminate or diffuse. By this we mean that the benefit which is gained from such products cannot be allotted specifically to individual consumers. For example, the provision of a police service will help society as a whole. If you are protected by a police service then criminals who are likely to commit offences against you are deterred or arrested. This public service not only guards you but also the rest of society who are similarly protected. To charge one individual for the benefit gained would be to ignore the fact that the rest of society is also gaining a benefit. The provision of this type of good through the market system would necessitate individual customers hiring personal body guards or hiring their own security systems. Whilst this may be feasible for those in society who have sufficient money to pay for such protection, there are many who have not and would find themselves without protection. The two factors which distinguish public goods from private goods are illustrated below:

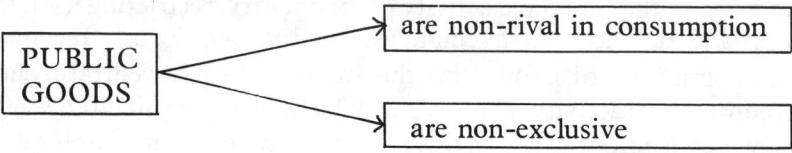

Non-rival in consumption

This means that if a given level of service is provided the fact that one individual consumes and benefits from it will not preclude others from similarly consuming and benefitting. Thus a number of people can consume the service simultaneously. The example we used of the police service illustrates the point. The protection of one person does not prevent others from being protected. Of course this does not mean that all individuals will benefit to the same extent. It simply means that all can consume the goods simultaneously to some degree.

Contrast this with most private goods. These are rival in consumption. If you were to eat a Mars Bar the one certain fact is that no one else will now be able to consume it! The consumption of such products by one individual means that less of the commodity will now be available to others and therefore some means of rationing the product in its allocation to rival consumers must be found. This is where the price mechanism comes in. Those willing to pay the price demanded will be able to consume the product. With public goods, however, the question is not one of rationing but of the State deciding what level of provision to make so that all can benefit.

Non-exclusive

The fact that they are non-exclusive is the second characteristic of public goods. This means that it is either impossible, or simply too expensive, to exclude certain individuals from gaining the benefits of public goods. With private goods, if a consumer is not willing to pay the price asked, he or she can be excluded from consumption, as the supplier will not sell the product to him. With public goods if an individual refuses to pay it is difficult to prevent him gaining the benefits from it. For example, if you decided not to pay that portion of your taxes which finance the police force, would the police then be able to distinguish between muggers who may attack you from those who may attack others whose tax has gone to pay for the service? It would be an almost impossible task. As individuals who elect not to pay for the service cannot be excluded from its benefits, the State resolves that all must be forced to pay through taxation.

The figure below shows how the distinction between the two categories produces a combination of four possible types of goods ranging from the totally private to the totally public.

The Distinction between Private and Public Goods

	EXCLUDABLE	NON-EXCLUDABLE
RIVAL CONSUMPTION	Private goods, an additional consumer will reduce the amount available to others. Product or service can be sold through the market system. (Examples would include most products we buy such as food, clothes, housing.)	Common property resource, where an additional consumer will mean less for others but there is no means of preventing or rationing consumption. (Few examples of this except perhaps common grazing land or a crowded seaside beach.)
NON-RIVAL CONSUMPTION	Goods where an extra consumer does not restrict others but where it is possible to seel the product through the market mechanism. (Examples would include a football match, cinema or theatre performance which is not full and so an extra spectator does not prevent others from gaining their enjoyment. If it is a full house it becomes a private good.)	Public goods which are supplied by the State but which cannot be sold because their benefits are diffuse or indiscriminate. (Examples such as national defence, law and order, roads and street lighting.)

We can see that once a public good is provided, individuals will benefit from it whether or not they have paid for it. This would make provision through the price system very difficult as private producers would be unwilling to supply it because they may be unable to cover their costs. They are faced with a serious problem known as the 'free rider phenomenon'. This occurs when some individuals, despite wishing to gain the benefit of the public good, refuse to pay for it as they believe others will provide the finance thereby allowing those who do not pay to enjoy a "free ride". When offered the choice,

> "if you want the provision of this service you must be prepared to pay for it; if you do not want the service you will have nothing to pay"

the meaner members of society (although some would refer to them as the shrewder members) will decide not to pay for the service in the hope that others will choose to do so and they will then gain the benefits free of charge.

. . . free riders . . .

The larger the group who are to benefit from the public good provision, the greater is the potential for the free rider and the less feasible it becomes to provide the service through voluntary contributions.

For example, if a fence dividing the gardens of two neighbours is blown down they may be able to reach an agreement to pay jointly for its repair as they are the two people who will benefit from this action. There are no "free riders" (unless of course we count those other neighbours who considered the broken fence to be something of an eyesore). If, on the other hand, we look at the larger issue of national defence, there would certainly be a number of "free riders". These would be the people refusing to pay simply because they know that others would finance the system anyway and they would still benefit. (Of course others may refuse to contribute to defence because they are opposed to nuclear weapons).

THE FINANCE OF PUBLIC GOOD PROVISION

There are two problems to be faced by the State in raising finance for public goods:

> (i)   the consideration of equity.
>
> (ii) externalities.

(i) Equity

One method of charging for public goods is by levying taxes individually so that, at the chosen level of provision ,each citizen pays an amount of tax equal to the level of benefit they receive. This approach is known as the 'benefit approach to taxation' in that it tries to equate an individual's tax bill with the level of benefit they receive from publicly provided services.

One major disadvantage of this method of taxation is that it may be regarded as inequitable since it disregards the distribution of income and wealth within society. An alternative means of taxation to this is based not on the benefits gained by an individual but on their wealth, income and personal circumstances. This is referred to as the 'ability to pay approach' and is essentially the tax system which is currently followed in the United Kingdom. While the financing of public good provision through general taxation does overcome the free rider problem it still leaves the difficulty of assessing correctly the most appropriate level of provision of public services.

(ii) Externalities

The second problem of finance results from the system used in this country for providing some public goods. It is known as the problem of externalities. The decentralisation of the provision of certain public services such as policing and roads means that they are financed to some extent from local authority rates. Thus the citizens of Derbyshire will be asked to pay through their rates for the Derbyshire Constabulary. This is fine in that it is the inhabitants of Derbyshire who will gain the benefits of the law and order provided. However, there may also be some spillover or external effects in that the Derbyshire police may also arrest criminals who, although living in that county, commit their crimes in neighbouring counties. In this way the citizens of adjoining areas are benefitting from a service financed by Derbyshire ratepayers. It may be the case that there is a reciprocal externality, in that neighbouring constabularies arrest criminals contemplating deadly deeds in Derbyshire. But nevertheless the fact remains that one county's ratepayers are providing a service which benefits other consumers who are not contributing to its cost.

There are a number of ways of avoiding the problem of externalities. Consider the following solutions:

> (i)   Public goods could be provided on a central basis financed through central government taxation. In this way the externalities do not matter as all citizens are faced with a tax bill according to their ability to pay.

(ii) The area benefitting from the service provided by its neighbour can be made to compensate the provider for the benefit gained. The difficulty here is in accurately assessing the extent of the benefit. For instance, can the Derbyshire Constabulary quantify the number of criminals they catch who intend to commit crimes elsewhere?

(iii) The level of service provided in adjoining communities could be standardised. In this way the taxpayers of one county enjoy the same level of provision as their neighbours, however this does not take into account the different levels of need in communities. For example, Derbyshire may be caught in a crime wave while the next county is relatively trouble free.

All of these solutions inevitably involve some element of central government intervention. The most commonly adopted method of dealing with externalities is for the central exchequer to provide part of the financing of those public goods. Thus the financing of the police force is on a fifty-fifty basis with half coming from the local rates and half from the Home Office. Similarly the cost of roads is divided so that main trunk roads are paid for by the Department of the Environment while the costs of minor roads comes from the local authority budget. Ultimately the provision of public goods is a matter of social choice expressed through the ballot box. The extent of provision is thus a reflection of how far an elected government fulfils the demands of its citizens.

(b) MERIT GOODS

The second category of products and services which are provided by the State in this country are those which are regarded as providing some element of benefit to society as a whole but which could be produced by private enterprise and sold through the market mechanism. These are referred to as 'merit goods'. Examples of such goods include education, the Health Service, parks and museums.

The characteristic which differentiates merit goods (such as education) from private goods (such as clothing) is that the benefit gained does not fall solely on the individual but on society as a whole. If you were to wear well-tailored clothing the rest of society would gain no benefit whatsoever. Yet with a trained and educated population, society can enjoy more production, research and innovation, all of which lead to a better standard of living for everyone.

THE STATE'S PROVISION OF MERIT GOODS

As with public goods, there are two reasons why the State should intervene to provide merit goods, and again the reasons are:

(i) the consideration of equity;

(ii) externalities.

(i) Equity

Let us concentrate our analysis on the provision of education. It is certainly feasible to have an education system which is solely provided by private suppliers. Individuals would have the freedom to choose the type and standard of education they regarded as being most appropriate to their children's needs and abilities. The private schools, colleges and universities would offer a wide range of educational methods and parents would be able to decide either to put their children through progressive schooling or they may prefer a more traditional approach. Institutions would in effect compete for pupils and students and those providing the most successful and popular modes of education would attract the biggest intake and of course make the most profit. Parents would have to pay for the services provided and the better-off sections of society would naturally have a wider choice in the education of their children. You may regard this as inequitable because the poorer sections of society would be faced with a lower standard of education than their more affluent contemporaries. You may even argue that education is a right and a necessity for life. Yet many more pressing necessities are provided through the market system and not by the State, food and clothing for instance.

(ii) Externalities

The concept of externalities was introduced when considering the financing of public goods. Externalities are the social benefits or costs gained or borne by society in general or by those who do not directly consume the service provided.

If we stay with our example of education, an educated electorate should, in theory at least, return a government whose policies are more in accord with the perceived wishes of society as a whole. Thus an education does not simply benefit you in enhancing your chances of obtaining a good job and enjoying the finer things of life, it will also be to the advantage of the rest of us in society. The argument is, therefore, that if society as a whole benefits from a service provided to an individual it should bear all or at least some of the costs of that provision.

If the state did not subsidise, perhaps some individuals would choose not to consume as much. Thus without free education some parents might choose not to send their children to school either because they believe that the benefit to be gained is not worth the price they are asked to pay or simply because they have insufficient income and choose to spend it on other things of more immediate benefit such as food or clothing. Whatever the reason, if some choose not to educate their children to their full capability then society in general will be the worse off. The State, therefore, intervenes in the market and provides certain services free or at a subsidised rate.

These social benefits (or as we shall see later, social costs) are often ignored by individual decision-makers who are not directly affected. This is somewhat understandable in that individials seek to maximise their own personal satisfaction even to the detriment of others. What is perhaps more worrying is when decision-makers in the public sector choose to ignore externalities in deciding whether or not the State should provide a particular service such as health or education. The difficulty is that externalities are often unquantifiable in that it is not possible to put an exact valuation on them. It is often more simple to ignore them. If the external effects of health care or education are undervalued or disregarded entirely, then one of the main justifications for State provision or subsidy is removed. It is then much easier to argue for the privatisation of these services.

Some goods or services will also result in an external cost to society even though they are individually consumed. Perhaps one of the clearest examples of this is pollution. Factories can belch out smoke and in so doing ruin the environment of others. Chemical effluent can pollute rivers and endanger wildlife. These external costs are not borne by the producers of the goods but by society as a whole. If the individual private producer was faced with bearing this social cost himself then total costs of production would rise and, as a consequence, there would be a reduction in the level of output. As a producer does not bear the cost, the government must intervene to protect other members of society, or at least to compensate them. Legislation could be passed to prohibit or limit these harmful side effects. In the case of pollution this had been done under the Control of Pollution Act 1974.

Alternatively, some form of taxation could be levied on the producer such as a hefty rate bill. The community could then use the revenue raised to provide a social benefit, for instance a lower rate bill for domestic ratepayers or a new sports centre, which in some way would act as compensation for the social cost caused by the pollution. The producer now faced with higher costs which more accurately reflects the true cost of production (as they would include the social cost) would be faced with the choice of either reducing production (and with it pollution) or passing on the higher costs in the form of price rises to the ultimate consumers of the product. In this way the consumer would be compensating those members of society harmed by the production of the product he wishes to buy.

THE EXTENT OF STATE PROVISION

The extent to which the State should intervene in this manner is something of a political debate involving the exercise of value judgements. It may be argued that education and health care should be the right of everyone regardless of their status or income. This is part of the rationale for the establishment of the State education system and the National Health Service. Others would argue that people with money should be allowed to spend it as they like and not have it taken from them in taxation to finance the schooling and health care of others. They should be allowed to send their children to "public" schools or enrol on private health schemes. The Thatcher Government has taken this view to some extent in its policy of encouraging the development of private education and health schemes.

The full scope of this debate is somewhat beyond the limits of this book and we shall satisfy ourselves in noting that where merit goods exist and society does benefit there is a justification for State finance and provision.

2. MARKET FAILURES RESULTING FROM THE DEVELOPMENT OF THE ECONOMY

Over the last hundred years the economy of the United Kingdom has developed in such a way that government intervention has become necessary in certain other areas:

      (a)   Monopolies and Market Concentration.

      (b)   Loss of Consumer Sovereignty.

      (c)   Growth of Large Scale Projects.

MONOPOLIES AND MARKET CONCENTRATION

As we saw in chapter 21 one of the most noticeable characteristics of the UK's changing industrial structure has been the increasing pre-dominance in most markets of a few very large organisations. This development has resulted in increasing concentration of output and resources into the hands of these organisations.

As was noted in Chapter 21 the market structure which has evolved has tended to be either monopolistic, in which there is only one major supplier or oligopolistic where a few large companies share the market between them.

A high degree of concentration in an industry is often used as a measure of the lack of competition. It can result in:

      (i)   excessive prices;

      (ii)   a lack of efficiency;

      (iii)   a lack of innovation;

and so be detrimental to both the consumer and public interest. Economists would refer to this as a welfare loss to society.

Whilst practically all organisations in private enterprise seek to maximise their profits it is the monopolist or oligopolist who has the power to push up price without fear of competition. You might assume that in an oligopolistic market, in which there are few suppliers, there would be fierce competition as each sought to extend output. However this is not always the case, as in many markets the few large scale producers are satisfied with their market share and would refrain from initiating a mutually damaging price war caused by one supplier dropping his price and the others being forced to follow suit.

It is difficult to be precise about the extent of the welfare loss to society which is attributable to market concentration. Various attempts at quantifying this welfare loss have suggested that it may be in excess of 10% of the Gross National Product (GNP). If this is correct, as some governments believe, then there is considerable justification for State intervention. A further consideration of this is undertaken in chapters 26 and 27.

LOSS OF CONSUMER SOVEREIGNTY

The growth and development of technology has meant that long-term planning and production processes are now essential for many products. For example, the launch of a new car requires:

    (i)   a research and development programme;

    (ii) considerable time and effort spent on design; and

    (iii) massive investment in capital and machinery;

before the new model can be unveiled. If a manufacturer has invested considerable time and money into the production of a new product then he is very reluctant to allow consumers to have the final decision on whether it will or will not be a commercial success.

Large scale producers, therefore, attempt to control the demand for their products by influencing consumers through advertising. If such advertising is found to be sufficiently persuasive then producers are able to develop products over the long-term and at considerable cost, confident in the knowledge that consumers will ultimately purchase whatever they, the suppliers, determine. This reduction of uncertainty in the future level of demand may be deemed necessary because of the money spent in production but it nevertheless can be regarded as an attempt at reducing the freedom of choice of individual consumers, one of the key features of the market system.

One might say that the potential of advertising to significantly influence consumer demand is debatable, and yet when we consider that total expenditure on marketing in the UK is in excess of 10% of GNP it is obvious that producers at least are convinced of its power to positively influence the demand for their products. The argument about the powerful influence of advertising is one for debate between economists and psychologists alike. As yet no conclusive agreement has been reached on its effects. The government does, however, regard it as necessary to regulate and control advertising to a certain extent. Whilst not seeking to manacle the entrepreneur, some advertising is still deemed to be undesirable.

With the establishment of the Advertising Standards Authority, the government has attempted to keep all advertisements "legal, decent and honest". Other products which are regarded as being harmful are restricted in their advertising. Thus cigarette advertising is prohibited on television. Yet tobacco companies are allowed to sponsor sporting events with the result that television viewers are regularly exposed to the names of different cigarette brands, thus possibly negating the effect of the ban on "direct" advertising.

(c) GROWTH OF LARGE SCALE PROJECTS

During the last hundred years, one of the most marked changes in the nature of industry has been the rapid growth in the scale of projects. The investment needed for large scale projects is immense. Often the risk involved is so great or the length of time before the realisation of any return on the investment so long, that private enterprise is unable or unwilling to provide the initial investment.

If there were considerable social benefit to be gained from the project the State may then deem it necessary to provide the finance. Often the criteria upon which the government bases its decisions are difficult to ascertain. Projects where the government is going to be the main consumer of the product are prime areas for State aid. Increasingly, though, the Thatcher Government has indicated that such projects should be financed by private enterprise or not provided at all. The Channel tunnel is an excellent example. Clearly in less economically stringent times the opportunity for State finance of large scale projects increases considerably.

3. FAILURES INHERENT IN THE MARKET SYSTEM

The final category of market failures is related to characteristics which are intrinsic to the system. We shall examine these under two headings:

(a) The unequal distribution of income and wealth.

(b) The effects of the business cycle.

(a) THE UNEQUAL DISTRIBUTION OF INCOME AND WEALTH

One of the foundations of the market system is that each individual has the freedom to dispose of his income in any way he may choose. However, this freedom is not unlimited. Each individual has a budget restraint, that is he is restricted by his level of income and wealth. The market system simply assumes a given distribution of income and capital and makes no attempt to rectify any inequality in the economy.

Within the UK, however, there is a very unequal distribution of wealth. Approximately 80% of the wealth of the nation is concentrated in the hands of 50% of the population, leaving the other 50% with only 20% of the wealth. The price system, by ignoring this problem in its basic assumptions, allows poverty to co-exist side by side with affluence.

The decision as to whether or not such a situation should be changed is very much a value judgement. Since the nineteenth century all governments have pursued a policy of redistribution to a greater or lesser extent through taxation and social benefits. The level of redistribution is often dependent on the particular hue of the government's rosette. A left-wing government is more likely to tax those in a higher wage bracket in order to provide more social benefits for those on lower income levels. A Conservative government is more inclined to lower personal taxation, justifying it on the grounds that individuals should have as much freedom as possible to spend their money in whatever way they choose.

Of course the redistribution effect of taxation is not solely limited to income tax. Indirect wealth taxes in the shape of Capital Transfer Tax and Capital Gains Tax also usually penalise the richer sections of society more than the less affluent.

(b) THE EFFECTS OF THE BUSINESS CYCLE

When left to operate freely the market tends to develop into a pattern which can be described as a business cycle. This means that it is subject to successive booms and slumps over a regular cyclical period. This pattern can be observed quite clearly if we examine economic activity in the UK over a long period. It has in fact been apparent since the industrial revolution.

In the nineteenth century the peaks (booms) appeared every seven to ten years. At these times the level of employment was usually fairly high relative to surrounding years. In between the booms were periods of lower economic activity usually falling to its lowest level roughly midway between the peaks.

After the First World War the pattern altered somewhat and the country was faced with nearly two decades of high unemployment with the slump reaching its trough in the depression of the mid-nineteen thirties. From the end of the Second World War until the start of the 1970s, the economy was running at a relatively high level of activity with little unemployment (it never exceeded 2.5% of the workforce and often ran as low as 1%). Concurrently with this period of high and stable employment levels, the economy experienced a much lower inflation rate than that which the country was to face in the 1970s.

With the 1970s came a return to the slump/boom pattern of the pre-war years. It must be emphasised, however, that the cycle in these later years was characterised by ever-deepening troughs in the slump years and much more modest recoveries in the booms. What was also apparent in the last decade was that the time span for each cycle had fallen from a seven to ten year period to one of only three to four years.

In this period, 1970 and 1972 were slight recession years. 1974 saw the peak of a mild boom followed in 1976 by a further period of growing unemployment. By 1978 the economy has started to pick up slightly but this was to be followed by the worst period of recession since the 1930s. The slump which started in 1979 has not been restricted to the United Kingdom but in this country it has been particularly far-reaching and the decline in output and growth in unemployment has been as dramatic as that of the early 1930s.

The breakdown of the market mechanism is most harshly illustrated from a social viewpoint in the case of unemployment. The general level of employment, it can be argued, is dependent on the overall demand for goods and services in the country as a whole. If there is a high level of demand then more jobs are available as producers seek to increase their level of output. Conversely if producers fear a fall in demand for their products they will invest less and in so doing create unemployment. The fall in employment will reduce demand and their worst fears will have been realised. They will then lay off or make redundant production staff and in so doing add to the level of unemployment and precipitate further consequent falls in demand. And so it goes on until some producers anticipate a potential increase in demand, invest more, and increase job vacancies.

The social horrors of the depression in the 1930s impressed on economists and governments alike the unacceptability of large scale unemployment. In response to these problems economists, and particularly the Cambridge economist, John Maynard Keynes, argued that the State must intervene in the economy to maintain and stabilise a certain level of aggregate demand and so reduce the risk of continued unemployment. Development of these theories led to the proposition that, when the economy is prone to inflation, governments should also intervene to curb rising prices. This theory as a whole was the beginning of macro-economics (control of the economy by the government) and the policies which have followed have been a consistent feature of post-war governments.

As with the other market failures the extent of government intervention is often a political value judgement and the relative costs to society of unemployment or inflation are regarded differently by the opposing political parties. In chapter 25 on Government Economic Policy we shall look more closely at the causes of these problems and alternative solutions to them. For the moment we shall simply conclude that while these problems do exist there is a justification for further State intervention in the economy.

FORMS OF STATE INTERVENTION

In the preceeding section we concentrated on an analysis of the market failures that have encouraged successive governments to intervene in the market economy. In this section we shall look at the ways in which the government intervenes. These can be divided into three basic areas:

1. Finance;

2. Legislation or Regulation;

3. Provision.

1. FINANCE

The state can intervene in the market through finance in two ways:

    (a)   positively through grants, benefits and subsidies;

    (b)   negatively by taxation.

(a) Positive finance

The government may seek to redistribute the wealth and income of the country in favour of those it regards as being most in need. It can do this through a system of grants, benefits and subsidies. Let us look at some examples.

(i) Pensions

One of the earliest forms of government financial help, the retirement pension, is provided to those who have contributed to the State scheme throughout their working life. The State, in effect, manages part of the income of individuals so that they will be provided for after their working days have ended.

(ii) Social Security

A similar contribution system to that of the State Pension scheme operates for unemployment benefit in that those in work are statutorily obliged to insure themselves through the State while they are in work against the eventuality of being unemployed.

Since the Second World War the Welfare State has expanded to look after those who, although not having contributed to a State scheme, find themselves in difficult financial circumstances. This system of social security was initially envisaged to provide a safety net for those relatively few members of society who would not be working, the assumption being that most people could and should find paid employment.

Circumstances have changed dramatically as the period of continuous full employment enjoyed in the 1950s and 1960s has come to an end. The social security system now finds itself having to cope with millions of people, many of whom have never worked and so have never accumulated sufficient entitlements to allow them to enjoy the benefit of unemployment pay. Many, it now seems likely, will never find paid employment and may be faced with the prospect of living off the social security system for the rest of their lives. The pressure that this extra number of unemployed has placed on the system has led to severe strains on its administrative and legal framework and has drawn considerable criticism and calls for reform. It has now become the largest single component of central government expenditure and there is little to suggest that this will cease to be the case in the near future.

(iii) Education grants

The State education system has developed a range of grants for students seeking to enter further and higher education. The student grant system is administered through local authorities and whilst many grants are mandatory there is also a considerable area of discretion in the offering of some grants. Clearly in these times of financial stringency for local authorities, there is an increased reluctance to be generous in such discretionary awards.

(iv) Grants and loans to industry

The Department of Trade and Industry is empowered to give grants and loans to some new businesses and as we see in chapter 25 also to those locating in the Development Areas. In so doing the State is directly intervening in the operation of the business market and choosing to subsid-dise the running of some categories of business in an effort to counteract the disadvantages they have in respect of other more established organisations or those operating in the more prosperous regions of the country. Other forms of grants, benefits and subsidies would include such things as rent and rate rebates, home improvement grants and grants to community or cultural organisations. Collectively this area of government expenditure is called transfer payments.

. . . *transfer payments* . . .

(b) Negative finance

Negative finance involves withdrawing money from the economy in the form of taxation. The taxation system in the United Kingdom has evolved with four major aims. These aims have developed as the State has increased its intervention into the economy.

The Taxation System:

(i)   Is the means by which the government raises revenue to finance the provision of goods and services.

The earliest taxes were raised to allow the State to fight wars both domestically and abroad. As the State's services expanded it needed to impose a wide variety of taxes on property and commodities. The Napoleonic wars saw the introduction of the first tax on income and significantly, it is often during periods of national crisis that the State is able to impose new or heavier taxes as the populace are willing to bear a heavier burden at such times.

(ii)   Is used by the State as the most important method of redistributing income and wealth.

By the last quarter of the nineteenth century the extension of the voting franchise increased the pressure on the government to re-distribute income and wealth by taxing the more affluent sectors of society in order to finance the provision of education and other welfare services and benefits.

(iii)   Is used to regulate the consumption of particular goods which are regarded by the State as being harmful to its citizens or which the State wishes to conserve.

It was also during the nineteenth century that the government began to use taxation to deter the consumption of certain goods, particularly alcohol, which it regarded as being harmful.

(iv)   Can be used as an effective means of controlling the economy.

This final use of taxation as a means of implementing government macro economic policy stems from the introduction of Keynesian demand management since the Second World War.

The complex requirements of these aims means that the government must attempt to impose a system of taxation which is both acceptable to the taxpayer and also achieves its own objectives. In this country tax is levied on three different categories of tax base:

(i)   Income

(ii) Expenditure

(iii) Capital

(i) Income

This is the most important in terms of revenue raised. The single most significant tax is personal income tax. Also included in this category should be National Insurance contributions (which are, in effect, a form of taxation). Corporation Tax also falls into this category.

(ii) Expenditure

The second category is tax levied on expenditure and this includes Value Added Tax and Customs and Excise duties. These have become an increasingly important source of revenue.

(iii) Capital

Finally, the government also levies taxes on accumulated capital in the form of Capital Gains Tax, Capital Transfer Tax and Stamp Duty on the sale of more expensive houses.

This brings in a relatively small amount of revenue and, as yet, there is no direct tax on wealth in this country.

The current yield for the different taxes levied by the government in 1986-87 is shown in the budget statement presented in chapter 12.

A more detailed analysis of the financial aspects of taxation and how it affects the individual and the organisation are covered in chapter 12, whilst the use of taxation as a means of controlling the economy by the use of fiscal policy is examined in chapter 25.

2.   LEGISLATION AND REGULATION

In order to control the workings of the market system, the State has enacted a vast array of legislation. We shall look at some examples of this.

(a) Restrictions on the power of the producer

One of the largest areas for State concern has been the concentration of industry. This has already been mentioned as the shift of economic power into the hands of a relatively few larger companies and the resultant fall in the level of competition. Monopolies and oligopolies can lead to a suppression of innovation and investment, and higher prices for the consumer.

Since the Second World War successive governments have embarked on a series of measures collectively known as Competition Policy. This has involved the establishment of the Monopolies and Mergers Commission which has the power to investigate an existing monopoly or a proposed merger likely to result in a monopoly. The criteria used defines a monopoly situation as existing if:

"25% of the goods or services in question in the UK are supplied by or to the same person (or group of interconnected corporate bodies)".

The Monopolies Commission has the authority to prohibit a merger or to insist that a monopolist sells off assets or shares. The government has also established two other bodies, the Restrictive Practices Court and the Office of Fair Trading. These are responsible for the policing of the behaviour of organisations which are thought to be exerting dominant market power against the public interest. Restrictive Trade Practices are defined so as to include producers' attempts to:

    (a)   fix retail prices;

    (b)   restrict the number of retail outlets; or

    (c)   force retailers to take all the goods in a manufacturer's range (known as full-time forcing).

Informal agreements are often difficult to detect and as such are much more difficult to control. However evidence suggests that the Restrictive Trade Practices Court has had a fairly significant effect as a result of its judgements. Over a sample of cases, 10% of agreements were completely abandoned, others modified and competition increased in about 50% of cases. On the other hand, many of the agreements condemned were simply replaced by some other form of restrictive practice which had yet to be defined as unlawful by the Court.

The success of the Monopolies Commission is perhaps more limited. Relatively few mergers have been reported to it and while some potential mergers have been abandoned through fear of action by the Commission, on the whole legislation has not had the significant effect on the concentration of industrial production that might have been hoped. The role of government competition policy is further considered in chapter 27.

Government legislation on restrictive practices is not limited solely to companies. The freedom of the individual to practice his trade or profession is also protected. The courts have attempted to prevent any restraint of trade. Legally if any restraint is placed upon employees it must be to satisfy certain criteria such as the need to protect the genuine trade interests of the employer enforcing it.

(b) Consumer protection

As we shall see in more detail in chapter 27 the government also seeks to protect the rights of the consumer through other pieces of legislation such as the Sale of Goods Act 1979, the Consumer Credit Act 1974 and the Consumer Safety Act 1978. In each case the law is being used by the government to influence the workings of the free market and to protect and enhance the interests of the consumer, who is normally the weaker party in any economic bargaining situation.

(c) Prices and Incomes Policy

A much more controversial area of legislation has been that involved in prices and incomes policy. In the post-war period several governments have sought both through statutory and voluntary policies to establish a means of limiting the increase of prices and/or incomes. This is a direct interference in the workings of the market as it aims to restrict producers in their attempts to charge the price for their products which they believe the market will bear.

In the case of incomes policy, the government attempts to circumvent the collective bargaining process to hold down what might be justifiably regarded as the market equilibrium level of wages and salaries. Governments have implemented these policies with the intention of reducing inflation, which they regard as being an economic ill facing the country as a whole. The success and failure of these policies will be evaluated in the chapter 25 on Government Economic Policy.

(d) Other legislation

A further area of government regulation and legislation is intended to influence the level of demand for certain goods and services. For example, cigarettes or alcoholic drinks cannot be legally purchased by young people. Pornography is deemed to be a social evil and its sale through the market is prohibited. In so doing, the government is limiting the effective demand and supply of these products. Whether a lifting of these forms of legislation would result in thousands of twelve-year-olds sitting watching Emanuelle whilst smoking Woodbines and drinking Scotch whisky is a matter of conjecture but nevertheless the government feels it has to protect society by restricting demand.

. . . protect society by restricting demand.

Alternatively consumers are forced by legislation to purchase certain commodities. It is illegal to drive a car without sufficient insurance or a motor cycle without a crash helmet. The law states that all children between the ages of five and sixteen must be educated. These are all examples of the government intervening in the market mechanism with a resultant increase in demand for these commodities. Clearly it is possible therefore and may well be desirable for governments to use legislation as a method of social control, as well as a tool for influencing positively or negatively the demand for goods and services. Without legislation the demand for the products mentioned above would certainly be lower but with a higher social cost in terms of injuries and lack of education.

The government also passes legislation to protect the environment. For example, there are controls on the amount of pollution allowed to enter the atmosphere and the erection of new buildings in restricted planning areas.

3. PROVISION

The government provides many services and products which it believes the market system cannot adequately supply. We have already discussed the necessity for the State to provide public goods such as law enforcement and defence. Earlier we also examined the more controversial area of merit goods where the government provides a health and education system which could be market supplied but which the government believes would be in such cases inadequately or insufficiently provided.

In this country we also have State provision of some goods and services which are produced by state owned organisations and sold to the general public through the market mechanism. This is sometimes referred to as 'public enterprise' and we shall now briefly examine the sector of the state's operation which falls under this heading.

(a) THE SCOPE OF PUBLIC ENTERPRISE

There is considerable debate as to which aspects of the State's activities should be included under the heading 'public enterprise'. The relevant organisations are often referred to as public corporations or nationalised industries but using such titles can also be somewhat misleading.

Even the Government itself has found difficulty in defining what it regards as a nationalised industry. For instance one official definition used in a National Economic Development Office Report (NEDO) in 1976 included under this heading only those public corporations operating in the market economy. It, therefore, omitted public corporations such as the BBC which does not charge for its service but gains revenue from the government who in turn raise it indirectly through the licence fee system. Earlier, in 1968, a House of Commons Select Committee had defined nationalised industries as having three characteristics which set them apart from other aspects of the government's activities.

These were:-

(i)   that the industries were wholly owned by the State or sufficiently owned by the State to be controlled by it;

(ii)   that the industries operated in such a way that the majority of their revenue came from sources other than from direct Parliamentary or Treasury subsidy;

(iii) that they are run by Boards of Directors appointed by the appropriate Minister of State.

By this definition, the major industries included in such a category would be such organisations as British Coal, British Rail, British Gas, the Central Electricity Generating Board and the Post Office.

This is not an exhaustive list and as you will see in chapter 25 on Government Economic Policy some of these industries, either in their entirety or in part, are regarded by a Conservative government as popular candidates for denationalisation. However, it is clear that nationalisation has tended to be concerned in the following areas:

(i)   Energy and water supplies

(ii)   Transport

(iii) Communications

(iv)   Basic heavy industry

There are also a number of other miscellaneous public corporations which do not fall into the definition of a nationalised industry previously cited. Among the most important of these is the Bank of England which reports directly to the Treasury.

The British Broadcasting Corporation, the Independent Broadcasting Authority and the Scottish and Welsh Development Agencies are also government controlled bodies but are financed directly from the central exchequer and so we shall exclude them in our main consideration of the performance of nationalised industries.

(b) THE JUSTIFICATION FOR NATIONALISATION

The arguments in support of nationalisation are many and varied and are matched by a number of arguments against public sector involvement in industry. In considering the scope of public corporations, it is therefore useful to become familiar with some of the arguments both for and against nationalisation.

(c) THE ARGUMENTS FOR NATIONALISATION

(i) Natural monopolies

Some industries may be regarded as natural monopolies or may require vast investment. A duplication of such industries would prove to be a waste of resources. Natural monopolies occur most frequently with the provision of public utilities such as water, gas and electricity. To have two electricity grid systems running parallel throughout the country would obviously be wasteful and so it is most economically efficient to have only one. Furthermore, it is argued that if a monopoly does exist it is better to have it under State control rather than to subject consumers to the possible abuse of monopoly power at the hands of a private industrialist. This reasoning obviously assumes that a government owned organisation will not abuse its position, probably a misplaced assumption!

(ii) National Security

Some industries should be controlled by the State for reasons of defence and national security. An example of this is the United Kingdom Atomic Energy Authority.

(iii) Job Protection

The State may wish to safeguard jobs by supporting industries which would otherwise close if left in private control. Such a decision involves the government making a value judgement that it is better to finance these loss-making industries than to incur the financial and social problems involved in large scale unemployment.

(iv) Consumer interest

As nationalised industries are not operated purely on a profit-making basis, the possibility exists for the interests of the workers in the industry and those of consumers to be put first. For example, people living in a remote village will be able to have telephone facilities which may not be provided by private enterprise, or which otherwise would be prohibitively priced.

(v) Economies of scale

Certain industries can be better managed on a large scale, with the possibility of gains from economies of scale. It is, therefore, in the interests of efficiency to have them nationally co-ordinated.

(vi) State control of the economy

If the State controls important sectors of the economy, such as transport, energy and communications, it will be able to implement its plans for the economy as a whole through its policies for these industries.

(d) THE ARGUMENTS AGAINST NATIONALISATION

(i) Disruption of the free market economy

Nationalisation is perhaps the first step away from the free market economy, with the balance of economic power shifting towards the State. Eventually a situation could be reached where all of the means of production are in the public sector and the State is the sole employer. This increases the monopoly power of the State in the supply of goods and services and also establishes a monopsony (a sole buyer) in the labour market, where the government is the only employer.

(ii) Reduction of competition and efficiency

It is argued that State ownership reduces competition, which in turn will adversely affect efficiency.

(iii) Misallocation of resources

Industries which are no longer economically viable should not be supported if the market for their product is in decline. This will lead to a misallocation of resourses with growth industries being "starved" of capital which they could possibly use to create more secure employment.

(iv) Heavy subsidy

Historically, the nationalised industries have required heavy subsidisation which increases the burden on either the taxpayer, the Public Sector Borrowing Requirement (PSBR) or both.

(v) Private ownership may still exist

A natural monopoly does not necessarily preclude private ownership, as can be witnessed in the USA where industries such as the telecommunications and electricity generation industries are privately owned but publicly regulated.

(vi) Undesirability

A monopoly, no matter who controls it, is undesirable. There is no guarantee that the government will not abuse its economic power by raising the price or limiting supply. The only legally protected monopolies are those in the public sector.

Sometimes government intervention shows a contradictory nature. The government has increasingly intervened in the market to make it more competitive through its competition policy. Yet it has simultaneously made other industries less competitive via its nationalisation programme.

This can all be conveniently covered by the phrase "in the Public Interest" but the term itself is open to wide interpretation by governments and the courts alike, all of whom are influenced to some degree by their own value judgements based on their political stance, moral attitude or social expediency as well as on economic factors. As one judge commented in a case involving the application of principles of public policy to resolve a legal dispute, "Public policy, like other unruly horses, is apt to change its stance . . . "

THE STATE AND ITS INSTITUTIONS

In the earlier part of this chapter we have considered the role of the State as an economic manipulator in its attempts at rectifying deficiencies in the market system. Before we go any further however, we really need to look more closely at what we mean by the State, in order to identify what it consists of and how it works.

WHAT IS 'THE STATE'?

Essentially a State is an organised political community which has a government recognised by the members of the community. A State will obviously have geographical location, with in most cases clearly defined and internationally accepted boundaries. In our case the State is the United Kingdom of Great Britain and Northern Ireland. In its turn the United Kingdom is a member of two major international communities, the Commonwealth, which is primarily a political and cultural association, and the European Economic Community which binds its members both politically and economically.

In order to understand the character of the organised political community we call the United Kingdom it is necessary to examine the institutions of State, for these tell us about the system of government that we have. Politically the State is described as a "Constitutional monarchy'. The Monarch's powers are constitutionally limited. The United Kingdom is also a democracy, for it is governed by the freely elected representatives of its citizens.

THE BRITISH CONSTITUTION

We can say that a Constitution is essentially a collection of principles and rules which define the composition and powers of the institutions of government, and which identify the relationship of these institutions not only as between themselves, but also to the individual citizen.

Two questions emerge. The first is where these fundamental principles and rules are to be found. In some countries such as the United States they are located in a written document, but in the United Kingdom there is no single document of this sort; the constitution is largely unwritten. On a first impression such a situation appears extraordinary; how can the country be governed if there are no rules laid down for doing so? Well in fact there are rules, but as we shall see, they are drawn from many sources, some of them remarkably informal. Our constitution only starts to make sense when it is viewed in the context of the historical development of the nation, and when one recognises the United Kingdom's undoubted political stability. The constitution is the product of many centuries experience of the problems of government, and if the test of its workability is measured by the incidence of constitutional crises we have experienced, then it is clearly a success for such events have been very rare in modern times.

Once having identified the character and content of the constitution the second question is whether there is any practical value to be had from obtaining such information. The answer is clearly an affirmative one; an examination of the constitution of a State provides us with answers to three further questions of fundamental importance, namely who makes the laws which regulate our society, who administers them and who deals with disputes arising out of them?

THE MAIN FEATURES OF THE CONSTITUTION

(i) It is largely unwritten

We have already seen that there is no single document or group of related documents that delineate the Constitution, but we do possess certain limited constitutional documents. One of the earliest is Magna Carta of 1215. More recently our constitutional position was notably altered by entry into the European Economic Community, and this was achieved by means of an Act of Parliament, the European Communities Act 1972. There are many other statutes of a constitutional character, but each of these is limited to a specific aspect, such as the powers of the House of Lords (the Parliament Acts 1911 and 1949) or rights in relation to voting (such as the Ballot Act 1872 which provides for secret ballots, and the Representation of the People Act 1969, which fixes the age of eligibility to vote at 18). In addition to statute the common law, that is law created by the courts, has also contributed to the content of the constitution. For example the courts recognised certain fundamental principles of justice, known as the rules of natural justice, which provide that when a matter is being judicially considered both sides should have an opportunity to be heard, that the proceedings should be conducted impartially and in good faith, and that the decision makers should have no personal interest in the matter before them. Similarly under the principle known as the rule of law the courts treat all citizens as being equal before the law whatever their social and economic status, have the power to overturn arbitrary decision making (especially by government bodies) when called upon to do so, and perhaps most importantly regard themselves as being able to declare the constitutional rights of individuals. These principles concerned with natural justice and the rule of law are, therefore, examples of the constitutional role of the courts, although as we shall see the practice does not always measure up to the theory. But probably the most remakable feature of the constitution is the importance of convention within it. By convention we mean rules which are observed for practical reasons but which are legally not binding. Many examples can be cited. Here are four of them;

(a) Legislation created by Parliament is only effective if the Monarch assents to it, thus the Queen could refuse her assent to, say, a Finance bill. However by convention, the royal assent is not withheld, and such refusal would be unconstitutional.

(b) Parliament must be summoned to meet at least once each year.

(c) The Monarch must invite the leader of the major group in Parliament to form a Ministry — the leader thus becoming the Prime Minister — and must accept those Ministers chosen by the Prime Minister.

(d) The Government's Senior Ministers make up the Cabinet, and are bound by the principle of collective responsibility, so that on major issues a Minister who cannot accept the

Cabinet's policy should resign. This occurred over the Westland Affair in 1986 where the Secretary of State for Defence, Michael Heseltine, found himself in disagreement with his cabinet colleagues.

(e)   If the government is defeated on a motion of No Confidence, the Prime Minister and the other government Ministers should resign.

Although conventions may emerge for different reasons they tend to share one central characteristic, they become established as being practical expedients in the effective organisation and operation of the business of the State. Thus it is a convention that a court is guided by earlier court judgements, and is bound to follow the principles established by them where the facts of the present case are materially the same as those dealt with under the earlier judgements. In this way the resolution of disputes is dealt with in a manner which is both consistent and relatively certain. Without it, judicial decision making would be largely random, and the uncertainty created by it would be damaging to individuals and organisations alike. We all have an interest in complying with legal requirements, if for no other reason than that to act contrary to the law carries financial penalties and even the loss of personal liberty.

(ii) Parliament has sovereign power.

Constitutionally Parliament has law making supremacy. It can make, amend or repeal any law, and with one exception there is no body that is superior to it. The exception is the EEC, which through its law making institutions can legislate for the United Kingdom, without reference to Parliament in Westminster, by the use of regulations. But the Community has no jurisdiction over most domestic matters and in any case if Parliament so chooses it can enact legislation by which the UK could withdraw from the EEC. However politically and economically damaging this might be, it is certainly not unconstitutional.

(iii) The Constitution is entirely flexible

This is because there are no special rules for creating constitutional changes.

THE INSTITUTIONS OF THE STATE

In order to operate an organisation it is necessary to determine the policies and purposes that it is to pursue, implement them, cope with any disagreements arising from the action taken and provide an administrative structure to manage the whole process. The government of the State is performed along similar lines. It has three basic functions. These are:

  (i)   legislative;

  (ii) executive;

  (iii) judicial.

We need to explain each of these functions and examine the institutions of the state which perform each role.

The functions to be satisfied are legislative (making the law), executive (implementing the law) and judicial (dealing with any dispute arising from the first two). Before any of their functions can come into play policy decisions must be made which become the substance of the legislative programme.

To peform these functions we have Parliament. This is the legislature responsible for enacting Statutes or Acts of Parliament as they are usually known. We next have the Government and the Civil Service which perform the triple role of policy decision making, statutory implementation and the administration of the apparatus of the State at a central level. Finally the judiciary made up by the judges in the courts dealing with public and private disputes. The traditional view is that for the state to operate democratically each function should be performed by separate organisations or individuals, to avoid any conflict of interest and role ambiguity. However in practice this 'separation of powers' does not occur. There is considerable overlap between the legislature and the executive, although the judiciary is certainly independent of both. The overlap occurs as a result of the political system operated in Britain, and it can be relatively simply explained.

THE POLITICAL SYSTEM IN BRITAIN

Constitutionally there must be a general election held at least once every five years. The purpose of this election is to enable the registered electors in each constituency to send their chosen representative to Parliament as an M.P. The United Kingdom is divided geographically into 650 constituencies, each having roughly the same number of electors although in some cases there is considerable population variation. Each M.P. is elected on a "first past the post" basis, so the candidate with the largest number of votes becomes the constituency M.P. The majority of candidates have an allegiance to one of the political parties, and it is normally on party lines rather than on the basis of personality that electors cast their votes. Prior to the election each party produces a manifesto which outlines the policies it intends to carry out if elected. The manifesto, election broadcasts and debates, general discussions, peoples' own personal convictions and social and cultural allegiances all go to determining how they will vote. There is however no legal obligation to vote. When the election process is completed the leader of the party which commands the majority of seats in Parliament (i.e. M.Ps of their party) is asked by the Monarch to form a Ministry, in other words organise the Government. This will involve choosing individuals to take responsibility for the various central government departments. These individuals will usually be M.Ps, members of the House of Commons (the lower house or chamber), although there is nothing to prevent the appointment of peers from the House of Lords (the upper chamber). For example, during Mrs. Thatcher's ministry, Lord Young has been a Secretary of State for Employment. Senior Ministers make up the Cabinet which forms the nucleus of the Government. Every Minister, or Secretary of State to use the title generally given today, is therefore a member of the legislature in his or her capacity as an M.P., and a member of the executive as head of a government department, a clear example of separate functions placed in the same hands.

THE LEGISLATURE

The legislature, Parliament, sits at Westminster. As we have seen it consists of a lower house, the Commons, in which M.Ps sit and the upper house, the Lords, which has a non elected membership that includes hereditary and life peers, law Lords and the Archbishop and Bishops of the Church of England. The primary responsibilities of Parliament are the enactment of legislation, which amongst other things involves the task of granting consent to the spending of public revenue, and the guardianship of the interests of the nation, which involves attempting to control the activities of the government when they are believed to conflict with the national interest. The control mechanism relies upon the accountability of Ministers to Parliament. They can be called upon to provide public answers during question time and during debates on proposed legislation. Furthermore they can be summoned to appear before Parliamentary Select Committees for more detailed and rigorous questioning. Undoubtably the broadcasting on radio of Parliamentary proceedings has increased the public awareness of the role of the legislature. Nowadays when the Government faces a severe test during Prime Minister's question time the occasion is built up into a significant media event. The general concept of accountability is considered in chapter 18.

What is legislation?

Technically, legislation is defined as the formulation of law by the Queen in Parliament, thus the Monarch and both Houses are involved in creating it. We have seen that the Monarch's role is limited to the granting of assent which is a formality; the real legislative power lies with the two Houses of Parliament of whom the House of Commons is constitutionally the most powerful. During this century two Acts, the Parliament Acts of 1911 and 1949 have reduced the power of the House of Lords. The 1911 Act provides that a money Bill (eg the Finance Bill) must be passed through the Lords without amendment, within one month following its passage through the Commons, whilst under the 1949 provisions the Lords are unable to 'block' any public Bill which has passed the Commons in two successive sessions. A Bill is the name given to legislation whilst it proceeds through the various stages which culminate in it becoming an Act after the Royal Assent is given.

A classification of Bills is contained in the figure below.

The Classification of Parliamentary Bills

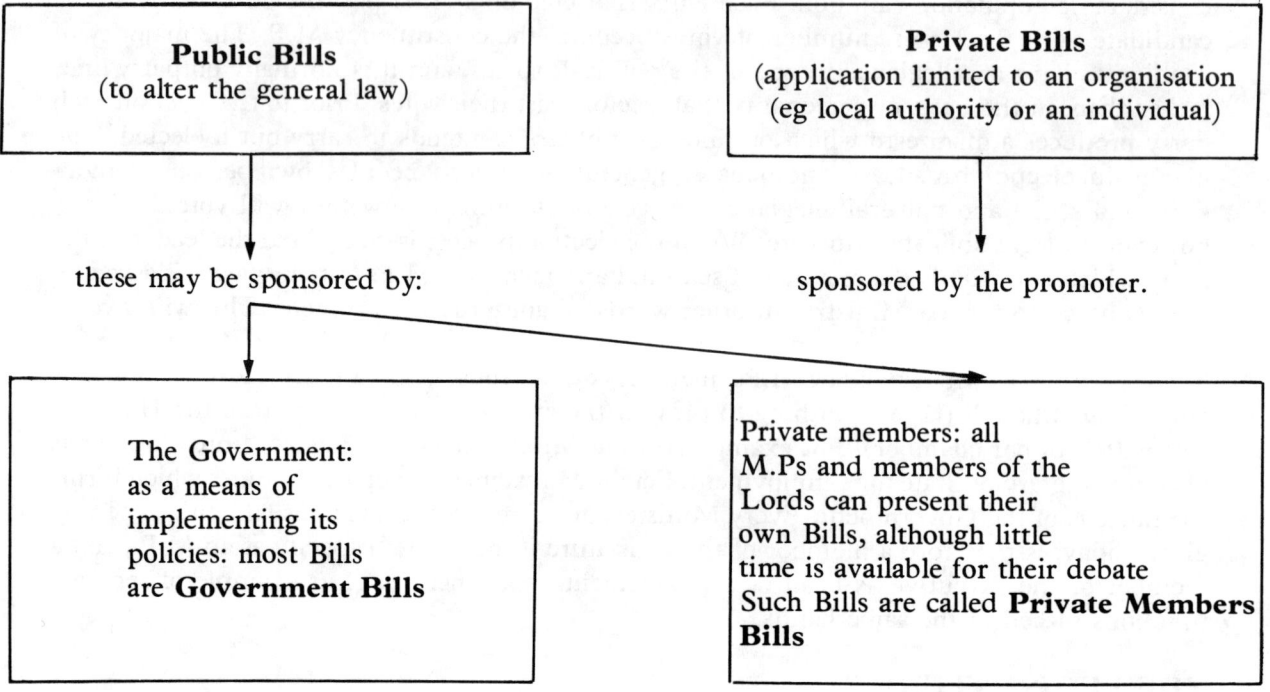

Something in the region of sixty or seventy Bills become law annually. Creating legislation is the most obvious way in which governments are able to implement their policies, whether they be fiscal, economic or social. The method of creating public legislation is described in the following figure.

Before the bill is presented to Parliament many events may have occured leading to its drafting. One possibility is given below.

The stages leading to the Proposal of Legislation

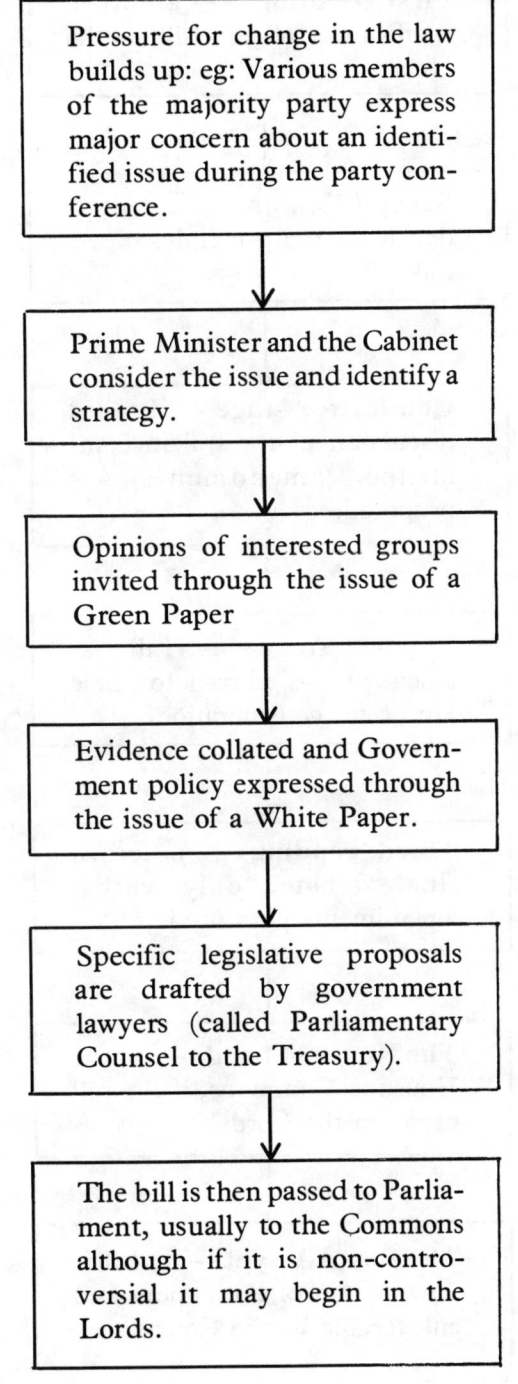

Pressure for change in the law builds up: eg: Various members of the majority party express major concern about an identified issue during the party conference.

Prime Minister and the Cabinet consider the issue and identify a strategy.

Opinions of interested groups invited through the issue of a Green Paper

Evidence collated and Government policy expressed through the issue of a White Paper.

Specific legislative proposals are drafted by government lawyers (called Parliamentary Counsel to the Treasury).

The bill is then passed to Parliament, usually to the Commons although if it is non-controversial it may begin in the Lords.

The Passage of Legislation

The procedure followed in both Houses is the same where public bills are being considered.

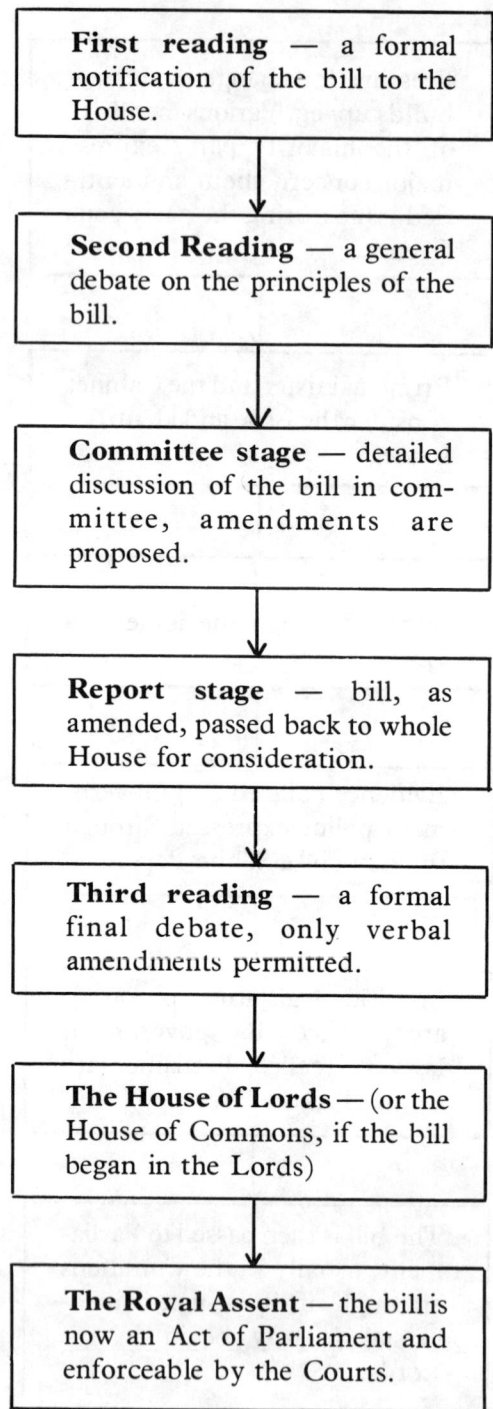

First reading — a formal notification of the bill to the House.

Second Reading — a general debate on the principles of the bill.

Committee stage — detailed discussion of the bill in committee, amendments are proposed.

Report stage — bill, as amended, passed back to whole House for consideration.

Third reading — a formal final debate, only verbal amendments permitted.

The House of Lords — (or the House of Commons, if the bill began in the Lords)

The Royal Assent — the bill is now an Act of Parliament and enforceable by the Courts.

Delegated or Subordinate legislation

It is not possible for Parliament to cope with all the legislative demands placed upon it. For one thing it lacks time due to the slow procedures; for another it does not always possess the technical expertise necessary to create detailed rules in specialised fields of knowledge. A further difficulty lies in anticipating, in the legislation being enacted today, what might develop in the future.

Parliament overcomes these inadequacies by delegating law making power to subordinates. These include organisations — local authorities are a prime example — as well as individuals, especially Ministers. Thus much of our statute law merely lays down general principles, while specifically granting the power to a Minister, in liaison with his or her department, to "finish the job" by legislatively filling in the details. Without such a system effective government could not be carried out in a country as complex as ours, but this does not mean that this method of legislating escapes criticism. Constitutionally the role of Parliament is weakened, as the executive obtains a law making capacity for itself; delegated legislation does not attract publicity sometimes the subordinate can legislate on matters principle. These criticisms are dealt with by control mechanisms which help us maintain a proper balance between effective government on the one hand and accountability on the other. The courts can be resorted to where it is believed that the delegated powers have been exceeded and, if this is established, the action taken by the subordinate will be declared ultra vires (beyond the powers) and void. Additionally Parliament has its own 'Scrutiny Committee' which examines statutory instruments (one form of delegated legislation) in order to report to Parliament on any matter requiring special attention such as lack of clarity in the instrument.

THE EXECUTIVE

During the twentieth century governments have taken upon themselves greater and greater responsibilities. A clear example can be seen in the development of the welfare state, which emerged at the end of the Second World War as a major product of social thinking, in which the State would care for its citizens from "the cradle to the grave". With a growth in responsibility has come an increase in the size of government, and an expansion of the role of the executive. Some 700,000 people are employed in this sector. The executive is made up of the Central government and the Central administration. The executive consists of the Privy Council, the Government of the day, the government departments and certain other government agencies.

THE PRIVY COUNCIL

The main responsibility of this powerful body is the issue of orders in Council, a form of delegated legislation. Its membership includes the Monarch and members of the Cabinet.

THE GOVERNMENT OF THE DAY

This is led by the Prime Minister. It includes the members of the Cabinet, most of whom head government departments, as well as other holders of government office including Junior Ministers, Parliamentary secretaries and under-secretaries. The heart of the Government is the Cabinet, and the Prime Minister has effective control over the Cabinet not only through chairing its meetings but also through the power to select and dismiss its members, subject of course to suitably talented replacements being available and such actions being acceptable within the party. The Prime Minister is therefore at the centre of British government.

GOVERNMENT DEPARTMENTS

Together the departments comprise the Central Administration — "Whitehall" as it is often known. The political head of each department is the Minister. He or she is assisted by a permanent staff of officials headed by a permanent secretary. These government employees are referred to as Civil Servants.

The most powerful of all the departments is the Treasury, for it is responsible for government spending and hence the budgets of all other Departments, whilst overseeing the general economic performance of the nation as a whole.

GOVERNMENT AGENCIES

As we saw earlier in the chapter the State itself provides certain types of goods and services. To briefly recap these are merit goods such as the health service and education, public goods such as the police force and the public enterprise sector which provides a national railway system, runs the coal industry and operates the national airline, to mention just a few of its diverse activities.

Different forms of organisations are used to provide and administer these goods and services, often at a local level. Thus education is provided by those local authorities having an education function. Others, like the various police forces, have their own organisations but are subject to local control, in the case of the police through local authority police committees, although ultimate responsibility lies with the relevant Ministers. In the case of the police this is the Home Secretary.

As regards the nationalised industries the legislation establishing State ownership of the industry also creates the organisation responsible for operating it.

Public sector goods and services that do not fall under the administration of local authorities are operated through government agencies such as British Coal, the Post Office and the MSC. Clearly these are not government departments such as the Departments of Health and Transport but they are ultimately subject to government control via supervision through the appropriate Ministers. The financing of the operation of government is examined in detail in chapter 12.

LOCAL GOVERNMENT

Whilst central government is responsible for policy making and implementation on a national basis, it is not possible nor desirable that politicians and adminstrators in London be responsible for providing local services, and thus a system of local government has evolved which fulfils this role at a local level. The present system of local government consists of local authorities on three tiers. Each tier carries out specific functions. County Councils for example are responsible for education and highways, whilst district councils deal with housing and social services. Parish Councils are responsible for granting allotments and the upkeep of village greens.

Local authorities are statutory corporations. The London boroughs were established under the London Government Act 1963, with all other authorities being created by the Local Government Act 1972. Legislation identifies the functions and powers of the local authorities, and determines the electoral arrangements under which councillors are elected by their local electorate as political representatives, in much the same way as M.Ps are elected. Local authorities have the limited power to create their own laws in the form of by-laws, which are an example of a form of delegated legislation.

Local authorities enjoy a considerable degree of autonomy, however since much of an authority's budget is met from central government funds there has always been a measure of central control, and in recent years the government's attempts at reducing public expenditure have led to central government in the form of the Secretary of State for the Environment asserting fiscal control over those authorities regarded as high spenders through 'rate capping'.

Furthermore the Metropolitan Counties, first created in 1974, were abolished in 1986 as a means of attempting to further reduce public spending on a local level, with the functions of these authorities being passed to district councils and to joint boards. The financing of local authorities is discussed in detail in chapter 12.

THE JUDICIARY

One of the most striking features of our constitution is the role of the judiciary in the person of judges. Whilst there is an overlap between the legislature and the executive, the judiciary remains independent of both, and this is regarded as a major constitutional safeguard. No one would feel confident in the impartiality of a judge in a trial involving a citizen's challenge to the legality of the actions of a Sectretary of State if the judge had been appointed by the Government, perhaps because of long standing public support given by the judge to the government's party. The independence of the judiciary is achieved in a number of ways.

(a)   It is a convention that judges do not express themselves politically. Likewise the judgements they issue are not matters on which Parliament or members of the executive should comment, although it is not unknown for this convention to be disregarded.

(b)   Judges are prevented by statute from becoming M.Ps. Senior judges who are appointed as peers can however sit in the House of Lords.

(c)   They enjoy immunity at common law from civil proceedings in respect of their judicial work. Thus no action could be brought against the trial judge by a convicted person aggrieved that his liberty has been taken away from him, even if the trial judge had mis-directed the jury. According to Lord Denning the justification for such immunity, "is not because the judge has any privilege to make mistakes or to do wrong, it is so he should be able to do his duty with complete independence and free from fear." (Sirros v. Moore 1975)

(d)   Finally, and probably most significantly of all, judges hold office during their good behaviour. This is provided under the Act of Settlement 1701. It means that a judge cannot be removed from office for giving a judgement which offends the Government, and thus judicial decision making even in matters that are politically sensitive, can be carried out without fear of political pressure or interference.

CONFLICT RESOLUTION

In any human society, whether a complex industrialised state like our own or a simple agrarian community such as are found in some third world countries, certain rules of conduct are necessary if the community is to co-exist in reasonable harmony. Some of these rules are purely social, but others are more formalised becoming rules of law, enforceable before the courts.

THE CIVIL COURTS

The court system in England and Wales is organised in a hierarchy. Minor disputes are dealt with by the courts at the lowest level of the hierarchy whereas more serious matters are dealt with in higher courts. In civil matters the seriousness of the dispute is generally related to the sum of money involved, the amount claimed in damages, or the value of property involved, and the jurisdiction of the courts is determined accordingly.

The County Court

The majority of civil disputes are dealt with by the county courts. Their main function is to act as local courts dealing with civil disputes relating to small claims. At present the country is divided into districts which are arranged into fifty-four circuits. Each circuit has one or more circuit judges assigned to it and the number of courts throughout England and Wales is in excess of four-hundred. Circuit judges are a creation of the Courts Act 1971 and are appointed from barristers of at least ten years standing. The administrative work of the county courts is carried on by a Registrar who is a civil servant and must be a solicitor of seven years standing. Registrars also have jurisdiction to try cases where the amount claimed is less that £500. The majority of civil disputes which lead to court action are now heard in the county courts as their jurisdiction has been extended to cover such matters as cases in contract and tort up to a limit of £5,000, housing and landlord and tenant disputes, hire purchase, undefended divorces, some employment disputes, bankruptcy and the winding up of small companies. The most important matters they deal with are:-

1. Actions in contract and tort where the sum claimed does not exceed £5,000 (no limit if both parties agree);

2. Matters which are equitable in nature and where the amount involved does not exceed £30,000, e.g. trusts, mortgages and dissolution of partnerships;

3. Petitions in relation to bankruptcy and the winding up of companies with a paid up share capital not exceeding £120,000 (limited to certain county courts outside London);

4. Under the Matrimonial Causes Act 1967 every matrimonial cause, e.g. divorce, nullity of marriage, must be commenced in the county courts and if not contested, heard there. Otherwise it must be transferred to the High Court;

5. Actions arising from disputes regarding the grant of probate or letters of administration where the estate of the deceased is less than £15,000;

6. Actions concerning title to land and actions for the recovery of possession of land where the net annual value for rating does not exceed £2,000.

The jurisdiction of county courts is also limited to their locality so that actions must normally be commenced in the court for the district in which the defendant resides or carries on business, or in the court for the district in which the cause of action arises. The importance of the county court can be seen by the fact that there are over three times as many proceedings commenced in the county court than in all the divisions of the High Court, which deals with all other civil disputes. It should be stressed however, that only a small percentage of the numerous county court cases that are begun ever go to full trial. This is often because when proceedings are actually commenced against individuals or organisations involving repayment of a debt, they simply fulfil the obligation.

In considering county courts, some mention should also be made of the small claims arbitration procedure introduced by the Administration of Justice Act 1973. As previously stated where one party to an action is claiming a sum of less than £500, the case is automatically referred to arbitration by the court registrar. Usually the arbitrator will be the Registrar himself and he will hear the case in private and decide the dispute on the basis of statements and documents submitted by the parties without the need for legal representation. This procedure, with the minimal cost attached to it, has proved of great value to the individual, particularly in consumer and landlord and tenant disputes.

The High Court

The High Court of Justice was created by the Judicature Acts 1873-5 and is based at the Royal Courts of Justice in London but may sit anywhere in England and Wales. It has a wide jurisdiction over civil disputes and, as a matter of convenience, is split into three divisions which are the Queen's Bench, Chancery and Family. Judges of the High Court are called puisne (younger) judges, and they are allocated to each division by the head of the English Legal System, the Lord Chancellor.

The Queen's Bench Division

This is the largest and most important division of the High Court and has jurisdiction over any civil matters not specifically allocated to the other divisions. In particular, the Queen's Bench hears contract and tort cases and has a separate Commercial court and Admiralty court within the division. The head of the division is the Lord Chief Justice and Queen's Bench judges also sit in Crown Courts where they hear criminal and civil cases. The court also hears appeals on matters of law from the Magistrates court and for this purpose the judges sit as Divisional courts. The Queen's bench has supervisory control over all inferior courts and tribunals and acts as a check on the abuse of power. The decisions of a public body therefore such as a local authority may in some circumstances be the subject of application for judicial review e.g. the abuse of statutory power.

The Chancery Division.

The division is in practice headed by the Vice Chancellor and is the smallest of the three. Its jurisdiction is related to specialist matters including company and partnership law, bankruptcy, mortgages, taxation, land and probate (disputes over wills).

The Family Division.

The Family division is the most recently established part of the High Court created by the Administration of Justice Act 1970 and is headed by the President. As its name suggests, the court is concerned with civil disputes relating to family law including divorce, nullity, legitimacy, wardship and marriage property disputes. Matrimonial jurisdiction is therefore shared between the High Court, County Court and Magistrates and this has led to calls for the creation of a unified family court which would standardise the legal approach and also integrate the social services involved.

THE CIVIL APPEALS COURTS

The majority of cases that are referred to in this book are decisions which have involved important points of law and have in some cases created precedents. In the main, these have been cases which have gone on appeal to the Court of Appeal or the House of Lords.

The Court of Appeal (Civil Division)

This court is headed by the Master of the Rolls and sixteen Lords Justices of Appeal. As an individual appeal court three judges preside, hearing appeals involving questions of fact and/or law. In practice, the evidence is not reheard but rather reliance is placed on the record of the previous trial. The majority of appeals comes from the High Court, county courts and the Restrictive Practices Court. The court has power to reverse, affirm or amend the previous decision and in some cases order a retrial.

The House of Lords (Judicial Committee)

As an appeal court (rather than a legislative body), the House of Lords is composed of the Lord Chancellor, who is head of the English legal system and a member of the government of the day and also the Lords of Appeal in Ordinary (Law Lords). It is the highest court of appeal for England, Wales, Scotland and Northern Ireland in civil disputes, and similarly in criminal cases (except for Scotland). Usually, five judges will form a court and the relatively small number of cases which go to it come mainly from the Court of Appeal. In cases involving a point of law of general public importance, an appeal may go direct to the House of Lords from the High Court. This is known as the "leap-frog" procedure and it was introduced by the Administration of Justice Act 1969.

CRIMINAL DISPUTES

The machinery that exists to deal with individuals or organisations that infringe the criminal law is the system of criminal courts. In addition to the many traditional criminal offences such as murder, theft, manslaughter, etc. there are thousands of statutory offences which are regulatory and are often of strict liability.

The Magistrates Court

Although it is the lowest of the criminal courts it nevertheless deals with the majority of criminal cases and indeed all criminal trials will start in the Magistrates Court. Judges in the majority of Magistrates Courts are laymen who have no legal training. They are Lay Magistrates, also known as Justices of the Peace. They have few formal qualifications except that they must be over 21 and under 60 and reside within 15 miles of the area in which they propose to act. Those appointed must be of good character but need no knowledge of the law and will normally have rendered good service to the community. While they are recommended for appointment by local advisory committees which interviews and assesses candidates, the final decision of appointment rests with the Lord Chancellor. An alternative to a bench of lay magistrates is the stipendiary, a professional laywer who is salaried and works as a full-time magistrate. They are now only appointed where there is a shortage of lay magistrates, usually in the larger cities.

In a criminal trial the role of the Magistrates is to determine guilt or innocence and if appropriate to pass sentence. As far as matters of law and procedure are concerned lay magistrates rely on the advice of the Clerk to the Court who is usually a barrister or a solicitor. The court's jurisdiction extends to dealing with summary offences (less serious offences), however Magistrates may also try more serious crimes known as hybrid offences for example, theft, if the prosecution and accused agree. Otherwise hybrid offences are triable in the Crown Court. As far as imposing sentences is concerned, the Magistrates are restricted to a fine of up to £1,000 and/or six months imprisonment. Alternatively they may commit the accused for sentence to the Crown Court.

Under s.35(1) of the Powers of the Criminal Courts Act 1973 the courts can made a compensation order in respect of personal injury loss or damage resulting from an offence. It seems however that compensation is only available in simple and straight forward cases where the amount can be readily ascertained. If substantial amounts are in question the matter should be left to the civil courts. Also the means of the defendant are to be taken into account in deciding whether an order is made. If a fine and compensation order are appropriate however, and the defendant's means are limited, then preference is to be given to the compensation order. Such an order is attractive to a victim who is unable or reluctant to institute proceedings. An alternative means by which the victim of a crime can recover compensation is the Criminal Injuries Compensation Scheme 1964 (as revised in 1979). Under this scheme the Criminal Injuries Compensation Board has the duty to distribute ex gratia payments to those who have sustained personal injury directly attributable to a crime of violence.

In addition to trying cases and sentencing, it is the role of Justices of the Peace to act as Examining Magistrates determining whether there is sufficient evidence against the accused for there to be a case to answer in an indictable offence. This is called a committal proceeding and if the Examinng Magistrates decided that a 'prime facie' case has been established, they must commit the accused for trial to the Crown Court and also decide whether he should be remanded in custody awaiting trial or allowed bail.

Finally, some mention should be made of the civil jurisdiction of Magistrates. This extends to hearing licensing applications, enforcing demands for rates and hearing domestic proceedings. The family jurisdiction extends to maintenance orders in favour of either spouse or children, exclusion of either spouse from the matrimonial home, custody and access orders, adoption orders and affiliation orders.

The Crown Court

Crown Courts were introduced by the Courts Act 1971 as a replacement for the ancient Assize and Quarter Sessions. They are situated in all major towns and cities in England and Wales and are responsible for trying all serious criminal cases known as indictable offences. For this purpose, the offences dealt with are classified into four groups ranging from the very serious (e.g. murders or treason) to the less serious (e.g. hybrid offences such as theft). There are also three types of judge who will preside over a Crown Court ranking in order of importance and the offences they deal with will reflect this. The hierarchy is from High Court judges then to Circuit judges and then to Recorders (barristers or solicitors of at least ten years standing who sit as part time judges). The role of the judge is to determine questions of law and evidence and generally to ensure a fair trial. It is the jury however, who will decide the guilt or innocence of the accused and if he is found guilty, the judge will fix the sentence. Juries are selected at random from the electors of the particular area. The Central Criminal Court (the Old Bailey) is the Crown Court with jurisdiction over the London area.

Criminal Appeal Courts.

We have already mentioned that the Queen's Bench Division of the High Court fulfils the role of criminal appeal court when appeals are made on questions of law from the Magistrates Court. The Crown Court also sits as an appeal court when appeals are made on questions of fact from the Magistrates court. Appeals in serious cases tried in the Crown Court however, are made to the Court of Appeal (criminal division) and in rare cases may go further to the House of Lords.

Courts of Appeal (Criminal Division).

For the purpose of hearing criminal appeals, the court is presided over by Lord Justices of Appeal and puisne judges of the Queen's Bench Division, three of whom will constitute a court. Appeals may be made as of right if a question of law is involved, such as the interpretation of the wording of an offence, but only with leave, (permission of the court or a High Court judge), if it is made on a question of fact such as insufficient evidence to convict. The court may allow the appeal and quash the conviction, substitute a conviction for a lessor offence, alter the sentence but not increase it, or in some cases order a re-trial.

The House of Lords

In rare cases, appeal may be made to the House of Lords from the Court of Appeal or also from a Divisional court of the Queen's Bench Division. Appeals are only heard where the court below certifies that a point of law of general public importance is involved and either the court below or the House of Lords grants leave to appeal.

ADMINISTRATIVE DISPUTES

Since the Second World War, ther has been a dramatic increase in the exercise of government functions involving an increase in social legislation (pensions, industrial injuries, sickness and unemployment benefits), an increase in powers to acquire land by compulsory purchase and increasing intervention in the private housing rented sector or by establishing a system whereby rent of dwellings may be controlled. In addition, there is a growing amount of statute law in relation to employment, covering such matters as redundancy, unfair dismissal, equal pay, sex and race discrimination. To resolve disputes arising in these areas machinery has been set up in the form of administrative tribunals. Tribunals are thought to be better equipped to deal with administrative disputes rather than the overloaded courts because they will include a specialist expert in the area concerned to help resolve the dispute, they are speedier and less costly than the ordinary courts, and they have wide discretionary powers which are necessary to enable them to resolve administrative disputes.

Administrative Tribunals

Administrative tribunals are set up by statutes which will also define the extent of their power. Different tribunals have been created to deal with the various types of administrative disputes. Social Security Tribunals hear disputes arising from individual claims for welfare benefits, e.g. supplementary benefit. For this purpose, the tribunal will consist of a chairman appointed by the Secretary of State and one representative of employers and one of employees. Similar local tribunals have been set up to deal with disputes arising from claims for industrial injuries benefit. The Lands Tribunal is a highly professional body whose main function is to decide questions surrounding the value of land particularly when land has been compulsorily acquired. Rent Tribunals are bodies which are created under the Rent Acts to determine the rents of certain types of private rented accommodation and also grant limited security of tenure to a tenant. Under the 1980 Act the functions of Rent Tribunals have been transferred to Rent Assessment Committees but when dealing with a Rent Tribunal function, the Housing Act 1980 provides that they are to be known as Rent Tribunals.

Special Tribunals

Certain bodies are categorised as special tribunals including Industrial Tribunals and Domestic

Tribunals. Both bodies have distinct and separate functions. Industrial Tribunals are bodies created under employment legislation and are not concerned with administrative matters but rather disputes relating to employment, such as unfair dismissal, redundancy, discrimination and health and safety. The Tribunal is constituted by three members, a legally qualified chairman and two lay members appointed after consultation with employers and trade unions. Decisions are taken by a majority, each member having an equal vote. An industrial tribunal sits as an 'industrial jury' and is the final arbiter on questions of fact. Appeal lies to the Employment Appeals Tribunal composed of a High Court judge sitting with two lay members. Domestic tribunals are simply disciplinary committees of particular professions, for instance doctors, lawyers or dentists, with power to discipline members of the various professions for professional misconduct.

Administrative Enquiries

Some areas of administrative action by government or local authorities, in particular housing and planning, provide no appeal route to tribunals from the process of decision making. Rather, provision is made under statute for an aggrieved individual to argue his case at a public local enquiry. The majority of such enquiries arise out of the compulsory acquisition of land by housing authorities. They are conducted before a Minister's inspector who, after hearing the evidence, will report to the Minister concerned. The final decision is made by the Minister himself.

Following a great deal of criticism of the workings of Tribunals in the late 1950's, the Franks Committee was given the task of inquiring into the criticism and, following its recommendations, the Tribunals and Inquiries Act 1958 was passed. Most of the law is now embodied in the Tribunals and Inquiries Act 1971. This statute provided for the setting up of a review body, the Council on Tribunals, which is given the task of reviewing the working of tribunals and reporting annually to Parliament. In addition, it is now a requirement that in most cases, if the parties request it, reasons for decisions must be given. This provision, of course, enables an individual who is aggrieved at a decision to more easily challenge it in the ordinary courts. The ordinary courts have power to supervise the decision making of Tribunals and administrators generally.

ARBITRATION

It is becoming an increasing practice for the parties to a transaction to provide by the terms of their contract that any dispute relating to the transaction should be referred to an independent arbitrator rather than the ordinary courts. This practice has obvious advantages of speed, less cost, and no publicity and also enables the dispute to be resolved by specialists skilled in the area of the dispute. An arbitrator may be specifically named in the contract or alternatively the machinery by which he may be appointed may be set out. Arbitration clauses are usually found in standard form contracts. Alternatively they may be expressly inserted into a contract voluntarily by agreement between the parties. In some cases the parties have no choice but to submit a dispute to arbitration. The law relating to arbitration agreements is contained in the common law and the Arbitration Act 1950 as amended by the Arbitration Act 1979. To be legally valid they must be in writing and stamped in accordance with the Stamp Act 1891. They are also subject to the courts supervision in relation to the conduct of the arbitration. If a dispute arises it is the duty of the appointed arbitrator to fix a hearing which he will do after defining the dispute. The procedure adopted is usually similar to a civil trial but it is held in private. The rules of evidence and incidentally the rules of natural justice, considered later in this chapter, are applicable to the hearing and difficult points of law may be referred to the High Court for determination. After hearing the evidence the arbitrator will make an award and also decide how the costs are to be paid. The Arbitration Act 1979 confers a right of appeal to the High Court on a question of law arising from the award and the court may vary, confirm or set aside the award.

THE EUROPEAN ECONOMIC COMMUNITY

This organisation, variously referred to as the European Community, the EEC and the Common Market, was created in 1957, under the Treaty of Rome. It originally had six members, France, West Germany, Italy, Holland, Belgium and Luxembourg. The United Kingdom, Eire and Denmark joined in 1973, Greece in 1981, and Spain and Portugal in 1986.

There are in fact three separate Communities; the European Economic Community; the European Coal and Steel Community; and the European Energy Community.

The United Kingdom's membership followed the passing of the European Communities Act 1972, by Parliament in Westminster. A subsequent national referendum, the only such referendum held so far in this Country, voted in favour of the UK's continued membership of the EEC. If the UK were to decide to withdraw at some time in the future this could be achieved by the same constitutional means by which it joined, namely an act of Parliament. Such a move, however, seems unlikely in the foreseeable future, since there is a general political support for continued membership. This is despite the adverse publicity attracted to the Community resulting from the food surpluses that have built up throughout the operation of the Common Agricultural Policy (CAP), a scheme under which farmers of the Community have been encouraged to increase their yield by the payment of EEC subsidies and the establishment of minimum prices. As a result "butter mountains" and "wine lakes" have developed, stockpiles that cannot be released because the market price would fall and the farmers' guaranteed prices could not be maintained.

THE AIMS AND OBJECTIVES OF THE EEC

As suggested by its title, the EEC has economic aims and objectives. These include: the creation of a single market within the member states that is available to all manufacturers and producers belonging to these states and which is free from tariff barriers; the maintenance of competitive practices within this free market; the standardisation of regulations governing the production and distribution of the goods; and the use of eurocurrency as a common form of currency. The aim of removing customs controls to enable the free movement of EEC nationals between the member states can be seen as having social as well as economic implications.

The EEC also has its long term political objective, political union between the members. Clearly, as for each of the member states, the economic and political objectives of the Community are closely related.

THE INSTITUTIONS OF THE EEC

The management of an international economic and political organisation geographically encompassing the major part of western Europe, and serving the needs of over two hundred million people from differing cultural backgrounds and varying stages of economic development, involves a variety of institutions, representing each of the three functions of government:

      (a)   the legislature: the Council of Ministers and the European Parliament;

      (b)   the executive: the Commission; and

      (c)   the judiciary: the European Court of Justice.

(a) THE LEGISLATURE

The European Parliament, quite unlike our own Parliament in Westminster, has limited law making powers. The real power lies in the hands of the Council of Ministers, but before considering the relationship between these two bodies, it is useful to look at the operation of the European Parliament in some detail.

The European Parliament

The Parliament sits for a period of five years, and the United Kingdom is divided into constituencies which elect and return "Euro M.P's" to represent them. The number of seats available is dependant upon the population of each member state. The first elections were held in 1979 and different electoral systems are used for electing representatives. In the UK the "first past the post" system is used.

Elected members sit together in political groups rather than by national grouping. There are six official political groups to which members can belong: Communists and Allies; Socialists; Christian Democrats; European Progressive Democrats; and Liberals and Democrats.

The headquarters of the Parliament is in Luxemburg, although some of its work is performed in Strasbourg and in Brussels. Most of its legislative work is performed by committees, and the largest political group is able to exert its influence by choosing the chairperson for these committees, and through being the largest single voting block in the Parliament. The work of the Committees reflects the various responsibilities of the Community generally. They range from the committees for Political Affairs, Legal Affairs and Economic and Monetary Affairs, to Regional Policy, Planning and Transport, Social Affairs, Employment and Education and Development and Co-operation. There is also, of course, a Budget Committee.

As under our own Parliamentary system individual members can raise publicly before the European Parliament matters raised by their own constituents, as well as issues of general European interest. Discussion is by means of public debate.

The Powers of the Parliament

These are closely controlled, however it can:

(i)   dismiss the commissioners who control the Commission (i.e. the executive arm of the Community, which is considered below). To do so however a censure motion must be passed by a $2/3$ majority.

(ii)   exercise certain powers in respect of the Community's budget, having a final say regarding some items of expenditure, and having the ultimate power to reject the entire budget, a power it has used. In such circumstances a conciliation procedure operates between the Parliament and the Council of Ministers. The passing of revenue for the budget depends upon each member state contributing its agreed contribution to EEC funds.
Wealthier member States contribute more than the poorer ones. The overall effect this will have on an individual member state can be that it contributes far more than it receives in grants and subsidies. Mrs Thatcher caused considerable political controversy over the United Kingdom's contribution to the budget when she sought to reduce the amount the United Kingdom was obliged to provide, on the grounds that it imposed an unequitable burden on the UK as a substantial net contributor.

(iii)   present its views on proposals submitted by the Commission to the Council of Ministers. The Parliament and the Commission work closely together on legislative proposals. It should be pointed out that although the Commission is an administrative body, the Commissioners can and do present policy proposals to both the Parliament and the Council of Ministers.

The Council of Ministers

It is this body which wields ultimate power within the Community. Each member state is represented by a single Minister, and the composition of the Council varies according to the issue being considered. Thus over a transport issue the membership will comprise the Transport Ministers from the government of each member state, and over agricultural matters, the

Agricultural Ministers. The most powerful member states have more votes than the others, thus the UK, France, West Germany and Italy have ten each. This weighting of votes is valuable in respect of the less important business of the Council, but on major matters, such as agricultural policy, a unanimous vote is required. As might be expected the Council of Ministers has not worked in notable harmony over the years, with individual Ministers seeking to protect their own national interests at the expense of broader European interests.

The Council can make major policy statements to Parliament, for debate there. Its strength lies in the fact that it has the final say over Community legislation.

(b) THE EXECUTIVE

The European Commission, based in Brussels, is the civil service for the EEC. The Commission operates under the direction of the Commissioners, each member state being represented by at least one commissioner. Some countries, including the UK, have two. The commissioners can present policy proposals to the legislative bodies of the Community, however their main responsibility is the control of the enormous bureaucracy, numbering many thousands of staff, who administer the policies of the Community. Like the Council of Ministers, the Commission has as its head a President. It is said of the Commission that it acts as a counter-balance to the Council of Ministers, taking a European view rather than a national one.

(c) THE JUDICIARY

The European Court of Justice

This court, which has eleven judges, sits in Luxemburg. The work of the judges is assisted by three Advocates-General, whose function is to present before the court impartial arguments on matters which are at issue. Unlike an English court, the function of the European court involves the discovery of facts using its own initiative, as well as reaching decisions through issuing judgments.

The jurisdiction of the court is wide. It can:

(i) hear actions brought against a member state by either the Commission (which enforces Community law) or another member state alleging non-compliance with Treaty obligations;

(ii) hear actions brought against the Institutions of the Community by member states, organisations and individuals; and

(iii) give a ruling on the interpretation of any of the Treaties. Such a ruling, which is a preliminary one, will follow a request to the court from a court or tribunal of one of the member states. After the ruling has been given it is left to the court or tribunal in question to apply the ruling to the facts of the case before it.

Under Article 177 of the Treaty of Rome the preliminary ruling of the European Court must be sought where a court in a member state from which there is no right of appeal is hearing a case which turns upon the meaning of one of the treaties.

Enforcement of the decisions of the court is satisfied through the enforcement systems of the courts and tribunals of the member states.

The Community Law

Community law is embodied in the treaties establishing it. The treaties confer law making powers on the two major organs of the Community, the Council and the Commission. It should be remembered that the Parliament is largely a forum for debate, and although it can produce legislation the Council of Ministers has the power to reject it.

Community laws come in the form of:

(i) **Regulations.** These are of general application and are automatically binding throughout the Community. No reference has to be made to Parliament.

(ii) **Directives.** These are also of general application, but are only binding on member states which bring them into force, i.e. they are not 'self-executing';

(iii) **Decisions.** These apply only to a particular state, organisation or individual.

Rulings of the European Court are also part of Community Law.

THE RELATIONSHIP BETWEEN COMMUNITY LAW AND ENGLISH LAW

The following points should be noted:

(i) Under s.2 European Communities Act 1972 the UK, in acceding to the treaties of the Community, adopted the laws made, and to be made, by the Community;

(ii) Because Community law is now part of our internal law, it is binding upon the English courts, and this may involve them, as we have seen, interpreting its various provisions;

(iii) In relation to Community law the jurisdiction of the House of Lords as the highest Court of Appeal in the United Kingdom is reduced; and

(iv) A gradual harmonisation of laws is taking place as Parliament brings UK law into line with Community legislation. Thus the Competition Act 1980 uses the wording of Article 85 of the Treaty of Rome to define anti competitive practices within the UK, harmonising domestic law in this area with Community law.

ASSIGNMENT — SUNDAY TRADING

Mrs Sheila Spence is a resident of the Hillview area of Sunderland. She is a council tenant and has lived in her present house at 7 Leighton Street for the past 15 years. When she first moved to Leighton Street there was a large area of derelict land on the other side of the street directly across from her house. In 1983 there was a proposal for a major redevelopment on the site including the building of a new 'Do It Yourself' super store. The proposed store was part of a national chain owned by DIY Holdings Limited. Before it was allowed to be built the council asked all local tenants if they had any objections to the planning application for the store. Several of Mrs Spence's neighbours were in favour of the store as it offered the chance of fresh employment prospects in an area of Sunderland that suffered high levels of unemployment. For that reason there were no objections against the planning permission from any local residents including Mrs Spence. There were however a number of objections from shop owners in Sunderland Town Centre who naturally feared that the new development would attract trade from their businesses in the town centre. Eventually the council decided to disregard the traders objections and planning permission was granted. The store was built and opened in a blaze of publicity in late 1984.

Initially there were no problems. The store prospered and several of Mrs Spence's neighbours were employed as part-time assistants in the store. In January 1986, however, DIY Holdings Limited decided to implement a policy of Sunday opening in all their stores and the Hillview store was opened every Sunday from 10.00 a.m. to 5.00 p.m. This proved to be an immediate success. The store began to do more trade on a Sunday than on any other day of the week. Shoppers were attracted from the whole of the surrounding area as it was the only store of its type in the town with Sunday opening. The increased custom, while proving beneficial to the store began to cause problems for local residents in general and Mrs Spence in particular. The store car park was not large enough to cope with the increased trading and Mrs Spence continually found people parking in the street and blocking her drive way. This was very inconvenient as it meant that on several occasions she could not get her own car out of her drive and her son, Bernard, and daughter in law, Ann, who often visited her on Sunday afternoons had to park two or three streets away from her house. Furthermore, the customers from the store who parked outside her house had a tendency to throw litter such as the packaging from their purchases into the street outside Mrs Spence's house. She had even found discarded DIY wrappings carelessly thrown over her garden wall. Mrs Spence became increasingly irritated by this behaviour. What made matters worse was that she was a very strict church goer and she believed that Sunday should be kept 'special'. The store customers behaviour was most upsetting to her.

TASKS

Assume the role of Mrs Spence.

1. Draft a letter of complaint to the Superstore's management in which you express your concern at the Sunday opening and the actions of the store's customers.

2. You have decided to take the matter further than a mere complaint and have devoted some of your spare time to looking into the situation. Before you do anything else you have decided to weigh up the pros and cons of the superstore opening on a Sunday. You have decided that the best way to proceed is to draw up all the advantages and disadvantages of the store's Sunday opening. You recognise that there are both costs and benefits of the situation and so you have chosen to classify them in terms of their private and social costs and benefits. To be able to do this you will have to determine what exactly is meant by 'private' and 'social' costs and benefits and, once you have done this to list in the appropriate categories your likely findings. Prepare a list of these in which you distinguish between private and social costs and benefits and summarise those that you are likely to find in this situation. Clearly you will not be able to put a monetary value on these but you may wish to summarise which you regard as major and which are only minor.

3.   In your research you have found that there have recently been a number of proposals to change the law on Sunday trading. In fact it has become an issue which has received considerale coverage in the national press particularly as the government sponsored the unsuccessful Shops Bill in 1986 which proposed a relaxation of controls on Sunday trading. So that you will understand what exactly happened in this process you decide to find out how legislation such as this progresses through Parliament. Prepare an outline of the stages through which a Government Bill would pass. Pay particular attention to the stages at which it could accepted or rejected for these may be the points in the legislative process where you as an individual, either through your M.P. or by the lobbying of a pressure group, could influence the legislation.

DEVELOPMENTAL TASK

4.   Undertake some research in which you collect information on the ill fated Shops Bill which was rejected by Parliament in early 1986. Such information could include newspaper and magazine articles and literature prepared by some of the interested parties. Using the material which you can collect prepare a short report in which you summarise objectively the case for and against the proposed legislation. You should remember that it was a Government Bill and so reflected the Thatcher government's philosophy of the free market. You may have to explain what is meant by this to fully understand why the government wished to support such controversial legislation.

ASSIGNMENT — THE BRANCH LINE

British Rail currently run a branch line in Somerset from the town of Taunchester to Framton, a small isolated rural community, 27 miles south east of the town. For the last 15 years the line has proved to be economically unprofitable. BR have recently suggested that the line should be closed in an attempt to save money. This has resulted in a considerable outcry from the residents of Framton, who argue that the railway is one of their main routes of communication with the rest of the county. If the line is closed they will be forced to travel by road to reach Taunchester and this will involve a considerable detour as there is no direct main road from the village to the town. Travelling time will increase from the present 45 minutes rail journey to a road trip of nearly 75 minutes. They argue that this will cause considerable hardship both for those who live in Framton and work in Taunchester and also for those people who see Taunchester as their main shopping centre. Local traders in Framton are very worried that the loss of the rail link will deter many of the tourists who visit Framton during the summer to see the local Abbey which is a beauty spot and tourist attraction. The Framton traders association state that the consequent loss of tourists will lead to a considerable number of businesses going to the wall as they depend on the increased summer trade to carry them through the quiet winter period.

British Rail have replied to this criticism by pointing out that the rail link currently is costing them almost a quarter of a million pounds a year in subsidies and there is little prospect of any increase in travellers using the line and so making it profitable. A spokesman for BR has published a statement in the local press in which he notes that the closure of uneconomic lines such as this is consistent with BR's national policy to seek a more profitable operation. The statement makes reference to the need to move towards a rail network based on marginal cost pricing and clearly, at present, more profitable lines such as the Bristol — London line are subsidising the unprofitable local services. The statement claims that the continued existence of unprofitable services requiring heavy subsidies will lead to substantial price increases for main line travellers and will reduce BR's ability to implement its ambitious electrification programme for the main inter-city lines.

Residents of Framton and Taunchester have formed a pressure group to attempt to engender support to keep the line open and the group is holding a public meeting to put forward its case.

TASKS

1. You have become a member of the pressure group and because you are known to study this type of problem you have been asked to prepare a briefing document for the main speaker from the pressure group at the meeting, Angela Brown. You are concerned that Angela is made aware of the arguments against closure, including a clear explanation of the private and social costs and benefits involved. You recognise, however, that it is important that she is able to rebut any arguments put forward by BR. You therefore need to include in your briefing document an explanation of the justification of BR's attempts to close the line. As Angela is not well versed in such arguments you will have to explain your points clearly and thoroughly. Produce the briefing document for Angela.

2. One of the major proposals that the pressure group is putting forward is that a cost benefit analysis of the problem is carried out. Produce a step by step plan for such a study indicating the costs and benefits which must be examined, the time scale which may be chosen and any other factors which you believe should be considered.

DEVELOPMENTAL TASK

3. Chose a particular project in your area, such as the building of a new sports centre, the demolition of a city centre area or the siting of a new shopping development and produce a simplified cost benefit analysis of the issues involved.

Chapter 25

GOVERNMENT ECONOMIC POLICY

THE ECONOMIC OBJECTIVES OF BRITISH GOVERNMENTS

The depression of the 1930s plunged this country into an unparallelled economic crisis. Mass unemployment, social deprivation, bankruptcy and economic decline faced the British people while the government sat back and allowed market forces to take their course. Policies were haphazard and piecemeal with little attempt at overall management of the economy because:

(a) the causes of the depression were not fully understood; and

(b) the government did not have the policy instruments capable of rectifying them.

THE SETTING OF OBJECTIVES

A major step forward in the understanding of the macro economic workings of the country came from the work of John Maynard Keynes, a Cambridge economist, who in 1936 published his famous book entitled "The General Theory of Employment, Interest and Money". From the beginning of the depression Keynes had been severely critical of the lack of government intervention to reduce the problem. In fact the governments of the time in this country made matters worse by reducing public expenditure on transfer payments and capital spending alike. Keynes made this point in 1931 when he argued:

> "The Government's programme is as foolish as it is wrong . . . Not only is purchasing power to be curtailed, but road building, housing and the like are to be retrenched. Local authorities are to follow suit. If the theory which underlines all this is to be accepted, the end will be that no one can be employed, except those happy few who grow their own potatoes, as a result of refusing, for reasons of economy, to buy the services of anyone else . . . "

> *(J.M. Keynes: "Essays in Persuasion", 1931)*

His point of view gradually became more influential in government circles so that by 1944 the National Coalition Government was willing to publish a White Paper which stated in broad but positive outline, the economic objectives which would be followed by post-war governments. The White Paper committed the government to the role of managing the economy and ensuring that certain basic objectives were sought. It stated:

> "The Government believe that, once the war has been won, we can make a fresh approach, with better chances of success than ever before, to the task of maintaining a high and stable level of employment without sacrificing the essential liberties of a free society."

> *(Government White Paper on Employment Policy, 1944)*

Together with its aim to ensure a high level of employment, the government also declared its intention to pursue a policy of price stability, economic growth and balance of payments equilibrium. These four policy objectives were the cornerstone for government macro economic policy from the mid-1940s until the late 1970s.

The major economic objectives of post-war governments became:

      (a)   a high and stable level of employment;

      (b)   price stability;

      (c)   economic growth;

      (d)   balance of payments equilibrium.

A major dilemma facing post war governments has been the question of whether or not all four objectives could be met simultaneously.

THE CONFLICT OF OBJECTIVES

The 1944 Coalition government and its successors recognised that these objectives are not necessarily compatible. For example, high levels of employment can increase the level of demand in the economy. This can then lead to rising inflation which may cause a fall in business confidence as businessmen are deterred by increasing costs. As their confidence in their future is weakened they are less likely to invest in new projects or re-invest in existing ones. This decline in investment results in consequent job losses. Similarly if the economy is growing it will usually mean a more prosperous population. In such circumstances this will often lead to a greater consumption of imported products causing a deficit in the balance of payments position. Therefore it has been very difficult for governments to pursue all of these policies simultaneously. It was necessary, therefore, for governments to choose a combination of policy objectives which would be politically acceptable and economically viable.

In fact the conflict between these objectives proved to be less problematic than had been anticipated, at least in the relatively stable and prosperous 1950s and 1960s. It is true to say that, while these decades did not produce for the United Kingdom the spectacular economic growth experienced by the USA, Germany and Japan, our productive capacity nevertheless gradually increased and the worst excesses of inflation and unemployment were not felt. The Balance of Payments did prove to be more of a recurrent problem but in a period of relatively low-priced energy and raw materials, the comparatively small trade deficits which occurred were but minor ripples on an otherwise tranquil economic sea.

The full impact of the problems facing the United Kingdom economy were not to be felt until the latter part of the seventies, when the objectives and targets expressed in the days of hope and optimism of the forties began to appear much more difficult to attain. In this chapter you should appreciate these four basic objectives as we move on to examine the major problems facing our economy and attempt to identify the underlying causes.

THE ECONOMIC PROBLEMS OF THE UNITED KINGDOM

UNEMPLOYMENT

The first of the economic objectives outlined earlier was the aim of government to create and maintain high and stable levels of employment. In the last fifteen years, however, the United Kingdom has faced the problem of rapidly increasing unemployment. By the early 1980s we had started to experience levels of unemployment unknown since the depression of the thirties. Perhaps more disturbing is the increase in long-term unemployment — people who have not worked for years, school-leavers who have never had a real job and may never find paid employment in their lives. These are the stark realities of modern Britain.

Let us now examine the causes of this unemployment which has affected the rest of the developed world to some extent, but has hit this country particularly hard. If we consider the unemployment figures for the United Kingdom for the last thirty years we may gain an insight into when the dramatic growth began and so be able to isolate some of its causes. The figure below, shows this change:

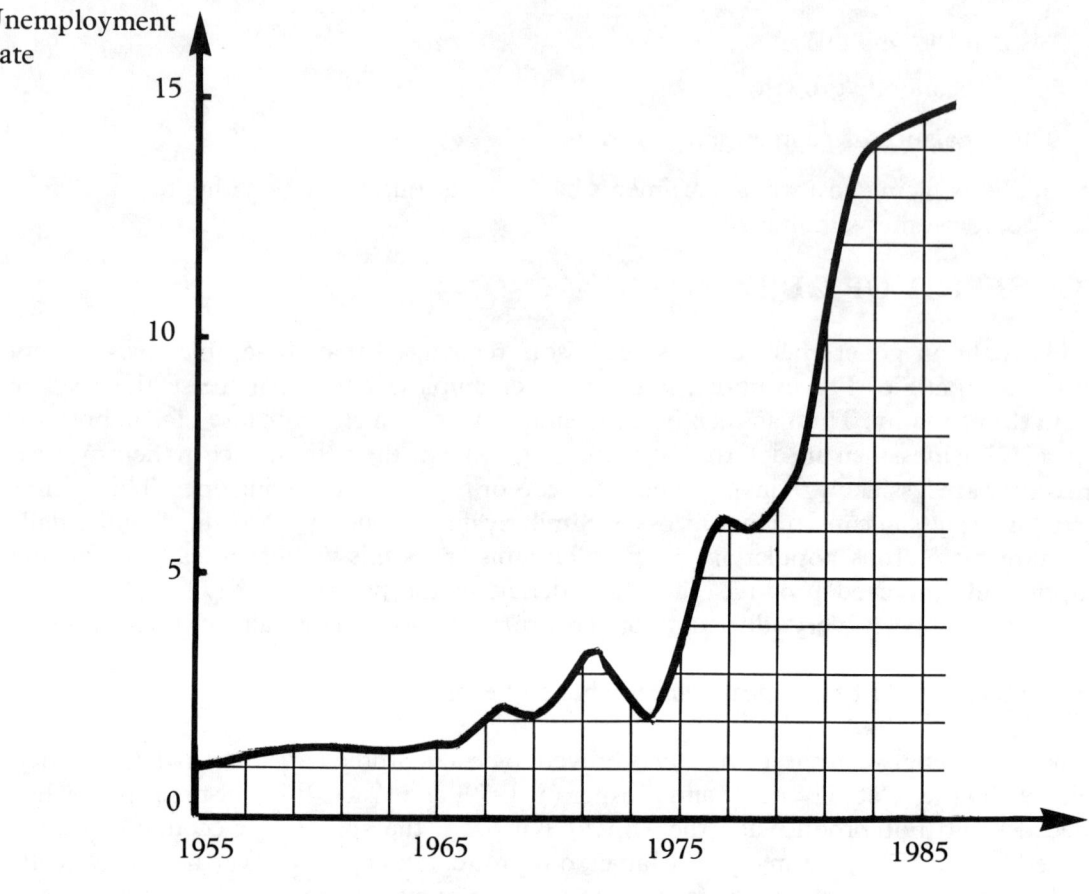

Unemployment in the UK 1955 to 1986

You can see that unemployment is shown as a percentage and that between 1950 and 1970 it was between 1% and 2%. This is a percentage of the workforce. It would be wrong, however, to assume that the government is attempting to place 100% of the workforce in employment. This would be unrealistic. When the government states that it seeks to achieve full employment, we could describe this simply as the situation where more vacancies exist in the economy than there are people looking for work.

Of course some of those who seek work will not always be able to find the exact job they seek, at the wage they require, or in the area that they live. Thus in the 1950s and 1960s when this country was described as having full employment there were still areas in the country such as Scotland, Northern Ireland, the North East and South Wales where unemployment rates were considerably above the national average. This is described as regional unemployment.

Unemployment can, in fact, be categorised according to the cause. There are four main categories:

      (a)   frictional unemployment;

      (b)   seasonal unemployment;

      (c)   structural unemployment;

      (d)   cyclical unemployment.

We will now examine each in turn.

(a) Frictional unemployment

In any dynamic and changing economy there will always be those who are temporarily unemployed. They may have left one job before they had found another or they may choose to have a short period of unemployment between jobs. This is quite common in such industries as the construction trade where workers are often on fixed term contracts. These temporary breaks from employment lasting a comparatively short time are known as frictional unemployment. It is not of the utmost concern to governments as it does not usually cause the social problems associated with long term unemployment. In economic terms, as long as it is only a relatively small proportion of the workforce that is frictionally unemployed then the effects on overall productive output are minimal. In fact the movement of workers to more efficient and rewarding jobs is to be encouraged.

There is a problem if there exists severe immobility of labour. This occurs when workers are unable to move to another area to find work because of family ties or housing difficulties, (this is known as geographical immobility) or when they are unable to change the type of job they do because of lack of expertise or training facilities, (this is known as industrial or structural immobility).

The government's policy to rectify such inflexibility in the labour market is through the introduction of retraining schemes for those wishing to change their occupation. It will also encourage people to move to areas of low unemployment through resettlement schemes and the advertisement of vacancies in Employment Offices and Job Centres in other parts of the country. In an attempt to discourage those who seek voluntary short periods of unemployment, the government does not pay benefits for the first six weeks of unemployment to those who have left a job without a sound reason.

(b) Seasonal unemployment

Some industries tend to operate seasonally and so those who work in such employment will find themselves temporarily unemployed in the "off season". This type of unemployment is most common among agricultural and building workers and those employed in the tourist industry. As with frictional unemployment, this particular problem is not of major consequence in the United Kingdom, although it does cause hardship for workers whose jobs depend on the season of the year and in those areas of the country where industries are predominantly seasonal. The government has made some attempts to attract year-round industries to these areas and pays State benefits to workers who face seaonal layoffs. These policies have been only partially successful.

(c) Structural unemployment

Structural unemployment is a long-term version of frictional unemployment in that it exists mainly because of immobility in the labour market. This results from basic changes in the demand and supply for goods and services in the economy. For example, the textile industry of the United Kingdom has suffered widespread unemployment as a result of foreign competition.

Much of the persistently higher regional unemployment can be explained by the decline in demand for the products of the basic industries which predominated in those areas. In areas such as Scotland, South Wales and the North East the decline of coal, steel and shipbuilding has been particularly marked. Such unemployment, resulting in deep structural changes in demand patterns, is often difficult to solve in the short-term given the existing immobility of labour.

Structural unemployment may result from supply changes, for instance, a reduction in the demand for a particular type of labour created by the introduction of robot machines. This is known as technological unemployment. Similarly, technological advances in the printing industry have meant that the computer typesetting of newspapers is now perfectly feasible, a process which has been bitterly resisted by the Fleet Street unions. Technological unemployment will always occur in a dynamic economy but often attitudes to change are much influenced by the general level of unemployment in the economy.

. . . *structural unemployment* . . . .

(d) Cyclical unemployment

Since the late eighteenth century, the United Kingdom's economy has followed a cyclical pattern alternating from boom to slump with levels of unemployment reflecting this cyclical trend. The cyclical pattern in the post-war era has been less well defined with peaks of economic activity occurring in 1951, 1955-56, 1965 and 1975-76.

Cyclical unemployment is the result of an overall lack of aggregate demand for goods and services in the economy. The business cycle, as it is known, has tended in the past to follow this fairly regular pattern. However, since the middle 1970s we have been faced with continuous and growing large scale unemployment. This is partly as a result of the world recession and is partly caused by our own government's attempts to reduce the level of inflation by lowering aggregate demand in the economy. Later in the chapter we shall be discussing the means by which the government regulates the level of aggregate demand in the economy.

PRICE STABILITY

The second major policy objective of post-war governments has been to achieve relative price stability in the economy. The general level of prices can of course change in either a downward (deflationary) or upward (inflationary) direction. Deflationary trends occurred in recent United Kingdom history when prices fell for much of the pre-war period, rising only after 1935. The post-war period, however, has been one of continuous inflation.

It is possible to measure the degree of inflation by several different sets of indices, but the most usual is the Index of Retail Prices.

Although fears were expressed in 1944 that achieving full employment might cause inflationary pressures, the decades of the 1950s and early 1960s were successful not only in achieving employment targets but also in attaining low levels of inflation. Between 1952 and 1955, retail prices averaged an annual rise of only 3.1% while between 1955 and 1960 it was even less at 2.7%. As the table below shows, the 1960s were also successful years in achieving relative price stability.

UK Inflation Rates 1960-1986

Year	% Increase	Year	% Increase
1960	1.2	1973	9.2
1961	2.7	1974	16.1
1962	3.2	1975	24.2
1963	1.7	1976	16.5
1964	3.9	1977	15.8
1965	4.7	1978	8.3
1966	3.7	1979	13.4
1967	2.4	1980	18.0
1968	4.8	1981	11.7
1969	5.2	1981	10.0
1970	6.4	1983	4.5
1971	9.4	1984	5.0
1972	7.1	1985	5.5
		1986	3.5

(Source: "Economic Trends", March 1975 and March 1986)

As the Table shows, the 1960s were also successful years in achieving relative price stability. Only from the late sixties did the pace of inflation quicken, reaching a peak of nearly 27% in August 1975. Since this peak the trend has varied upwards and then downwards again to its level of around 3.5% in 1986. Inflation has been a world-wide problem in the post-war era although the rates have varied widely. While the facts about inflation are relatively precise and clear, the causes of the inflationary process are much less so.

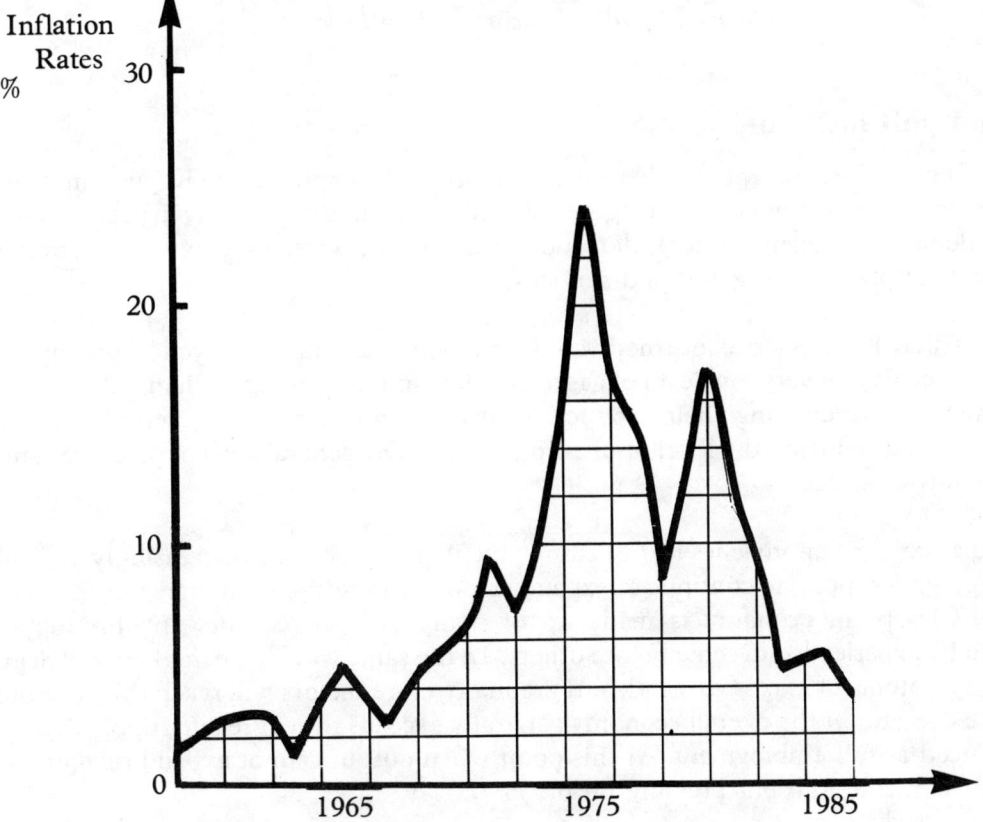

UK Inflation Rates 1960 - 1986

In the same way in which unemployment has been categorised according to its cause, there has been much debate in recent years about the cause of inflation and two basic theories have emerged:

(a) demand pull inflation; and

(b) cost push inflation.

There are, in addition, several other explanations including that of the monetarists who see the cause of inflation in a much wider social and economic context. We shall next examine the mainstream theories and see to what extent they can provide explanations of the recent trend in inflation in the United Kingdom.

. . . demand pull . . . cost push inflation

(a) Demand pull inflation

One view of inflation widely accepted is that which was originally expressed by Keynes, in which changes in the price level are linked to changes in aggregate demand and supply in the economy. By aggregate demand is meant the total demand for goods and services. Aggregate supply is simply the total supply of such goods and services.

As explained earlier, Keynes was concerned with a situation where massive cyclical unemployment exists as a result of a very low level of aggregate demand. As aggregate demand expands, producers respond by increasing their production of goods and services, thereby increasing aggregate supply and reducing the level of unemployment. The general level of prices remains unchanged as output increases.

However, as the economy approaches its full employment level it becomes increasingly difficult for output (aggregate supply) to continue to expand smoothly in response to increases in aggregate demand. Clearly an economy is made up of many different sectors and production difficulties will be experienced in some before others. In the same way, some markets will begin to experience symptoms of excess demand, and gradually more sectors will reach this situation until aggregate demand in the overall economy generally exceeds the aggregate supply capable of being produced at full employment. At this point when output cannot expand further, the effect of excess demand is to put pressure on prices.

The mechanism by which the excess demand results in prices being increased can be briefly illustrated as follows:

If overall aggregate demand exceeds aggregate supply in the economy this will manifest itself in a number of ways which can be observed in the various sectors, for example, unemployment is low, numerous job vacancies exist, overtime is offered and worked by employees and shortages of goods exist.

These conditions will affect producers in two ways:

(i) There will be a vigorous demand for labour which enables the trade unions to press for, and obtain, higher wages for their members. Employers concede these increases which are then passed on to consumers as higher prices.

(ii) A response to market demand is sometimes made directly by producers raising their prices to what the market will bear.

Prices then begin to increase in the overall economy and as the inflationary process begins someting else starts to happen, expectations reinforce price rises. This effect is created by both the worker and the consumer. In wage negotiations unions naturally demand a higher settlement if they anticipate a rise in the level of prices in the coming year. This reinforces the increase in wages and once again prices rise. If consumers anticipate rises in prices, the obvious reaction is to purchase goods immediately. They will either spend the cash they have or borrow, and in either case it will simply add to overall aggregate demand in the economy.

(b) Cost push inflation

An alternative explanation of inflation is to be found in the view that the inflationary stimulus does not come from the demand side of the economy as with demand pull, but arises from the supply side. Inflation is caused by increases in the costs of the factors of production which in turn leads to producers passing on these cost increases as higher prices to the consumers. The original increases in costs may be caused by:

(i) trade unions pushing up wages ahead of what is justified by productivity; or

(ii) independent increases in the costs of raw materials such as that caused by a falling exchange rate.

This analysis of inflation is one which has the twin attractions of common-sense simplicity and easily identifiable "culprits" in the inflationary process. We must be careful, however, not to accept this view simply because of its simplicity. Successive governments of differing political persuasions have tried to lay the blame for inflation at the door of the trade unions. Recent empirical evidence on the effect of trade union pressure for higher wages has, however, indicated that for most of the 1970s the objective of trade unions was one of simply trying to maintain wage levels in line with inflation rather than to outstep inflation with their pay demands.

MONETARY CAUSES OF INFLATION

A third cause of inflation is proposed by "monetarist" economists such as Professor Milton Friedman of the Chicago School of Economics. This cause is a variation on the demand pull theory. Monetarists see the cause of inflation as an excessive increase in the money supply. In doing this they are the modern exponents of the ideas of earlier economists who believed in the quantity theory of money. Put simply, any increase in the quantity of money in circulation leads, after a time lag, (during which real output may change), to increases in the level of prices, and vice versa.

If the money supply increases by a greater proportion than the increase in the output of goods and services then inflation will result. To say this another way, the value of money has fallen. To maintain stable prices the growth of the money supply must keep pace with the expansion of output. If output (measured in terms of the country's economic growth) only increases by say, 2% then the money supply must be controlled so that it too only increases by 2%.

To support this analysis, monetarists have produced empirical evidence, over a long historical period and from many countries to show a cause and effect link between an increase in the money supply and a resultant increase in the level of prices.

The section began by noting that this was an area of considerable debate among economists. To a non-monetarist economist very little of the previous explanation is valid. The areas of conflict are numerous. To these economists changes in the money supply do not always result in inflation. Even the empirical evidence, which seems so conclusive to the monetarists, is not entirely accepted as providing practical evidence of the theory. The monetarist explanation of inflation is one example of an area where economists disagree fundamentally on the causes of the inflationary disease which results inevitably in widely different prescriptions for its cure.

CAUSES OF RECENT INFLATION IN THE UNITED KINGDOM

Now let us see how these theories stand up when examining the major economic and social problem of inflation in the United Kingdom in the 1970s and 80s. Several factors can be suggested as the possible cause(s) of this inflation.

First let us examine the evidence for demand pull inflation. By all the statistical indicators of excess demand, such as the level of employment and job vacancies, this period has been one in which it appears hard to find evidence of excess demand. Look at the figure and you will see that unemployment levels have been extremely high and rising in the 1970s and 80s compared with earlier decades. The conclusion must be that it is hard to pin the blame for inflation on excess demand.

Alternatively we could consider the cost push theory. There are two possible explanations under this heading:

      (a)   wage push inflation; or,

      (b)   a rise in import prices.

(a) Wage push

The 1970s and 80's have certainly seen an increase in wage levels. These are illustrated in table below: opposite.

Percentage changes in wage rates 1960-1985

Year	% change	Year	% change	Year	% change
1960	2.6	1969	5.3	1978	14.1
1961	4.2	1970	9.9	1979	14.9
1962	3.6	1971	12.9	1980	11.4
1963	4.8	1972	13.8	1981	12.9
1964	4.8	1973	13.7	1982	9.4
1965	4.3	1974	19.8	1983	8.4
1966	4.6	1975	29.5	1984	6.1
1967	3.9	1976	19.3	1985	8.5
1968	6.6	1977	6.6		

Source: "Economic Trends" (Annual Supplement) 1985, and
"Dept. of Employment Gazette".

At first sight the statistics seem to suggest evidence of a wages explosion from 1970 onwards which resulted in higher prices after an appropriate time lag. Other statistics, such as those detailing industrial disputes, seem to suggest a more militant attitude on the part of the unions. There is no doubt that, superficially at least, the evidence for wage push is inviting. But on closer inspection this is not so compelling. For example, once inflation gets underway (fuelled by other factors such as import costs) it becomes difficult to determine cause and effect so clearly. It may have been that wages were merely responding to anticipated inflation rather than causing it. Furthermore, monetarist economists conclude that monetary expansion is essential to permit wage push inflation to continue. But, even if this is true in principle, in practice governments may not react in this way by allowing unemployment to rise to levels sufficient to damp down wage settlements.

(b) Rise in import prices

An alternative or complementary cost-push cause is seen by many in the rise in import prices which has occurred since the early 1970s. One major element was the rise in oil prices introduced by OPEC (Organisation of Petroleum Exporting Countries), following the 1973 Arab-Israeli war. This led to increased production costs, which in turn resulted in higher prices, which could have had a feedback effect in terms of stimulating wage demands and thereby fuelling wage push inflation.

The UK was also faced with massive increases in the price of other imports. The loss of the Empire as a source of cheap raw materials forced us to pay the going world market rate. Also the floating of the pound in 1972 and its subsequent dramatic fall in value led to the cost of imports going up.

The Monetarist view of inflation

The final element of the inflation analysis is evidence for the monetarists view of inflation. There is no doubt that in the early 1970s there was a marked increase in the growth of the money supply as shown in the table below.

The statistics provide yet more proof to the monetarists of the validity of their explanation of inflation. At this point the debate between economists sharpens. To the non-monetarist any increase in the money supply leads to lower interest rates and credit which is more freely available, both of which add to spending and boost aggregate demand. In other words, the monetary expansion works via the excess demand process explained earlier. Lack of excess demand in the 1970s seems to rule out this cause. The evidence can thus be used to support either view of the inflationary process.

Percentage annual change in the Money Supply Measure, M3 1970-85

Year	% change	Year	% change
1970	9.5	1978	15.0
1971	13.9	1979	12.6
1972	24.5	1980	14.3
1973	26.3	1981	17.7
1974	10.2	1982	8.7
1975	6.6	1983	10.0
1976	9.5	1984	9.4
1977	10.0	1985	12.8

Source: Financial Statistics, Bank of England

In conclusion, the truth is probably that inflation is caused by many factors which interact with each other. This complexity makes identifying the cause extremely difficult and probably gives rise to governments looking for easy, obvious targets, whether these be irresponsible trade unions or excessive growth in the money supply. It is this difficulty in determining the underlying cause of inflation which results in the conflicting approaches to solutions which are discussed later in the chapter.

ECONOMIC GROWTH

The third policy objective of governments has been economic growth. Only by achieving a satisfactory rate of growth in its productive potential can the United Kingdom economy produce more goods and services to provide its citizens with an increase in their wealth and standard of living. One of the most disturbing features of the United Kingdom's post-war economic record has been the relatively low economic growth when compared to rival economies. The United Kingdom's growth rate has tended to be of the order of 2 - 3% in good years and zero or even negative in poor years.

The table below illustrates the varying growth rates between 1980 and 1984 for selected economies.

Average % annual growth in Gross Domestic Product
1980 - 84 (selected countries)

Japan	4.2%
USA	1.9%
France	1.2%
W. Germany	0.9%
Italy	1.1%
U.K.	0.8%

Source: The British Economy 1985 (Lloyds Bank)

The reasons for the United Kingdom's relatively poor performance are tied in with the reasons for economic growth itself. This is by no means a clearly understood process. Long-term growth represents an increase in potential aggregate supply, and so initially is determined by the economic resources available to the economy, together with the efficient and full utilisation of these resources. Capital, and how it is used, is probably the most decisive factor of production in determining growth rates.

It has often been suggested that the United Kingdom's poor performance has been due, in part, to a failure to re-invest and modernise its capital stock. The use of machinery which is older and less efficient than our rivals has produced slower rates of growth. Why this reluctance to invest has happened is another difficult question and the search for an answer produces a very wide range of hypotheses. There are those who suggest that the United Kingdom's investment spending has been wrongly directed and that we should have been putting more money into factories and machines rather than houses and welfare. Leftwingers argue that it is the basic capitalistic structure of the economy which is to blame or that the lack of investment policy and lack of lending by the banks which is the root cause of the problem. Others argue that it is the variations in the political and policy targets inherent in the Labour/Conservative political pendulum in the post war period which has led to a discontinuity in business planning and confidence which is essential to industry and commerce. This vagueness in understanding the conditions necessary for growth tends to lead to economic growth being something to be hoped for rather than a specific policy target.

BALANCE OF PAYMENTS EQUILIBRIUM

The United Kingdom has experienced fluctuating fortunes in its attempts to achieve the fourth of its economic objectives, Balance of Payment equilibrium, since the Second World War. By limiting the analysis to the period of the last twenty years, a distinct pattern emerges in relation to the Balance of Payments. In the early 1960s, the United Kingdom's balance of trade deteriorated into increasing deficit. The conclusion of this trend was seen in the devaluation of the pound in November 1967. The position changed dramatically thereafter and resulted in a trade surplus. This strong position in the United Kingdom's Balance of Payments did not last beyond the early 1970s however. The major trend in the early 1970's was the movement of the current account into massive deficit, reaching almost £3,500 million in 1974. This was the result of many factors, most important of which were the price rises in primary products (especially oil) and the decline in the growth of world trade. To some extent, these deficits were alleviated by surpluses on the investment and capital flows account, but still left the United Kingdom with the problem of financing an unfavourable overall deficit flow. This was resolved by relying on both overseas borrowing and drawing upon official reserves of foreign currency.

The United Kingdom achieved a turnaround in its payments position in the late 1970s. The years after 1977 showed a considerable improvement (despite temporary distortions in the 1979 figures), reaching a position in 1980 where a current account surplus of over £2,500 million was recorded. An important element in this improvement has been the effect of North Sea Oil in reducing the petroleum trade deficit. Overall, however, the period cannot in any sense be described as one in which equilibrium in the economy has been generally achieved. This is especially true considering that the recent improvements in the Balance of Payments have been attained against a domestic background of rising unemployment and poor economic growth.

THE MANAGEMENT OF THE ECONOMY

In the previous section we examined the nature of the economic problems facing the United Kingdom. We must now analyse and evaluate the basis upon which the economy has been managed in the post-war period and the theory and concepts which have contributed to the economic policy of successive governments in their attempts to remedy these problems.

The most distinctive feature of government economic management in this period is that it can be divided into two distinct eras.

(i) The Era of Keynesian Policy

In the thirty-five years or so following the government's White Paper of 1944 on economic objectives, governments of both political persuasions pursued policies basically founded on the ideas of Keynes and the economists who followed in his footsteps.

(ii) The Era of Monetarism

In the late 1970s there emerged a strong challenge to Keynesian thinking. This has been described as the "monetarist revolution" in which the four basic economic objectives stated in 1944 have been reduced to one over-riding aim, the elimination of inflation.

Monetarists believe that this should be the single paramount target of economic policy and that in achieving it the other problems will subsequently be solved. This switch has been accompanied by a re-appraisal of the basic causes of inflation and the appropriate methods of economic control. We shall begin with an analysis of the Keynesian approach and its means of application.

KEYNESIAN DEMAND MANAGEMENT

As has already been noted, the basis of Keynesian economics is that the problems of unemployment and inflation are the result of disequilibrium in the economy's demand for goods and services and its ability to supply them. A series of simple diagrams may illustrate these concepts. Firstly, consider a state of equilibrium:

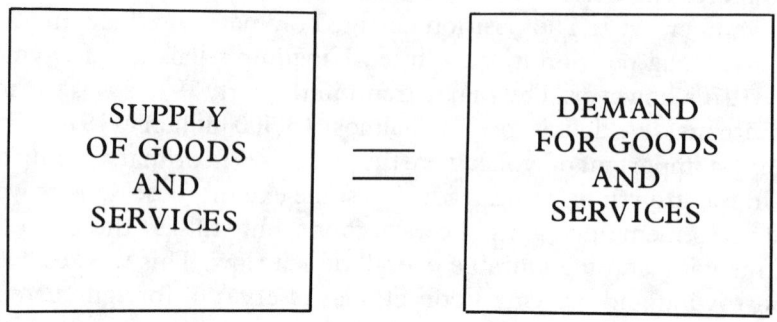

Here we have a situation where aggregate (or total) demand for goods and services equals the supply. In such circumstances it is argued that there are no upward or downward pressures on the level of prices. There is an equilibrium. Prices remain stable and as such there is no inflation. In such circumstances it is argued that there are no upward or downward pressures on the level of prices. There is an equilibrium. Prices remain stable and as such there is no inflation. What the diagram does not illustrate, however, is whether or not there is unemployment in the economy. We do not know the number of workers (or other resources) required to produce the level of supply shown.

What if there is unemployment?

In a situation where there is unemployment, Keynesian economics would:

(i) prescribe an increase in demand, and thereby;

(ii) precipitate a corresponding increase in the supply of goods and services, and thereby;

(iii) require employers to hire more workers, and so reduce the level of unemployment.

Let us follow these stages through in the form of diagrams. Firstly, we have the economy in equilibrium but with an unacceptable level of unemployment:

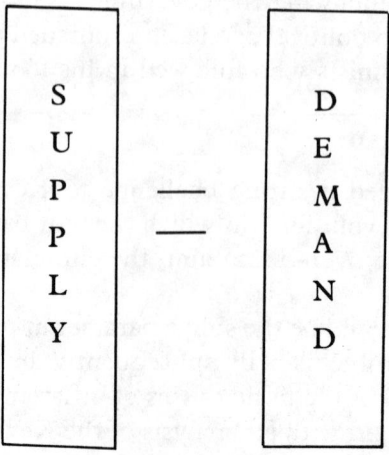

The government therefore stimulates demand so that it is now greater than supply :

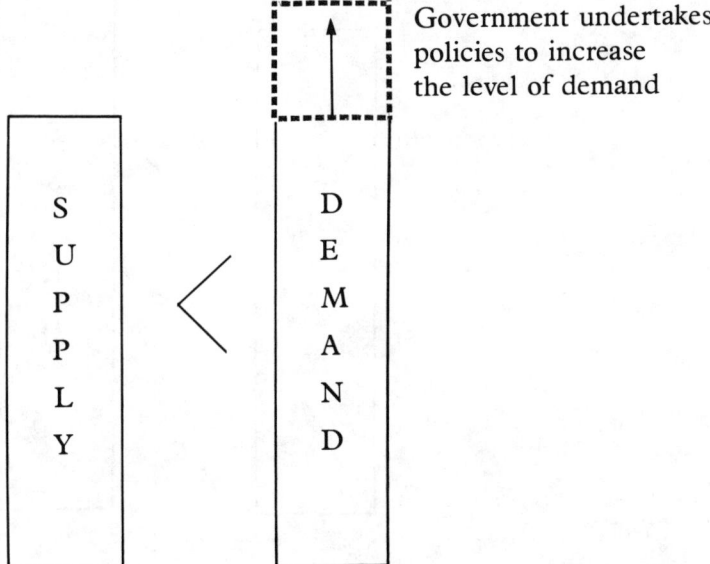

Government undertakes policies to increase the level of demand

Producers then respond to the higher demand by increasing output to achieve a new equilibrium but at a higher level of employment. Once again, supply equals demand:

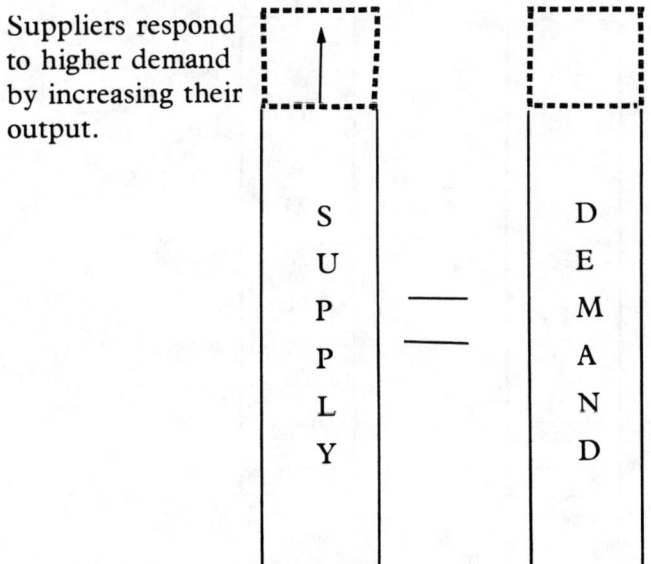

Suppliers respond to higher demand by increasing their output.

What if there is inflation?

If the country is facing the problem of inflation but without unemployment, Keynesian economics diagnoses this as an excess of demand over supply. Again this can be illustrated with the aid of diagrams. We begin where demand exceeds supply. Producers are unable to increase output as there is no spare capacity within the economy. Instead they respond by increasing prices:

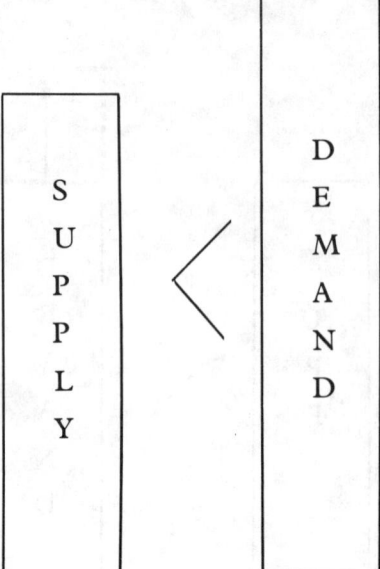

To counter this inflationary tendency the government must depress the level of demand in the economy until it again matches the ability of suppliers to produce and so equilibrium is regained with stable prices:

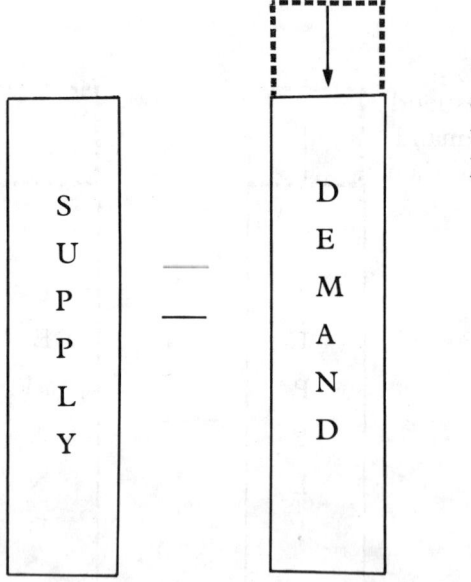

Government applies measures to reduce the level of demand

Is demand management really so simple?

The relative simplicity of this analysis made it attractive and easy to understand. Governments would first identify the problem they wished to rectify and then adjust the level of demand accordingly. Critics noted, however, that in practice the mechanics of supply and demand in the economy often did not work as smoothly as the theory would predict. For instance, let us return to our first example in which the government sought to reduce unemployment by increasing demand and so encouraging a rise in output. What if the increased demand is for products made by those sectors of the economy which are already overstretched? Here no amount of demand pull could induce an increase in employment in those industries. The result is that producers simply respond to the excess demand by raising their prices. And then you've got inflation!

. . . deflate the economy . . .

What if the increased demand is not channelled towards domestically produced goods and services? Then you will have a situation where consumers demand more imports, and instead of the United Kingdom's unemployed finding work, it will be the workers of other countries who benefit. Obviously the art of demand management lies in being able to influence those elements of demand which can be directed towards domestically produced goods in industries which are capable of expansion. This leads us to the problem of defining and evaluating the components which collectively comprise aggregate demand.

THE CONSTITUENTS OF AGGREGATE DEMAND

Aggregate demand may be described as the total effective demand or expenditure of all buyers of capital or consumer goods within the economy as a whole. Put simply this means that it comprises all the money that is spent on goods and services by all the individuals and organisations within the country within a specified period (such as a year). Clearly this includes

     (i)   individuals;

     (ii) businesses; and

     (iii) the government;

and so we sub-divide aggregate demand into these three sectors then distinguish the type of spending made in each sector. The figure below illustrates one way of making this division. The process of division allows the government to identify more clearly the areas within which its policies may be applied. The two most significant elements of aggregate demand in terms of the amount of spending they represent are:

(i)   personal consumption; and

(ii)   government consumption.

Relatively small changes in either of these have a substantial influence on overall demand, and so it is these two areas that together form the main focus of Keynesian demand management. (As we shall see in the next section this revolves around the use of fiscal policy which involves changes in taxation and government spending.)

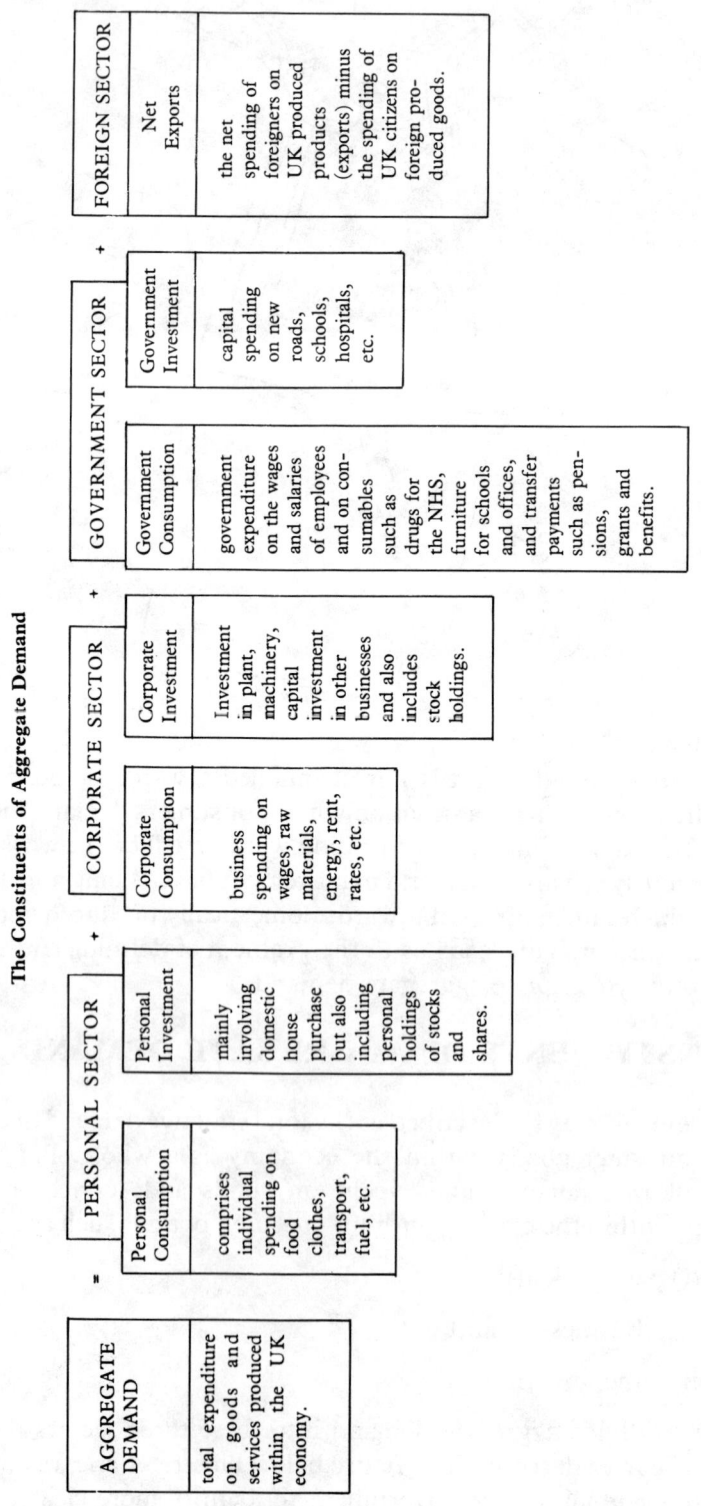

The Constituents of Aggregate Demand

AGGREGATE DEMAND		PERSONAL SECTOR		CORPORATE SECTOR		GOVERNMENT SECTOR		FOREIGN SECTOR
	=	Personal Consumption	Personal Investment	Corporate Consumption	Corporate Investment	Government Consumption	Government Investment	Net Exports
total expenditure on goods and services produced within the UK economy.		comprises individual spending on food clothes, transport, fuel, etc.	mainly involving domestic house purchase but also including personal holdings of stocks and shares.	business spending on wages, raw materials, energy, rent, rates, etc.	Investment in plant, machinery, capital investment in other businesses and also includes stock holdings.	government expenditure on the wages and salaries of employees and on consumables such as drugs for the NHS, furniture for schools and offices, and transfer payments such as pensions, grants and benefits.	capital spending on new roads, schools, hospitals, etc.	the net spending of foreigners on UK produced products (exports) minus the spending of UK citizens on foreign produced goods.

(+ signs appear between sectors: PERSONAL SECTOR + CORPORATE SECTOR + GOVERNMENT SECTOR + FOREIGN SECTOR)

The government faces clear policy alternatives in order to solve either unemployment or inflation.

PROBLEM TO BE SOLVED	GOVERNMENT ACTION TO BE TAKEN
UNEMPLOYMENT	Increasing aggregate demand by cutting taxes and increasing government spending
INFLATION	Reduce aggregate demand by increasing taxes and lowering government spending

The important factor to note here is that the two problems require alternative and contradictory courses of action. Keynesian economics held that it was unlikely that the economy would face both problems simultaneously. For a Keynesian economist inflation was a consequence of excess aggregate demand while unemployment was caused by insufficient demand. However, the governments of the post-war years recognised that there could be circumstances in which there existed substantial unemployment with a small level of inflation, and vice versa. These possible differing combinations of inflation and unemployment led to the development of a framework of analysis which demonstrated the relationship between the two. This is known as the Phillips curve, and that is what we shall look at in the next section.

THE TRADE-OFF BETWEEN INFLATION AND UNEMPLOYMENT — PHILLIPS CURVE ANALYSIS

In 1958 A.W. Phillips presented an analytical framework which would allow governments to choose their preferred combination of inflation and unemployment. It was known as the Phillips curve and a simplified version is shown in the figure below.

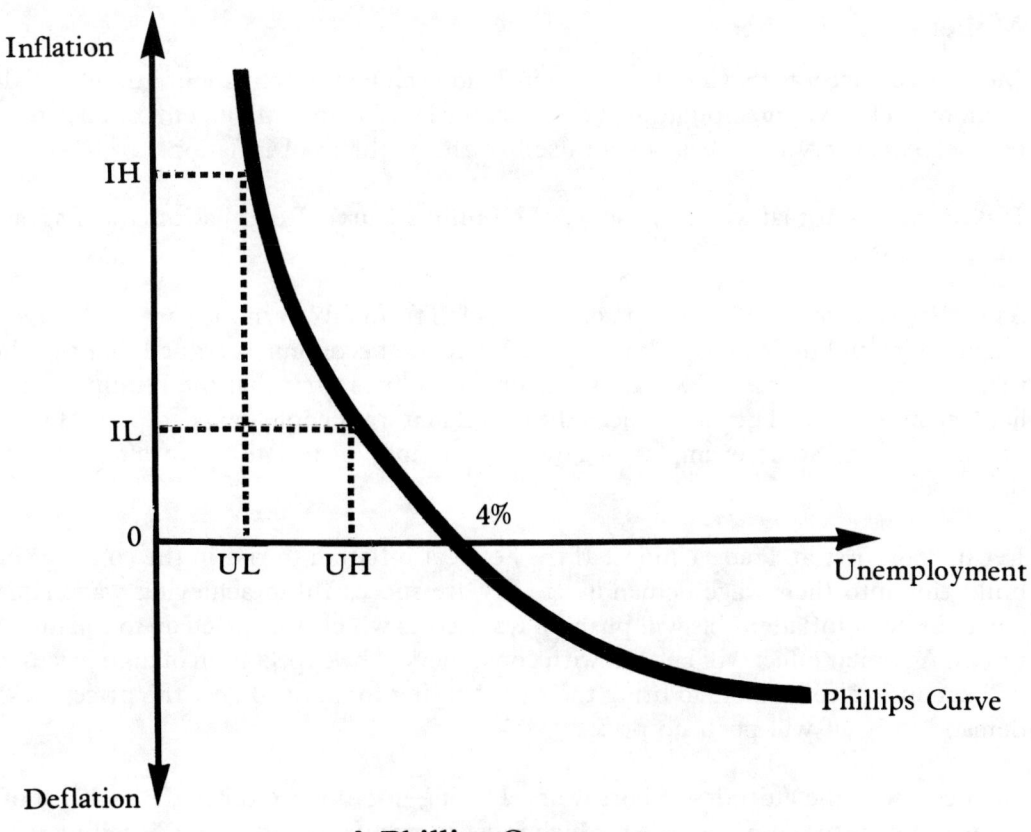

A Phillips Curve

The Phillips Curve shows the policy trade-offs open to government. For instance, a relatively low level of unemployment UL (indicating a high level of demand), may result in significant inflation rates, IH. Conversely, weak aggregate demand producing high unemployment, UH, may be accompanied by low inflation IL. Phillips predicted in 1958 that an approximate unemployment level of 4% would mean that demand was so low that there would be no inflation whatsoever. If unemployment rose further, as had been the case in the depression years of the 1930s, then prices would actually fall (deflation) and this was witnessed as the overall price level fell from 1929 to 1936.

Most governments in the 1950s and 1960s pursued policies which meant that unemployment was kept below 3% and inflation below 5%. However the 1970s saw much higher inflation rates than those which should accompany the prevailing levels of unemployment, according to the Phillips Curve prediction. This decade proved to be a time of major challenge to traditional Keynesian ideas. By 1976 the country faced the joint problems of 5.3% unemployment and 26.5% inflation. The Phillips relationship no longer appeared to hold true.

The country had inflation and economic stagnation and this led to a new term being coined, "stagflation". What was worse, the traditional Keynesian remedies contradicted each other. To increase aggregate demand and solve unemployment made inflation worse and to decrease demand and to hold down prices resulted in rising job losses. This then was the dilemma of Keynesian economics in the mid 1970s. As a counter to the apparent failings of Keynesianism there then emerged the economic doctrine of Monetarism.

THE EMERGENCE OF MONETARISM

The attractiveness of the monetarists' ideas are that they are conceptually simple (although considerably more complex in practice). As we have already noted in the previous section, monetarists regard inflation as the paramount problem facing any economy. Its cause lies in an increase in the money supply in excess of the growth in the economy's productive output. In the next section we shall examine the mechanics of monetary policy. Here we shall concentrate on the implications of the monetarists' theory on overall economic management.

Monetarism in theory

Monetarism accepts that a reduction in inflation can be brought about initially by deflating the economy. This will precipitate an increase in the level of unemployment, but it is regarded as the cost which society must bear to rid itself of the problem of inflation.

It is at this point that we re-introduce the Phillips Curve. Refer back to the diagram shown on the previous page.

As we have already seen, this form of analysis fell from favour in the early 1970s as inflation and unemployment both rose simultaneously. Monetarist economists argued that this did not mean that the underlying theory was basically unsound but rather that the Phillips Curve itself was liable to movement. They introduced the idea that it was people's expectations of inflation which had this effect. Some examples of how expectations of inflation can alter the situation will illustrate this.

Let us look first at Trade Unions. If they expect inflation to rise in the coming year they will build this into their wage demands. If they are successful in achieving wage rises above the current rate of inflation this will push up wage costs which are passed on to consumers in higher prices. A similar effect will be seen with consumers. The expectation of high prices in the future will encourage consumers to bring their purchasing forward to beat the price rises. This extra demand in itself will push up prices.

Next consider the attitudes of borrowers. During inflationary times the real cost of borrowing tends to fall as the sum borrowed, which must subsequently be repaid, is falling in value in real terms. Thus if borrowers think inflation will continue they will raise the level of their borrowing and this has inflationary consequences. Finally look at the view of lenders. Those in society who seek to lend money will want an acceptable return on their loan in terms of the interest they will receive. If inflation is rising they anticipate this and try to protect the value of their loan by seeking higher interest rates and so force up the cost of borrowing.

All of those individuals, by anticipating inflation, actually make it occur. It is almost a self-fulfilling prophesy — in other words, if you think there will be inflation, then there will be inflation.

The effect of this anticipation of inflation is to shift the Phillips Curve to the right as shown in the figure. This new curve is known as the Expectations Augmented Phillips Curve. The extent of the shift to the right will depend on the level of inflation which people expect and the extent of the actions they take to anticipate it and to compensate for it.

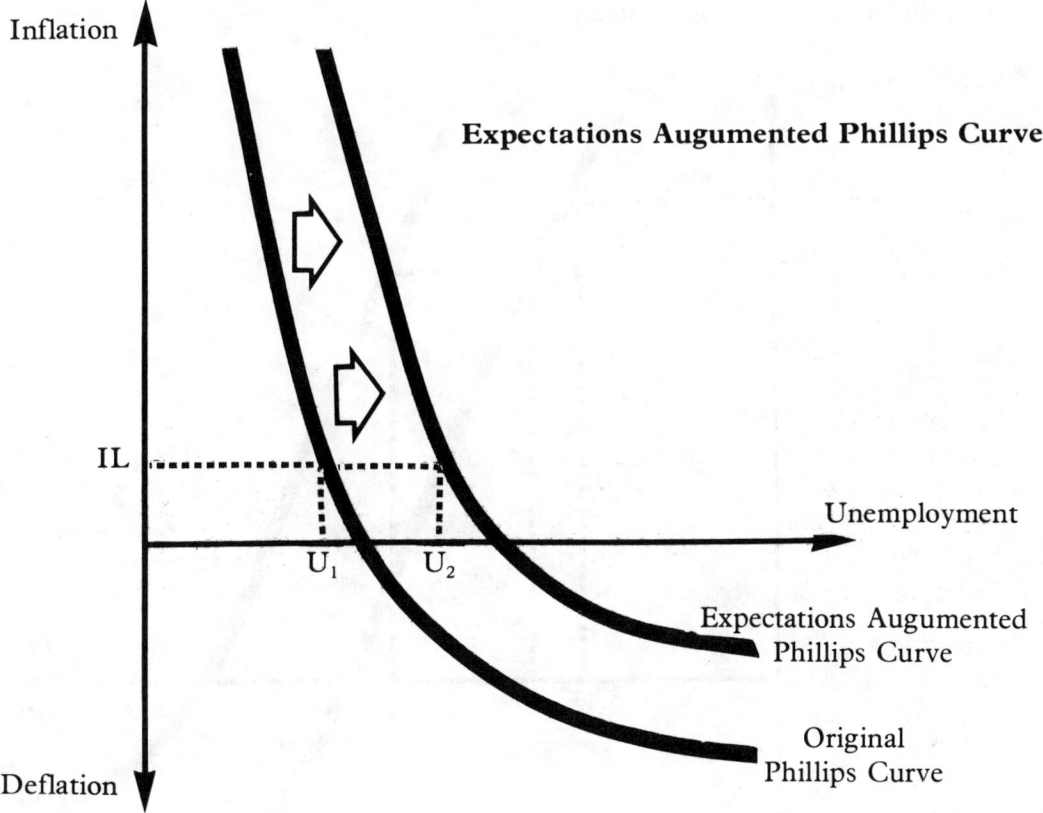

This poses a number of problems for the government in their attempt to reduce inflation:

(a) The country must bear a higher level of unemployment if inflation is to be brought down than it would have done had the curve remained stable. (In the figure the rate of unemployment, which is necessary to achieve inflation rate IL, is U1, with the original Phillips Curve, but has increased to U2 as expectations of inflation have pushed the Curve to the right.)

(b) The greater the level of inflation expected by society then the further to the right will the Curve be shifted, so making the first problem worse. The government, therefore, must make people believe that inflation is going to fall and that their policies to achieve this will succeed.

(c) If the government does not make the people believe that their policies will succeed then they will be even more costly in terms of unemployment to implement. In fact the more inflation people expect, the greater will be the level of unemployment which must be endured to bring inflation down.

In order to relate this theory to the United Kingdom economy we shall examine some of the thinking behind the economic policies of the Thatcher Government from 1979 to 1986 in the light of the previous comments.

MONETARISM IN PRACTICE — THE UK EXPERIENCE 1979-86

When Mrs. Thatcher's Government came to power in 1979 it was faced with an unemployment rate of 5.4% (1.5 million), and an inflation rate of 13.4%. In addition, the trend of both these rates was upward and people expected inflation to rise. The government's stated primary policy objective was to reduce inflation to single figures as soon as possible. In order to achieve this they believed that unemployment would have to rise to about 7.5% (2.2. million). They recognised that this was a high price to pay but believed that such a rise in unemployment was politically acceptable as long as inflation did in fact fall. Unfortunately, they had under-estimated the shift to the right of the Phillips Curve so that by 1981 inflation had been reduced to 11%, but unemployment has risen to 10%.

This is illustrated in the figure below.

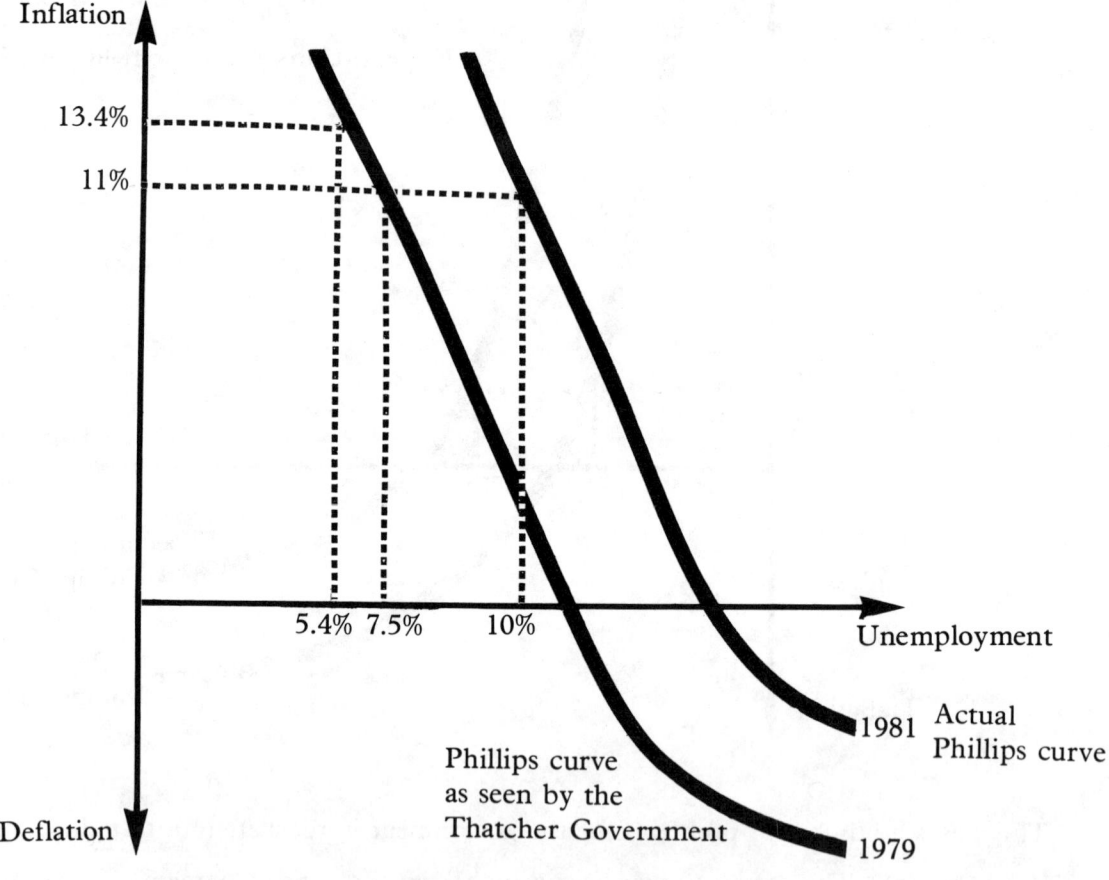

Shift of the Phillips Curve from 1979 to 1981

As unemployment rose beyond the expected level, some members of the Conservative government believed that it would produce a significant decline in the government's political popularity and as such could result in the next election being lost. They urged the government to ease its policy and allow the country to reflate, even at the cost of high inflation. However, as we have already noted, a key factor of monetarism is that the government must be seen to be determined to reduce inflation and in so doing reduce expectations. Fortunately for the Thatcher government the political impact of rising unemployment was not sufficient to seriously damage their popularity. This was due to a number of diverse factors such as:

    (a)   the weakness of the Opposition

    (b)   the rise of the SDP/Liberal Alliance splitting the Opposition, and

(c)   the undoubted popular appeal of Mrs. Thatcher's foreign policy.

The government was thus able to continue to reduce inflation and, despite the rise of unemployment to above 3 million, inflation has fallen below 3%, The government's hope is that people's expectations of inflation will go into reverse. If they will anticipate falling inflation their actions in making wage demands, consuming and investing, will lead to a leftward shift of the Phillips Curve in the coming years.

The government believe that if inflation can be held in low single figures then:

(a)   business confidence will revive;

(b)   investment from both domestic and foreign investors will increase; and

(c)   the rate of unemployment will consequently fall.

The figure shows what the government hopes will happen to the Phillips Curve.

The belief is that the anticipation of relatively stable inflation rates at low levels will result in a significant shift in the Phillips Curve so that, by perhaps 1987, inflation can be held at 3% or below, and unemployment will fall to 7% or below. Whether or not this will happen will depend on a variety of factors, some of which are within the government's control, while some are not. Inflation in the United Kingdom, as was noted in the previous section, is crucially influenced by changes in the world economy and by factors such as fluctuating oil prices. If the Thatcher Government's overall monetarist strategy is to succeed many external influences will have to play their part favourably.

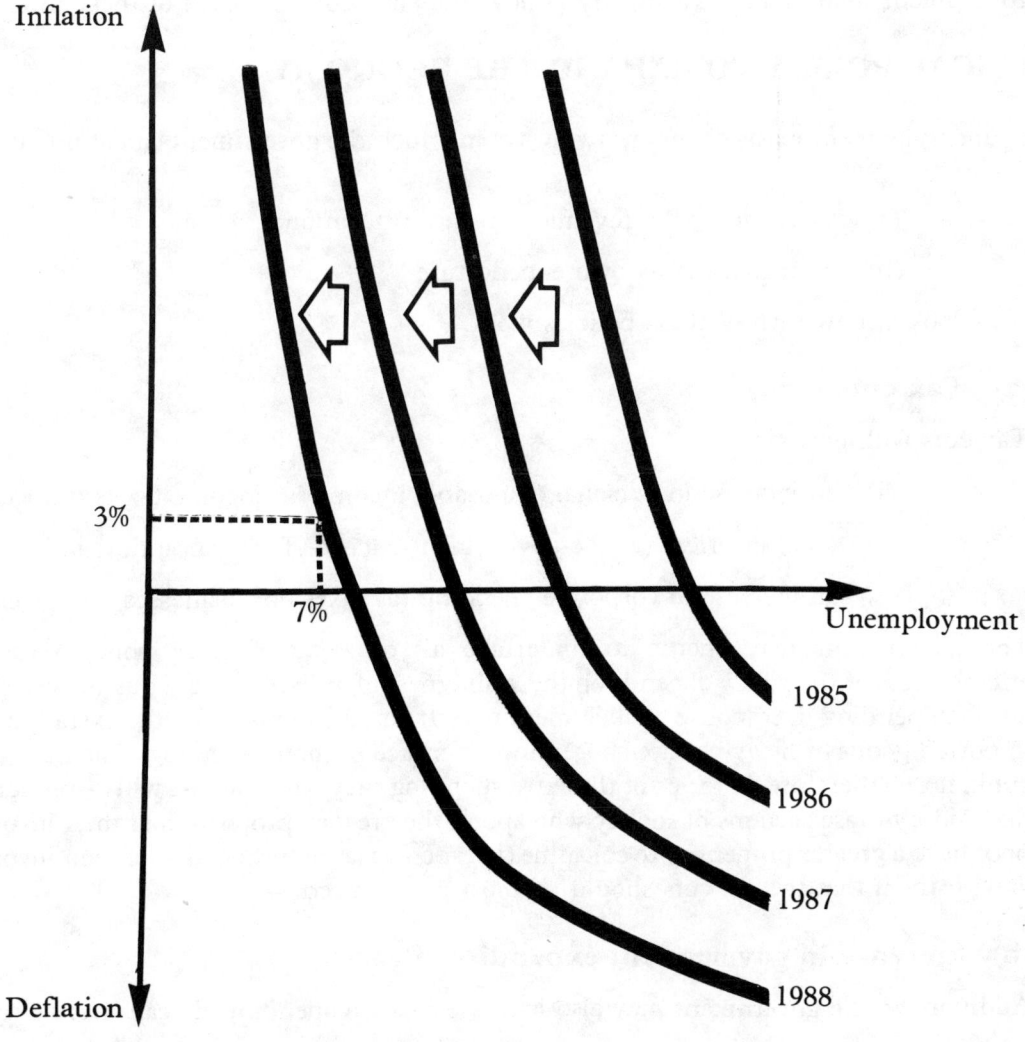

Government's Hopes for Shift in the Phillips Curve

Many critics of this policy would also argue forcibly that the cost of reducing inflation has been too high in terms of the unemployment and social distress it has caused. They believe that falling inflation may increase business confidence but it is not certain that this will lead to more jobs. Instead it could result in greater mechanisation and higher levels of efficiency. Thus output may start to increase but unemployment rates will not necessarily fall in the way the Thatcher Government would predict.

This section has concentrated on an overview of the differing theories underlying the Keynesian and Monetarist approaches to economic management. The next section will examine the alternative methods of control and evaluate their relative merits.

POLICY OPTIONS AVAILABLE TO THE GOVERNMENT

FISCAL POLICY

This policy option has been applied by governments in an attempt to control the economy since the 1940s. It is based on the principles of Keynesian Demand Management. We have already seen that Keynesians argue that unemployment and inflation are the result of disequilibrium in the economy's aggregate supply and demand. The assumption is that the economy tends to experience a series of booms and slumps with the fluctuations of the business cycle. Thus fiscal policy is essentially counter-cyclical, that is when the ecomomy is in recession the government pursues expansionary measures and conversely when the economy becomes "over-heated" the government follows a contractionary policy. We shall consider each of these in turn.

FISCAL POLICY TO EXPAND THE ECONOMY

If unemployment exists there are two ways in which the government can stimulate aggregate demand:

> (a)   by reducing the revenue it raises in taxation;
>
> (b)   by increasing its own expenditure.

Now look at how each of these policies work.

(a)   Tax cuts

Tax cuts will mean:

> (i)   an increase in personal disposable income (as income tax is reduced); or
>
> (ii)   a fall in prices (as the government cuts VAT or excise duties); or
>
> (iii) an increase in corporate spending (as taxes on businesses are lowered).

The government may choose to undertake all or some of these policy measures. The effectiveness of the policy depends on the willingness of individuals and businesses to raise their level of spending in response to such measures. It could be nullified if the extra spending is on imported goods or if savings are chosen in preference to more spending. The most productive cut in taxes, therefore, in terms of the extra spending they will generate will be reductions in the tax paid by those sections of society who spend the greatest proportion of their income. As the poor have a greater propensity to consume (i.e. spend a larger proportion of their income) then it is with them that the tax cuts should be most pronounced.

(b)   Increase in government expenditure

Additionally the government may also increase its own spending. It can do this by:

> (i)   greater expenditure on goods and services or by employing more people in the

public sector. This will create an immediate and direct increase in the level of demand; or

(ii) increased expenditure on transfer payments (benefits, grants, etc.) which will result in positive changes in consumer spending; or

(iii) a higher level of capital investment by building more schools, hospitals, roads, etc. While this type of spending may provide tangible benefits to society, it does take longer to bear fruit as projects must be planned, designed, and approved before implementation. There may, therefore, be a time lag in the period between electing to proceed with such expansion and the positive effect being felt in the economy.

The overall impact of such changes is that the government should face a budget deficit. Revenue falls while expenditure rises. This is known as budget deficit financing and will lead to increases in borrowing by the government to allow the implementation of such a policy.

FISCAL POLICY TO CONTRACT THE ECONOMY

If the policy objective is a reduction in inflation the government must pursue methods which are the reverse of those outlined above.

(a) Tax increases

Taxes should be raised to discourage spending. Here the most effective means of reducing expenditure is to tax more heavily those people who spend the greatest proportion of their income (for to tax those who save heavily may simply result in a reduction in savings rather than expenditure). This means that taxes on the poor should be increased. Of course this may conflict with considerations of equity and fairness and as such the most effective means of reducing spending may not always be seen as the most acceptable.

(b) Reduction in government expenditure

Reductions in government spending may also be undertaken and this may mean a fall in public sector employment, cuts in transfer spending and a fall in the government's investment programme. The overall outcome should be a budget surplus. This would withdraw income from the economy and so reduce aggregate demand.

One of the major difficulties with fiscal policy designed to influence demand is that it may contradict the other aims of taxation and government spending. One of the primary objectives of taxation is to act as a means of redistributing income and wealth. Yet as we have noted the most effective method of reducing spending is to tax the poor more heavily. Similarly government spending is the process by which a wide range of public and merit goods provision is financed. Thus to cut spending in order to reduce demand will also be detrimental to the level of supply of such services. The basic difficulty with fiscal policy is not that it does not prove effective in countering inflation or unemployment. Rather it is its inherent weakness in reducing both at the same time. This flaw led to the development of the government's alternative means of control, monetary policy.

MONETARY POLICY

The emergence of monetary policy has perhaps been the most significant change in economic management in the post-war period. The crux of monetary control is the need for the government to regulate the expansion of the country's money supply so that its growth does not drastically exceed the increase in the economy's productive capacity. To understand this we must first be clear about what the government is trying to control.

The money supply

The money supply or stock of money in its widest sense is the amount of notes and coins and bank and other financial deposits in the economy. While it is obvious that currency can be regarded as 'money' it is less easy to recognise that bank deposits, often in the form of figures in accounts, are also money. Most transactions involving large amounts of money undertaken in the economy rely on cheques as the means of transfer. This will result in the commercial banks readjusting their accounts as money is drawn from an account in one bank and moved into an account in another bank. In most cases there is no need for a physical movement of notes and coins to accompany this as there will be similar transfers occurring in the opposite direction. Thus banks do not need to hold currency to cover all of the deposits they hold, only sufficient to allow them to meet their customer's demands for notes and coins.

Therefore, depending on the measure of the money supply we use, bank deposits account for between two-thirds and three-quarters of the money supply.

The creation of money

The government, through the Bank of England, is responsible for the printing and minting of notes and coins and so it has direct control over this part of the money supply. But in addition the commercial banks through their activities of accepting deposits and making loans, also play an active role in creating money. A simple example will illustrate this:

(a)   If an individual deposits £100 into his or her bank account the commercial bank will have an increase in its liabilities (the money it owes) of £100;

(b)   The bank will then hold a percentage of this as a reserve;

(c)   The bank will lend the rest out to a borrower;

(d)   The borrower will then spend the money (it is unlikely that someone will borrow simply to save). In most cases this will result in a seller receiving cash for the sale of some goods or services to the borrower;

(e)   The seller then deposits the money received into his or her bank account. This has the same effect as the initial deposit because the bank will again hold some of the deposit in reserve and lend out the rest.

This process of deposit, reserve, lend, spend and deposit will continue with the original £100 in notes circulating through the economy. After each cycle in the process, the deposits of the commercial banks have risen by the amount of the deposit made. The depositors rightly regard their deposits as money and as such the money supply is increased. This process is called the money or bank multiplier.

The figure shows a simplified version of this process.

The Money or Bank Multiplier

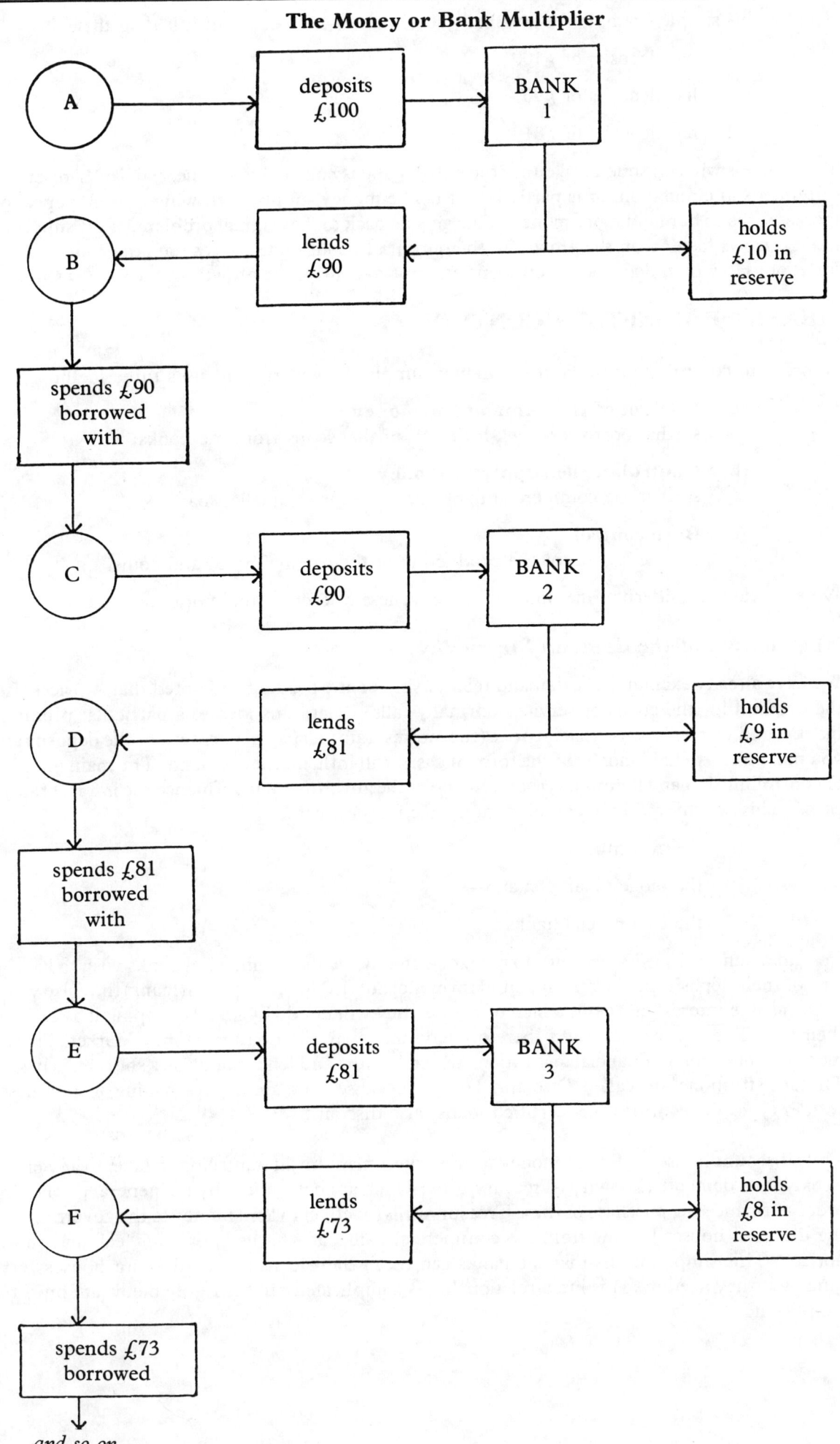

and so on.

Even in this simple example the original £100 in notes has been multiplied so that:

A   has deposits of £100

C   has deposits of £90

E   has deposits of £81

This process will continue until either the entire £100 is held in the commercial banks' reserves, or remains in circulation, or is partly in both. The money supply is growing as each depositor increases his or her holding of money. This gets us back to the original problem. If the supply of money grows faster than the growth in the output of goods and services then the result will be inflation. How then does the government attempt to control the growth in the money supply?

MEANS OF MONETARY CONTROL

In order to control the growth in the money supply the government uses three methods:

(a)   **Control of the demand for money**
so that borrowers seek fewer or smaller loans from the banks;

(b)   **Control of the supply of money**
so that the commercial banks make fewer or smaller loans;

(c)   **Base control**
i.e. the control of the production of the original notes and coins.

We shall now consider the method and effectiveness of each of these options.

(a)   Control of the demand for money

We have already examined the demand relationship of any product and noted that as prices rise the demand for the goods or services normally falls. Relate this idea to a particular product, money, and you will realise that its price (the interest rate you pay to borrow it or the deposit rate you must forgo to hold money in the form of cash) will influence its demand. The main method of controlling demand for money, therefore, is for the government to influence the interest rate it earns. This is achieved by a complex inter-reaction between:

(i)   the government;

(ii)   the money markets; and

(iii)   the commercial banks.

To understand this, it is necessary to recognise that while the commercial banks wish to keep a part of their deposits in a relatively liquid form (i.e. not tied up in long term loans) they also wish to earn some interest on them, which of course they will not do by merely keeping it as cash in their tills. The commercial banks therefore lend money to the London Money Market. This is merely a collection of financial institutions which borrow and lend money on a short term basis. These institutions are called Discount Houses because they are always willing to purchase certain types of securities (i.e. certified loans) at a discount.

Thus discount houses will lend money to the government by guaranteeing to take up any of its weekly loan demands, known as Treasury Bills, which are not wanted by the general public. In order to finance the purchase of these Treasury Bills (in effect to lend money to the government) the discount houses borrow from the commercial banks at what is known as "call and short notice". This simply means that the banks can recall their loans to the discount houses very quickly if they need to. This inter-relationship is complicated but the figure below attempts to simplify it.

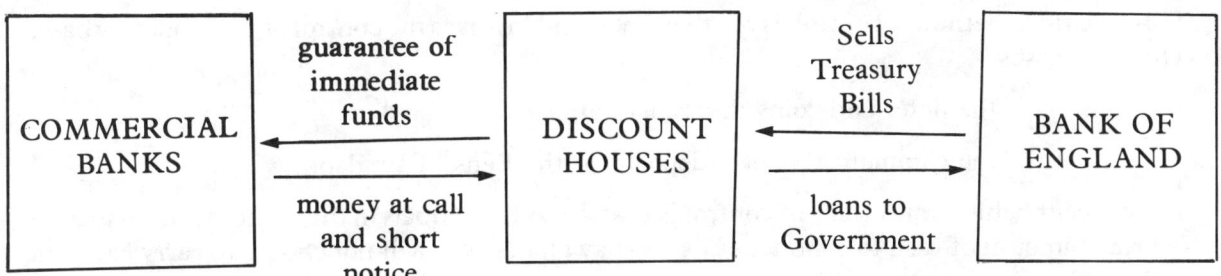

**Inter-relationship of government, money market
and commercial banks.**

This process allows the government to influence interest rates throughout the economy. If the Bank of England offers a high rate of interest on its loans from the discount houses this attracts money. To finance these loans to the government, the discount houses offer high rates to the banks for 'call' money. The banks transfer funds to the money market leaving less to lend out to ordinary borrowers and so the price (interest rate) to borrowers goes up. Conversely, to the lower interest rates, the Bank of England makes its rates lower, attracting less money to the government and so allowing more to be borrowed elsewhere in the economy.

The Bank of England also acts as 'lender of the last resort' to the discount houses so that if they are short of funds, should the banks require an immediate payment of a loan or to discount a treasury bill, the discount houses borrow from the Bank of England. It will set its lending rate according to the level of interest rates it seeks to achieve in the economy. In this way the discount houses know what rate they should charge to commercial banks seeking immediate cash.

The effects and effectiveness of interest rate policy will be considered after we have examined the other means of monetary control.

(b) Control of the supply of money

The supply of money is controlled by the Bank of England monitoring and regulating the amount of money the commercial banks can, and are willing to, lend out. Until 1981 the Bank of England specified a certain percentage of the commercial bank's deposits which the banks had to hold in reserve and so could not lend out to the general public. Now, however, no specified reserve ratio is required. Instead the banks are required to be 'prudent'. This means that they should take account of the type of deposits they hold and when they could be withdrawn (i.e. with long-term deposits accounts there is no risk of an immediate withdrawal). The reserves they hold should reflect the imminence of likely withdrawals of deposits. For example, a current account can be withdrawn 'on sight' (i.e. at once) and the banks must, therefore, hold a higher percentage of this type of account in reserve in readiness than they would deposit accounts. So, how then, can the government influence the amount the banks choose to lend out?

The method employed is called Open Market Operations. This involves the government borrowing money from the general public (by the sale of Treasury Bills or Gilt Edged Securities). The lender (the public) pays the money to the government in the form of a cheque. The Bank of England acts as a banker for all the banks who are required to keep $1/_2$% of their deposits there, and at this stage, the Bank withdraws the amount it is owed from these deposits. Because the commercial banks' deposits at the Bank of England are now reduced, they must transfer funds from elsewhere to maintain their $1/_2$% balance at the Bank. This means that they have less money to lend out. In this way the Bank of England can influence the ability of the commercial banks to create loans.

(c) **Base control**

This, the final method of control, is relatively new and involves the control of the monetary base. This comprises:

      (i)   the notes and coins in circulation; and

     (ii)   the commercial banks' deposits at the Bank of England.

The concept behind this means of control is that we, as individuals in the economy, need to hold a certain amount of cash to conduct our everyday affairs. We will not choose to carry less cash around simply because the government asks us to do so, and the Bank of England uses this demand for cash to influence bank lending. Clearly the banks also need cash to be able to meet the possible withdrawal demand of their customers. If the Bank of England reduces the amount of notes and coins in circulation in the economy this will not influence an individual's money holding and so the banks feel the squeeze. They must 'top up' their cash reserves by reducing the amount of money they lend out and in so doing the expansion of credit and the growth of the money supply is reduced.

The explanation above has been purposely simplified to allow you to grasp the concepts behind monetary control and some of the finer detail has been omitted because of lack of space. The important point to understand is that the government reduces the growth of the money supply by holding down borrowing from the commercial banks and so limiting the process of credit creation.

We shall next examine the effectiveness of these monetary measures.

The effectiveness of monetary control

In the early 1980s the government forced up interest rates in an attempt to deter borrowing but this policy was less than successful. The lack of success can be explained by looking at the different categories of borrowers.

(a) **Personal borrowers**

In theory, higher interest rates should deter us from borrowing money for a new car, video, or summer holiday. In fact, it was found that personal borrowing was relatively interest inelastic. This meant that as interest rates rose we continued to seek loans and were willing to pay the higher price. It was the growth of unemployment which dampened the level of personal borrowing rather than higher interest rates.

(b) **Corporate borrowing for investment**

Businesses are much more conscious of the cost of borrowing money and so higher interest rates did have a pronounced effect on borrowing for this purpose. Industry slackened its new investment and in so doing made the problem of unemployment worse. Workers were laid off as investment projects were either abandoned or rejected before they began.

(c) **Corporate borrowing to finance cash flow difficulties**

As the government tightened the monetary screws, businesses found their debtors took longer to pay because credit from banks became more expensive and less easy to obtain. Many businesses faced cash flow problems because while such items as employees wages must be paid regularly, the firms debtors may withhold payment for as long as possible. The options facing a business were often either to go under by not paying its bills or to borrow from the banks even at the higher interest rates. This led to a dramatic increase in business overdraft borrowing as firms fought desperately to survive.

Because these three categories of borrowers reacted differently to high interest rates, the combined effect was that the desired reduction on credit creation was not as positive as the government had hoped. They attempted to push up rates even higher and in so doing accelerated the growing unemployment as businesses collapsed, or reduced their workforce to cut costs.

The other means of money supply control are also somewhat suspect in application. Attempts to control bank lending have not always proved effective. The commercial banks as money-making enterprises seek to avoid restrictions on their lending (and the ability to make profit) and so the government has had to introduce changes in their control which are yet to be seen as fully successful.

Base control is still somewhat in its infancy and while in theory it does have the attraction of giving the Bank of England and the government direct influence on the money supply through the printing of money, its drawbacks are that interest rates tend to fluctuate and the government loses its indirect control over the mortgage rate which it has used in the past as an effective electioneering tool. At the present time the government is combining elements of all three methods of control in an attempt to find the most suitable and effective mix. However, one major hindrance to its money supply policy lies in the extent of its own borrowing and that of the rest of the public sector.

THE IMPACT OF GOVERNMENT BORROWING ON MONETARY CONTROL

As we outlined earlier, one of the means by which the government can influence commercial bank borrowing is by attracting money to itself by offering higher interest rates. This leaves less in circulation in the economy to be loaned and borrowed. However, this process assumes that when the government does borrow it hold the money and so keeps it out of circulation. If instead of holding the money, as it were 'in limbo', the government simply spends the money it borrows, then it goes back out into the economy to be loaned and borrowed as before and in so doing increases the money supply. The answer to this problem of monetary control then is, on the surface, quite simple — the government should not spend the money it borrows. Unfortunately, the problem is not that easy to solve. Increasingly governments have been facing budget deficits (i.e. their revenue is less than their expenditure). They must borrow to spend and pay their way. The difference between government revenue and expenditure is called the Public Sector Borrowing Requirement (PSBR) and its size will play a large part in determining the effectiveness of monetary policy.

Advocates of monetarism argue that the larger the PSBR is, the less powerful the policy can be. Thus the suggestion is that public expenditure must be cut to reduce the PSBR. This to some extent explains the Thatcher Government's determination to trim the public sector. Later in this section we shall briefly examine the government's attemps to control local authority spending and how privatisation of the public sector is used to reduce government borrowing and increase its short term revenue.

Opponents of monetarism argue that it is not the size of the PSBR which is crucial but how it is financed. This can be examined by looking at the sources of government borrowing:

(a)   The commercial banks

If money is borrowed from the commercial banks they can use these loans as part of their reserves (short term loans to the government in the form of Treasury Bills can always be turned into cash immediately at the discount houses) and so lend out more, adding to money supply growth.

(b)   The private sector

If, instead, the borrowing is from the private sector this reduces commercial bank deposits and so they have less to lend out. Even if the government immediately spends the money borrowed from the private sector, this merely re-establishes the amount of money in the economy in a neutral, non-expansionary, non-inflationary way. Another problem with borrowing from the private sector is that normally it does not save sufficient funds to meet all of the government's PSBR needs. Such government borrowing may also prove detrimental to economic growth by diverting investment away from private industry.

Those who advocate a short-term increase in government spending, even at the cost of a greatly enlarged PSBR, suggest that as expenditure on jobs, services and government investment rises this will reduce unemployment and so lower the government's transfer benefit payouts. It is almost a case of swings and roundabouts. The government should pay out now (to create jobs) to avoid having to pay out in the future (in the form of social security and unemployment benefits). This line of thought has not been in favour with the Thatcher Government who have pursued a policy of reduction and privatisation. One area which has felt the effects of this policy most severely has been local government.

CENTRAL GOVERNMENT CONTROL OVER THE LOCAL AUTHORITIES

As local authorities are dependent on central government funds in the form of grant aid as a major proportion of their income, it is here that the central administration has chosen to implement its policy of retrenchment. Each authority receives an annual grant depending on its notional rateable income and the predicted level of its spending needs. Its rateable income is determined by the quantity and quality of rateable property it has in its area, and its spending needs reflect its demographic and geographical make-up of the area. Since 1979, local authorities have seen a continued cut in the central government's estimates of their spending needs and a consequent fall in grant aid. Some councils have responded to this by maintaining the level of their services and transferring the cost from grant income to higher rates.

The government countered this continued higher spending by introducing a policy of cash limits on higher expenditure tied to a system of penalties by which, as council spending increased, their grant was proportionately reduced. This had the required effect in some areas — some councils did introduce spending cuts. Other authorities chose to bear the penalty burden rather than slash services.

The ultimate step on the part of central government appears to be to 'cap the rates' of the 'overspending' authorities. By this, central government will actually specify the rate an authority is able to levy and, if that authority then chooses to set a higher rate, ratepayers will be entitled by law to refuse to pay any rate in excess of the government's 'cap' limit. Councillors who vote through rate increases above the government limit are personally liable to be penalised. The likely outcome of such a move is difficult to predict but some government critics see it as the sacrifice of local autonomy in terms of local authorities' revenue and expenditure for the sake of an overall monetary policy.

PRIVATISATION

A further policy to reduce the PSBR and increase short term government revenue has been privatisation. The present Conservative Government is committed to the sales of some of the public corporations either in their entirety or in part, in an attempt to reduce the State's involvement in industry. This is certainly a controversial move and there is strong opposition from both the Labour party and the trade union movement, as well as from certain elements within the Conservative party itself.

The Arguments against Privatisation

There are three major arguments put forward against privatisation:

    (a) **Financial**

        It is said that the government has not considered the long-term implications of such a move. The industries which are currently being sold or are to be sold off are necessarily the more profitable areas of the public sector, for it is unlikely that private investors would wish to take over a loss-making concern. The possible result of such a policy could be that the government will be left with only the major loss-making nationalised industries and with no possibility of cross-subsidisation.

(b) **Private monopoly**

It is also argued that the government is in danger of merely transfering a State monopoly to private monopoly, with no attempt made to introduce competition to improve efficiency.

(c) **Job losses**

A further criticism is suggested by the trade unions. They claim that privatisation will be accompanied by large job losses and that this is hardly desirable in times when unemployment is already high.

Methods of Privatisation

The government has a number of methods at its disposal to privatise the nationalised industries. We shall examine the main three:

(a)   the sale of shares;

(b)   the introduction of private capital;

(c)   the use of private contractors.

The sale of shares

In the same way that the government requires legislation to nationalise an industry, it must go through a similar procedure in reverse to transfer it back to private ownership. A new company must be formed. The assets of the nationalised industry are transferred to the new company. The company is given share capital to sell on the open market. It is very important that the assets of the new company are given a realistic value. The government's first real venture into privatisation of this kind was in February 1982 with the sale of Amersham International. The value of the company's shares was greatly under-estimated, and the lucky buyers who purchased the initial issue quickly made a large profit by re-selling them on the stock market. This incident led to considerable criticism of the government, who effectively lost out by selling the shares too cheaply. However, when the government later sold shares in Britoil, it over-priced them, and found that it was short of buyers.

Other examples of equity sales (sale of shares) include:

(a)   Cable and Wireless;

(b)   British Rail Hotels;

(c)   Associated British Ports.

Other targets for privatisation have included British Telecom which raised around £4,000m and British Airways. The government, however, is faced with a problem in the sale of the latter public corporation. It is generally agreed that the introduction of more competition is a desirable element of privatisation. However, if the government allows competition at present, for example in permitting British Midland to compete with British Airways on the London-Glasgow shuttle service, then this will reduce the profitability of the nationalised industry and as such it will become a less attractive proposition to private investors. Indeed, the government has been criticised for failing to take the opportunity to encourage more competition by keeping monopolies as strong as possible in order to obtain a good price when they are sold off.

This system of privatisation ensures that the government will receive a healthy boost to its funds and will also be relieved of the financial and administrative burdens of running the public corporation. However, the State is also giving up its rights to future profits, which in the long run could prove more lucrative than the once-only injection of cash to government funds. Another contentious issue within the sale of shares is the question of who actually buys the new equity. The government favoured encouraging small investors, and 65,000 people obtained shares in Amersham and 158,000 in British Aerospace. However, the initial number of shareholders has rapidly dwindled, and the vast majority of shares in privatised industries are now held by the large financial institutions. A notable exception to this is the case of the National Freight Consortium, which was sold in its entirety to its management and staff, who have found the value of their shares has virtually trebled in price since privatisation.

The introduction of private capital

This system involves the introduction of private risk capital, either directly into nationalised industries or into joint projects, such as the Channel Tunnel. The government attempts to attract private money into a project which it feels it cannot afford to finance alone. Success in this sphere is inconsistent. For example, in an effort to finance a new gas gathering system in the North Sea the government sought the assistance of private financiers and the major oil companies. In return, the financiers demanded a guarantee on gas prices and the oil companies asked for their investment expenditure to be offset against tax. The government would give neither assurance, and as a result, the project was scrapped.

In order to tempt private money into such ventures it may be necessary for the government to adopt a policy of give and take. It will be interesting to see if projects such as the Channel Tunnel proceed in such circumstances.

The use of private contractors

A form of privatisation which is currently favoured is to allow certain services presently provided by the public sector to be put out to contract in the private sector. One of the pioneers of this field was Southend's Conservative Council. Their refuse collection service was successfully transferred to private contractors, with a saving estimated by the council in the first year of some £600,000. The workforce received higher wages, but their numbers were reduced by one-third. However, this so-called 'success' story has been matched by instances of failure, with standards falling and jobs being lost on a large scale. This is one of the major reasons for the strong trade union resistance. It is also vital that a strict control on standards is maintained if private contractors are introduced. If they do not fulfil the expected standards, then the contract must be reviewed and alternatives considered. One interesting example of this form of privatisation has arisen in Birmingham. The council's refuse collection service was put out to tender and the council's own refuse collection staff formed a workers' co-operative and successfully bid for the contract, albeit with a reduced workforce. The co-operative has proved so successful that it is actually taking on additional business, in the field of commercial and industrial waste from established private organisations.

Overall, it remains to be seen whether privatisation will work. The government has predicted its success but at the same time it has been accused of missing an opportunity to break down monopolies and to strengthen competition, in favour of simply cashing in financially on the sale of profitable parts of the public sector. Only future developments will show whether the quest for privatisation has been based on sound economic criteria or merely on ideological rationale.

REGIONAL POLICY

The policies previously discussed have been aimed at solving problems in the country as a whole by seeking to reduce the aggregate rate of inflation or unemployment. However, in the UK there are some regions which have specific problems of unemployment above the national average, low growth rates and many associated social problems such as crime, poor housing, etc.

Successive governments have made various attempts to alleviate these particular problems through Regional Policy. They have attempted this by two different types of policies:

1. encourage unemployed workers to move to more prosperous regions;

2. induce companies and firms to move to the regions of high unemployment.

1.   Encouragement of the Mobility of Labour

Some workers are less able to move from one area to another in search of work because they have a high immobility of labour. The government has tried to help by giving financial incentives (travelling and resettlement grants), encouraging retraining (through Skill Centres and Government Training Schemes) and improving workers' knowledge of opportunities in other regions (through the Job Centres and Department of Employment). A policy such as this may well alleviate unemployment in the short term, but it tends to have the longer term effect of moving workers away from their traditional home areas, leaving these regions to decline and so to some extent reinforcing regional inequality in the UK.

2.   Encouragement of Organisations to Resite in the Regions.

The government has sought to give financial assistance to organisations willing to locate in the regions. Certain regions such as the North East, Merseyside and West Cumbria have been designated Development Areas. In these areas, Regional Development Grants are available which help towards the purchase of new capital assets and also provide a grant for each new job created. Additionally other areas are designated as Intermediate Areas. These include the West Midlands, Humberside and parts of Yorkshire, Lancashire, South Wales and the South West. In these regions lesser grants are available for businesses creating new jobs.

The EEC is also an increasingly important source of funds through its Regional Fund. This provides money to finance specific projects in the poorer areas of Europe. Unfortunately certain of the UK's regions now fall within that category.

Regional Policy — Success or Failure

This type of policy has been used in some way for 50 years and yet there are still considerable inequalities between the regions. Does this mean that the policy has failed? Certainly the policy has not achieved its objective of a fair distribution of industry throughout the country. Nevertheless, it has created and maintained many hundreds of thousands of jobs in the regions. The policy itself has been very costly to promote and it is estimated that the cost of each job created is well in excess of £2,000. Clearly the problem of regional unemployment has grown in the last six years as national unemployment has also risen. Many critics of the government now believe that an overall policy of reducing mass unemployment together with a reinforced regional policy is necessary if the growing inequality in the regions is to be reduced.

INCOMES POLICY

A further method of government control which we must consider is that of incomes policy. An incomes policy is intended to reduce the level of wage increases and so moderate the inflationary consequences of rising costs of production. Essentially, incomes policy is a means of tackling cost push inflation and as such is not favoured by monetarist economists who see inflation's cause as excess monetary growth. Incomes policy has, nevertheless, been extensively employed in the post-war period in a variety of forms. We can distinguish incomes policy by its type and by its degree of implementation.

Types of income policy

(a) Voluntary incomes policy

Here agreement is reached between the government, trade unions and employers to limit wage rises to a mutually acceptable level. To 'sweeten the pill' the government may be forced to offer other concessions to the unions such as a more sympathetic labour legislation or social policy in accord with their wishes. (Such a policy was in force in the late 40s and middle 1970s under Labour governments.)

(b) Statutory incomes policy

In this instance, the government passes legislation which imposes a specified maximum wage increase and enforces such legislation for a certain period of time. Such policies are normally opposed by trade unions who regard them as an unacceptable restriction on free collective bargaining. (Statutory policies were imposed in the middle 1960s and late 1970s by Labour and in the early 1970s by a Conservative administration.)

Degree of implementation

(i) Full on

This refers to a total wage freeze usually lasting for a short period such as six months or a year. No wage increases are permitted.

(ii) Half on

This policy imposes a certain increase either in percentage terms (e.g. 5% maximum wage rise) or in money terms (e.g. £6 a week across the board). Some previous policies have combined elements of both percentage and poundage increases as well as attempts at index-linking wage increases to inflation.

The effectiveness of incomes policies

The underlying concept behind incomes policies is that inflation is caused by excessive wage demands. If there are other contributory factors such as:

      (a)   money supply growth;

      (b)   rising import costs; or

      (c)   a falling currency;

then simply holding down wages may have little effect on the overall inflationary position.

What is worse is that if an incomes policy is imposed and inflation does continue to rise, then workers are continually suffering a fall in their standard of living. This can result in frustration and resentment building up and increasing pressure for wage increases once the constraints of the incomes policy are removed. Past experience suggest that there is an almost immediate catching up period when the policy is relaxed and any discrepancy between rising prices and wages which has occurred during the life of the policy is immediately compensated for, as trade unions push for higher wages.

A second major disadvantage of incomes policy has been that it has tended to polarise the government and the trade union movement. This has been particularly true of statutory policies such as that adopted by the Heath government from 1971-74. Concerted efforts by trade unions to break the policy can introduce political instability and can be causal in the defeat of governments. This was seen in Heath's fall in 1974 after the miner's strike in opposition to his incomes policy, and in the demise of the Callaghan administration in 1979 after the so-called "winter of discontent". Governments are therefore justifiably wary of introducing a policy which may be politically unwise and at the same time based on a premise that is economically unsure.

The reluctance of the Thatcher Government to introduce such a policy reflects both its belief in the monetarist causes of inflation and a desire to avoid the kind of industrial conflict experienced by the previous two governments. Instead the Thatcher administration has elected to pursue a more restricted policy regarded by some as "incomes policy in disguise". This has involved attempts to impose wage restrictions on the public sector and, as such, the government acting as an employer in a wage negotiating situation rather than being seen to impose an overall wage limit on all sectors of the economy.

AN ASSESSMENT OF THE SUCCESS OF GOVERNMENT ECONOMIC POLICY

This chapter has concentrated on an examination of the major economic problems facing the United Kingdom.

If we compare the situation facing the country in the 1980s with that which existed in the 1950s and 1960s we may draw the conclusion that overall economic policy has not been particularly successful. To achieve a rate of inflation close to that of those earlier decades we have had to suffer mass unemployment not experienced since the bleakest years of the depression. Economic growth has been at a sluggish rate for most of the 1970s and 1980s, and if it were not for nature's benevolence in providing us with North Sea Oil we would be facing our traditional post-war balance of payments deficit.

The policies of Keynes and his followers proved an adequate if erratic means of control until the early 1970s. It was only then that the twin evils of inflation and unemployment managed to surface simultaneously. There are clearly a number of reasons why this has happened. They include:

(a) Britain's changing role in the world economy;

(b) the growing strength and confidence of the trade union movement in the 1960s and 1970s;

(c) the shifting balance of economic power in the post-OPEC world,

(d) the increased sophistication and accessibility of a banking and financial system opening up the availability of credit to the masses.

The rejection of Keynesian ideas and the headlong charge into the monetarist experiment has produced its traumas. The concepts and theories of monetary policy, all so clear and logical in the sterility of the class or seminar room, have proved much more complex to implement effectively in a dynamic economy less willing to respond to the prod of an interest rate movement than would have been hoped.

The monetarists predict that the economy is undergoing a transition which will make it leaner, more efficient and more able to react to a changing world environment. This remains to be seen. What is clear is that the major problem of unemployment remains and appears, at least at present, unresponsive to the efforts of Keynesian and monetarist alike.

ASSIGNMENT — THE IMPACT OF MONETARY POLICY

The government's monetary policy has had a considerable impact on the economy in the 1980s. It has affected individuals and organisations in both the public and private sectors. One such organisation is Weller Finance Ltd, a company engaged in providing finance to individuals and businesses. The company has an agency for a major building society as well as acting as a broker for a number of insurance companies which provide both domestic and commercial mortgages linked to endowment policies. Alan Weller, the managing director of the company, is a competent businessman but readily admits that he is unclear on the rationale for monetary policy and the precise methods the government employs to implement it. He is particularly concerned about changes in the interest rate and its effect on borrowing.

TASK

1. You are employed by Weller Finance Ltd and Alan has asked you to prepare an outline of the rationale underlying monetarism, the main methods of monetary control and the economic effects of monetary policy on the economy. Whilst you may have your own views on the appropriateness of such a policy, you should try to make these notes as objective as possible. To help in the preparation of these notes you should refer to the tables on unemployment, inflation and growth of the money supply included in the chapter.

DEVELOPMENTAL TASK

2. Obtain a copy of the government's Financial Statement and Budget Report for the current year. This is published immediately after the Budget in the spring. From this document identify the main aspects of the government's current economy strategy and analyse and evaluate any changes in policy which are included in it.

ASSIGNMENT — PRIVATISATION

Contract Cleaning Ltd is a large private company specialising in office and factory cleaning. It is based in Barnet, Hertfordshire and has mainly dealt with cleaning contracts in the North London area. The managing director of the company is Nigel Hill and he is keen to see the business expand. He is aware that in certain areas of the country, local authorities and area health authorities have privatised their cleaning operations. Nigel wishes to investigate this further as a possible avenue for expansion but is aware that there is considerable public opposition to the government's policy of privatisation.

TASK

1. You are employed as a management trainee by Contract Cleaning Ltd. Mr Hill has asked you to prepare a report for him on the issue of privatisation. In the report you should consider the following points:

    (i)   the different ways in which the present government has interpreted the term 'privatisation';

    (ii) the benefits the government claim will result from putting privatisation into practice;

    (iii) the economic arguments against the policy of privatisation.

DEVELOPMENTAL TASK

2. Investigate examples of privatisation in your own area or in the public sector as a whole. Identify examples where privatisation has occurred or has been proposed. Evaluate the arguments for and against such privatisation.

Chapter 26

PRICING AND MARKETING

THE DETERMINATION OF OUTPUT AND PRICE

In this chapter we will examine the different market conditions that may face an organisation and how these, in relation to its costs, will determine its price and output. We have already considered in chapter 21 the range of market forms which can exist. We saw that in theory, this ranged from a perfectly competitive market with many buyers and many sellers to a monopoly with a single supplier. However, as we noted, the most common market form in the UK is oligopoly, in which a small number of major suppliers dominate a market. In this chapter we will use the extreme market forms to explain simply how price and output is established before looking at the pricing policies in oligopolies. Our first task is to analyse an organisation's revenue, in other words the money it receives from the sale of its products or services.

AN ORGANISATION'S REVENUE

Any trading organisation must ensure that its total revenue from sales exceeds its total costs of production. If total revenue does exceed total cost then the business will make a profit, if it does not, then the organisation will make a loss. From this we can see that:-

$$\text{Total Revenue} - \text{Total Cost} = \text{Total Profit}$$

Total Revenue (TR) is all the money earned by the organisation from the sale of its products or services. In order to calculate TR, we simply multiply the selling price per unit of the product or service by the number sold.

$$\text{TR} = \text{Price} \times \text{Quantity Sold}$$

If the organisation sells a variety of products or services, or sells different products at different prices, then TR is the sum of all the quantities sold at each price. For example assume that an organisation produced three products (A, B and C) and sold them at three prices (P1, P2 and P3) then TR would be:-

$$
\begin{aligned}
&\quad\text{Price of A (P1)} \quad \times \quad \text{Quantity sold of A (QA)} \\
&\qquad\qquad\qquad\qquad + \\
\text{TR} \;=\; &\qquad\qquad \text{P2} \;\times\; \text{QB} \\
&\qquad\qquad\qquad\qquad + \\
&\qquad\qquad \text{P3} \;\times\; \text{QC}
\end{aligned}
$$

An organisation's average revenue is found by dividing the Total Revenue by the number of units sold. Therefore average revenue is TR/Q where Q is the total quantity sold.

The important factor to recognise is that, in most cases, the supplier's revenue is the price for which the product is sold. Most suppliers do not charge a range of prices for a particular product at any one time. In fact, they set one price for a particular product or service and sell as much as they can at that price. So, the supplier's average revenue curve is in fact the demand curve for the organisation as it shows how many units are sold at a specified price. A simple example will explain this.

> A producer makes 30,000 units a year and wishes to sell them all. He does not know what price to ask. If he asks £5 each, he sells 10,000. At £4 each he sells 20,000 and at £3, he sells 30,000. This demonstrates the demand curve for his product.

Now calculate the average revenue. If he sells 10,000 at £5 each, then total revenue is £50,000 (10,000 x £5).

$$\text{Average Revenue} = \frac{\text{total revenue}}{\text{quantity sold}} = \frac{£50,000}{10,000 \text{ units}} = £5$$

Similarly, if he sells 20,000 at £4 or 30,000 at £3, TR (£80,000 and £90,000 respectively) divided by Q (20,000 or 30,000) equals AR (£4 and £3) which is equal to price. Thus the average revenue curve of an organisation is also its demand curve.

Marginal Revenue is the extra revenue gained from the sale of one extra unit. For example, if the Total Revenue gained from selling 5,000 units is £30,000 and total revenue from 5,001 units is £30,005.50 then the marginal revenue gained from the 5,001st unit is £5.50.

It is important to be able to calculate the Marginal Revenue gained from the sale of an extra unit because, as we will see later, no organisation should manufacture a unit of production if the cost of producing it (Marginal Cost) is more than the extra revenue they will earn if it is sold (Marginal Revenue). This is because if it did so the supplier would be losing money on the production of the extra unit, and for most organisations it would be wrong to produce anything (even one unit) at a loss.

The revenue that the organisation gains from the sale of its product in relation to its costs of production will determine whether it makes a profit or a loss. If revenue is greater than costs, it will result in a profit, if it is less then the result is a loss.

A distinction may be drawn when considering the profit of an organisation between:

    (i) 'normal' profit; and

    (ii) 'supernormal' profit.

(i) Normal Profit.

Normal profit is the sum of money sufficient to keep the organisation operating in the same type of production. This may be a relatively small profit margin but it will be greater than that which it would gain in an alternative form of production.

(ii) Supernormal Profit

If the organisation makes a much greater profit than it could earn in another industry, this is termed "Supernormal Profit". However, if producers in a particular industry continue to make supernormal profit, this may be sufficient to encourage other organisations to enter the industry and compete for this higher level of profit. If new suppliers enter a market, this will tend to bring profits down as competition will lead to lower prices and consequently lower revenue as the new producers attempt to win over some of the existing suppliers' customers.

. . . attracts new suppliers into the market

A producer cannot survive for long in an industry in which it makes a loss and so continual loss making will tend to reduce competition and therefore allow efficient suppliers, who are profitable, to remain and increase their market share. Some producers will attempt to bear a loss which they regard as temporary, in the hope that market demand will increase in the future so allowing them to increase revenue. This may mean carrying costs in excess of revenue for a period by either:-

    (a)   using accumulated reserve capital to pay costs;

    (b)   borrowing to pay costs; or

    (c)   subsidising the loss making product.

This type of market behaviour is only feasible in the short term for long term losses will clearly mean that the organisation will go out of business as a result of insolvency. Exceptions to this may be the case of public sector organisations. Some of the major nationalised industries, for example, British Steel or British Coal, have continued to be unprofitable for a number of years. Such industries are not closed because the government regards the social loss to the economy of creating even more mass unemployment as being so great that it will continue to subsidise these industries from public funds. In other industries, such as British Rail, the government may be willing to subsidise loss making sections of the industry because it believes that they provide social benefit. In other words that such provision is good for society and so such undertakings are allowed to continue despite the fact that the revenue received (in the case of British Rail, its ticket sales) is less than costs of its operation.

So far in this chapter we have assumed that organisations always seek to make the biggest profit possible, in other words that they are profit maximisers. As we saw in chapter 21 this is not always true. In many public sector organisations profit is clearly not always the prime objective. This may also be true in the private sector. Some businesses in the private sector prefer to earn only sufficient profit to allow the enterprise to continue in existence and so may not seek to expand the level of their production to make supernormal profit. There are a number of possible reasons for this. The growth in output may increase the likelihood of greater management problems in a bigger operation particularly with industrial relations. Furthermore a higher level of profit may encourage increased competition from new suppliers entering the market and so could actually lead to a lowering of profit as prices are forced down. However, to explain the theory of price and output determination we will assume that the organisation will seek to achieve at least normal profit and will be hoping to profit maximise.

PRICING AND OUTPUT DECISIONS TO ACHIEVE PROFIT MAXIMISATION

We will now examine the different types of market structure and consider how each type will affect pricing and output decisions.

A PERFECTLY COMPETITIVE MARKET

Earlier in chapter 21 we noted that perfectly competitive markets are rare in the U.K.today. However, the concept of perfect competition is useful to explain simple pricing and output decisions.

The characteristics of a perfectly competitive market are that:

(i) there are many buyers, all seeking to purchase the product;

(ii) there are many sellers, all of whom are competing for potential customers;

(iii) each producer is offering a relatively similar product to those of his competitors;

(iv) both buyers and sellers have full knowledge of the prevailing market conditions; and

(v) there is freedom of movement into and out of the market by both producers and factors of production.

Such a competitive situation influences the demand for an individual producer's product by ensuring that there is no one supplier with a dominant market share. If a single producer were to begin to make supernormal profits this would be likely to attract new producers and suppliers into the industry.

As we saw in chapter 21 often the reason why a market remains competitive is that it is impossible for any supplier to gain economies of scale from large scale production. This is because of the type of product that is being produced. Consequently the optimum level of production for each organisation represents only a relatively small portion of total market sales. Accordingly no individual producer is able to independently influence overall market price. An individual supplier cannot put price up independently of other suppliers as consumers would simply buy elsewhere. Similarly a supplier would be foolish to drop its price below that of its competitors because all its output at optimum level of production can be sold at the prevailing market price. So each supplier must accept the equilibrium market price which is determined by the interaction of aggregate supply and aggregate demand. Each individual supplier is known as a Price-Taker. This can be shown in graphical form as follows:-

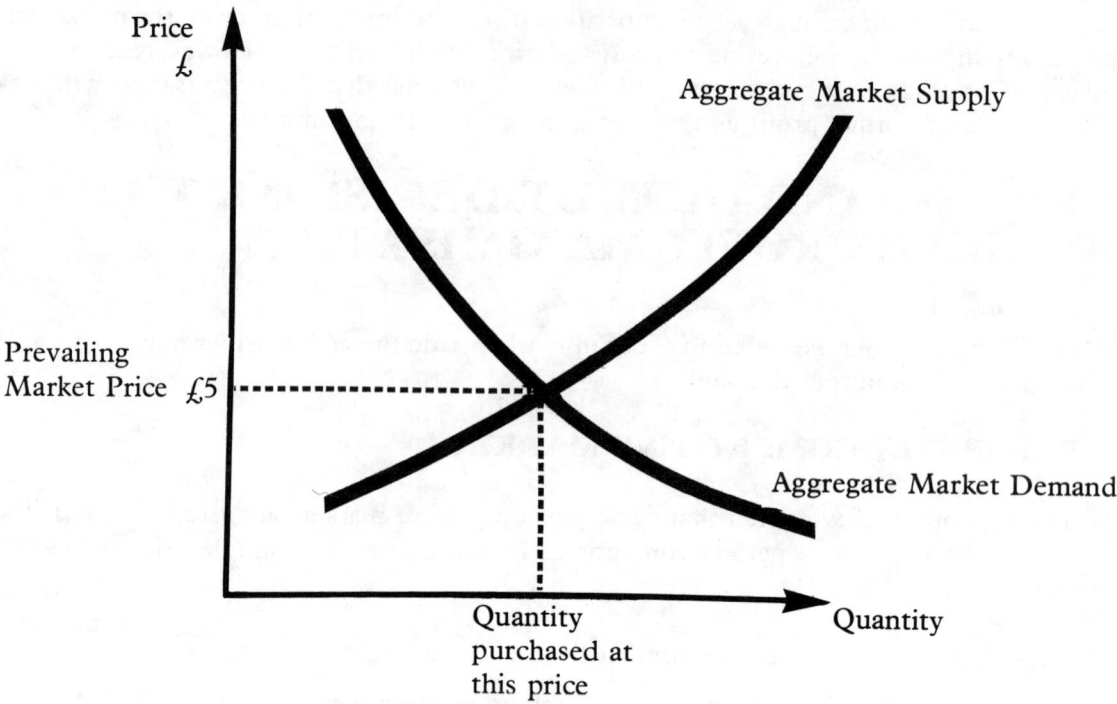

**Market Supply and Demand determining the Prevailing Market Price
in a Highly Competitive Market**

Each producer must accept the prevailing market price and is able to sell all that he can produce
at a cost which is below the market price. In effect, this means that for each individual supplier
the demand curve is horizontal. This does not mean that the demand curve for the industry as a
whole is horizontal, rather that for an individual supplier the price for which output is sold will
not have to fall to sell all the output. Accepting the prevailing market price will also mean that the
average revenue curve will also be horizontal, for each unit is sold at the same price. Similarly the
marginal revenue curve will also be horizontal as each extra unit sold will always produce the
same amount of revenue. In fact, the demand curve will equal both the average revenue and the
marginal revenue curves and will also represent the prevailing market price. A simple example
will illustrate this point.

Market Price	Units Sold	Total Revenue	Marginal Revenue	Average Revenue
£		£	£	£
5	1	5 (1 x 5)	5 (5 - 0)	5 (5 ÷ 1)
5	2	10 (2 x 5)	5 (10 - 5)	5 (10 ÷ 2)
5	3	15 (3 x 5)	5 (15 - 10)	5 (15 ÷ 3)
5	4	20 (4 x 5)	5 (20 - 15)	5 (20 ÷ 4)
5	5	25 (5 x 5)	5 (25 - 20)	5 (25 ÷ 5)
5	6	30 (6 x 5)	5 (30 - 25)	5 (30 ÷ 6)

And shown graphically:-

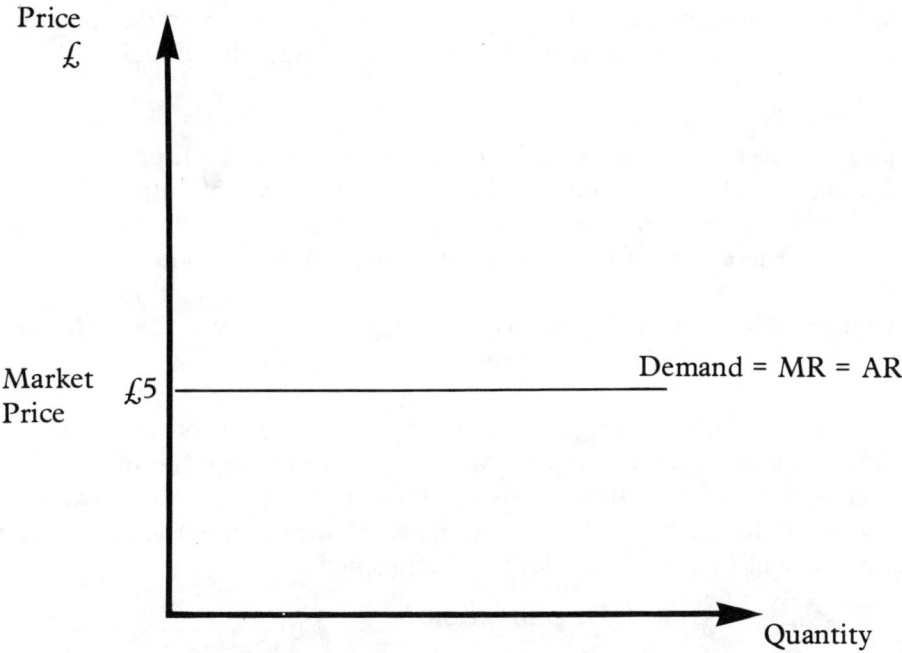

**Individual Demand Curve for an Organisation in a
Perfectly Competitive Market**

We can now introduce the costs of production which we considered in chapter 16. It is then possible to determine the most appropriate output level for the organisation.

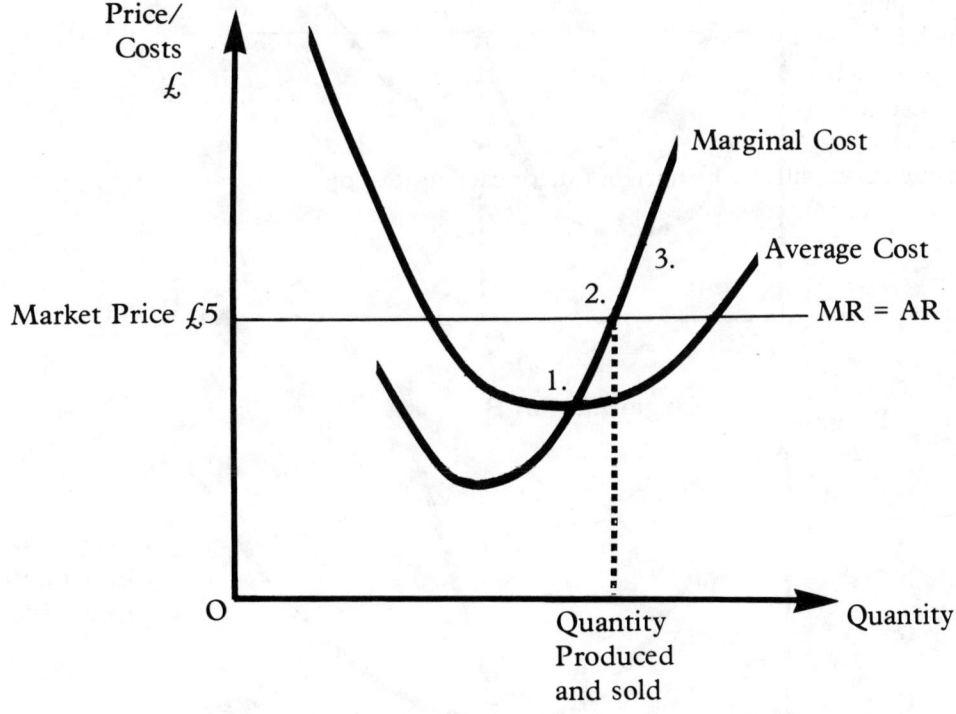

**Maximum Profit achieved by a Producer in a
Perfectly Competitive Market**

The most profitable level of output is where Marginal Costs equal Marginal Revenue. (This is shown as point 2 on the diagram). However let us try to confirm this by considering other possible levels of output.

First consider the position at the optimum level of production, where average costs are at a minimum, (Point 1 on the diagram). If the organisation produced at this point it would not be earning all the profit that it could. There is still output which could be produced where MC is less than MR. Each of these units would produce a profit for the manufacturer. Although each extra unit is not produced as cheaply as the last they are still profitable and so still worth producing.

A second potential level of output could be a situation in which the supplier produces at a point where MC exceeds MR, (Point 3 on the diagram). At this level of output each extra unit costs more to produce than the extra revenue gained from its sale. Therefore each unit produced at any level of output in excess of the point where MC = MR is produced at a loss.

So, as we confirmed initially, most profit is made by producing (and selling) the output achieved where MC = MR, (Point 2 on the diagram).

Now we consider three different suppliers each producing similar products in the same market but with differing levels of efficiency and consequently differing levels of cost. In this example all three producers should set their levels of output at the point where marginal cost equals marginal revenue if they seek to make maximum profit. But consider the different levels of profit they make because of their differing levels of efficiency.

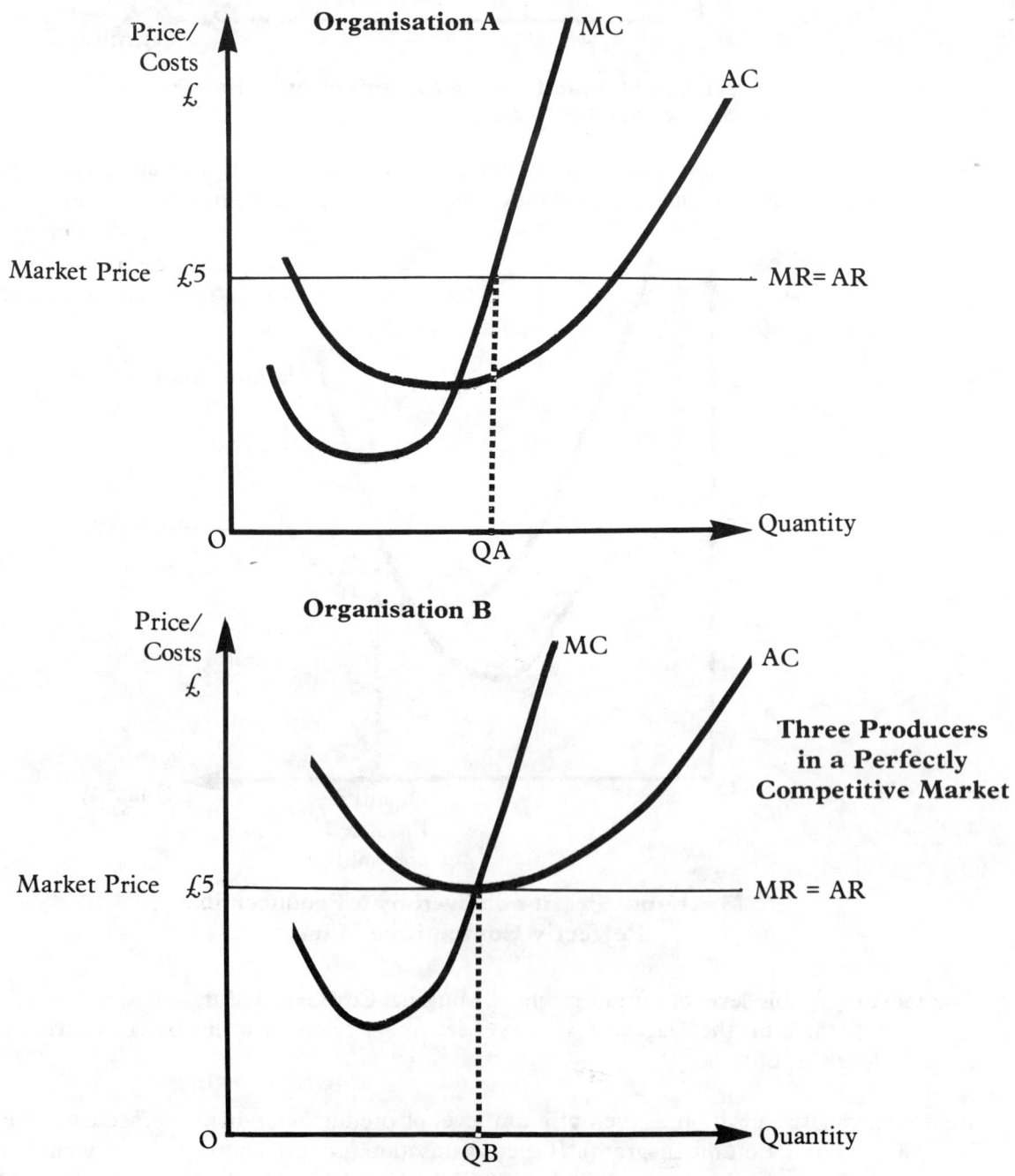

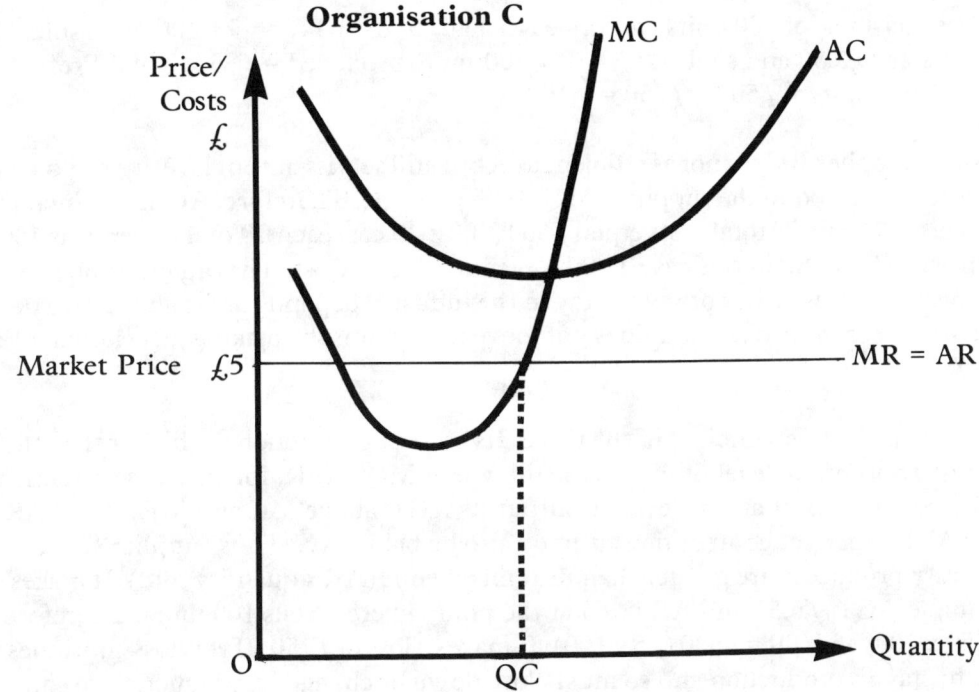

Organisation A is the most efficient and so its costs are lowest. It produces an output at QA where MC = MR. At this output its total profit can be found by subtracting Total Costs from Total Revenue. Total cost can be found by multiplying the average cost at this level of output by the quantity sold. Total Revenue can be calculated by multiplying average revenue by total quantity sold. (Refer back to the definitions of AC in chapter 16 and AR earlier in this chapter if you are unsure of this). As AC is below AR at the point where MC = MR, then the producer will make a profit. His profit level is shown by the diagram below.

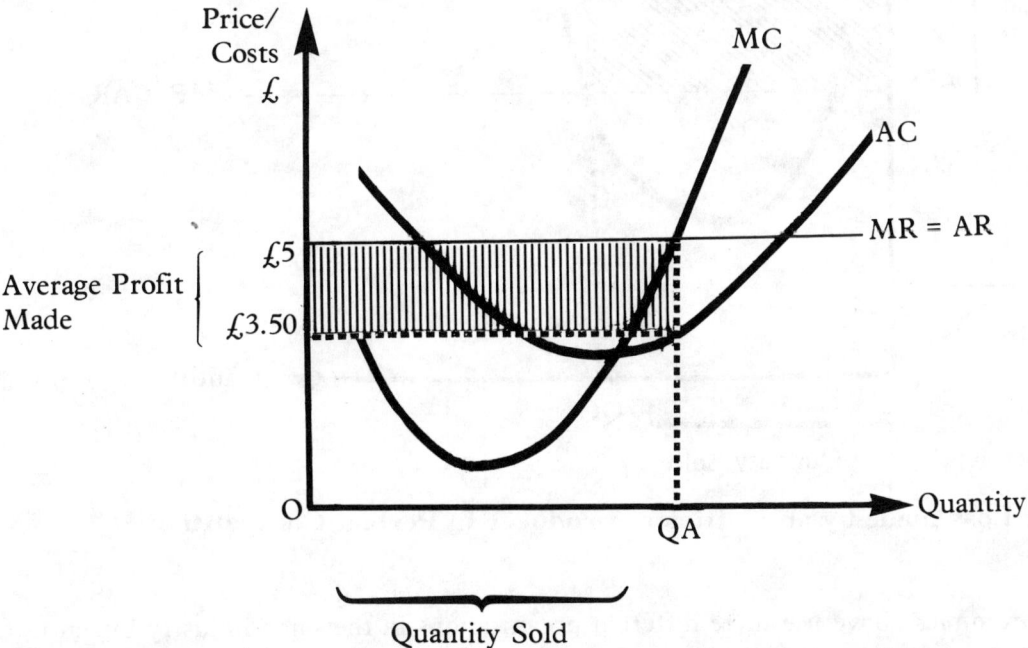

Profit made by an efficient producer in Perfect Competition

If QA represents a sale of 100 units and price is set at £5, then TR = £5 x 100 units sold = £500. Average costs are £3.50 and so TC = £3.50 x 100 units produced = £350. Total Profit = Total Revenue - Total Costs = £500 - £350 = £150.

Now consider supplier B. It is not as efficient as A but still sets its output level at the point where MC cuts MR. At this point the suppliers MC also equals AC. Therefore, AC must equal £5. If it also produced 100 units its total costs equal £500 (100 x £5 cost each). Total Revenue is 100 units sold x £5 price = £500. So in this case Total Revenue = Total Cost. The organisation just breaks even. The decision on whether or not to stay in the industry depends on its alternative potential profit levels in other industries. If it does not move then it must be making just enough to stay in production.

Organisation C is the least efficient of the three. Its costs of production are higher than the other two. Its most appropriate level of output is still where MC = MR, for the same reasons which were discussed above. But at this level of output its AC is above MC and MR. As its AR is the same as its MR in perfect competition, it must also be below AC. Thus supplier C's total costs (AC x quantity produced) are greater than its total revenue (AR x quantity sold). It makes a loss. In the example AC is £6.50 and AR is £5 at the point where it sells 100 units. Therefore TC = £650 (£6.50 x 100) and TR = £500 (£5 x 100). It makes a loss of £150. If this loss continues it will be unable to stay in production and so must close down or change its production to some more profitable products.

The following diagram illustrates its loss making position.

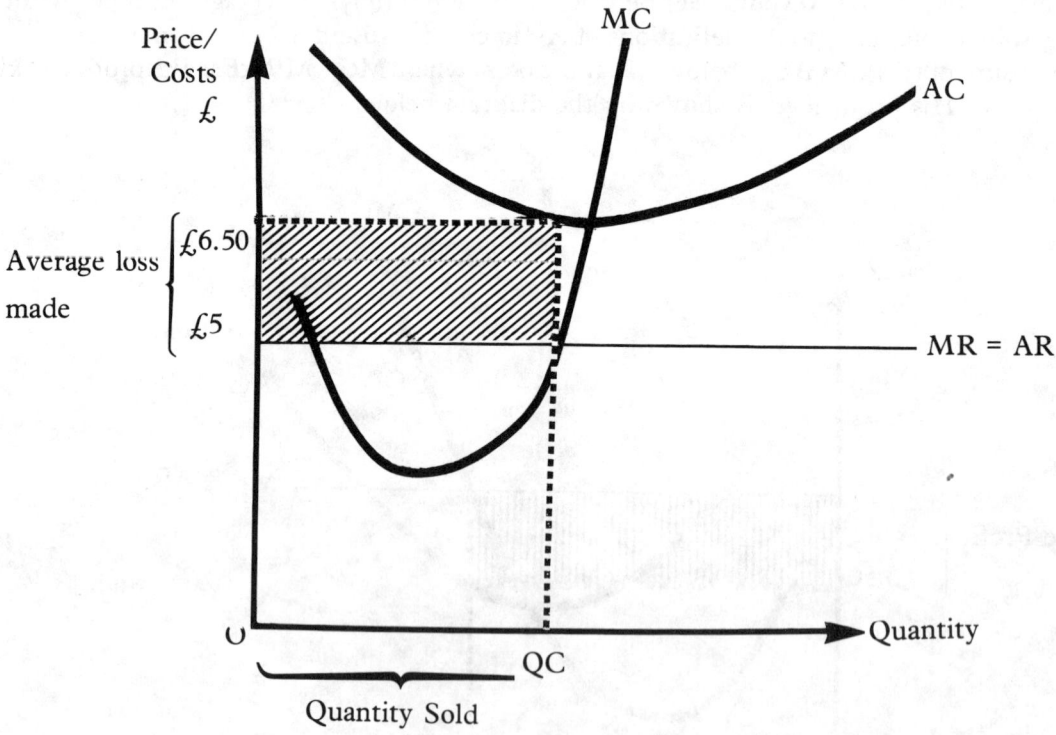

Loss made by an inefficient producer in Perfect Competition

The three examples above use three different organisations in the same industry but in fact changes in overall demand and supply can determine whether a single individual supplier in a perfectly competitive market can change from being in a profitable position to a loss making one or vice versa.

In the case of our least efficient producer (C) it could become profitable if market demand for the product increases and so moves price up. The changing market supply and demand curves will illustrate this point.

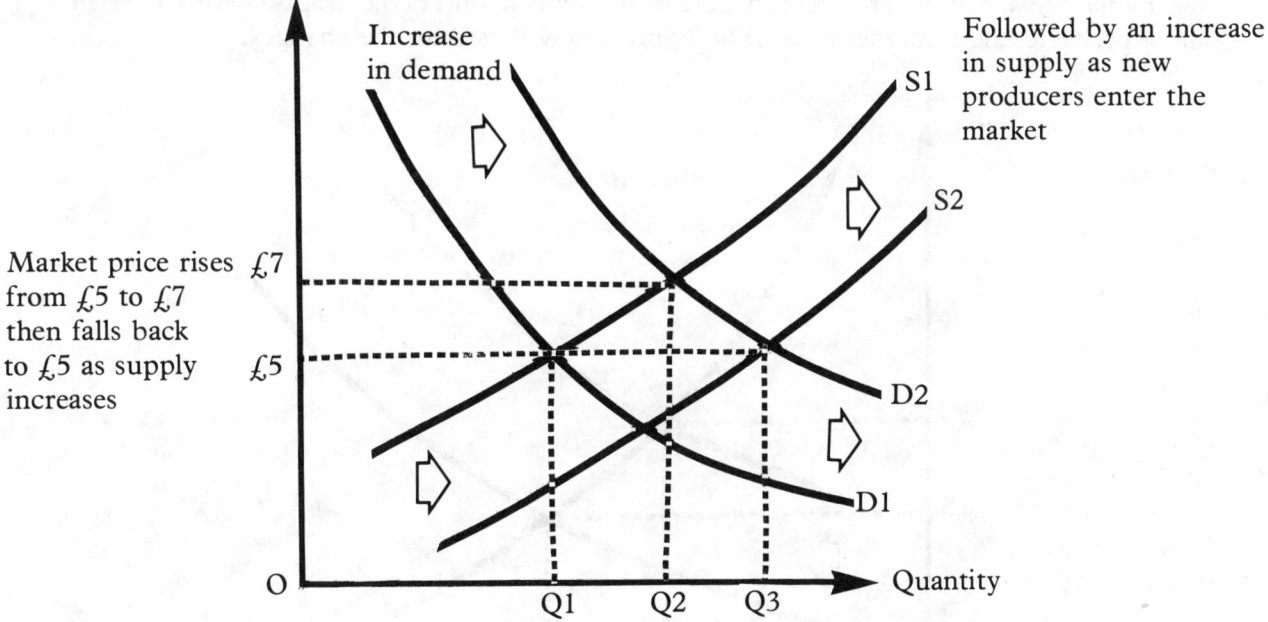

Increase in Aggregate Demand followed by an Increase in supply returning the Market Price to Equilibrium

This increased market price means that organisation C now gains an average revenue of £7. This is above its average cost of £6.50 and so it becomes profitable.

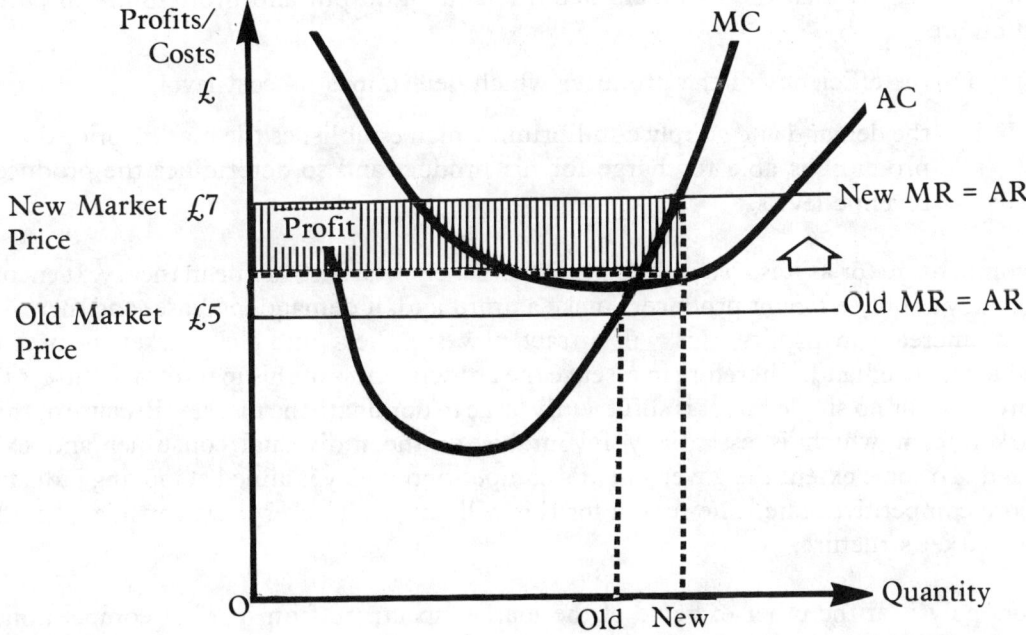

New Market Price Making Previously Inefficient Producer Profitable

If the market price did rise to £7, then both producer A (who was profitable at a market price of £5) and Producer B (who was just breaking even at £5) will now make substantially more profit. Perhaps this will be sufficient to induce new suppliers to enter the market in the hope of making substantial gains. This will result in an increase in supply (a shift in the supply curve to the right) and a probable fall in market price. The figure below illustrates the changes.

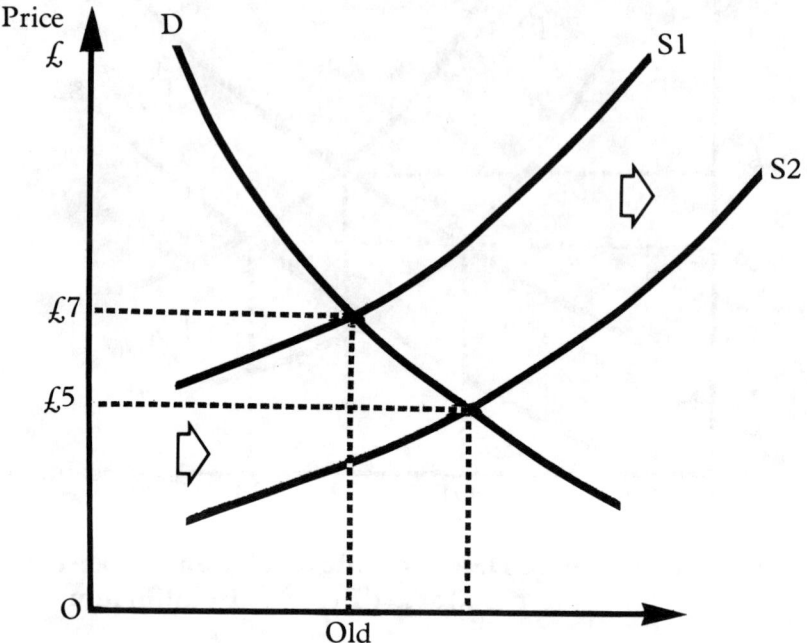

**Shift in Supply curve as a result of New Suppliers
entering the market forcing Market Price Down**

From this you can see that the two main determinants of output and profitability in perfect competition are:-

a.   the efficiency of the producer which determines its cost level;

b.   the demand and supply equilibrium which establishes the market price that the producer is able to charge for his product and so determines the producer's revenue levels.

Perfect competition (or as it is also called 'the Price Takers Market') is fine in theory. It encourages efficiency as only efficient producers make a profit and, if demand increases and there is no consequent increase in profits, this will attract new suppliers into the market to meet the increased level of demand. Therefore in essence the attractiveness of this market structure is that no one producer or no single buyer is sufficiently large to dominate the market. Because of this it is a market form which is essentially favourable to the individual consumer and to be encouraged. To some extent the government's competition policy is aimed at moving industries into a more competitive state. The reason for this will become clearer if we consider the other forms of market structure.

Pure monopoly is at the other extreme of the market spectrum from perfect competition. It means that a single supplier dominates the market. Consumers have no choice (other than not to buy the product at all) but to purchase from the monopolist.

As the monopolist is the sole supplier in the market then the market demand curve is, in effect, the monopolist's demand curve. We know from chapter 21 that market demand curves tend to slope from top left to bottom right as the higher is the price, then less of the product is normally bought. In the case of the monopolist, the demand curve is also the organisation's average revenue curve. From the AR curve it is possible to determine the supplier's marginal revenue curve. This must also continue to fall as the price is reduced to sell more. A simple example will illustrate this:-

Market Price	Units Sold	Total Revenue	Marginal Revenue	Average Revenue
£		£	£	£
10	1	10	10 (10 - 0)	10 (10 ÷ 1)
8	2	16	6 (16 - 10)	8 (16 ÷ 2)
6	3	18	2 (18 - 16)	6 (18 ÷ 3)
4	4	16	- 2 (16 - 18)	4 (16 ÷ 4)
2	5	10	- 6 (10 - 16)	2 (10 ÷ 5)

As you can see, MR falls at a faster rate than AR. This is because each additional price cut to induce more sales will mean that the extra units sold add less and less to total revenue (because the price of all previous units must also be cut if the producer wishes to set one price for all the products sold). This means that the monopolist's revenue curves will look like this:-

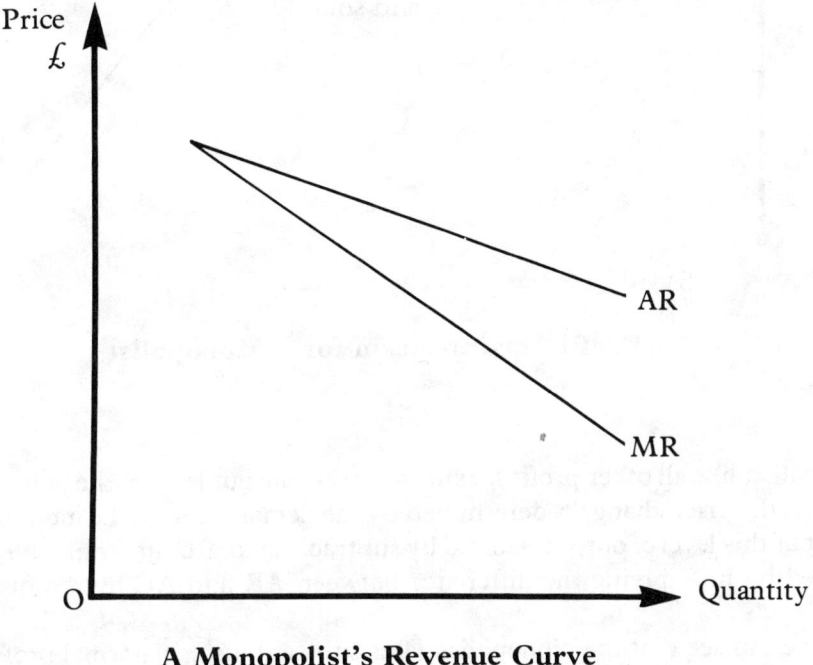

A Monopolist's Revenue Curve

From this we can see that the monopolist would actually lose money if the fourth and fifth unit were to be sold as MR is less than 0. This is because the average price has to be reduced to sell more by so much that total revenue is actually falling.

Now add the costs of production to determine the level of output and the price that the monopolist will set.

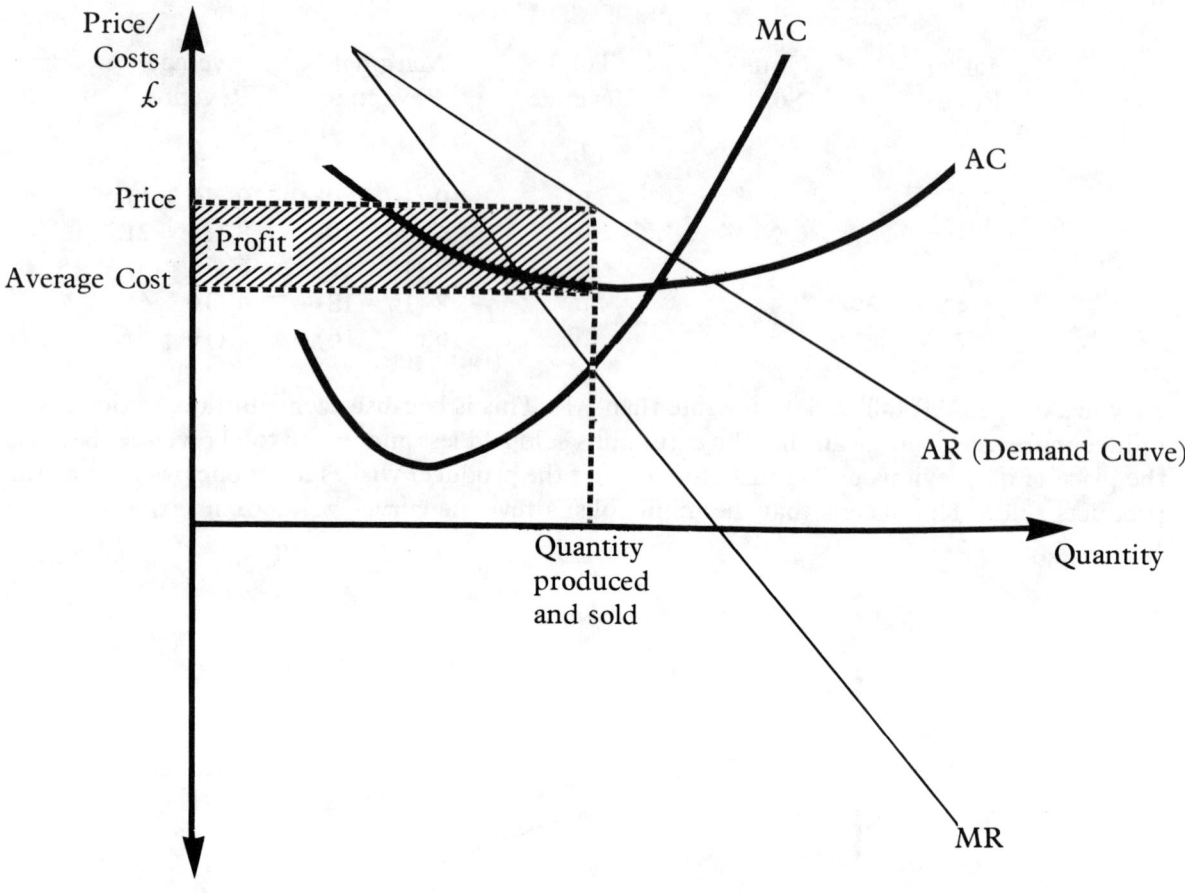

Profit Maximisation for a Monopolist

The monopolist, like all other profit maximisers, sets output level at the point where MC = MR. At this point, the price change is determined by the demand curve (the monopolist's AR curve). Total profit at this level of output is found by subtracting total costs from total revenue. This can be calculated by multiplying the difference between AR and AC by the quantity sold.

From this we can see that the monopolist gains substantial supernormal profits. In other more competitive markets such profits would be sufficient to attract new suppliers into the industry. Why then do other producers not attempt to enter this market attracted by high profit levels? The answer is because a major characteristic of a monopoly is the difficulty encountered by new suppliers if they wish to enter the market. Therefore the existing monopolist can continue to make substantial profits in the long term without fear of competition. Of course, if demand for the product falls this will shift the demand curve (the AR curve) to the left and could result in the monopolist making a loss — but only if AR falls below AC.

PRICING AND OUTPUT IN STATE OWNED MONOPOLIES

Most of the monopolies in the U.K. are state-owned, such as the Post Office, British Rail, and the Electricity Boards. This gives them many of the advantages of a monopoly supplier. In fact, some of the nationalised industries make extremely large profits. Some of this profit is reinvested into industry to provide a better product or service for the community in the future. Much of the remainder goes to the government as extra revenue to supplement the revenue from taxation. However, as we saw in chapter 18 many of the nationalised industries do not have profit maximisation as their prime objective. They aim to provide as extensive a service as possible to consumers by keeping prices as low as they can. Of course, they are usually expected to at least break even. In order to do this an organisation merely has to equate average costs with average revenue. Thus, if TC (AC x output) = TR (AR x output) the organisation breaks even. As average revenue is the price the organisation charges then this must be set equal to average costs. This can be illustrated in the diagram below:-

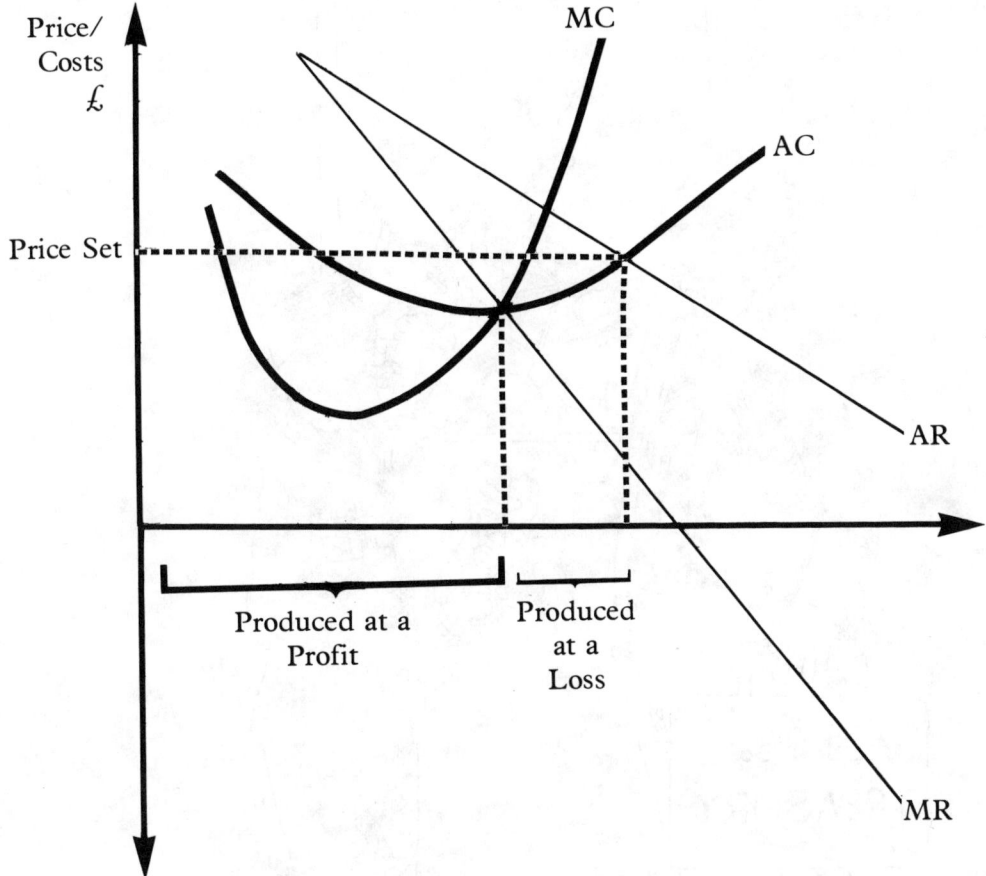

Average Cost Pricing by a Nationalised Industry

You can see from the diagram that the organisation is producing some of its output at a loss (all production where MC is above MR). However, this is balanced by profits from output where MC is below MR. So overall, no profit or loss is made. If it had set output level at the point where MC = MR, it would have produced less that it is currently supplying. Thus, the extra output is being supplied (at a loss) to the community as a service — because the government has decided that the benefit to the society from its provision (the social benefit) outweighs the actual cost of production. Examples of this would be unprofitable railway lines, post delivered to the far reaches of the country at the normal average rate and electricity and gas supplied to outlying homes without charging extra.

benefit outweighs the cost of production

In reality most nationalised industries charge a price which is somewhere between the point where MC = MR and AC = AR. While they do not make excessive profit, therefore, they do a little better than just breaking even and so provide working capital and money for reinvestment for profit.

PRICING AND OUTPUT IN OLIGOPOLY MARKETS

The extremes of perfect competition and pure monopoly were helpful in explaining why a profit maximising organisation should set its level of output where MC = MR and enables it to determine its profit level, (AR - AC) x Quantity Sold. But you will recall the most important market form in the U.K. today is the oligopoly, an industry which is dominated by a few major suppliers.

The Pricing Policy of Oligopolists

The assumption that a market which is shared between a few major suppliers will necessarily be competitive is not supported by the evidence of the real world. Despite the fact that non-price competition may exist, for example, in the form of advertising, it is common to find that the prices set by oligopolists competing in the same market are often very similar. An oligopoly market tends to evolve because of the type of production involved, the extent of the economies of scale which can be gained and the most efficient operational size for the organisation. If the major producers in the industry have reached this optimum level of production, then any substantial increase in supply will increase their average costs. Consequently none of the suppliers may be keen to raise their level of production. Each is satisfied with its existing market share. Their marketing efforts are directed towards maintaining existing market sales rather than increasing them. If this is the situation with all suppliers, none will be likely to drop price in an attempt to increase market share. A stable market price will evolve which will give a satisfactory profit level to all producers.

Possible Changes in Price Levels

Price changes obviously do occur in oligopoly markets and we shall now examine how these may come about. A reduction in price by one supplier will attract his competitors customers and so lower the competitors' level of sales. This may mean that the competitors lose some of the cost advantages of economies of scale and so are forced to try to regain their previous market share by following suit and also dropping price. The result of this is that market shares return to their previous levels but at a lower price and consequently at a lower level of profit. Therefore it is in none of the producers' interests to reduce price and set in motion such a downward price spiral. A brief illustration may help to explain.

> A market is divided between three suppliers with the following market shares: A, 30%; B, 30%; C, 40%. 'A' tries to increase its market share by lowering prices, resulting in an initial realignment of sales. A now has 38%, B now has 26% and C's share falls to 36%. Both 'B' and 'C' are now producing below their most efficient level and so are forced to lower prices to a comparable level with that of 'A'. The market shares then return to their initial distribution with no producer gaining any marked benefit. In fact all are now worse off because the price has fallen.

This price stability is usually broken by the action of one producer raising price because of inflation, increased labour costs, or other increases in the cost of production. Competing producers will find that their sales increase as they take customers away from their higher priced rival and if they are producing below their capacity this may be welcomed. However, if they are already producing at their optimum level and have no spare capacity, they might not wish to increase sales and so they simply increase price in line with the competitor and gain the benefit of higher profit levels. This type of behaviour is known as price leadership. Clearly, it is the consumer who loses out because he is faced with a higher overall level of prices.

PRICING POLICY DURING A RECESSION

When total market demand is falling because of a recession, price leadership will be less prevalent as all producers may be losing sales and so have output falling below their optimum level. In an attempt to maintain flagging sales, they may drop price, step up advertising campaigns and generally improve their terms of sale. This could lead to a "price war" in which all producers try to undercut each other in order to retain their market share. Consequent lower profit margins must be accepted for the period of the recession. Examples of price wars during the present recession can clearly be seen in the car and petrol industries. Falling demand for cars during the middle 1980's led major producers like BL and Ford to substantially cut prices, offer better trade-in-deals and add many "free" extras to their cars. The petrol industry suffers periodic price wars when demand falls below available supply. The major oil companies lower pump prices in order to compete with smaller companies who purchase their oil on the world market at the cheaper rate.

The Entry of New Suppliers into the Market

If new suppliers attempt to enter the market, this may also result in price competition. Existing producers may undercut the new entrant's price in order to prevent him from becoming established in the market. Existing suppliers will try to squeeze out any new producer before he has attracted sufficient regular customers. Original producers are willing to bear a period of relatively low profits in order to maintain their existing market share.

PRICE DISCRIMINATION

Another aspect of the pricing policy of dominant suppliers is their ability to price discriminate or differentiate. If a supplier is able to sell the same product or service to different customers at different prices, it may be able to increase total sales and thereby utilise excess capacity. For example, a cinema owner may set different admission charges for adults, children and old age pensioners if he cannot fill all his seats with adults paying the full rate. Other examples can be seen in the sale of railway tickets, electricity, gas, etc. Price discrimination enables the dominant producer to make full use of its capacity and so is of benefit. However, it may be seen as unfair competitive practice in some circumstances such as when suppliers or wholesalers give preferential prices to some retailers in an effort to prevent them from turning to other rival producers.

There is a tendency towards price leadership rather than competition. All producers have a share in the market which they may be satisfied to maintain. This is because they are producing at or near their optimum level of output. Attempts by an individual supplier to increase market share by price-cutting can result in additional output being produced at a rising cost which may mean falling profit margins. Other producers, who seek to maintain their share of the market, retaliate by cutting their price and so the original market share of the first producer is not increased but merely maintained (but at a lower profit level). Similarly, an increase in price by one producer may be copied by the others who can still sell the same share of the market — but at the higher price. The result is price stability for certain periods which is followed by price leadership as all producers raise prices to a similar level almost simultaneously.

Will a general increase in prices by all producers not lead to a drop in the total market sales? We know from our analysis of market demand that price increases result in a decline in quantity demanded. However, the extent in the fall in demand will be a major determinant in establishing which prices may be increased and must be of major concern to the suppliers. This is known as the elasticity of demand.

ELASTICITY OF DEMAND

This term simply refers to the responsiveness of demand to a change in price. In effect, how far will quantity demanded stretch or shrink if price is lowered or raised? It is of importance to a producer in two respects:-

   a.   if the producer wishes to raise price he needs to know the extent of his loss of sales;

   b.   if the producer decides to increase output he needs to know by how much to lower his price to gain the required extra sales.

If a product has a demand which does not respond to variations in price it is said to have an 'inelastic demand'. Price rises or reductions will have little effect on the quantity sold. This is a characteristic of most necessities. A substantial price increase for bread will mean people will still buy bread and have to make do with less of other things. If a product does not have any close substitutes, then a price rise cannot result in consumers switching their purchases to alternative products. The achievement of an inelastic demand curve is an objective of suppliers because it means they can raise price without substantially losing custom.

Elasticity of Demand

The reverse is true if the product has 'elastic demand'. This means that even a relatively small price increase will result in a substantial reduction in sales as consumers either no longer buy the product at all (this is known as the income effect) or they shift their purchasing to an alternative, (this is called the substitution effect).

We can illustrate elasticity graphically through the slope of the demand curve. See the diagram below.

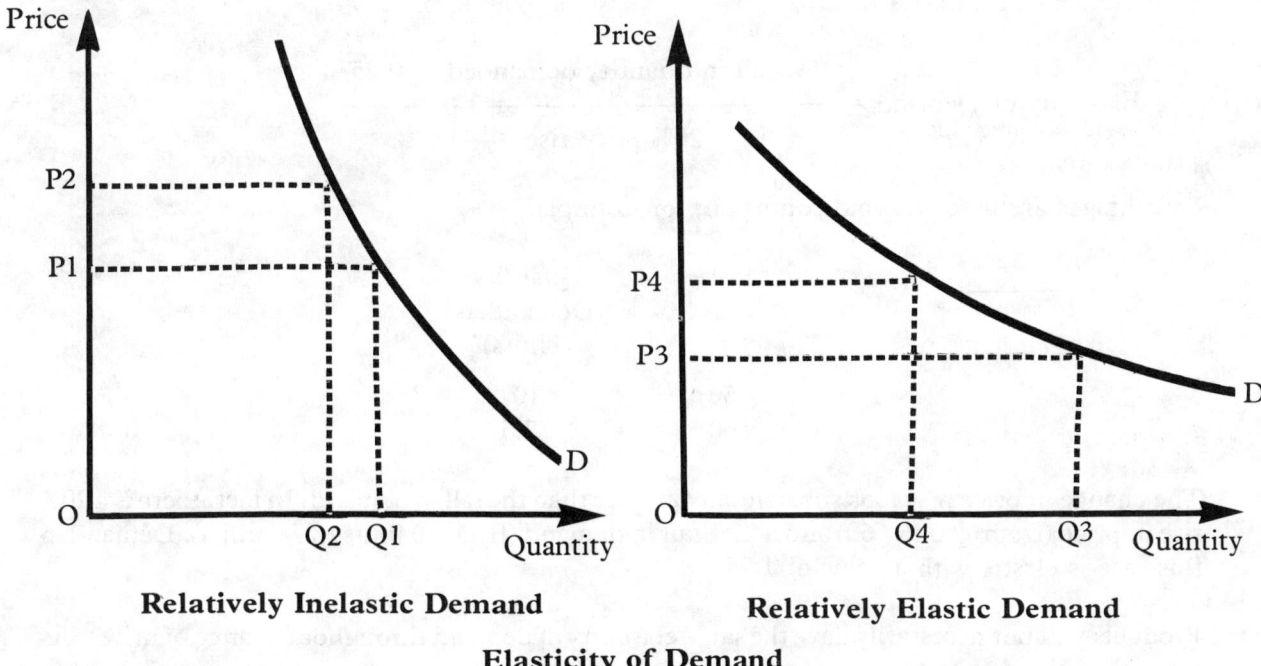

Relatively Inelastic Demand   **Relatively Elastic Demand**

Elasticity of Demand

The diagram on the left showing a product with inelastic demand illustrates that a relatively large price increase (from P1 to P2) will have only a limited effect on the quantity purchased (a fall in quantity from Q1 to Q2). While the diagram on the right, of the product with elastic demand, illustrates a much smaller increase in price (price rise from P3 to P4) and a much more dramatic reduction in demand (quantity purchased falls from Q3 to Q4). Expressing this numerically we can see that:-

$$\text{Price Elasticity of Demand} = \frac{\% \text{ change in Quantity Demanded}}{\% \text{ change in Price}}$$

We use a percentage change for quantity demanded and a percentage change in price. If we did not then the scale of the change in quantity demanded or the price change may be deceiving. A simple example:-

Price	Quantity Demanded
£	Units
5	100
6	75

In this case an increase in price of 20% (from £5 to £6) results in a 25% fall in demand (from 100 to 75 units). This is a more than proportionate fall in demand. (Expressed simply demand shrinks more than price stretches.) Thus demand is said to be elastic. The equation would show:-

$$\text{Elasticity of Demand} = \frac{25\%}{20\%} = 1.25$$

If elasticity is greater than 1, that is demand changes in a greater proportion than price, then it is said to be elastic. A less than proportionate change would result in a figure less than 1, for example if price rose 20% and demand fell only 5%, this would indicate inelastic demand. The example below illustrates this.

$$\text{Elasticity of Demand} = \frac{5\% \text{ fall in quantity demanded}}{20\% \text{ price rise}} = 0.25$$

Percentages are used to avoid confusion, for example:-

Price	Quantity Demanded
£	(Units)
50	10
60	7.5

The change in price may look substantially greater than the fall in demand. In fact, there is a 20% rise in price (from £50 to £60) and a 25% fall in demand (from 10 units to 7.5 units). Demand in this case is elastic with a value of 1.25.

Products will not necessarily have the same elasticity of demand throughout a range of prices. As price rises the demand for a product usually become more elastic because consumers tend to switch demand to cheaper substitutes. This switch in demand from one good to another can also be calculated by using what is called 'cross elasticity'. This simply illustrates how a change in the price of one product affects the demand for another product. So:

$$\text{Cross Elasticity of Demand} = \frac{\text{\% change in Quantity demanded of product A}}{\text{\% change in price of product B}}$$

This can occur as consumers switch to cheaper substitutes but it is also of importance when considering the effect of the price changes of one product on its complements (remember these are products whch tend to be purchased together such as cars and petrol, electricity and electric central heating). Here a rise in the price of one product will result in the fall in demand for the other, for example as petrol goes up in price so demand for large petrol hungry cars falls and vice versa.

A further variant of elasticity is that which relates to a rise or fall in income and its effect on demand for a product or service. Thus, an increase in a person's income will usually result in an increase in the demand for a product. This is more pronounced for what are referred to as 'superior goods' such as holidays and consumer durables. Alternatively an individual whose income rises may well demand less of an 'inferior good' such as poor quality food. This would be because they are now able to purchase better quality products as they now have a higher income available. So for instance as income rises a person may buy fewer sausages and more steak. Income elasticity can be defined as follows:-

$$\text{Income Elasticity} = \frac{\text{\% change in quantity demanded of a product}}{\text{\% change in income}}$$

When the quantity demanded of a product increases positively in response to a rise in income, this is a normal response to a rise in income and would indicate a normal or superior product. If the quantity demanded of a product actually falls when income rises, this indicates a negative income elasticity and so the product is an inferior good.

It is not only the producer who will benefit from a knowledge of the elasticity of demand. The government is obviously extremely influential in the raising and lowering of prices through its taxation policy. The Chancellor of the Exchequer must be aware of the likely effect of either a change in the general level of taxation (such as increases or decreases in V.A.T. or income tax) or of specific tax (for example, a change in the duty on petrol, alcohol or tobacco). If it is the government's objective is to increase its tax yield from petrol duty then it must be confident that the tax increase and the consequent price increase will not result in such a reduction in the demand for petrol that overall tax revenue from petrol falls. The most appropriate goods to tax specifically are therefore those with inelastic demand, as a tax increase will not deter consumption. These products are those with no close substitute and so inevitably the Exchequer taxes products like petrol, alcohol and tobacco.

MARKETING

For any producer to be successful he must be able to sell his product. It is not sufficient for a manufacturer to decide what he can make, he must also determine what are present customer demands and how they are likely to change in the future. Therefore the art of marketing is finding out what customers want to buy, setting objectives to meet this need and ensuring that this can be done at a profit. We discuss the process of establishing customer needs as the prime objective of the enterprise in chapter 7 and in this chapter we will concentrate on the means by which consumer demand can be determined and influenced.

THE ESTIMATION OF DEMAND — MARKET RESEARCH

The importance of determining both the extent and the elasticity of demand for products has meant that organisations must attempt to estimate existing demand and potential changes in the demand for their products. This is achieved by the process of market research. This involves the collection and analysis of information relating to consumer requirements for the product, the price they are willing to pay for the product, where the product is purchased and the factors which influence the consumers' purchasing decisions.

The use of sophisticated statistical sampling techniques, in which responses from a small section of the potential market of consumers is used to estimate total demand, can provide organisations with a clear indication of the relationship between price and other factors.

Market research may be carried out either by the organisation's own marketing department or by market research specialists, hired to undertake surveys on specific products. The types of survey used include personal face-to-face interviews, telephone and postal questionnaires, and analysis of the products sold at retail outlets. Increased expertise in the application of such methods has resulted in a much greater degree of certainty on the part of producers as to what the consumer actually requires. This is particularly important when large scale production is being considered. Millions of pounds may be invested in the development and manufacture of products such as the launch of a new model of car. The risk involved in a capital outlay of such proportions is reduced by the producer being informed by market research that the product which will eventually be marketed will actually meet consumer demand. Despite this many new products fail because they do not adequately meet consumer needs and this is often the fault of poor initial market research.

THE STAGES IN MARKETING A PRODUCT

There are essentially four stages in marketing a product.

1. Assessing the market;

2. Ensuring that both the product and its price are right for the market;

3. Advertising and promoting the product;

4. Selling and distributing the product.

1.   ASSESSING THE MARKET

It is important to recognise the market from the customer's point of view. Thus a supplier must identify what consumers want and whether their needs are already being catered for by existing suppliers. It is almost impossible for a small company to 'create' a market unless it has developed a product that is so unique and inventive that customers did not recognise that they needed it. Large companies can develop such products such as compact discs or home computers but essentially these producers were sufficiently confident that a market would evolve, that they were willing to invest millions of pounds in research, development and promotion.

Most other businesses will be faced with supplying a product for which a market already exists. They may believe that they can produce a product which is superior to that which is currently available. Nevertheless they should satisfy themselves of the state of the market. Obviously it is much easier to sell in a growing market in which existing suppliers are finding it difficult to meet expanding demand than to enter a declining market in which existing suppliers will fight to hold onto their shrinking market base. In most instances it is foolish to try to go against the tide of market forces. It is better to consider moving into a healthier area rather than entering a declining market.

Information is available on most market sectors in the U.K. This may come from simple, easily accessible sources such as a local library or a trade association. The Government regularly publishes data on many markets in its Business Monitors which are available in good reference libraries. Organisations such as Dunn and Bradstreet will provide information on individual companies or market sectors. Other census information will provide figures on the number of customers and, if a company is to trade in a local area, the simple expedient of checking competition in yellow pages and even touring an area to 'weigh up' the competition should not be overlooked.

Once the competition has been identified it may be possible to assess their trading performance to find out the level of profit being made in a particular business. If the competitor is a limited company their annual accounts are available from the Registrar of Companies in Cardiff and can be examined for a small fee either direct from the Registrar or by using an agency which will find out such information.

As we note in chapter 7 the importance of good business information on the market, customers and competitors cannot be too highly stressed. Knowledge is power. It will not only reduce the risk involved in establishing a new business or product, it could also prevent a business from making costly mistakes.

Mention should be made of the similar survey techniques used in the estimation of need for public services. Clearly the government needs to be aware of potential demand for such services as housing, education, medical care and help for the aged or handicapped. The most widespread survey of this kind is the General Census of Population which is undertaken once every ten years. It provides the government with not only information on the numbers of population but also useful data on age and sex distribution, housing, employment and level of qualifications in the country.

Local authorities have also tried to produce structure plans for their area based either on a sample or on the total population of their area. These are normally undertaken using questionnaire techniques although data from diverse sources such as school records and unemployment returns are also utilised.

Before leaving market research it is worth noting that many organisations, particularly smaller ones, do not attempt to scientifically analyse potential demand. The cost of such surveys may be prohibitive and so the entrepreneur's own estimation on the marketability of his product may have to suffice. However as we have said simple market research need not be expensive and the effort involved in digging out such information will invariably pay dividends.

2. THE RIGHT PRODUCT AT THE RIGHT PRICE

A business needs to be aware of what attracts potential customers to its product rather than those of its competitors. Is it the quality of the product or service which is attractive or is it merely that its price is cheaper than anyone else? This is important, for if the price is the only deciding factor then the supplier must ensure that production is as efficient as possible. Should competitors recognise that price is a major determining factor in market share they may attempt to cut their prices and unless the company is efficient it will not be able to respond.

If it is the quality of the product or service which is attractive to customers then the managers of the business must concentrate on maintaining such high levels and emphasising it in their advertising and marketing. Often it is the special distinguishing features of a company's product which makes it successful. It should be seen by the customer to be somehow different. This may be an actual difference in terms of quality or performance or merely a perceived difference in the view of the customer. This may be created by imaginative packaging or presentation or by creating an image for the product.

There is always the possibility of developing a new product but as we noted earlier this involves considerable risk, both in development costs and in the likelihood that it may be rejected by the consumer. It is sometimes wiser to develop and improve existing ideas. The Japanese are the world masters at taking other people's initial concepts and developing and marketing them successfully.

The price that a business is able to charge for its product will be dependent on a number of factors. As we saw earlier in the chapter the three most important are the level of market demand, the structure of the market and the costs of production facing the supplier. It is essential to assess what price customers will bear. If the market is highly competitive then the business will be a 'price taker' and have to accept the prevailing market price. In other market conditions care must be taken to examine the prices offered by competitors and also the state of their business. If competitors are already overstretched then it may be possible to impose a higher price but if there is already a considerable spare capacity in the market this will tend to force prices down. Producers need to be aware of the demand for their product so that they know whether to produce more or less and the appropriate price to charge.

3.   ADVERTISING AND PROMOTING THE PRODUCT

An individual's taste or preference for specific goods or services is determined by the amount of satisfaction the person believes he will get from that product. For example, one person may get considerable satisfaction and enjoyment from wearing a formal white shirt because he thinks it looks smart. Another individual with differing tastes would not be seen dead wearing a white shirt. He regards them as boring and they remind him of Persil advertisements. That is his own personal preference. If both were given identical shirts, each shirt may be indistinguishable from the other in its material and make up and yet they would give different amounts of satisfaction to the two people. Therefore we should recognise that it is not just the product itself (its quality, price, manufacture, etc) which makes it desirable but also the perception of the potential customers and whether or not they wish to buy it. Clearly there are a number of different influences on taste or preference. Obviously factors such as age, personality, upbringing, will be important and it is normal for a consumer's tastes to change during his life. For example tastes usually tend to mature as we get older. Similarly an extrovert will get more satisfaction from colourful, outlandish clothes than a shy person would. The influences develop either naturally or because of environmental circumstances in which we live.

However, taste and preference can be manipulated, either directly or indirectly, by various sections of society. The friends and acquaintances with whom you mix may influence the things you like by their own preferences and action. If it is necessary to go to a particular pub or club to be "in the crowd", then you might go and so your consumption of drinks or disco visits may increase. Similarly, producers are going to try to influence your taste and preference. This is part of the process of marketing a product. This may be done in a number of ways. For instance, by advertising, which is a clear attempt by the manufacturer to increase the consumers awareness of the product. The supplier may also try to set a trend or fashion for the product which will indirectly affect the consumer's perception of it.

a.   Advertising

There are numerous advertising media including television and radio, billboards, newspapers and direct advertising. All have their particular advantages and disadvantages. The key to good advertising is not to waste it on people who are not potential customers. There is an old saying that "Half the money spent on advertising is wasted — but we don't know which half." Therefore advertising should, wherever possible, be directed towards particular customer segments. It would be a very unwise toy manufacturer who concentrated all his advertising in an engineering trade journal. Essentially the equation is to reach as many potential customers as possible for the lowest cost per head. It is for this reason that newspapers and commercial television and radio stations are continually emphasising their readership, viewing or listening numbers. In this way potential advertisers will be persuaded that they are going to reach a specific audience.

The next important factor is to decide on the content of the advert. Should it stress the quality of the product, its price, or attempt to create a particular image? This really depends on the needs of the supplier. As we shall see later the company may wish to sell a lot more at the same or a slightly lower price or it may wish to increase its price without losing customers. Each message must be put over in a different way. The type of advert used and its impact will also determine how often it need appear. Some adverts are so immediately impressive that they need to be seen only a few times to get over the product message. A good example is the advertisement for the Fiat Strada which showed the car being manufactured by robots to the sounds of a famous opera score. This advert is remembered by many people despite the fact that it appeared on television a mere handful of times. Other advertisements appear so often that they not only lose their impact they can also become positively irritating and so create a negative image for the product.

Advertising is carried on for many reasons — to bring a product to a consumer's attention, to advise of a price change, but most often try to persuade the consumer that he will get a certain level of satisfaction from the product.

'Smartie people are happy people' implies that if you eat a certain sweet you will be happy. A ski chalet with a party of people drinking Martini suggests that you could end up with the "jet set" if Martini becomes your tipple. The list is endless, each one raising the level of your perception of the product.

We note in chapter 27 that the law protects consumers from untrue or misleading statements in the sale of goods or services. However, advertisers can lawfully use superlatives and innuendoes which may mislead the unsuspecting. For example, a perfume advert which has handsome young men risking life and limb to present a young lady with a bunch of flowers may mislead a poor unsuspecting innocent into spending her hard-earned money on the spray. Can she then sue the advertiser when, after liberally dousing herself in perfume, she finds that men do not in fact immediately fall under her spell? Clearly not, because a normal customer would not be influenced to such a degree that she would actually believe that such scenes shown in advertisements are anything but acted out fantasies. Of course, any factual claims made in adverts must be able to be substantiated to satisfy the Advertising Standards Authority. So the toilet paper carried in the mouth of the puppy must be the length represented in the television advertisement.

b. Trend or Fashion Setting

Some products such as records and clothes can be influenced by a trend or fashion. It is an objective of any manufacturer of such products to try to make them 'trendy' or 'fashionable'. With clothes, this is done when the fashion houses, magazines and writers tell consumers that what was "in last year is now out". The result of this is that clothes bought last year and which have not lost any of their inherent characteristics (warmth, durability, well-fitting, etc.) may have immediately lost there fashion value to the style conscious consumer as he or she does not wish to wear them and look "old fashioned". Instead the consumer will go out and buy new clothes which are invariably made by the same manufacturer. This is clearly a producer's ideal, for his products have built-in obsolescence and must be replaced after a relatively short period, not because they have worn out but because they no longer provide satisfaction to the consumer. Imagine if a producer sold a consumer durable product which was supposed to be long-lasting and yet broke down within a few months so forcing the consumer to buy a replacement. The producer may well be made liable under the law of contract. Yet with changes in fashion exactly the same thing is happening. The products do not break but simply become 'useless' because fashion has moved on.

Other producers may influence fashion in different ways. The music business is one in which trends influence consumer purchasing. Clearly an imaginative promotion company can "hype" a less than talented singer to super stardom by outrageous acts or expensive videos and thus encourage consumers to buy not only records, but badges, T-shirts, and everything else that goes with the music business.

GOVERNMENT INFLUENCES ON DEMAND FOR PRODUCTS

The government also tries to influence consumer demand for goods and services by actively encouraging or discouraging their consumption. Government-sponsored bodies such as the Health Education Council will promote advertising campaigns to discourage smoking or drinking. They try to influence the amount of satisfaction that the consumer thinks that he will get from these products. Other forms of advertising by the Government may encourage consumers to insulate their houses, lag pipes in winter and get new tyres for their cars.

There is also a trend in advertising to compare a manufacturer's product with that of its competitors. "Persil washes whiter" implies "Brand X" does not. Increasingly in new car ads, the virtues of a manufacturer's model are compared favourably to the less than perfect characteristics of other cars. This is aimed at reducing the consumer's opinion of the other cars. They hope to cause a fall in demand for competitors' products and create a substitution effect.

THE EFFECT OF ADVERTISING ON THE ELASTICITY OF DEMAND FOR A PRODUCT

The elasticity of demand seriously influences the freedom of producers to raise and lower prices. However, the advertiser can influence the consumers perception of his product and so change the elasticity of demand. This may be achieved in two ways:

      (i)   advertising to make demand more inelastic;

      (ii) advertising to make demand more elastic.

(i)   Advertising to make demand more inelastic

A manufacturer may wish to make his product seem more indispensible to the consumer. In other words he wants to make demand more inelastic. This will allow the producer to increase his price without losing sales. The advertiser will attempt to do this by showing that his product is unique, has no substitute and is the best of its type. In this way if the manufacturer increases prices, consumers will feel that they cannot transfer their purchasing to the other products. This type of advertising is trying to reduce the substitution effect. Examples of this sort of advertising include adverts which say "Probably the best lager in the world" or "Sunday wouldn't be Sunday without the Sunday Times.

(ii) Advertising to make demand more elastic

Alternatively a manufacturer may not be so interested in showing that its product is better than everyone elses merely that it is as good as the rest. This may be because the supplier does not want to increase price but instead wishes to drop price and increase sales. The producer does not want consumers to believe that simply because they are paying a lower price that they are receiving inferior quality. The producer wants them to think that its products are every bit as good as those of the competition — but cheaper. This type of advertising campaign will stress the comparativeness in quality but the differences in price. Volvo do this by listing the attributes of all the competitors' cars, showing that the Volvo has at least the same features and then emphasising that the Volvo is the cheapest of the bunch.

THE EFFECT OF ADVERTISING ONCE AN INITIAL PURCHASE OF A PRODUCT HAS BEEN MADE

In the previous sections, it has been stated that advertising aims to raise a consumer's perception of a product, in other words to persuade him that the product will give him more satisfaction than he presently thinks it will. But what if, after purchase, the consumer realises that in fact, the product does not provide this enhanced level of satisfaction? Firstly, there is the effect on the producer's hope of future sales. The producer's primary aim in advertising is to increase the person's anticipated satisfaction from consuming the product. However, if after the consumer has purchased the product, what if it does not meet the customer's expectations. If the product does actually provide an acceptable level of satisfaction, in other words if it is worth the money paid for it, then even though it is not as good as he thought it might be, the consumer will still make further buys. But if the consumer is disappointed then the advertising has only achieved the result of one sale. The consumer would not be persuaded twice that the product is good value and consequently will not buy again. It is important to note that the consumer has no legal redress simply because he thought that the product was better than it actually was — as long as the seller has not made false or misleading statements.

Complications can occur however if the product or service that the consumer buys can, because of its very nature, be of variable quality. For instance, a football fan may pay money to see his favourite football team in the belief that the enjoyment he will gain will be worth more than the admission charge. However, if the team plays below standard he will have no legal right to sue the football club (otherwise most of the clubs in the Football League would face innumerable law suits). Instead, all he can do is to register the fact that he has not gained value for money (the value of the admission charge plus the time spent is greater than the enjoyment gained) and so he may not go to matches again. However, as the quality of the football match is likely to vary, he may return in a fortnight in the belief that this time the team will play well and it will be worth time and money to watch them. If the fan is a supporter of Sunderland Football Club and is continually disappointed at the standard of play, his continued support surely defies rational analysis.

4. SELLING AND DISTRIBUTING THE PRODUCT

(i) Selling

A company may have faithfully followed all the steps in the marketing process and yet may go out of business simply for the reason that it could not sell or distribute the product to the ultimate customer. The consumer may be desperately demanding the product but this will be of little use to the supplier unless the product is handed over and the buyer's cash is received in return. Often manufacturers find that while the final consumer may want to purchase the product the difficulty lies in persuading the retailer to take sufficient stock to satisfy demand. Retailers are generally by nature a cautious breed and want to make sure that they do not get left with unsold goods on their hands. Therefore it is up to the manufacturer to ensure that it not only persuades the ultimate consumer that the product is right, but that all the middlemen in the distribution chain believe that the product is worth stocking. For many manufacturers this involves employing sales representatives whose responsibility is to ensure that the product is always on the shelves when the customer comes to buy. Such representatives must be persuasive but must also be able to establish working relationships with the retailers.

(ii) Distribution

The distribution of the product is dependent on its nature. Most large organisations have their own distribution network which could involve fleets of vehicles and depots strategically placed throughout their market areas. Smaller organisations make use of commercial carriers, British Rail and the Post Office. Whatever method is used the essence of good distribution is to ensure speed and certainty. The product must reach the customer as quickly as possible, for time spent in transit costs the manufacturer money as the sale has not been made and the revenue has not been received. Nonetheless the product must also get to the right person and in a saleable condition. For this reason many companies pay great attention to their distribution networks for it would be extremely unfortunate if a business failure was caused by the business' inability to supply the customer with the product which it had worked so hard to produce and market.

ASSIGNMENT — THE TALL SHIPS RACE

The Tall Ships Race is to be held this year at Laten Head, at the mouth of the River Drey. This spectacular event has attracted entries from throughout the world, and up to 250,000 spectators are expected to attend.

One of the prime viewing sites is the local cricket ground, sited on the cliff top with a view across the whole of the river mouth. The Local Authority has decided that this site will be used as a vantage point for the event for the day. Laten Cricket Club, who use the ground, are prepared to rearrange their fixtures for the three weeks surrounding the event to allow for preparations and also repairs to the ground after use. In return, the council have agreed to pay them a £500 'disturbance fee' plus a donation of 50p towards the 'pavilion fund' for every car which uses the facility.

The council has estimated that the capacity for the area would be 1000 cars, and, using a sample of its own council employees, has produced the following estimates for demand for a combined car parking and entrance fee at a variety of prices:

Price £	Demand	Price £	Demand
0	1000	6	545
1	950	7	425
2	890	8	290
3	820	9	150
4	745	10	0
5	650		

The only other cost that the council anticipates is that of the Stewards. Local students can be hired for this task at a rate of £20 for the day. The Safety Committee have suggested that the following numbers of stewards will be necessary:-

Number of cars	Number of stewards	Number of cars	Number of stewards
1 - 50	1	701 - 750	12
51 - 100	2	751 - 775	13
101 - 200	3	776 - 800	14
201 - 300	4	801 - 825	15
301 - 400	5	826 - 850	16
401 - 450	6	851 - 875	17
451 - 500	7	876 - 900	18
501 - 550	8	901 - 925	20
551 - 600	9	926 - 950	25
601 - 650	10	951 - 1000	30
651 - 700	11		

The debate is now centred on what price to charge. At a recent meeting of the full council, the Conservative Leader of the Council, Reg Moseley, proposed that a price be charged to maximise profit. Kevin Batley, leader of the Labour Group was outraged and said that the facility should be provided free of charge. An Independent councillor, Timothy Browne, suggested a compromise whereby the council should merely attempt to break even if possible. The matter was deferred, and a special meeting of the council was called in two weeks time.

TASKS

1. As a local government employee in the Recreation and Leisure Department, you have been asked to prepare a report on the pricing debate and the result of each proposal, using figures and diagrams where appropriate. Prepare this report in which you recommend which price will make maximum profit, which price will result in a break-even position and what costs the council will face if it makes no charge and still has to pay the cricket club for the use of its facilities and also has to pay the wages of the stewards.

2. Your NALGO representative calls you and expresses grave misgivings that non-union labour is to be employed. He asks if you could supply him with calculations for costs/profit etc assuming unionised Labour is employed, at a minimum rate of £35 per day. You agree to call him back. Prepare notes for this telephone conversation.

3. Your own Section Head mentions to you that he believes the sample used for the demand estimates is unrepresentative of the local populace. He asks you to supply him with notes on the problems involved in statistical sampling and suggestions for an improvement in the council system of market research. Prepare these notes in the form of a memorandum.

ASSIGNMENT — 'GET UP AND GO'

Harford Council, troubled by rising levels of unemployment, have launched a campaign to help small businesses called 'Get Up and Go'. This will provide certain financial assistance to new businesses and advice on business matters to both new and existing organisations.

The Business Assistance Office is located in Harford Civic Centre and the service has immediately proved to be popular. One of the most popular features of the service for both existing and newly established businesses is the Office's Marketing Section which provides advice on market research, pricing, advertising and other aspects of marketing.

Speedi-Kleen, a dry-cleaning business, was established two years ago, but is facing financial difficulties. Trade levels stand at approximately 1,500 garments per week at an average price of £2 per garment. However, costs are extremely high, and the organisation is losing almost £200 per week. The two partners in the firm, Terry Binks and Alan Forster, have written to the Business Assistance Office seeking advice as to the wisdom of a 'Special Offer' they are planning. The offer is to clean four garments for the price of three. Market research surveys of the current customers have indicated that demand would rise to approximately 1,650 garments per week.

In contrast, System Service Ltd is prospering. Established only one year ago, the company repairs and services computer systems, and is the sole provider of this service in the locality. The Managing Director, Vince Russell, has written to the Business Assistance Office to enquire whether it would be advisable to increase his prices by 10%, without having carried out any market research.

Special Kitchens Ltd. is the idea of Andy Nattrass. He intends the company to be designers and suppliers of custom-built kitchens. Andy is unsure how to approach the initial marketing of his company, but has earmarked a budget of £4,000 for the initial launch. Requiring help, he has contacted the Business Assistance Office for advice.

Sarah Martin has recently completed an Advanced Secretarial Diploma course at Harford College of Further Education, and has decided to set up in business on her own as Toptime Typing, providing a typing service from her home for local businesses. She has a very limited budget, and can only initially afford to spend £200 on promotion. She is seeking advice on how best to spend this money.

TASKS

1. You are employed as Assistant Advisor in the Marketing Section of the Business Assistance Office. The Chief Advisor has asked you to reply in writing to the letter from Speedi-Kleen, offering advice on their 'Special Offer'. Write this letter.

2. You have also been asked to write to Mr. Russell, offering advice on his proposal to raise his prices. Your Section Head thinks it would be a good idea for the Office to attempt to explain the concept of Price Elasticity of Demand to Mr. Russell, who has no knowledge of economics, and also how this concept applies to his particular case. He asks you to provide some brief notes on this subject.

3. Both Andy Nattrass and Sarah Martin require full reports on how to launch their respective businesses. You have been asked to prepare these two separate reports, with recommendations to each 'entrepreneur'. In doing so, you must bear in mind that full research into the available advertising media, and their actual and relative costs and benefits is essential. It may also be useful to provide an outline of a proposed advertising campaign for consideration by your superiors.

Chapter 27

COMPETITION POLICY AND CONSUMER PROTECTION

While it is perfectly understandable that suppliers of goods and services will wish to pursue their own interests, unfortunately this may be to the detriment of competitors and often the consumer. Certain markets for goods and services tend to develop in a way which is in conflict with the broad public interest, in other words which can be seen as economically or socially undesirable. To some extent the courts have sought to overcome these tendencies, but the scope of market activity makes it more appropriate that the government should intervene and legislate to curb what it may regard as unsatisfactory trading practices, and governments of all political persuasions have indeed done so. In this chapter we consider the approaches that have been adopted, concentrating mainly on legislative intervention in the operation of the market. These approaches are examined under three headings:

1.   The regulation of market structure through monopolies and mergers legislation;

2.   The control of anti-competitive practices through restrictive practices legislation; and

3.   Consumer rights.

1. THE REGULATION OF THE MARKET STRUCTURE THROUGH MONOPOLIES AND MERGERS LEGISLATION.

As we noted in chapter 21 one of the most certain ways of ensuring a high level of competition in a market is for there to be many buyers and many sellers, none of whom have such a significantly large market share that they can influence the price. They must all accept the market price, in other words they are price takers. However, as we have already noted in chapter 21, the UK market, since the second world war, has developed a more concentrated structure. The most prevalent market form is oligopoly. Producers are described as price searchers. The government has attempted to lessen this trend towards concentration by passing legislation designed to control the growth of dominant suppliers.

The increase in merger activity

Much of this concentration has been the result of mergers, with one major organisation taking over or merging with another. In fact giant mergers have become a major aspect of the commercial scene. In 1984 there were 89 takeovers of major public companies in the U.K. The value of the bids exceeded £4.4 billion. This record was exceeded in 1985 when 94 takeovers of such companies occured with a value of £5.3 billion and by 1986 this figure will be far exceeded again. In this period many household names have been taken over. For example: MFI, the home improvements chain were taken over by ASDA, the supermarket group; Debenhams, the department store company, was acquired by Burtons, the clothing chain; Arthur Bell, the Scotch whisky company were taken over by Guinness, the brewing giant; and the Imperial Group, the food, drink and tobacco combine were taken over by the Hanson Trust, who are essentially financiers but who are expanding into many areas of industry and commerce. Other even larger takeover bids are currently in the pipe line. At the time of writing these include a bid by Elders IXL brewing, farming and finance group and manufacturers of the famous 'Fosters' lager for Allied Lyons, the food and drink company which has been referred by the government to the Monopolies Commission and a potential £3 billion merger between Unilever, the Anglo-Dutch food and detergent multi-national and the Beecham Group, the drug and food company. An example of other takeovers which involve much smaller amounts but are also significant is the takeover at a cost of a mere £5 million by Amstrad, the home computer and electricals company, of Sinclair, perhaps the most famous name in U.K. micro electronics. In several of the above examples both producers are in the same market and so such mergers will lead to commercial control becoming centred in fewer hands. U.K. governments have since 1945 shown concern over this type of behaviour and legislated accordingly.

Legal Control of Monopolies and Mergers

The first major piece of legislation was the Monopolies and Trade Practices Act 1948, which created the body now known as the Monopolies and Mergers Commission. Legislative powers were strengthened by the Monopolies and Mergers Act 1965. The Commission's main responsibility is to act as a watchdog enquiring into possible monopoly or oligopoly situations and report its findings to the government for possible further action. The Fair Trading Act 1973 repealed and re-enacted the 1948 and 1965 Acts and established the Office of the Director-General of Fair Trading. The Director-General was given authority to refer to the Commission possible areas where market concentration could be detrimental to the public interest, and was also given authority to assist the Commission in its investigation of such situations.

The 1973 Act:

- (a) defines both a monopoly situation and a merger situation;

- (b) grants investigatory powers to the Monopolies and Mergers Commission;

- (c) grants powers to the Secretary of State for Trade and Industry to issue orders to deal with monopolies and mergers.

A Monopoly/Merger Situation.

The 1973 Act defines a monopoly/oligopoly/merger situation as existing if the following circumstances arise:-

either a single enterprise has (or through a merger, is likely to have) control of 25% of an individual market (a monopoly share);

or if the total assets of the merged organisation exceed £5m.

The Monopolies and Mergers Commission

This body is technically independent of the government. It has the duty to "investigate and report on any question . . . with respect to the existence of a monopoly situation . . . or with respect to the creation of a merger situation." Both the Secretary of State and the Director General of Fair Trading can report matters to the Commission for investigation.

In its report the Commission will decide if either of the above circumstances exist and, if so, whether or not there are any factors which could justify the government in allowing them to continue. There are many instances of industries in which there is one company with more than 25% of the market, for instance in the biscuits market, United Biscuits have a 40% market share, and in baked beans, Heinz have a 64% market share. The fact that these have not been referred to the Commission reflects the belief of successive governments that competition was nonetheless adequate in these industries. If a referral is made, the Commission will consider whether or not the merger or the level of concentration operates in the public interest. To decide this, the Commission must bear in mind factors such as:-

(a)   the need to promote effective competition within the U.K;

(b)   the need to protect consumers' interests regarding the price and variety of goods;

(c)   the need to minimise the costs of production;

(d)   the need to develop new techniques and products;

(e)   the need to ensure unrestricted entry for new competitors into existing markets; and

(f)   the need to ensure a balanced distribution of industry and employment within the U.K.

These factors may be somewhat contradictory in that some, for instance (a) and (c), seek to improve economic efficiency either within organisations or within the economy as a whole, while others such as (f) aim to restrict the free movement of industry and so impose certain constraints on it, thus making it less efficient. For instance a manufacturing business may be most cost efficient if it is situated in the South East of England close to its major markets yet the Commission would encourage a more balanced distribution of industry throughout the U.K. and so would encourage it to locate in the regions.

If the Commission's report indicates areas of concern, the Secretary of State for Trade and Industry on behalf of the Government has the following options open to him. He may by order:

(i)   require the transfer of property from one organsiation to another;

(ii)   require the adjustment of contracts;

(iii)   require the reallocation of shares in an organisation;

(iv)   prohibit a merger taking place.

The above orders are enforceable by court action through an injunction, that is a court order prohibiting or requiring specified action.

Examples of mergers which were rejected by the government have been those between Boots and Glaxo, and Lonrho and the House of Fraser. In the first case the two companies attempted to argue that Research and Development would be enhanced in pharmaceuticals as the joint company would have much greater assets. However the Commission did not accept that there was sufficient evidence to justify this and having considered the other possible consequences of market concentration in this industry rejected the merger. In the second case the Commission felt that by taking over the House of Fraser, Lonrho would have had too great a share of the department store market and so would not permit the merger to proceed.

2. THE CONTROL OF ANTI-COMPETITIVE PRACTICES THROUGH RESTRICTIVE PRACTICES LEGISLATION

One of the major factors which will ensure a competitive market is that there should be no barriers to prevent the establishment of new organisations in the market. It is in the consumers' best interests that, if high profits are being made in a particular market by existing suppliers, there should be no restrictions on new organisations entering the market and so achieving healthy competition. The reality is that many markets are oligopolistic, and the producers who control them can effectively prevent new competitors entering the market by price control. In addition, free market entry may be restricted by the use of restrictive trade practices by organisations.

Examples of restrictive practices include:

(a) Agreements between Suppliers.

Suppliers often form agreements or associations with other suppliers in the same industry with the aim of either:-

(i) limiting the supply of goods or services;

(ii) fixing a standard price;

(iii) standardising contractual terms of sale;

(iv) purchasing raw materials through a "common pool" at an agreed price.

(b) Agreements between Suppliers and Distributors or Retailers

Suppliers who are dominant in a market may enter into agreements with distributors or retailers under which a minimum price is set for the resale of the supplier's products. These agreements may also restrict the distributor who may be required to exclusively stock the supplier's products. In return the retailer may be granted sole dealership over the product in a particular area and substantial discounts on the supplier's standard price.

(c) Other Anti-Competitive Practices.

Examples of other restrictive practices include:-

1. full-line forcing.

This involves a supplier requiring a distributor or retailer who wishes to stock the supplier's major product, to carry the full range of his products. For example, a shopkeeper wishing to sell a major brand of baked beans may be required to carry the full range of the supplier's tinned products.

2. tie-in sales.

This is a less extreme form of the same arrangement, whereby the sale of one product is tied to the sale of others. Thus, a purchaser of a certain type of photocopier may also have to enter into a service agreement with the supplier to purchase all photocopying paper from him.

3. reciprocal trading.

This involves organisations agreeing to purchase each other's products exclusively. Thus other competitor's products cannot be purchased where such an agreement is in force.

4. long-term contracts.

Here a distributor agrees to carry the supplier's products exclusively for a long period and therefore effectively restricts competitors from entering the market.

The individual practices mentioned are all examples of the means by which dominant suppliers may exert pressure on distributors or retailers. The ultimate sanction which may be used against distributors or retailers who fail to agree to such practices is a withdrawal of supplies.

THE LEGAL CONTROL OF ANTI-COMPETITIVE PRACTICES

Legislation specifically designed to prohibit anti-competitive practices is contained both in EEC law and the United Kingdom's own domestic statutes.

EEC Competition Law

The main provisions are found in Articles 85 and 86 of the Treaty of Rome, and they prohibit trade agreements that endanger freedom of trade between member states by preventing, restricting or distorting competition within the Common Market. Examples of such agreements are those which:

    (a)   fix prices or trading conditions;

    (b)   limit production, markets, technical developments or investment;

    (c)   share markets or sources of supply;

    (d)   apply dissimilar conditions to equivalent transactions with other trading parties;

    (e)   make the conclusion of a contract subject to the acceptance of unconnected supplementary obligations.

Fines can be imposed by the EEC Commission on the parties to such an agreement. However, an agreement that otherwise infringes the Articles may be allowed to continue in certain circumstances, for example where the agreement exists in order to promote technical or economic progress which will also benefit consumers.

U.K. Competition Legislation

The Competition Act, 1980, echoes the language of EEC competition legislation. Under the Act trade practices, other than those registerable under the Restrictive Trade Practices Act 1976, which "involve a course of conduct which has, and is intended to have the effects of restricting, distorting or preventing competition in connection with the production, supply and acquisition of goods and the securing of services in the U.K." are treated as 'anti-competitive practices'. Whereas EEC legislation deals with competition within the broad geographical area of the Common Market, the 1980 Act is obviously restricted to U.K. markets.

A detailed investigation procedure is set out under the 1980 Act and is shown in the figure below. Essentially all the alleged anti-competitive practices are subject to preliminary investigation by the Director General of Fair Trading. If the practice is proven to be anti-competitive, action can be taken by the Secretary of State for Trade and Industry.

Particular practices by individual organisations may now be investigated and if necessary prevented without the need to investigate the industry as a whole. However, only large organisations are brought under scrutiny, that is companies with a turnover of more than £5m or more than a 25% share of their particular market.

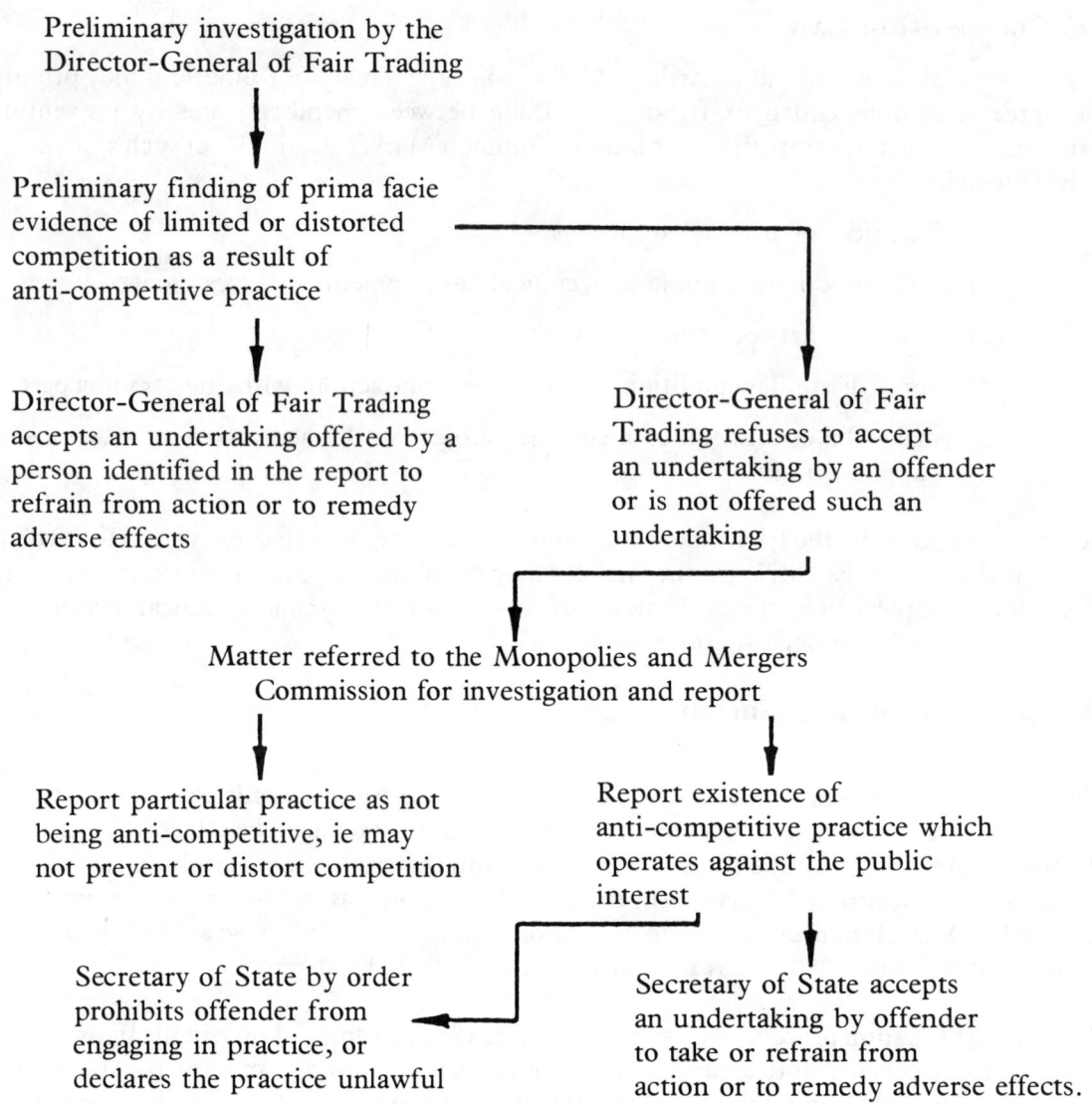

Investigation procedure under the Competition Act 1980

Unlike the Restrictive Trade Practices Act 1976 there is no presumption under the 1980 Act that an agreement referred to the Commission operates against the public interest. In determining this question of public interest, the Commission simply takes into account all matters which appear to it to be relevant in the particular circumstances. For example, a manufacturer may offer his product to supermarkets at much bigger discounts than he offers to corner shops. The practice of offering such discounts could be referred to the Commission as being "anti-competitive" in that the number of corner shops is likely to be reduced because of this practice. The Commission in deciding the question of 'public interest', would have to balance the advantage to the consumer of obtaining lower-priced products against the convenience to the consumer of local shopping.

Having reached a conclusion on a reference, the Commission must then report to the Secretary of State for Trade who has the power, by order, to declare an anti-competitive practice unlawful if the offender refuses to refrain from that type of conduct. The Act expressly excludes restrictive practices already registerable under the Restrictive Trade Practices Act 1976 to prevent an overlap of proceedings.

The types of practice which may be investigated by the Director-General of Fair Trading under the 1980 Act would include the giving of specific discounts, rebates and allowances, full-line forcing, tie-in sales, reciprocal trading and long-term contracts.

Additionally the Act grants the Secretary of State for Trade and Industry the power to refer to the Monopolies Commission any matters concerning the cost and efficiency of public corporations if they act as monopolists. These corporations include the Post Office and British Rail. This is an example of the government using an independant body to keep its own house in order, although of course the government does still retain the discretion as to whether or not to make a reference to the Commission.

It must be stressed, however, that such individual practices will only be regarded as "anti-competitive" and declared unlawful after a consideration of all the circumstances relating to their economic effect in the particular market situation. Of course, if this were taken to the extreme 'competition itself' could be regarded as anti-competitive, because if it is successful it could have the eventual effect of reducing the number of competitors by eliminating those which are least successful.

The Restrictive Trade Practices Act, 1976

It was mentioned above that the Competition Act 1980 does not apply to agreements registered under the Restrictive Trade Practices Act 1976. Under this Act, duties are imposed on the Director-General of Fair Trading. He is required to compile and maintain a register of restrictive agreements, and also to bring such agreements before the Restrictive Practices Court, which has the function of deciding whether they are contrary to the public interest. The types of agreement registerable under the Act are those made by suppliers of goods which lead to a restriction relating to:

    (i)   the price charged for goods;

    (ii)   the terms and conditions of supply of goods;

    (iii)   the quantities or descriptions of goods to be supplied;

    (iv)   the process of manufacture to be applied to any goods;

    (v)   those who may obtain the goods;

    (vi)   the area in which the goods may be obtained.

A registerable agreement is presumed to be contrary to public policy and therefore the Director-General of Fair Trading must bring such agreements before the Restrictive Practices Court. If the parties can satisfy the court that the agreement does not harm the public interest then it may be declared valid. To assist the parties there are eight grounds, called the "eight gateways", set out in the Act. If they can establish any one of the gateways then the agreement will be treated as a valid one.

. . . *protect the public*

Such gateways include the need to:

    a. protect the public against injury;

    b. counteract restrictive measures taken by anyone not a party to the agreement;

    c. enable the parties to negotiate fair terms with a monopolistic supplier or customer;

    OR the removal of the restriction would:

    d. deny the public as purchasers other substantial benefits;

    e. have an adverse effect on unemployment or exports.

In fact, relatively few agreements have been approved by the court, and this indicates the tough line that it has taken with regard to restrictive practices.

> In *Re Net Book Agreement 1957*, the court considered an agreement by book publishers not to permit the retailing of books below published prices. The agreement was justified on the grounds that its removal could lead to unfair competition from large supermarkets and department stores only carrying a limited number of best-sellers, which could mean that specialist book sellers were forced out of business.

Alternatively,

> In the *Chemist Federation Agreement 1958*, an agreement by this Federation to limit the sale of patent medicines to the public, only by qualified pharmacists, was declared void. The court was unimpressed by the argument that the restriction was necessary to protect the public against injury in view of the potentially dangerous nature of the goods being sold.

The Resale Prices Act 1976

One of the most fundamental aspects of competition between retailers is that they should have the ability to charge whatever price they wish. Yet one of the most widely used restrictive agreements was the practice by dominant suppliers of imposing standard prices for their goods on all their retail outlets. These 'resale price maintenance' agreements were forced on distributors and retailers by suppliers, who could always threaten to withold supplies to ensure compliance. Such agreements were initially controlled by legislation in 1964, their regulation now being contained in the Resale Prices Act 1976. Under this Act it is unlawful for suppliers to make agreements to withhold supplies from, or supply on less favourable terms to, distributors who do not observe resale price conditions. As with other restrictive practices, the Restrictive Practices Court has power to grant exemption on one or other of the grounds specified in the Act upon an application made by the Director-General of Fair Trading.

So far, only three exemptions have been made, relating to books, drugs and maps. Apart from these exemptions it is 'prime facie' unlawful for a manufacturer to withhold supplies in an attempt to enforce a minimum resale price. Such a refusal to supply goods could, however, be justified if the producer shows that the dealer in question has, within the preceeding 12 months, been selling the same or similar goods as a 'loss leader', that is selling at a retail price below wholesale cost in order to attract custom for that and other products.

> In *Oxford Printing Ltd. v. Letraset Ltd. 1970* the defendants withheld supplies from the plaintiffs, who had cut the price of the defendant's products and also used them to promote the sales of a competitor's product. Such withholding of supplies was held to be lawful in the circumstances.

It is through the machinery of the Director-General of Fair Trading, the Monopolies Commission and the Restrictive Practices Court that the legislation discussed above is enforced and the behaviour of dominant suppliers may be controlled. The extent to which governments are committed to competitive markets may be measured by the level of activity of these enforcement agencies. Certainly in relation to mergers there is a growing concentration of industry in the economy which may not be in the public interest despite government competition policy. More success has been achieved in countering specific adverse behaviour of dominant suppliers. The ability of governments to exercise some degree of control over the market structure is fundamental to the requirement of protecting the public interest and ensuring that the position of consumers is not prejudiced. In the next part of this chapter we will consider the government's position on consumer protection in some detail.

CONSUMER PROTECTION

Consumption of goods is a fundamental characteristic of economic activity. In the remainder of this chapter we consider some of the legal issues associated with the process of consumption, concentrating particularly upon two of them. Firstly the rights consumers have in relation to goods they use and services they receive, and secondly the steps they can take if these rights are not respected by producers and suppliers.

The caveat emptor approach

It is said that the traditional attitude to consumers' rights can be summed up by the expression 'caveat emptor', let the buyer beware. Whilst it is doubtful that this principle has at any stage in our commercial development provided a completely accurate description of the relationship between buyers and sellers, it is certainly the case that in the past the business world, and consequently the courts, tended to the view that the onus should be on buyers in commercial transactions to satisfy themselves that they were striking a just bargain. Over time there has been a gradual erosion of this view, so that today it is more realistic to describe the market as one in which 'caveat venditor', let the seller beware, is the prevailing philosophy. There are many factors which account for this shift. One of the most obvious is the enactment by Parliament of legislation aimed at strengthening the consumer's position.

'Caveat emptor'

Consumer legislation has employed different methods to achieve its objectives; for instance by preventing sellers from attempting to exclude or restrict their legal liabilities through the use of suitably drafted contractual clauses, seller's private rights have been reduced. Also the imposition of criminal liability for false and misleading statements accompanying the making of a contract subjects sellers to the public humiliation of possible fines and even imprisonment. Underlying these legal developments has been a recognition of the increasing importance throughout the twentieth century of the role of the private consumer in the domestic market, and an awareness that nineteenth century attitudes towards consumers' rights are simply no longer socially acceptable today. Consequently all political parties have demonstrated a willingness to respond to pressure for legal change where a strong enough case has been put forward on behalf of consumers for doing so. Consumer programmes on television and radio have been effective in highlighting many of the abuses suffered by consumers at the hands of unscrupulous businesses and traders.

The fact that legislation has been necessary to effect changes in the market methods employed by sellers also demonstrates the unwillingness or inability of the market to meet the changing social demands placed upon it through the mechanism of self regulation. Of course it is not only in the business world that statute has been used to modify behaviour. Other examples include the efforts made at outlawing discriminatory practices of a sexual, racial and religious kind.

What is a consumer?

Before examining in more depth the rights enjoyed by consumers we need to consider the term 'consumer'. Whereas from an economic standpoint the expression is used broadly to describe those who 'use' goods or services, efforts at defining the term from a legal standpoint have found it necessary to go on to distinguish between private consumers and business consumers.

This is because it has been felt that greater legal protection should be granted to private consumers than to business consumers. In theory at least the latter should be better placed in terms of their experience and knowledge and bargaining power to look after their own interests than the ordinary private person. In practice a small business organisation that trades with a much larger organisation may be in no stronger an economic bargaining position than you or I would be in the same position. The fact is that in commercial contracts the reality of relationships between parties who are not bargaining equals is that the stronger will invariably dictate terms to the weaker, whose real choice is whether to "take it or leave it", rather than to reopen the negotiations to obtain a better deal. Such an option is simply not available. This type of trading approach typifies a major part of United Kingdom's trading activities, and it appears to strike at the very notion of what an agreement is always said to represent — a 'meeting of the minds' of the parties arrived at through a process of negotiation.

The true face of commercial activity is that most contracts are 'contracts of adhesion', agreements under which one of the parties is obliged to adhere to the other's terms. For the sake of accuracy it should be said that sometimes the stronger party will be the consumer, not the supplier, and so it may be the consumer who is imposing terms, but this is less common than the dominant supplier situation.

The Unfair Contract Terms Act 1977, which is considered later, provides us with an important example of how the legislation defines the private consumer. Such a person, the Act says, is someone purchasing goods of a type ordinarily supplied for private use or consumption who is not making the contract in the course of a business, but is buying or hiring the goods from someone who is selling in the course of business. This tells us that it is not just the underlying purpose for which the goods are being bought, but also the nature of the goods themselves which distinguishes a private consumer transaction from a business transaction. So if you buy a ten ton lorry under the Act this would not necessarily constitute a product "ordinarily supplied for private use or consumption". Similarly if you purchased a lawnmower, which you were going to use in your work as a landscape gardener, you would be purchasing in the course of business. In both cases the legislation would not treat you as a 'private' consumer, with the effect that your legal rights are reduced.

The nature of product liability

Generally the goods we use, for example a washing machine, or that we consume, such as a meal, are items we have actually bought. But we can act as consumers in other ways. A person whose washing machine has broken down may use a friend's as a temporary measure, and maybe the meal that you have eaten has been bought for you in a restaurant. The fact that you do not own the goods does not prevent you from using or consuming them, but it may have an effect upon the nature of your legal rights. The reason for this can be explained quite simply.

If you buy goods from a commercial seller the contract automatically includes a number of major undertakings, in other words promises, that the seller has to fulfill. They include undertakings which relate to product standards. If the goods do not match up to these standards the consumer has the contractual right to reject the goods and sue the seller for damages. There has been in fact a breach of contract. The undertakings in question are imposed upon the seller under the Sale of Goods Act 1979, and the seller remains liable even if he has taken all reasonable care to ensure that the products he is selling meet the standards required by the Act, and therefore he is not at fault if they fail to do so. An illustration of this principle would be where a shop sells a catapult to a child, who is injured when the catapult snaps. The shopkeeper will be liable under the contract even if he carried out sample inspections of the catapults before buying them himself from the supplier.

This actually happened in a case called *Godley v. Perry 1960*. Lawyers call liability of this sort which arises without fault or blameworthiness 'strict liability'.

If follows that a buyer who suffers physical harm from a purchased product can recover compensation for the harm by alleging a breach of contract. But let us suppose that the seller has gone out of business. Is the buyer then left with no remedy?

And what about other people who might be affected? What if the catapult had not injured the little boy who bought it, but his friend who was standing beside him? Earlier we mentioned the washing machine a friend had let you use, and the meal bought for you in the restaurant. Would you have any rights if you received a serious electric shock from the washing machine because the manufacturer had not properly earthed it, or if the meal caused you food poisoning because it was not properly cooked? In all three cases the problem seems to be that as the injured parties have no contract with anyone, they cannot therefore pin liability on anyone. Even the buyer who finds that the seller is now out of business seems to be in the same predicament.

It seems unjust that the injured parties should be denied any legal rights simply because they are not parties to a contract, and in fact in each case it is possible for them to seek compensation for the physical harm that they have suffered. The law recognises the existence of a duty, which manufacturers and producers who owe to anyone they might reasonably expect to be harmed, as a result of their negligently manufacturing the goods or providing the service. This is not 'contractual liability', but 'tortious liability'; it arises under the tort of negligence.

A tort is a civil wrong, and torts are imposed as a part of the general law. We are all subject to them, whether we like it or not.

> The principle that a consumer, whether or not he is an actual buyer, who suffers harm as a result of a manufacturer's negligence can sue the manufacturer for damages, was established by the House of Lords in *Donoghue v. Stevenson (1932)*. In this case a woman suffered physical illness and shock after discovering that the contents of a bottle of ginger beer she was in the process of drinking included the decomposed remains of two snails. The bottle had been bought for her by her friend. The court decided that the manufacturer owed her a duty of care, therefore putting him under an obligation to use reasonable care in the manufacture of the product.

This duty of care is sometimes said to be a duty owed towards the 'ultimate consumer'. It is a very important aspect of the law regarding product liability. It is especially important to note however, that it is liability based upon fault. If a manufacturer can demonstrate that the manufacturing process, the design of the product, and other production aspects have been performed with proper care, he will not be liable. A manufacturer must therefore ensure that he acts as a reasonable manufacturer would have acted in the circumstances if he is to fulfil the duty of care which he owes to the ultimate consumer of his products.

> In *Vacwell Engineering Ltd. v. BDH Chemicals Ltd. 1971* the defendants, who were chemical manufacturers, were held liable under the tort of negligence when one of their products caused an explosion. Their liability arose through a failure to warn prospective users that if the product came in contact with water it could lead to an explosion.

Sometimes it may be very difficult for a person to prove that a manufacturer was in fact negligent, because it will not be possible to identify precisely how the breach occurred. How, for example, did the snails come to be in the bottle of ginger beer? It may be possible for the consumer in such cases to rely upon a rule of evidence known as 'res ipsa loquitur'. This means 'let the facts speak for themselves'. Under this rule the courts will infer negligence of the defendant where there is no reasonable explanation for the damage caused, for example a new car with faulty brakes which cause the owner to crash, or a television that explodes. However the activity causing the damage must be something totally within the control of the defendant, which would not be expected to occur if reasonable care had been exercised. The rule has the effect of shifting the burden of proof to the manufacturer to prove the absence of negligence.

The Donoghue v. Stevenson principle extends to a wide range of subject matter, from hair dye in *Watson v. Buckley 1940*, to lifts in *Haseldine v. Daw 1941*, and even a tombstone in *Brown v. Cotterill 1934*.

The EEC has issued a directive requiring the United Kingdom Parliament to introduce legislation to impose strict liability on producers. When this legislation is introduced much of the present fault based system will disappear.

It is argued that this increase in liability will be very costly for producers, although there is evidence that the resulting increase in insurance premiums when passed on to the consumer will generally increase unit costs by only a fraction of 1%. To a limited extent strict liability has already been introduced in this country under the Consumer Safety Act 1978, which is considered later in the chapter.

THE TERMS OF A CONSUMER TRANSACTION

A consumer who buys goods or services does so by means of a contract with the seller or supplier. As with any type of contract, rights and corresponding obligations will come into existence when the contract is executed. The nature of these rights and obligations depends primarily upon what the parties have expressly agreed. It may be for example the seller's stated responsibility to deliver the goods on a certain date to a specified destination. These obligations are terms of the contract. They should be carried out, for if they are not this will amount to a breach of contract. The remedy in such circumstances is an award of damages, the technical expression for an award of money compensation to the injured party.

It is the court which makes the award when the plaintiff establishes that the defendant is in breach of contract. The fundamental aim in awarding damages is to put the innocent party in the position he or she would have been in had the contract not been broken. So as an example, the basic award where a seller fails to deliver goods is the difference between the contract price and the market price or current price prevailing at the time the goods should have been delivered. It may be that when the breach occurs, equivalent alternative goods are available on the open market at a lower price than the contract price, in which case damages would be nominal, that is a token amount, but there would be little point in suing in such circumstances.

Clearly breaches of contract vary in importance; the remedies available in the event of a breach vary accordingly. As we have seen damages will always be available, but if the breach is regarded as a major matter, in other words something which is vital to the substance of the contract, the injured party has the additional remedy of repudiation. This means that he has the right to reject the contract.

Major terms in contracts are known as 'conditions', while minor terms are referred to as 'warranties'. It is for the parties themselves to decide which terms are the major ones and which the minor ones. In the event of a dispute, if they have failed to identify the importance of a term the court will endeavour to do it for them, for only in this way is it possible to gauge the seriousness of the breach.

Sometimes it is impossible to say whether a term is a condition or a warranty when it is first created because it will be so broadly framed that it could be broken in a major respect or a minor respect, and therefore it is only possible to say after the event what effect the particular breach should have on the contract. Such terms are referred to as 'innominate', meaning intermediate terms.

> The position is illustrated in *Hong Kong Fir Shipping Co. Ltd. v. Kawasaki Kaisen Kaisha Ltd 1962.* Here a ship was chartered on terms that stated that it would be 'in every way fitted for ordinary cargo service'. Inefficient engine-room staff and old engines contributed to a number of breakdowns so that during the first seven months of the charter the ship was only able to be at sea for eight and a half weeks. The charterers repudiated the contract. The Court of Appeal decided that this particular breach did not entitle the charterers to repudiate. Diplock LJ stated that the term in the contract was not really either a condition or a warranty but rather "an undertaking, one breach of which may give rise to an event which relieves the charterer of further performance . . . if he so elects and another breach of which may not give rise to such an event but entitle him only . . . to damages."

> Thus in the *Moorcock 1889,* a term was implied by the court in a contract between a ship owner and a firm of wharfingers. The contract was to use their wharf on the Thames for the discharging and loading of his vessel, the Moorcock. He was going to pay a charge for the use of the cranes alongside the wharf. While the vessel was moored there she was damaged when the tide ebbed and she came to rest on a ridge of hard ground. The Court of Appeal held that the wharfingers were liable for breach of an implied term that the mooring was safe for the vessel. 'In business transactions such as this,' said Bowen LJ, 'what the law desires to effect by implication is to give such business efficacy to the transaction as must have been intended at all events by both parties who are businessmen.'

> In *Irwin v. Liverpool City Council 1977*, the defendant council let a flat on an upper floor of a block of flats to the plaintiff tenant. A term was implied by the court into a tenancy agreement between the plaintiff and the defendant Council to the effect that the defendants had an obligation to keep in repair the stairs and the lift in the block of flats which they owned.

When a condition is broken, although the remedy of repudiation is available, there may be good reasons why the consumer would wish the contract to stand. For instance goods of the particular kind may be in short supply, or it may take a long time to obtain a replacement. Thus it is open to the consumer to treat the breach of condition as a breach of warranty and look for damages only. This is known technically as an 'ex post facto warranty'.

The terms of a contract may arise in any of the following ways:

By express agreement. The parties to the contract may expressly agree their mutual obligations. For instance the terms as to the time and place of delivery may be expressly stated.

By implication. This can occur in two distinct ways, namely through the actions of the court and by means of statute.

TERMS IMPLIED BY COURTS.

The courts will sometimes imply terms into a contract to make the contract 'work'. The justification for doing this is the view that had the parties actually addressed their minds to the matter they would have agreed that the term was an obvious and necessary component of the contract.

Contracts of employment provide a very vivid illustration of the common law implying terms into contracts. This is discussed in Chapter 19.

Arguably in consumer law, of much greater significance than the role of the court is the fact that statute implies terms into contracts. As in the case of common law implied terms, there are many examples that can be cited as illustrations. Here we shall concentrate on the statutory implied terms which are designed to benefit the consumer.

Terms implied by statute

For the sake of simplicity we can examine such terms under the following headings (i) terms in contracts of sale; (ii) terms in contracts for services; and (iii) terms in consumer credit transactions.

(i)   Contracts of Sale

Contracts of sale, or sale of goods transactions as they are usually referred to, are the most common types of transaction made. Millions of them are entered into every day. They are regulated by the Sale of Goods Act 1979. This Act determines the rights and duties of the buyers and the sellers of goods. Amongst its provisions are rules regulating the time at which ownership passes from the seller to the buyer, what the rights of the parties are if the contract is broken, what the obligations of the seller are, and, of course, how a contract for the sale of goods is defined. Here we examine the last two aspects.

Under s.2 of the 1979 Act a contract for the sale of goods is defined as one in which the seller transfers or agrees to transfer the property in goods to the buyer for a money consideration called the price. The term 'property in goods' means ownership, so the Act does not apply to transactions such as hire-purchase agreements where there is merely an option to purchase rather than a binding obligation to buy. It also does not apply to transactions which involve pure barter, that is where goods are exchanged for other goods. Furthermore if a contract is one where the substance of the undertaking is the supply of skill and labour by one of the parties, such as the carrying out of rewiring work by an electrician, then another Act, the Supply of Goods and Services Act 1982 will apply.

The term 'goods' covers a wide range of property including all personal property such as cars, clothes and household appliances, but it does not extend to non-tangible property such as a patent.

The Act in sections 12-15 imposes a set of conditions upon sellers which taken together make up a very stringent trading code highly beneficial to all consumers, and particularly to private consumers.

Under s.12 of the Act there is an implied condition that the seller has the right to sell the goods. If this obligation is broken because the goods belong to someone else, the buyer will be able to recover in full the price paid. A person may of course be authorised by the owner to sell goods for him. Corporate bodies can only trade through human agents in this way. Right to sell really means 'legal power' to sell.

> Thus in *Niblett v. Confectioners Materials Co 1921,* the purchaser of a quantity of tins of preserved milk could not resell it without infringing the Nestle Company trademark. This infringement arose because the labels placed on the tins by the manufacturer bore the name "Nissly Brand". The manufacturer was held to be in breach of s.12.

Under s.13, where goods are sold in accordance with their description, there is an implied condition that the goods shall correspond with the description. Description extends to weight, size, quantity and ingredients.

> In *Re Mooore & Co. Ltd. v. Landauer & Co. 1921,* the buyer purchased a quantity of canned fruit. The contract stipulated that each case should contain 30 tins but on delivery about half the total quantity of tins were packed in cases of 24. The court held that the buyer was entitled to reject the goods, even though there was no evidence that the buyer would suffer any loss.

When dealing with questions of weight and dimensions, whilst there must be strict compliance by the seller, very small deviations from the specifications can be ignored, for instance when a consignment of 100 tonnes of potatoes is 2lbs short.

Buyers should beware when using specialised trade terms to purchase goods.

> The buyer in *Grenfell v. E.B. Meyrovitz 1931,* was held to have no remedy under section 13 when a quantity of glass he had purchased under the description "safety glass" proved unsuitable for use in goggles because it splintered under certain conditions. The glass conformed with the technical meaning of safety glass.

> In *Peter Darlington Partners Limited v. Gosho Limited 1964,* the seller supplied canary seed to the buyer. The seed was sold on a "pure basis". In fact it was only 98% pure. This was in fact the highest quality of purity possible, and the court rejected the buyers' claim that the seller was in breach.

. . . sold on a "pure basis" . . .

Under s.14(2) 'where the seller sells the goods in the course of a business there is an implied condition that the goods supplied under the contract are of 'merchantable quality'. 'Merchantable quality' means as fit for the purpose or purposes for which goods of that kind are bought as it is reasonable to expect having regard to any description applied to them, the price (if relevant) and all the other circumstances'.

Clearly the standard that is expected of goods under this section is a flexible one. Goods must be able to do the job they have been bought for, but only to the extent that this is consistent with:

(a)   Description. Goods described as "shop soiled", "manufacturers rejects" or "seconds", or simply as "second hand" cannot be expected to demonstrate the quality of a new or perfect product;

and

(b)   Price. A person could not reasonably expect the same standard of quality and durability from a pair of shoes costing £5 as a pair costing £45, although if the shoes costing £5 had been reduced from £45 in a sale the price would probably not be relevant in determining the standard of quality.

The major benefit of s.14(2) to the consumer is that it provides a remedy beyond the scope of s.13. A leaking kettle is still a kettle, even though it is not of sound quality. The breach in such a case occurs under s.14(2) rather than s.13.

The case law on merchantable quality appears to have been generated by the more extreme examples of defects, rather than the mundane complaints most of us have from time to time. They range from woollen underpants containing a chemical that caused dermatitis as in *Grant v. Australian Knitting Mills 1936,* to "Coalite" that included a detonator from the mine, which exploded when thrown onto the household fire, (*Wilson v. Rickett & Cockerell & Co. 1954.*)

There are a number of important features of merchantable quality which should be noted:

(i)   the seller must be a business seller. The implied condition does not apply to private sales.

(ii)   the seller need not be the manufacturer, but may be anyone in the chain of distribution, such as a wholesaler or retailer;

(iii)   the condition does not apply where the defect has been drawn to the buyer's attention prior to the sale, or where the buyer has examined the goods before buying them and ought to have discovered the defect;

(iv)   if the seller is to seek to comply with this section, some system of quality control will need to be introduced, increasing costs of production; this is particularly relevant where the seller is also the manufacturer;

(v)   liability under the section is strict. In *Frost v. Aylesbury Dairies Ltd. 1905*, the dairy supplied milk contaminated with typhoid germs. The dairy was held liable despite establishing that it had used all reasonable care to prevent such contamination.

Under s.14(3) "where the seller sells goods in the course of a business and the buyer, expressly or by implication, makes known . . . to the seller . . . any particular purpose for which the goods are being bought, there is an implied condition that the goods are reasonably fit for that purpose, whether or not that is a purpose for which such goods are commonly supplied, except where the circumstances show that the buyer does not rely, or that it is unreasonable for him to rely, on the seller's skill or judgement". *Fitness*

Sometimes consumers, whether they are private consumers or business consumers, place reliance on the expertise of the seller. We can see this happening when a customer goes into a shop and asks whether the shop has something that will perform a particular task, say fixing a broken ornament or removing stains from a carpet. Or a business may describe its accounting procedures to a supplier of office equipment, relying on the supplier to supply a suitable computer system to cope with these processes.

It is in such cases that s.14(3) imposes liability upon the seller, if the goods supplied, even though of merchantable quality, do not fulfil the purpose the buyer requires of them.

> In *Cammell Laird & Co. Ltd. v. Manganese Bronze & Brass Co. Ltd. 1934* the buyers supplied the sellers with a specification for ships propellors which they were to manufacture for the buyers. Reliance was placed upon the sellers regarding matters outside the specification, including the thickness of metal to be used. The propellors were found on delivery to be too thin. The buyer's action was successful on the ground that the unfitness concerned a matter on which the buyers had relied upon the seller's skill.

Often sections 14(2) and 14(3) overlap. The contaminated milk in *Frost v. Aylesbury Dairies 1905* was both unmerchantable and unfit for its purpose, namely to drink.

Finally, under s.15, when goods are sold according to a sample, there are implied conditions that:

1.   the bulk of the consignment shall correspond with the sample;

2.   the buyer shall have a reasonable opportunity of comparing the bulk with the sample;

3.   the goods shall be free from any defect rendering them unmerchantable which would be apparent on reasonable examination of the sample.

This is a useful provision, since commercial and non-commercial consumers alike often purchase goods on the basis of a sample they have examined. For instance this is often how we buy a carpet, and is the way in which the buyers and the sellers of many raw materials trade.

(ii) Contracts for the supply of goods and services

The Sale of Goods Act 1979 does not apply to contracts under which a consumer receives not only goods but also some form of service associated with the goods. Such contracts arise when you employ a builder to re-roof your house or where a firm of electricians are brought in to install a wiring system in a new shop. Contracts which include these two components, that is the sale of goods plus the provision of a service, are referred to as contracts for work and materials. They are dealt with by the Supply of Goods and Services Act 1982. The Act also covers contracts exclusively concerned with the service element, for instance where a garage adjusts your car brakes without replacing them, or a heating engineer cleans and inspects your central heating boiler without providing any new parts.

Whether a contract is simply for goods or is in fact for work and materials is not always easy to identify, although if the value of materials is less than the labour costs the contract is likely to be one of sale. For instance a contract to prepare and supply a meal in a restaurant was held to be a contract of sale in *Lockett v. A.M. Charles Ltd. 1938*, as was a contract to supply and lay a carpet in *Philip Head & Sons Ltd. v. Showfronts Ltd. 1970*. However in *Robinson v. Graves 1935*, a contract to paint a portrait was regarded as a contract for work and materials.

Under the Act any goods supplied must meet any obligations as to title, description, quality, fitness for purpose and sample, which are virtually the same as those under the Sale of Goods Act 1979. So if a central heating system is installed and it fails to work properly because the pump on the boiler is defective, the installing engineer will be in breach of contract.

With regard to the service element three important provisions apply:

1.   section 13 specifies that "where the supplier is acting in the course of a business there is an implied term that the supplier will carry out the service with reasonable care and skill". The standards to be maintained will be those prevailing in the trade or profession at the time.

2.   section 14 requires that if the contract does not specify the time for carrying out the work, or it is left to be determined in a manner specified in the contract or by the course of dealing between the parties, there is an implied term that the supplier will carry out the work in reasonable time.

3.   section 15 states that if the contract price is not fixed and there is nothing in the contract making provision for fixing it, then, in the absence of any course of dealing between the parties which would determine the price, there is an implied term that the consumer will pay a reasonable price.

It is also important to be aware that a supplier who carries out the work without due care and skill may be liable to anyone suffering physical harm and additionally, following the case of *Junior Books Ltd. v. Veitchie Co. Ltd. 1983*, any economic loss which is reasonably forseeable. Once again such liability arises under the tort of negligence.

Credit transactions

These are examined later in the chapter, but here we can note that hire purchase agreements contain a set of implied undertakings on the part of the creditor. (i.e. the supplier of goods to which the agreement applies). These implied undertakings again follow those contained in the Sale of Goods Act 1979 with regard to description, merchantable quality and fitness for the purpose, and corresponding with any sample provided. Thus the debtor, the person purchasing the goods on credit, enjoys rights of the same kind as those of a buyer, the implied terms in this case being contained in the Supply of Goods (Implied Terms) Act 1973.

The exclusion and restriction of liability

No examination of a consumer's contractual rights would be complete without considering how the law deals with the practice of excluding and restricting the seller's liabilities. We have seen how a contract creates obligations which the parties making it are obliged to meet, and that failure to do so constitutes a breach of contract which can possibly lead to a claim for damages. It follows that a prudent person, recognising the potential liabilities involved in entering into a contract, will try to reduce or entirely remove any such risk. How far this is possible depends upon whether the clause in the contract excluding or restricting liability is successfully incorporated into the contract, and if it has been, whether it satisfied certain tests of validity laid down by both Parliament and the courts. Let us consider these two aspects separately.

Incorporation and drafting of the terms

To become a part of a contract a term must be included in the contractual offer. We saw in Chapter 21 that a term is only valid if it is certain. In other words it must have a clear meaning which a court can, if needs be, specifically identify. So if a term either does not form a part of the contractual offer, or is in some way unclear, it will be ineffective.

A good example of terms failing to become part of the contract occurs where terms are introduced after the contract has been made.

> This happened in *Thornton v. Shoe Lane Parking 1971*, where the terms of the contract were contained on the back of a parking ticket. They could only be read therefore after the customer had inserted the money into the machine, and thus subsequent to the making of the contract.

. . . accepted no responsibility . . .

> In *Olley v. Marlborough Court Hotel Ltd. 1949*, the plaintiff was staying in an hotel with her husband and her furs were stolen from their hotel bedroom. A notice on the back of the bedroom door stated that the hotel accepted no responsibility for lost or stolen items unless they were deposited with the manageress for safe keeping. The notice was held to be ineffective, since it was not brought to the plaintiff's attention until after she had booked the room at the reception desk.

Where the term is contained in an unsigned document, or on a notice, it will be effective only if the person relying on it took reasonable steps to bring it to the attention of the other party, and where the document or notice containing it might reasonably be regarded as contractual and likely to contain contractual terms. Of course if a document containing contractual terms has been signed then the signatory will be bound by its terms as was the case in *L'Estrange v. Graucob Ltd. 1934.*

The need to express contractual terms clearly is very important, especially when the term is an attempt by one of the parties to exclude liability. As Scrutton LJ pointed out in *Alison (J. Gordon) Ltd. v. Wallsend Shipway and Engineering Co. Ltd. 1927*, "if a person is under a legal liability and wishes to get rid of it, he can only do so by using clear words".

Thus the courts use the following tests for determining whether the exclusion is valid:

(i)   does it, clearly and unequivocally cover the breach of contract in question. This is a rule of strict interpretation;

(ii)   is it ambiguous or doubtful? If it is, it will be construed against the person who is relying on it. This is known as the 'contra proferentem' rule.

Furthermore it will be presumed that an exclusion clause was not designed to defeat the main purpose or object of the contract. This is however only a presumption and it is legally possible to draft an exclusion clause to cover the most fundamental breaches of contract. Compare the following cases.

This case has gone in favour of the defendant

In *Karsales (Harrow) Ltd. v. Wallis 1956*, the defendant purchased a second-hand car on hire-purchase terms from a finance company. A clause of the agreement stated "No condition or warranty that the vehicle is road-worthy or as to its age, condition or fitness for any purpose is given by the owner or implied therein". Following the agreement the car was delivered to the defendant at night. It was totally incapable of self-propulsion, and many parts were either missing or had been replaced by older parts. When the defendant found it in this condition the following morning, he refused to accept it. The Court of Appeal held that the exemption clause was not intended to cover such a fundamental breach as this. "A car that will not go" said Birkett LJ "is not a car at all".

In *Photo Productions Ltd. v. Securicor Transport Ltd. 1980*, the defendant company had contracted to provide a night patrol service for the protection of the plaintiff company's factory. An employee of the defendant company entered the factory while on patrol and created a fire which caused over £600,000 worth of damage. The defendant company sought to avoid liability by relying on a clause in the contract which excluded liability for "any injurious act or default by an employee of the company unless such an act or default could have been forseen and avoided by the exercise of due diligence on the part of the company" and "any loss suffered by the customer through . . . fire or any other cause, except in so far as such loss is solely attributable to the negligence of the company's employees acting within the course of their employment". The House of Lords held that the clause covered the breach of contract in question even though it was a fundamental one. The parties were in an equal bargaining position and were therefore free to determine the extent of the obligations owed under the contract. The language of the exclusion was clear and it was not for the court to reject what the parties had agreed.

Statutory control of exclusion clauses

One of the most disturbing features of exclusion clauses is that they are a common feature of contracts of adhesion, the 'take it or leave it' contracts mentioned earlier in the chapter. A person who is in a weak bargaining position may have no effective control over the power of the stronger party to insert such exclusion clauses.

Under the Unfair Contract Terms Act 1977, Parliament has come to the aid of the weaker party. The Act applies not only to contractual exclusions but also tortious ones, for example a notice at the entrance of a public park that attempts to exonerate the council from liability for any harm suffered to the members of the public whilst in the park.

Under s.2 a person cannot, either by a contractual term or by notice, exclude or restrict his or her liability in contract or tort for death or personal injury arising from negligence. Liability for other loss or damage arising from negligence can still be excluded, provided the exclusion can be shown to be reasonable.

> An example of this second part of the section is found in *Phillips Products v. Hamstead Plant Hire 1983*. The hire company hired out a JCB to the plaintiffs under a standard term agreement. A driver was included, but the company excluded any liability in negligence for the driver's acts. In the event whilst he was working under the plaintiff's directions the driver damaged their factory through his own negligence. The court held the exclusion clause to be unreasonable and therefore invalid. It was unreasonable because the hire was for a short period giving the plaintiffs little opportunity to insure. They did not select, nor effectively control the driver, and moreover their experience of such hiring arrangements was very limited.

Under s.3, where a person inserts in his or her own written standard terms of business any term purporting to exclude or restrict liability for breach of contract, the term must satisfy the test of reasonableness. If the other contractual party is a consumer the rule applies even if the contract is not based upon the other's written standard terms. An example of the application of this section would be where a time limit is placed upon the period for making claims.

Section 5 of the Act deals with guarantees. It provides that where goods are of a type ordinarily supplied for private use or consumption, a term contained in a guarantee of the goods cannot exclude or restrict liability for loss or damage caused by the negligent manufacture or distribution of the goods, where the defect occurs when the goods are in consumer use.

Finally section 6 deals with exclusions of the implied conditions of the Sale of Goods Act 1979. Originally it was quite permissible for a seller to exclude the statutory implied conditions from a contract of sale, but under the 1977 Act the position is very different. S.6 provides that if there is a sale to a consumer any clause excluding the terms implied by sections 12 to 15 of the Sale of Goods Act is ineffective. A person buys as a consumer if the goods are of a type ordinarily sold for private use or consumption by a seller in the course of business to a person who does not buy them in the course of business. In a non-consumer sale, for instance between two businesses, any attempt to exclude s.12 of the Sale of Goods Act is absolutely void, although sections 13, 14 and 15 can be excluded if the seller can show that this is reasonable. Whether it is reasonable to do so is determined by a number of guidelines laid down by the Act. These are:

a)   The respective bargaining strengths of the parties relative to each other. This involves considering possible alternative sources of supply. For instance a monopolist seller may have difficulty in establishing the reasonableness of a widely drafted exclusion clause.

b)   Whether the customer received an inducement to agree the term, or in accepting it had the opportunity of entering into a similar contract with other persons but without having to accept a similar term. The reference to other persons involves account being taken of the suppliers within the market and their terms of trading. Sometimes suppliers combine to produce standardised terms of trading, giving buyers no opportunity of finding improved terms. An example of an inducement would be a reduction in price.

c)   Whether the customer knew or ought reasonably to have known of the existence of the term. This involves the customer's knowledge of the trade in general, its terms and customs, and knowledge of the seller, with whom the customer may have previously traded on the same terms.

d)   Where the term excludes or restricts any relevant liability if some condition is not complied with, whether it was reasonable at the time of the contract to expect that it would be practicable to comply with the condition. It might not be practicable, for example, to require the buyer to notify the seller of defects occurring in a large consignment of goods within a limited time period with a proviso that failure to notify in time will relieve the seller of any liability.

THE ADMINISTRATIVE MACHINERY OF CONSUMER PROTECTION

Successive governments have recognised that individual consumers of goods and services are in a vulnerable position in relation to producers and suppliers. The manufacture and supply of goods and services often involves complex processes and it is difficult therefore for consumers properly to assess their true quality or acceptability. Also consumers are often far detached from manufacturers and suppliers and are usually in a position of economic weakness. The risk of exploitation has led to the creation of numerous consumer associations and organisations whose aim is to give advice and support, and report alleged malpractices to the appropriate agencies empowered to enforce the law.

The protection of the interests of consumers generally has led to the gradual introduction of the criminal law into consumer protection so that there are a large number of consumer statutes generating regulations and orders which create numerous offences. In the main such offences may be categorised as:-

1. Those connected with the methods and conditions of sale of goods or supply of services such as misleading advertising, consumer credit offences and offences relating to aggressive sales techniques; and

2. Those resulting from the dangerous nature of services offered or the dangerous, deteriorated and adulterated nature of products for sale, for example innaccurate or incomplete descriptions of dangerous products or lack of safety in the provision of services and the supply of dangerous goods.

The Fair Trading Act 1973 created the post of Director-General of Fair Trading, the main watchdog for consumer affairs. The responsibilities and powers of the Director-General include:

a. the protection of the economic interests of consumers. This involves collecting information relating to commercial activities in the UK with a view to discovering practices which adversely affect consumers;

b. the protection of the general interests of consumers. This involves receiving evidence of commercial activities which may adversely affect consumers general interests, such as health and safety interests;

c. the obligation to assist the Secretary of State for Consumer Affairs. The Act imposes a duty on the Director to give information and assistance to the Secretary of State in respect of matters connected with his duties and also to recommend action;

d. the obligation to seek orders in respect of detrimental courses of conduct. The Director has power to seek orders from the Restrictive Practices Court against persons who persistently maintain conduct which is unfair to consumers. Such conduct includes persistent breaches of the criminal law or civil law covering consumer protection. The Director must first attempt to obtain an assurance from the person that he will refrain from the conduct but if none is given or observed the Director should seek a court order to direct the person to refrain, or accept his undertaking that he will refrain from the course of conduct. Breaking the court order will place the individual in contempt of court and make him liable to imprisonment.

The Fair Trading Act 1973 also created new administrative machinery for consumer protection, the Consumer Protection Advisory Committee, with the aim of discovering and preventing adverse 'consumer trade practices'. Such practices are concerned with the manner of supply, promotion, packaging, salesmanship and securing payment. The Director General can refer a consumer trade practice to the Committee to decide whether it adversely affects the consumer's economic interests. The Committee then reports to the Secretary of State who has power by statutory instrument to make a ministerial order.

An example of an Order made under this procedure is the Consumer Transaction (Restrictions on Statements) Order, 1976, (as amended) which makes it a criminal offence for a seller in the course of business to unlawfully, by notice, attempt to exclude his liability for breach of the implied conditions of the Sale of Goods Act. Hence the administrative machinery created by the Act helps to prevent unfair trading practices by dealing with persistent offenders and acting as a deterrent to others. In addition, the delegated order making power available to the Secretary of State means that consumer law may be changed quickly without the need for new legislation to deal with fresh abuses as they occur.

Local enforcement of the 1973 Act is delegated to individual local authorities. The Consumer Protection, Trading Standards, or Weights and Measures departments within County Councils are obliged to enforce most consumer legislation as well as to provide advice and support to members of the public. The volume of consumer legislation is enormous particularly when you bear in mind that each consumer protection statute generates numerous regulations and statutory orders. The major consumer offences are contained in the Consumer Safety Act, 1978, the Food Act 1984, the Unsolicited Goods and Services Act 1971, the Consumer Credit Act 1974 and the Trade Description Acts 1968 and 1972. The following is a brief guide to the above legislation so that you may appreciate the role of trading standards officers in relation to enforcement.

1. The Consumer Safety Act 1978.

This is a broad statute passed with the purpose of consolidating all the previous legislation on consumer safety in relation to certain products which are regarded as being potentially dangerous. Under the Act, the Secretary of State is given wide powers to make regulations for ensuring that goods are safe, and appropriate information is provided. Existing regulations relating to oil heaters, electrical goods, toys, pencils, night dresses and children's clothing will eventually be replaced. Many of the regulations will simply specify existing safety standards, for example the approved British Safety Standards, in respect of particular categories of goods. If the Secretary of State believes there is a risk of danger connected with the supply of goods, he has power to make a prohibition order, serve a prohibition notice or notice to warn. This restricts the manufacturer in the supply of the specified goods. A supplier in breach of the regulations commits an offence and is also liable under civil law if anyone is injured as a result of the breach. The Act provides that it is a defence for the supplier to show he took all reasonable steps and exercised all due diligence to avoid committing the offence. Trading Standards officers employed by local authorities fulfil the dual role of advising traders and enforcing the legislation. To assist them in the task of enforcement wide powers of entry search, seizure and testing are conferred by the 1978 Act.

2. The Unsolicited Goods and Services Act 1971.

This Act was passed to impose criminal and civil sanctions on traders carrying on the practice of 'inertia' selling. This involves sending goods or providing services which have not been ordered and demanding payment or threatening legal action if payment is not made. The Act provides that unsolicited goods and services need not be paid for and unordered goods may be retained by the recipient if not collected by the sender within six months of delivery. It is an offence for the sender to make unlawful demands for payment.

. . . sending goods . . . which have not been ordered

3.   The Food Act 1984.

Under this Act administration and enforcement powers are conferred on local authorities in relation to the preparation and sale of food. The principal objectives of the legislation (previously the Food and Drugs Act 1955) are (a) to prohibit the sale of food which is adulterated or which contains harmful additives, foreign bodies or mould, for which there is misleading labelling or advertising, and (b) to prescribe standards of quality for certain foods. The latter power has led to minimum standards of quality being prescribed by regulations made under the legislation for many foods, such as meat and dairy products. The principal offences under the Act are the making of food which is unfit for human consumption, the selling of food which is either injurious to health, or is not of the nature, substance or quality demanded by the purchaser, or is falsely or misleadingly described.

Accordingly in *Shearer v. Rowe & Rowe 1985,* an offence was committed when a purchaser, who was a trading standards officer, was sold what was described as minced beef but in fact contained 10% pork and 10% lamb.

A conviction under the Food Act can lead to fines, imprisonment and even a closure order in the case of food premises.

4.   The Consumer Credit Act 1974.

To a large extent this Act contains the law in relation to consumer credit transactions such as hire purchase, personal loans, overdrafts, credit cards, credit sales and budget accounts. The Act provides for criminal, civil and administrative sanctions which may be imposed on persons who infringe its provisions. Protection is conferred on the credit consumer by imposing a system under which those organisations involved in providing or arranging credit must be licensed to do so. These licensing arrangements are under the supervision of the Director-General of Fair Trading but local enforcement is carried on by Consumer Protection departments. Credit agreements are further regulated by requiring that they must be in a prescribed form and that the consumer is supplied with all necessary information such as his rights of rebate on early settlement and right of cancellation and termination of the agreement.

5. The Trade Descriptions Acts 1968 and 1972.

These Acts introduced criminal sanctions against those who make false statements in the course of business. The Act does not apply to private sales and so a purchaser in a private deal who is induced to contract by means of a false description can only rely on civil law actions for misrepresentation or breach of contract to provide a remedy. For the Act to apply the transaction involved must be an integral part of the person's trade or business.

> In *Davies v. Summer 1984*, therefore, the House of Lords held that the sale of a car by a self employed courier could not be regarded as a sale of stock in trade or the disposal of a business asset for profit, and so the Act did not apply.

However where goods or services are supplied in the course of a trade or business the Trade Descriptions Act creates the offences of either:-

applying a false trade description to goods or supplying goods to which a false trade description has been applied;

giving a false indication as to the price; or

making a false statement knowingly or recklessly as to the provision of service accommodation or facilities.

In relation to enforcement, wide investigatory powers are conferred on local trading standards officers to purchase goods or services, enter premises to make checks and require suppliers to produce documents. Before a prosecution is brought the local authority is required to inform the Department of Trade in order to prevent numerous prosecutions for the same false trade description.

> The legality of bringing a second prosecution where there are a number of victims of the same unlawful act was in issue in *R. v. Thompson Holidays 1973*. Here a false statement in a travel brochure constituted an offence under the Trade Descriptions Act and the Court of Appeal held that a separate offence was committed every time someone read the brochure.

In relation to goods, the first offence mentioned may be committed by a supplier who applies a false trade description to goods, or supplies goods to which a false trade description has been applied. An example of this would be a manufacturer's label. A trade description includes any markings on the goods or packaging which covers matters such as quantity, size, method of production, composition, fitness for purpose, testing, approval, place or person who manufactured, etc. It can include an oral description of the goods by the seller and even one applied to the goods by the consumer if it is reasonable to infer that the goods supplied correspond to the description, for instance where a consumer requests a wool jumper and is supplied with one containing cotton.

> In *Sherratt v. Geralds Jewellers Ltd. 1970*, the defendant committed an offence when he sold a watch described as a "diver's watch" and engraved "waterproof" which stopped once it was immersed in water.

. . . described as a "diver's watch" . . .

Also in *Fletcher v. Bludgen 1984*, the court held that an offence equally can be committed by a trader when he is buying, as well as when he is selling. Here a private seller, having been told by a dealer that it was not possible to repair his car, sold it to the dealer for £2. The dealer repaired the car and advertised it for sale at £135. The court held that an offence has been committed.

To be 'false' the description must be false to a material degree. In *Robertson v. Dicicco 1972*, the court held that the expression 'beautiful car' was false when applied to an unroadworthy car for it constituted a reference to the mechanics, and an offence had been committed. Similarly, in *Kensington and Chelsea B.C. v. Riley 1973*, it was held that the description "in immaculate condition" was false when applied to a car which needed £250 spent on it in repairs.

The second offence mentioned relates to pricing so that a supplier who gives a false indication of the price of goods also commits an offence. Such a false indication could arise by either:-

a)   making a false comparison with a recommended price, such as by advertising "Recommended Price £200, our price £150;"

b)   making a false comparison with the trader's own previous price, for example by stating "was £60, now £20";

c)   indicating that the price is less than actually being charged, for instance, advertising "Elsewhere £210, here at only £160".

In relation to false comparisons, the Act stipulates that the goods may be regarded as having been offered at a higher price previously, if they were so offered within the previous six months for a continuous period of not less than 28 days. Unfortunately, this offence has been difficult to prosecute successfully mainly because of the obvious problem of proof, and the practice of some owners of chains of retail outlets, who evade this section of the Act, by displaying the goods for sale at one shop in the chain for the required period and then maintaining that they have dropped the price in all the shops.

In *Westminster City Council v. Ray Allen (Manshops) Ltd. 1982,* there was no offence committed by a trader who having had his goods on sale for more than 28 days at the Leeds and Rotherham shops, put them on sale in London at an advertised reduced price.

As far as the suppliers of services such as tour operators, dry cleaners, taxi services, etc. are concerned, in order to commit the third offence mentioned, it is necessary to show that the supplier made a false statement 'knowingly or recklessly'. This offence is not one of strict liability.

In *Sunair Holidays Ltd. v. Dodd 1970,* a travel brochure described accommodation at a hotel as having "all twin bedded rooms with bath, shower and terrace". Holidays were provided in rooms without terraces. The court held, nevertheless, that no offence had been committed because at the time the statement was made it was true, since the accommodation existed and nothing which happened afterwards could make the statement reckless.

It is at the time that the statement is made that it is necessary to judge whether it was false and whether the supplier knew it was reckless. Subsequent facts cannot make a false statement true, and vice versa.

In *Cowburn v. Focus Television Rentals Ltd. 1983* the false statement was "hire 20 feature films absolutely free when you rent a video recorder". This was false for a customer who rented a video was required to pay postage and packaging for the video films and only six were delivered. Despite the fact that the defendant subsequently tried to honour the advertisement by refunding the postage and packaging costs and sending 20 free films, they were nevertheless guilty of an offence of recklessly making a false statement as to a trade description.

Furthermore in *Wings v. Ellis 1984,* the false nature of a statement in their travel brochure was not known by the tour operator when the brochure was published, and when the mistake was discovered, reasonable steps were taken to remedy it. Nevertheless a holiday was booked on the basis of the false information and a subsequent complaint was finally upheld by the House of Lords. As the tour operator was aware that the statement was false when read by the complainant an offence under the Act had been committed.

In *Baxters (Butchers) v. Manley 1985,* offences had been committed under the Trade Descriptions Act 1968 and the Weights and Measures Act 1963 in relation to the pricing and weight of meat exposed for sale in a butchers shop. The claim that the offences were due to the act or default of the shop manager concerned was accepted. Nevertheless the defence of the owners that they had taken reasonable precautions was not accepted by the court. Relevant circumstances indentified by the court included the failure to give the shop manager any detailed instructions or guidelines on the relevant statutory provisions; the lack of staff training; the inadequate supervision by the district manager and the failure to establish positive precautions to prevent the commission of an offence.

Reasonable precautions could include adopting a code of practice drawn up by the relevant Trade Association or the Office of Fair Trading.

This was the position in *Lewin v. Rothersthorpe Road Garage 1984,* where this defence was offered in response to a prosecution for selling a car to which a false trade description was attached. By adopting the Motor Agents code of practice and instructing the staff in its content the employer established the defence of taking reasonable precautions where the offence was due solely to the default of an employee.

An obvious way to avoid committing an offence under the Trade Descriptions Act is to disclaim responsibility for a trade description. Thus a car dealer who is uncertain as to the validity of a mileometer reading on a car could simply display a notice disclaiming its accuracy. Provided the disclaimer is as bold, precise and compelling as the trade description itself, it will be effective. The Motor Trade code of practice approved by the Director-General of Fair Trading in 1976 recommends the use of the following form of wording:-

> "We do not guarantee the accuracy of the recorded mileage. To the best of our knowledge and belief, however the recording is correct/incorrect".

In relation to misleading pricing, further offences were created under the Price Marking (Bargain Offers) Order 1979 made under the Prices Act 1974. The order is aimed at misleading comparative price statements relating to goods or services. Unlawful statements include indications that the goods for sale are at a price lower than goods of the same trade description such as "price elsewhere £25, our price £13." Also an indication that the goods for sale are at a price lower than the value ascribed to goods would constitute an offence, for instance, "worth £15, our price £9.50". Such price comparisons are banned even if they are true for they are regarded as misleading to the ordinary shopper.

> In *West Yorkshire County Council v. M.F.I. Furniture 1983*, however the expression "Britain's lowest price" did not infringe the order, for the statement did not necessarily lead the ordinary shopper to believe that the price offered was lower than any other price for goods of the same description.

Certain price comparisons are permitted by the Order. Notably where the trader makes a comparison with a price he previously charged or he proposes to charge, or one charged by an identified trader or one recommended by a manufacturer or importer.

CONCLUSION

The law relating to consumer matters is dynamic, and there are a number of trends that can be identified in the present market system.

There is a move towards placing the basis of producers' liability on a no fault footing, as well as increasing emphasis on awarding compensation in the event of successful convictions for trading offences. Small claims in the courts are being dealt with using cheaper, quicker and more simplified procedures, and arbitration is being used as a device for dealing with consumer disputes.

Finally codes of practice are increasingly emerging as a means of regulating trade activity.

A code of practice is a voluntary statement by a trade association of the standards of business it expects from its members. While such codes are not legally binding, where a complaint is made as to the quality of the work done, the fact that a code has been broken is useful evidence. The Office of Fair Trading has the responsibility for encouraging trade associations to draw up codes, will advise on their content and may even give a code its approval. A trader who belongs to a trade association and is in persistent breach of the association's code of practice will normally be disciplined by the association itself. The majority of existing codes provide for inexpensive conciliation and arbitration in the event of disputes. Codes relevant to services and approved by the Office of Fair Trading include those relating to car repair, dry cleaning and laundry, electrical servicing, post and telephones, travel, photographic processing, glass and double glazing. Some of the nationalised industries have agreed codes of practice with the Office of Fair Trading, and they include the electricity councils and the Post Office who have established consumer councils.

ASSIGNMENT — HANNAY MANUFACTURING

Hannay Manufacturing plc is a major national company based in the City of Manchester. It has been in existence for more than fifty years and is one of the City's largest employers. It has recently been leaked in the national press that the company could be the possible target of a take-over bid by Wilding Engineering plc. This company is the main competitor in the market in which Hannay Engineering operates and Wildings hope to consolidate their position in this market and become the dominant supplier. The proposed take-over has become a topic of considerable public debate in the city.

TASK

1. You are employed as junior reporter on the Manchester Evening News and have been asked by your editor to prepare an article for publication in the paper. In the article you should explain the following points:

    i)   the problems which could result from a take-over such as this in which one company becomes dominant in a particular market;

    ii) the procedures which the government might employ in attempting to decide whether or not the proposed merger is in the public interest;

    iii) the benefits that Wildings might claim to justify the merger.

DEVELOPMENTAL TASK

2. Examine the financial pages of one of the quality newspapers for one month. List all the mergers or takeovers which are mentioned as actual or potential. Analyse the action of the government and the Monopolies Commission in each of the cases.

ASSIGNMENT — GREENCROFT GREENHOUSES

Tom Cooper, a keen gardener and a member of the local gardening club, has for a number of years specialised in growing show tomatoes on a small scale in the "lean-to" on his allotment. He sees the following advert in the April edition of "Gardening World".

Introducing the

"GREENCROFT"

A new revolutionary greenhouse which will bring Mediterranean conditions to your garden. This greenhouse is ideal for growing all types of hot house fruit and vegetables. Each greenhouse is supplied in kit form with full instructions for easy erection within three hours.

Size —   Length 12 foot
Width 5 foot
Height 6 foot

giving 360 cubic feet of growing space.

Price: £375 inclusive of delivery.

Available from your local gardening centre.
Manufactured by J. Sandford Ltd.

Tom, having recently won on the premium bonds, is considering purchasing a new greenhouse as he hopes to improve the quality and size of his tomato crop.

The two reasons for this are:-

a.   he is keen to exhibit show tomatoes at his local gardening club.

b.   the price of commercially grown tomatoes has recently increased substantially and he hopes to make savings on the family food budget.

Tom visits Todd's, his local gardening centre, who have the "Greencroft" in stock and he is advised by the manager, Mr. Massey, as to the suitability of the "Greencroft" for growing tomatoes. Tom decides to take the plunge and buy the greenhouse, which the gardening centre agrees to deliver the next day. He also purchases 10 dozen tomato plants from the gardening centre.

The greenhouse and plants are delivered the following day and Tom and his friend, Jim, a market gardener, spent the morning erecting the greenhouse paying close attention to the manufacturer's instructions.

After completing the erection, Tom and Jim install heating equipment, a propogating frame and then the tomato plants. On standing back to admire the finished job, Tom and Jim suspect that the dimensions of the greenhouse are not as specified and, on checking this, they discover that its dimensions are in fact — length 10ft, width 6ft and height 6ft.

Tom immediately returns to the centre and complains to Mr. Massey that the greenhouse does not match the advertised dimensions. Mr. Massey, however, maintains that there is really no problem as the cubic footage of the greenhouse, is in fact, equivalent to that advertised and, in any case, Tom should take it up with the manufacturer. Determined to take further action on the matter, Tom returns home to find to his horror that the greenhouse has totally collapsed for no apparent reason, completely destroying all his installed equipment and tomato plants.

Tom has written to the local Consumer Protection Department of his council explaining that neither the garden centre, nor the greenhouse manufacturer, are prepared to respond to the complaints he has made to them. In his letter he has provided the Department with all the information contained above.

TASK

1. In your role as an assistant to the Trading Standards Officer you have arranged to interview Tom in order to advise him as to the legal position in relation to his complaint. You are required to produce a set of notes for your own assistance in the interview with Tom. These notes should deal with:

    (a) Tom's contractual rights against the garden centre;

    (b) any legal rights he may have against the manufacturer;

    (c) the possibility of the Department taking legal proceedings against the garden centre or the manufacturer in relation to the Greencroft advertisement.

DEVELOPMENTAL TASKS

2. Undertake a role play exercise in which the interview is simulated.

3. Write a letter to the manufacturer, J. Sandford Ltd, indicating the basis upon which legal proceedings are being considered by the Department against the manufacturer.

INDEX